# TRIUMVIRATE

*Indian Hill, the house of Ben: Perley Poore; Colonial America meets* Waverley, *as drawn by Stanford White.*

# TRIUMVIRATE

## McKim, Mead & White

*Art, Architecture, Scandal, and Class
in America's Gilded Age*

## MOSETTE BRODERICK

ALFRED A. KNOPF  New York · 2010

*This Is a Borzoi Book*
*Published by Alfred A. Knopf*

*Copyright © 2010 by Mosette Broderick*

*All rights reserved. Published in the United States*
*by Alfred A. Knopf,*
*a division of Random House, Inc., New York, and in Canada*
*by Random House of Canada Limited, Toronto.*
*www.aaknopf.com*

*Knopf, Borzoi Books, and the colophon are registered trademarks*
*of Random House, Inc.*

*Library of Congress Cataloging-in-Publication Data*
Broderick, Mosette Glaser.
Triumvirate : McKim, Mead & White : art, architecture, scandal, and class in
America's Gilded Age / by Mosette Broderick. — 1st ed.
p.   cm.
Includes bibliographical references and index.
ISBN 978-0-394-53662-0
1. McKim, Mead & White.   2. McKim, Charles Follen, 1847–1909.
3. Mead, William Rutherford, 1846–1928.   4. White, Stanford,
1853–1906.   5. Architects—United States—Biography.
6. United States—Civilization—1856–1918.   7. United States—
Civilization—1918–1945.   I. Title.   II. Title: McKim, Mead & White :
art, architecture, scandal, and class in America's Gilded Age.
NA737.M4B76 2010
720.92'2—dc22    2010026988

*Manufactured in the United States of America*
*First Edition*

To Kayla Baker Stotzky—one in a million and away too soon

# CONTENTS

# ILLUSTRATIONS

# AUTHOR'S NOTE

This work began with a kind offer from Victoria Wilson at Knopf. I set out to learn as much as could be known about McKim, Mead & White, their friends, clients, and fellow artists. The initial research was carried out in existing collections, particularly those given to the New-York Historical Society over the years. Just as work began on the book, the family of Stanford White donated a large collection of letters and responses in press books to the Avery Library of Columbia University. The letter books had clear signs of removed items, with whole pages missing or neatly cut tissue pages. Someone had edited these books. In her book on her family and Stanford White, *The Architect of Desire,* Suzannah Lessard offers the specific time and identity of the "editor." At the beginning of the Depression, when commissions were falling off in the practice of McKim, Mead & White, Lawrence Grant White went through the papers of his father with an eye to history, removing items that caught his eye and could have brought further shame to a family already burned severely by the manipulation of the popular press and the legal system orchestrated by the mother of Harry K. Thaw, White's murderer. Clearly and understandably, Larry White intended to protect the family from sensitive parts of Stanford White's life.

Running through the world of McKim, Mead & White was a sense of the exploration of life's pleasures. A circle of bisexual and homosexual entertainment can be traced within the office. The circle included Stanford White, Saint-Gaudens, Joseph M. Wells, Frank Millet, Whitney Warren, Thomas Hastings, probably Mead, and many others. The other partner, Charles McKim, was clearly aware of this world and comfortable in it. Lawrence White did not want letters with open references to such gatherings to be found, nor did he wish letters with romantic expressions to be looked at by the next generation of scholars, who might aspire to write a book more probing than the puff piece Charles Baldwin wrote in 1931 as a pendant to the biography Margaret McKim Maloney had hired Charles Moore to write. Lawrence Grant White expunged the letterpress books and then seemingly "lost" much of the correspondence Joseph Wells wrote to McKim, Mead & White during his first and only visit to Europe. The letters Wells wrote early in his journey remain, but the entire correspondence after he reached Florence has been lost. Were the letters written from Italy of a more personal nature? Did they refer to specific individuals? Why would all the letters be saved except for those written as Wells was preparing to return home?

As anecdotal memories of the circle of gay life in New York at the end of the century have not survived, we have only the clues found in a careful study of letters Lawrence Grant White missed, or those written to others such as Augustus Saint-Gaudens, which do survive in collections elsewhere. Any person reading the letters can observe the current running through the office in the 1880s and 1890s. Aline Saarinen, while working on her proposed biography of White over thirty years ago, came to the conclusion that White was homosexual. It seems clear that White was bisexual, but there are batches of letters unmistakably revealing times in his life when he was part of an active gay circle—evidence that is still present despite Larry White's sharp blade. The goal of this study is to focus on the image-making presentation made by the architects; the sexual orientation of White and the circle he favored is of no importance to the work he did and is best left in simple form here.

The office of McKim, Mead & White continued to be recalled in the professional press for two decades after White's death, as a number of the men who had worked with the principals wrote their memoirs of life in the office. The English press, particularly those from the Liverpool School of Charles H. Reilly, praised the American architects on the eve of the arrival of the modern movement. By the mid-1920s, modern work in European architecture was threatening the values McKim had inculcated as he helped to fashion the American definition of beauty, art, and architecture. In a short time, McKim's carefully wrought vision was put on a shelf and forgotten. No longer would all ambitious young architects stream to the McKim, Mead & White office. A strong new cultural passion swept the art world.

As the world of McKim, Mead & White lay dying, McKim's daughter commissioned the reluctant Charles Moore—whom she would pay a goodly sum—to write about her father. Moore had known McKim in Washington, D.C., in the architect's later years, but did not intend to commemorate him with a book. Margaret McKim and her husband, Dr. Maloney, made it pleasant to write this book of closure to an era. Immediately after this, White's family probably asked Charles Baldwin to write his innocent biography of White. By the late 1920s, it had become acceptable to speak positively about White again; indeed, the great set of doors on White's Gould Memorial Library at the old New York University campus in the Bronx honoring the architect's memory were created in this decade. White's persona had become safe again, and a light book about the architect could be written and published. Poor Mead, alas, had no heirs to commission a book about him.

For the next half century, McKim, Mead & White lived in a negative twilight, disliked now for their architecture, not their personal behavior. The architects were dismissed as mere copyists, not original thinkers. In the 1960s, as the great writer on art historical subjects Aline Saarinen researched a study of Stanford White, the architect's life and work began to come out of the shadows. Saarinen abandoned her study when she became disillusioned about the Stanford White she found; on reading the letters still in the family barns, she realized that she didn't admire the man anymore. Saarinen's drafts for her books are remarkable, and one regrets only that she walked away from White, then died far too young. Saarinen's papers and the draft of her study are in the Smithsonian's Archives of American Art; they would form the basis of a great book on a woman who could have created a genuine taste for the arts in America, had she lived to become the CBS network's cultural anchor. America's interest in the arts would have been far different had Ms. Saarinen done the television stories she was asked to provide.

The first modern scholar to work on the careers of McKim, Mead & White was Leland M. Roth, whose fine dissertation was later made into the indispensable monograph on the firm. Mr. Roth's work is the best study of the careers of the architects and is especially notable for his work identifying the Italian sources of the architects' later buildings.

Richard Guy Wilson has brought the architects' work to life with numerous books on the firm and the era. His wonderful account of the Mackay house has just appeared. The chapters on the service side of the Gilded Era are a great contribution.

Of the three partners, however, only Stanford White has had a proper modern biography. Paul M. Baker's excellent *Stanny* is a masterpiece of research and indispensable for a study of the architect. Mr. Baker uncovered a wealth of new material and must be considered the definitive biographer of White. White's descendants have produced several new books on the architect. Suzannah Lessard wrote about her family in the vale of tears three generations after White's humiliating death. Claire N. White published a volume of White's letters with their charming sketches, and Samuel G. White created the most beautiful books on the architects ever made. Mr. White is the very best of colleagues, loving toward his great-grandfather and yet not too defensive about his peccadilloes. Samuel G. White is himself an architect, and his practice deals superlatively with the old and the new. His great-grandfather would be pleased with his work and that of Elizabeth White.

The family of Stanford White suffered after White's murder, becoming the victim of an orchestrated defense trial of the most sophisticated kind. Many old friends disappeared as the ordeal began. Many of White's treasures had to be sold, and questions were raised about the authenticity of some objects he had purchased. The family felt the dark cloud of perceived disgrace for two generations, yet remained gracious to scholars wishing to see family papers.

I first came to know of McKim, Mead & White in my last year of college, when the instructor leading an American art class along Madison Avenue at Seventy-eighth Street after a trip to the Metropolitan Museum asked the small group if anyone had ever heard of the architects. The question was posed at the end of the era of modern architecture, when white-walled houses and glass skyscrapers were still the apogee of good design. The class remained silent as the instructor indicated two McKim, Mead & White houses on opposite sides of Seventy-eighth Street. Finally, a student raised her hand and replied to the question. "Sure," she said, "I know who Stanford White was, my grandfather shot him." Indeed, the young woman was named Thaw. I mentioned this startling conversation to my mother, who had been a beautiful Virginia belle in the 1920s. "Oh, yes," she remarked, "Harry Thaw lived in Virginia and pursued me in the summer while I was in school at William and Mary," adding that he had a flunky greet young girls and attempt to arrange dates with Thaw. Thaw's reputation had put him beyond the normal range of human interaction even with young people in a different state from his birth and crimes. After college, when I went on to graduate school, it was on McKim's campus at Columbia. Even though the classroom buildings and campus were much changed from his early vision, the work of McKim and his colleagues was inescapable. Once aware of the architects, one could hardly walk about the city without noting their presence. In their day, McKim, Mead & White more than any other architects put their stamp on New York. We have now lost a number of the buildings done by the firm—Madison Square Garden and Pennsylvania Station were two notable destructions that should never have taken place—but one still feels Stanford White's rapid short steps on the streets near Madison Square and McKim's sense of scholarship at the Morgan Library. The architects are gone, but, for a time, this was their New York.

THIS BOOK STARTED OUT as a full building-by-building catalogue of the entire work of the architects. Years were spent tracking down and visiting houses throughout the region. Real estate ads often connected the architects' names to houses. Investigations followed to determine if the claim had any validity. New York City Buildings Department archives were thoroughly searched, and I was able to uncover many unknown commissions in the city of a minor sort—some even extant. Eventually, however, I realized that a definitive survey of all McKim, Mead & White buildings could take a lifetime and would need to go on to another volume. Therefore, this is not a study of all the work of the office, but rather a study of the path of the architects. In the end, many buildings, even a few important ones, were not included. Perhaps someday a gazetteer of McKim, Mead & White's work will follow.

The complex layer of architectural history as seen in the work and stylistic innovation of McKim, Mead & White appears at the end of the book. Lengthy discussions of architectural styles will be found in the notes rather than the text.

New York City, March 2009

# INTRODUCTION:
## McKIM, MEAD & WHITE

In the early 1890s Columbia College and New York University moved to the northern region of the city to create campuses that they hoped would give them academic credibility. Two Roman domes built upon upon hilltops in New York, two libraries built to preserve the thoughts of the ages; two magnificent buildings meant to shape the identity of recently acquired wealth in the nineteenth century. The two colleges prepared to take themselves seriously. For their physical presence, both college presidents turned to the most prominent architectural firm in America, McKim, Mead & White, to give their respective schools a vision for the future.

One might think that each school would want a different architect, but the partnership had two distinct personalities, that of McKim and that of White. Stanford White's commission came first from his father's college, New York University, which had given him an honorary degree despite the fact that Stanford had not even completed high school. McKim's work at Columbia followed as he edged out the other competitors for the new campus. McKim, whose college career was limited to a single year at the Harvard Scientific School, had no Columbia connection. The two men designed for what were, in reality, impoverished institutions hoping for a donor to make at least the central temple of learning, the library, a centerpiece of the new schools. Who were these men who transformed the colleges of New York?

The name of the architectural firm McKim, Mead & White is almost a household word in America. The practice, which was synonymous with bringing American buildings to a level of design equal to that of contemporary Europe, helped to establish the creation of beauty as a goal for builders of individual structures as well as of whole cities during the Gilded Age. These men who played a major role in shaping the ethos of beauty in America grew, as did the nation, from modest native stock to figures of international reputation.

Charles Follen McKim, William Rutherford Mead, and Stanford White hardly seemed destined for fame. All were born a half generation before the Civil War, all were of intellectual but modest backgrounds, and all had personalities sufficiently flawed to make their destiny seem a surprise. Perhaps it's even true that none was for long a talented designer. It was the synthesis of their association and their lifelong loyalty to one another that made this firm almost the brand name of architecture in turn-of-the-century America.

The eldest of the three, William R. Mead, remains enigmatic to this day. Known to his partners, affectionately, as "Dummy,"* Mead described himself as the rudder of the ship, the man who kept his partners from making "damn fools" of themselves. These comments were correct. It was Mead who kept McKim, Mead & White afloat from its first days, guiding the firm through a major disaster and into the modern world.

A taciturn soul deliberately insistent on keeping a low profile, Mead avoided the social life pursued to a frenzy by his partners. Moreover, he married out of the loop, selecting as a bride a Hungarian-born woman, Olga Kilyeni, who had no connections to potential clients in the United States. The couple had no children. Mead had no burning personal cause; indeed, he humorously noted in old age that his partner McKim, who stressed that physical exercise was the key to good health, died young, while his partner Stanford White had been true to his motto of a short life and a happy one. Mead just worked hard, had a quiet, perhaps boring life, and long outlived the others.

Abolition was the cause that united many of those in the parental circle of McKim, Mead & White, and brought them some early clients. No one fought the good fight better than James Miller McKim, whose role in the abolitionist movement was his life. Stanford White's narcissistic fop of a father also embraced the antislavery cause. Among the firm's early con-

---

*The nickname probably came from the game of whist, in which three can play a dummy version rather than the expected four players. While we are not clear about the exact meaning of the term to the three partners, the name is certainly humorous and self-mocking. It probably refers to Mead's lack of loquaciousness as well as the constantly changing moves of the three men.

tacts, Augustus Saint-Gaudens, William Henry Furness, Henry Villard, Frederick Law Olmsted, Frederick F. Thompson, Theodore Roosevelt, and Russell Sturgis all knew each other from events connected to the rejection of slavery. Indeed, only Mead's family's position toward slavery is unknown, although it was probably liberal. As children, McKim, Mead and White grew up with the war's noises just out of earshot. They were to turn the fervor of their parents' abolitionist zeal into the cause for beauty, carrying the banner of art forward as their parents had done with that of freedom for the slaves.

# TRIUMVIRATE

# 1. McKim

Charles Follen McKim, the architect who would achieve international recognition as a high-minded educator, succeeded in his goal of bringing the United States up to the cultural standards of contemporary Europe. McKim, who would work to professionalize and expand the artistic quality of American architecture as well as make Washington, D.C., into a major international capital, began life as a bit of a "loser." He was a weak student without a driving ambition. His father was James Miller McKim, one of the leading figures of the abolitionist movement. When his mother, Sarah McKim, gave birth to her second child and only son (there had been two daughters), Charles Follen, on August 27, 1847, she was staying at Isabella Furnace in Chester County, Pennsylvania, at the home of her sister and sister's husband, Colonel Potts. At the time, Charles's father, driven by abolitionist fervor, had gone to Britain to raise funds for the movement—duty before family.

Naming two of the McKim children Lucy and Charles was itself an act of reverence to those engaged in the abolitionist cause. Lucy was most likely named for Lucretia Mott, and Charles was named for the great German idealist Karl Follen, although the McKims Americanized the spelling of Karl to Charles.

The late 1850s saw the family in Germantown with the young Charlie struggling for his education in local schools while his parents became participants in major pre–Civil War events. By 1859 the two McKims and William Lloyd Garrison had taken an active role in freeing slaves. Indeed, the McKims were the hosts for a famous incident involving the release of a slave, Henry "Box" Brown, who, in a desperate bid for freedom had himself nailed into a crate in Richmond, Virginia. He was then express-mailed to the McKim home, where somehow, after the twenty-seven-hour journey, he was able to clamber out of the cramped space having survived his ordeal. Shortly thereafter, the McKims had the sad and brave task of accompanying the remains of John Brown, along with his widow, from Charleston to the burial site in North Elba, New York. The fervor of the national debate fully occupied the McKim family, as Miller McKim and William Lloyd Garrison championed the cause of providing education for the slaves.

The Garrisons and McKims, close since they fell under the influence of Karl Follen, now found their lives becoming even closer. Two of Garrison's sons were buddies of the young Charlie (the spelling of Charles's name varied in the letters, morphing from Charlie at first to Charley later on). Garrison and McKim, while being immortalized by John Rogers for a work of pedestal statuary,* decided to educate the boys by sending them to view the battle site at Gettysburg just a few weeks after the battle had ended. This long tramp to Gettysburg was made by Frank and Wendell Garrison, Charlie McKim, and Will Davis, a grandson of the idealist Motts who grew up at their home. In this way the group of young men became the heirs of the key figures of conscience whose work caused the battle. One might wonder if Charlie or the other boys had a sobering moment on this pilgrimage, but they seem not to have had a sense of the horrors of battle. The account of the trip in the sixteen-year-old Charlie's diary for his family is like that of a teenager on vacation remarking about the meals, accommodations, and people he saw. "Arrived at Harrisburg and stopped at Herr's Hotel; Hotel first-class and accommodations good," he wrote. "We went in swimming and had a pleasant bath and walked back to Herr's." It includes only a matter-of-fact account of the scene on the actual battlefield. "We visited the Cemetery and Round Top. Dead horses, shallow graves, shells, cartridge-boxes, etc., were the principal features."

Shortly after the trip, Annie McKim, Charles's adopted sister, married a Union soldier, James Frederick Dennis, and moved to Auburn, New York, where her husband worked for the local newspaper. The household, now with only Lucy and Charlie at home, revolved around Miller McKim's work with the American Freedmen's Relief Association, which was

---

*McKim was initially part of the group who modeled for Rogers's *The Fugitive's Story* (1869), but he was dropped before the work was completed. Rogers depicted many social issues of the day.

devoted to the education of the freed slaves. As Miller McKim became the corresponding secretary and the war drew to a close, his activities centered upon New York City.

The abolitionist movement had its heart in Philadelphia and Boston, but at the end of the war it was clear that both business and philanthropy would be administered in New York. During the week, Miller McKim lived in a boardinghouse in Manhattan, returning to Philadelphia on weekends. In New York, he, Frederick Law Olmsted, and Charles Eliot Norton joined the Irish-born journalist E. L. Godkin in discussing plans to create a weekly journal of politics, literature, art, and science. Miller McKim liked the idea of this journal as a sounding board for his work for the Freedmen cause, and he seems to have personally secured the needed capital to assure its launch as *The Nation* on July 6, 1865. The founding of this journal, which is still being published today, provided the McKims with an extra perk: better employment for Lucy's new husband, Wendell Phillips Garrison, son of William Lloyd Garrison, whom she had married on December 6, 1865. Wendell Garrison, who had been working in New York City as the literary editor of the New York *Independent,* became the managing editor of *The Nation* just months before his wedding. We don't know where the newly married Garrisons lived in the spring of 1866. Perhaps, like Miller McKim, they lived in a boardinghouse, a common accommodation for newly married couples in mid-nineteenth-century New York.

On weekends Miller McKim returned to Germantown to his family. The commute by train was relatively easy, but the McKims decided boarding in New York City was not appropriate for the now-middle-aged Miller. The Pennsylvania family made a gesture of acknowledgment to the new national order and decided to remove to New York. The plain-speaking Sarah was not up to the city itself, an overly active and expensive place, so the McKims purchased a small house in the first planned American suburb, Llewellyn Park, New Jersey. Llewellyn Park was on a hillside above the town of Orange, only about twelve miles west of the Hudson River, making it an easy distance from the city. "The Park," as the McKims called it, was a wonderfully picturesque community created by Llewellyn S. Haskell, who had ties to Miller McKim's world (and that of Stanford White's father). Lushly planted and with winding but well-paved roads, Llewellyn Park created a rural setting within the growing New Jersey town of Orange. Several houses in the gated community were built by Haskell's friend and neighbor, the architect Alexander Jackson Davis, who may have also had a role in the layout of the park. Llewellyn

Park had just been completed when the McKims moved in. They purchased a modest Gothic cottage built by Davis for a painter six or seven years before.

Modest though it was, the house proved a financial strain for the poorly paid Miller McKim, who shared the house and expenses with his newly married daughter Lucy and his son-in-law. The families set up households in June 1866, and their descendants would remain in the house for four generations, celebrating the good of life while seeing an overly generous share of tragic early deaths within its walls. We do not know how the young Charlie felt about the Davis-designed house, which he would live in for only two months. In August, at the age of nineteen, he was off to Cambridge, Massachusetts, where he had elected to enter Harvard University, though he would not join the socially ambitious young men reading classics at the college.

It had taken him an extra year's study to attain the level of accomplishment needed to take the Harvard entrance exams. From the end of the walk to Gettysburg until the summer of 1866, he had studied in the Philadelphia public schools and at home with a tutor, trying to get his Latin up to Harvard expectations. He wrote his friend Frank Garrison in the spring of 1866, "I am not going to enter the classical school at Harvard, I am fitting for the Scientific School and Propose to enter next September." Probably in the same letter, Charlie continued:

> I never meant to pursue one of the learned professions for a livelihood and hence it was a mistake from the very beginning to think of college; but I fall into the common error which many boys do of thinking what a fine thing it was to go to college, and what a splendid education I should have, and all that, without ever looking ahead and providing for the future, or if I did give it a passing thought now and then it was only to say to myself, how easily I could live, and how my Latin and Greek would elevate me. And perhaps they would were I lawyer, doctor, or minister, but what practical account would they be to me as a merchant, chemist or engineer? Now look at the advantages which the Scientific School offers. In the school of mining, one studies Chemistry, Geology, Metallurgy, French and German in addition to thorough instruction in mathematics.

He goes on to say that only a student from a well-off family could take a college degree and then start a career in which advancement was slow. A student graduating with professional training could start immediately at a higher salary.

The language of this letter is so stilted and mechanical that it comes as no surprise to us to read the final words, which confirm that these opinions on professional training come from the advice of others whose wisdom he has sought. Miller McKim had no fortune to leave his children, and he puzzled over how to improve the prospects of his underachieving son. The profession of engineering, he had heard, could advance a youth quickly. Especially given the opening of the American West, mining engineering seemed the best ticket of all. Charlie had never shown much inclination for science, but pressure was now placed on him to go to the best American college and to enroll in the program with direct employment prospects.

This mistaken decision set the boy up for a year of misery. Ironically, the world of scholarship, the path not taken, would be the keystone to McKim's career. In the last two decades of his life, he would work as an educator more than an architect.

In August 1866, a nervous Charlie McKim arrived in Cambridge to begin his admissions examination for the fall term at the Lawrence Scientific School. He was to live with Tom Morgan Rotch and his mother in their house on Kirkland Street near the university. Tom Rotch was going into Harvard College in September. The world of Cambridge was made more comfortable as his old friends the Garrisons were nearby in Roxbury, and Charlie's friend from the walk to Gettysburg, Will Davis, had already begun his second year at the college. After a frantic month of cramming, Tom Rotch and Charlie McKim each took the entrance exam for their schools in the university. Tom sailed through the exam and went on to a distinguished career as a physician, teaching in the Harvard Medical School until his death in 1914. (Charlie's boyhood friend Will Davis also had a distinguished career as a professor of geology at Harvard.) Charlie gained admission to the Scientific School. But he was quickly to learn that he had little aptitude for engineering and that there was a wide social chasm between Harvard College and the Scientific School. His friends were in the classical school, and socially he felt "his" world was there. The Scientific School was a bit déclassé. Added to his miseries was an uneasy sense of being shabby genteel. He wore many clothes made by his sister and his mother at home, while his friends had the luxury of purchasing exquisite items in men's haberdasheries.

The world of the Scientific School quickly showed McKim his weaknesses. Despite constant study, long preparations, and goodwill, he fell behind in all classes except drawing and French. His letters home have an air of quiet defeat as he tries maturely to plot a future to please his family, focusing on European schools of engineering. At first, the mining and engineering school at Freiburg tempted him. Then he learned that one of the Rotch boys had gone to the mining school in Paris. Since his French was vastly superior to his German, he began trying to steer his family around to the idea of sending him to Paris for a year. "School goes awfully hard," he wrote on October 19, 1866, "and I am only now beginning to make headway. If thee should be in the way of getting any knowledge of the Mining School at Paris (now said to be the finest in the world) I should be very glad to know it." He claimed that being a year older than many of his fellow students made it important for him to get into the workforce quickly, and that he could finish the mining school in Paris in one year, thus saving his family the two extra years of tuition at Lawrence Scientific School. The real story, clearly, was that he was on the verge of failure and preferred to leave college rather than be sent home in defeat.

Charlie's academic difficulties and his misery in being at a secondary part of the university made the year an anxious one. "I have to keep up the study by myself, which is very hard work, since from my window I can hear them laughing and talking below . . . and by next Thursday night I shall either be happy or disgraced. The latter is a fearful thought and one which can't be kept out," he wrote. In his letters we see the great highs and lows often associated with depression. These problems appear with increasingly debilitating results as he ages. One can only wonder if Charlie's extra preparatory year may have been a result of the beginnings of this condition and if his parents sensed a problem ahead for their son. But his family did all they could to collect information and guide him to a career he could enjoy. After some research and letters to all the people Miller McKim could think of consulting, the family decided Charlie's plan was reasonable and earmarked an annual sum of seven hundred dollars for him to live in Paris. Miller McKim put great confidence in the opinion of his cousin Joseph Parrish, who had been a teacher before becoming an engineer, and in the son-in-law of William Lloyd Garrison, Henry Villard, a German-born journalist and abolitionist with great ambition. Villard, as a European, was consulted on the practical aspects of living abroad. Unlike most Americans, Miller McKim had been to both Great Britain and France, so he could accept his son moving so far from home.

Somehow, at just the moment when the McKims surrendered to Charlie's plan, he abruptly gave up the idea of the mining school, the École

Centrale des Arts et Manufactures, and set his sights on the architecture school, the École des Beaux-Arts, giving absolutely no explanation for this sudden change. In the scanty accounts of McKim's childhood, we learn of no drawing aptitude. The decision to turn to architecture seems almost impulsive, as if his one successful subject at the Scientific School, isometric drawing, had persuaded him to consider architecture school, just as his skill in French had made him light on Paris. Perhaps McKim's experience of a new house in Llewellyn Park made him think of architecture as a career. We do know that Miller McKim considered building two small, inexpensive suburban houses as an investment for his family and that his abolitionist circle included the architects Russell Sturgis and George Fletcher Babb. The strongest push to architecture, though, may have come from his Harvard experience.

*Henry Villard, a far better abolitionist than railroad baron. His house changed the American aesthetic in domestic urban architecture.*

In the spring of 1867, the first Harvard College graduate to go to architecture school abroad, Henry Hobson Richardson, had a much-reported wedding to a local girl in Boston. Richardson had been very popular as a student, and his marriage may well have brought him to Harvard again. A more likely report of Paris probably came from Robert S. Peabody, a fellow student at Harvard. Peabody was off to the École des Beaux-Arts in Paris in the fall of 1867. He may have introduced McKim to another young man also bound for Paris, Francis W. Chandler. With friends, Paris and the École seemed a lot safer. McKim could escape from Harvard without failure and go abroad with people he knew, making it possible for him to save face in his education.

McKim's only triumph at Harvard was in athletics. Influenced by Karl Follen and his emphasis on the importance of a sound mind and body, Charles McKim was a fine skater, gymnast, baseball player, and cricket batsman. As a student at the Scientific School, McKim spent an hour each day in sport and became well known at Harvard for his skill in baseball. Harvard had an excellent team, the Harvard Nine, but to McKim's regret, Scientific School students were not permitted to join the team. The Harvard trustees may have learned of McKim's baseball skills in the fall of 1866, since the following spring Miller McKim received a personal letter from James Russell Lowell, pleading with him to let his son postpone withdrawal from Harvard and remain at the school for an important match between the Harvard Nine and the Lowell Club. His father acquiesced and allowed Charlie to play the vital game. In this way he ended his Harvard career at a blissful high moment as a star of the triumphant Harvard team. McKim's baseball talents remained a Harvard legend for the rest of the century.

McKIM'S HARVARD GLORY was rapidly replaced by drudgery in the office of an architect, Miller McKim's old ally Russell Sturgis, in New York City. Though Charlie still wanted to study abroad in Paris, his parents insisted that he first have some training in an office in the United States. They probably did not pay for Charlie to join the office; they merely wished their son to try the profession during the summer to prevent his making a blunder, as he had with the Scientific School program. In Sturgis's office, McKim rapidly sized up his prospects without training abroad as nil. Family friends were unlikely to provide him with orders for new building, and so he would remain forever behind a desk as an unimportant person. He wanted escape and advancement prospects which only study abroad could provide.

To Charlie, France seemed the natural choice. America's first architec-

*The Harvard baseball team in the late spring of 1867. McKim is standing at the right. The triumph of this game was the high point of his year at the school.*

tural program in a university (MIT) was just beginning and did not yet have a reputation. England had no system of architectural training open to foreigners. Germany had programs, but his attempts at learning the language were not as successful as his study of French. To add to the attraction, Paris was at the height of its glory as the most admired city in Europe. America as well was consumed by frenzy of admiration for things Parisian, with the French mansard roof crowning fancier buildings and upwardly mobile people imitating life at the court of Louis Napoléon. The wealthy folk at the Second Empire court in Paris included members of the French *nouveaux riches* from industry and the modern world. In other words, the Parisians at court were very much like the American class of newly wealthy people trying to improve their social standing by mingling in higher circles. The court of Napoléon III happily opened up to Americans. Socially aspiring citizens, especially those from the Southern plantations, were recovering from the devastation of the Civil War in the gay scene of Paris. The city McKim wanted to visit was on everyone's lips in 1867, as the third of the great international expositions was taking place that year, making the glamour of Paris an even greater lure.

The McKim family watched their sensible idea of a trial period in Sturgis's office devolve to routine participation and finally gave in. Charlie would not accept anything but a sojourn in Paris. So at the end of the summer, he sailed for Europe. Before he left he begged Russell Sturgis for a letter of introduction to the famous French rational Gothicist E. E. Viollet-le-Duc. But though Sturgis had studied in Europe, he had gone to Munich in 1859 and had no French experience. Perhaps to feel important, he promised the letter, but contrived a series of excuses to delay it for the next three years. No letter ever was written. Probably he was not acquainted with Viollet-le-Duc. Much disappointed, Charlie hoped to encounter the French master in person. But Viollet-le-Duc's lectures at the École des Beaux-Arts two and a half years earlier had culminated in a serious skirmish following which he abandoned the school. McKim never met his idol, but his studies abroad would leave a lasting imprint on his work.

# 2. "A Mighty Serious Thing"

In May 1867, a few months before McKim left for Paris, his sister Lucy and her husband Wendell Garrison welcomed their first child, Lloyd McKim Garrison. As he set off on his voyage Charlie still had ringing in his ears the new mother's appraisal of his decision: ". . . going to France is a mighty Serious Thing." The Atlantic crossing in this day was a major ordeal, but McKim was cheered by the companionship of Peabody; their friend Chandler was to follow just behind them. These friends came from that better social class McKim felt to be his natural associates at Harvard's classical school, although neither man was there while he was in the Scientific School.

Robert Swain Peabody (1845–1917) had already graduated from Harvard the year before McKim arrived. Like the Rotches, he was from New Bedford. After college he had trained in the Boston office of the prominent architects Ware & Van Brunt, and he had decided to go to the École des Beaux-Arts in Paris the next fall. One can only speculate on the source of Peabody's Parisian decision. Certainly Ware knew of the École and its teaching system, even if he had not attended it himself. Ware, who was asked to become the professor of architecture in the first academic course in America at MIT, did travel to Paris to study the methods of instruction at the École. Did Peabody notice the publicity of Richardson's wedding in January of 1867? Probably learning of his planned voyage to Paris, the Rotches may have introduced Peabody to McKim. It may even have been Peabody who convinced Charlie to give up the École Centrale for the Beaux-Arts.

Peabody must have been a persuasive person, as he also brought along his office mate, Francis W. Chandler (1844–1926), a slightly older man who had served with the Massachusetts volunteers in the Civil War after only a year at Harvard. Chandler was placed as a paying student with Ware & Van Brunt in 1864, rising to the position of draftsman by 1866. He set sail for Liverpool on September 25, 1867, on the boat *City of Washington,* arriving in Paris on the fourteenth of October to join Peabody and McKim, who had been there about a month. The friends shared rooms at 1 Rue des Fleurs for the next two years as all three studied at the Atelier Daumet, which was the day-to-day part of the educational process.* The three young men then sought admission to the École des Beaux-Arts, becoming, it seems, the fifth, sixth, and seventh Americans to go on to study architecture after Richard Morris Hunt, Henry Hobson Richardson, Sidney V. Stratton, and Alfred H. Thorp. Hunt and Richardson had returned to the United States and set up practices in New York City; each was on his way to a career as one of the two major architects of post–Civil War America. Alfred Thorp settled in New York City as a Frenchified dandy. Of Sidney Stratton more will be read in a moment.

The success of Hunt and Richardson showed that the École could yield career dividends beyond those an American boy could achieve by paying to work in the office of an established local man—a practice that had not been widespread in America anyway. "European training" brought a special cachet to the architect. As Americans still felt culturally inferior, a lick of European polish could greatly impress those who found the transmission of that tradition important. Hunt and Richardson returned to the United States able to discuss not only the architecture and art of Europe, but also its music, language, gastronomy, and manners. This air helped them to convince monied Americans that they could put some of this European gloss on their designs. Both the architect and the client would bathe in a brighter light, and show cultural superiority over native-trained, often provincial architects and their clients, who tended to receive watered-down replicas of perhaps slightly out-of-style European precedents. The architects trained abroad could bring their patrons into the world of high contemporary Europe by drafting new designs in keeping with the latest work in Paris. Such architects could also bring well-off Americans interpretations of older European buildings calculated to give clients a sense of fitting in with the greatness of the past through a sophis-

*Pupils worked within an office and received critical reception from older students and the master (Daumet here); lectures and competitions were held at the École itself.

ticated Americanization of a classic moment in European architecture. McKim, Peabody, and Chandler were to do precisely this for their clients—make finer buildings to help Americans see themselves as joining the sophistication and culture of Europe.

The American third man to enter the École, just half a year before the arrival of McKim and Peabody, was the seemingly brilliant young man from Natchez, Mississippi, Sidney Vanuxem Stratton. Though Stratton's star would climb for a time, unlike the other early men at the École, he would see it extinguished quickly, leaving him relatively unknown to the world.

IN PARIS, PEABODY, CHANDLER, AND McKIM lived together, worked together, inspired one another, and traveled together, taking vacations as architectural tourists and bracing each other at life's pitfalls until the Franco-Prussian War sent them home, Peabody and Chandler to Boston and McKim to New York. Peabody and Chandler remained lifelong best friends, but despite the closeness of the Parisian years, McKim did not keep up with Chandler and only slightly with Peabody. Rival practices killed the friendship formed in the fields and on the frozen ponds of the parks, where the Americans amused the Parisians with their skating expertise and innings of baseball.

The fourth member of their circle was Stratton, who would go to New York as McKim did. He became a best friend, client-supplier, almost partner, and trusted advisor until mental illness forced him home to Natchez about twenty years later.

The Paris that Stratton, Peabody, Chandler, and McKim experienced was wildly exciting, indeed dazzling to these Americans. The city was large, and replete with royal, palatial, and civic buildings far in excess of what they would have seen before. The street life, cafés, theaters, music, food, and museums all energized these visitors. It seemed to them that almost anything they wanted to see, do, or eat was possible. McKim pushed Peabody to join his health routine, rowing on the Seine in the summer and flying through the air on trapezes in an acrobatic course the friends enjoyed in winter. They played baseball in the Luxembourg Gardens, and on the few cold days of winter when the lakes of the Bois de Boulogne froze over, McKim executed perfect figure eights for the awestruck viewers. He was a superlative skater, graceful and fluid, able to glide in long sweeping movements which made him fascinating to the French, and a magnet to Americans visiting Paris.

Those who flocked around McKim included wealthy young women "finishing" their education in the court of Louis Napoléon. Lucy Oelrichs, the daughter of a Baltimore shipping magnate, was given skating lessons by young Charlie, whom she described as fine and noble, already discoursing on the role of beauty in life. The young McKim was very interested in finding a woman to share his life. It is even possible that his insistence on going to Paris might have had to do with following a lady going abroad, as cryptic portions of his letters allude to romantic liaisons. Perhaps "Mackim," as he was known to the French, had a crush on Lucy Oelrichs. On his return, the humble remuneration of his first job was used to purchase a pair of lady's ice skates with silver-plated hardware, which were nestled in a small leopard-skin bag trimmed in brown velvet. He had them monogrammed with her initials by Tiffany's, then sent to Miss Oelrichs. This romance went no further. Lucy Oelrichs married an American of patrician breeding, Augustus Jay, and the couple were among McKim's best friends in his last years. A more serious romance in Paris, promoted by his old friend Tom Rotch, took place between McKim and Tom's sister Anne Morgan Rotch, his senior by two years. The lure of financial support from the Rotch family to continue his study abroad may have been an inducement. But McKim's family, reacting strongly and rapidly, forbade the liaison, as the age difference seemed important to them. Names of other young women who would figure in future events float by, including the beautiful young Annie Bigelow, a friend of the Rotch family. At this time she was much sought after by McKim's friend Will Davis.

During the summer holidays of 1868, McKim, Peabody, and Chandler spent the week of July fourth paddling an outrigger along the Seine to Rouen. The young men found the buildings of the distant past a revelation. Schooled by the taste of the day in the United States for the High Victorian Gothic, the three were inspired to seek out real medieval buildings, which they did with joy. Seeing buildings made so long before was intoxicating to the young men, and this orgy of architectural inspiration would continue to guide their careers back home. They became the interpreters of European architecture to rich Americans, able to describe fluently buildings from the Middle Ages to the eighteenth century and to customize them for a new audience who believed the torch of Old World greatness was now being passed to the deserving and achieving shores of the New World.

We learn of the life of a student in the Atelier Daumet as seen through McKim's eyes in a letter written to his adopted sister Annie's husband,

Fred Dennis, who then owned and ran a small paper in Auburn, New York. In this letter of August 31, 1868, one of very few that survive, McKim tells of his daily walk:

> Imagine, reader, that you and I are walking along one of those great boulevards which divide Paris like so many arteries . . . and get into the old town, as yet untouched by Napoleon III, and still ancient in appearance and manners and as foreign to the side we have just left as centuries could make it. . . . Our destination is on the Rue du Four St Germain. Beyond that . . . and away to the rear of the quadrangle, is our studio, or *atelier,* from which every two months, competitive designs are sent to the School of Fine Arts [École des Beaux Arts], placed on exhibition, and awarded prizes. . . . On a series of long tables are stretched the designs; and now if you will figure to yourself above each board a cigarette sticking into the mouth of a long haired, unkempt "scrub," dressed in a gray blouse, you may gain some idea of a French student. . . . But over in yonder corner is a fellow, who in his way, is a genius. . . . Taking a T-square in his hand and mounting a box . . . begins the opera of "Don Giovanni."

It was at the back of quadrangle that the French architectural master Honoré Daumet ran a studio in rooms facing the courtyard. Daumet was given a fee by his students for criticizing the work they did during long hours at the studio tables. Usually some twenty to thirty of them worked on a competitive design in the studio to be sent to the École des Beaux-Arts, put on exhibition, and judged for prize-worthiness. The studio was a tall square room with excellent sunlight, but it was far from a peaceful environment. Pranks by students against each other punctuated the day on a regular basis in the cigarette-smoke-laden air. Many students sang as they worked, with the more aggressive ones putting on a version of a full-scale opera and gesturing dramatically with a T square. This particular signature of life in the Paris atelier was to become a feature of artistic life in the United States, as American artists took up singing in their studios. When the day ended and the light failed, McKim related that the students flocked to the café Estaminet du Senat for a long, pleasurable evening.

Among his fellow students in the atelier, McKim seems to have formed a friendship with the young Frantz Jourdain (1847–1935). Frantz-Calixte-Raphaël-Ferdinand-Marie Jourdain was just McKim's age, born to a musical family in Antwerp, Belgium; his father was a singer, his mother a musician and poet. The family was quite similar to McKim's—a gentle, intellectual couple in straitened circumstances with strong ties to social causes. Ferdinand Jourdain, Frantz's father, had been much involved in the social unrest in Europe of 1848, which was to its place and time a political statement akin to Miller McKim's involvement with the abolitionist cause. The young Jourdain entered Daumet's studio in 1866 and the École in the same years as McKim.

Just before the academic year began, he asked McKim to join him on a trip down the Loire to the château of his aunt late in September as the harvest came in. McKim accepted happily and wrote the trip up for the Auburn newspaper, leaving out all the names of those involved. The account began with a description of the two men in the French train bound for a twelve-hour journey to Château Neuf near Angers, capital of the province of Anjou. It is likely that the château they visited is that known as Angers, a museum of tapestries today, with a core going back to the thirteenth century. To McKim this was an amazing experience worthy of a book—a tale of the courtly eighteenth-century manners of the château owner and her servants. The letter offers a wonderful tidbit of social history as the American views truly old-fashioned rural French custom and agriculture.

The friendship between McKim and Jourdain did not survive over time, although perhaps we can assume that the "small inheritance" Jourdain refers to—enough for him to set himself up as an architect in Paris in 1872—came from the fat, old Aunt M whom he had visited so courteously four years earlier. Jourdain became a journalist and an advocate of contemporary metal architecture such as the Galerie des Machines of the 1889 Paris Exposition. Jourdain and McKim shared an admiration for Viollet-le-Duc, but in later years it became clear that Jourdain was interested in the structural issues raised by that author, while McKim was interested in his lectures on history. From Viollet-le-Duc they would veer off in two directions, Jourdain to the structure of buildings, McKim to the façade.

Paris for McKim was wonderful as an adventure in living, but tedious in the atelier. The École had been torn apart in the winter of 1864 over Viollet-le-Duc's role, and his sacking resulted in severe economic constraints for the school. The forces gaining control were not to McKim's liking, sharing neither his taste for medieval precedent nor the message of rationalism given by Russell Sturgis at home. He also found the program at the École unsuitable for what he imagined would be his practice in the future: It was too grand, too focused on governmental building for a young man expecting to build small suburban houses back home. Most devastating of all was his failure to win even a mention in the competitions sponsored by the École. His friend Peabody did gain this honor in the spring of 1869, while McKim again fell short. The constant mediocre reception of his work was distressing, but life was so good and his family at home so understanding that he soldiered on.

The only other noteworthy moment in McKim's student career was the closed-mindedness he displayed when his brother-in-law, Wendell Garrison, sent him a letter of introduction to Hippolyte Rodrigues, a leader of the Jewish Reform movement in Paris. Wendell attempted to get him to meet Rodrigues and his circle, but Charlie brought the letter back unpresented. Unlike his parents and sister Lucy, who was then trying to preserve Negro dialect by recording the songs of the former slaves, McKim did not embrace the world of "others." Perhaps Miller McKim noticed this, as he makes a point of mentioning his socializing with his Jewish neighbors, two families living in Llewellyn Park, in his letter to Charlie; later he tells his son to study synagogue design in Paris and England, as it may become a useful skill in the United States. Miller McKim was friendly with William Henry Furness of Philadelphia, whom he knew from abolition meetings years earlier, and he notes in another letter to his son that Furness's son, the young architect Frank Furness, had just begun a good-sized synagogue. Miller McKim was quite astute in noting the need for training in synagogue architecture and suburban house design, since Americans had little knowledge of how to fill the growing requests for buildings of this kind.

In the spring of 1869, letters from the McKims urge Charlie to travel to England and enter an architect's office for half a year to gain some of the British experience considered supreme at home. His father had acquired the impression that English architects were the finest, while those from France and Germany were "only draftsman." This must have been discouraging to Charlie, who had felt unless he went to Paris he would always be a draftsman in Sturgis's office. Then, in another discussion with the Furnesses, Frank Furness said that Paris was gaining status in the profession. This caused Miller McKim to update his advice. The new idea became for Charlie to accompany Peabody and Chandler, who were going home via England, on a visit to that country, but then to return to Paris and reenter school in the fall. This he happily did.

In the late spring of 1869, Charlie crossed the Channel with Peabody, armed with a letter from the Anglo-American architect Frederick Clarke Withers to his brother Robert Withers, who was in architectural practice in the city of London. This introduction McKim was willing to use. He had a wonderful summer in England, receiving hospitality from many and forming a bond with English people whom, he remarked in his letters home, he greatly liked. One such Englishman was R. Phene Spiers. Spiers was an Oxford-born man from a mercantile family who had gone to Paris as the first English student at the École des Beaux-Arts. In Paris, he had formed a close friendship with H. H. Richardson when the latter entered the school. He now befriended McKim. They met at the new Architectural Association in London. The friendship blossomed over their mutual enjoyment of cricket. Spiers invited McKim to join in games, where the young American, a hero in a cricket match in Philadelphia in the spring of 1866, put on an excellent performance. Spiers is said to have done a major professional favor by introducing the young McKim to the work of the English architect Richard Norman Shaw and his partner W. Eden Nesfield. Although there is no direct evidence that Spiers actually did this, the two Englishmen were then beginning to build houses that were starting to attract the notice of the younger designers; the work of Nesfield & Shaw was so important to the young McKim that it seems likely he knew of Leyswood or Glen Andred, then at an early stage of construction. With Miller McKim's insistence on learning what was new in England in his

*R. N. Shaw's Leyswood in Sussex, England, designed 1866 and executed 1868–69.*
*Mostly demolished, this house was reproduced in periodicals of the day and had a broad influence on English and American architects in the early 1870s.*

mind, McKim may have concentrated on Nesfield & Shaw, whose designs would have a profound influence on his work in the United States throughout his lifetime. McKim traveled in Britain, visiting the Gothic sites before returning to France, alone, on August 1, 1869, now an honorable member of the Architectural Association.

When McKim reached France, he began a ten-day tour of Normandy, the northern French region so popular with the court of Louis Napoléon. Along the Channel coast, summer visitors now flocked to what had once been a quiet agricultural region. Tourists had come to Normandy from the 1830s onward, and English architects sketched the giant vernacular farm buildings and the manor houses. Deauville and Trouville became resorts. The trip to these villages had been arduous until the railroad pushed through from Paris to Rouen, and again in 1854 to the coastal towns. Visitors found cool breezes, picturesque vistas, and great fishing in the region in the early days. The area especially attracted the newly made men of wealth in industrial France who did not have the loyalty to their home districts of the landed aristocratic class. They would build commodious, wooden-framed summer villas along the coast from the mid-century forward. The new houses often used elements of the vernacular buildings of the region, such as brick infilling between timbers and decorative woodwork, to create a harmonious appearance and reflect the older buildings nearby. Such coastal houses were also being built in northern Germany. The new villas appear taller and more vertical in contrast to the horizontal appearance of the older farm complexes and manors of the region, which sprawl heavier and lower to the land.

In Normandy McKim also saw a few stone châteaux not too dissimilar from those he had visited in the Loire. The château as a grand house type was undergoing a revival at this time in France, particularly among newly wealthy families in the vineyard regions, where successful wine production seemed to mandate the building of a château on their properties. McKim must have noticed that the new Normande villas in the wooden vernacular style were similar to those he would have seen Hunt building in Newport during his college visit. But he was looking mainly at the older farm complexes with their asymmetrical massing and aggregate appearance. He must have reveled in their picturesque and ample roof areas, which appealed to the medieval taste he had developed in the Victorian Gothic world of Russell Sturgis's office.

McKim was surely also aware of the grand new Hotel des Roches Noires built atop the bluffs over the ocean at Trouville. The great resort hotel, considered the king of local hostelries, would be painted by Monet

LEFT: *Vernacular Norman house at Thiers. The English and Americans flocked to the coast of Normandy in the summers of the mid-nineteenth century.*

BELOW LEFT: *A Norman street in a snapshot probably taken by McKim.*

BELOW RIGHT: *McKim photograph of a twin-towered house from his study tour of Normandy, ca. 1869.*

and other artists who flocked to the Norman coast in summer. It was in the coastal cities that McKim would encounter the casino—a center for entertainment in the town that attracted tourists and seasonal visitors alike. The casino was originally a center for theater, dance, and music: a place for amusement and social connections, not gambling. The gambling casino would develop in the mid-nineteenth century far to the south on the Riviera in Monte Carlo. In due course, McKim would help bring the pleasures of the European social casino to the East Coast in the 1880s.

Following his sojourn in this fashionable resort region at the height of its season, McKim traveled alone to Germany, Austria, and down to Florence in Italy. Now deeply committed to the profession of architecture, he studied, drew, and photographed buildings, keeping a record of what he had seen for his future work back home. Money as ever was tight, and he had to return to Paris without seeing Venice or Rome, a serious omission in his years of study. Back in Paris, he roomed with a Robert Shaw of Boston while returning to the École in the vain hope of a mention in one final *equisse,* a competition held at the school. His time abroad was now coming to an end, as Miller McKim pressed his son to return home in the spring of 1870, setting a May 1 deadline. It was the Franco-Prussian War that would finally persuade McKim, forcing him back across the Atlantic and to Llewellyn Park. There he had a joyous reunion and bonding with Lucy's son, Lloyd McKim Garrison, who was to be his favorite nephew. His affection was returned by the child, who listened to his uncle's adventures and amused the family by telling his childish versions of his uncle's stories from his trip to Europe.

# 3. To Become an Architect

Once McKim had returned to Llewellyn Park, he had to make a final decision about his future base. Taking his father's advice that their old home, Philadelphia, was a great but provincial city, he selected New York; in his father's words, it was a real metropolis. This decision meant passing up a certain job with Frank Furness, who by now was making a name for himself in Philadelphia as an innovative and idiosyncratic designer. Since McKim was far more traditional than was Furness, it is surely fortunate that they did not join forces. The obvious New York City choice, after his European preparation, was the office of his father's friend, Sturgis and Babb, where he had begun his career three years earlier. Sturgis was now free from his early partner, P. B. Wight, and was bringing in plenty of work doing "color" interiors for his clients with great success. Mid-century interior design extolled strongly painted colors and patterns on the walls. This was indeed the height of Sturgis's career, so why did McKim not return there? Probably, McKim calculated that since George Babb was there as a powerful second to Sturgis, it would take a long while to advance from under the wings of two such accomplished figures.

Instead, he chose to go to Henry Hobson Richardson, the Harvard graduate who had preceded him at the École. Richardson's wedding trip to Boston has already been mentioned and may have resulted in the two meeting in Cambridge. We also know that Frederick Law Olmsted, then at the height of his career and at work on Central Park in New York, was a friend of Miller McKim's. Olmsted was part of the Freedman's Relief

Association and was active in the creation of *The Nation.* He also knew
Richardson well, and the two could have met through this mutual friend.
In any case, McKim promptly presented himself to Richardson, now at
the onset of his great and short career, at 6 Hanover Square in New York
City. Richardson received him kindly, but in his deep stutter told McKim
that he had a single draftsman and no work. He offered a glimmer of hope,
however, noting that there was a competition entry still alive for the Brattle Square Church in Boston. If he won, he promised to take the young
man aboard. When news of his success in the competition leaked out, he
was true to his word, and McKim joined Richardson on May 1, 1870, at a
sum of eight dollars a week.

RICHARDSON SHARED McKim's training in Paris and had also made a
deep study of European architecture, including the manors of Normandy.
It is likely that he was becoming aware of the work of Richard Norman
Shaw and William Eden Nesfield, which McKim may have seen only ten
months earlier. The two must have discussed these residential buildings,
as they would become the stepping-stones to the new domestic vernacular
houses the two were to create. We know that there were photos of Shaw's
buildings of the 1870s in the Richardson office, but we cannot be certain
when they were brought in or who brought them. There were also photos
of Norman farm complexes, but again we do not know if these date from
the early years of McKim's stay with Richardson.

Richardson was a great architect with a fertile visual sense, but, surprisingly perhaps, he had no interest in drawing his designs. His method was
to make small conceptual designs on paper, then turn over the work to
others to be completed. Often he would then give oral instruction to his
assistants, who would develop the master's ideas. McKim was there for
this phase in the Brattle Square Church project and would be there to help
draft the competition entry for nearby Trinity Church in Boston's Back
Bay. For two years he labored for Richardson, who was now growing phys-
ically and professionally into "the Great Mogul," as he was nicknamed.
From Richardson's example he would gain the confidence to work with
assistants, having seen what it was to give instruction as the hands of others produced one's own design. Also from Richardson, McKim learned the
importance of socializing and working with clients. Richardson was very
skilled at getting his way with both clients and building committees, and
McKim would follow his lead; in later life his nickname was "Charles the
Charmer."

One can only wonder how McKim's parents took to the choice of

Richardson. The elder McKims were pragmatic about the need to help their son launch himself and overcome his weaknesses, which probably kept them from objecting to a connection to the architect from Louisiana. Richardson's family had settled in the South in the early nineteenth century and become affluent in the days of slave ownership. Indeed, the Richardson family were slave owners, the natural enemies of Miller McKim. Richardson himself went north in his second year of college to enroll at Harvard, and from the days of the Civil War on he never returned to the South. He did not return home even for the death and funeral of his mother. Though popular at Harvard, he seems to have remained politically neutral in the Cambridge of the period. It appears that Richardson faced the issue of his family's involvement in slavery by ignoring it totally. The McKims followed suit, and we see no evidence of any discussion of the issue in the family papers.

Into the office of Richardson just after McKim's arrival came a fresh, new, and very young face: that of Stanford White. Then seventeen, he came in the articled fashion of the day, but without any payment to the master. The son of an impoverished New York City intellectual and dandy, he had had a poor education in the New York public schools and could not afford college. With an introduction to Richardson from the painter John La Farge, and from Frederick Law Olmsted, young Stanford White came to Richardson as a lowly beginner. He did have one advantage: he was a natural, self-taught artist who could draw far better than either Richardson or McKim. White's father often wrote for journals and newspapers, was a regular at *The Nation,* and had taken on the abolitionist issue as the Civil War neared, writing strong letters to newspapers abroad castigating Southern plantation owners' labor practices. Thus, White and McKim came from similar belief systems.

McKim saw himself as a qualified architect at this point and had a card made with his name, identifying himself as an architect with Gambrill & Richardson (Gambrill being a New York partner of Richardson at the time) at 6 Hanover Square, New York. These business cards were made for distribution to Miller McKim's circle, as Charles hoped for his own commissions to start an independent practice. He began his personal career with a barn for his father in 1870, designed in the manner of the architect of the family house, A. J. Davis, but no longer extant. Was this perhaps an omen for a career which in time was to base everything on precedent?

For Richardson, McKim drew up the Brattle Square Church, which still stands in Boston and is affectionately known as the church of the "Holy Bean Blowers" after the sculptural detail of the trumpet-blowing angels on its tower. It was built for a Congregational community with a long history in Boston, which was now moving to the newly created land-fill district in the Back Bay. Many architectural critics believe that this design ushered in a cohesive period in Richardson's career and credit McKim for his part in making a clear and integrated design. McKim also drew up plans for the Buffalo State Asylum for the Insane, while White acted as a site man in Buffalo. He did the drawings for alterations to New York City's "horse set" hotel, Hotel Brunswick on Twenty-sixth Street at the top of Madison Square Park, now demolished; and for Richardson's Hampden County Courthouse in Springfield, Massachusetts. In addition, McKim worked on the Phoenix Insurance building in Hartford and the Andrews house in Newport (both demolished).

McKim worked hard for Richardson, learning the practical ins and outs of an artistic office. Richardson put a high premium on finishing the buildings according to the Beaux-Arts principles they had learned in Paris, with muralists, sculptors, glassmakers and other fine arts men incorporated into the program if the budget allowed. The sharing of work

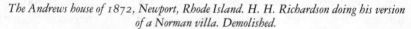

*The Andrews house of 1872, Newport, Rhode Island. H. H. Richardson doing his version of a Norman villa. Demolished.*

with sculptors began at Brattle Square Church. The tower of the church was designed to have sculpture by F. A. Bartholdi, soon to be known in the United States for his Statue of Liberty. Richardson had hoped to hire the painter John La Farge to do the interior design, but a tight budget ruled out an "artistic" interior. Both Richardson and McKim were wedded to the concept of beauty and to the cooperation of artists in American buildings. McKim would bring this goal to a crescendo in his later large commissions.

In 1872 Richardson decided to try his luck with another Boston ecclesiastical competition—this one for a church to accommodate the preaching of the late nineteenth century's great broad-church Episcopalian minister, Phillips Brooks. This tall clergyman, whose sermons were said to be electric, had pulled in great numbers to the old church on Summer Street. The growing crowds proved the correctness of the church committee's decision to invite Phillips Brooks to Boston from his old parish in Philadelphia, where in 1868 Brooks had written the Christmas carol "O Little Town of Bethlehem." Brooks was such an asset to his Boston congregation that the vestry purchased land in the new Back Bay and held a competition for the design of the new church.

On June 1, 1872, Richardson's firm won the competition on the strength of McKim's drawings for the church. These original drawings do not seem to have survived, but they may have outlined a forceful stone building with a high corner tower not dissimilar to the Brattle Square Church then rising nearby. As the summer of 1872 arrived, the idea of the prominent tower over the lantern seems to have been added to the plans. The decision was made after Richardson inspected the the planned church plot and noticed an enticing neighboring empty triangle of land. He saw the possibility for a much larger and more impressive building complex if the church were to purchase it, and therefore pressed the vestry and congregation for rapid action. Richardson's wishes were honored, and the property was bought. This rolled the ball back into the architect's court, as he now had to redo the church and complex to make better use of the whole property.

At this moment Richardson became ill, beginning what would be a lifelong battle with renal disease, and he was confined to his home in Staten Island for the summer and early fall. Richardson, whose design skills would be legendary, was attaining notable physical proportion. He loved the good things of life, including food and wine in great abundance. Wags would compare the increasingly massive size of his work to his own enlarging girth. The physical problems arising from Richardson's gas-

*Richardson's office.*

tronomy exacerbated the chronic nephritis, or Bright's disease, which would claim his life in 1886. His assistant on this job, Stanford White, would be afflicted with the same disease in his later years.

The expectation of work in the office and then the dampening of that prospect with Richardson's illness helped McKim pull away from the firm; he would strike out on his own in 1872. McKim's work on the first Trinity design would be eclipsed by the Trinity we know today. The revised design was handled for Richardson by Stanford White, who, with only two years in the office, was now able to take over McKim's role as the person who could transform Richardson's words into a drawing. White also had the benefit of some experience as a site man, which McKim did not have. As an apprentice, he had traveled for Richardson to Buffalo, Hartford, and other locations to study the work and be prepared to brief Richardson about the progress of new jobs. He assumed this role rapidly despite having no formal education for it. In the fall of 1872, White would work with Richardson to rethink Trinity, then assist him in creating the "art" church of his Beaux-Arts ideals, using John La Farge and others to assemble one of the United States' greatest buildings.

IN 1871, WHILE THE BRATTLE SQUARE CHURCH was under way, Richardson moved his office to 57 Broadway at Exchange Place. The new offices were in a five-story iron-fronted building favored by architects. It had generous windows on each floor of the Broadway frontage; they were so big that they swung out on a central metal dowel. The building must have been fairly new when Richardson took space there; the upper floors, reached by a wooden staircase, were probably hard to rent, and as the rooms were well lit and cheap they were a haven for architects. But behind the staircase were small dark rooms facing the back, which few would want. It was into these dim rooms that Charles McKim's ambition led him as he secured his first commissions. He informed Richardson that he would begin his own practice in these back rooms while giving over his place to the young Stanford White, who had so rapidly moved into a trusted position in the office.

Though McKim was taking a risk by striking out on his own, he felt it was justified by his recent work. Completing the plans and entry for the Trinity Church competition was a large responsibility. McKim had labored over it in friendly rivalry with his old friend from his Paris days, Sidney Stratton, who on his return from Paris had gone into the *other* École office, the more established practice run by Richard Morris Hunt. As Hunt's head draftsman, Stratton had worked over Hunt's entry. We can only assume McKim and Stratton did not discuss specifics of the competition with each other as their friendship grew, but McKim must have been pleased when the church vestry selected the Richardson design. The commission for the Boston building would galvanize Richardson's career and

*Francis Blake house, 1875, an early and awkward house by the youthful McKim. Demolished.*

give him parity with Hunt as a leading American architect. As Richardson received this prize job, McKim must have felt he had finally won the "mention" he had longed for in Paris. With such a success and an able man like White to be handed the Trinity work, McKim felt confident that he was leaving Richardson at a good time.

Newport played a major role in McKim's life in 1872, as the young man's life changed on another front. All thought of a union with Miss Rotch had faded, but through the Rotch family, with whom McKim had remained intimate, he now found a new love, the beautiful and very young Annie Bigelow of New York and Newport, daughter of John William Bigelow and his wife, Anna Maria Bigelow. It seems clear that with work now coming directly to him, McKim felt emboldened to take on a new romance. The Bigelows came from Worcester, but had settled in New York when John became a cotton trader. We cannot be certain where John Bigelow found his cotton during the Civil War, but by 1864 he had made a great profit, enough for him to buy Bayside, the biggest house at the Point in Newport, where he and his family would summer. The house had a large porch facing the water, which McKim described as a "bully piazza." Directly to the north of the Bigelow house was the house of John and Elizabeth Auchincloss on Washington Street. Can this have been the house altered or added to by McKim in 1872?

By 1874, McKim had received several commissions from friends of his father in New Jersey, one in New York, and, perhaps, an alteration in Newport. His year at Harvard led to a request to build a house at Worcester, Massachusetts.

The practice was beginning well, but McKim could not handle all the work coming to him. It must have seemed an ideal opportunity when William Mead returned from study in Florence in 1872. Mead paid a call on Russell Sturgis, for whom he had briefly worked at 57 Broadway, hoping to be hired by his old mentor. Sturgis was out of town, and Mead wandered into McKim's office. The two had never met, as Mead had gone to Sturgis just after McKim went to Paris, but Mead knew McKim's name. He must have expressed to McKim his hope that an old Amherst buddy would be sending him some work; when McKim indicated that he could use a bit of a hand, the two decided to share space and work in a loose and amicable way. There was no formal partnership at this time.

The two men worked together on a competition entry of 1874 for the City Hall in Providence, Rhode Island, but did not win (later, the firm would build the State Capitol in Providence). Mead brought in a job at Lake Cayuga in upper New York State for the Cayuga Lake Hotel. The

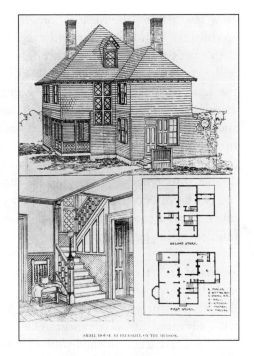

RIGHT: *A house at Peekskill, New York, perhaps the one built for Dwight Herrick, a friend of Mead and McKim, in 1877. The design is rather conventional.*

BELOW: *An early commission for McKim and Mead at Amherst, Massachusetts, likely for William Fearing, ca. 1878. Again, a rather banal building. It would be a stretch to believe McKim and Mead would become stellar figures as architects.*

single image of the hotel in the firm's records shows a building whose corner resembled the contemporary domestic commission McKim was completing for Francis Blake. Mead's only other known commission of this era was the house for his Amherst classmate and lifelong friend, the attorney Dwight S. Herrick. Members of the Herrick family lived in Chesterfield,

New Hampshire, the Meads' hometown. The personal relationship Mead established with Herrick would pass to McKim as well. Herrick served as both men's private attorney throughout his life and made out McKim's will. The Herrick house in Peekskill is extant and is characteristic of the buildings each man was designing in the early 1870s. The steep, angular roofs are a major feature of the houses, which have a purposeful and plan-driven asymmetry. Bargeboards and wooden trim provide signature touches that distinguish McKim and Mead's work from that of the builders' houses of the day. Almost all their designs feature large usually double-story fenestration behind the interior staircase. Despite the touches the two architects used to elevate their work, few would find their designs much beyond those available in the pattern books used by carpenters and builders of the period. They were not off to a great start as innovators.

A FORMAL ENGAGEMENT between the twenty-six-year-old architect and the much younger Annie Bigelow was announced in April 1873, despite the worrying health of Miller McKim, who was declining rapidly with advanced prostate cancer. The joy of a successful engagement to a beautiful and accomplished woman whose family could advance McKim's career was tempered by his father's terminal illness and increasing national economic difficulties. The economic depression that began in 1873 would last five years.

The work on the Blake house advanced, and Charles spun between the Manhattan office, Llewellyn Park, Boston, and Newport, visiting home as much as he could. In early June 1874, Miller McKim seemed to improve, and Charles traveled east, but about the tenth of the month, his father sank into a painful final stage, with morphine being administered in the house in Llewellyn Park. A frantic message did get Charles and the Garrisons to McKim's bedside, and Charles was there when his father died on the morning of June 13. Lucretia Mott came to the house to prepare the body for the funeral, while family friend Mrs. Kenyon Cox took Wendell and Charles away as the burial was arranged. Miller McKim was buried in Rosedale Cemetery in Orange, New Jersey, where members of Stanford White's family may also have been interred.

# 4. THE MARRIAGE AND NEWPORT

John William Bigelow (1824–1883) and his wife Anna Maria (Barton) Bigelow, the couple soon to be McKim's in-laws, lived on a sheltered drive in Newport. Their house, Bayside, was the largest and grandest in the area, with a view of the harbor. Built in 1861 for a Mrs. Murray, the big house with its lovely porch provided the setting for the parties that accompanied the wedding, which was held on a Thursday, October 1, 1874. The wedding on a weekday may reflect the sadness of the mourning period for Miller McKim or, perhaps, the non-Episcopalian values of the groom's family.* Sarah McKim had raised her two children in Quaker tradition—indeed, Charles used the idiom of "thee" and "thou" in his letters until just about this time. McKim selected a Unitarian clergyman, the Reverend O. B. Frothingham, to lead the service at the wedding, while the bride's family asked the local minister William S. Child to perform the ceremony. McKim would repay Reverend Child by designing for him a small schoolhouse that still stands at the Point, a few blocks south of the Bigelow house.

Little is known about the wedding other than that there was a wonderful reception given in the crisp fall weather on the porch of the house. Annie was a beautiful bride with a perfect face, long hair, and a calling to the arts nursed by private school in New York and travel to France as a teenager. During the reception, Annie was joined on the porch steps by

*There does seem to be a custom of Thursday weddings at this time.

*McKim project for a schoolhouse published in* The New York Sketch Book
*of 1873. McKim affected an elaborate logo in the lower right-hand corner.*

her elder brother, William Blake Bigelow, then twenty-two and about to
set off for Paris to study at the École des Beaux-Arts, doubtless influenced
by his new brother-in-law. William Bigelow was well known as a sailboat
enthusiast in Newport; he had begun college in 1868, then transferred to
MIT in 1869 with the class of 1872, but left in 1871 without a degree. It
is unclear if Bigelow took any classes in the new architectural program
at MIT.

While courting Annie in Newport in 1873, McKim designed a schoolhouse project published in *The New York Sketch Book*. It resembles a big
dovecote, similar to those McKim had seen in France. Though not built in
this form, the plan may have resulted in the more modest school building
McKim later designed for Child at the Point.

After the wedding McKim and Annie lingered in Newport—the economy was now weak, and little work was likely to come into McKim's
hands. For his father-in-law, McKim built a barn and stable, still standing
on Second Street behind what was then the family house. McKim's Newport neighbor asked him to turn the eighteenth-century Hunter house,
which had become a boardinghouse, into a private residence again.

The young couple would return to New York to an apartment house
built by George Da Cunha, about whom we know little but who seems to
have been a pioneer in the development of apartment houses in New York
City in the 1870s and 1880s. Richardson had a connection to Da Cunha

through his office, so the young Charles may have already known the developer when he rented an apartment for his bride. McKim had lived at 236 East Thirteenth Street. The couple moved to 46 West Forty-fifth Street. In the summer, the McKims would reside in a small cottage near Annie's family on Washington Street in Newport.*

THE POINT IN NEWPORT, once the home of Quakers, now had fancy new homes of the Auchinclosses, Bigelows, and Stanfords, but it was still the location of a good number of eighteenth-century town houses built by Newport's leading figures a century earlier. The eighteenth-century merchants and artisans liked the protected inner bay shore where storms did not do great damage. The Newport gentry built wooden versions of British buildings—indeed the Newporters were an Anglophilic lot. Newport had sided with the British during the Revolutionary War, which effectively killed business for this fourth city of the Republic after the Revolution. Those Newport families trying to con-

*The schoolhouse as built for the Reverend Child at the Point, Newport, Rhode Island, 1873–74.*

tinue in the economic mainstream moved to New York City to improve their fortune. Newport was left behind with no economic engine for rebuilding. Thus, poverty proved to be the great preserver. The eighteenth-century houses of the Point were left alone.

In the 1830s, a group of summer people, many from families earlier transplanted from Newport to New York, began to spend summer days in the cool, breezy, inexpensive, and fairly empty Newport. Joining the New Yorkers were planters of the Caribbean and the American South who remembered the pleasant weather their ancestors had enjoyed in the eighteenth century when they sailed to Newport for the summer. Similarly in France, the 1830s saw the fishing villages of Deauville and Trouville fill

*The Bigelow house was demolished years ago, although the stable still stands. The porch of the Bigelow house was placed on a neighboring property. Oddly enough, the "bully piazza," as McKim called it, still exists even though the house is gone.

*The Bigelow stable designed by their new son-in-law, McKim, ca. 1875.*
*Although the house is gone, the stable remains.*

with vacationers. The first twenty years of life in these new summer colonies were easy, with many visitors residing in local houses as boarders or renting vacant cottages from farmers or sea captains. By the 1840s hotels began to appear at Newport, but not in pasturelands or at the Point. The commodious wooden hotels were built above the business district of Newport, on a high rocky bluff midway between the protected wharf area and the open ocean, close to the old Jewish cemetery.

THE SOCIAL LIFE OF THE DAY was simple but comfortable—sailing in small boats in the harbor or taking to the ocean below the cliffs. Picnics in the country also provided amusement, especially for the women and children who spent a large part of the summer in Newport while their husbands took the Fall River Line's new steamers back and forth to Manhattan. Businessmen commuted to Newport on the overnight boats for the weekend, while academic and clerical families, as well as some plantation families, remained the entire summer. Atop the bluffs south of the Ocean House hotel, just beyond the curious seventeenth-century stone mill incorrectly thought of in the nineteenth century as a Viking outpost from the days of Leif Ericson, a new section of Newport began to develop.

In 1839 George Noble Jones, a Savannah plantation owner, asked the architect Richard Upjohn, then based in New York, to build him a "cottage" just beyond the Viking Tower. The Jones family had summered at Potter's Boarding House before deciding to build a new home about the same size as the local rentable cottages, thus giving the term "cottage" to wooden summer houses in Newport. The appellation would continue for the rest of the century, becoming a somewhat silly conceit as modest houses gave way to enormous mansions that their owners still called "cottages." Soon after Jones built his Carpenter's Gothic house, Edward King would call Upjohn back to Newport for his cottage in the towered Italian style (also called a Tuscan villa style), built of brick near Jones's house. In the mid-nineteenth century the summer people were beginning to want their own houses designed to enjoy nice breezes and, perhaps, a view of the water. The bluff between the Touro Cemetery and the Viking Tower—near the old ropewalk, now Kay Street—proved to be just the place for some new houses to be built. The new structures included both private homes and houses constructed as rental units for summer visitors who wanted to rent an entire house. This new district of Newport high above the old safe area of the Point and daringly near the ocean became the center of residential life. Thus, when John and Elizabeth Auchincloss moved to the Point in the 1850s, they were going back to the "old" quarter, not the new district. When the Bigelows purchased their house just south of the Auchinclosses, they also put themselves in the old quarter, as did the young McKims.

Charles McKim must have felt a bond between the eighteenth-century Georgian houses at the Point and the old districts he had found in Paris just before Baron Haussmann cut wide boulevards to modernize the French city. McKim's interest in the older buildings of Newport was

*The Thomas Robinson house in Newport. McKim's early venture in restoring an old house.*

*The interior of the Robinson house, perhaps rented to Reverend Child in the early
1870s. This is an early "Colonial" restoration by McKim, who added door
surrounds, worked on the fireplace, and supplied furniture.*

probably aided by meeting the local father-and-son architects and antiquarians George Champlin Mason senior and junior. The elder Mason was
building many of the new cottages in the Kay Street area in Newport.
Mason senior remembered old Newport and cherished local history. For
Charles McKim, who walked daily by the venerable Hunter, Robinson,
and Dennis houses in Newport, Mason's antiquarian attitude was intriguing. So very much was changing in New York City, the bay side of Newport seemed quaint. In 1874, McKim hired a local photographer to follow
his instructions and make a beautifully done set of pictures of eighteenth-
century buildings in Newport. McKim, who had once photographed
European buildings himself, now sought high-quality pictures with a
hope of perhaps publishing his views of Newport as a book.

The photographs seemed to lead to the job of making these buildings
"old" again. The young bridegroom McKim was asked to bring the
eighteenth-century Hunter house back to its earlier appearance as a
single-family house. In the mid-nineteenth century it had been used as a
boardinghouse, and moldings had been removed and the configuration of
rooms changed. The Thomas Robinson house at 64 Washington Street
was restored to an earlier day by McKim in this same year. The house,
built in the first half of the eighteenth century, was redone and given a
Jacobean chair (called a Colonial chair by Americans at the time) and
other more sophisticated late eighteenth-century Newport furniture. Two

years later on nearby Poplar Street, McKim also "Colonialized" the so-called John Dennis house, built in the mid-eighteenth century.

The interest in Colonial America was growing, stoked by antiquarians like the elder Mason and McKim. H. H. Richardson had taken a nominal editorial role in a new architectural publication called *The New York Sketch Book*. Richardson turned over the job of doing the journal to the young McKim, who at once published in it a view of another historical building—the rear of the Bishop Berkeley house at Newport, with its massive sloping roof. McKim participated in this American antiquarian group as curiosity grew about the vocabulary needed for a full-fledged set of Colonially detailed houses and the possibility of a revival movement. McKim would move from restoring a Colonial house to designing a new house in this venerable fashion.

The following summer saw the birth of the McKims' daughter, Margaret, on August 13, 1875, at Newport. The first two years of Margaret's life may well have been spent in the New York City apartment in winter and in Newport for the summer, although one account states that Annie and Margaret never returned to New York City. The perfect circle of intellectual pursuits and beautiful surroundings on the porch at Bayside had already begun to decline. The "bully piazza," once the setting for social and literary entertainment, was left empty. Mrs. Bigelow would miss the meetings of the literary Town and Country Club, which had included the Civil War hero Colonel Higginson, the author Helen Hunt, and perhaps Frances Tracy Morgan, the second wife of J. P. Morgan, among many others; members remembered hearing McKim read aloud during a tranquil meeting of the Club. It would seem the economic downturn of the 1870s affected the Bigelows, putting pressure on the marriage, and on Annie, who apparently wanted to remain in Newport. Rumors must have flown over this split between the young couple; people seem to have known the cause, but the gossip never appeared in print.

The couple was clearly unsuited for each other, but as the biographer of McKim wrote much later on this ticklish point—after carefully vetting the phrase with Annie Bigelow McKim Day through her grown son— "malign influences" broke up the marriage. McKim's biographer, Charles Moore, was commissioned and paid to write the book by Annie and Charles's daughter, so the phrase was run past several parties. The ambiguous phrase seemed to be a veiled reference to a woman friend of Annie's, Rose Wagner, who came to New York with Annie before the wedding to help the bride set up and decorate the couple's future apartment. In this period McKim himself was doing interiors, so giving the decoration over to Annie and Rose was a concession. Rose Wagner seems never to have left Annie, becoming the baby's nurse. The implication in whispered tradition was that Annie and Rose had a love affair, which excluded Charles from the picture.

However miserable Charles was, the family ties were not yet broken. William Bigelow had just returned from Paris and the École and was clearly still friendly with McKim. In the summer of 1877, McKim, Mead, Bigelow, and Stanford White took off to the New England coast for what would become their famous Colonial Tour. It was inspired by an article in *Harper's Monthly* two years earlier (July 1875) called "Newburyport and Its Neighbors," which highlighted the route they four men would follow. They toured the coast very happily, stopping at Indian Hill, the ancestral home of the Poore family in West Newbury, Massachusetts. (See White's drawing of Indian Hill on the frontispiece.)

The Poores had lived at Indian Hill from the early eighteenth century on. The house was now home to an old newspaper man with connections to the abolitionists, who insisted that his name be written with a colon as Ben: Perley Poore (1820–1887). Poore's father had been well off and able to take his son to Europe in 1831, when crossing the Atlantic was a difficult voyage. In France, Ben: Perley Poore met General Lafayette and visited Sir Walter Scott's house, Abbotsford, in Scotland. Poore returned to Athens, Georgia, where his father bought him a newspaper, *The Southern Whig,* which he ran until he was arrested for being "tainted" with abolitionist notions after dancing with African American slaves at a rather wild party. Poore was fined four hundred dollars and expelled from Georgia. The young man settled in malaria-ridden Washington, D.C., for the remainder of his career. While Poore worked, he collected antiques for his summer home, Indian Hill, creating there a cross between a French *manoir* and Scott's antiquarian house. Poore considered his house Colonial. He was said to have a Colonial kitchen, a feature treated with great reverence the previous year when such a kitchen was a shrine at the Philadelphia Centennial.

The men's visit was enhanced by the presence of Poore's two beautiful, if frail, daughters, and it extended to four days as the jovial Poore and his daughters entertained the enthusiastic amateur antiquarians. Although Poore's house was a fantasy, this "Colonial" trip became a legend of McKim, Mead & White, and one cannot help wondering how the four got along (seemingly well) and whether they saw signs of the early decline of Poore's beautiful girls, who would soon die, preceding their father. The young men left Indian Hill to continue looking at century-old New England.

Indian Hill would burn in the twentieth century, with only a portion of the house and collection remaining.

THE YEAR 1877 WAS a propitious one for the association of McKim and Mead, as Mead's cousin Rutherford B. Hayes had just won the presidential election. Although Mead knew his cousin well, no tale of White House visits has survived.

It is certain that Annie did not return with Charles and her brother to New York that fall, but Charles and Bigelow continued to get along well, with Bigelow drawing and doing some interior work for McKim. Bigelow also seemed able to bring in some customers to the practice, leading to the creation of McKim, Mead & Bigelow sometime in late 1877 or early 1878, a partnership with headquarters at 57 Broadway.

All should have been well in the office that year as the economy had improved, jobs were appearing, and the partners were working well together, but Annie was undergoing a period of mean-spiritedness. A separation and divorce were under way, a rare event in the social scene of the day, especially after so short a union. Was Annie feeling the pressure of people's attitudes? In 1878, with Rose Wagner's assistance, Annie turned the divorce action into a messy situation. She began spreading rumors about McKim, filing papers accusing him of "unnatural acts against the bounds of Christian behavior." Annie seemed to be implying that McKim engaged in homosexual activities, and thus could not be allowed to see his daughter unless accompanied by the Bigelows in their Newport home.

The range of the accusations must have been magisterial, as they sent McKim into a full-scale depression, with a second breakdown to follow as the reality of the divorce and custody battle took his youth away. The charges were terrible. They circulated widely in Newport and New York and should have ruined the architect's career. In truth, few must have believed Annie's words.

The charges did rupture the partnership in 1879, when family pressure forced Bigelow to withdraw from the firm. It can certainly be judged from the continuing relationship between McKim and Bigelow to the summer of 1879 that McKim had done nothing terrible, or the two could not have worked closely together for two more years. Annie Bigelow pressured her brother to leave, perhaps realizing that her accusations were not credible if her brother continued to work with the man she was insisting was culpable for the breakup of the marriage. By forcing him to leave the partnership, Annie pretty much ended her brother's architectural career. The Bigelows retreated to Newport, where John William Bigelow would die on the verge of bankruptcy. The house was sold in 1886, and Mrs. Bigelow moved to Boston. In the following year, Annie married the Reverend John Williams Day of the Channing Memorial Church in Newport. She would have three sons, move to the Midwest, and die deeply hurt that the words she used against McKim were thought to be unduly influenced by others. Annie must have realized in her last years that she was perceived as the person who broke up the marriage and kept their daughter from seeing her father until the girl reached maturity and demanded to see McKim.

With Bigelow's withdrawal from the office, a place now existed for a man who could draw and do interiors.

# 5. McKim and Mead in the Early Years

C lients and how to find them were a major concern of McKim and Mead as they contemplated their future in 1876. The international depression had not yet ended and money was scarce, although a few people did seem able to afford an architect. The McKim family's friend from Miller McKim's years in the Presbyterian Church, Moses Taylor (1806–1882), had risen to great prominence in business. His career followed the economic growth of the nation from the simple agrarian world of Cuban sugar to shipping, then to the railroad boom, gas and coal companies, and, finally, to banking in New York City as president of National City Bank. In the years after the Civil War, his was one of the great fortunes of the age.* It must have been with joy that McKim received from Taylor his very first well-funded commission—for a summer house in Elberon, New Jersey, with a budget of almost sixty thousand dollars, a great sum for the bottom of an economic slump period. McKim's dreams of gaining a reputation through a prominent job were being realized. We can only wonder how Taylor had the confidence to give such a big job to a young man, but he and his children would remain fond of McKim and give him many commissions over the next thirty years.

The location for the new house was one of the America's first seaside resorts, greater Long Branch on the Atlantic coast in New Jersey, about an

---

*Moses Taylor is worthy of a modern biography as an early and important figure in the development of businesses from sugar to banking in the mid-nineteenth century.

*Moses Taylor gave McKim his first big break. Taylor and his children stayed loyal to the firm for their lifetimes.*

hour's trip on a fast boat south from New York. While Newport with its cool bathing waters had become a resort in the later 1830s for returning families once connected to the city, Long Branch became popular only from about 1870. Part of it was called Elberon, a contraction of the name of an early cottager and developer, L. B. Brown. Elberon is located atop a high bluff cooled by gentle breezes in summer. Its friendlier water temperatures made it a comfortable rival to Newport. Getting to Elberon from New York City was far simpler than getting to Newport. Indeed, Elberon was the Deauville of America—the summer center for the nation's newly self-made men with commercial, not hereditary, fortunes. It was easier to rise socially in Elberon than Newport, where newcomers were subject to scrutiny. It therefore became a magnet for the newly rich, particularly those associated with the circle of President Grant.

Elberon had a three-mile strip of bluff above the ocean, flanked by a north-south road called Ocean Drive. The thin strip of houses, the hotels, the so-called casino, and a church or two sat along the drive. The summer colony had two methods of transportation: boat service from New York, quick and cool in the summer; and the railroad, which brought residents directly to town, giving them the convenience of being able to walk to their houses.

The attractions of Elberon were sailing in catboats and bigger craft, ample beaches, croquet, archery, and later tennis. The American male interest in horseflesh found satisfaction at the nearby Monmouth track. The summer life painted by Winslow Homer in his *Breezing Up* of 1872 was idyllic enough to attract General Grant to the wooden houses on Ocean Drive during the season. Ingenious at real estate promotion, L. B. Brown offered Grant the gift of a summer house to enable him to live near members of his cabinet. The arrival of Grant's circle added to the New York City folk on the beach.

UNLIKE IN NEWPORT, in Elberon there was no older building stock to inspire a young architect such as McKim. The design of these houses could then be fanciful. For inspiration, McKim now turned to his sketch and photograph album to summon up houses from Norman coastal villages, as the other American architects who had studied at the École des Beaux-Arts had done. Resort houses in Normandy were primarily wooden structures, which were what American clients requested. McKim's two role models, Richard Morris Hunt and H. H. Richardson, had returned from Paris and built resort houses for their clients in the style known as the villa Normande, wood framed with a set of features common in northern European vernacular houses. The primary identifying feature of these houses was exposed areas of wooden truss work of a decorative and nonstructural nature. Hunt used these northern European houses as models for his new resort houses at Newport in the 1860s. Richardson, in his wooden resort house for F. W. Andrews in Newport, of which McKim had made a drawing, also used this mode.

With the big commission at Elberon, McKim could have done a version of these Norman houses, but he must have wished to make a reputation. He decided instead to step beyond the Norman villa and make a beach-worthy house using forms he had likely seen in Britain in the work of Richard Norman Shaw. The idiom McKim selected was the great gables of Shaw's country houses. On upper stories Shaw used a rough surface covering, which in photographs or engravings appeared to be shingle, but in the English houses almost always consisted of hanging slate tiles, not wood. Richardson had shared McKim's interest in Shaw—indeed Richardson, as we know, owned a number of photographs of Shaw's work, and McKim was now in a Shavian period. The young architect took

*Moses Taylor house at Elberon, New Jersey, 1876–77.*
*McKim's first important house. Demolished.*

Shaw's gable to the seaside and let the wind blow breezes into the house. For the Moses Taylor house of 1878, McKim built a double-decker, arched open porch to welcome in the air of the beach. It was a large house, open and filled with summer scents.

The Taylor house produced rapid results. McKim now quickly built houses in Elberon, New Jersey, for George H. Prentice, George Sloan, and John D. Wood. Notice of his work had even reached L. B. Brown. The local developer had purchased Charles G. Francklyn's open cottage of 1873, which had been designed by Edward Potter, with the idea of expanding it into the Elberon Hotel. McKim was asked to create the new hotel in the guise of cottages grouped around the main building. The commission for the Elberon Hotel helped to establish McKim's reputation there for the next decade, until the resort suffered a social decline.

If Elberon was indeed the summer colony of the newer movers and shakers, Newport was at a higher social plane, with established families of several generations' standing. Newport in the Civil War era had a New England intellectual flavor. Rather as in the Norman resorts, writers, artists, and idealists dominated the social life. At Newport Mrs. Bigelow

*L. B. Brown house in Elberon, New Jersey, at right. Cottages were added to an earlier house to make a resort hotel in 1877. The small houses were in a pre-hotel, independent cottage tradition. Americans' first summer stays were in boardinghouses, followed by renting a local cottage. The Elberon Hotel likely provided meals and laundry service to the cottages. The resort was laid out along a spinal road.*

*Charles G. Francklyn house, 1876, absorbed into the Elberon Hotel. The house has a drive-through passageway on the north side — an unusual arrangement in American houses.*

had helped to found the literary Town and Country Club; its weekly readings, attended by writers and artistic people, kept the resort at a level above other post–Civil War summertime watering places. As McKim read poetry from the piazza in 1875, the writer Katherine Prescott Wormeley noticed the aesthetic young architect, and she asked him to design her house in the Kay Street district at Red Cross Avenue in 1876. Ms. Wormeley, who was the American translator of Balzac, got a house rather similar to those McKim had built in his earliest years as an architect. The small wooden house with strong bargeboards and a simple appearance adds only a tower at a right angle for novelty.

IN THE FOLLOWING YEAR, McKim and Mead collaborated on a welcome-home house for William Dean Howells in Belmont, Massachusetts. Howells, who had married Mead's sister in Paris a decade and a half earlier, was now establishing himself as an editor, writer, and literary figure in Boston. McKim knew Howells in another context, as Howells had begun his career with *The Nation* when Miller McKim helped create the magazine.* For the couple, McKim and Mead built a house in a rather conventional style topped by a great redwood shingled roof, which gave the house its name, Redtop. It reminded the Howellses of Colonial Amer-

*The young Henry James, a friend of Howells, also began his literary career with *The Nation*.

*The Wormley house at Newport, 1876–77. McKim's awkward design is obvious here.*

ican houses, prompting McKim to present to Howells his now-abandoned book project of photographs of Newport houses as a housewarming gift. Since Howells was connected to the Boston publisher Ticknor & Fields, McKim may still have held out a shred of hope of future publication when he gave Howells the volume. If so, nothing came of it. The Howellses did not remain at Redtop more than a few years, moving to Beacon Street in 1885.

WITH A GOOD NUMBER OF JOBS coming in, McKim's confidence in his own business seemed to increase, even if he might still have been concerned about his design skills. When he was summoned to build a big house in Newport, he was elated. Dr. and Mrs. Thomas Dunn called on McKim in the spring of 1877 and asked him to design a large stone house for them. The couple, who were full-time residents, requested a house of a size not seen by recent builders in the city, with a solidity requisite for winter warmth. Mrs. Dunn was a member of the Newport family whose eighteenth-century house is today a major visitor's site, the Hunter house. McKim knew Kate Hunter, as the Hunters were old friends of the Rotches. McKim would have been aware that the Hunter family had lost family members in an Atlantic-crossing tragedy three years earlier, and he was surely respectful of Mrs. Dunn's tender state.

McKim cheerfully worked up a set of drawings for a big English-looking house in a half-timbered style. His presentation came a bit late, but it was the projected cost that cooled the client's interest. The design for the Dunn house, conventional by British standards, seemed to be acceptable, but the cost and architect's fee made the couple angry. The Dunns wanted a house for less than fifteen thousand dollars, and McKim could not get the figure below twenty-five thousand dollars. McKim asked only 2½ percent on the commission (the level of architects' fees had yet to be standardized in the United States), but the Dunns resented even this. As a result of their outrage, McKim lost the job. The Dunns hired the local architect and antiquarian George Champlin Mason to build their house. This marked the end of McKim's involvement with Mason. But he would get his revenge in the next decade, when McKim, Mead & White became the premier house builders in Newport, more or less putting Mason out of business in his hometown.

IN THE FALL OF 1877 McKim, Mead & Bigelow seem to have made a formal partnership out of the loose arrangement in which the three men's work had been intertwined for several years. McKim and Mead continued as usual, leaving Bigelow the special assignment of producing the renderings and details. The partnership's commissions consisted of a small amount of city work and a host of wooden summer houses. All of it was strictly residential, with Bigelow doing some interiors in New York City, while all three worked on backyard extensions of New York row houses, extra floors on brownstones, and other such small commissions.

One larger commission was McKim's first New York row house, built for Edward N. Dickerson (1824–1889), a patent lawyer. Dickerson had lived at 62 East Thirty-fourth Street in a typical brownstone for twenty-three years when the house next door came up for sale, probably at a good price, as New York had just come out of a boom cycle and was now in a stagnant period. Dickerson hired McKim to build a wide double house with an observatory atop the skylight, as his hobby was astronomy. For this splendid opportunity, McKim abandoned the old-fashioned brownstone of a typical New York house for a venture in a bold new taste. Ignoring the late Victorian styles of the few individual row houses of the day, he turned to the work then gracing the pages of the British architectural periodicals eagerly read by young American architects—the style of England's latest generation of designers, the so-called Queen Anne. The young Turks in London's architectural world wanted their new buildings to look historical yet different from those of their Gothic Revival forebears of the previous generation. If the High Victorian Gothic blended Medieval features, they would substitute different time periods in a non-Gothic hybrid building. They wanted a new set of historical sources—not Greco-Roman, not Gothic, not Renaissance. As the exclusions removed all the periods used in earlier revivals of the century, the young men turned to the recent past, the seventeenth and eighteenth centuries, allegedly the time of "Good Queen Anne."

The characteristics of the Queen Anne style included scrollwork, small panes of glass in the fenestration, and often a northern European stepped gable. Houses of this style were being built in London, in the developing sections of northern Chelsea and Knightsbridge. The building material favored was brick, and the references to history in the stepped gables may indeed hint at the beginning stages of a preservation movement, as those traveling to Holland and northern Germany had seen such gables.

The Queen Anne style crossed the Atlantic and was picked up by a few men, including McKim, who saw it as a way to get noticed in New York for his currency in the latest work. With a willing client, McKim built what seems to have been the first Queen Anne row house in New York. Yet when the house was put before the public, only its elaborate, English-styled ebonized interior received praise. A mysterious figure, Remigio Laforte, is credited with the design of the interior features, which included a fireplace in the newest form of industrial fabrication of material—polished steel. Although steel fireplaces were common in England, Laforte must have been selected by the client, as his name is not connected with McKim's firm at any other time. As for the exterior of the Dickerson house, the major architectural critic of the day, Montgomery Schuyler, deprecated the façade in the nation's new professional magazine, *American Architect and Building News,* by comparing it to furniture and called the design, with some acuity, "a monumental sideboard." McKim would have taken the criticism to heart, as he needed people to reassure him. When on his own, McKim was not a confident designer. He needed design assistance. In due course he would turn to an old friend, Sidney Stratton, and to his first employee—arguably the genius of the office—Joseph M. Wells, who was hired in September 1879.

# 6. STRATTON AND WELLS

Among the most intriguing figures in McKim's circle of artistic friends was Sidney Vanuxem Stratton, whom McKim had known from Daumet's atelier in Paris in the fall of 1867. It seems plausible that Stratton and McKim knew about each other before they met in Paris. Stratton's father, a renowned Presbyterian clergyman, Joseph Buck Stratton, and Miller McKim shared many likely meeting places, although Stratton came from a family with higher social standing and far more affluence than did McKim.

Joseph Buck Stratton of the Easthampton, Long Island, Strattons was born in Bridgeton, New Jersey, in 1815 to a family of well-off merchants. He attended Princeton College, graduating in 1833. After college Stratton must have been apprenticed in a law office before setting up as an attorney, first in his hometown and then in Philadelphia. In 1840 he gave up law and entered Princeton's Theological Seminary, graduating three years later. One can only wonder if while still practicing law Stratton may have met Miller McKim in Philadelphia. Stratton's first and lifelong post was in Natchez, Mississippi, in 1843, and he was to die in that city in 1903 as a highly revered figure. Stratton brought with him to his new church his bride, Mary Vanuxem Smith of Philadelphia, whose family was well established in the insurance business. The couple's first child, Sidney Vanuxem Stratton, named for his maternal grandfather, was born August 8, 1845, in Natchez.

When the Strattons arrived in Natchez, that city was reaching the height of its economic prosperity. This region of antebellum Mississippi had made millionaires out of many planters, and life had become quite sophisticated for those affluent enough to build large plantation mansions and gracious city houses. The great houses had an impact on the Strattons, father and son. Joseph Buck Stratton took up furniture making, and Sidney would become an architect with a specialty in private houses for wealthy clients.

Just three years after Sidney's birth, Mary Stratton died of yellow fever. Joseph Buck Stratton was then married again, to Caroline M. Williams, a sister of the wife of Haller Nutt, the builder of the great octagonal house, Longwood. The Strattons had two more children who died young: a daughter who was a victim of the deadly fevers that periodically swept the South and a son who died in 1888. In the end, of all the children, only Sidney Stratton would survive.

Joseph Buck Stratton's second wife was connected to Stephen Duncan, who came to Natchez from Miller McKim's hometown of Carlisle, Pennsylvania. Duncan made a fortune and built a fine house, Ashburn, in Natchez. The land Duncan purchased for his house was bought from John Bien of New Orleans, who would become H. H. Richardson's stepfather, another possible point of connection between Richardson and Stratton.

In the circle of Duncan was Dr. John Ker, a Presbyterian physician who along with Duncan was involved in a major Natchez case concerning the freeing of slaves. A local plantation owner had freed his slaves at his death, providing them with funds to go back to Africa. Despite local consternation Duncan and Ker saw to it that the plantation owner's wishes were respected. Surely Miller McKim would have known of this story.

We know little about Joseph Buck Stratton's position on slavery. He did minister to a black congregation and attended to many fever victims in the slave communities, but his position in the war may have been a bit pro-South. Sidney Stratton was eighteen in 1863, and his father was fortunate enough to discover a former partner from his old Philadelphia law practice who was now an officer in the engineering division of the Trans-Mississippi Department in western Louisiana. Stratton secured a safe wartime duty for his son in this division. Sidney Stratton joined the Engineering Corps in July 1863, returning home two years later.

Happy to have his son survive the war, the elder Stratton now had to assist the young man in his search for a profession. Sidney was clever, well versed in piano, and already an expert on the opera. The young man seems to have traveled in Europe with his father and stepmother in 1859, when the congregation of the church sent the family abroad to "rest." Sidney had learned a bit in the Engineering Corps but did not wish a future in science or even a stint in college, so the family decided to try architecture as a profession and to send Sidney to the École des Beaux-Arts. Both Stratton and Richardson were fluent in French from life on the Mississippi delta, so the language would not be an obstacle as it was to McKim and others. Sidney left for New York on September 23, 1865, to voyage across the Atlantic and spend nearly four years in France. In Paris, he entered the École and the Atelier Daumet, perhaps becoming the contact and model for McKim and Peabody, who would soon join him there. Stratton and McKim became good friends in Paris; their relationship would last thirty years in New York City.

Stratton, a better student than McKim, returned home on June 30, 1869, ten months before his friend. He joined, as we know, the office of the only other École-trained American architect at this date, Richard Morris Hunt. Hunt was older than Richardson, socially better connected in New York, and far better established at this date. Thus Stratton got the more established job with Hunt. McKim on his return was obliged to apply to the embryonic office of Richardson. The careers of Stratton and McKim ran parallel at their New York offices. Stratton remained with Hunt a little longer before setting out on his own, and indeed was there when the young Louis Sullivan visited Hunt's office seeking advice about the profession. Sullivan was later to recall a discussion with "Friend Stratton."

Stratton began to work in high social circles well beyond those of McKim. He was soon accepted at the University Club and got some help from family connections among the Strattons and Vanuxems and Lenox Kennedy. He was a man on the rise: young, a Parisian sophisticate, an opera fan, witty and single, a perfect dinner guest and clubman.

Stratton's Natchez connections included Stephen Duncan, who took him to meet a relative, William Butler Duncan, then prominent in New York City, and to visit the Cuban-American family of great social-climbing skill, the Yznagas. The elder Yznaga delle Valle was a well-off sugar merchant from Cuba who had married an ambitious American woman from Louisiana. The couple settled in Natchez, where they built a modest plantation house, Ravenswood; they also made periodic forays to New York City and Newport. Their three children, Consuelo, Natica, and Fernando, were beautiful, fun-loving, and brought up with a direction to marry well. Consuelo would do this with some aplomb, landing the eighth duke of Manchester and making a grand, if unhappy, marriage to this English peer in 1876. Brother Fernando, who played the dapper bachelor well, was to marry the sister of the archetype of all social climbers of the mid-nineteenth century, Alva Smith of Mobile, bride of the young and hapless William Kissam Vanderbilt. Later in the century the Yznagas fell on hard times, but in the 1870s the witty and amusing family were the toast of high society.

Stratton, whose family was sent to summer in Newport, surely knew the Yznagas, who also spent the hot weather in the resort. The Natchez group must have stuck together, and Fernando must have helped bring Sidney Stratton into New York's highest circles of fashionable clubmen.

Once Stratton had his connections in place, he was able to leave Hunt to set up an independent practice, taking over a section of McKim's rooms from 1877 to about 1889. Stratton would pay a quarter of the office rent, which was $188 annually. His jobs went into the McKim, Mead & White bill books with a pen notation marked on the entry "check to Stratton," indicating that the payment was for his own work. Indeed, from about 1880–84, the letterhead for the office showed the names of the partners with a bold black line below, then Stratton's name in the same typeface.* Stratton was an "almost" partner and enriched the firm's reputation by bringing in families such as the Colgates, Kings, Roosevelts, Iselins, and Barneys, as well as the brother and sisters Breese, John Cleve Green, Stuyvesant Fish, and Daniel Lord Jr. Stratton's clients helped boost the practice up the social scale, bringing work to the firm that continued after his breakdowns ended his career. He played a major role in propelling the architects into a higher social class than they could have reached on their own. The debt to Stratton was a big one, as this "almost" partner made McKim, Mead & White architects to the *Social Register.*

McKim was plagued by self-doubts, and in his most anxious moments he continued to call upon Stratton through the 1880s. By the end of that decade, Stratton retreated to Spring Lake, New Jersey, with a friend, perhaps the Brooklyn engineer Henry Brevoort, also a bachelor.

Soon after, Stratton's health declined. He began to suffer from delusions, and his body developed tremors that forced him to give up playing the piano. Stratton had fashioned McKim's initials, CFM, into a monogram for McKim's Steinway, which he had previously enjoyed playing. He also found that work had become a challenge. In the early 1890s Stratton took to Bridgeton, New Jersey, where he spent extended periods of time with his father's family. His friend Dr. Charles Hitchcock, who would become McKim's personal physician, suggested he seek the care of a Dr. Wurts. Wurts proved to have some skill at calming Stratton's system, but still Stratton lost confidence. In the summer of 1894, he left New York for

---

*About 1882, the letterhead actually has Stratton's name above that of Stanford White.

*The office at 57 Broadway with pictures of the work of the firm, ca. 1888. Sidney Stratton is seated at left, while Mead leans upon a chair.*

*The Frederick Roosevelt house in Skaneateles, New York, 1879–81. Stratton's design suffers from a lack of focus.*

*Stratton's house for J. K. Gracie at Oyster Bay Cove, New York, 1884, extant but altered. Stratton had excellent social connections in these years.*

Natchez and the security of his father's care. Sidney Stratton built several houses in Natchez before settling in as an insurance salesman. He was well known in Natchez, a president of the local club, and in the decades he spent there he outlived most of his early friends in New York. After McKim's death, Mead wrote to Stratton, remarking that the two of them were the sole survivors and enclosing copies of McKim's obituaries. Stratton died on June 17, 1921, apparently never having returned to the New York architectural world.

One early client brought to McKim by Stratton was Samuel Gray Ward (1817–1907), the Boston businessman who was in charge of the U.S. interests of the merchant bankers Baring Brothers. In 1877 Ward asked McKim to build a large summer house in the intellectually oriented western Massachusetts community at Lenox. The expensive house (it cost thirty-three thousand dollars) would be McKim's first in Lenox, a place where he would later briefly keep a summer home of his own.

Samuel Gray Ward (often confused with New York City's famous man

*S. G. Ward house in Lenox, Massachusetts. McKim and Mead's first house in the resort community, 1877–78. An early and important commission, it is long gone. The commodious wooden houses proved impossible to winterize and went out of style. These shingle-clad houses were demolished or had "accidental" fires in the first years of the twentieth century.*

of letters, Sam Ward) moved to New York City from Boston as Baring Brothers expanded their presence in the United States. Stratton and McKim came to know him at about this time. Ward continued to summer in Lenox, a community favored by Bostonians. The Lenox house McKim built was of wood, long, low, and with great gables covered in a variety of shingles cut in patterns. Rather than have a uniform shingle covering, the different textures in the ground-hugging house provide a sense of time's passage, with sections of the building clad over time. Ward's house was a fine example of McKim's study of the eighteenth century and of the Queen Anne style, but with a deep American flavor. This house may have been McKim's first good design—a house in America's Colonial style but also a modern home with all the conveniences then expected, such as a modern kitchen, service rooms, and closets.

A TURNING POINT in McKim, Mead & Bigelow's career had been reached. The economy had rebounded, big houses were being built, and the architects had work in New York City and the three summer resorts of Elberon, Lenox, and Newport. When the strain of Annie Bigelow's accusations against her former husband pulled the partnership apart, Bigelow retired and joined the decorative firm of Herter Brothers as a house architect. He also continued his own commissions, some still done through McKim & Mead's offices and appearing on their bill books. Since McKim and Mead could no longer count on Bigelow as a draftsman and creative force, the architects took on their first paid assistant, a Boston-born architect of great talent who would transform the design level of their work—Joseph Morrill Wells (1853–1890). McKim hired Wells in the fall of 1879, although Wells may have worked for McKim and Mead as a part-time office assistant before becoming an official employee in September.

Wells, who could trace his ancestors directly back to the great Samuel Adams, was one of two sons of a Boston printer of modest means, Thomas F. Wells, who instilled in his boys a pride in heritage and intellectual attainment but lacked the funds to send them both to college. The elder son, Webster Wells (1850–1916), was a mathematical genius and did manage to enter and graduate from MIT in the class of 1873. Webster would become a member of the MIT faculty, but there was not enough money to help young Joseph receive a higher education.

Joe Wells was drawn to architecture in high school. He then spent a period of time in the office of the well-born architect Clarence S. Luce, whose specialty was wooden suburban and resort houses in Massachusetts and Rhode Island. Wells was probably unable to afford a place in the office as a paying pupil, but rose through ability in Luce's firm.

Wells's education, then, was in wooden houses. This would later make him an ideal assistant to McKim and Mead, who were working in a parallel vein. In due course he left Luce's office to join that of McKim's Parisian companion Robert S. Peabody, then already successful in Boston and in partnership as Peabody & Stearns. Wells rapidly distinguished himself at Peabody & Stearns, becoming the chief designer by 1874. Peabody, whose career had taken off more rapidly than McKim's, already had in hand a commission for a big insurance building, the Boston headquarters of Mutual Life Insurance of New York. The tall building designed at Peabody & Stearns had a tower capped by a pyramid. Wells was laboring over the proportions of the cap when Peabody came by and insisted that Wells detail the cap with ornamental crockets. Wells felt this to be an unneeded bit of historicism and protested the detail, but Peabody insisted on the flourishes. In a fit of rage, Wells left the Peabody office for New York, where he worked on the design of a Boston house for Martin Brimmer in the employ of Richard Morris Hunt. We do not know if Wells worked on any other project with Hunt. He surely knew Stratton in Hunt's office. There is a four-year gap in Wells's career between 1875 and 1879 when we cannot account for his activities. He must have worked in the offices of established men until he was officially hired at McKim & Mead in September 1879. Over the next eleven years Wells was to have a profound effect on McKim and Mead, and indeed on American architecture.

WITH A FIRST EMPLOYEE now in the office, McKim and Mead were nervous and reluctant to expand further. They debated the return to New York of their old friend and occasional collaborator Stanford White, who had been with Richardson since 1870. Richardson had now fully moved his operations to Brookline, Massachusetts, and White wished to remain in New York. McKim and Mead considered the possibilities. Wells was already at work, but he was a concept and design specialist, needed for the more ambitious projects McKim and Mead were trying to garner. The architects also required someone to do those pesky interiors McKim had given up and to make rapid sketches for new work. But could they afford another person in the office? White had little training beyond Wells's level, but he had higher social cachet and would not join the firm as an employee. So, with reluctance, McKim and Mead offered White a position as a third and lesser partner. White responded rapidly, and in the second week of September 1879 McKim, Mead & White began with Joseph M. Wells as chief designer.*

Today that younger partner, Stanford White, is the best-known member of the firm. Weekly real estate ads proffer homes and apartments from Stanford White's hand—yet many were done before or after White's lifetime. Stanford White was a major designer in the United States, especially in his youth. Appending his name to buildings seemingly created in his style lent them a certain cachet, and could lead to better sales. His great achievement was to unite wealthy businessmen with a vibrant and new American artistic community and thus help create the arts side of America's Gilded Age.

---

*The official document of partnership would not be concluded until the next year.

# 7 . STANFORD WHITE

S tanford White was the only partner in the firm to be born in New York City. The youngest of the three, he was born on November 9, 1853. He was also the least well educated, with no known attendance in any special school and no higher education in schools beyond his sixteenth year. His father's family had been in the United States longer than that of any of the other members of the firm, preceding Mead's ancestors to New England by a year. Rather as in Mead and McKim's homes, intellectual and cultural accomplishment were expected, but in the White household life was a constant struggle between expectation and a true lack of resources. The Meads were the best off financially; money was a vital issue in the McKim home, but funds were found for major goals such as education. In the White house, the cupboard was always bare.

The Whites were proud of their forebears, who had arrived in Cambridge, Massachusetts, in 1632 before moving westward to be among the founders of Hartford, Connecticut. Many Whites served the Bay Colony, as Meads had served in Vermont and New Hampshire. In the boyhood of Stanford White, pride in belonging to a very old family in a nation now filling rapidly with newcomers was a major theme. Stanford's father, Richard Grant White, felt himself still to be English, and loved to pontificate about their 225-year-long sojourn as an English family in America. Richard Grant White blamed his fellow Americans for having struck out on their own. His position in regard to his country and time was retrogressive and resembled that of his paternal grandfather, the Reverend Calvin White. Calvin White, a fourteen-year-old student when the American Revolution occurred, felt the action was an extreme error. He wished the United States to remain British. As this did not occur, he turned to religion for escape, moving from traditional New England Congregational theology to Presbyterianism, and then to Episcopalianism, followed by an improbable conversion to Catholicism. The long-lived Calvin White had an impact on his grandson, who did not play with successive theologies, but did bounce from career to career while maintaining himself to be an "out of continent" Englishman.

Richard Grant White's own father was less eccentric. He was born Richard Mansfield White in 1797 in New Jersey. R. M. White brought his family to New York City, where he became a shipping and commission merchant in the seaport—a business dominated by the elite families in New York in the first half of the nineteenth century. With a good position and the correct ancestry, R. M. White moved quickly into the top circles of New York's mercantile elite, settling in a commodious house in Brooklyn and bringing up his children as patrician New Yorkers. But complacency kept many shipping merchants of his class from recognizing the threat of English steam vessels. White was among those who ended up in bankruptcy, and he died in poverty in 1849. The fall of these merchants became material for the writers Henry James and Edith Wharton, whose grandparents had been in that tier. Many families had to rent out their properties to strangers and live in cheaper places on the proceeds. Richard Grant White's family was hardly unusual, but in his eyes, the rug had been pulled out from him and would never be put back, leaving him feeling betrayed and displaced.

Richard Grant White tried out a series of professions after completing his studies at the University of the City of New York (later New York University) in the class of 1839. He did well in public speaking, graduating as the class marshall. Tall for his day and rather handsome with a drooping mustache, Richard Grant White was a dandy with affected clothing and musical tastes. As a young child he attended the opera in the old Park Theater, and went on to sing in choirs and to play the violin and cello. White collected these instruments, stringing them himself and often buying damaged but good instruments in the hopes of restoring them, which he was usually unable to do. Music and literature were White's passions, but a happy career eluded him from his earliest days. After graduating from college, he studied medicine under the eminent physician Dr. Alfred Post, but he soon recognized that he was not cut out to be a doctor. He then studied law as he had medicine, working with a practicing professional and managing to get admitted to the bar before

*Richard Grant White painted by Daniel Huntington at the time of his marriage.*

giving that up as well. White finally settled on a literary and journalistic career, although neither his newspaper criticism nor Shakespearean studies could really support him. Thus White joined the ranks of other nineteenth-century authors who worked by day in the U.S. Custom House and wrote at night.

White styled himself as a debonair man about town, but his studied superiority kept him from good friends and a wealthy wife. Soon after his literary career began, White met the Mease family of Charleston, South Carolina, who were living in New York. One of the Mease girls was a children's book author known as "Aunt Fanny" (Frances Elizabeth Mease Barrow). "Aunt Fanny" introduced White to her younger sister, Alexina Mease, whose middle name, Black, was a signal of courtesy to an uncle thought likely to leave her a fortune. This was never to happen, as the Civil War wiped out these prospects. The Mease women were clearly awaiting something, as was Richard Grant White, who married Alexina in 1850, hoping for her inheritance. The bride was barely twenty. At the time of their engagement, the two sat for America's greatest portraitist, Daniel Huntington, who immortalized the couple as they awaited a better day—which never came.

On Christmas Day 1851, Alexina White gave birth to a son, whom she named for her husband's father, Richard Mansfield White. Richard Grant White may not have been the baby's father. In a letter written shortly after the baby's birth, R. G. White asks his wife to kiss the "dear little monkey . . . for his reputed father and tell him I could not love him more if I really was his father." This peculiar remark cannot be explained. If Alexina Mease were already pregnant and married R. G. White as a cover, we would not have a fourteen-month delay before the birth of the child. One can only wonder who the father of the child was and why it would not have been her husband. Almost two years later, Stanford White was born, truly the son of his father and named for a wealthy piano dealer, David Stanford.

The two boys grew up in rented houses near Washington Square, attending not private schools, as had their father, but ordinary public ward schools. From his house at 173 East Thirteenth Street Richard Grant White wrote for the *Courier and Enquirer* and other journals while studying and preparing his own edition of Shakespeare. These literary pursuits gave White a feeling of superiority over his fellow citizens commensurate with his feelings of unjust poverty. At least while writing, he felt better than others. In 1858 White fought with his editors at the *Courier and Enquirer* over his payment and resigned; this rash act left him in a terrible financial pinch. He appealed to Moses Grinnell, one of the port of New York's premier merchants, for a loan of five thousand dollars (which he would never repay), and took the money to buy stock in the new *New York World,* hoping for an editorial position there (which did not come). Grinnell was the collector of the port

*Alexina M. White painted by Huntington.*

until questions regarding his honesty forced him out of the job in 1870. White had to move his family out of Manhattan to Ravenswood, Queens, to lower his annual rent; he finally admitted failure and again took a position in the Custom House, working in the Revenue Cutter's office, where he would remain while writing at night. The U.S. Revenue Cutter Service was a division of the customs operation in which small boats were used to ferry the customs officers back and forth to the ships anchored in the harbor. Once employed there, White was able to move his family back to Manhattan, settling a block east of his old rental house at 186 East Tenth Street, where his family would live for six years.

Richard Grant White's position in the Custom House was modest, but he took care to dress well, amass one of New York's most important private libraries, collect musical instruments, and live in a fashionable part of the city while his sons were in the ward schools. The choices in the family seemed to be all his own, as he felt his opinion to be the only one that mattered. We learn nothing about Alexina in these years; R. G. White dominates all. In 1861, he put 644 of his volumes up for sale, which brought in about a thousand dollars, less than he had hoped to realize. It is not clear what White intended to do with the proceeds of the sale. He had been cultivating a relationship with Dr. Howard Crosby of the University of the

City of New York and may have hoped to give a donation to his alma mater, badly in need of cash, and solicit a teaching position in literature, but an offer was never made. White hated the Custom House position and would no doubt have loved the improvement in status implied by an academic job, especially with a son ready to go to school. In about the same year he attempted to gain membership in the Century Association, New York's venerable social club, where talent was supposed to mix with money in order to encourage the arts. He was soundly blackballed and never admitted to this or any other club. White was not the most popular of people and would never be a clubman—a failure that Stanford White would reverse, as he became the ultimate clubman.

The Civil War exploded a few months later. Richard Grant White took up the Union cause despite the fact that his wife and her potential inheritance were in the South. He joined the New York Rifles, helping to train men in New York, but never went into battle. Meanwhile, he offered tactical advice to Lincoln and also wrote letters in support of the Union cause to *The Spectator* in London. White signed his letters to England only as "Yankee," in an obvious if anonymous reference to his forebears in New England. They were widely read and gave White a reputation that he would make use of a decade later when he finally traveled to Britain and identified himself as the "Yankee."

In the course of the rifle drilling and the benefit evenings in support of Union troops, Richard Grant White mingled with Miller McKim; the great landscape architect Frederick Law Olmsted; Bernard Saint-Gaudens, the city's great bootmaker; and a German-born lithographer, Otto Boetticher. All these men would circle around each other in the next decade. Indeed, R. G. White would even join *The Nation* in its first days.

The constant issue in the East Tenth Street house was shortage of the money that White believed was necessary to keep the family in its proper social position. White was preoccupied with his family's downward slide, yet his personal decisions made their financial situation ever more precarious. After the war, any thought of money from South Carolina had completely disappeared, yet he continued to buy books and instruments. Even an enormous book royalty on a satirical novel White wrote about politics in America in the early 1860s, *The New Gospel of Peace,* said to come to ten thousand dollars, seems to have made little impact on the debt at home. The family later came to think that R. G. White had a second family whose needs broke the budget of the East Tenth Street house, but no proof of this has ever been found. White did boast to Julian Hawthorne, the son of Nathaniel Hawthorne, in a sacred confidence that he had an English woman friend in New York, but this is hardly enough to explain his family's poverty.

In 1871, when both his sons were on their own, Richard Grant White began a curious novel, *The Fall of Man,* a humorous tale satirizing Charles Darwin's *The Descent of Man* with an odd twist. White's novel made a play on the search for Dr. Livingstone and for the source of the Nile sponsored by J. G. Bennett's *New York Herald. The Fall of Man* involves a mass meeting of gorillas and concludes with the protagonist, White himself, being pursued by a female gorilla. In the final moment, when the novelist kills the gorilla, it turns out to be a man. One can only wonder if R. G. White had another life with men in the city. George Templeton Strong, the great diarist of New York, knew him as a "decorated and flamboyant gent," while Julian Hawthorne writes that "in some respects he [R. G. White] was Old Maidish; though he was the father of two little boys."

After the war, White's journalism moved toward a virulent rejection of the nation's increasing materialism as great wealth began to appear. As American values changed, he felt his own position was sinking even faster, which caused him to spew out reactionary articles and books decrying the loss of the "old" America. White's journalism and books of the 1860s and 1870s made some money for the family, and they saved on rent again by moving to Bay Ridge in Brooklyn, where they lived from 1867 to 1870. As the boys were not in private school, this move may have been a face-saving gesture for White; his sons would be in public school there, but no one he knew would notice.

Richard Mansfield White, the elder son—known as Dick—was not a student. The boy had a short temper, lack of follow-through, and not many intellectual skills. Indeed, finding something for Dick to do was a major problem, as the young man seemed to get into trouble at every turn.

Stanford was less of a burden. The young redhead was quick and had better judgment than his elder brother, but he seemed to find his greatest enjoyment in drawing. Julian Hawthorne remembered him as a handsome lad who was fond of drawing fantastic houses on bits of paper. The question of his future education arose in 1870, when Stanford White might have considered college. The family returned again to East Tenth Street, but no college application was made. Did R. G. White wish he could afford to send his son to his old school, the University of the City of New York? At just this moment in the university's history, Dr. Crosby was considering opening the college as a virtually tuition-free institution, a gesture that ultimately did not take place. The idea of an almost free tuition carried a taint of the charity student with which the Whites did not wish to be associated. Did the young Stanford refuse to go to college? Did R. G. White insist there were no funds available for tuition and expenses? We do not know.

The elder White again sold many of his books in October of 1870, but we do not know where this money went. We do know that R. G. White consulted Frederick Law Olmsted as well as John La Farge, a painter and son of a city hotelier of means, on what to do about Stanford's future. Having loved to sketch since he was a lad of six or seven, Stanford expressed a desire to study painting. R. G. White brought his son to visit La Farge and to show the painter some of his work. La Farge was known to give advice and had also offered guidance on a future career for the young Henry James. La Farge had been left a million dollars a decade earlier at the death of his father. But he was now broke, having had to sneak out of his Newport house just ahead of the debt collectors. He felt that painters were not properly appreciated or even able to earn a living. In an embittered mood, La Farge therefore advised the Whites not to consider a career in painting. Remembering that the young Stanford had designed an ingenious drainage ditch for the family during their time in Bay Ridge, the elder White mentioned this to La Farge, who suggested a career in architecture.

R. G. White might have articled his sixteen-year-old son to an architect, but he did not use his resources for this purpose. Instead he let the

*Stanford White watercolor of a French manor, perhaps the Manoir D'Ango.*

*The young Stanford White on the roof of a building near the New York seaport.*

boy go to an architectural practice as an entry-level employee, perhaps not even a paid one.

Frederick Law Olmsted, a friend of Richardson's, agreed to take Stanford to Richardson and introduce the two. Thus, Stanford White, an untrained youth with a painterly bent, was now on a path to the future in the office of "Mr. R," as White would call him.

IF WHITE WISHED TO BE A PAINTER, he did not appear to have taken lessons from any of the nearby places where he might have received some tutorial assistance. But he would have had the benefit of his father's library, which was rich in books about painters.

When Stanford White joined Gambrill & Richardson, the firm was still at 6 Hanover Square, and Richardson was just beginning his mature career. This was probably White's first encounter with the architectural profession, although he may have known the earlier generation of English-trained or English-influenced architects who were part of the circle of White's beloved aunt, Laura Fellows Dudley of Balmville (now Newburgh), New York. White's aunt would take the family for extended vacations in her large house near the Hudson. She was married to Henry Dudley, who had settled in Newburgh and was often part of committees with the architects and landscape designers of the late 1850s and 1860s.

The firm Gambrill & Richardson was a loose arrangement of convenience for the two partners. Each kept his own work, and Charles D. Gambrill seems to have run the office. The firm dissolved when Richardson moved to Brookline, Massachusetts.

Stanford White joined Gambrill & Richardson in an entry-level position, while the Paris-experienced McKim entered as a chief draftsman. It would seem White spent the first year getting accustomed to the world of architecture. In his second year he began to take a more visible role. White could draw, which Richardson did not do naturally or easily, so by the end of his second year, White had begun to fill the artistic role in the office, which he would fully assume when McKim left in 1872. White then took on another area Richardson disliked: interior decoration. In this period, the profession of interior design was still in its infancy in the United States, with only a handful of people willing to undertake decorative work. White would become a decorator more, perhaps, than an architect.

In the early phase of White's entry into interior design, he and McKim pored over contemporary British work in the two British architectural journals. Professionally made photographs of work on interiors done by English architects such as Richard Norman Shaw were only then becoming available for sale, and the young men studied these carefully. Richardson's office had a number of photographs of Shaw's recent interior work. White and McKim would also have been interested in the Pre-Raphaelite painters and the decorative work being done by William Morris's company in London, which would parallel their own work later on.

Once in the Gambrill & Richardson office, the novice White often worked under the command of McKim, who must have relished the role of mentor. In Russell Sturgis's office McKim had been under the tutelage of George Fletcher Babb, and now he held a position equivalent to Babb's and was himself able to dispense advice and help.

Probably through McKim, Stanford White established a relationship

with Babb, which would have great importance in White's aesthetic formation during the 1870s and early 1880s. Although White worked for
Richardson and McKim, Babb's visual judgment on proportion and detail
became Stanford White's standard. White constantly tested himself
against Babb's judgment, marveling at the older man's ability to conceive
how a design on paper would truly appear once made in three dimensions. Babb would be as close to an educational instructor as White would
ever see.

From Richardson and McKim White learned the practical matters of
the profession. After assisting McKim in the New York office for two
years, the young man, now barely nineteen, was given his job when
McKim resigned. It was now White's duty to travel around the Northeast
in advance of Mr. R, preparing for the architect's visits to the Buffalo State
Asylum and the Hampden County Courthouse in Springfield, Massachusetts. For about three years, White was constantly on the go, checking on
the progress of new buildings, keeping Richardson informed, and seeing
how construction worked. From Richardson, White learned the value of a
rapid conceptual sketch, which would be given over to assistants to trans-
late into a presentation drawing. Richardson's office method was to talk
through a new building while sketching the idea, and then to transfer the
actual creation of the plans to his assistants. Both McKim and White, who
were part of this process in Richardson's office, would later use the technique in their own practice. The key to the method was to have good assistants. Richardson picked his men well and was blessed with many
talented assistants. When McKim and White went into practice, it would
be Mead who would keep them supplied with able fresh blood.

The style White would pick up from Babb, McKim, and Richardson
would rely on a picturesque interest in medieval European prototypes.
Shaped by his three mentors, White would be attracted by compositions
with medieval detail, forced asymmetry, preeminent rooflines, and artistic
flourishes. Two of these men would also inspire White to fantasize about
seeing real European buildings with his own eyes. It does not seem that
Babb ever left the United States, but McKim and Richardson had traveled
in northern Europe. Stanford White could still only dream of seeing
Europe, but in 1876, his father finally had the culminating experience of a
lifetime. With the money he had not spent on his son's education, Richard
Grant White prepared for and made a trip to England. White, in his own
eyes the literary lion of the New World, fitted himself out with clothing
and an elaborate silver toilette kit, then embarked for England, where the
out-of-step American found the nation to be as civilized and respectful of

his values and person as he had hoped. He proudly wrote home that in England R. G. White was immediately recognized as a gentleman and always escorted to the first-class areas of the railroad. He indulged in a festival of self-importance, writing home for money, which young Stanford probably sent along. R. G. White did not share Miller McKim's preoccupation with getting his son launched in a good career; he never notes anything of interest to his son in his letters from Britain, even though Stanford had by then spent six years in architectural training. With the example of his father's trip, Stanford White must have decided to try to go abroad. He had saved his money for such a purpose, living at home and using funding from Richardson's office when he traveled.

As White mastered McKim's job in Richardson's office and work slowed due to the economic downturn of the mid-1870s, he amused himself by working on his drawing skills. Inspired by the work of English interior specialists of the mid-century, he began to focus on interiors, an aspect of building creation Richardson disliked. From 1876 or so onward, White carved out his own place in Richardson's office as a draftsman and interiors specialist. His interest in interiors stemmed from the work under way at Richardson's office in 1873, particularly the preaching space within Trinity Church. White was kept busy on many of Richardson's jobs, including the interiors of the Newport houses of F. W. Andrews and the Watts Shermans.

As money was a key ingredient in the making of a good interior, Richardson and White were happy that adequate resources were found to do at Trinity what Richardson had not been able to do at the Brattle Square Church—that is, create a total work of art. The European ideal of a building as a synthesis, a virtual symphony, of all the skills and crafts, could be realized in Boston. Richardson could do justice to his École training, which had stressed the inclusion of printers, sculptors, and woodworkers in a major building campaign.

At Trinity, Richardson was finally able to call upon John La Farge, the French-trained painter now interested in the decorative possibilities of glass. La Farge shared Richardson's interest in the building as a total work of art and was delighted to create murals on the walls of the church. The interior work was a golden opportunity for the artists connected to the project. Everyone seemed to recognize that this collaboration of muralists, architects, decorative specialists, and the like could foster the careers of many, even if work in the unheated church was unpleasant during a cold winter.

Along with La Farge, who was well known to White, the Trinity project included Augustus Saint-Gaudens, who would rise to become America's foremost sculptor; Kenyon Cox, the painter; Frank Millet, another painter; and Francis Lathrop, brother of the journalist, an artist who like La Farge would also work in stained glass. Here at Trinity the pattern of White's life was made. A group of artists was formed who put art above all and who would make up the heart of White's circle for his lifetime. All these men were devoted to creating beauty together, an endeavor it was the duty of America's wealthy to support. The goals of Trinity's design and the friendships solidified here would be the core of White's life.

THAT THE ARTISTS knew each other is a certainty. Some twenty-five years ago, when the painter Allyn Cox was discussing the career of his father, Kenyon Cox, and his contemporaries, a naïve query about one of the artists knowing another brought a bemused laugh from Cox. Everyone, he told us, knew everyone else then. In a society not attuned to art, those interested in beauty found each other rapidly.

Augustus Saint-Gaudens had traveled more widely than White before their paths brought them together. The Irish-born sculptor, whose French father was a renowned bootmaker in Manhattan, had gone abroad to Paris for training. With the Franco-Prussian War nearing Paris, Saint-Gaudens had fled to Rome, where he enjoyed all aspects of life from the fountains to music and ice cream. Saint-Gaudens returned home to New York briefly in 1872 to work on a few projects and visit his family and had met Richardson at that time. Three years later, Saint-Gaudens returned to New York, engaged to a Bostonian woman he had met in Rome, Augusta Homer. Saint-Gaudens had been very poor and had few connections in Europe; the visit of the intellectual Bostonians to Italy had provided the student sculptor with a touch of home and the prospect of commissions. An engagement to Augusta Homer, a cousin of the painter Winslow Homer, would bring great cheer to Saint-Gaudens.

The sculptor returned to New York in 1875. In March, he joined David Maitland Armstrong, an artist and glassmaker who was a member of a patrician American family, in a studio in the German Savings Bank building at Fourteenth Street and Fourth Avenue. Maitland Armstrong and Saint-Gaudens shared rooms on an upper floor of the bank. While alone in the studio, Saint-Gaudens liked to make a bit of noise as he worked. He would leave water running in the sink to simulate the fountains of Rome and amuse himself in the manner of the ateliers at the École des Beaux-

Arts, which he knew well, by vigorously singing all the andante of Beethoven's Seventh Symphony. This pastime helped the sculptor work but did not please the building superintendent, who became furious with Saint-Gaudens's fountain as it led to water problems in the building. The loud singing brought Saint-Gaudens and White together. As White was walking by the building, he heard Saint-Gaudens's voice and recognized the music from his father's musical discussions. White rushed up the stairs to meet this redheaded fellow, who would become a lifelong friend.

Shortly after this encounter Saint-Gaudens met La Farge and Charles McKim. McKim may have known Saint-Gaudens's father, Bernard P. E. Saint-Gaudens, as he had been active in abolitionist circles. The reacquaintance was probably made through an early patron of Saint-Gaudens's, William Maxwell Evarts (1818–1901), who had commissioned a portrait bust in Rome. Evarts was a member of a distinguished American legal firm with Charles C. Beamen, Joseph Choate, Charles Southmayd, Charles E. Butler, and Butler's son, Prescott Hall Butler, who became a close friend of McKim's. Evarts's firm would be the attorneys for McKim, Mead & White, and the partners would commission many jobs from the architects. Evarts was a Bostonian but apprenticed in law in Windsor, Vermont. He would be appointed secretary of state by Mead's cousin, President Rutherford B. Hayes—confirming Allyn Cox's small world statement.

McKim and Saint-Gaudens would sustain their lifelong friendship and collaborations with a self-described "devouring love of ice cream." McKim, Mead & White and Saint-Gaudens would be forever united with the goal of bringing the heritage of European culture to America.

The bonds of an artistic friendship at Trinity would keep Lathrop, Millet, Saint-Gaudens, and at times La Farge with McKim, Mead & White. Only Kenyon Cox, who was in Miller McKim's friendship circle, would not have constant commissions from the architects.

The interior collaborations of artists who were peers was partly inspired by the example of the artists associated with the Pre-Raphaelites in London. The influence was primarily the work of Morris, Faulkner & Co., who would be role models for artists who hoped to carry out interior work organized in a less authoritarian way than was practiced at the École, where the architect was in charge. The arrangements McKim, Mead & White would develop the precedent in America of treating artists as peers in the architectural endeavor. Italy, too, would inspire all these men. If the arts had combined during the Renaissance with the backing of wealth and influence to the good of all, so too could they be chosen to bring a new Renaissance forward, this time on the soil of the New World.

STANFORD WHITE'S FATHER was far from immune to the delights of romance, and young Stanford inherited this propensity. It seems that the young man's first serious involvement was with a beautiful, red-haired neighbor, Anaïs Casey, who lived at 133 West Eleventh Street. The parents of Anaïs, Henry H. Casey and Anaïs Blancet Casey of Quebec, were friends of R. G. White. Though the Caseys lived close to the Whites on the other side of Fifth Avenue, the families appear to have had little else in common. The Caseys were not part of the old mercantile gentry, and unlike R. G. White, who was a nominal Episcopalian, the Caseys were ardent Catholics. It is possible that the Whites and Caseys met when their children, who were of similar ages, were in school together, but one assumes the elder Casey children, Henry and Anaïs, went to parochial school. Most likely, the Whites and Caseys met when Henry Casey entered Gambrill & Richardson soon after White had, and the boys formed a friendship. Henry Casey may then have introduced White to Anaïs, and the parents met afterward.

Anaïs Casey was a rare and beautiful person. Lovely to behold, she was also kind, noble, and high-minded. The young Stanford seems to have fallen in love with her in the mid-1870s, when Anaïs was at home caring for her younger siblings after the death of her mother. That the relationship between the two was close enough to bring the families together is obvious, but in the end, it would seem White's lack of religious conviction kept them from marrying. Charles Rutan, who would later be a partner in Richardson's successor firm, joined Gambrill & Richardson at about the time White was there. Rutan reported that Stanford was deeply religious at that time. He recalls White making elaborate genuflections at the altar of a church they were sent to measure, then severely lecturing Rutan for his lack of faith. The religious phase even extended to the issue of payment for work done on Sunday, which elicited a festival of negative oratory from White. After a while, Rutan reports, the religious phase passed, never to return.

White did seem to be caught up with Anaïs, but her intense religiosity got in the couple's way. She tried to bring her conviction to her boyfriends, hoping to show them the light. Stanford must have tried to see if he could follow Anaïs and become a Catholic but failed to do it. White and Anaïs broke off their relationship, but the families continued to be close. When White traveled, he would ask his parents to share the letters home with the Caseys. In 1879 Henry Casey left Richardson's office to go to San Francisco to design houses. Casey had been diagnosed with TB and told to go west and enjoy an outdoor life in the hope of surviving the disease. In San Francisco Casey met a young painter from Concord, Massachusetts, Edward Emerson Simmons, whose mother was a sister of Ralph Waldo Emerson. Simmons and Casey embarked on a health-improving venture that included pitching a tent and camping near a waterfall in northern California, but the trip proved the opposite of what they had hoped for. Casey fell victim to pleurisy, ran out of food, stayed damp, and declined dangerously. It was all Simmons could do to get him on a train to the East Coast and his sister. Anaïs Casey summoned Stanford, and the two took turns nursing the dying man, who succumbed to TB in three weeks' time.

Anaïs Casey continued to offer guidance to those of her set contemplating conversion to Catholicism. Mrs. Samuel G. Ward, the wife of the client of the McKim, Mead & Bigelow house in Lenox, was similarly given to good works. In 1883 Anaïs Casey met Mr. and Mrs. George Bliss in Washington, D.C. George Bliss (1830–1997) was a Massachusetts man in the circle of E. D. Morgan, a powerful figure in New York in his day whose life would intersect with McKim, Mead & White. George Bliss's wife, Kitty, was dying, and Mrs. Samuel Ward helped Kitty accept Catholicism before her death. In 1887, Anaïs Casey married George Bliss at her own church, the Church of St. Francis Xavier in New York. Bliss had become a Catholic before the wedding. It would seem that George Bliss was able to do what Stanford White had not.

After the breakup with Anaïs Casey, Stanford White paid attention to Julie Richardson, the daughter of Mr. R, in Brookline, but this romance also fizzled. About this time White began to court young Sara Delano, of the highly esteemed mercantile family. The Delanos had a house on the Hudson not far from White's aunt Laura Dudley. White may have met Miss Delano through David Maitland Armstrong, whose family home was nearby. The romance was short-lived. Miss Delano would marry another man, and her son would be Franklin Delano Roosevelt. In Stanford White's last years with Richardson, he was still unencumbered, making it possible for the young man to consider further educating himself with a trip abroad.

Going to see the buildings of Europe was becoming a goal for all young American architects at this time. Travel abroad was easier than in the old days, with safer, slightly larger boats to cross the Atlantic, although the

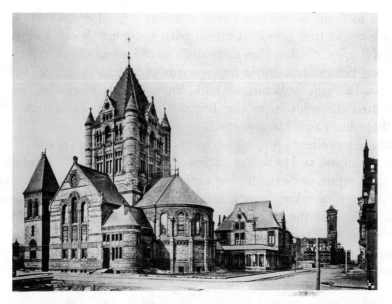

*H. H. Richardson, Trinity Church, Boston, 1872–77. The tower is often credited to Stanford White.*

crossing could still be perilous. The cost of living in Europe was modest, enabling a person like White to see with his very own eyes the buildings and paintings he had studied from book plates and photographs.

White was now maturing in Richardson's employ to the point of being his trusted assistant and even a near equal in some portions of Richardson's design process. Just a few years after the Trinity Church in Boston had been designed, as construction proceeded in the watery landfill of Back Bay, the builders Richardson depended on, the Norcross Brothers of Worcester, Massachusetts, informed him that the tall lantern tower he and White had planned for the church would be far too heavy for the supports used in Back Bay. Richardson was forced to rethink a key element of his design.

The importance of White's design sense was clear when he suggested the Spanish tower from the Old Cathedral at Salamanca as a source for a new Trinity tower. Stories flew that La Farge had sent White a card with this tower on it as an inspiration, but it is equally plausible that White's awareness of this source can be traced to paintings and watercolors made by American artists traveling in Europe and being shown in the first wave of art galleries in New York City. One such American painter who depicted Spanish scenes was Samuel Colman (1832–1920), who was known to Stanford White's father and had a good reputation. Indeed, White would later provide Colman with a summer home. Colman had shown a series of watercolors and paintings of Spanish scenes in New York not long before, including a large picture of Salamanca painted in 1870. Perhaps La Farge or White, or both, knew Colman's painting, and that suggested the solution to the Trinity Church crossing lantern, which would be built as White designed.

White was already playing a large role in Richardson's domestic work. Richardson was said to be less interested in this genre than he had been in his early, reputation-establishing career. White probably had an increasingly easy time taking on the residential work. Following Richardson's lead, he learned the importance of charming the clients—especially, in residential work, the wives. White's growth as an architect can be measured by his role in the design of Gambrill & Richardson's house for William Watts Sherman (1842–1912) and his bride, Annie Wetmore Sherman (1848–1884).

William Watts Sherman came from an Albany, New York, family and was trained as a physician in New York City, where his father settled and became a partner in the investing house of Duncan, Sherman & Company. Watts Sherman, as he liked to be called, had a fine education, including time spent at a German university, which was considered important for sons of wealthy New Yorkers maturing at this time. Watts Sherman abandoned medicine for his father's investment banking house; cultured and with large sums of money at his disposal, he became a respected figure in New York society and a great clubman. In 1871 Watts Sherman married the daughter of William Shepard Wetmore (1801–1862), an important business figure who owned a large tract of land in the newly enlarging summer colony at Newport. Wetmore's son, George Peabody Wetmore (1846–1921), lived in the family house located on that ridge of Newport extending southward from the Viking Tower. William Shepard Wetmore had built a substantial and permanent house on his property in 1851–52, using the building talents of a local contractor, Seth Bradford. When the elder Wetmore's house was finished, it must have seemed odd. It was the largest new house at Newport, it was made of stone rather than the usual wooden frame, and it was located on this isolated projection of the island south of the center of town. Out along the Wetmore property there were only two neighbors, the owners of the Upjohn villas George Noble Jones and Edward King, whose summer houses were on the protected, harbor side of the ridge. Wetmore's house made a year-round statement about living in Newport, but in the 1850s when it was built, Newport's growth was only as a summer place. Wetmore and his house stood out as atypical but helped to create the sense of prosperity that would enable Newport to grow rapidly after the Civil War.

George Peabody Wetmore inherited his father's home and immediately decided to improve its appearance. To work on the house, Château-sur-Mer, he would call an increasingly familiar architect back to Newport: Richard Morris Hunt. Hunt would work with Seth Bradford's stone walls but would Frenchify the house, making it appear grander and more up-to-date, since the popular venue for traveling Americans in those days was the Second Empire. Hunt's work at Château-sur-Mer must have been seen as a blessing by Wetmore's neighbors and the local real estate developer Alfred Smith, who was pitching Newport to New Yorkers with a fierce tenacity.

IN 1870 ANNIE WETMORE was finally able to call her own a parcel of the southern end of her father's large tract, used at this point as pastureland. After her marriage the next year and a tryout of summering at Newport in rented quarters, Mr. and Mrs. Watts Sherman decided to build a "cottage" on the southern side of the Moon Gate on her family property. This lovely fence with a round hole at the closure of the gate still survives today. The obvious choice of an architect would have been Hunt, who summered in Newport and had built for others of a similar social ilk and whose brother, William, maintained a painting studio in that city. Instead, however, the Watts Shermans selected the less well known, younger man, Richardson, for reasons not recorded. Watts Sherman needed only a summer home, not the stone pile his brother-in-law had craved. Perhaps Watts Sherman needed to establish himself as his own man, not the brother-in-law of Wetmore. Perhaps he had learned of Richardson's work through Richardson's established clients in Albany, Watts Sherman's familial town. Perhaps the two knew each other from the Century Association, that New York club devoted to putting artists in touch with patrons. Perhaps Richardson was known to Watts Sherman for the recently completed large wooden house at Newport, the F. W. Andrews house. The final possibility is that the Watts Shermans were Anglophiles—they were known to spend a lot of time in England—and wished for an English, not a French, house. If this is so, why did the couple hire another École des Beaux-Arts product? The possible answer lies in the importance Richardson's office attached to the work of the English architect Richard Norman Shaw.

As we know, Richard Norman Shaw and his partner, William Eden Nesfield, practiced in mid-century Britain as Nesfield & Shaw. Richard-

*William Watts Sherman house, Newport, by H. H. Richardson 1874–76. Located just off Bellevue Avenue, the house is of the scale of the pre–Gilded Age cottages.*

son, we remember, while at the École had made friends with an aspiring English architect, R. Phene Spiers. Spiers was active in the young architects' club, the Architectural Association, and would remain the conduit from Richardson to Shaw, serving that purpose most notably in 1869 by hosting the young McKim in London for the summer.

At the time of the Watts Sherman commission, architects did not work in other countries. The Watts Shermans might have wished for a house in the new Shavian Manorial style then being shown in the pages of the British professional journal, *Building News,* which seemed socially appropriate to young, wealthy people like themselves. If not Shaw, the next best thing might be an American firm with a library of Shaw's work, and Richardson's in McKim's day was just such a place.

By the time the commission came into Richardson's office, McKim was on his own (but just next door at 57 Broadway), and White was McKim's successor at Gambrill & Richardson, where he was still poring over the photos of Shaw and the plates in *Building News.* McKim transferred his appreciation of the new domestic work in England to White, and the two became the creators of Shavian work in the United States. For Watts Sherman in the years between 1874 and 1876, Richardson and White created a house with a richly textured wooden surface made from American shin-

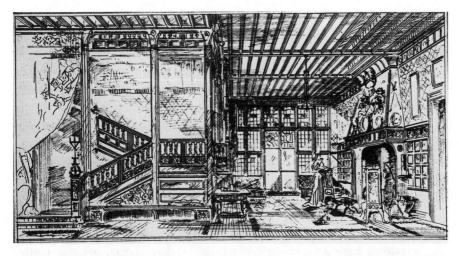

*Sketch of the living hall at the Watts Sherman house, said to be drawn by Stanford White. The La Farge window has been removed. The social life of the day took place in the living hall.*

gles rather than the tiles their British precedents had employed. The development of the plan may have been Richardson's, but the gabled façade of the entry looks very Shavian and is surely the work of McKim and White. The detail in the ornament of the gable comes directly from a recent Shaw house, Grim's Dyke, in northwest London. Although a case

*Stanford White drawing for Richardson's Cheney house in South Manchester, Connecticut, 1876. This is White's version of Shaw's drawing for Leyswood.*

has been made for a Colonial element in this house, it was begun the year McKim did his photographs of old Newport.

The interior of the Watts Sherman house revolves around a large open public space to one side of the main staircase. This open area with benches and a fireplace, known as the living hall, appears in English country houses from 1859 forward, as seen at the country house Chesterton, by the British architect Alfred Waterhouse. This living hall—a social space, not a decorated area—became a feature of the new summer houses that were being built in the the United States from the 1870s through 1890s.

The flow of the space in the living hall and the definition given the reception area by the ceiling beams is always said to be from the hand of Stanford White. The living hall culminated in a floor-to-ceiling leaded-glass wall with windows by John La Farge. The opalescent-glass decorative windows here are the first example of that special artistic genre, stained glass, in American domestic architecture. The inclusion of an artist's work in a house begins here, as White adapts the goals of the Pre-Raphaelites in England, and the role of artists in interiors will continue to grow in the following three decades.

White made friends with Mrs. Watts Sherman, and in a few years he would be called back on his own to add a large wing to the house: three floors of new rooms with a fine library on the ground floor. Mrs. Watts Sherman would die young, and when her socially well-connected husband remarried and contemplated a ballroom extension, he turned to another architect, thus assuring us that Annie Wetmore Sherman was the interested party in the relations with White.

After the Watts Sherman house was completed, White continued to design homes in the Shavian style for Richardson's potential clients. His friend McKim saw to it that these drawings would gain recognition by having them printed in *The New York Sketch Book* in 1875.

As White's reputation increased and some small decorating jobs began to come his way, he seriously considered leaving the Great Mogul. With a romance over, some savings, and no pressing obligations, White decided to go to Paris to see the much-touted Exposition being mounted there in the summer of 1878. His friend Augustus Saint-Gaudens was already there, with an apartment and a studio set up for work, including a joint project or two with Stanford. White was to provide a base and Saint-Gaudens the monument for the first important commission the two would receive—a tribute from friends of Admiral David Farragut of Mobile Bay Civil War fame, to be placed in a New York City park. This commission had been passed along in kindness by the man expected to have the job, the sculptor J.Q.A. Ward. Ward, one of the nation's leading artists, gave the job to Saint-Gaudens in order to help establish a career for the young man. Saint-Gaudens and White recognized that this would be a make-or-break experience. White along with Ward had helped Saint-Gaudens get the job. White's father knew men on the committee and put in a word for the boys, although one can only wonder if this really was a help or a hindrance. Job in hand, Saint-Gaudens took to Paris to create a great work.

In the Exhibition in Paris that summer were examples of American art selected by Saint-Gaudens's New York studio mate, David Maitland Armstrong, who was both a well-connected diplomat and an artist and who headed the selection committee deciding on the works to go to Paris. White and his friends may well have felt that the trip was even more worthwhile than before, since European fairs were now considering American artists as part of the mainstream art world. This may have been the extra lure that prompted White to depart from Richardson's employ. Richardson, who had been in his Brookline office for four years, was most gracious as he wished White a good sojourn. He surely knew White had not been happy spending an increasing amount of time in Brookline as the New York City practice closed up. White was attached to his home city. The polite severance left open the chance for White to return to Richardson, but the young architect had tired of the New York–Boston commute he had made for four years. White had outgrown a job in Richardson's office, but was he ready to see the Old World?

# 8. WHITE IN EUROPE

The awakening of Stanford White to the artistic richness of Europe began as a short tour to be done alone, but expanded wondrously into a sojourn of more than a year that would establish White's place in the world for the remainder of his life.

Although White had become the disciple of Norman Shaw in New York and had listened to his father's repeated assertions of English superiority, the first stop on his European travels was France. The Exposition was already in progress, and Saint-Gaudens with his wife, Augusta, would be there to meet White, who spoke no French. Saint-Gaudens's father had taught the sculptor his mother language, so Gus, as he was known, could assist White in his travels.

White's voyage from New York on the French steamer *Periere* promised to be a lonely one, but at the last moment Charles McKim, experiencing immense pain after the breakup of his marriage, decided to accompany him. Annie Bigelow McKim had begun her legal action in Newport; it was filled with accusations against Charles aimed at keeping him away from their baby daughter. McKim was also grieved by the death the year before, at a young age, of his sister Lucy, who left behind three young children. He was now suffering the beginning of what would be lifelong bouts of anxiety and depression, and he hoped to cheer up by visiting the Exposition. McKim had gone to Paris eleven years earlier for the last Exposition, that of 1867; this was most likely his first trip to Europe since the Prussians had advanced on Paris, sending him home eight springs earlier.

The transatlantic voyage was not to be notable for either the company or the weather. The men found their fellow passengers a bit of a bore. McKim became terribly seasick as he always did, and the total absence of fresh food made the men yearn for vegetables and fruit along with the bath they craved when they landed at Le Havre. In Paris, the young men roomed together in McKim's old building from his student days. McKim had to shepherd White through the city, taking him to feast on a dinner at Foyot's in the student quarter, where patrons could have a fine and inexpensive meal. White's initial responses to the Old World seemed to relate to his person, not the architecture. White ate and found French food a sensory revelation, then went to the theater and saw Sarah Bernhardt. He attended a student ball and took on some slightly adventurous nightlife in Paris. White went to the legendary Café Mabile, which had been illustrated in *Harper's Weekly* in March 1867 and become known for scandalous dancing, but he found it to be tame. His early letters home read rather like those sent by a college student on his first semester abroad. For the first few weeks and with McKim as a roommate, his behavior was virtuous.

*Stanford White's sketch of McKim doubled over in seasickness as the two men began their voyage across the Atlantic.*

White reported on the 1878 Exposition, noting its size and the fact that every artist from 1850 forward was represented, but gave no sense of the pictures or artists he liked, or of the fair itself, other than to remark that it was larger than the Philadelphia World's Fair of 1876. His failure to mention the new French painters is a curious comment on his then provincial taste in painting, though in his letter home of July 30, 1878, he writes: "As far as pictures go, it is by far the greatest exhibition of modern paintings ever held. They date from about 1850 to the present time, and include all the important works of the best men of all countries." No mention is made of Monet, Manet, Degas, or other modern painters of the day, who, while not at the Exhibition, painted the opening celebrations. In the Salon of 1878, which White described in his July 30 letter as not at all interesting, was the lovely Renoir painting of Madame Charpentier, now at the Metropolitan Museum of Art.

White's letters from Europe are lively, amusing, and well written considering his poor education; they are often illustrated with witty sketches.

The young White in these letters is loving to his family, especially his mother, and well able to put himself into other people's places and empathize with them in a genuine way. One is struck by White's humanity, on this first trip to Paris, in suffering for his mother, then at home nursing her husband's sister in a final, painful illness. There seems to be a great change in White's character in a decade, when he becomes so self-absorbed that he can no longer relate to the nuances of other people's actions. At this time, however, White seems sincerely concerned about his friends and family.

In Paris in late July, the Exposition's fame drew more New Yorkers. White and McKim visited with David Maitland Armstrong, then dined with McKim's chum from his days in Paris, Sidney Stratton. Stratton had come to Paris to see the Exposition, traveling with the elderly New York City socialite and scholar Robert Lenox Kennedy (1822–1887). Kennedy was a patron of the arts and enjoyed the company of McKim, White, and Stratton, taking the young architects to restaurants. The group had such a fine time that White wrote home of feeling a bit spoiled, as such meals in restaurants were not possible for his parents. In a letter to his mother of November 21, 1878, he wrote, "I wish I felt sure of your getting as good a dinner as I do everyday. It usually consists of ten courses."

By August serious touring began, and White now wrote home about the buildings and regions he visited. After White and McKim criticized Saint-Gaudens's first attempt at the body of Farragut, they decided to behave like teenagers and run away to the south. On smashing the unsuccessful first model for the Farragut, Saint-Gaudens sensed relief and promised to go to Hades with the other two, which was not quite their destination. On the second of August the three men, who were all redheads—at least then: McKim's hair disappeared early—jumped a train and headed for Fontainebleau, Sens, Dijon, and Beaune. They had not gone far on their journey before looking at buildings had dropped to a solid third among their priorities, just after food and pretty women. Their voyage was enlivened by ample amounts of wine, which kept the three friends in a festive state as they traveled in an assortment of vehicles, including a broad barge down the Rhone to Avignon.

The trio visited St. Gilles, which White described as having the best piece of architecture in France: the triple marble porch of the church. The porch at St. Gilles du Gard would come to Boston when Richardson's successors placed it at the front of Trinity Church, and later on to New York, when White himself re-created the porch for a memorial to Cor-

nelius Vanderbilt. In terms of aesthetics, White shows
his decorative viewpoint immediately. The porch at St.
Gilles is a fine detail of a bigger building, but it is of
almost theatrical detail. White's comment identifies his
interest in decoration above pure architecture, which
would be his special touch throughout his career.

*Augustus Saint-Gaudens's humorous
relief of McKim, White, and
himself as the three redheads
traveled through France.*

On arrival at Nîmes, McKim and Saint-Gaudens
enjoyed the splendor of the Roman theater from atop its
benches, while White, absorbed in the setting, ran down
to the center of the arena and did his best gladiatorial
impressions. This lighthearted frolic would make a lifetime memory for all. To cheer the depressive McKim,
Saint-Gaudens created a commemorative medal of the
journey, replete with pig Latin inscribed around the edges as a defense
against the vocabulary the young men employed on the voyage. The words
were meant to be a secret shared among the three participants. Their band
of friendship was now cast in bronze. Toward the end of August, McKim
and White toured Brittany.

Saint-Gaudens would also make a companion small relief of Charles
McKim, perhaps to further cheer him during this stressful time. At the
end of September, McKim returned to New York to face the wreck of his
personal life and go on with his work.

White, now thoroughly on his own, lived in Paris for a few days before
traveling again. He absorbed and sketched France and the Low Countries
that fall, going to all the tourist sites and museums. For White the trips
were a visual orgy of beauty that would deeply influence his future career.
A man from the New World was now reveling in the Old—anything
old. White loved the antique. As McKim, Babb, and Richardson had,
he adored the Middle Ages. He studied the Renaissance and had special
affection for big Baroque paintings. White loved objects, towns, buildings, opera, music, theater. Missing in his accounts, however, are references to contemporary buildings. He did not seem to notice the new Paris
now emerging out of the old city. White never remarked on recent work
of any kind. He had fallen in love with art of the past, preferably of a
highly decorative sort; sculpted Gothic portals became the apogee of his
criteria of judgment. The Stanford White emerging as an adult was one
with a strong love of the decorative design that would characterize his
thirty-year career.

While Stanford White was in Europe, the Richard Grant White household in New York would also lose its first son, as Richard Mansfield White decided to move out of the house and live on his own. Dick was beset by emotional problems that kept him from being able to hold a job. His parents had long realized that he would never be a success, and they were always concerned about his future. Dick was sent to study hydraulics with the inventor of the hydraulic water pump and probably learned to use some technical systems, but he would be unable to apply the skill to any group activity. There was an incident in Philadelphia in the summer of 1878 involving a Mrs. E. F. Loiseau of North Eighth Street, which was very difficult for Richard Grant White to clear up for his son. It was obvious Dick would have to work alone, as he could not cooperate with others. With the United States expanding, there were many glimmers of hope for a profitable career in the new West, particularly in the technical fields of engineering and mining. With Dick's knowledge of hydraulics and his independent streak, the prospect of a mining career in the Southwest suggested itself. Exactly how Dick White came to purchase a series of mines near Hermosa in New Mexico is unclear, but in the fall of 1878, he left New York City for a solitary life in the rough new territories.

White noted the empty house in his letters to his mother and wished her well as he continued his travelogue of all the medieval sites in France. Periodically he would return to Paris for a dose of city life, staying in Gus Saint-Gaudens's cavernous studio for a few days, then rushing back to his sightseeing. In the late fall of 1878, White visited Normandy, but the letters from this important resort area do not survive. We know White would have been primed for this experience, as both Richardson and McKim were well aware of this favored watering hole of fashionable Parisians, with its pleasurable and theatrical casino (though White saw it off-season). White's thoughts about the region are lost but visually alive, for when he returned to the design of wooden summer houses, the Norman agrarian complexes with their asymmetrical angles, diverse textures, and idiosyncratic gestures would appear in his next decade's work.

White visited sites in Normandy and drew the complexes in his rapid sketch style. Some of White's drawings were done on unbleached paper and others on the pages of a blue sketchbook. The drawings are usually unlabeled, making it difficult for us to identify the exact *manoirs* White visited, although a drawing of a complex in Normandy made at this time and recently sold by White's family looks to be the Manoir d'Ango, an important source for Richardson and Wells. White apparently also drew the Château de Compiègne, as Cass Gilbert would later copy the drawing while he was in the office. The sketch in Gilbert's notebooks at Avery

Library has an annotation indicating that it was copied from White's pencil drawing of "Compiegne."

WHITE RETURNED FROM NORMANDY at Christmas to have an excellent holiday dinner with the Saint-Gaudenses at their apartment. The joyful feast was a relief for a person traveling alone in Europe at a holiday time when little public hospitality was available. It was very generous of Augusta (Gussie), Saint-Gaudens's wife, to take the traveler into her home, as she did not much care for White, who returned her sentiments. The thin, rawboned Boston woman married to White's closest friend did not engender warm feelings in White, who thought her "a regular clothes rack" of a person, unattractive and annoying with her slight deafness. Gussie resented the time her husband spent with Stanford.

Augusta Homer had married the tall young sculptor in Rome. She had seen his promise and must then have been dazzled by his European charm. It seems that she did not recognize how humble his background was. Augusta Homer was proud of her ancestry. The marriage would founder fairly quickly once the couple returned to America. Gussie implied her husband wished to spend more time with White than with her, which was probably correct. Although the marriage survived, it remained a troubled one, with Gussie's family trying to keep her from her husband as much as possible and Gus open to a lifetime of extramarital affairs of all sorts.

To White, Gussie represented a burden on Gus, and his way of venting his dislike for her was to refer to her using the German word for a mature or married woman, "Frau." The word carried negative implications for White and would later be used for others who displeased him. White preferred male companionship and often dismissed wifely women as "Frau." White recognized that Gus had married for relief from his terrible financial straits, which were keeping him from a great career. Gussie's financial assistance would allow Gus to devote his time to his sculpture, but did not buy White's affection. Gussie surmounted the negative attitude, feeding White many meals and even repairing his clothes, a favor hardly called for by the warmth of their relationship.

Stanford and Gus had gone beyond their initial meeting to a private collaboration that would continue for their lifetime. Soon after they met in New York, the two worked on the interior of Trinity Church. Just as White was preparing to go off to join Gus in Paris, he was able to convince Richardson to consider Saint-Gaudens for the interior of the New York State Capitol at Albany then being finished, but this juicy commission escaped them. By the time White went off to Paris, Gus did have two

*Admiral David Farragut at Madison Square. Figure by Augustus Saint-Gaudens working closely with Stanford White, who did the bench/base. The collaboration of artists would be a theme of both men's immensely successful careers. White's Madison Square Garden tower is in the background. This is a commission that launched the men's careers. Their lives were spent in and around this park, where the McKim, Mead & White office would move, the antique dealers held court, and many theaters and clubs were located. A replica of the Farragut statue stands in the park today, but in a different position.*

jobs, the tomb for the family of E. D. Morgan in Hartford, Connecticut, and the tribute to David Farragut to be placed somewhere in New York City. With both commissions awarded to the sculptor, White rode Saint-Gaudens's coattails, shepherding the job through McKim and Mead's office and putting himself forward as the designer of the base or architectural elements. The White/Saint-Gaudens collaboration would produce a host of monuments done by architects and sculptors in good Beaux-Arts style, promoting the idea of public monuments in the United States as a means of beautifying the nation. The public monuments of White and Saint-Gaudens are among the best in the nation, and the influence of their example helped add momentum to the civic improvement goals of the City Beautiful movement.

Once in Paris, White and Gus had focused on Farragut, which was a work to make each man famous. The commission came with only enough money for a basic monument and stipend for the sculptor, but the ambitions of the two men would call for more money to make a better work. White was willing to do anything to make a reputation with this monument. He labored on a base which was unlike any other in New York and would also serve as a seat. In Gus's Paris studio, Stanford went so far as to make a full-scale paper mock-up of the monument to check its proportions. White's bench was decorated with two female figures, one on either side of a central sword. The women represent loyalty and courage and were done in a high Pre-Raphaelite-inspired manner. On the far sides of the bench, White created fish in a watery drapery, a theme he would continue in later work.

Back home in the early fall of 1879, White would agonize about the shape of the bench, showing his design to his old mentors, La Farge and Babb. At the height of his uncertainty, McKim ambled by and told White to trust his own best thoughts. This sharing of ideas and personal reinforcement would characterize the next decade's working relationship between the two men. Once the design was settled and the issue of cost resolved, a location for the statue had to be determined. In the end, White's intuition again prevailed, and the site near Fifth Avenue at the top of Madison Square Park was chosen for the monument.

On a glorious day, May 25, 1881, with a military band, abundant flags and bunting, and a large crowd of spectators the unveiling of the monument took place. The dedication began with a speech by the silver-tongued attorney, Joseph Choate, whose life and partners would intertwine with White's for many years to come. A beaming, proud Richard Grant White witnessed the event, which would make Saint-Gaudens the nation's most prominent young sculptor. Although it had been a battle, in the end the quest for beauty and the creation of art had won. White and Saint-Gaudens had triumphed over the parsimonious committee members and had created the most sophisticated public monument yet seen in the nation, one that was a far cry from the traditional Civil War variety then being built.

White and Gus were a bit worse for wear at the ceremony and the poorer for the effort, which had indeed cost them money, but White and Saint-Gaudens were now established artists.

The bond between the two men that had sorely tried Gussie's patience had grown in Paris during the winter of 1878–79. A telegram from White, off in the country, could command Gus better than could the requests made by his wife. At one point, a desperate Gussie tried to interest White in her sister, then living with the couple in Paris. A friendship would bloom, but White immediately realized the intellectually honest Eugenia Homer was not the girl for him. In his letters concerning Miss Homer, White began to use a phrase he would repeat for years: "I am sure that she—or any other girl—is not for me." White's remarks about women and marriage seem to indicate a lack of interest in any serious relationship. Indeed, beyond a generic series of references to "pooty" girls, there is little other indication of ending his bachelor status.

In the spring of 1879, Gus contracted a harrowing intestinal infection, and it took round-the-clock nursing by Gussie, White, and Gus's brother Louis to pull him through. After he had recovered, Saint-Gaudens joined White in Italy for an Italian summer. White got around Italy more than had McKim, spending time in Rome and even Naples. McKim had only got to the north. The heat was difficult to endure, but White did have a chance to explore the nation, which would be more important to him than France, before going north to England and home.

While in Italy alone with Gus, who had been in Italy twice before and could act as a guide, something happened between the two that cannot be fully ascertained. White's letters, which were carefully edited by his son in the Depression years 1931–32, contain references to an incident that almost cost the men their friendship. With an ocean between them in the following months, each writes the other admitting blame and urging the other to not be too serious about what happened. Gus seems to do the bulk of the apologizing for his behavior. The language used by the two—who address each other as "beloved" and even "doubly beloved" and sign missives as "ever lovingly thine"—indicates a possible pass made at White by Saint-Gaudens. Although probably the act was rejected, an ambiguity toward homosexual moments appears in their letters from this point forward; both words and drawings seem to indicate a shared experience, and their old motto *Kiss My Ass,* used as an ending for letters, becomes more serious when signed with graphic cartoon drawings.

It would appear that Saint-Gaudens, who had married for security, had numerous affairs with women and probably with men as well. In this world of "bumming" or "sprees," as they called it, the two men shared an interest in liaisons and sensations beyond those expected of married men at the fringes of proper New York society. Both men would have active lives outside the veil of marriage. Saint-Gaudens would even have an out-of-wedlock child with his model Davida. White is not known to have had any illegitimate children, thanks, probably, to Dr. T. Gaillard Thomas, New York society's best-known solver of "women's problems."

In July 1879, White headed northward from Italy to return home via England. His thirteen-month sojourn was now almost over; White was thoroughly out of money—indeed, for his winter and spring 1879 expenses, he owed Gussie a good sum, which he would be unable to pay for over a year. Though the need to return home was pressing, this was his first trip to England, so he rushed in a visit to London, which he would discover far outshone his expectations. Perhaps the Anglophilia of Richard Grant White had caused Stanford to reject England and put it off for the end of his adventure, but once there he fell in love with the city and its museum collections. White compellingly urged Saint-Gaudens to see London and the museums as soon as possible. Either in France on the way to England or in England itself, White finally let down his guard and committed some indiscretion. We have no idea the kind of trouble White experienced, be it financial or personal, but legal action was taken against him; this trouble would follow him to New York, where a year later it was still dogging him. Prescott Hall Butler, a figure known well to McKim, an attorney and junior in his father's office of Evarts, Beaman & Southmayd, would do a great favor for White and resolve the problem. This involved a voyage to England in the summer of 1880, made with the very depressed McKim, who needed to be cheered by a change of surroundings yet again.

McKim had fallen back into a helpless state of depression and was unable to work. As had happened two years earlier, the realization that a friend was traveling to Europe prompted him to seek comfort in a change of scene, and he arranged to join Butler. In fact, both men suffered from depression, and the journey to England and Paris was a vacation for each. While abroad, Butler repaired the damage White had caused and returned home carrying two very expensive Scottish Highland outfits for his children. As a thank-you gift, White asked Saint-Gaudens to make a relief of the Butler boys in their Scottish rig. He paid Saint-Gaudens for the work and had a cryptic message carved in this relief panel for presentation to

Butler, whose new house in St. James, Long Island, he was now helping to decorate.

AS WHITE ARRIVED in New York harbor aboard the *Olympus,* he had only a limited set of possibilities for returning to the working world. He was not eager to go back to Brookline and Richardson, and he may have hoped that McKim and Mead in New York—now without Bigelow, who had retired—might offer him a place, as Mead may have implied while visiting Paris a few months before. The offer McKim and Mead made, now lost, was a nervous and ungenerous one. The economy had picked up and there were a number of jobs, but their recent hiring of Wells probably made McKim and Mead reluctant to make a formal offer. Stanford White had no academic credentials, and his family would not be likely to supply commissions. His only strong points were his decorative skills and the fact that, as McKim noted, he could "draw like a house afire." The proposal came to White in England as he was about to board the *Olympus.* The offer was a for quasi junior partnership, with his name on the masthead but a very small percentage of the firm's profits.

The financial aspect worried White, who probably realized that a big office would pay a draftsman equal or more, but an offer of a partnership was all he could hope for. As he knew he could summon up some small decorative commissions that would pay him directly, he decided to accept the offer. In 1878, McKim, Mead & Bigelow had been created. A year later the partnership ended, and the legal entity of McKim, Mead & White was formed, with McKim getting the lion's share of profits at 42 percent, Mead at 33 percent, and White 25 percent. The following year, when it was clear that White was bringing work into the firm, the final deed of partnership, with a third for each, was recorded. The partnership continued until 1905. Under the agreement, all work was to go into the firm's bill books, already complicated by Stratton's quasi partnership. Despite these arrangements, White, like Stratton, put his own "private work" list in the firm's books (although not all the jobs). The rules of architectural practice in the day were for all work to be considered company work. White's private jobs were even taken care of by McKim and Mead when he was out of the office. Like Stratton, White put his name next to private decorative work in the bill books, to indicate that these were his personal commissions and the fee should go to him directly.

When White returned to the United States and entered the offices of McKim & Mead, he was certain of a small amount of extra work selecting wallpapers for parlors and creating dining rooms for people he knew in

New York. He was also expecting a share in the work of the Associated Artists, which had been founded that year by Louis Comfort Tiffany, the painter turned decorator (and soon to become glassmaker). The painter Samuel Colman was a consultant to Associated Artists, and the wood-carving expert Lockwood De Forest was then abroad. White knew Colman and had been asked to join the three in a project. Associated Artists had been given work at the Veterans Room of the Seventh Regiment Armory on Park Avenue.

The large brick Armory building had been finished in 1879 and was now awaiting decoration of its special rooms. As the Seventh Regiment was a "society" militia, well-connected interior specialists were brought in for the important spaces. McKim's old friend Sidney Stratton worked on rooms here, and Tiffany, Colman, and De Forest turned to fellow artists for help in decorating the Veterans Room. This episode in collaborative artistic design produced the most original décor yet seen in the United States and reached a level of design well above the work of the nation's most expensive firm, the Herter Brothers, who were then completing their last full design project, the lavish triple house for William Henry Vanderbilt and his daughters at 640 Fifth Avenue. The Vanderbilt commission, though splendid and rich, was largely based on precedent, while the Associated Artists ventured into new territory with the Veterans Room. The Herter firm was well enough connected to also be given a room to decorate at the Armory—the Board of Officers Room.

The Associated Artists modeled themselves after the interior decoration firm begun in 1861 by William Morris and known until 1875 as Morris, Marshall & Faulkner. The Morris group considered themselves a brotherhood of painters, designers, architects, and amateurs who could work together to achieve more artistic results. The group had the opportunity to do some splendid work, but the number of clients was small and the work was unpredictable. This rather unremunerative club was reorganized as Morris & Co. in 1875, and a shop with their designs was set up in Oxford Street in 1877. Tiffany, Colman, and De Forest knew and copied Morris & Co., mirroring the goals of the firm with the confidence that such a high level of taste could be achieved by Americans.

The work White did for Associated Artists was independent and never appeared in the bill books of McKim, Mead & White. Along with White, the artists Frank Yewell and Candace Thurber Wheeler joined in the collaboration with Tiffany, Colman, and De Forest on the Veterans Room.

The large room that Associated Artists created was indeed unusual and splendid. A military theme was involved, with much work done in a silver metallic color and chains as a motif—the veterans, it was expected, could relate to a theme of chains and entrapment. The frieze recounts the history of warfare. The idea was to hark back to a warrior theme of the distant past. Suits of armor and chain mail were then a popular item for collectors and were often placed as a decorative gesture in homes of the period. Indeed, Stanford White later purchased a suit of armor, which he would wear from time to time to elaborate costume balls. The Veterans Room has exotic touches, incorporating details of Asian and North African decorative art. These were favorite themes for Tiffany and his artistic mentor, Samuel Colman, who had together visited the countries on the southern rim of the Mediterranean. Most interesting of the ornamental themes is the artful handling of the Celtic forms then popular in England. White may have been responsible for this detail, as he, through his father, surely had kept abreast of the Pre-Raphaelite and succeeding Arts and Crafts vogues in England.

Happily, the Veterans Room still awes visitors today, as do the other function rooms created for the gentry who sponsored the Seventh Regiment Armory. For Associated Artists and the other designers, the public rooms in the Armory were intended to showcase their interior skills. Obviously the decorators hoped for wonderful new commissions to flood into their offices from clients who had paid for the Armory rooms.

The idea of using multiple decorators for a single commission is a bit of politesse left over from the mid-nineteenth century. At that time, when houses needed interiors done up, many tactful home owners asked a small number of firms each to do a room. Perhaps this was a gesture of grace for the husband's family artist, the wife's family decorator, or those who were club and social peers. The house owner may have had a rather disjointed set of rooms, but peace was achieved. As the donors to the Armory building had favorite decorators, the showcase nature of the hiring of multiple decorators made particular sense. Although White did no further work with Associated Artists and the firm reverted to one of its principal figures, Candace Wheeler, in 1883, White went on to build houses for Tiffany and Colman and to work with the other artists of this short-lived brotherhood.

WITHIN A DECADE, White himself was to become more a decorator than an architect, happily taking on entire decorative and art-buying schemes when a rich and trusting patron could be found. This vision for his interiors mixed the goals of artistry promoted by William Morris and Tiffany with those of the opulent Herter Brothers (who actually created

*The interior of the Veterans Room of the Seventh Regiment Armory designed by Associated Artists, 1880. A creative milestone of American design blissfully still intact.*

furnishings, while White did not). Like the original Herters, White turned himself into a supra-Atlantic figure striding between the antiquities of Europe and the needs of America's new barons of business. His role was to set up self-made Americans as cultured and sophisticated players in an international aristocracy.

As if the "private" list of Stanford White's work was not enough, he frequently did favors for fellow artists and friends, dashing off house plans and designs on envelopes and dinner napkins. These off-the-books designs probably helped give rise to the myth of the "Stanford White house," so happily kept alive by Realtors in the greater New York area. There is always the chance that such a house really did have its origin in White's drawing on a linen napkin. He was fortunate that his partners did not object to this practice and looked the other way to avoid an argument. Frank Lloyd Wright would not be as fortunate in his relationship with Adler & Sullivan in Chicago.

# 9. THE BUTLERS, THE SMITHS, AND THE STEWARTS

Tightly woven into the partnership of McKim, Mead & White were the Butlers of New York City and Stockbridge, Massachusetts. The Butlers were part of a prominent legal practice who were both clients and counsel for the architects. Charles E. Butler (1818–1897) came to New York City from Virginia with his family at the age of ten. In the customary preparation for a career in the law in the first two thirds of the nineteenth century, Butler set out to learn from a well-respected figure in the profession, apprenticing himself to J. Prescott Hall. Admitted to the bar in 1839 and continuing to work with Hall, he rose to become a leading attorney in New York. When Hall retired to Newport in 1840, he joined William M. Evarts, the patrician New Englander, to establish the firm Butler & Evarts.

The remarkable Charles Ferdinand Southmayd (1824–1911), a throwback to the eighteenth century, joined the team in 1852. The severe Southmayd bridged the gap between the old way of practicing law and the new, corporation-serving firm Butler, Evarts & Southmayd would become. He came from the old New York set, having been born in 1824, when the city's small number of gentry still lived at Manhattan's tip. Southmayd disliked the changes that had taken place in the world following his admission to the bar and as a partner even refused to abandon his quill pen, "scrivening" his briefs and working only by candlelight. Southmayd may have been a bit odd in his behavior, but he had brilliantly defended John Jacob Astor, the original real estate magpie of New York, and kept the Astor family's loyalty through two more generations. Southmayd's lonely tenacity—he seems never to have married—produced clever solutions to difficult problems, earning him steady loyalty, though he never argued a case in court. He was highly respected and admired by all the young men who undertook the study of law in his office. The trial work was taken by Joseph H. Choate (1832–1917), the city's finest orator. Choate, long on charm, even in after-dinner speeches (his were notable), could relate to almost any jury; his well-chosen words and diplomacy were legendary. The combination of Southmayd and Choate was enough to frighten off frivolous cases.

The partnership, which would change names as partners arrived, left, and returned, included several other men with their own specialties. The nervous Charles C. Beaman, who spoke rapidly and not very well in public,

*Charles E. Butler, attorney and heir to the Stewart estate, thought by all others to have messed up the case.*

was a master at private negotiation and able to work well with difficult men. He was known as the great conciliator. The Butlers, Choate, and Beaman all became clients of McKim, Mead & White, and all the partners in this first large legal practice in New York had work done by Saint-Gaudens.

If Evarts, Choate & Beaman, as the firm in due course became, were the first law practice of size and varied skills, how appropriate it was that they should be intermeshed with McKim, Mead & White. William Evarts, a founding partner, was also, as we remember, a key client in the creation of Saint-Gaudens's career. Another partner, Charles Tracy (1810–1885), was a specialist in estate law and railroad law at a time when American growth in railroads was at its peak. Tracy also practiced real estate law. His daughter was the second wife of the young J. P. Morgan.

Charles E. Butler, perhaps the least loved of the partners, had much to do with McKim, Mead & White. He had married Louise Clinch, the daughter of an old New York mercantile family that appears repeatedly in McKim and White's lives. Their four children included a son, Prescott Hall Butler (1848–1901), named in honor of his father's old legal mentor. The boy was born in the family summer home on Staten Island, a location

*Prescott Hall Butler, McKim's friend and White's future brother-in-law, with his sons, ca. 1880. The boys are wearing their Scottish attire bought on Butler's trip to defend Stanford White.*

then at the height of fashion as a residential retreat for New York's mercantile gentry.

At that time Staten Island was a short breezy boat ride from Manhattan. It provided a summer respite for the New Yorkers then living at the southern tip of Manhattan near St. John's Square. A quick sail from the lower Hudson River would bring them and their families to the northern banks of the island, where wooden summer homes could be built with magnificent prospects of the waters of the port. The farming districts on the southern part of island supplied the house builders with excellent produce all summer. Many of the city's up-and-coming gentry summered on Staten Island in the 1840s. But the buildup of port activity and steamboats began to extinguish the community by the middle of the century, and many families left for Newport and other more distant watering holes. Some stayed on Staten Island, however, and even tried to live there year-round. These included Frederick Law Olmsted, who tried farming on the island; William Henry Vanderbilt, also involved in farming at this time; and H. H. Richardson, who built a house there after his marriage and treated the island as a suburb. A few baronial residences were built on Staten Island just after the Civil War, including a great stone towered pile lived in by several wealthy New Yorkers, among them the well-known yachtsman Thomas Garner. Staten Island had lost its chic summer-home status by the time of the Civil War, but remained a place in the country until it was built over in the twentieth century.

Having lost his wife in 1852, Butler left Staten Island for Stockbridge, Massachusetts, where he built Linwood, a house still standing today. Butler absorbed himself in Stockbridge, even briefly retiring from his legal practice, only to return to New York a few years later when he married Susan Ridley Sedgwick. Butler and his family would live in New York, making Linwood their vacation home. Back in New York Butler would move in Miller McKim's circle, and he prepared the legal papers for McKim's Freedman's Relief Association in 1865.

Butler's son, Prescott, attended the Hoffman School in Stockbridge before going to Harvard, where he graduated in 1869. He was one of the "fortunate fellows" able to go to Harvard College while McKim was restricted to the Scientific School.*

At graduation there was little choice for Butler to do anything other than practice law. But he had a strong interest in matters artistic, shared with his Harvard friend Walter Tuckerman, whose particular focus was sculpture. The two young men socialized often in Tuckerman's Manhattan studio, which broke up the monotony of Butler's days in his father's office, where he'd gone to learn the legal profession. He kept a diary for portions of his life, and on reading through the pages, one sees little interest in the law or legal matters. It appears that Butler was pushed into the profession, the office, and probably even marriage by an irascible father. His true love was the theater, and he later became the host in America to a number of celebrated actors and actresses. Butler's life would be a rather sad one: his father dominated him to such a degree that he fell victim to psychological troubles, probably including depression. Charles Butler did not die until 1897, giving Prescott true freedom to live as he liked for only four years before his own early death. In his last years Prescott Hall Butler recognized his true love in his wife's sister, who was married to another man.

As an aspiring, if reluctant, law student, the young Butler took time from the office of his father to apprentice with a notable jurist, Judge John Lawrence Smith (1816–1889), who regularly kept a bevy of law students in his Smithtown, Long Island, house. Smith's wife was a cousin of Butler's mother, and through Butler's introduction the Smith family were to become vital contacts in the lives of both McKim and White.

THE APPRENTICESHIP to Judge Smith had come easily, and although Butler may have found Smithtown refreshingly rustic, he was eager to get back to New York City. Judge Smith and his family had deep roots in the Suffolk County town of Smith's ancestors, which had even been named for the family. Although he preferred Smithtown, Judge Smith also kept open a house just above Washington Square at 101 Clinton Place on the Clinch/Stewart estate properties in New York. He and some of his children spent the grimmest winter months in the city.

Before Sarah Nicoll Clinch married Smith, who was a second cousin, she had been cared for by an aunt on the Clinch side, Cornelia. In 1825 Cornelia had married a northern Irish immigrant, Alexander Turney Stew-

---

*At Harvard with Butler were Dr. William Bull, who would later be McKim's surgeon; Frank Millet, later the friend and collaborator of White and McKim; and Frank Appleton of Boston, whose family would also mingle with McKim.

art, who had recently arrived in the United States with his widowed mother, a nurse. Stewart and his mother quickly settled into American life, and Mrs. Stewart found a new husband, Mr. Martin. While supporting his mother, Stewart had taught in city schools, but when his mother remarried in the 1820s, he started in the retail trade. His system was to buy slightly damaged dry goods, particularly ladies' accessories, have them repaired, then sell them at an off price. Stewart's better prices (one doubts his customers knew he was selling repaired merchandise) established him as a figure on New York City's first retail boulevard, Broadway. With help from his wife and her family, who had been acquiring Manhattan land, Stewart built up his store and bought property with his profits. He probably received excellent advice in the early 1830s, as both his father-in-law, Jacob Clinch, and his mother-in-law's family, the Irelands, were clever about property, making them among the city's prominent new real estate owners.

British settlers such as the Clinches and the Irelands were now after land once the sole purview of the Dutch families. The real estate purchases made by the Irelands, Clinches, and A. T. Stewart were directly based on their working patterns in the city. They bought in the lower portion of Manhattan, within the existing city, whereas the land king in early nineteenth-century New York was a German named Jacob Astor, who bought land well above the city to await development. It was indeed a surprise to the Astors just how rapidly their uptown lands became part of the city. Stewart both knew and admired Astor. As his shop prospered and he was able to undertake the nation's first department store at Chambers Street, just above City Hall, he began to emulate Astor in buying properties on the northern edge of town.

The success of Stewart's store, which opened in 1846 and was popularly known as the Marble Palace, was superb. The multi-department store, with its interior glazed courtyard, prospered and expanded, yielding a fine profit. By the Civil War Stewart had become the second-richest man in America, surpassed only by the Astors. He was a good businessman, buying an interest in his suppliers' businesses when he felt they made a good product. He bought mills that produced textiles and factories that supplied his well-known carpets. He even bought the Westchester quarry that yielded the stone for his marble store. In 1861 Stewart opened a second, larger department store, a white cast-iron building on Ninth Street between Broadway and Lafayette, often compared to a cloud as Stewart had sky blue shades in the store windows. The big store also featured a large open atrium with an organ to provide music for the customers. He

*Probably portraits of A. T. Stewart and his wife, Cornelia Stewart, the second-richest couple in America. Stewart was a successful dry goods merchant, but the money came from the large real estate holdings of his wife's family.*

and his wife would make frequent trips to Europe to purchase stock for the store. In England he particularly visited Manchester, where he bought fashionable items. Stewart sometimes went up to Scotland, then to Paris and Germany, where he would examine new goods in the light of the interior courtyards of the factory and warehouses. These examples of industrial architecture surely inspired him to include a glazed atrium in his two stores.

Stewart purchased not only commercial buildings off Broadway above City Hall but also residential properties off Bleecker Street in the West Village. As the big store began to thrive, he expanded his properties to nearby Clinton Place. Before the Civil War Stewart lived at Depau Row, a row of fine houses south of Washington Square, but before long he began to consider moving uptown. Soon after the second store opened, he moved to Thirty-fourth Street and Fifth Avenue, buying the northwest corner of Thirty-fourth Street, just across the street from the newly developed Astor houses built by Astor's grandchildren. He bought a gaudy house recently finished by "Sarsaparilla" Townsend, a soda-pop magnate who had fallen victim to a reversal of fortunes.

Stewart's first intention was to redo the house for himself and his wife. But within a few months, his architect declared the Townsend house to be beyond redemption and set to work replacing it with the largest, most

*The Stewart Marble House at Thirty-fourth Street and Fifth Avenue, John Kellum, architect.*
*Demolished. America's first opulent urban palace.*

expensive, and showiest new house yet built in New York. In keeping
with his first store, this was known as the Marble House. Stewart shoe-
horned himself into Astor land and one-upped the Astors with the huge
house he built for himself and his wife. Mrs. Stewart was often described
as being, by her later years, a bit simpleminded, but surely a plain and
good woman. She and her husband had no need of this huge house, especially as the two had no surviving children. The house was built as a vessel
for establishing socioeconomic rank in the city and nation, not as a home.
The huge palace was filled with treasures. As the flattering author of an
appreciation of the interiors seemed unable to repress, the décor appeared
to have been intended only as a means of display: "Items were chosen only
for their expense . . . or, rather, only the most costly seem to have been
selected."

From this noteworthy palace Stewart was able to entertain the Astors,
Boss Tweed, and General Grant, who as president attempted to install his
wealthy friend as a member of his first cabinet. Opposition proved so
strong, however, that Stewart's name was withdrawn the very next day.
Stewart's vast wholesale and retail empire and his large real estate holdings had made him a very wealthy man. He enhanced his role in the city

by owning the most popular nightspot of the age, Niblo's Garden, as well as the Broadway hotel in which it was located. He enjoyed the August racing season in Saratoga, New York, a rougher resort than Newport or Elberon. In Saratoga, overt gambling and serious matchmaking were the priority activities; Stewart therefore purchased large properties in there, including the hotels and stables. Increasingly he became interested in trophy properties.

John Kellum, the architect of Stewart's Marble House, who had grown up in the flat middle section of Long Island just twenty miles east of Manhattan, inspired in Stewart the idea of buying a huge tract of the Hempstead Plains and turning it into a "Garden City" served by a spur of the Long Island Railroad. At Garden City, Stewart planned to build pleasant, freestanding homes, which he would rent to genteel types—in other words, he would create a development in a park-like setting similar to Llewellyn Park. In this vision there was a role for himself and his wife: king and queen of Garden City. He began the community with orders for a hotel and set of mansard-roofed houses near the central train station.

Stewart had expressed little interest in the charitable institutions of New York until he undertook the building of a respectable hotel for working women on Fourth Avenue several blocks below Grand Central Depot. The idea here was to have a place for women that would be safe and reasonably priced; many of them were to work in his store. Critics contended that Stewart's hotel for women would be a front for the building of a new hotel for ordinary paying guests. (This would indeed happen; in the 1890s, McKim, Mead & White would convert the hotel for the carriage trade.)

STEWART WAS A RICH and mighty figure in the post–Civil War city—and the butt of jokes inspired by his crude behavior. Stewart's brother-in-law Charles Clinch was head of the Custom House in New York City. Richard Grant White worked for Clinch. At a time when Americans were beginning to buy furnishings and clothing abroad on a grand scale, there were constant stories—well known to Richard Grant White—about favored status granted at the Custom House for imports addressed to Stewart, thanks to Chief Clinch. The case against Clinch was serious and brought out future president Chester A. Arthur, who took over the post in the 1870s and tried to oust those at the Custom House who engaged in such favoritism (only to do it himself). The customs duties paid in New York's port were a major source of revenue for the federal government; reform was difficult, and it continued to be an open secret that duties could be "negotiated." Indeed, as Stanford White's career as an importer of household and artistic works matured, he spent many hours calling on all his friends to help him battle the Custom House.

The Clinch family was strongly bonded together. Jacob Clinch and his first wife, Susannah Banker, had a daughter, Cornella, who married A.T. Stewart. Clinch and his second wife, Louisa Ireland, also had children. Louisa's grandson, Prescott, grew up with the legend of the Stewarts, and thus when a dinner at the Stewart's house was arranged, the Butlers would push him forward. Surely Prescott could pin his life on the Stewart coattails if he managed to land one of Judge Smith's daughters. Cornelia Stewart had helped raise Judge Smith's wife, Sarah Nicoll Clinch Smith, but at a time when the Stewarts were less wealthy. Aunt Cornelia, whose children had died, took a strong liking to Sarah Nicoll Clinch Smith and her daughters. The Smiths had eleven children, six of whom reached maturity. The Stewarts would let the Smiths live in a Stewart property during the winter. They helped to educate the girls and even brought the family abroad on buying trips. Judge and Mrs. Smith traveled with the Stewarts to Rome in 1866, and the Stewarts came to trust only Mrs. Stewart's family. As Mrs. Stewart aged, she selected various great-nieces as social secretaries or companions. Mrs. Smith had too many children and was in Smithtown for much of the year, so Aunt Cornelia requested the elder Smith daughter, also named Cornelia but called Nellie, as her ward. Nellie was given a room in the Marble House, taken to Europe for her education and to write letters for the Stewarts, given some finishing in a New York school, and turned into a very likely heir, along with Mrs. Smith, for the vast Stewart fortune.

Charles E. Butler understood this well. He pushed his son into courting Nellie. The courtship appeared loveless, but resulted in an engagement after Prescott proposed to the two-years-older Nellie in a reception room of the Marble House. He must have felt himself selling out totally to "Mogy," as he called Stewart, a nickname for Mogul. The palatial "Marble Shanty," as Butler called the house, was clearly looked down upon as gross in its appearance. The wedding was scheduled to take place in 1874, when Butler passed the bar. Some three hundred guests witnessed the marriage on June 2 of that year, in the old St. James' Church in St. James,* a small section of Long Island just north of Smithtown. It was the social event of the season. A flag-covered train brought guests from the Smith's ancestral home to New York City. The wedding party

---

*The service was conducted by Aunt Cornelia's favored Episcopal clergyman, Bishop Littlejohn, and a relative of Judge Smith's who was the rector of the Episcopal church in Stockbridge, Massachusetts, the home of Charles E. Butler.

included the youngest Smith daughter, Bessie, who was a flower girl to her sister. The guests and Mrs. Stewart showered the couple with lavish gifts to begin life together.

A year after the wedding, a house was prepared for the family, probably part of the Stewart holdings near Thirty-fourth Street. Until then the couple did as many other young people would do in the 1870s and lived in one of the new apartment houses then called French flats. Once, newly married couples had resided in boardinghouses until they could afford a row house, but now they took an apartment until they could manage a house. There were a number of new flats being built near Second Avenue between Thirteenth and Eighteenth Streets. The newly married Butlers moved into a flat at 244 East Thirteenth Street, in a building run by Rutherford Stuyvesant, a prominent figure in old New York society who virtually invented and made correct the concept of the apartment for fashionable people.

On October 1, 1874, just as the Butlers were moving into their apartment at 244 East Thirteenth Street, McKim was being married to Annie Bigelow in Newport. Amazingly enough, McKim and Annie would move into the same building and onto the same floor as the Butlers. The friendship between the two men was renewed and matured into a close relationship. Butler would take a strong interest in decorating a second apartment in the Albany on West Fifty-seventh Street, then being rented out by George Da Cunha, an apartment developer who had connections to McKim and Richardson in their early days in New York. McKim spent the winter season of 1874–75 helping Prescott design furniture for the new apartment. Nellie Butler was left out of the decisions, only participating in the selection of carpets, which she would order from Stewart's store. McKim and Butler worked through furniture issues, and in this early day McKim actually designed many pieces for Butler's residence. McKim designed a sideboard, dining-room table and chairs, and a bookcase. The sideboard was in an Italian Renaissance style, while the chairs were old-fashioned high-backs, and the bookcase was based on a Nuremberg choir stall in a medieval form.

McKim's foray into interior design was short-lived and seems to have occurred only in the years of his independent practice, although late in his career, McKim worked closely with Frederick Vanderbilt on furnishings at Hyde Park, New York. These were rare instances of McKim involving himself in interiors, although he did, for his own personal use, often buy a pitcher or such household item when he traveled. In the 1870s he favored the taste of the Aesthetic movement promoted in the books of Clarence

Cook and Charles L. Eastlake, men who wrote primers for the decoration of artistic homes. McKim's furnishings were usually of ebonized wood. When the Butlers had a baby in May 1875, McKim designed a crib with a side rail that could be lowered. One only wonders if he had two made, as his own daughter was born just a few months later.

Among Prescott Butler's closest friends was Walter Tuckerman. The Tuckermans had been friendly with the Butlers for at least two generations; through the Butlers McKim joined this circle, and he was to build twice for the family. Walter Tuckerman's father, Lucius, traced his friendship with the Butlers back to their neighboring houses on Staten Island in the 1840s. Lucius Tuckerman was the manufacturer of a high grade of iron ore known for its exceptional tensile strength made in Saugerties on the Hudson. He joined Charles E. Butler in Stockbridge when Staten Island began to appear passé. At the Butler wedding, Walter Tuckerman met Florence Fenno, who was a cousin of Nellie's, and they married at the Emanuel Church in Boston in June 1875.

Although married and seemingly settled, neither McKim nor Butler was very happy at the end of the 1870s. As their respective businesses consumed their energies, both men became closer to Stanford White than to each other.

IT WAS IN 1878 that McKim, Mead & Bigelow moved into a larger office at 57 Broadway, just above the Battery at the tip of Lower Manhattan. The narrow five-story building was only twenty-nine feet wide. That year a New York architect specializing in commercial buildings, Emile Greuwe, redid the interior for the Charter Oak Insurance Company, inserting a small metal cage elevator in the stairwell. Then, when Bigelow retired, the firm of McKim, Mead & White took over the entire top floor, with its three big windows on Broadway providing a view of the seaport and its back windows looking out over the Hudson. Each of the three partners had a little cubbyhole room about six feet square as an office, so all of them spent more time in the pleasant drafting room on the Broadway front of the building. A big leather-covered swinging door separated the spaces and was always dangerous, as White would come through at a great speed, paying little mind to a possible person on the other side of the door.

The next employee after Joseph Wells in the office was probably unpaid—Maxwell E. Butler, the brother of Prescott. He was a draftsman of uncertain ability who eventually went into real estate about 1900. This self-described intellectual may have even paid for space with McKim,

Mead & White, as Stratton did, conducting a private practice from his desk at 57 Broadway, as we never see his name attached to the work of the office.

Office space in the greater Wall Street region, then Manhattan's only recognized business area, was rather casual, with a mixture of businesses occupying the five- and six-story buildings. Shops and restaurants were on the ground floor, such as the architects' favorite lunch place, Braguglia & Carreno, which they always referred to as "SPAIN" (probably a joke as the food was likely Italian). Rents on the upper floors of the buildings decreased as the floors rose, thus explaining the insertion of the rickety lift in the stairwell as a justification for increasing rents on the top floors. Life at McKim, Mead & White could be amusing, with paper-ball catch often played in the office and plenty of humor to make the long days pass faster. It is likely that the presence of the Pinkerton Detective Agency on the floor just below made for amusing moments.

The office space for attorneys in the Wall Street area was not much better, with most legal offices tiny and in oddly placed corners of buildings. One firm, Man & Parsons, had an office that could be reached only by walking in from an iron balcony resembling a fire escape on the outside of the building. Clients had to brave rain and "Spain" to enter the office. At 10 Wall Street, lawyers had rooms with primitive amenities and no elevator at all. The two most customer-friendly buildings were the Brown Brothers building and 52 Wall Street, where Evarts, Southmayd & Choate had space. The offices of the latter were on the third floor, and as at 57 Broadway, employees were expected to walk up the stairs. An elevator existed at 52 Wall Street, but a ride cost ten cents. In the Evarts, Southmayd & Choate office, legal papers were laboriously penned and copied by poorly paid scriveners. A primeval "law telephone" was placed in a closet, where one tried to get through to another telephone with a tricky process of matching one's telephone with the number wanted.

Most forward-looking businesses were trying telephones and typewriters by the late 1870s, and they became commonplace in the next decade. As businesses expanded and grew more complex—Evarts, Southmayd & Choate became a big office, as would McKim, Mead & White—employees and modern conveniences were added. By the early 1880s businesses would move from the old practices of small numbers and personal visits to clients and suppliers toward a modern office of employees with specific tasks and up-to-date machinery that would gradually eliminate the need for constant personal contact. In this decade, as business becomes recognizable to us, the tall building served by an elevator also became increas-

ingly necessary in New York. The tall office building was a natural corol-
lary to the growth of a more complex business office. Both Butler's and
McKim's firms would ride this change as their companies became the
leaders in the corporatization of their professions.

Change from the old ways seemed attractive to McKim in the 1870s.
He claimed to have been one of the first to ride on the new elevated line
once it opened, perhaps to help Prescott with plans for his move to an
apartment in the Albany. McKim was happy to build the second of a new
building type in America—the artists' studio building.

In 1878 Lucius Tuckerman asked McKim to build a studio building at
the east side of Washington Square. His son Walter Tuckerman had been a
classmate of McKim's at the Lawrence Scientific School, though the two
seem not to have known each other there. Walter began as an engineer, as
McKim had originally intended to do, but wanted to be a sculptor. In due
course, however, he succeeded his father in the Ulster ore factory, and he

*The Benedick/Tuckerman building at 79–80 Washington
Square East. This great artists' studio building still stands,
although the windows have been dramatically altered.*

was to die young, at forty-four, without ever achieving his goal of becoming an artist.

Walter Tuckerman's interest in the arts in America was part of a family tradition. An uncle, Henry T. Tuckerman (1813–1871), had devoted his life to the study of art, and he wrote one of the early books on American artists. Lucius Tuckerman admired his brother's devotion to the arts and decided to improve the lots at 79–80 Washington Square East as a tribute to Henry by creating a studio building for bachelor artists.

Henry Tuckerman, who never married, lived in a small apartment in the first studio building for artists on West Tenth Street, just a few hundred yards from Fifth Avenue. This venerable block of studios had been designed by Richard Morris Hunt soon after his arrival in New York in 1857–58. The building provided space for artists to work in pleasant, north-lit studios, plus a central exhibition space where the resident artists could display their work to the public and thus gain sales. Many well-known American painters lived, worked, and exhibited there. The Tenth Street Studio Building was influential in creating a positive climate for American artists in their own nation.

Tuckerman's decision to empower American artists further came about as the economy picked up in 1879. The commission was for a cheap, quickly built residence of six stories in red brick, intended to provide living and working spaces exclusively for bachelors like Henry Tuckerman. Indeed, the building was given the name the Benedick in reference to the bachelor figure in Shakespeare's *Much Ado About Nothing*. The Tuckermans justified the need for such a building for single men by arguing that boardinghouse landlords did not like single male tenants, a bias that had led to a shortage of available spaces for men. In reality, carving up the building into minimally comfortable spaces without multiple toilets, kitchens, or family accommodations kept the cost of the building down and allowed for more apartments to be inserted, thus generating more rent—the Benedick had thirty-three apartments on its six floors. The building management had a concierge at a desk near the arched entry, employed a janitor, and provided elevator service. With rents of $350 to $550 a year, it proved a fine investment. The clever concept of the "bachelor flat" would be used repeatedly for the next twenty years; these spaces built with minimal expenditure could be carved up and marketed as living quarters for single men. The principle seems to have been that bachelors did not care about their abodes. McKim, Mead & White built several such buildings offering bachelor flats in unusable areas.

The Benedick came into the office of McKim, Mead & Bigelow but was finished by McKim, Mead & White. The principal designer was McKim, who enlivened the building with a few Queen Anne decorative touches. It still exists. There were two swelling iron bow windows facing toward the park (new materials have replaced the original iron of the bows). Above the bow fronts a row of nine round-arched windows on the top floor creates a unified front, echoed at the cornice by a blind arcade. The top of the Benedick appears very much like a contemporaneous building by George Fletcher Babb at 173 Duane Street (extant), which was constructed as a loft building for the Ireland estate.

It is certainly no surprise that the Benedick looks like Babb's commercial building, as the two designers were working side by side at 57 Broadway. McKim had known Babb virtually his whole life. George Babb was one of twelve children of William George and Anna Earle Babb, who by the time of the Civil War were living in Orange, New Jersey, where Miller McKim probably met them. George Babb had been with Russell Sturgis during McKim and Mead's time in that office, and he had a profound influence on Mead. As Sturgis turned to writing and away from the practice of architecture, Babb struck out on his own. But he needed a partner to bring in work. Although a well-established figure in the architectural world of New York City, respected for his sense of proportion and good design, Babb was not charming. He often made shocking pronouncements in discussions, then maintained total silence and refused to explain his remarks. Despite his credibility within the profession, he could not attract wealthy patrons. Thus, in about 1877 he formed a partnership with Walter Cook, an architect just back from France and a cousin of Prescott Hall Butler. In due course Babb & Cook took over a portion of McKim's premises at 57 Broadway.

Walter Cook was a mixed-up youth—rather like McKim at the same age. He had moved about rather dramatically, studying literature first at Yale and then at Harvard before going off to Munich for a year to study architecture. He finally went to Paris to enroll in the École des Beaux-Arts, arriving just as McKim was leaving. It is possible that the two met there, as in his last months in Paris McKim roomed with a man who was in Cook's class at Harvard and had gone to Munich with Cook. Cook stayed on in Paris until 1877 when he returned to New York. At the time he teamed up with Babb, Cook was new and untried but fairly good on charm, making him the more client-oriented of the pair. And Cook had a built-in patron—his mother, Catherine Ireland Cook of the Ireland-Clinch New York City real estate world. Mrs. Cook would own a good portion of the Ireland-Cook properties below Fourteenth Street, A. T.

Stewart and his wife being the owners of the other portion of the family holdings. Prescott Hall Butler and Walter Cook were peers and cousins. By introducing Babb to Cook, Butler helped create a firm that did notable work from 1877 to about 1890, when Babb's taste proved old-fashioned and austere and Cook became the dominant partner.

Babb & Cook (later Babb, Cook & Willard) shared not only space with McKim, Mead & Bigelow (later White) on the top floor of 57 Broadway, but also social and professional lives. Babb was close to the original partners, and then to White. Indeed, it is Babb who served as the arbiter of design in White's first work. White frequently repeated that he valued Babb's judgment over all others in the early days. His circle at McKim, Mead & White included Stratton, Wells, Babb, and the artists who collaborated with them; Augustus Saint-Gaudens and his slightly loony brother, Louis; Frank Millet, Prescott Butler's old Harvard chum; Frank Lathrop, an acquaintance from Trinity Church Boston; and some painters. This group, often called "the old gang," formed the friendship core of McKim and White, and the men socialized at numerous dinners and parties. Mead and Cook did not take part in this social core, and Babb would pull away when he and White fought over a commission for West Point. Babb was an embittered man. He was often dirty in his personal appearance and displayed some indications of a psychological disorder—for instance, he was phobic about being photographed. Although he often took pictures, there are no known images of Babb.

The commercial work of Babb & Cook and McKim, Mead & White in the 1880s, with their use of round-arched windows in groups of three, blind arcade cornices, and subsuming arches on red brick buildings, is quite similar and reveals collaborative exchanges between the neighboring firms. Indeed, Babb would build 55 Broadway, the iron-fronted building just south of 57 Broadway, as the firms worked side by side. Sadly, all these modest-sized buildings on Broadway are long gone.

If the solution for a dignified and reasonably priced building at the Benedick may have borrowed some of its inspiration from Babb & Cook, it would provide the city with a wonderful residence to create a new generation of artists. On the upper floor of the building were four large studios which had north light as the Asbury Methodist Episcopal Church, the neighboring building on the north, was low enough to let light in over its roof. Until a taller building replaced the church a dozen years later, the Benedick had a bevy of artists in its halls.

The first year's register shows a Tuckerman in the building, along with Charles Butler. The then-unmarried Mead had a room there also, as would

Olin Levi Warner, the sculptor, and the painters Albert Pinkham Ryder, Winslow Homer, J. Alden Weir, George Maynard, and W. Gedney Bunce. Even John La Farge briefly lived in the building. Life in the Benedick would create the aura of an artistic bohemia for Washington Square.

Two years after the Benedick was completed, Lucius Tuckerman had the firm build him a modest hotel (now gone) around the corner that backed on the Benedick at 41 West Fourth Street. The area from Broadway to Bleecker Street had a series of modest hotels for tourists, particularly those from European nations, with specific hotels for Spanish, Swiss, and visitors of other nationalities. Tuckerman's seven-story hotel did not seem to be aimed at a single nation's tourists but fit in with the modest hostelry characteristic of the neighborhood. The hotel commission was the first for McKim, Mead & White in New York City and would usher in a small genre of their work, as New York began to attract more visitors and needed bigger and grander hotels.

For Walter Tuckerman, now married and accepting of his father's determination that he should take over the business, a summer house seemed a retreat from the grind of work. Like Prescott Butler, he felt the weight of carrying on the family tradition when he might have preferred an artistic career. Tuckerman and Butler both searched for a country house and ended up on the North Shore of the thinly populated farming region, Long Island. The commute for Tuckerman and Butler to their family summer homes in Stockbridge was long and confining, although Butler did love

*Cass Gilbert's watercolor of the Walter Tuckerman house in Oyster Bay Cove, New York. An early victim of the shift in taste away from the seaside style in the first years of the twentieth century.*

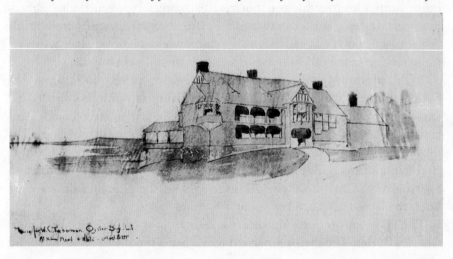

the peacefulness of the town. The trip to the Berkshires, which involved first a journey by steamer up the Hudson, then travel over land into Massachusetts, was for too arduous for a regular weekend visit. Butler began building his Long Island home first, and then Tuckerman followed, selecting a waterfront community about halfway across the island from Butler's area in St. James.

In 1882, Walter Tuckerman asked McKim, Mead & White to build him a good-sized wooden summer home on the peninsula facing Oyster Bay harbor at Cove Neck. A few New Yorkers were already planning or beginning to build homes in this unspoiled area, including Louis Comfort Tiffany, W. R. Grace, a Roosevelt, a Gracie, and, across the harbor, the Beekmans. But the real magnet to Oyster Bay was the Weeks family, long fixed to the area and friendly with the Butlers. Prescott often visited Frank Weeks in Oyster Bay on his way to St. James.

McKim, Mead & White would build Tuckerman a commodious house in so-called shingle style, popular in this period for seaside/resort architecture. The house was big, airy, and surrounded by open porches. An open loggia on the second floor of the harbor side of the house provided cool breezes for sleeping, a feature much used in later houses in the area. Tuckerman would also arrange for the building of a stable and coachman's house, which still exists. The big shingle-covered houses of this seaside mode would prove too large and difficult to make into year-round houses, and many would be demolished early in the twentieth century for more up-to-date styles of homes. The Tuckerman house did not long survive its designers.

The Tuckermans, as we know, had a disagreement with their builders, Mead & Taft, who were contractors often used by McKim, Mead & White. Butler would represent Tuckerman in a suit against the builders, which also ended the Tuckerman relationship with McKim, Mead & White.

The friendship of Prescott Butler and McKim was close in the middle years of the 1870s, as Butler escaped from home and McKim tried to bury his misery. The two ate dinner together frequently, collaborated on Butler's decoration project, and visited the Butler residences. Prescott complained that McKim didn't like to eat in "Christian" places, which meant Butler's club, preferring public restaurants, but McKim was trying to avoid embarrassing moments encountering Bigelow friends in the clubs. McKim surely preferred the anonymity of a public restaurant in a day when well-connected people seldom ate in one.

McKim took Butler along for evenings in Elberon, including a dinner with Charles Franklyn, whose newest house was just being built in Elberon in 1876. Butler brought McKim to Stockbridge in 1877, establishing his friend in a community where he would be active for a decade. Even Butler's father fell under McKim's spell, giving him a large commission for a twenty-thousand-dollar job. The specific location of this work is no longer known—was it a new building next to the Butler house, Linwood, or the beginning of the Stockbridge church, St. Paul's, which the Butlers would build and use as a family memorial? In 1883 McKim worked on this church gratis. The Butlers loved Linwood, but Prescott recognized that time to travel to the Berkshires was difficult to come by and that the place was not always relaxing, inhabited as it was by his domineering father who was showing no sign of dying young. Butler was also pressed by his wife's family, the Smiths of Smithtown, who were deeply rooted to their namesake home on Long Island.

THE SMITHS ARE THE ANCESTRAL FAMILY of the town on Long Island's North Shore that bears their name. The tale that their patriarch "Bull" Smith claimed all the land he could circle in a day's ride upon the farm animal that gave him the nickname is likely fictional. The Smith family came to Boston from Gloucestershire in England in 1630, settling at Narragansett in what is today Rhode Island. They tried to purchase land from the local Native American population, but a dispute arose, forcing the Smiths to Long Island. There the family purchased the land from Lyon Gardiner. As for the story of the bull ride, there may have been a shortage of horses in the region and the Smiths may have surveyed their purchased land atop a bull. The family has remained on their land to the present day—a record by American standards.

The head of the family in the late nineteenth century was Judge Lawrence Smith, who had come before the New York Bar in 1840 and practiced in New York City for four years before returning to Smithtown. In 1858 Smith become a county judge, which he would remain until his death. Smith built a regular office in his Smithtown home and often took in students, whom he would illuminate while allowing them to live in the house with his wife and children. The father-dominated household was run by Smith, but he did allow some time for amusement, and the life of the house was pleasant for the fledgling attorneys, who would sometimes marry a Smith daughter. Nellie, as we know, married Prescott Butler, who had come to Smithtown to study law with her father. The next daughter, Louise, would marry Frank Osborne, another student of her father's.

As the family grew, the judge and his wife enlarged their holdings of Smithtown properties. Their deep love of the region was passed on to their children, who loved the seasonal pastimes of the country captured in the Setauket pictures painted by a neighboring artist, William Sidney Mount. The local season stretched from the spring plantings to the cider-making and pig-killing festivals of fall. In winter, the Smiths lived in houses at 101 Clinton Place (modern Eighth Street) and 355 Fifth Avenue, which belonged to the Clinch-Stewart estate. With Butler, McKim would see both the Stewarts' marble palace and visit Judge Smith in Smithtown about 1877.

After Prescott Butler married Nellie Smith, he often brought his friend McKim to visit the Smiths in Smithtown. McKim had no sailing skills, and indeed was subject to seasickness on Atlantic crossings, but Butler taught him the basics of sailing a small boat as a sport. McKim would have to work hard to conquer the art of the sail. When he triumphantly negotiated Long Island Sound on his own, Butler and the Smiths created a stuffed duck trophy called the "quak." McKim was absorbed into the fresh-gingersnap-cookie world of the Smith girls, establishing a closeness that he would never lose. Since McKim had just lost his own sister and would outlive most of his family members, the Smiths became a surrogate family. McKim loved all the girls from Nellie to baby Bessie.

McKim was delighted in 1878 when Prescott brought him to a high point north of Smithtown where he was about to buy land for a weekend house. The architect enthusiastically offered to design a country home for Nellie and Prescott. McKim immediately began to design a wood-frame house in the form of a big gable covered above the base with shingles. The Butler house was initially a modest one, which kept some of McKim's components of a bigger house in line, as only a simple shape was needed here. As ever, McKim's stairhall was lit by a tall window, which became a design feature in the road-facing façade of the house. The house had some ornamental detail on the staircase window, done in Queen Anne style.

The construction of the house kept Prescott and McKim together and kept McKim in the Smith household, deepening his love of the Smith girls. The friendship between McKim and Prescott may have included a trip in 1878 or '79 to the Atlantic coast of Nova Scotia. Prescott made a journey to the Northeast and Canada; judging from the sketches kept, McKim may well have been with him.

McKim's enthusiasm for the new house, which would be begun 1878, prompted him to introduce Stanford White to Butler at about this time. White would form his own friendship with Butler, as they both enjoyed theater and going out at night, which McKim had been too depressed to do. The friendship between Butler and White would grow close enough

*The Prescott Hall Butler house, Bytharbor, in St. James, Long Island.*
*Watercolor likely by Stanford White.*

for Butler to agree to go to England in 1880 to solve White's legal problem.

The friendship with McKim and Butler by 1879 brought White to Smithtown and into the Smith household, where he met the Smith girls. White enthusiastically joined in on the Butler house design, helping to detail the ornament and even personally carving a wooden motif on the façade. The work White did at the house would give it a Continental air, which we can see in an 1884 watercolor probably painted by White. There are awnings on the windows, and even an ancient Roman touch— a fabric curtain draped over the main doorway.

The Butler house needed a name, and during the summer of 1880 Nellie and her sisters came up with one that described it: "Bytharbor." The girls wrote Prescott to suggest the name, which he immediately rejected as being overly "Hebrew." Nevertheless, the name stuck and the house would always be called by it.

When the first phase of construction came to a temporary halt in 1881, Butler bought a neighboring property in a curiously devious way. Clearly he did not want to buy property under his own name, perhaps fearing the price would be higher. Butler enlisted White in his scheme, and the penniless White briefly purchased the land, which he then sold to Butler a few days later. White and the Butlers were now the best of friends, as we can see when White thanks Butler by having Saint-Gaudens create a relief panel for the spot over the fireplace at Bytharbor.

The expansion of the house may have stopped about 1882, but only briefly. The Butlers, and indeed all the Smiths, expected shortly to be very rich. After the Civil War they had watched the enormous Stewart fortune continue to grow. Since the judge's wife, Sarah, had been effectively adopted by the childless Cornelia Stewart and the Smith girls were favorites of the old lady's, they could expect this money eventually to come to them. There is little evidence that Judge Smith and his wife cared very much about the fortune they might soon have, but the children were brought up knowing that they would be the second- or third-wealthiest family in the nation. The Butlers certainly recognized the future sums Nellie would be likely to possess. The only thing that the Smiths and Butlers did not adequately recognize was the devouring nature of a cousin's husband.

Cornelia Clinch Smith Stewart preferred her Clinch-Smith relatives, but she also showered attention on a niece who had married a lawyer with connections to Boss Tweed, Judge Henry Hilton. Hilton was an aggressive figure who seemed to offer helpful advice to the aging Stewarts. He was able to keep his thoughts of the Stewart fortune repressed during Stewart's lifetime. Hilton and his family lived in a row house just west of the Stewarts so that he could drop in often on his wife's elderly aunt and uncle. Stewart misjudged Hilton's level of greed and put his trust in the man, whose Tweed connections would assist Stewart in his real estate and dry goods empire.

When Stewart finally died in April 1876, the world waited to learn the size of the estate and its disposition. With Stewart buried in the family vault at the old St.-Marks-in-the-Bowery graveyard and his widow wandering aimlessly in the cheerless Marble House, Hilton saw his opportunity. If he could fool Stewart, who was a rational thinker, surely he could control Aunt Cornelia. The family-oriented Hilton, whose children had socialized with the Smiths and Butlers, suddenly became Hilton the monster.

The will of "Mogul" Stewart left a generous benefaction to Judge Hilton, whom he wished to oversee the care of his wife. For his work, Hilton would be given a million dollars. The remaining estate would go to Cornelia. Hilton rapidly cornered Mrs. Stewart, who was ignorant of all Hilton's promises to Stewart, and set about putting the assets of the Stewart estate into his own hands. He convinced Mrs. Stewart that her late husband's estate, his stores, the very lucrative mills and factories that he had owned, the marble quarry, and the hotels in New York and Saratoga were of little value, and he offered to trade legacies. Hilton would give the million-dollar legacy to Mrs. Stewart, and he would take the useless businesses and properties off her hands. Mrs. Stewart agreed to this arrangement, putting all her trust in Hilton and his financial acumen.

Hilton rapidly took control of Mrs. Stewart and the empire and managed to keep the old lady's trust. Mrs. Stewart, devoutly Episcopalian, began building a cathedral in Garden City in honor of her late husband. Gestures such as cathedral building and continuing residence in the Marble House attracted public attention, both the good and the bad. The curious members of New York's money-oriented society wondered why the widow Stewart was wandering around in the marble barn, virtually alone, and who would be given the house in the end. Stewart had intended it to be a fine arts gallery and hoped to give it to the City of New York, as the family did own a notable collection of contemporary European and American painting and sculpture. The plans Stewart had entrusted to Hilton would never be carried out.

The Stewart aura would attract a criminal element just two years after the old merchant's death. A desperate group of thieves stole Stewart's remains in the dark of night from the vault at St. Mark's, transporting the bones to Canada, where they secretly buried Stewart in a potter's field, then presented Mrs. Stewart with a ransom note. Mrs. Stewart, little able to cope and hysterical about her husband's remains, again put her faith in Hilton, who promised to pay the demanded sum, retrieve the body, and give it a proper Christian burial. No one is certain what happened next. Hilton claimed to have followed Mrs. Stewart's direction and had someone's body brought to the new cathedral in Garden City for burial, but most people believed Hilton did not pay the ransom and simply substituted someone else's remains, leaving Stewart in an anonymous grave in Montreal.

Hilton and his children took on the A. T. Stewart store, which he had promised Stewart he would close, giving the proceeds to Mrs. Stewart. Instead, he kept it open and ran it himself, badly, and drove it out of business in short order. Hilton then ruined the excellent mills Stewart had owned, driving Stewart's empire into bankrupcy. Mrs. Stewart lived another decade, unaware of Hilton's betrayal of her husband's trust. As Mrs. Stewart bought nothing for herself in these years, she was blissfully unaware of Hilton's actions. The Stewart heirs in Ireland and the Smiths and Butlers must have watched with horror the siphoning off of the estate they had expected to inherit, but the family could not convince Mrs. Stewart that her trust in Hilton was mistaken.

Mrs. Stewart finally died, rather unexpectedly, forcing Hilton to scramble up the stairs and seal off the house, allowing only his own family access. Once Mrs. Stewart's remains had joined the pauper in A. T. Stewart's grave, the legal scramble began. Charles E. and Prescott Butler pounced on the assets in the name of Cornelia's relatives—the Smiths primarily, and the families of two other Clinch children, the Merillons and Boreels. The Butlers and Judge Horace Russell (who was the husband of one of Hilton's daughters) acted for the Clinch family. A. T. Stewart, who had had little contact with his homeland and relatives there, would have been astonished at how quickly his relatives in Ireland made a case for some of his estate. But there was not much left. Hilton had succeeded in losing a huge sum in his businesses, perhaps some twenty to forty million dollars, and it seems Hilton had not given Mrs. Stewart even the million he had promised in trade for the assets of the estate. The heirs must have been greatly disappointed to find all that remained was Stewart's real property, but that was a hefty parcel, including properties all over Lower Manhattan; all of Garden City, as yet undeveloped; and property in Saratoga.

Judge Hilton had liked the fast track and fast crowd of Saratoga. He had built himself a large private home and park near the city and attempted to manage Stewart's hotel with some new policy changes. It was Judge Hilton who put up signs in the lobby forbidding rooms be let to Jews and dogs. The resort, which had been attracting a wealthy and mixed August guest crowd, had been a stop on the vacation trail of Jewish banker and philanthropist Joseph Seligman and his family. The coarse new policy created a thunderous response in the weekly German-language humor magazine *Puck,* which had a festival at Hilton's expense. The Hilton affair damaged Saratoga's reputation as well as the value of Stewart's properties. Thus, the Stewart heirs would have to redo the hotels to try to revalue the properties. In 1880 Prescott Butler dispatched Stanford White to one hotel in Saratoga, the Windsor, where White fitted out the hotel with Japanese screens and new décor, hoping to hide the scandal behind a renovation. The Stewarts were gone from Saratoga by 1887, but the settling of the estate would be a slow process with far less value than the heirs expected.

WHEN STANFORD WHITE FIRST MET the Smiths, he was most aware of the wealth of the Stewarts; his father knew Mrs. Stewart's brother, who worked at the Custom House with him and also studied Shakespeare. In a letter home from France on November 21, 1878, White made a joke about not caring if Stewart's body was really in the "shameful" mausoleum in Long Island. White must have recognized in the Smith family a link to the dry goods king of his father's dinnertime stories.

When Stanford White began to visit Smithtown, most of the Smith girls were taken. The only girl left at home was Bessie Springs Smith, the youngest of the children, who had been rather like a kid sister to Prescott Hall Butler; she returned the sentiment by naming Butler as her favorite of all her father's law students. Bessie loved the rural life of Smithtown even more than her siblings did. She rejoiced in swimming, fishing, and sailing in the harbor; she loved seasonal feasts and particularly enjoyed the fall pig slaughter. Bessie greatly respected her powerful father and may have been the most like him of his children. As a student, she was not a bluestocking and did not enjoy the New York City finishing that Aunt Cornelia had provided. Bessie was taller than most girls in her day, with a long straight nose, wide mouth, and a good figure.

When Stanford White met Bessie in 1879 or 1880, she amused him with her ability to sing and whistle at the same time. White began to try to establish a relationship by searching for the sheet music for a song the two had sung, sending the music with a basket of fruit. Although flattered by the attention, Bessie was still young and uninterested in the red-haired architect she had first seen in her father's office as she spied on the grown-ups through a keyhole. White would invest two years in trying to gain Bessie's favor. After his love for Anaïs Casey had been unsuccessful, he briefly tried to court girls who might further his career, including Richardson's daughter and Miss Delano. White recognized the value of a well-off bride. Saint-Gaudens had advanced his career with his marriage to a woman of some means and good connections. White, who many times had repeated his disinterest in women and marriage, clearly recognized the value of a great-niece of the great mogul. Was White really in love with Bessie? One cannot be certain, but the tone of his letters to her suggests the case was rather more as it was with Prescott Hall Butler: a courtship made with an eye to the fortune of Mr. and Mrs. Stewart.

Bessie did not respond well to White's first attempts at courtship, prompting the architect to try to give Bessie some time to miss him as he set out to check up on his brother, Dick. Three years earlier, Dick had gone west to New Mexico in the hope of establishing himself as a mining specialist. From the Southwest, Dick wrote home with enthusiasm about several mines he had discovered and begged his family assist him in purchasing the properties. Stanford agreed to help, and Aunt Laura Dudley's husband also invested in Dick's mines. After a lot of hyperbole about the fortune he would soon make, the family decided to see if Dick might really have come upon a good property. Stanford opted to go west and check on Dick's prospects. The family seemed to hope that a real find had been located, as White told the Smiths that there was hope of a fortune to come from these properties.

Getting time off from the office was not easy. McKim, Mead & White had numerous jobs at hand, including a substantial commission for a palatial town house complex that might really establish the reputation of the architects beyond the personal-recommendation level. For White to extract himself in this time of promise required a substantive explanation. White assured McKim and Mead that he needed to oversee his troubled brother—if Dick really had found a potential load of ore, he would have to be supervised or he would let the opportunity slip away. White probably also recognized that should a fortune not arise, he would have to get a job for Dick in the West, where all concerned realized he was far better off. White may also have informed his partners that he had some hope his absence and the prospect of wealth might ignite Bessie's interest in his courtship.

As only army engineers and desperate men traveled overland, White prepared to head west by visiting the city's toniest purveyors of adventure clothing, Park & Tilford, fitting himself up for his journey as his father had done to go to England six years earlier. In February 1882, Stanford White set off for New Mexico.

When White arrived in Socorro, he was immediately plunged into his brother's rough-and-ready life. Dick took him to a shanty, a real one, outside of town, where he could live with fewer bugs than in the wooden buildings of the town. As the region was still vulnerable to attack from all sides, the Whites were armed to the hilt with guns and knives. In rapid order, while making fun of White's New York Western attire, Dick set out to toughen up the tenderfoot, subjecting him to endless hours in the saddle, forty-mile walks in a day, sleeping outside in storms, and eating meals out of cans. The grub must have been a real comedown for White after Europe and the restaurants of New York, but rather amazingly, he got into the routine. They spent a month at Socorro, probably with Stanford trying to confirm any potential in Dick's claims, which did not seem to emerge. Dick must then have spoken up about the Black Range some 150 miles away, another area he thought might promise riches.

The Black Range must also have been a dud, as White promptly embarked on his backup plan, hatched in New York before he departed for the West, of finding a new profession for his brother. This mission was to involve a trip to Mexico.

Stanford White was a good family member to engage in this elaborate
job search for his highly flawed brother. He undertook a miserable and
dangerous journey to visit Dick, followed by an even riskier adventure
into Mexico. White's letters home in the 1870s and early 1880s consistently reveal him as a decent, thoughtful, self-questioning, and appreciative person. He went out on a very thin limb to try to establish Dick in a
career, and one can only admire the Stanford White of this period.

Writing home to his parents and to Nellie, Prescott Butler's wife,
White gives details of this rough trip. It involved making his way into
Chihuahua via El Paso, taking a stagecoach, then riding a mule in a steep
descent for the final 150 miles to the tiny, remote, and dangerous town of
Batopilas in the Sierra Madre range. Once in Batopilas, White and his
guide hiked three miles along the river to the Hacienda de San Miguel,
with its mansion, offices, and metal-refining plant. The object of this journey was to meet Alexander Robey Shepherd of the District of Columbia.
Shepherd was a native of the nation's capital who rose to the top political
office there in 1873, only to fall from favor within a year when a series of
major charges of corruption were made against him. He ended up in
Batopilas, Mexico, opening a great silver mine in 1880 and living very
well. Shepherd built a grand house and entertained lavishly. Food and
wines were brought in from the Pacific side of the Sierra Madre, rather

*The White brothers, Richard and Stanford, in the middle,
on horseback in the American Southwest.*

than the difficult route White took in from the east. Perhaps White knew of Shepherd through Prescott's father's partner, Evarts, who had been in Washington. Another possible connection to Shepherd might have been Anaïs Casey, who was in and out of Washington, D.C., often in the 1870s and 1880s. Shepherd graciously brought White and his unnamed traveling companion to the house and entertained them lavishly for a week. The hacienda Shepherd built was not at all Spanish in form, but a Gothic house made of adobe—surely an incongruous apparition. Whatever idea White presented was not realized, and he left the same way he had arrived, enduring a week of miserable travel to return to his brother in Socorro.

During the New Mexican adventure White had kept in contact with his partners in New York, asking his parents to send books on English furniture to the office and recognizing he was more useful there than in helping with Dick's search for a future. By late May of 1882, just three months after he set out for the West, he dropped his original plan to travel to Oregon, where he had intended to work on buildings planned for the new route to Portland being built by the Northern Pacific Railroad. The railroad was run by McKim's somewhat annoying "Yarman" (German) brother-in-law, Henry Villard. Villard, who was an old-time abolitionist and friend of Miller McKim, had married Lucy McKim Garrison's sister-in-law, Fanny Garrison. Villard had brought several nice jobs to the office, including a hotel in Portland, Oregon, but White decided the difficulty of trip outweighed the value of job, and abandoned all thought of more travel, heading directly home to absorb himself in his work. We don't know if White had any contact with Bessie Smith while he was in the Southwest or if his absence made any difference to her that spring. Curiously, while on his travels White had been thinking of Anaïs Casey again, or perhaps he was sending her a message from Mexico, as he sent his father a letter for Anaïs and asked him to locate her and deliver it.

Back in New York by the beginning of June 1882, White rejoined the office. McKim and Mead had managed to keep going quite well in his absence, and the ever-useful Joseph M. Wells had taken over much of his work while he was gone.

# 10. JOE WELLS

J oe Wells had settled into 57 Broadway, assuming a major role in the detailing of buildings. With Mead handling practical matters and McKim bringing in clients and making the presentations, Wells fell into his natural role of designing many of the buildings for the partners. Although socially inferior, Wells was a far more able architect. He had few managerial skills and was terrible with clients, as he could not control his remarks, which had more than an edge of dry humor. He was not a man who suffered fools gladly. Wells was at his best left alone at a desk; he was often quiet for a time as he worked through ideas in his head before pouncing on paper to delineate the solution to a difficult problem. Those who worked with him always gave him full credit as the firm's premier designer from 1879 to his premature death in 1890. Wells was the force who would lift McKim and Mead into a confident design stage and leave them with the tools to continue after his death.

One piece of evidence for Wells's role in the firm came from the great architectural historian Henry-Russell Hitchcock, who just missed knowing the architects. In the 1920s Hitchcock moved in a circle at Harvard run by alumni of the McKim, Mead & White office. He also knew William King Covell of Newport, who would become a local history teacher and architectural photographer. Hitchcock's drafting instructor at the Harvard School of Design was C. Howard Walker, an architect who was in and out of McKim, Mead & White in the firm's earliest days. "Howdie" Walker was Joe Wells's best friend. Walker, a fellow Bostonian, relates that in the late 1870s Wells shyly appeared at his door, carrying a

sheaf of large rolled drawings. Walker believed that
these exquisite works were the first large renderings
done in America. Wells kept the drawings with him in
New York, putting them up at 57 Broadway. He gradually nudged McKim, Mead & White over to the drawings, pointing out the subtle beauty of symmetrical and
well-proportioned buildings. As picturesque asymmetry played itself out in the 1880s, Wells helped the
partners find detail for new works needing a special
touch. Surely the bits of Renaissance detail at the Edgar
house in Newport and at J. Coleman Drayton's house in
New York City came from Wells.

*Joseph M. Wells in an oil sketch by*
*Thomas Wilmer Dewing, ca. 1884.*
*Mead kept the image of the fourth*
*"partner" on his desk throughout*
*his life.*

It is hard to know if Walker spoke of Wells to Hitchcock in the 1920s or if Hitchcock, who had amazing
visual skills, just recognized it himself, but he correctly
notes that McKim, Mead & Bigelow's work picks up in
quality when Wells arrives and falls into repetitive and
formulaic competence after Wells's death. He attributes
the great decade of design during the 1880s to Wells.
Stanford White thought in decorative flashes while
Wells thought architecturally. All the former office men
who knew Wells or even knew of him echo the same conviction. McKim
emphasized Wells's premier importance, while Mead from retirement
spoke of the early days of the partnership and of four partners, stressing
his sense of Wells as a coequal. Indeed, Mead kept an oil sketch of Wells
painted by Thomas Dewing on his desk out of respect for the almost partner snatched away too soon.

Only one person who was in the office while Wells was there denied his
prominent role. This was William Mitchell Kendall, a Massachusetts
native like Wells, who joined McKim, Mead & White early on, serving
White for several years before becoming McKim's right-hand man, a position he retained. Admitted to the firm as a partner in 1906, Kendall took
a personal delight later in life (once White and McKim were dead) in
insisting that Wells had no role in the office other than doing detail flourishes. Kendall ran the firm in the years before and after World War I. The
death of White opened a Pandora's box of negative publicity; rumors flew.
The principals in the firm attempted to counter the scandal by extolling
the partners' design skills to save the firm's reputation. Kendall always
insisted McKim and White were the only designers, but his was a single
voice. Indeed, anecdotal accounts stress his mean temperament. One gets

the sense that he may have tried to have the final word by ruining the reputation of the other draftsman in the office of the 1880s, who was far more respected than he was. He must have felt inferior, since Wells was offered a partnership after a decade, while Kendall had to wait twenty years for the offer.

Once Wells appeared, two idioms of design flourished. Wells was gifted in the picturesque and could pull the beach-resort, shingle houses into an attractive whole. He also maneuvered a reluctant team trained in the school of Richardson into an admiration society for the Italian Renaissance. Wells had the ability to synthesize forms from history and put them together in ways that had never been seen before, either in the past or in contemporary work in Europe. He grafted together historical precedents and mixed them with new forms to make successful new buildings with honesty, a sense of proportion, and intelligence.

Even before Wells was officially hired by the firm in 1879, he may have been helping out with suggestions and doing the drawings. Within a few years, his confidence and the level of respect he commanded had grown so much that when White went to New Mexico, Wells was given White's jobs. From 1882 to 1890 he was a professional coequal in the office, but neither socially nor in remuneration—he remained poor his whole life. By 1884 or so, when Mead married, Wells moved into the Benedick (perhaps to Mead's old rooms), but he was always financially strapped.

Wells came from a family with a deep love of music, as had Saint-Gaudens and White. He was absolutely passionate about music, believing that it was better in Europe. On an evening's stroll in the fall of 1882 the three friends heard a musical group playing in a beer garden on Broadway. The architects were most impressed and invited the musicians to Saint-Gaudens's studio to play for their friends. Wells kept working on the musical performances that followed the initial one, improving on musicians and selections from the great composers. About forty-five men came regularly, with Richard Grant White joining his son in the first two years of the concerts. Guests were free to sit comfortably and puff away on tobacco products, making the studio gray with smoke. The regulars were New Yorkers interested in the arts—mainly men, but women did occasionally drop by. In the circle of artists who enjoyed music in New York in the 1880s, Wells was the ringmaster, and in the smoky studio, a fraternity of artists thrived.

Wells was the master of music and architecture for the office. He was good at little else. A defensive hide of anger cloaked the young man, who got on poorly with most people and could quickly stir up a controversy with a caustic remark. Wells was not capable of working with clients, which made him the opposite of McKim and White, who had well-developed layers of charm. Wells fell into the backroom role and had only one full job that involved meeting alone with clients. While at work, he penned witty remarks rather like the repartee of the writers of the Algonquin Round Table in New York City in the 1920s. Wells could cut to the quick and sniff out sham in a moment. Content in the end to sit and work in the shadows, he was the person who created the mature career of McKim, Mead & White, but he was also the person who snuffed out the creativity of his partners. Wells finally educated the office on the joys of Renaissance architecture. He taught the partners how to find precedent in the volumes of Letarouilly and others in their growing library—and by showing them that the pages of books contained all the answers, he removed their life force. By the end of the century, everything came out of books.

Wells replaced Babb as the man McKim and White turned to for review of their work. He kept standards of design in the office high while solving the difficult problems. Stories about his work habits abound. One frequently repeated tale recounts how White burst in excitedly on Wells at a

*The office of McKim, Mead & White at 57 Broadway.*

solitary breakfast, holding a drawing he had just made. White said something to the effect that he felt his design was as good as the Parthenon—to which the sour Wells replied, "So too, in its own way, is a hard-boiled egg." Wells was the arbiter of quality who at times conceived his designs by hanging out over the street front of 57 Broadway for days, dangling a chenille monkey on a string from the fifth-floor window while not putting a pencil to paper. When the solution finally came together in his mind, he would jump inside and furiously draw his idea.

Wells's abilities in architecture were superior to those of the partners, and having such a superior employee made McKim, Mead & White into an office that placed great trust in their workforce. Wells conditioned the partners to gather the first thoughts about a new project and then let him pull it together. By the later 1880s the partners were heavily—at times even totally—dependent on their assistants. As McKim and White took off on their own paths, the other men in the office effectively were McKim, Mead & White. The office became the prototype of the modern large architectural practice, where many produce work in the name of a few. Without an assistant as skilled as Wells, the firm might never have developed this model, which enabled them to take on many projects in a limited time.

Although we do not know what Wells's initial contributions to the office may have been, the competition entry for the 1879 Union League Club building may reveal his hand. The competition ushered in a series of New York club designs, many to be accomplished by McKim, Mead & White, who became clubmen as well as club architects.

The British gentlemanly interest in men's clubs, especially urban clubs, crossed the Atlantic rather suddenly. British clubs began in an individual's home; in the next stage of enlargement, they took on a house for club use; then, when finally successful, they would build a clubhouse. These clubs implied a certain position and were frequented by men who identified with the views known to be held by that club. The British tended to belong to only one club, which would secure the loyalty of its members. New York clubs modeled themselves on those of London in implying a purpose, but did not necessarily hold the exclusive interest of their members. The first club in New York City, the Union Club, was founded in 1836, followed by the Century Association in 1846–47.

The Union Club was a social club that met in houses on Broadway until 1855, when Griffith Thomas, a prolific architect in mid-century New York, built a new clubhouse in the Renaissance palazzo style on Twenty-first Street at Fifth Avenue. This was the first U.S. club built and used exclusively as a club. The style had been used in the 1820s in London by the architect Charles Barry for his clubs in Pall Mall, so Thomas's importing of the Pall Mall–type clubhouse was a sincere copyist's tribute to the suitability of an Italian palace for a nineteenth-century club.

In the early years of the Civil War, a dispute arose in the rooms of the Twenty-first Street club over sides taken by Union Club members on the issue of slavery. So in 1863 the Union League Club was formed as a breakaway from the static Union Club support of the Union cause. Those looking for an end to slavery moved to the Union League, which began life at 26 East Seventeenth Street. Here the club members organized the Sanitary Fair, an effort to support Union soldiers, in which Richard Grant White (though not a member) was much involved. The Union League Club also sparked the discussions that led to the creation of the Metropolitan Museum of Art. Its original house on Seventeenth Street was remodeled by Gambrill & Richardson before the club moved to a palatial house on Madison Avenue at Twenty-sixth Street, formerly the home of horseman and bon vivant Leonard Jerome. Jerome turned his house into a club building after his flamboyant behavior had embarrassed his wife sufficiently that she left for Europe with the couple's children (the Jeromes' daughter Jennie would marry in Britain and become the mother of Win-

*The ill-fated competition entry for the Union League Club by McKim, Mead & Bigelow, 1879. Perhaps the hand of Wells can be seen in the design.*

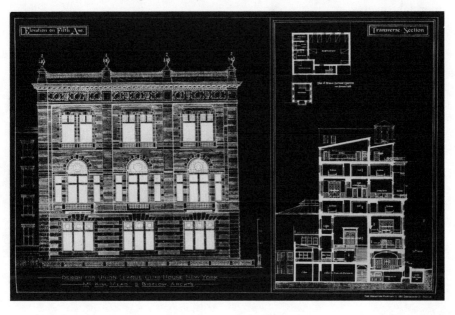

*Joseph M. Wells drawing of the Farnese Palace, ca. 1878. Created in the United States before Wells went abroad and said to be the first important architectural rendering made in America.*

ston Churchill). The house, one of the city's first mansions, would serve as a headquarters for a series of clubhouses until the 1960s, when the newly formed New York City Landmarks Preservation Commission proved too weak to prevent its demolition in favor of a banal, modern commercial tower.

In 1879 the Union League Club was sufficiently strong to consider building its own clubhouse. Since the Union Club was on Fifth Avenue, the Union League decided it would be as well, with property on Thirty-ninth Street. A competition was held and was won by the Boston firm of McKim's old Parisian friend Robert Peabody, Peabody & Stearns (the clubhouse has been demolished). The McKim, Mead & Bigelow competition design had some Renaissance-inspired features and a unified cornice line, for which Wells was likely responsible.

To Wells, who had left Peabody's office in a huff, his old firm's success must have been galling, especially as the Peabody & Stearns design was rather pompous and incoherent. The McKim, Mead & Bigelow design, which used an arcade in Renaissance style on the main floor and loggias above, may have come from Wells's personal study of Italian palaces. The Italian palazzo form was not new in New York. Renaissance details had traveled to the United States through book plates in the 1840s and '50s

*Joseph M. Wells drawing of the Louvre. Wells is known for two great drawings shown to his friends, but not this image. These drawings have not been seen in a century and were unknown except to the office.*

and had been the design form for the brownstone row house.* After some twenty years of fashion the palazzo form became tired, leading younger designers to new styles such as the mansard-roofed French Second Empire, a contemporary form then being used in France and England. The other imported styles were the English High Victorian Gothic and later Queen Anne. Peabody's firm worked in the Queen Anne style, as had McKim. But Wells's design was different. In his evening hours he turned to European architecture, which he had never seen with his own eyes, studying book plates of French and Italian buildings intently and making careful drawings of their inspiring forms. Wells made at least three elaborate elevations of such buildings: the façade of the building housing the École des Beaux-Arts in Paris, the Palazzo Farnese, and the Cancelleria in Rome. These drawings sat over his drawing table and may well have led to the Union League design. Wells was not officially on the payroll at this date but may have been in the office full-time, receiving payment in cash. Neither Mead nor McKim had much interest in Renaissance buildings at this time; they were still in a picturesque mode and were unlikely to have cre-

---

*The use of brownstone as an exterior cladding on a traditional brick row house began in the 1840s, just as the Renaissance door frame, window, and cornice detail became fashionable. Thus, the brownstone-fronted row house came to be equated with Renaissance idioms.

ated the Union League design. The Union League Club façade seems to evoke that of the École des Beaux-Arts building, which would likely have been an acceptable precedent to McKim.

Wells based his study of buildings on the plates of books such as the three-volume illustrated set by the French architect Paul Letarouilly, *Édifices de Rome Moderne* (1840), which was filled with beautiful images of Renaissance buildings. Wells much envied those who could afford a higher education, since his own economic position had made this impossible. His dissatisfaction with his provincial education finally boiled over in the summer of 1880, when he threw caution to the winds, borrowing money and sailing for Europe. Although travel in Europe was reasonably priced, Wells did not have the resources for it, nor did McKim, Mead, or White have the money to send him at this time. He may have had some small savings gained from extra work drafting for other architects.

Wells set out in June 1880 for Britain, France, and Italy, armed with a sketch pad and camera and intent on a sojourn of about a year. He arrived in England with a young man, a student at Harvard, who seems to have found Wells's cynicism unbearable and soon deserted him in Britain. Wells saw Liverpool, Chester, then London, observing it all while nursing a terrible toothache. British architecture bored him, and he found only domestic building and the Norman remains worthy of his attention. He would already have been familiar with the recent work in the High Victorian Gothic and Queen Anne, which evidently held little interest for him. In July, Wells traveled across the Channel to Paris, where he was equally bored by the recent Second Empire work. But he found the ornament on medieval buildings, especially at Rheims, overwhelming, and truly liked the picturesque composition of anonymous old streets and their rooflines. He wrote to White that he had recognized a street from White's notebooks of two years earlier as he toured in his friend's footsteps.

In the fall of 1880, Wells fell in with a group of young architects in Paris, which included some men he knew from other offices, such as William H. Whidden and Alexander Wadsworth Longfellow, nephew of the poet. In the group was an Isaacs, and a Chamberlin, probably William E. Chamberlin, and a Stickney. Some of these single young men were in ateliers connected to the École, but others were in Paris solely for the experience. By day, the young men viewed buildings. In the evening there was a lot of socializing, musical performances, theater, and eating, especially at a place known as "Chez Blots." One cannot be sure if this was a nickname for a restaurant where they ate, as the group did seem to descend into the demimonde of Paris, often dancing until the small hours.

The definition of "blot" in the day would refer to a failing in backgammon, or a stain, or even a sin. The café seemed to be a center of the young men's life.

In September, the handsome Thomas Hastings of New York appeared and spent time with Wells. Hastings would join McKim, Mead & White, as would Whidden and Chamberlin. From the early fall until Christmas, the young friends explored Paris and made jaunts to tourist sites amid a party atmosphere of sometimes amusing, sometimes nasty behavior. The world Wells joined and thrived in has many similarities to the Left Bank atmosphere Americans thronged to Paris to experience over the next sixty years. The lives of this group of young men were chronicled in the diaries kept by Alexander Wadsworth Longfellow from July to December 1880. They contain no references to women the men socialized with, and the word "queer" to describe abnormal male behavior is used frequently; however, no definitive comment can be made about the actual activities of the group.

After Christmas Wells headed off to Italy, which he hoped would be a crowning experience of Renaissance palaces viewed in warm weather. He was not properly prepared for Italy in winter and took snow as a personal affront, but he got into the swing of things once he found Larkin Mead and was able to socialize a bit more. Italy was not the triumphant heaven Wells had expected, although he noted, "Italian architecture is great, grand and dignified . . . Another excellence is their magnificent style of execution. They are the most skillful artists in the world—but they are inferior to the French in the free handling of detail or design . . . I see very little to sketch. There are no picturesque groups of roofs. No Italian ever made a crazy design like some of these in Brittany."

# 11. THE SUMMER HOUSE AND THE SEASIDE HOUSE

Wells returned home to settle in at the office in spring of 1881, never to go abroad again. Back in New York, he would assist the partners in the rich flowering of the resort style of wooden houses they had begun a few years earlier. Wells, McKim, and White had now all seen the picturesque buildings of the northern French coast in Brittany and Normandy.

Normandy and the coast were resort areas attracting the new money of industrial France, much as Elberon and Saratoga attracted the same social rank in the United States. Americans had already observed the wooden vernacular houses of these French resort towns, and architects like Richard Morris Hunt had built in a similar style at Newport and in other country places. As we know, the French Normande style had inspired the design of many East Coast cottages in the 1860s and '70s. These houses, occupied for only half the year, were often quickly and somewhat cheaply built, but the Normande style gave them a look of permanence as the vernacular detail was associated with older residences. A new house could appear timeless.

The wooden domestic architecture of American resorts had a further characteristic. The verandah, also called a piazza or porch—that open response to the human desire to bask in summer breezes—appeared as a dominant characteristic in the American adaptation of the type. Often it included a wraparound porch, which served as an outdoor living area for summer. The verandah had been brought to the North by the plantation owners of the West Indies and American South, who knew the value of a big, wind-catching porch in the tropics. As the plantation families summered in Newport, the large porch began to appear on the cottages there before becoming a characteristic of all sea- or lakeside residences in the United States in the second half of the nineteenth century.

Before the Civil War, the cottages of Newport could as easily have been found at the edge of a town, in the country, or at a resort. They had few local seaside features and did not yet emphasize the verandah or porch. When Hunt and others brought in Norman-style cottages, wooden porches of increased dimension became a feature of the ground floor, often taking up a full face of the building. Among the vernacular European prototypes used for summer houses in the 1860s was the so-called Swiss chalet, a type for smaller middle-class homes across Europe, which featured a second-floor porch surrounding one or more faces of the building.

The tall roof shaped like a witch's hat and the use of the porch became part of McKim's first summer ventures in Newport and New Jersey. When after his marriage McKim tried to update the two eighteenth-century houses that adjoined the Bigelow property at the Point, he gave

*Elberon cottage by McKim, ca. 1876, for Charles G. Francklyn, seen from the ocean side. Some slight allusion to the contemporary work of R. N. Shaw in England. The heavy slope of the roof recalls the back side of the Bishop Berkeley house in Middletown, Rhode Island. For the street side of the house, see page 47.*

each of the houses a big porch. The Robinson house needed to be enlarged for modern use, so here McKim made an interior in the Colonial manner, reproducing moldings and panels for the parlor/sitting area of the house. As we remember, he brought in some furniture he thought appropriate, including chairs likely made in Paris by Carlhian & Baumetz and intended as reproductions of Colonial chairs. He gave the small Colonial house a large porch to catch the breezes of the bay. The client here was Benjamin R. Smith, a descendant of the Robinsons and one of the Philadelphia Smiths so friendly to Miller McKim. McKim added another porch to his next Newport Colonial restoration, the John Dennis house (also owned by the venerable Benjamin Smith).*

At the Francklyn house in Elberon, New Jersey, McKim pulled together the three features that defined the next summer cottage style formulated in his circle. The style synthesized the asymmetrical extensions, textured surfaces, and occasional shingle covering of Colonial American houses with features from Norman farmhouses and touches from Norman Shaw. It came to be known as the Modern Colonial or the American Queen Anne, or, as the architectural historian Vincent J. Scully dubbed it in his important 1955 book of that title, *The Shingle Style,* the name being a salute to the prevailing material of these houses—the shingle covering. But the most interesting work of McKim's early career was the second summer cottage in Elberon for Charles G. Francklyn, heir to the Cunard line. In 1873 Francklyn had built a cottage on the beach in a Swiss chalet, double-porch variant of the northern European villa type, according to the design of New York architects Potter & Robertson. When Francklyn decided to leave it, the house was quickly purchased by the local Long Branch developer, Lewis B. Brown, who as we know hired McKim to transform it into a hotel with small cottages. At the same time Francklyn hired McKim to build his new cottage on land purchased from Brown just up Ocean Avenue, also facing the sea. The second Francklyn house pushed McKim to the highest design level of his early years. He made the new house idiosyncratic, with a double-story porch on the beach-side gable and a high, exposed porch with a top deck to the south. McKim continued his bargeboard gable treatment, but did an astounding thing here: he opened the house with a large square carriage driveway directly under the big gable on the north side. The drive-through passage, a sort of internal porte cochere, allowed visitors to alight and enter the house within the covered

---

*The two Colonial houses were being prepared for rental, and the porch was probably meant to attract a good tenant. One can even wonder if the newly married McKims might not have rented the Robinson cottage.

drive. A separate unit connected only above the driveway completes the composition. This open passageway is novel in the United States and may represent a feature McKim had noticed in the rustic complexes of Normandy, which were altered and added to over time. McKim's inspiration here was likely these agrarian Norman structures, not the seaside villas of the region. Farms in Normandy could give a sense of having been built over time; and the idea helped to give a new dimension to these wooden cottages sitting out on the back of a sand wall. The big, asymmetrical gable with its downward-sweeping roof coming to the first story of the smaller part of the house derives from McKim's interest in Colonial architecture, particularly the sloping, heavy roof of Bishop Berkeley's house in Middletown, Rhode Island.

McKim had had the rear of Bishop Berkeley's house photographed in 1874 and published the view in *The New York Sketch Book*. This was itself unique, as it was one of the first photographs to appear in an architectural magazine. McKim held the long, textured roofline of Berkeley's house dear and incorporated its hunchback gable into many future projects.

Although the Francklyn cottage had the elements of the new, seaside shingle style, the house was still angular and compressed. It had its

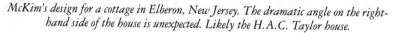

*McKim's design for a cottage in Elberon, New Jersey. The dramatic angle on the right-hand side of the house is unexpected. Likely the H.A.C. Taylor house.*

*The H.A.C. Taylor house and the Talbot house on the bluff of Elberon, 1878.*
*Talbot would sell his house to the son-in-law of of Moses Taylor, giving Taylor's son*
*and daughter adjoining residences.*

moment in history when President Garfield was brought to the house to die in 1881. But it burned in 1914.

In 1878 at Elberon, McKim designed the H.A.C. Taylor house and the Richard Talbot house side by side on the bluff. The Talbot house was soon sold to Robert Wintrop, who was Taylor's brother-in-law. Rather Shavian, it had specific repeated gables, a covered porte cochere, and a sleeping porch above. Interrupting the shingle covering were eighteenth-century oriel windows to the sleeping porch, an overscaled scroll gable over the door frame that seemed to scream "Colonial," and a screen covering part of porch overlooking the driveway. Features of the new shingle seaside style appear here, but the house is a contained cube. Its cost was double that of the Talbot house, so it could afford to be open and large, while the Talbot house seemed to hold its breath.

The H.A.C. Taylor house was the first of three houses designed by the firm for this client. Here the irregular gables of different sizes also recalled the work of Richard Norman Shaw, while with its forced asymmetry and an angular porch, the large rambling house began to breathe the sea air. The surface texture was cut up with patterned shingles, asymmetrically positioned windows, and wings, gables, and porches all over the place, arranged as in a Norman farm complex built over time.

ANOTHER SUCH CLIENT was Dr. Richard Derby, a well-known eye surgeon in New York City. Dr. Derby was a New Englander and graduate of Harvard (class of 1864), where he had become especially friendly with his college roommate, Robert Lincoln, son of President Lincoln. Richard Derby's mother, a New Yorker, was a strong-willed widow who had inherited land at Lloyd's Neck on Long Island's North Shore. Dr. Derby married Sarah Coleman Alden of Cornwall, Pennsylvania, a daughter of Anna Coleman Alden, another forceful widow. The Colemans of Cornwall had made a fortune from coal mines and furnaces in Pennsylvania and were probably friends of the Miller McKim's. Both Anna Coleman Alden and her brother Robert Percy Alden commissioned houses from Charles McKim within a year of each other. For Robert Percy Alden, McKim built a big year-round house in Cornwall in a restrained, Shavian style. The other house, designed for the overwhelming Mrs. Alden, her daughter Sarah, and Sarah's new husband, Dr. Derby, was a summer resort cottage on Mrs. Derby senior's property. It sat atop the ridge of land at Lloyd's Neck overlooking the inlet that leads to Cold Spring Harbor and Oyster Bay. The site was a historic one, Fort Hill, a legendary lookout in the American Revolutionary War. The Alden Derby house was one of McKim's best early houses. Built over the battlements of the old fort, it was a very long, thin house, only one room wide for two thirds of its length. The house was entered from the land side at its widest portion at

*The Alden Derby house, Lloyd's Neck, New York, 1879–80. This wonderful house was encapsulated in a masonry castle in the early twentieth century.*

the south end, where there was a big, asymmetrical gable, resembling Prescott Hall Butler's house, also on Long Island's North Shore.

In the composition of the Alden Derby house, Normandy once again meets Norman Shaw, but here there is a stone base with a lower floor of clapboard under upper shingled areas. The house was probably designed by McKim and refined and balanced by Joseph Wells, who brought order to McKim's architectural ideas. The result was one of McKim's first masterful works.

Mrs. Alden and her daughter's family at first lived together in Lloyd's Neck when not in New York. Later she moved to the venerable Lloyd Manor House close by, but the families continued to be together in New York. Soon after White joined the office, Mrs. Alden had him assist her in decorating the main entertainment area at 3 East Fortieth Street. The second floor contained her own space at the front of the house, while her daughter and son-in-law had the back of the house and the children occupied the third floor. Dr. Derby set up his office practice in a row house he purchased at 9 West Thirty-fifth Street. He saw his patients (P. T. Barnum was one) on the main, parlor floor of the house and at first intended to rent out the upper floors to paying tenants. McKim, who needed a place to live now that it was clear his marriage was fully over, asked for the second floor and moved in. He was to stay there through the end of the century.

Two other jobs materialized through this set of connections. J. Coleman Drayton, one of the Colemans of Cornwall, had married an Astor granddaughter, and he was allowed to build on the Astor estate at 374–80 Fifth Avenue. He asked McKim, Mead & White to do the house. Another Coleman of Cornwall was married to Archibald Rogers, who lived at Hyde Park in a country house called Crumwold Hall, where Sidney Stratton did some work. The Rogers asked for plans for a church from McKim Mead & White for Hyde Park, but it was not built. They also commissioned the firm to do some work, probably internal only, on their New York town house at 340 Madison Avenue in 1883–84. Through this family, the architects met the young Franklin Roosevelt and the Newbolds, who owned the house on the other side of Crumwold Hall. The Archibald Rogers family was much admired. Rogers himself was the master of a hobby of the 1880s and '90s—ice boating—and Mrs. Rogers was extraordinarily gracious. They entertained without an eye to social advancement and cared about people based on merit. She was a marked contrast to Anna Coleman Alden, an imperious woman who looked, acted, and dressed like Queen Victoria. After Mrs. Alden's death in 1897, the Derbys immediately sold their Long Island house, and the new owner built a stone castle over the shingles. The castle still stands. The Derbys moved to Islesboro, Maine, where they entertained Charles Dana Gibson, the illustrator, who bought land on a nearby island, and the young Ruth Draper. The Theodore Roosevelt daughters, Alice and Ethel, visited. Dr. Derby's son later married Ethel Roosevelt.

Knowing presidents was important to Dr. Derby. His youthful trips to Lincoln's White House were renewed when his friend Grover Cleveland invited him over; he visited a third time with Theodore Roosevelt's girls. Very formal and old-fashioned in his manners, Dr. Derby suffered from bouts of depression. In 1906 he had to go to Dr. Bull's private sanitarium in Litchfield, Connecticut, where patients were given residential treatment. Charles McKim also spent time there, and both men exhibited symptoms of what seems to have been severe depression. Although the two men had much in common in their youth, in later years they did not get along well, as McKim felt Derby had let 9 West Thirty-fifth Street deteriorate. McKim electrified the house in 1894, but two years later he decided he wanted better accommodations. He then moved farther east into an Astor estate rental house on Thirty-fifth Street, rejecting Dr. Derby's offer to sell him the old house for forty thousand dollars. It must have been very odd for the two men to be in the same sanitarium in their last years.

THE ADMIRATION FOR NORMAN ARCHITECTURE was shared in the McKim and Mead circle at the time. We know that Joe Wells particularly admired the Norman complexes. He wrote to White from his Italian visit on January 18, 1880, that Normandy was still on his mind and he was going to have photographs made of the Manoir d'Ango, an early sixteenth-century complex in Varengeville. The Manoir d'Ango was a prime inspiration for the seaside style. Richardson, White, and many others in their circle admired this Norman farm complex and another they attributed to the same architect, the Manoir d'Archelles. Wells hinted that he could not afford to have the photographs made himself and asked the office to share the expense. He felt that the Manoir d'Ango—especially its loggia, the exterior of the building, a corner of the courtyard, and the colombien (dovecote)—was so important a source that large-scale photographs rather than simple snapshots needed to be made. Wells and his peers seem to have been especially drawn to the complex stone patterns on the dovecote, which probably influenced the patterns of shingles used in their American houses. Wells regarded this complex as an outstanding exemplar. He would send Longfellow and his other Parisian friends out to see and draw it. He wished to have the nearby complex at Archelles, especially the corner tourelles, photographed for future study, and he also sent a photographer to take a picture of an early Renaissance porch at Ry near Rouen and a chimney at the Château de Maintainville near Ry.

The planning of the seaside houses was also novel. Intended for good weather use only, and planned for numerous guests, they had an ample number of bedrooms and generous indoor and outdoor social space. The house seemed to move around a central hall used as a circulation space with the principal staircase rising beside it. Such a hall had already been seen in the work of Richardson and McKim and White, but it was now enlarged as a point of greeting and social exchange. Summer houses were filled with guests: some were there for fishing, others for sailing, others for horseback riding, and the exchange of plans for activities could be conducted on the staircase. For more complex negotiations, people could sit down for a few moments on benches in this "living hall." On cool evenings, the fireplace in the hall provided comfort and a focus for a congenial visit. All this implied a lively social and sporting life. The social world at this time was more open, friendly, and vigorous than it became toward the end of the century, when pretense and acquisition became more common themes of conversation. The seaside cottage was the apogee of the "bully" life that young Theodore Roosevelt so exemplified. Such habits and such domestic architecture survived for just a single generation; then a more monied and Eurocentric lifestyle led to houses of which McKim, Mead & White would be equally the masters.

The seaside style would migrate to the inland summer communities as well. For those uninterested in marine activities, summer colonies developed in hill and mountain regions. The most prestigious of the inland social centers was the Lenox-Stockbridge region of the Berkshires in western Massachusetts, long popular with Bostonians. The hills had picturesque town centers, with a traditional core that did not exist in some seaside resorts, and vast rolling lands which when not in agricultural use made ideal grounds for a country house. From Boston came a literary crowd, well-off academics and clerics who gave the towns an intellectual quality. New Yorkers came to Stockbridge, among them, as we have seen, the Butlers. McKim and Stratton visited the Butlers there frequently enough to make connections for future work.

Commissions at Lenox included one we know, the big Samuel Gray Ward house (1877–78), which combined Shavian gables clad in American shingles with Colonial details. The Ward house straggled over its site, reflecting that built-over-time look McKim promoted as appropriate for the area. Although the house does not seem to swell out from the inside as does the full-blown shingle style, it is on the verge of doing so.

*The Carey house, Gusty Gables, in Lenox, Massachusetts. The house is a rare survivor of this style of building.*

By contrast, Gusty Gables is a big, gabled, shingle-clad house built by McKim a year later than the Ward House. It seems to blossom out from the inside to achieve the shingle style. This was built for Miss Carey, whose mother was a de Peyster, a Dutch Colonial family from New York. Though Scully's term is useful to describe the appearance of the houses, there is a shade of difference between the shingle-clad houses in the country, in the new suburbs, and at the seaside. The fullest flowering of the shingle houses seems to be the seaside version.

THE FIRST OF THE CLASSIC EXAMPLES of this seaside style began to be built on the East Coast in the spring of 1879, when several architects took up their own versions of the seaside cottage form. Perhaps the masterpiece of the genre was the huge Black house at Manchester-by-the-Sea, Massachusetts, designed by Peabody & Stearns. But the most consistent work in the style was done by McKim, Mead & White in the decade from 1879 to about 1890. Even if the office never produced anything as perfect as the Black house, overall McKim, Mead & White must be considered the masters of the seaside style.

The blossoming of the wooden house into the shingle seaside style

*Victor Newcomb. His was one of the greatest houses of the summer seaside style. Sadly, his tragic life led to madness.*

involved the collaboration of all members of the firm. The principals spent a lot of time out in the main drafting room, where details could be refined as each partner and Wells suggested improvements. A Norman dovecote, a grain tower, perhaps a solid or void in the massing—all these ingredients came together in a festival of imagination. The decade of this collaboration between the partners and Wells marked the firm's high point of creativity. Indeed, the shingle seaside style seemed truly to come together only after Wells joined the office, with White adding flourishes and Wells putting the mass together so that the house flowed.

McKim, Mead & White slowly now came to be thought of as the premier architects of the nation, as Richardson's health became precarious. Richardson's biographer, and America's first important woman to write on architecture, Mariana Griswold Van Rensselaer, turned her eye to McKim, Mead & White's work in a series she wrote on new architecture in America from 1884 to 1886 in *The Century Magazine*.

By this time the firm's reputation was made; clients appeared without family prodding and work grew. As the volume in the office increased, the staff had to be enlarged. The drafting tables filled with young men, some with architectural training, some without, creating an vibrant atelier life that outdid the Richardson office at its height. Mead assigned one or two new men to draw up McKim and White's projects from initial sketches. Wells floated from desk to desk, nervously invigorating the office with his caustic jokes, musical selections, and generally admirable judgment on architectural composition. The office was a fusion of the ateliers of the École with the American need for closets and bathrooms. For about forty-five years, young architects beat down the door to Mead's office, wanting to put time at McKim, Mead & White on their record. Eventually, the young men became the firm and began to repeat its trademark style, but in the energetic period of Wells's days, the office was at its height of creative and original work.

In 1880 the firm designed a large and important house in the resort style, perhaps one of McKim, Mead & White's masterpieces in this genre. On the Ocean Avenue dunes near the Elberon Hotel, Victor Newcomb commissioned a house at the massive figure of thirty-five thousand

*Interior of the Newcomb house. This great design for a client with new wealth and no family furniture shows Stanford White at his most creative as an interior designer.*

*The Victor Newcomb house, Elberon, 1880. A fine example of the seaside style long submerged into a new residence. Newcomb commissioned windows from John La Farge for this house.*

dollars, a great sum in those days.* A Southerner, Newcomb had come to New York to represent his railroad interests and had fallen in with the circle of General Grant. He is thought to have bailed out Grant when the former president's son-in-law failed with Grant's investments. Newcomb kept his ties with political figures; indeed, Mrs. Garfield was being entertained in Elberon when she was informed of the shooting of her husband.†

The Newcomb house at Elberon was a low rectangle with a full pitched roof broken only by a single dormer. Yet on the ocean side, a gable popped out of the mass, topped by a porch and deck. The Ocean Avenue side had a wing in a single-story gable housing the service area. The most notable feature was the half-round Norman tower marking the interior staircase.

The interior of the house was equally impressive. Here White probably had a hand in the design. The principal sitting rooms were a proto-modern open space with individual chambers marked by ceiling beams in varied directions. The crosshatched detail of brick and cork displayed White's playfulness. A polar bear rug sat on one of the floors, adding a wintry touch to the cool summer parlor. White loved these polar bear rugs and used them in many schemes. Wicker furniture vied for attention with the Asian bronzes favored by Newcomb. If the interior looks busy to us, it was clever for its day, displaying a sense of openness and informality for a family with no inherited furniture. The assembly of items was meant to display the Newcombs as artistic people. White already recognized that interior design set businessmen's images onstage, and for those who were self-made men with no heritage to proclaim, artistic was as good as it could be.‡

The firm's last big job at Elberon was for Tiffany & Co.'s president, Charles Cook. At the time McKim, Mead & White were completing the Tiffany family mansion in New York, so Cook logically turned to the owner's architects. The picture of the Cook house reproduced in Scully and other books is not the correct house. Cook's house was large, ornate, and had a rather fat Norman tower; it was not a triumph of design. The photo called the Cook house may really be a house built by McKim, Mead & Bigelow for C. M. Packer on Ocean Avenue.

---

*McKim, Mead & White built two more Ocean Avenue cottages in Elberon the same year, one for James A. Garland, an old friend of McKim's family, and another for Horace White. Images of these two houses have not been found.

†Newcomb was also a frequent guest at A. T. Stewart's table during the years he worked with Governor E. D. Morgan in New York.

‡After the Elberon house, Newcomb hired McKim, Mead & White in 1881–82 to build him a town house at 683 Fifth Avenue, and ten years later, a stable on Fifty-fourth Street. In later years he was afflicted by madness, which caused his fall from grace. The Elberon house was sold to Lyman Bloomingdale of the Third Avenue department store in New York.

Elberon did get some better-quality houses in the early 1880s, but its day was over. The houses lined up on either side of Ocean Avenue had a certain boring tree-like regularity. In addition, the publicity for the resort and the lure of presidential summer visits worked too well. If house owners could take the train and walk to their homes, so could day-trippers. Hordes of Saturday visitors walked right along Ocean Avenue and peered in the doors and windows of the summer colony. The annoying presence of ordinary people coupled with Grant's illness and death in 1885 made the seaside resort passé. Those still in good financial shape such as H.A.C. Taylor moved on to Newport, a resort with higher tone. Others stayed, but many sold houses to a new group, New York's recent Jewish elite, who were to make Elberon their summer colony.

THE FALL OF ELBERON put pressure on Newport to widen its social borders, something houses—particularly showy ones—could do. Indeed, William Kissam Vanderbilt and his ambitious wife Alva managed to crash Newport's defensive wall when Alva set out to construct her Marble House. For the new money unable to fit in at Newport, Narragansett Pier offered a nearby alternative. Many who built or rented in Narragansett were unlikely to succeed at Newport.

Summering in Rhode Island demanded wealth and social pretension as well as leisure. The original, rather more intellectual community at Newport was once filled with Southern plantation owners able to leave home for the entire summer. The very wealthy could also do this, as managers handled financial affairs back home. Other seasonal colonists were fancy clergymen whose parishes would send their pastor away for the summer, and academics with family money. Men at the helm of business, physicians, or people who needed to be in the office even in an oppressive summer, were less able to go to Newport or Narragansett for the season. Instead, many men worked all week in the city, then took the Fall River Line steamer overnight, waking up to Newport on the horizon. Such businessmen came up for weekends, leaving the city to join their families at Newport for short spells. A closer destination was Southampton on Long Island's eastern end. The summer colony here was small at the time of the Civil War but grew rapidly in the mid- to later 1880s, with people coming directly from New York as well as from Elberon.

With the social mortality of its rival, Newport was confirmed as America's premier resort. The popularity of the place brought delight to its real estate men and the father-and-son architects the Masons, who had enjoyed a first-class business in their hometown.

Modern Newport's growth into a mecca for the well-to-do can be placed at the feet of the greatest of its real estate promoters, Alfred Smith (1809–1886). Smith came from humble Newport people, and was not related to or of the same class as Benjamin R. Smith, whom we have already met as the owner of the Robinson house and of cottages at the Point. Alfred Smith was a working-class local lad who found the economy moribund at the beginning of the nineteenth century, after the town's allegiance to Britain in the Revolution had cost it its financial core. Many Newport families left and moved down to New York. Prominent New-porters went into banking, but Alfred Smith came to New York in the 1830s as a tailor. He rose at Wheeler & Co. on Broadway, perhaps then New York's most fashionable tailor; he mastered the art of smooth talking and became a well-paid salesman. As he helped to fit the garments, he found it easy to speak of his hometown, where land prices were low and men with capital could purchase property cheaply. Smith's clients lis-tened, and one, William Beach Lawrence, bought a sixty-acre farm. As he followed the laying out of Kay Street for rental houses in Newport, Smith longed to return and join in the slow resurgence of the city as a summer capital. He had worked hard in New York, saving each penny; indeed, rumor had it that he slept in the shop to save rent money.

With savings of about twenty thousand dollars, he left Wheeler & Co. in 1839 for Newport, where he married and built an old-fashioned white clapboard house. He set to work selling real estate but did not at first suc-ceed. Refusing to abandon his promotion of the city, he switched to land-scaping until the market improved. In this way he discovered the value of landscape in creating interest in development. So far did Smith believe in his goal of creating a great resort that in 1845 he joined other investors in purchasing land on the middle ridge of the island at farm prices. Two years later the Fall River Line began its service, and a large hotel, Ocean House, opened. Smith and his fellow investors hoped that the hotel stay might cause some visitors to consider purchasing land nearby on his acres. Within a decade his intuition proved true.

Smith became wealthy rapidly after managing to convince the town council to build an avenue down the ridge to the beach at the southern end of the island, which he and a coinvestor, Bailey, happened to own. The highway to Bailey's Beach was built fifty feet wide, and Smith lined it with trees to make a grand avenue. He then drove his carriage from one hotel to another looking for potential land purchasers. It was always said that if you got into Smith's carriage you would buy the land, so good were his salesman's techniques. He was unwilling to let a passenger disembark without a purchase. Smith himself created the Newport of villas and cottages by forcing sales on his lands to either side of the new highway, called Bellevue Avenue. Under Smith's aggressive promotion, summer cottages began popping up around the King and Jones cottages and down around Wetmore's house and along Bellevue Avenue to Bailey's Beach. During the Civil War, he was even able to persuade the city government of Newport to create another broad avenue on the southern portion of the peninsula, Ocean Drive. Alfred Smith and his ceaseless promotion made Newport more than the two-mile road with houses on either side that we saw in Elberon. It was he who made Newport happen, put people on properties and made the roads beautiful. He and his family had no interest in social mobility and did not join in the life of the town. The Smiths lived quietly with their family until their health failed about 1880. When Mrs. Smith died, McKim, Mead & White designed a fine tombstone for this kindly, plain woman, known for her good deeds.

But it was the gentry at Newport who kept the resort vibrant with activities, clubs, and parties. In earlier days Newport had been a literary summer colony, and it still had its social club tied to that tradition. The only club, the Newport Reading Room, was difficult to join and had an all-male membership. The more casual reading group founded by Mrs. Bigelow on her piazza kept the tradition, but the audience was broader and included women. These small groups fitted well with the cottages of the mid-century, as the summer population was small enough for everyone to meet. Social life—if one was accepted—was carried on at home, on picnics, atop horses on Smith's new avenues, and at the beach.

Into the literary Newport of the 1870s came New York society's bad boy, James Gordon Bennett Jr., son of the creator of the *New York Herald*. James Gordon Bennett Sr. had arrived in New York from Scotland and after a great struggle managed to start a tabloid paper in a basement in 1835. Bennett's paper grew in an era when steam-printing equipment lowered the cost of newspaper pages. He knew just what to put in his pages—scandal and ads. He took advertising of all sorts and filled his paper with gossip, a perfect formula for success. He was a rough-and-tumble, rather crude bachelor until the Irish-born Henriette appeared before him. He rapidly fell in love with the much-younger woman, marrying her and fathering two children. James Gordon Bennett Jr. was born in 1841 at 114 Chambers Street, followed later by a daughter, Jeannette.

Henriette was beautiful, young, and Catholic. Bennett senior was coarse, old, and a Protestant. The marriage soon fell apart, leaving Henriette to seek solace in drink. After a few years of trying to manage in New

York, she picked up the children and took them to Europe for an education. Bennett junior mastered three languages and gleaned sophistication rapidly, but he displayed a personality flawed by rapid mood swings, enhanced from his teenage years by large measures of alcohol. Bennett junior wished to stay in France, but his father wanted to give his son the newspaper. He began to spend half the year in New York with his father in a house on Thirty-eighth Street and Fifth Avenue and at a country house in the hills of Washington Heights at 181st Street, where a few successful Scotsmen had residences.

It turned out that the young Bennett had a flair for sensationalism. It was he who was to send Stanley on a search for Livingstone, who turned out not to be lost. Later he named a boat for his baby sister, then sent it to the Arctic where it became icebound and people froze. Between his moments of attention to work, Bennett junior played sports with a dangerous intensity. Returning to New York from his mother's world in Europe, he quickly joined the New York Yacht Club. He made a wager to sail the Atlantic in the worst of winter and did so. Bennett junior even tried to be a naval hero in the Civil War; he bought his own boat and presented himself to Lincoln for duty, only to become angry when denied a command. In his determination to help his only son, Bennett senior then hired the German-born journalist Henry Villard to lobby Lincoln and Salmon P. Chase. Villard is said to have threatened Lincoln with retraction of editorial support if the president refused to accept the service of the untrained Bennett. Instead he was sent to Port Royale, the place where, coincidentally, Miller McKim and Villard had worked on the freedmen's cause. Fortunately, Bennett survived and did no harm.

After a year, he was back in New York, where his father surrendered to him the newspaper and the Fifth Avenue house before dying in 1872. Bennett did have a way with news stories, which he managed in between bouts of drinking and rough behavior with his friends at the Union Club on Twenty-first Street. He took all his meals at the club and made it his turf.

Bennett built a new building for the *New York Herald* on the site of P. T. Barnum's burned-out museum. For this iron-fronted creation he went to a rather staid architect, Arthur Gilman, whose task was to outdo the decade-old New York Times building nearby. The result was income-producing but not as pioneering a building as the contemporary Equitable Life Asssurance building, also by Gilman with assistance from George B. Post, the master of the New York skyscraper. Soon afterward Bennett was trumped by his rival, Horace Greeley, who made his New

York Tribune building rise taller and more impressively than the Herald building.

By the 1870s Bennett was rich and debonair enough to be a social figure, though a sinister one. About 1875 he met the beautiful Caroline May of Baltimore, and the pair became engaged. Caroline and her brother Frederick lived in New York on Nineteenth Street, just two blocks below the Union Club. Fred May was as erratic as Bennett. In a dispute in Baltimore, he had for spite ridden his horse up the stairs of the Barnum Hotel, considered the city's best. This excessive gesture sent Fred May to New York. He later went to Europe, where the actress Lillie Langtry was said to adore him. The Mays sailed, as did Bennett, who in 1875 asked the young and then unknown Augustus Saint-Gaudens to create the Victory cup for the New York Yacht Club. Caroline May was friendly with the man who won the trophy, the young yachtsman and cotton king Thomas Garner of Staten Island. Proudly, Garner kept the trophy aboard his boat. But in 1876 it capsized, drowning the Garners and several others, although Caroline May's sister, who was aboard, survived the accident. The trophy must have gone down with the boat.

Bennett should have been happy at Christmas 1876. He had recovered from his mother's death in Saxony three years earlier, was a great success in journalism, and had become engaged to one of the belles of America. At the close of the year it was still the custom for friends to wear themselves out making New Year's Day calls on their acquaintances. On January 1, 1877, Bennett arrived at the Mays' drunk and perhaps terrified at the thought of marriage. He handled his extraction from the engagement rather badly by urinating into the fireplace before all of New York. A scandal ensued. Bennett was challenged to a duel by Fred May, but this was only a face-saving event as May fired into the air. Bennett then left for France, where he spent most of the rest of his life.

He continued to run the paper, usually by cable from his boats or from Paris, and came back to New York only for sports. There he kept three places to call home. He retained his father's brownstone on Thirty-eighth Street, but it was too far away for a drunken man to walk after leaving the Union Club. He therefore bought 28 West Twenty-first Street, which he ran as a bachelor establishment, keeping a set of rooms for himself there in staggering distance of his club. For sentimental reasons Bennett also kept his father's house in Washington Heights, where he thought he might build his own mausoleum.

Though Bennett was now unwelcome in New York, Newport, where he had begun to summer in about 1875, still loved him. He had a member-

*James Gordon Bennett Jr., from* Vanity
Fair, *January 1884. Bennett was a
newspaper publisher and society bad boy.*

ship in the haughty Reading Room and purchased
a house built of stone—thus a villa, not a "cottage"—at the top of Bellevue Avenue, just across
the street from William Travers's commercial
block. The house fittingly was called Stone Villa,
and Bennett personalized it by putting blinking
owls' heads atop the fence. In 1877 he bought
property nearby on Cliff Street for building some
rent-producing cottages before returning to Paris.
Then, in the summer of 1879, Bennett brought
over polo equipment from England and a few polo
stars to teach Americans the game. Among them
was a certain Henry Augustus Candy, who through
Bennett acquired a visitor's card for the Reading
Room. For whatever reason, Bennett persuaded
Candy to repeat Fred May's stunt of riding his horse
up the steps of the Reading Room. The incident
ended his acceptance there.

Bennett promptly reacted by proclaiming Newport too dull and lacking a social center. He
already owned land across from Stone Villa. He
now decided to donate this vacant land for a new social center, the Casino,
which he backed heavily. Intent on showing up the Newporters of the old
guard, he decided that Newport needed to have less reading and more
people-watching. To complete his assault on the city, Bennett selected
McKim to design his casino in 1879, though they had begun discussing
the project as early as February 1878. This was the moment when the
Bigelow accusations were swirling around McKim, who was in some disgrace in Newport and thus perfect for Bennett's work, as he wished to
annoy precisely the people who were listening to the Bigelows. The
Casino transformed McKim's standing in the community and led to the
firm getting enough jobs in Newport to put a serious hole in the practice
of the local architects, the Masons. McKim, Mead & White became inti-
mately associated with the growth of Newport in these years.

The Newport Casino offered shares to summer people at five hundred
dollars each. It was a joint-stock speculation, though Bennett was turned
to for financial help when it was needed. McKim had a difficult job. His
idea was to design a new building type based on the casinos of seaside
Normandy, those socially centered places to see and be seen. Gambling,
other than friendly wagering on a game of cards, played no part in the

Norman casino, nor in the American version; entertainment was the aim. This was the first of four or five casinos to be built by the architects in the 1880s, and it was also the biggest and most important. It had a storefront entrance block almost two hundred feet long available for commercial rental, and deep interior spaces with places to walk, play lawn tennis, drink, eat, and even watch plays. The building had to be ready in less than a year. The awarding of the job to McKim, probably agreed on in the late summer of 1879, may have been a factor in McKim and Mead's decision to bring White into the firm. Someone had to design the interior spaces, the theater, and the public lawn spaces. McKim and White labored on this building for almost two years to get the Norman forms and shingle covering right, and thus bring their design work to national prominence.

McKim's first job was to design the long street front and line it up with an already existing block of Norman-influenced wooden buildings designed a decade earlier by Richard Morris Hunt for the horseman William Travers. Half-timbered work to blend with Hunt's building would hardly be assertive enough. Puzzled as to how to proceed, McKim borrowed the façade from an inn Norman Shaw had just completed in the London suburb of Bedford Park, which had been published in *Building News* early in 1880. McKim put this tribute to Shaw on Bellevue Avenue with a wonderful narrow, tiled entry where visitors could be seen coming through the entrance to the pleasure areas to the east. On either side of the entrance were to be shops. Initially, no one knew how to use the upper floors, which became bachelor appartments.

The lawn side of the Casino looks far more Norman, with an echo of the court at the Manoir d'Ango. The sense of accretions over time is captured here in a splendid balance of shapes, designed largely by McKim with the help of Wells and carried out in Newport under the supervision of a new young office assistant, Cass Gilbert. The spectator areas were brilliantly handled by White, who chose to use lattice-like screen work, creating a perfect balance between wall and air. The weaving together of wooden elements has an Asiatic feeling, Japanese perhaps, or Chinese. The screens contain space but allow just the kind of visibility that Bennett wanted for the the voyeuristic resort he was now helping to formulate. How better could a Newport hopeful test the waters than to gauge reaction to one's appearance at the Casino? Bennett felt the resort needed beautiful young people, and the Casino was a perfect place for high visibility. Although it was a club, the public was allowed in the courtyards. Within a year, the Casino realized some privacy was needed, and McKim, Mead & White were recalled to transform the bachelor rooms into club

*The Casino at Newport. McKim's exterior of the street face of the central social point in Newport.*

rooms. Now New York City grandees like Cornelius Vanderbilt (who had just bought the wooden Breakers from the Lorillards and wanted a place he could retreat to) were able to find refuge at the Casino.

The rush to completion was impressive. The building was ready enough for public inspection by the end of July 1880. A big opening to the public followed in early August. By then the lawns were a lush, thick green, the flower beds in full bloom, the pathways completed and perfect for pedestrians. Lander's orchestra provided a "choice" program of music, and huge numbers of visitors came to ogle the pleasures available. Activities for men and women made the Casino an easy place for newcomers to ease their way into the community. A newer group with younger people now made Newport their summer resort. For younger women, the game of tennis was just becoming acceptable, replacing the earlier, proper female sport of archery. Tennis was a major part of the Casino's entertainments.

Many of the new house renters and owners now swelling Newport in the summer were New Yorkers with enough social cachet to find a place in America's most exclusive colony. Each year a directory of cottage owners in town and of those renting empty houses was published. The lists were so impressive that many men decided it was worth the lengthy boat ride to be with the anchors of the economy of the nation. Newport was our

*The courts at the Casino. The street entry opens to a large internal set of social spaces.*

summer social capital, as popularizers liked to boast. From the 1870s to World War II, Newport was at its most social, and attractions such as the Casino kept people's interest.

Among the New Yorkers transplanted to Newport was the remarkable Catharine Lorillard Wolfe (1828–1887), the woman who brought the first paintings to the new Metropolitan Museum and devoted her days to good deeds for Grace Church. Catharine Wolfe was the daughter of John David Wolfe (1792–1872), a hardware merchant, and a daughter of the Lorillard snuff business. The Wolfe and Lorillard fortunes grew during Catharine's lifetime, creating a fortune for this unmarried lady. The Wolfes had connections in Lenox, so when Miss Catharine asked several architects to design a big house for her in Newport, the change of location was significant. On this occasion McKim, Mead & White's design lost out to McKim's old friend and rival Peabody. The drawing McKim did for this house seems to have been important to him; he later gave it to his assistant, the architect Henry Bacon.

The Wolfe house was one that got away. Nevertheless, in 1887 three new commissions from New Yorkers came into the office. The first was from Theodore Havemeyer (1839–1897), a member of a sugar family and Austrian consul in New York. Havemeyer purchased the Newport house

*The Game Room at the Casino, designed by Stanford White. A rainy-day retreat.*

the Masons had built not long before for Loring Andrews, a rich leather tanner and a major supporter of the University of New York. Andrews was then about to build one of the cottages in the Montauk Association that McKim, Mead & White designed about this time. Havemeyer liked the vernacular wooden appearance of his new purchase, which he renamed Friedheim. He was a friend of Bennett, so the suggestion of the young New York architects to build a large addition he envisioned may have come from Bennett.

The second of the new clients was Levi Parsons Morton (1824–1920), a Yankee from Vermont who moved first to Boston and then to New York. In Boston, Morton had joined Junius Spencer Morgan before the latter went to London with George Peabody. Morton then went down to New York, where he briefly joined Moses Grinnell in dry goods, then set up L. P. Morton & Co. during the Civil War, specializing in specie payments and financing the war effort. His financial success was partly due to his awareness of the importance of political figures to aspiring capitalists, and in due course he began to contemplate political office for himself. In 1878 Morton won a seat in Congress as a Republican, and President Hayes appointed him a commissioner to the Paris Exposition. After three years in Washington, he was sent by President Garfield to France as the American minister. Morton would accept Bartholdi's Statue of Liberty for the United States while serving in that position.

In 1869 Morton bought Fairlawn in Newport, an Elizabethan-styled house with a curiously patterned, zigzag slate roof. Within a few months, he was entertaining Grant there. This house, too, may well have been designed by the Masons. The young New York architects may have been known to Morton through the time they all spent in Paris in the summer of 1878, when they went to the Paris Exposition. Morton asked McKim, Mead & White to build him a stable on the north side of his driveway. The stable does not reflect the main house in style, as it was in the firm's current wooden mode. The architects designed several such stables for existing houses, which were proof of a serious commitment to living in style, even if only for a season, in Newport. Morton was a satisfied client who would come back a decade later to ask first for a new New York City town house, and later for that town house to be converted to commercial use.

The third commission involved a return to the Watts Sherman house. Stanford White had declared when he began as a junior partner in McKim, Mead & White that he could live on a smaller share of profits as long as he could do some decorative work on the side.

*Levi Parsons Morton, a man whose presence in the politics of the nineteenth century is too little known today. Morton served as vice president and governor of New York State and toyed with the presidency. As minister to France, he accepted the Statue of Liberty in Paris.*

The decorative work begins immediately in 1879 on his return from Europe, and is often legitimized as a small commission on the firm's books. White would offer modest advice often done on a flat-fee basis. After the Casino success, White received several new commissions in Newport.

During the building of the Watts Sherman house in 1875–76, White's abilities had been clear to Annie Wetmore Sherman. In 1881 she therefore asked him to build a three-story addition to the house. It is likely that she saw White as the major force during the construction a few years earlier, which is why she did not return to Richardson. The proposed wing added a bedroom and more space for entertaining, as well as a new library, the focus of the enlargement.

The creation of a library as a center point for a house addition was new to White at this time. A room for quiet introspection was unusual in Newport, although those who went there were still thought literary and it was a conceit for wealthy businessmen to display a private scholarly side. White's library for the Watts Shermans was unlike anything he had done before and was more in the spirit of McKim's various Colonial revival works a few years earlier at the old Quaker Point. It might be called antiquarian in McKim's manner, down to the carved wooden shell motif often used by McKim; however, there is a clear, crisp definition to the room, marked by its grid, dark green walls, and incised gilt trim, that seems more English Queen Anne than American Colonial in feeling. With its ornate ceiling, formal suite of furniture, and small-scale detail, it seems almost to belong to a refined English home. White had returned to the United States in 1879 with books on English interiors purchased just as he left Liverpool. A year later he asked his father to send these volumes to the office. R. G. White sent Stanford's books from his New York City bedroom. All this may indicate the use of these books in the detailing of the Watts Sherman library.

Less studied and more American is the addition of a wing creating a larger dining space for David King at Kingscote, the former Noble Jones house. This commission predates the Watts Sherman addition slightly. The Noble Jones house, which we have already noticed, had been designed by Richard Upjohn and was Newport's first new cottage. It was used by the Jones family until the Civil War, when the furnishings were taken out and shipped back to Georgia. After the second Southern exodus caused by the Civil War, a Newport neighbor, William H. King, purchased the cottage in 1863. The Kings were an established local family, many of them physicians or businessmen. Several of the Kings were in the early nineteenth-century China trade. William H. King was dispatched to Canton, where he found himself caught by the opium usually sold to the Chinese. Shortly after buying the house he suffered a breakdown and spent the rest of his life in a mental hospital. The house was taken care of by the executors of his estate and may have been rented in summers.

In 1875 King's nephew, David King III, became guardian of his uncle, and began to rent the Noble Jones house for himself and his new wife, the former Ella Louisa Rives, who came from a dashing Virginia family. King hired the local firm, the Masons, to build a wing on the house in 1878, which enlarged the dining room and provided service areas. The work was not as fashionable as the Kings would desire, and so, in about 1880, they turned to Stanford White to take over the addition and decorate the din-

*Stanford White's library at the Watts Sherman house of 1881. The library is a distinct departure from earlier work at the house. Delicate moldings detail this room.*

ing area. It was at this date that the name of Kingscote was attached to the house. The commission probably came to White as the Casino had just been begun and was almost across the street.

Though in a different material, shingle, the new three-story addition to Kingscote attempted to blend with Upjohn's earlier house. When adding to an earlier structure, architects at this time made a real attempt to blend with the original building. Here McKim, Mead & White pulled the addition back from the line of the house and even added a detail from the Upjohn house, a raised drip mold over the windows in their new wing.

The addition brought new bedrooms to the upper floors, but it is White's new dining room that is the highlight of the house. It reveals the architect at the height of his creative prowess. The dining room is entered through a spindle screen of the type being used to define inner and outer rooms in the Newport Casino's courts at just this time. Such latticed spindle screens are also seen in the upper walls of the Newcomb house and in other houses. They were very popular at this moment in American architecture, but White used the open-and-closed effect better than others. Indeed, the room is a series of contrasts: The upper areas of the walls are

*Kingscote, the Newport house of David King. A new addition of 1880–81
includes a dining room designed by White. The Kings had family furniture,
so White's fanciful interior concoction was not needed here.*

covered with flat, smooth, nonreflecting cork, an innovative use of a novel
material in the year 1880–81.*

The dining room has mellow mahogany wood offset by the glimmer of
silver in a cabinet custom-made with a note of Colonial detail in the
triple-shell motif. The dull, rich gleam of the Sienna marble fireplace, perfectly flat in form (a signature of White at this time), contrasts with the
Tiffany glass tiles which admit and transform light. As the day passes to
evening, the tones in the glass move through the rainbow. An antique
spinning wheel, the ultimate symbol of the Colonial America, sits in the
room, anchoring the Kings to the Newport heritage. But to show that the
young couple had up-to-date tastes, the lamp backs made by Archer &
Pancoast have an enlarged floral motif almost suggestive of the Aesthetic
movement; a similar flower is cast in the Tiffany blocks. White caught
every detail in this room from the hinges to the drawer pulls and made
them small works of art.

---

*We cannot be sure White was the first to have the idea of using cork as a decorative material. At
this very time, just as sheets of cork over shiny glass appear on the dining-room walls at Kingscote,
Richardson and Saint-Gaudens would use cork on the walls of Richardson's gatehouse for the Ames
family at North Easton, Massachusetts. One can only suspect that White assisted Richardson with
the interior of the gatehouse.

The glories of Kingscote are still with us, thanks to the generosity of the heirs, who left the house to the Preservation Society of Newport. David King's daughter married David Maitland Armstrong's son, and it is their family that left the house to the public.

The attention given to McKim, Mead & White as the Casino rose led to entire house commissions. One of the best early houses by the firm is the Samuel Tilton house—a masterpiece among the firm's summer cottages. The house is sited in the mid-nineteenth-century Kay Street area east of the Jewish cemetery. McKim, Mead & White were familiar with the district, as they had already built two small houses in the mid-1870s hereabouts and would now build two larger houses close by. The neighborhood already had a slightly intellectual character and smaller, less showy properties. The Tilton house was an experiment with Norman Shaw's big gable and the northern European use of wet stucco embedded with objects, combined with a shingled gable and latticework screens. Because the house was inland and the setting suburban, it was more self-contained than some oceanfront examples of their work. The open porches

*Samuel Tilton house, Newport, in the denser Kay Street district, 1880–82.*

and balloon-like swellings of seaside cottages are absent. This is an older person's house, reflecting a more stable household life with fewer guests.

Similar to wooden houses of the period, the Tilton house sits on a strong raised base, here of cut stone rather than the usual brick. Some of the stucco panels have random stones embedded in them. There are also two large found-object mosaics created out of coal, glass, and stone: a sunburst effect and a heraldic shield. The windows here reflect interior symmetry of placement or size. Patterned shingles cover the upper walls. The entrance to the house features a double Dutch door, often used by the firm at this time. The Tilton house is notable for the interior hall, where a fireplace with benches (an English inglenook) provides a cozy place to sit and talk. Flanking the hearth is a spindle-braced staircase. The living hall was a key feature of the 1870s and 1880s houses; it could be open and socially oriented for resort houses or snug and able to husband warmth for more suburban houses like this one. Latticework in the spindles vies for attention with the paneling detail. The benches and wooded overmantel add the Japanese Aesthetic tone much the vogue at this time.

Farther down Bellevue Avenue from Kingscote is a residence more oriented toward guests, the Bell house. Isaac Bell (1846–1889) came from a

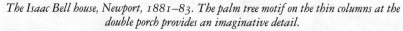

*The Isaac Bell house, Newport, 1881–83. The palm tree motif on the thin columns at the double porch provides an imaginative detail.*

family that had settled in the United States in 1640. He was the thirteenth member of the family with the name, and like his father had been involved in the cotton trade in Savannah, Georgia. Bell seems to have established a novel method of using New York capital to stimulate cotton growing after the Civil War and made a handsome profit from it. Indeed, he did so well avoiding the fate of the ruined cotton plantation families that he was able to retire in seven years. By 1877 Bell seems to have fully reestablished himself in his home city as a wealthy and eligible bachelor. At about this time he met Jeannette Bennett, probably in France where she was completing her education.

Jeannette Bennett was the younger sister of the headstrong James Gordon Bennett Jr., who following his parents' deaths in 1872 and 1873 was in charge of his sister. He was bound to support and educate Jeannette until 1880, when she reached her twenty-fifth year and could manage her own inheritance. As being Bennett's kid sister was not an enviable position, Jeannette may have been eager for a husband to free herself from her brother's rule. Having selected Isaac Bell, she returned to the United States in the summer of 1878 for the wedding. Jeannette had not been in America since 1872, when she and her mother returned to see her father during his final illness. But James Gordon Bennett seems to have suffered at the thought of giving away the bride in America. The prospect must have brought back memories of his brush with marriage in New York. Bell and Jeannette would have preferred a New York wedding, but James Bennett took the couple to Newport instead, where he rented Levi P. Morton's house while the latter was in Europe for the Paris 1878 Exposition. Having done so, he set about preparing for a fall wedding for his sister. September and October were considered perfect months for a wedding. The Bells were duly married and probably returned to New York City for the winter.

James Gordon Bennett may have wished his sister well in her new life, but he managed to make her name synonymous with death. In July of that year, he had another one of his bursts of journalistic creativity. With Henry M. Stanley in tow, he bought a steam yacht, christened it the *Jeannette,* and fitted out an American expedition to the Arctic. But when the unlucky ship reached the frozen north, it became embedded in an ice pack, killing the captain and most of the crew. The *Jeannette* became a notorious disaster, surely not a happy omen for Jeannette Bennett Bell.

In 1880 Jeannette Bell reached her maturity under her father's will, and the Bells began to think of building their own house in Newport as a summer residence. Isaac Bell bought the lots very close to James Gordon

Bennett's Stone Villa from Alfred Smith the following year and called in his brother-in-law's architects. The choice gave birth to rumors that Bennett paid for the house or the land or both, but there is no evidence that he had any role in the matter. With Jeannette Bell now in charge of her own funds, Isaac Bell was able to live without working. The couple had three children by the time the Newport house was well under way in the spring of 1882. Their pattern was to live in New York City and travel abroad. But at about the time the house was ready, Bell decided to use it all year round. He was bored and had begun to absorb himself in Republican politics. To avoid annoying the New York Republicans, he decided to begin his political career in Rhode Island where he would not get in the way of old friends. As the house neared completion, it was equipped with a furnace so that it could become the family's main home.

Just as the family moved in, Isaac Bell partnered with the Western mining millionaire John W. Mackay to invest about a million dollars in the Commercial Cable Company, a venture that would lay another set of transatlantic cables to rival Jay Gould's monopoly in the cable business. The company was sometimes called the "Bennett facilitator" because Bennett used its lines constantly; it provided the means for him to be able to live in France and run his New York paper by cable. Years earlier, in an effort to save his failing marriage, Bennett's father had tried to run the *Herald* from Europe, but returned to the United States. The son, by contrast, was able to closely manage the paper from another continent.

In 1885 Bell's party loyalty brought him a perk: he was appointed as the American minister to the Netherlands by President Cleveland. He set off for The Hague with his family but fell ill on arrival. The young ambassador eventually returned home in an effort to recover his health, but to no avail—he died just after the New Year in 1889 at the age of forty-two. The surviving Bells spent little time in their Newport house, often renting it out until they decided to sell it.*

The Bell house was begun as a summer resort house with the usual brick base and the requisite summer porches, set in a purposeful asymmetrical manner reminiscent of Norman farm complexes. A Norman tower identifies the entry to the house, which is clad in shingles cut in a variety of patterns. Fish-scale shingles mix with wave-like shakes cresting in two great gables on the front.

The Bells' decision to live in the house year-round was probably made

---

*One renter was William Collins Whitney, who did not build in Newport. Whitney was on the other side of politics, a stalwart of the New York Democrats.

after the exterior was completed. When McKim, Mead & White designed a year-round house, they would enclose it more and tighten it into a box form. The full-time expression of this house can be seen in the interiors, which were elaborately done in the Aesthetic style. The interior shares elements of Anglo-Japanese taste with the work at Kingscote, but here there is rattan on the walls rather than cork. The Bell house was purchased by the Preservation Society of Newport, which has completed a meticulous restoration.

With much of the work of McKim, Mead & White being done in Newport, the partners spent a fair amount of time on the Fall River Line boats coming and going by sea. When three more commissions came in for houses to be built in 1883, the pace must have been frenetic. It was all the more arduous because Cass Gilbert, an excellent young man who worked in the office from 1880 to 1882, had just left to start a practice in St. Paul, Minnesota. Gilbert was only twenty-one when he arrived at McKim, Mead & White, but he showed such great promise working on the Walter Tuckerman house design and the Casino that the office had positioned him in Newport for a good part of the year in 1881 and 1882. Gilbert became the site man for Newport-related work. Ross Winans, son of the railroad builder Thomas Winans, lived in his father's large wooden cottage in Newport built by the Masons early in the 1870s. When Ross Winans decided to build a house in the emerging northern neighborhood around the railroad station in Baltimore, he asked McKim, Mead & White to design the house, and the architects dispatched Cass Gilbert to oversee the building. But by the end of 1882, Gilbert, anxious to start his own practice, had returned to the Midwest. The architects had to scramble to replace him.

The three new commissions in Newport of 1882–83 were all shingle houses: one modest, one medium, and one grand. The smallest of the group was the Charles M. Bull house, a restrained and gabled composition just above Newport proper on Dudley Avenue at Broadway in Middletown. The Bulls were an old Newport family, and Prescott Hall Butler was a classmate of the renowned physician William T. Bull. The name of the house was Karlsruhe, or "Charles's nest," a humorous reference to the princely resort in Germany, but the house was an expected gable shingle house with the almost mandatory double Dutch door beloved by Stanford White. Unpublished in its day, it survives under a coat of white paint and with its ground-floor interiors stripped of any detail.

The somewhat larger house was begun in the spring of 1882 for an old friend of the White family, the artist Samuel Colman. Colman's father had been a successful bookseller and publisher. His painter son, of Richard Grant White's generation, had gone off to Europe to study art in the mid-nineteenth century, traveling, among other places, to Spain, where Americans had not then much ventured. Colman was also one of the first artists to travel to the American West.

The site for Colman's house was on Red Cross Avenue, in that almost suburban quarter behind the Jewish cemetery inhabited by many artists, writers, and intellectuals. Colman's place was just down the street from the houses of Katherine Wormeley and Samuel Tilton. Here was an established neighborhood with a specific character, not the new and open lands popular with the richer people of the day. If Colman hoped to meet potential patrons in Newport, they did not materialize. Most of the major spenders in Newport favored contemporary French Academic painters and did not support American artists.

The Colman house is less a shingle-style resort cottage than a country home. It has no Norman features and few touches of Richard Norman Shaw. The main body is kept within in a huge roof mass rather like a Dutch Colonial gambrel roof or a much-broadened mansard roof. There even appears to be a New England widow's walk atop the roof like a royal crown. The house base and entry wall are of dressed stone with a slightly raised stone surface. The block of the house is contained and regularized.

Colman was seeking a home in Newport. Since it was to be his primary residence the house appeared homogeneous and contained, not reaching out to accept summer guests and weather. As he had some financial resources, he was able to acquire a fine painting collection, which he installed here, including a Corot and canvases from the recently dispersed collection of one of America's first great collectors, John Taylor Johnston of New York. But although Colman did up his house to perfection (the library was published in the book of books for proud house-owners, the sumptuous 1883–84 subscription folio *Artistic Houses*), he did not find Newport to his liking and soon returned to permanent residence in New York. The house was then sold and acquired by J. Coleman Drayton, yet another client of McKim, Mead & White.

The major house of 1882 at Newport was Southside, a vast summer seaside cottage for Robert Goelet built at the top of Cliff Walk facing out across the Atlantic. The Goelet house was in the new section of the island where the larger houses would be built, an appropriate location, as the American millionaires who would build here faced toward the Old World, where they could eye it for its titles, artworks, and culture. The

Atlantic bank of Newport would be the setting for many marriages made between wealthy Americans and titled Europeans.

The Goelet family were old New Yorkers who had landed in the seventeenth century as Huguenot refugees. In the eighteenth and nineteenth centuries, they steadily and quietly purchased land, which they usually then leased rather than reselling. They owned significant properties in Manhattan. Indeed, Grand Central Terminal sits on Goelet land extracted from the family by the ruthless Commodore Vanderbilt with a little help from the New York State Legislature.

In the nineteenth century, Peter Goelet had built himself a freestanding town house at Nineteenth Street and Broadway, where he kept peacocks in his garden. The asthmatic young Theodore Roosevelt, growing up on nearby Twentieth Street, took a modicum of enjoyment in watching Goelet's birds while doing breathing exercises out of doors. Peter Goelet was a bachelor and a bit eccentric; two nephews were his primary heirs: Robert (1841–1899) and Ogden (1846–1897). On inheriting their uncle's estate, they found the properties Peter had hoarded now to be worth a great sum, as New York City moved northward onto Goelet lands. As a result, they became wealthy young men. The death of their father almost doubled their land and capital.

The Goelet brothers were well-brought-up young men, educated and mannered, indeed a cut above most of America's newly rich families. When they married, they moved to 591 and 608 Fifth Avenue, where each had built a fine home by the established New York architect E. H. Kendall, who had specialized in commercial buildings. They began to visit Newport with their families in the 1880s, probably renting houses until 1882, when Robert Goelet asked McKim, Mead & White to design a summer house for him.

We do not know why Robert Goelet selected McKim, Mead & White. The Goelets had had no prior relation with the architects, having used Kendall just a few years earlier; they continued to use him for commercial work in New York. Robert Goelet's commission must have been one of the many the architects had received in the wake of building the Casino. Indeed, the Goelet house turned into almost as big a job as the Casino; there were virtually countless rooms in this vast family house.

The site for the new mansion was on the Atlantic side of the island, just south of the Kay Street area, making the name Robert selected, Southside, appropriate. Begun in 1882 and completed in 1884, Southside sits atop the usual red brick base floor before rising to its shingle-covered height.

*Southside, the Robert Goelet house at Newport, 1882–84. The street side of the house.*

*Southside, the garden front, boarded up for winter.*

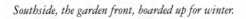

The inland side of the house with its entrance is more contained than in many earlier shingle seaside cottages. The principal door is balanced by equal-sized fat Norman two-story rounded towers. The door and window arrangement on this façade seems symmetrical except for the southern sitting-room wing, which extends closer to the driveway than does the service wing on the other side of the house. The ocean side of the house has a vast piazza supported by slender columns. The "big gulp of air" resort house is now brought into a reasoned order, as if more disciplined taste has influenced the design. The Goelet commission tamed the shingle house.

In 1883 as the Goelet house rose, Stanford White's difficult courtship of Bessie Smith at last seemed likely to be successful. With the hope now of an improved financial position, White was able to join Robert Goelet in some of his social and pleasurable pursuits. Goelet was to become one of White's closest friends, and the two spent many evenings together each month until the former's premature death at the end of the century. Robert Goelet was a member of one of the most exclusive sportsman's clubs, the Restigouche in Quebec, Canada, which was devoted to salmon fishing from June through August. Club members, who had put down a hefty sum to belong, would travel to the Gaspé Peninsula for what was usually three weeks of complete retreat from the daily ordeal. At Restigouche, members took to the river with rod and reel to do battle with giant toothy fish. The sportsmen were well treated by local Native Americans and service people, who made certain that visitors won against the salmon. Goelet brought White to Restigouche in June 1883 in the very first year of the club. Four years later he gave White a loan to pay for his membership. Perhaps the weeks of the year when White could truly relax were at Restigouche, and he enjoyed retreats there for the rest of his life. Many of White's current and future clients fished with him, as did the debonair John L. Cadwalader, who became McKim's best friend and was a club founder.

White could joyfully lavish detail on the interiors of the Goelet house, as he now had both a client he enjoyed working with and a patron with a nearly unlimited purse. Here he took the drawing rooms of the Victor Newcomb house and raised their ceiling beams to the top of the great hall, which functioned as a double-height circulation space. At Southside he refined some of his signature details; the entry door—a double Dutch one, of course—was embellished with a bold sun. White liked the sunburst and zodiac and used these forms on doors, safes, and book covers. He had a great love of textured materials for wall surfaces—he used cork at some locations, Japanese embossed papers in other houses, and tooled Spanish leather when a client could afford the cost. He was fascinated with patterns made by steel-headed nails driven, as here, into wall and door surfaces. The same zodiac designs, nail-head patterning, and frieze areas of "illuminated" Spanish leather occur in his exactly contemporary design for the Villard houses in New York.

Here was a space with a more European sensibility. Stanford White had spent more than a year in Europe just four years before, but the Europe he saw then was not an insider's world. Now, when he had a cooperative patron, he began to see himself as an interpreter of the European aesthetic heritage, bringing his limited knowledge of classical detail to flatter the sophisticated Goelet or Henry Villard in New York. White increasingly fashioned himself into a one-man band, transporting the riches of eight hundred years of design to the new inheritors of the mantle of achievement: the American robber barons.

His capacity for creating a traditional Old World interior was limited at this point; much of his knowledge came from book plates. White's expertise would grow on future trips as he gained entry to houses and to dealers and their displays, and as he began to travel in much higher social circles.

Exactly how and when White began to purchase European antiquities is uncertain. He bought a few textiles and rugs during his "student" trip,

*Southside, interior of living hall. This remarkable house, still owned by the family, surely should be declared a national treasure.*

but began buying in earnest only on his next voyage, in 1884. In the interim he came to know dealers in European objects who had beautiful items for sale in New York. Probably the first place where White found such things was on John Street a few blocks from 57 Broadway. According to one anecdotal account of the origins of the House of Duveen in the United States, "Uncle" Henry Duveen had a shop above an artist's supply house on John Street; McKim and White came in search of pencils and wandered upstairs, where Duveen, it is said, dazzled the architects with his huge supply of Dutch tiles. Duveen was also able to provide Tudor-like antique chairs, which he brought over from Paris where such items were being made. White and McKim, it is claimed, grabbed these items for use in their Fifth Avenue mansions. This story specifies the year as 1877, well before White was even in McKim's practice and a decade before the firm was building mansions on Fifth Avenue. Clearly the date here is an issue. Russell Hitchcock remembered that King Covell, an old Newport resident, had told him that the first of White's houses into which he put European antiques was the Goelet house in Newport. Hitchcock had been told Carlhian of Paris supplied the fireplace overmantel for the great hall. Carlhian records do not support this attribution, however.

Other European acquisitions began to feature in these houses of the early 1880s as well. Around the mirrors in the Isaac Bell house are Breton bed panels, but we do not know where they came from, just as we cannot determine the provenance of the overmantel at the Goelet house. It is tempting to try to see in these elements the first inklings of White's increasing obsession with passing on European artworks and architectural elements to Americans.

The American great house of the late nineteenth century had to have large tapestries hanging in the main spaces. At Southside we see the beginning of this fever. Old woven panels could be purchased quite cheaply in Europe at this time, and damaged areas could be reasonably repaired. Their great sizes gave them boldness of pictorial value for far less than Old Master paintings, which were as yet not prevalent in large numbers in American collections.

A final feature found in these Newport houses was the colored leaded glass window. Samuel Colman designed his own, but a sort of restrained rectilinear window design appears in many of the houses of this era in Newport and New York. Windows of this type appear at the entrance of Southside. Are they fillers from the mass-produced workshops within Tiffany or John La Farge? Or are they the work of David Maitland Armstrong? Or, again, a favored artist now in New York and working closely with the architects, Francis Lathrop? The bill books for the houses give no clue.

The formula for the next decade's work appears full-blown at the Goelet house, the only McKim, Mead & White house in Newport still in the original family. It survives in flawless condition and should be treasured as a major monument of American architecture. But wooden summer houses of this kind quickly go out of style. When Ogden Goelet built his house nearby in 1888, he opted for the château style and called on the architect for French baronial form, Richard Morris Hunt. In terms of architectural style, the Ogden Goelet house was *retardataire,* Hunt having already designed a number of similar houses. But the material used—stone—provided baronial dignity. Stone houses were to put wooden houses out of style.

A further Newport client of the 1880s was H.A.C. Taylor, son of the Moses Taylor who employed McKim at Elberon. Moses Taylor had two sons, the high-minded H.A.C. Taylor and a genuine ne'er-do-well, George C. Taylor, who spent his life tormented by alcohol abuse and other problems. Both sons were loyal to McKim. George C. Taylor asked McKim, Mead & White for a large shingle house in 1884, which was initially to be at Moriches, Long Island, just west of the Hamptons. It seems he may have then taken the drawings and actually built his house on the Atlantic Ocean near Islip. H.A.C. Taylor had purchased land outside Newport just after the Civil War to create a model farm. He must also have been eyeing Newport for his own residence, but he stayed in Elberon with his aging parents until Moses Taylor died. The model farm needed a director and Taylor hired Colonel George Waring, the sanitary expert. Colonel Waring spent the winter in New York and the summer in Newport running Taylor's farm and living in a small Norman-style villa near the Jewish cemetery called the Hypotenuse. Taylor spent time in Newport looking at Waring's developments at the farm and often joining the members of the Town and Country Club for literary afternoons which sometimes included McKim. In 1882 Taylor asked McKim for drawings for a big house on Annandale Road, but he did not build the house until 1885–86, when his father was breathing his last.

Newport was still snobbish toward newcomers, especially the people who had been key figures at Elberon. Taylor, therefore, probably wished to make a statement about his social status. His house was intended to project his good breeding and superior ancestry to the Grant administration people in Elberon, so he asked McKim to make him a big, modern, but Colonially styled house. He had known McKim a decade before when

McKim had been an early and prime advocate of the Colonial style in America and had enlarged those three old Newport houses at the Point. But the Taylor house was something bigger, an entire essay in the Colonial style, not a set of mere Colonial details in seaside cottage mode. The design evolved gradually over two years until the house was refined into a new style that would become a major component of McKim, Mead & White's practice. The Colonial style the architects put forward was usually built of wood, with eighteenth-century detail, genteel entry porches, a widow's walk, and increasingly symmetrical form. It was based on old New England houses, but the houses had taken Alice in Wonderland's magic pill and grown huge.

The H.A.C. Taylor house, now gone, was rather unresponsive to the resort location. Perhaps Taylor had enough of resorts at Elberon. Missing in the Newport house were piazzas and summer details. Instead it stressed the earlier Newport and implied that Taylor could claim Colonial American ancestry.

The house was not yet contained in a big rectangle but relied on an earlier plan, like that of the Goelet house, where wings of the house flank the central entrance at different angles. It is clear that McKim, Mead & White were launching fresh historicisms. They had contained the novelty of their earlier work and were beginning to revert to a more

*The H.A.C. Taylor house at Newport, 1882–86. An early venture in the Colonial style, sadly gone. View from the street.*

*The H.A.C. Taylor house, back of the house.*

symmetrical form. The creation of a more ordered style probably owes a debt to McKim's interest in earlier American architecture and his fear of unguided design. The group dynamic at 57 Broadway had produced excellent results in the period between 1879 and the early 1880s, as the partners, Joseph Wells, and occasionally Sidney Stratton and George Babb, helped one another to create original and balanced compositions. One can almost hear Wells's acerbic comments as he softened and rounded McKim's angular forms and balanced the asymmetry of the seaside cottage. Wells had a fondness for the picturesque and the variety of roof forms found in European vernacular buildings. But he also had a love for the order of the Renaissance; witness his drawings of two carefully measured elevations of Roman palaces, which he had seen in books and then visited.

It was Wells who nudged his colleagues into more regularized composition. His constant justification for form and proportion were the volumes of Letarouilly then becoming the firm's bible. McKim took Wells's lesson to heart. As work in the office increased and the collaborative effort began to decline, he turned to architectural history books as his inspiration and guide. He became book- and precedent-bound, even if each work was tailored to its client and purpose. For country houses and institutions with a heritage such as Harvard, the Colonial style seemed to be the answer for him. The H.A.C. Taylor house was the great step into the safety of the past.

In 1884, as the Taylor house design was completed, McKim, Mead & White had another request for a Newport house in the Colonial spirit from Commodore William Edgar, who wanted a home of substance in the Kay Street area on Old Beach Road. McKim's old friend from the Town and Country Club, Edith Wharton, may have suggested the architects. Commodore Edgar's wife was Edith Wharton's aunt, a Rhinelander. Several Rhinelanders asked for a McKim, Mead & White house, and one suspects Wharton encouraged the Edgars here.

Edith Wharton trod an uneasy line between the older, high-minded, literate society of Newport and its smarter set, increasingly focused on Europe. She walked this tightrope for some years but eventually sought more comfortable values in Lenox, Massachusetts. Wharton lived in a Newport cottage, Pencraig, and never asked McKim to design for her.

*Joseph M. Wells drawing.*

The Edgar house is brick rather than the usual wooden clapboard. Indeed, it is McKim, Mead & White's first brick house in the Colonial

*Commodore William Edgar house, Newport, 1884–86. A tawny brick house that harks back to the eighteenth century.*

Revival. It stands in a rather dense mid-nineteenth-century neighbor-hood, not on the ocean, and so does not need to be replete with porches. It has a central entrance with fat, bowed two-story towers on either side that have an eighteenth-century flavor. Here is an essay in Southern Colonial style rather like a Virginia house. The thick chimneys with pierced arch openings also recall the American South, as does the use of a Palladian window over the main entry.

Yet the Edgar house is not very Colonial at all. The bricks are not the red ones of the American eighteenth century, but thin, tawny bricks that Stanford White helped to create with the Perth Amboy Terra Cotta Company. They are thinner and more golden than American bricks, indeed almost Italian. In the western wing, the main block manages to confront Newport summers in the form of an open loggia above the drawing room. Here there are resemblances to Wave Crest, a house McKim, Mead & White built in 1885–86 in Far Rockaway for John H. Cheever. In the Cheever house the wing was open on two levels, but in both cases the upper loggia is supported by four columns.

By 1884 or so, McKim, Mead & White had begun to repeat successful parts of buildings in other commissions. The Edgar house has similarities to the Goelet house in the main façade and an open-air loggia resembles that of the Cheever house. The repeat of architectural notes is common in a practice when commissions flood in. When pressed, the designer recalls a feature that has been successful and uses it to complete a new work.

The work in Newport slowed down as the national economy ebbed in the mid-1880s. McKim, Mead & White had all but taken over the Masons' wooden house trade. Besides their new houses of the 1880s, they had built stables and barns for existing houses and undertaken the odd flat-fee job. In their early days, when eager for work, they sometimes did a job for a flat-fee payment, particularly when Stanford White decorated a single room on a modest budget. Occasionally, a larger work was done for a fee without supervision; the architects supplied only a drawing and plans. There is one such work in Newport, the John H. Glover house up above Ocean Drive on Moorland Road, then a fairly empty part of town. In 1886 the firm supplied the drawings for the house for five hundred dollars. It was built and still stands today as a rock-bound, somewhat clumsy version of a McKim, Mead & White design.

Following the Glover house, work at Newport fell off for a year or two, until the Vanderbilts barged their way into society there. Alva Smith Vanderbilt led the attack along with her architect, the now aging Richard Morris Hunt. Alva Vanderbilt's Marble House (1888–92) raised the stakes in the game, since the stone house carried a hefty price tag. Hunt's name won acceptance at Newport, and the new houses of the late 1880s and early 1890s would be Hunt-style châteaux on suburban plots. The summer house was supplanted by the house as accessory to a social gamble with high stakes and elaborate rules. The new stone houses became trophies used for the planning of dynastic and international marriages. McKim himself did not return much to Newport, preferring to go to Narragansett nearby, though White continued to make brief visits at Bob Goelet's. The architects returned to build and improve the palaces, but this was now a different town.

The wooden houses for the smaller or more modest resorts produced variations of the work done in Newport. At Richfield Springs in New York State, where a sulfur water point provided healthful benefits to its believers, McKim, Mead & White produced a variation on the Isaac Bell house for the Chicago magnate Cyrus Hall McCormick in 1880–82. The house, Clayton Lodge, sat atop a stone base with a single large dominating gable rather than the parallel plane of the two gables at the Bell house—a more expensive affair. There were symmetrical oval windows set in ornate frames on either side of the big gable. But the sulfur springs did not help McCormick, and he died after only three years in the house, which has now also turned to dust.

*Clayton Hall, the Cyrus McCormick house in Richfield Springs, New York, 1880–82. The house has collapsed.*

In the 1870s at Wave Crest in Far Rockaway, McKim and Prescott Hall Butler enjoyed a warm fall, swimming in the Atlantic Ocean as late as October when they visited Charles C. Beaman, a partner in the law firm of Evarts, Butler, Choate et al. They met there John Cheever and his daughter, lately married to the handsome John Cowdin. The bride's father built the couple a seaside house with a remarkable butterfly plan, where right-angled regularity gives way to wings like those of a butterfly. McKim had begun to work on the hinged plan in the early 1880s, and he would use the shape in 1885–86 for the ocean house of the Cowdins. McKim would do a variation on the butterfly plan for the Appleton house at Lenox and the Osborn house at Mamaroneck.

# 12. THE SUBURBAN HOUSE

A different version of the shingle-covered house of the 1880s was produced for the full-time residence of people who lived beyond the city but traveled to work there. In the years after the Civil War, Miller McKim advised his son to learn the English and French methods of building such inexpensive wooden houses. Having himself taken such a house in Llewellyn Park, he recognized the potential of this genre. His son's firm was to become so eminent that in due course the architects had no need to continue to build these modest dwellings. But in the early years, McKim designed several smaller suburban houses.

The first such house surely came about thanks to Miller McKim's assistance. Stewart Hartshorn, a businessman who made roller-blind window shades, wanted to build an ideal commuter colony at Short Hills, near Millburn, New Jersey, on the Erie-Lackawanna line. He bought thirteen acres with gently rolling hills and planned an ideal community as Llewellyn Haskell had done earlier, but he had a more realistic approach to commuters' needs, placing the railroad station at the center of the community and thus making it a perfect town for a businessman and his family. After convincing the railroad to put a station in Short Hills, Hartshorn hired McKim, Mead & Bigelow in 1879 to create a model house in a cheap but sturdy style. It was to be a small family house for rent at $750 a year or for sale at $3,000. McKim's prototype actually cost almost double the sale price, but Hartshorn wished to carry out a social experiment. He realized no profit on the development until just before his death in 1937.

*The Short Hills Civic Center, focus of the community, 1879–80.*
*Burned in a fire to the distress of the community.*

As a focus for the community at Short Hills, Hartshorn also asked McKim, Mead & White to create a suburban centerpiece, a music hall, next to the train station. It functioned as an all-purpose building for decades, and gave Short Hills a visual and civic identity. The music hall was a Norman *manoir* with a very picturesque tower in the form of a rook-

*William C. Chapin house, Providence, Rhode Island, 1881–83.*
*This picture, taken just before the house was demolished, shows*
*the property as a used-car lot.*

ery or dovecote. This fanciful building presented a smiling face to the community until it burned down in 1976. The loss was locally mourned.

In July 1881, McKim, Mead & White designed their only house in Providence, Rhode Island, for William C. Chapin. At the edge of the city, it is a venture in the shingle-style suburban mode. The Chapins, who were well established in Providence, had lived on High Street, later renamed Westmister Street. In 1881, William C. Chapin purchased a lot near the family house, which was occupied by a substantial early clapboard house of 1820—the Grant-Tyler house by the prominent local architect John Holden Greene (1777–1850). Despite McKim's pious words about Colonial architecture and his much-touted love of older American buildings, he clearly was willing to look away when a house of the early Republic might hold back a job. The Grant-Tyler house was duly demolished.

The new house, three stories tall and timber framed, replaced the old one quickly. It rose on an ashlar base to a clapboarded first floor with a lattice screen concealing the entrance. A fully exposed brick chimney climbed above the house on the main façade topped by a small dovecote. The second and third stories were shingled, and a full hipped roof with eyebrow windows sat firmly atop the house. Unlike the seaside cottages in the resort mode, the suburban house is much more contained, limited to a basic rectangle. The Chapin house had a peculiar double gable over the primary entrance, with two rounded bows in the second story on either side of a Jacobean panel. On the third floor, covered with fish-scale shingles, were two more bows and an "opus sectile" panel (a design made from materials larger than tesserae) with stones set in cement in a sundial pattern. The Chapin house is very odd for the architects, as it is a Normanflavored house built over the body of a real American house. The house did not have a happy history: It was used as an old car lot by the 1930s and demolished at the beginning of World War II.

Perhaps the height of the suburban house was the Metcalfe house of 1882 in Buffalo, New York. Sadly demolished in 1980, it was a most unusual commission and about the last of the suburban McKim, Mead & White houses to survive.

The Buffalo house was the first and most significant of the firm's houses in that city. It was commissioned by a woman, Arzelia Stetson Metcalfe and her son, James. Mrs. Metcalfe, who had lived next door to the site where she would build the house, had been widowed in 1879. Her late husband had made a success of his career in banking and a local railroad. He had been dead for the requisite three years, so that his widow could shed her mourning role and take on life again. She had three sons and a daughter whom she raised in an intellectual household, where reading and literature dominated winter life in the cold city. All four of her children had inherited their mother's interest in artistic matters; indeed, the selection of the architects seems to have been made by Mrs. Metcalfe's daughter, who had sought out the great critic of the time, a well-born woman, Mrs. Mariana Griswold Van Rensselaer (1851–1934).

Like Frances Metcalfe Bass, Mrs. Van Rensselaer found America's first European-trained artists more pleasing company than members of her own social class. She was a New Yorker by birth—both sets of her grandparents had lived side by side in the wonderful houses at the north of Washington Square—but she had also spent time abroad. Many mercantile families whose businesses had been eclipsed by European shipping companies were forced by the rise in the cost of living in mid-nineteenth-century New York to sojourn in Europe, living well on rents paid for the city properties they had vacated. Mariana Griswold had enjoyed a European education but within an American community. On her return to the United States, she married a man who went into mining engineering and died prematurely. As Mrs. Griswold Van Rensselaer, she began to write frequent articles on the arts and architecture for *The Century Magazine* in the 1880s. She knew Augustus Saint-Gaudens, John La Farge, and McKim, Mead & White. Her championing of the firm's work of the early 1880s in a series of articles for *The Century Magazine* on the current state of American architecture provided their first critical endorsement and helped to establish their reputation before Richardson died.

They were not the only new American artists whom she supported. In 1888 Saint-Gaudens honored her with a profile done in bronze relief, for which Stanford White designed a frame. Frances Metcalfe Bass admired and visited this remarkable and accomplished woman, who probably steered McKim, Mead & White toward her friend.

The Metcalfes watched from their old home as their new house was built by local Buffalo craftsmen. The severe weather extremes were beyond the range of knowledge of New York City builders. The Metcalfe house was a restrained rectangle with rounded extrusions, more tightly geometrical and placid than the seaside shingle houses of the same date, though it shares some features with them. Buffalo has cold winters and a tight house with cold-resistant materials was imperative, so the Metcalfe house had a dressed ashlar stone base and a pressed brick second floor, and instead of wood the "shingles" were really terra-cotta tiles. McKim, Mead & White here conformed to the hung tiles or slates used in England by Nesfield and Shaw and in some work in Normandy. Even the brown and

*The Metcalfe house, Buffalo, New York. Sadly, this rare remaining
suburban McKim, Mead & White house was allowed to be
destroyed, leaving two far more common later houses by the firm
standing around the corner.*

red colors of the house seemed to register fall and winter. A small single-
story portico let the Metcalfes greet visitors, but here it was a shelter
against weather, not (as in the seaside cottage) a way to extend a cool
breeze. The dining room incorporated the curve of a Norman tourelle, but
the protrusion was modest and ended at the second floor. Under the big
hipped roof, a great tile-hung gable reminiscent of the gable in the Tilton
house at Newport sounded the note of the English Queen Anne architects.

The interiors, fitted out by local woodworkers, made up about a third
of the price of the house. As winter in Buffalo was spent indoors, it was
logical to emphasize the inside of the house. The rich, warm woods used
in the principal rooms can be seen today in the elements of the house that
were saved and now are found in the collections of the Buffalo and Erie
County Historical Society, the Buffalo State College, and the Metropolitan Museum of Art.

# 13 . CITY HOUSES

New York City was the location of much of McKim, Mead & White's early work. Before White joined the partnership, McKim, Mead, & Bigelow already had the Benedick under way and had started their second row house, a big one, at 283 Madison Avenue in what was a rather old-fashioned genteel neighborhood. The commission arrived just as Wells went on the payroll and White joined the office. The client was Frederick Ferris Thompson (1836–1899), whose father was a founder of First National Bank and ran Thompson Brothers, a private bank. Thompson had a direct connection to Miller McKim as he, too, was an ardent abolitionist. He had married a wealthy woman from the Clark family and summered in Canandaigua, where he became a fine photographer. But though Thompson began life with ideals and made a point of specifying in his New York house a warming area at the entrance for messenger boys to thaw out in winter, he later met with financial reversals and was accused of embezzlement by the Clark family. The Thompson house is a McKim exercise in the Queen Anne complete with a scrolled gable on the fifth-floor dormer, but the rest of the front is more subdued than the earlier Dickerson house.

In 1880, Mead and White were asked to design another big, urban town house, the Charles Tracy Barney house at 10 East Fifty-fifth Street. The client was to become a close friend. Charles T. Barney was born in Cleveland, Ohio, in 1851, the son of Ashbel Holmes Barney and Susan Tracy Barney. The elder Barney was president of the U.S. Express Company in Cleveland. In 1875 his son married a Whitney girl, a sister of the soon well-known William Collins Whitney, settled in New York, and went to work at the American Sale Deposit and Columbia Bank. He then commissioned McKim, Mead & White to build a wide town house for his family. Barney was a patron of contemporary American artists. Not only did he buy works by Winslow Homer, Edwin Austin Abbey, James McNeill Whistler, and John La Farge, but he put a stable he owned on West Fifty-fifth Street at the artists' disposal as a studio space, charging modest rent. Barney's introduction to his architects could have come through the young artists he encouraged or through Sidney Stratton, who was friendly with Barney's father and built him a house at Bar Harbor, Maine.

*The Frederick Thompson house, 283 Madison Avenue, New York, 1879–81; demolished. Thompson, initially a considerate businessman, ended up as a figure of ill repute.*

The Barney house was quite wide and built of red brick over a stone base. The stonework on the house was cut in a deliberately rock-like way to contrast with the smooth brickwork laid in an intricate pattern. The main block of the house ended with a balustrade, with dormer gables appearing above the balustraded cornice. Montgomery Schuyler uncharitably called the house a "mad orgy of bad architecture." The interiors at the Barney house were quite splendid, with rooms given over to different themes. There was a Renaissance room, an Arabic room, and a Colonial room. Indian shawls were used as wall coverings for the parlor. The dining-room ceiling was covered in leather—doubtless the work of Stanford White, who was probably also responsible for the Indian fabric. White arranged for his old mentor, George Babb, to do a grand room in a catacomb style, where Barney displayed a new painting acquired from

*Barney drawing room on Fifty-fifth Street in New York City.*

*J. Colman Drayton house in New York at 374–380 Fifth Avenue, part of the vast Astor rental property in midtown. Demolished.*

the artist Thomas Wilmer Dewing. White designed a special frame for the painting.

Barney stood by the architects despite Schuyler's comments and gave them further work. In 1895 he left Fifty-fifth Street for a different house at 67 Park Avenue, which McKim, Mead & White remodeled and decorated. Joseph Pulitzer, the Hungarian-born publisher of *The New York World,* took over Barney's former house and lived there until a fire drove him out. Pulitzer then had his new house designed by McKim, Mead & White.

After John Jacob Astor died in 1847, his heirs inherited a large portfolio of property, and in the 1850s they began to develop houses on and off Fifth Avenue above Thirtieth Street. Upon marrying, two of the Astor grandchildren built their own houses on this property at Thirty-third and Thirty-fourth Streets. In 1879 the Astor estate continued the family connection by building a house for an Astor great-granddaughter at 374 Fifth Avenue. Until then the Astors had favored the style of the brownstone builder Peter Kissam, who worked for the estate, or of the more self-important master of the row house, Griffith Thomas, who did the Caroline Schermerhorn Astor house on the corner. But this new generation wanted their own architects. Miss Astor's husband was J. Coleman Drayton, who suggested McKim, already his family's architect.

The original house must have been substantial, as it came in at eighty-three thousand dollars, a very large sum for that period, especially considering that the land was given to the couple. In the fall of 1882, Coleman Drayton rehired the architects to expand the house northward through two more row houses to make a mansion of triple width. There were several elaborate interiors, including the library, which was illustrated in *Artistic Houses* and hung with a Beauvais tapestry. Placed on the ceiling were ebonized strips displaying the marks of the sixteenth-century printers, casting Drayton as a gentleman-scholar. A photograph of the exterior shows what seems a wide house but not a triple house, so perhaps the work at 378 Fifth Avenue was internal only. The exterior of the house at 374 Fifth Avenue seems more restrained and dignified than McKim's earlier row houses, faintly suggesting an Italian town palace down to the heraldic shield set in the upper façade.

But Drayton's princely status rapidly plummeted when his wife ran off to Europe with a handsome insurance executive in the early 1880s. He endured some terrible festivals of gossip in the papers as well as threats of a duel followed by long legal battles. For a time, he settled in a country house in Bernardsville, New Jersey, then bought from Samuel Colman the McKim, Mead & White house in Newport, before finally relocating to Surrey, England. The Astors had to try to keep the peace and the family name out of the headlines.

Although Richardson had moved from Staten Island in New York back to greater Boston when his college friends gave him work, we have seen that McKim and White kept in touch with him. The climax of the relationship, or perhaps its swan song, came in the town houses that Richardson, McKim, and White built next to each other for F. L. Higginson and Charles A. Whittier in Boston in 1880–83.

THE HIGGINSON FAMILY of Boston were among the city's premier capitalists, and McKim knew them from the old Town and Country Club

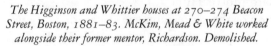

*The Higginson and Whittier houses at 270–274 Beacon Street, Boston, 1881–83. McKim, Mead & White worked alongside their former mentor, Richardson. Demolished.*

sessions on the Bigelow porch. Colonel Thomas Wentworth Higginson was part of the old intellectual circle at Newport, where he spent most of his time, and had been an abolitionist in the circle of Miller McKim and William Lloyd Garrison. When his cousin, F. Lee Higginson, wanted some work done on his house at Beverly Farms, Massachusetts, McKim got the job in May 1879. The next year, F. Lee Higginson asked Richardson to build a house for him at 274 Beacon Street, Boston. Higginson's partner, Charles A. Whittier, asked McKim, Mead & White to build a companion house on the same block at 270 Beacon Street. In this way McKim, Mead & White got to work with Richardson one last time to build a pair of houses attached to each other.

The investment firm of Lee, Higginson & Co. was at the top of the economic ladder in Boston, and the partners, Francis Lee Higginson (1841–1925) and Charles A. Whittier, wished to convey as much in their residences. On a block facing the patrician Beacon Street, Whittier and Higginson and their friendly rival architects built what were really two double-width houses with stone bases and upper floors of brick. Richardson and McKim, Mead & White agreed to share the same cornice and roofline, materials, and window type, and to build an urban, square-headed window version of the turreted château style made popular in the 1870s by Richard Morris Hunt.

The invocation of the château on the streets of a city was meant to link the client with European aristocracy, particularly the French noble class. Hunt, Richardson, and McKim, Mead, and White all knew châteaux well from their journeys in the Loire. In 1870 Hunt had proposed a château at Seventieth Street and Fifth Avenue for Josiah Fiske; this was not built, but eight years later he began the famous French house for Alva Smith Vanderbilt, the ambitious wife of William Kissam Vanderbilt. The success of this house probably influenced the McKim, Mead & White design for Whittier in Boston. It was said that Charles McKim had a particular fondness for the Vanderbilt house and in his later years would take an evening stroll past its location on Fiftieth Street for reassurance before going to sleep at night. But the château style preferred by Hunt was far more ornate and decorated. The evocation of a castle here in Boston was very much simplified, and the two houses were built of brownstone and brick, not the white stone that Hunt preferred.

The Charles Whittier house is dominated by a tall central château tower topped by a sharp conical roof. Here is McKim, Mead & White's first urban version of the tower they had used in their wooden-shingled country houses. The partners looked to a later version of the Loire château than had Richardson. The tower's position at the center of the house overwhelms the composition. The projecting covered entrance porch at the outer edge of the house met the street wall, while the staircase wall above the door recedes. The entry to Higginson's house, by contrast, was much more Old World, resembling a great stable door. The conventional portico to Whittier's house made a more comfortable entrance. Even allowing for the fact that the Higginson house never received the series of sculptures Saint-Gaudens had been asked to create for it, Richardson did not work as well in such restrained circumstances of collaboration as McKim, Mead & White. The younger men had here upstaged the Great Mogul.

The three partners were sufficiently pleased with the Boston house to design a second version of it in Baltimore for Ross R. Winans in 1882–83—a great, freestanding, brick and brownstone house on a lot near the Baltimore railroad station. The Winans fortune went back two generations to the Ross Winanses, who made mechanical innovations for the first railroad lines in the United States, notably the Baltimore and Ohio. Other B&O line investors, among them the Garretts of Baltimore, were to be steered into the McKim, Mead & White office by the grandson. Ross Winans I had two sons who went to Russia in the early 1840s to develop the railroad line linking Moscow and St. Petersburg. Thomas DeKay Winans married there Celeste Revillon, a Russian woman with Italian and French ancestors. Ross Revillon Winans was born in St. Petersburg in 1850. Thomas and Celeste Winans returned to the United States the next year, establishing themselves in Baltimore. In 1871–72 they built a summer house, called Bleak House,* in Newport on the then-empty Ocean Drive; it was through Newport that Ross R. Winans came to know of McKim, Mead & White.

In 1879, Ross Winans married his first cousin Neva Whistler. The bride also had a Russian childhood, as the Winans took their relatives with them to assist in their Russian railway-building venture. One of Thomas Winans's sisters was married to Major G. W. Whistler. The Whistler children included Ross Winans's bride, Neva, and James Abbott McNeill Whistler, the painter. But J. M. Whistler was never part of the artists' circle favored by McKim, Mead & White.

TO DEAL WITH THE WINANS HOUSE, McKim, Mead & White dispatched to Baltimore their young and able assistant Cass Gilbert. This

---

*Perhaps a reference to the house in Broadstairs, Kent, where Charles Dickens summered while writing his book about the British judicial system.

*Ross Winans house in Baltimore, Maryland, 1882–83.*
*A late work in the Richardson mode.*

was Gilbert's final work in the office before going off to St. Paul, Minnesota, where he developed a thriving practice (he would return to New York City at the close of the century). Gilbert acted as site man for the Winans house, as Baltimore was too distant for a higher-ranking person in the office to make the frequent inspections needed to carry out construction and finish the interior to the standard required here.

The Winans house is a splendid work. The cobalt blue wall tiles inside the entrance may not be Tiffany tiles as in Kingscote, but the effect is rich and rather like the great Holland Park house in London recently completed for Lord Leighton. The bright blue effect may also acknowledge the room Whistler had done for the Leylands in London, known as the Peacock Room. At the Winans house, we also see the small, square, glass bricks, transparent but tinted, that adorn the dining-room wall at Kingscote. Two inventive interior features display the most creative side of White: the pierced copper panels on the dining-room sideboard, unique in detail, and the door of Ross Winans's safe with its double sunburst panels—ever a White signature. Here at the height of his creativity, White has picked up an Old World conceit, metal nailheads embedded in panels to create a raised texture and design. As we saw, such nailhead details appeared in Newport as well as in New York City in the Villard interiors.

The Winans house retains the materials, tower, roof profile, and square-headed windows of the Whittier house but, freed from the constraints of attachment to another dwelling, becomes a long rectangle. Ross Winans's last days were brought almost to madness by the nearly simultaneous deaths of his wife and two of his children in 1907. The house, luckily, does survive, the only McKim, Mead & White town house of this style and early date to remain standing.

The final urban version of the McKim, Mead & White castle style was begun in the spring of 1882 in New York for Charles L. Tiffany, a founder of the jewelry and silver store still trading today. Tiffany's business was successful enough for his son, Louis Comfort Tiffany, to be afforded a fine education. By the time Tiffany matured, he was able to launch himself as a painter studying with Samuel Colman. As a decorative artist, Tiffany briefly joined ranks with the young Stanford White in 1879 in the decorative firm called Associated Artists. Two years later, the Tiffany family decided to live together to create a private family residence of heroic size. Louis Tiffany met with Stanford White and showed him his idea for a big house on the corner of Madison Avenue and Seventy-second Street, far above the fashionable portion of the city. Tiffany's sketch shows a medievalizing block rather too tall to be a private house but in keeping with Richardson's work. The boulder-based, round-arched entrance design Tiffany proposed really should have gone to Richardson in Brookline, but it was a big, expensive house, and McKim, Mead & White bit the bullet and agreed to do a house in the style of their former master.

*The Tiffany house, once on Madison Avenue at the northwest corner of Seventy-second Street, 1882–85. Demolished, it is one of the city's greatest losses of the 1930s. This picture was taken just as the house's life came to an end.*

In terms of design, the house is out of the run of the office. To keep Louis Tiffany happy, the architects (particularly White, who was then still friendly with Tiffany) let the artist have the upper hand. Tiffany knew what he wanted, and his father had the money to carry through the artist's desires. When Tiffany later rebuilt his summer home, the Briars (later Laurelton Hall), in Oyster Bay Cove, he designed much of the house himself.

Where the design most honored the basic desires of Tiffany was in its size and shape: its boulder ground floor, its corner tower, and yawning, mouth-like entry. In the upper levels White tried to control Tiffany's hefty instincts with brick elevations, using a light-colored, speckled brick of a tawny hue that White had made in McKim's school town, Perth Amboy, by the Perth Amboy Terra Cotta Company. This brick, essentially White's invention, was to be popularly known as Tiffany brick. White

*The entry to the Tiffany house. The metal gate at installation.*
*The pulpit is the height of a carriage, so guests could enter the*
*elevator without stepping to the ground.*

collaborated with the Perth Amboy company for a decade as he moved toward and then away from a thin Roman brick. The brickworks prospered, producing many of White's designs in subtle hues, and other architects followed his lead by going to New Jersey to create a signature brick.

White further tamed the Tiffany sketch by adding some Norman Shaw and Colonial features to the block. The two gables on the south-facing

*The hall of Charles L. Tiffany's apartment in the Tiffany house.*

façade were each given a triple Palladian window to break out of the medieval mold. The central gable in the middle of that façade rather resembled Shaw's work, as did the upper gable on the Madison Avenue frontage.

Upon completion, the house was quite imposing, with its North River bluestone base (it was actually a brownish-green color) and its golden, flecked brick. It stood like a giant over the emptiness between the chic area of Fifth Avenue in the Fifties and Seventy-second Street. Inside it was a triple residence, with three vast apartments. The entrance was through the great Richardsonian arch, which had a portcullis that could be raised or lowered at will, allowing visitors to alight from their carriages on a pulpit-like circular platform made of stone before walking to the elevator. The elder Tiffany was supposed to live on the lower floors, but since he did not like the apartment, it was rented out to affluent families. Tiffany's daughter had the middle section of the house, and Louis Comfort Tiffany himself was at the top in a huge, magical, exotic, aerie that defied description. Alma Mahler Werfel wrote of her almost opiate visit in her book *And the Bridge Is Love,* describing a huge boulder fireplace that looked like a giant, hand-cut wooden pipe. The fireplace could be seen through the glazed central gable of the house, signaling Tiffany's residency to the city below when the fire was kindled.

In 1936 the Tiffany family sold the house, and it was demolished. Its replacement, an apartment building by Rosario Candela and Mott B. Schmidt, is one of New York's great buildings of the period. But the loss of the Tiffany house, years before the Landmarks Preservation Commission was proposed, was one of the worst that New York architecture has sustained.

# 14. THE END OF THE PICTURESQUE

The phase of McKim, Mead & White's Norman or Breton-inspired towered style was completed by two buildings done in the boulder style of the Tiffany house base, a style associated with the work of Richardson more than McKim, Mead & White. One of these tower complexes was essentially a resort and country house, the other the focal point of a summer community.

In 1883–85 Charles J. Osborn selected McKim, Mead & White to build his huge summer and winter home at Mamaroneck, in Westchester

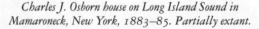

*Charles J. Osborn house on Long Island Sound in
Mamaroneck, New York, 1883–85. Partially extant.*

*Osborn interior designed by White. White purchased*
*objects for this house on his honeymoon.*

County, perched above the Long Island Sound's North Shore. Osborn was the broker for the scourge of Wall Street, Jay Gould. There was little connection between Gould and his associates and McKim, Mead & White, who tended to serve clients at least claiming to be more high-minded than Gould. The Osborn commission may simply have come from the client watching the Tiffany house go up.

Unusually, Osborn wanted a house that was partly shingle-covered in a resort mode and partly boulder-like and rough. Though its main purpose was as a rambling summer home, which would be closed up for winter as such houses always were, he asked to have a portion of the house made suitable for winter living, a sort of snug apartment for year-round use.

The Osborn house was set on a rock-and-boulder cliff at the edge of the water. It's first floor matched the setting with a rock-faced course of masonry in a long H-plan and a huge piazza on the southwestern side extending out in a dogleg bend. McKim revised a device from the Francklyn house in Elberon, where the driveway was cut through the ground floor of the house so that carriages could advance and drop off passengers under shelter. At the Osborn house visitors could alight on the western side of the driveway in the summer, or step into the eastern apartment in the winter. The small winter quarters were rather like an old movie camera in plan, a rectangular box with twin corner towers on the outside angles. The summer house rambled to the west asymmetrically, while the eastern wing was tight, contained, and protected. The summer side

*Osborn interior with a ceiling painted by
Thomas Wilmer Dewing.*

caught the prevailing winds; the winter side was protected from the storms. The Osborn house married urban and resort versions of the houses the architects were then building.*

Money was ample—White was able to purchase items for the Osborn

*The Osborn interior.*

*The Norman towers, all of the same shape and size, predominate, in particular toward the water. As in the Newport house for Robert Goelet, a raised platform set off the base of the house.

*The Narragansett Pier, Rhode Island. A great work for a summer colony in a consciously historical style by McKim. The casino would be built on the inland side by Louis Sherry. The pier was the center of social life, with a Sherry's restaurant along its flank to the right in the photo.*

house during his second trip abroad in 1884, his first real shopping trip in Europe for a client. But Osborn did not live long in the house, dying a few years after it was completed. His widow and children sold it and moved to Virginia, taking the furnishings that White had bought for them, but in a letter they sent to the architects' office, remembering the joy of the Osborn house interiors.

At the Mamaroneck house, White had his first success in getting a fellow artist a commission—in this case his painter friend Thomas Wilmer Dewing, who was brought in to paint a ceiling panel. Many extensive ventures with other artists followed for homes of the American princes of commerce. But his hope for permanent, fine, artistic houses like the hotels and châteaux of France was dashed as styles and times changed. Many such paintings were later lost to changes of taste or to fire. The Osborn house itself was gutted by fire, though a good portion of the building and outbuildings remains as a yacht club.

The final incarnation of the picturesque reverie came at Narragansett. Here on the inland coast of Rhode Island across from Newport, another summer colony had risen. But with its modest sense of noblesse, it needed a social anchor. Charles McKim took the lead in the work done at Narragansett, creating the casino that would make the town in the same year as the Osborn house: 1883.

NARRAGANSETT WAS NOTED for fine beaches and a protected harbor, once lined with piers, which had been used as the region's commercial trading base. The town was often called Narragansett Pier. Its transformation into a resort was greatly enhanced in the mid-1870s when railroad connections made travel there easier. The town needed a center, however— a summer resort touch of the type McKim, Mead & White had provided a few years earlier across the bay at Newport. McKim may have landed the job because of the Newport Casino, or perhaps some Philadelphia friends recommended him. In any case, at Narragansett he made a lifelong connection with Dr. Charles Hitchcock, a Providence-born physician with a New York City practice. Hitchcock spent his summers in Narragansett, caring for patients there before returning to New York for the winter. He became McKim's trusted personal physician as well a friend and neighbor. Hitchcock was an active promoter of the Rhode Island resort and personally paid for the wonderful small stone lifesaving station he had McKim build just under the casino. McKim himself returned often to Narragansett in the summer, taking cottages for his own use, building for the New York caterer Louis Sherry, and happy to be so close to Dr. Hitchcock.

The Narragansett Pier Casino is the image of the town seen on souvenir paperweights, ashtrays, and cigarette boxes. It is like something from one of the Norman sketchbooks of McKim or White or Wells, a Mont Saint-Michel giving a sense of age to a new resort, conjuring up a past that was not there. With its great roofline, its loggia, and its drive-through arch, it seems like an entire village by the sea.

To complete the roof effect, favored by Wells for a picturesque romantic appearance, McKim is said to have taken an active role at the end of the tile-laying, climbing on the roof with a crowbar to pull away a few newly laid slates. This would give a timeworn look to the new building. With its looping plan akin to that of the Osborn house, the Pier Casino brings the practice's love affair with the vernacular buildings of coastal France to an end. A decade of imaginatively arranged features from the Old World blended into a new building for the New World had run out of ideas. A fresh wind had blown in with Joseph Wells's interest in Italy. Wells had written that he also had a love for the casual arrangements of buildings, roofs, and additions that he saw as he looked out the window of his hotel while in Europe. But the architecture of intellect, not emotion, was in Italy, he insisted. By 1883 he had his office convinced of this truth.

# 15. SUCCESS

B y 1883, McKim, Mead & White had achieved an impressive list of commissions in important places from Boston to Baltimore. They were now building houses that cost over three hundred thousand dollars, a goodly sum for the period. They had designed and built two casinos, and were about to undertake two church commissions. At this stage Mead lived at the Benedick and McKim far to the north in the city's most affluent section, Thirty-fifth Street, on Dr. Derby's second floor.

As for Stanford White, he lived still with his parents, but his life had gone beyond the old family patterns. The older lifestyle of Richard Grant White with its dark rooms and old-fashioned clothing and literary taste was no longer commonplace. The couple still kept the values of the 1830s and '40s, when their mercantile class was at the top of New York's social order. Even the music the father played for his visitors had an old-fashioned quality. Prescott Butler and his wife remarked that as they left the house they felt as if they were walking out of a picture. Stanford White avoided the issue by living in the present. Every night he dined out with friends, clients, or fellow artists. He kept up with Saint-Gaudens when he was in the country, and spent much time with the artists who lived in the Benedick, where Mead still did and Joseph Wells soon would. White knew many artists from the old days with Richardson, but more new faces joined his set when he became a "Tiler."

The Tile Club was a group of artists and writers who decided to spend an evening a week in each other's company. Founded in 1877, this small band of New Yorkers (including Winslow Homer and J. Alden Weir) held a social evening once a week in each others' studios and homes. The ostensible common element was the creation of hand-painted tiles. The group bought blank white tiles, which they painted during their club meetings. The tiles were eventually glazed, and the week's host got to keep them. These meetings were more social than creative, with everyone giving one another nicknames and relaxing into an environment of smoke, cheese, and alcohol. Eventually music—particularly Beethoven—was added to the mix and would filter down to the weekly studio concerts Joseph Wells planned for Sundays in the winter; they were held in Saint-Gaudens's studio in the late 1880s.

The Tile Club expanded to include Saint-Gaudens, Elihu Vedder, William Merritt Chase, Francis Millet, John Twachtman, Francis Hopkinson Smith, and Edwin Austin Abbey. The curious dwarf-like fashion photographer Napoleon Sarony hosted the club for a time in his studio, which was decorated with stuffed reptiles and suits of armor. There was a mummy by the door, which was opened by Madame Sarony, dressed in the latest fashion.

Saint-Gaudens probably brought Stanford White into the club at about the time of the Farragut unveiling. White found the group wonderful, and became good and lasting friends with many of the painters. He even took inspiration from the work of other Tilers. His base for the Farragut statue, with its fish motif at the edges, came at least partly from Winslow Homer's 1879 Tile Club fireplace surround of fish. In about 1882 the painter Edwin Austin Abbey, who had been living in England, returned to New York with an English friend, Alfred Parsons, also an artist, and the two men took a studio at 58½ West Tenth Street. The studio was entered through a dark passageway that led to a small rear courtyard and a house that Abbey opened to the Tilers. The rear house later became their exclusive home. Among the Tile Club members White was nicknamed "the Beaver," perhaps as a salute to his constant energy or to the building characteristics of the hardworking animal. Once the rear house became the Tile Club studio, he decorated the space, designing white-tiled fireplaces for either end of the clubhouse and paneling the walls in redwood. It was then hung with pictures done by club members and exotic metal objects in a Tiffany-like taste.

Once the club had a house, better food appeared. The Wednesday-night events evolved into full dinners, and for several years members took summer barge trips together. This cosmopolitan club might have gone on for a generation, but in 1887, a year after it published its own self-congratulatory volume with a cover designed by White, its members, now successful, were no longer keeping up the meetings. Nevertheless, the Tile Club consolidated White's friendship with the artists Millet, Weir, Abbey, Chase, and others. Clubmanship was the backbone of White's artistic life. He joined clubs in profusion and often designed them.

As White began to mingle in New York's artistic nightlife in 1880, he began to feel his lack of an academic degree. He had no professional or collegiate credentials. When he started to seriously court Bessie Springs Smith, he may also have felt his lack of degrees under Judge Smith's gaze. McKim's friend Sidney Stratton kept his place in New York society in the 1870s and early 1880s through his membership in the University Club. Stratton could probably speak for White's admission to the club, but one needed a university connection—not necessarily a degree. Perhaps an honorary one would do.

At this time, 1880, the University of the City of New York was in difficult straits and almost facing bankruptcy. A desperate request was therefore made by the university's chancellor Dr. Crosby to E. D. Morgan for a million dollars. Richard Grant White had a slight relationship with Mor-

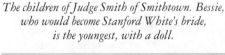

*The children of Judge Smith of Smithtown. Bessie, who would become Stanford White's bride, is the youngest, with a doll.*

gan and had gotten Saint-Gaudens and Stanford White the commission for the Morgan family tomb at their home near Hartford, Connecticut, when the Morgans' son lay very ill and E. D. Morgan was preparing for his death. White and Saint-Gaudens's great memorial for the Morgans in Hartford had just been completed when a fire destroyed all of their work. The memorial was never rebuilt. The elder White may have used his acquaintance with Morgan to help Dr. Crosby gain favor with the wealthy man. A few years later, as the university president felt the warm breath of the community on his back and recognized he would be forced out of his job, Richard Grant White asked Crosby for a returned favor. White, at Dr. Crosby's last moments in office, asked for his son to be given an honorary master's degree. The degree was bestowed in June 1881, making the young White eligible for admission to the University Club. Perhaps his father had given the needy university one good royalty check from his Shakespeare editions.

Stanford White's honorary degree was awarded at the right moment, since the University Club rules had just been changed to require a five-year post-college waiting period for all new members except those with honorary degrees. White did have excellent connections at the club, as Stratton was long a member and Russell Sturgis had brought McKim in earlier. Indeed, McKim even designed the club flag in 1879 (the flag has been lost). White could now fit in with the architects who had already discovered that the men's club was a most natural route to finding potential clients. Richardson's move to Boston was based on his recognition that the backbone of his practice was jobs that came from friends made at the Harvard clubs he had joined during his college career. White had long been aware of the club as an agent to put poor but talented artists together with men who could buy their work; this was the promise of the Century Association, a club that his father had wished to join.

McKim had made contacts at the University Club by serving on the library committee along with Prescott Hall Butler and four other men, all of whom had work done for their houses by the firm: Brayton Ives in Seabright, New Jersey, in 1886; Frederick Stevens, who commissioned a complete redecoration of his Newport house in 1882; the publisher Henry Holt, for whom a house in New Rochelle was begun in 1883; and William Collins Whitney, a major McKim, Mead & White customer at the end of the 1880s. The steering committee of the club included another client, J. Coleman Drayton.

Joining the University Club brought the architects onto a more level playing field with leaders of business. Although Prescott Hall Butler, who often took his meals at the club, had complained that McKim had an almost "congenital dislike for eating in the club," McKim now was to design the building. In the decades after the Civil War, dining at a restaurant in the evening caught on slowly. Men were expected to be at home for dinner. But the new category of bachelors often could not be at home or as in White's case, preferred not to eat with their parents, and the club offered a respectable alternative. The clubhouse, with its integral theme of sociability, was a place where single men or bachelors for an evening could go and expect to find a likely companion for a meal and conversation. The University Club became a refuge for McKim, Mead, and White, since none had a place for dinner as enjoyable as the club had become. As the nation prospered, the custom of joining multiple clubs arose. Even many married men who found evenings at home with the family tedious could escape by going to the club, and the more clubs one belonged to, the more nights spent in convivial and undemanding circumstances. Clubs would become a defining factor in late-nineteenth-century life, and McKim and White would take active roles in a number of them. By the early 1880s, White could call the loose association of Tilers his home on Wednesdays and could drop in at the Fifth Avenue clubhouse of the University Club on other evenings.

White now seemed to belong to a higher world, a world his father had hated. Stanford made it to fewer dinners at home than he had before. Richard Grant White missed his son's companionship and was totally disconnected from Dick, who was still trying to establish himself in the Southwest without success. In an effort at backing up Dick's future, Stanford White and the boys' uncle, Henry Dudley, of Newburgh, New York, invested in mines that his brother had been certain contained major lodes. They turned out to be worthless and unstable, putting Stanford in a bad humor. He was doing well financially for the first time ever, but was helping his parents and was not happy to throw away money. Frustrated, he decided on a last visit to the Southwest to sign over the mines to Dick. The trip became easier when McKim's former brother-in-law, Henry Villard, asked White to help design the Northern Pacific Railroad's Northwestern terminus buildings in Portland, Oregon, and Tacoma. As the Northern Pacific, which Villard then ran, would pay for the trip across country, White detoured to see Dick in August and September 1883 before going to the Pacific Northwest.

THE SUMMER OF 1883 had been a good one for White. After much back and forth, and a fair amount of Smith family uncertainty, Bessie

Springs Smith finally agreed to his offer of marriage. Following secret dis-cussions, with Prescott Hall Butler and his wife, Nellie, Bessie's elder sis-ter, playing the role of matchmaker, the Smith family agreed to let White enter their world. White celebrated with his first visit to the world of sport clubs in June, when Bob Goelet took him to the Restigouche for a round of man against salmon.

That August, Saint-Gaudens and White were promised a major public sculpture commission to be a centerpiece for Lincoln Park in Chicago: a standing Lincoln in bronze. The two had to be in Chicago to look over the site on August 15, 1883. White began preparations for his trip to the West Coast and coaxed Saint-Gaudens into joining him to see the new world of the American West. White managed to convince Gus that there was something to see in the new districts of the nation. One cannot fully imagine what White promised Saint-Gaudens to get him to go along on this rather rough journey beyond the relative civility found in Chicago. Villard's work at the end of the line would not include sculpture, so there was no commission likely to enrich the sculptor. Rather, White must have spun a yarn about the beauty of the Western sky and the rugged life of the cowboy. Saint-Gaudens—now married for six years and with a son, Homer, almost three—had begun a search that he and White would con-tinue together later in the 1880s: a search for new sensations. Saint-Gaudens's home was often empty, as the Massachusetts Homer family sat rather heavily on his wife, Augusta, especially after the baby was born, insisting that she and her son stay with them, leaving Gus alone. Most likely Gus decided that spending the late summer alone in his Manhattan apartment at 22 Washington Place was not as interesting as seeing the new West, which White was extolling. Gus may well have thought of Bierstadt, Samuel Colman, and other artists who had also raved about the West.

In the first week of August 1883, White left Bessie with her family out in St. James to enjoy the happy summer life in which she thrived: the small Episcopal church and Sunday lunch; the week spent swimming, clamming, sailing, and fishing in the Sound. These were all pursuits of limited interest to White, who was no churchman and did not love nature other than the salmon region of Quebec Province. White boarded a train for St. Louis with Gus and their adventure began.

The train ride west was the easiest part of what would become a rather nightmarish journey for Gus. It was not until the two men were in Kansas that White revealed to Gus the details of his pursuit of and then engage-ment to Bessie. He had remained oddly secretive, not saying anything about such an important matter until this moment. White must have added that the planned wedding would not interrupt their relationship any more than had Gus's marriage. Saint-Gaudens, a bisexual, clearly had an intimate relationship with White in which Gus was the ardent partner. The letters between the two in the 1880s and early 1890s contain details of business or collaborative work followed by amorous and even pornographic words and images. The correspondence between them is often augmented by sketches and their lifelong greeting to each other—"K.M.A." Gus's letters to White in the decade or so of their affair contained continual references to their secret relationship, with Gus often longing for White's kisses. On the train ride in Kansas, White must have told Gus that their affair would continue, a detail left out of White's version of the story to Bessie. As the two men sat on the train watching what Gus insisted was the same corn patch and fence for seven straight hours, White admitted to Gus the reason for his preoccupied state. Gus responded by remarking that White had indeed been cross, moody, and unbearable for the last three years. White then showed Gus a picture of Bessie, adding that all his troubles were now over, a comment Gus had made some years earlier when he was about to marry. Gus, happy about White's improved temperament, humorously replied that his troubles had just begun. For both men, the marriages were as much about economic security as anything else. In an era when many socially prominent people married for bloodlines, titles, and consolidation of property, romantic love was not always part of the package. White tried to sound serious about Bessie, but in fact they were not terribly compatible: Bessie was a person of simple country pursuits, while White was a man of complexity, deeply urban. Bessie, though not unintelligent, was not particularly interested in design, art, Europe, antiquities, or anything that was part of White's life. She and her mother were devout Episcopalians, while White failed to do more than pay lip service to the church. Indeed, White and Bessie, rather like Gus and Gussie, were unsuited to each other; both marriages were more about economic stability than deep romance.

When Stanford and Gus arrived in the desert region called the Jornada del Muerto, or Journey of Death, the two disembarked from the train, ending up in a mud hut that served as the local inn. Gus found his room was to be shared with two strangers, rather murderous-looking fellows who even slept armed to the teeth. In the deepest part of the night, the only other building in the New Mexico Territory town of Eagle caught fire, frightening everyone, since it was the mining supply store and was filled with explosives and gunpowder. The locals' attempts to prevent an explosion only added to the chaos. The fearful howling of local animals and the roaring of two huge bears that had been captured and chained near the store made for a terrifying night. Fortunately, most of the stock was prevented from exploding.

The next day Gus and White rode off to the mountains some thirty miles away. The strain of the night and the long ride took their toll on Gus, who, after wishing he had never come west at all, fell over in a dead faint before they reached Dick's cabin. Poor Gus's Western adventure only got worse: The local cowboys kept them awake for hours on their first night sleeping outdoors, telling wild beast stories; before bidding the sculptor good night, they urged him not to fear if snakes crawled over him while he slept, which he did not at all. These bad experiences culminated in a sixty-mile stagecoach ride between Chloride and Eagle, with Gus seated next to the driver, who was thoroughly drunk. After a few hours the driver passed out, giving the reins over to Gus, who had never driven in his life, though he managed to keep them alive.

The two friends abandoned Dick with his hopeless mines and headed west to Los Angeles, then north through California to Oregon. There Stanford was to meet Henry Villard, who had made a major public relations journey to Portland to inaugurate his new railroad link to the Northwest. White was dragooned into going up to Tacoma with Villard and his invited group of European noblemen and investors. Tacoma, much touted by Villard, was in White's words "a god forsaken place . . . of board shanties and tree stumps," where Villard intended to continue his Pacific empire. Villard saw promise, but the investors and indeed his architect saw emptiness. White and Gus returned to New York at the end of September, never to visit the West again.

# 16. STANFORD WHITE GETS MARRIED

Once White was back in New York, he and Bessie formalized their betrothal on October 11, 1883, with an official engagement announced by the bride's father. The wedding was planned for February 7, 1884, at the old Church of the Heavenly Rest, a highly refined-looking Gothic building located just above Forty-fifth Street on Fifth Avenue (long since replaced). On the Saturday night before the wedding, Stanford's artist friends staged a bachelor dinner, rather tame by later standards, at Martinelli's restaurant at Fifth Avenue and Sixteenth Street. Large restaurants were just becoming acceptable places for entertainment; the question of social tone among the guests was less pressing there than at a club, which was convenient in this case, as some of the artists were not perfect club types. Stanford White's friends J. Alden Weir, Gus, Prescott Butler, McKim, Mead, Wells, Babb, and the painters William Merritt Chase, Wyatt Eaton, J. Carroll Beckwith, Albert Pinkham Ryder, and Thomas Dewing—as well as some writers, including Richard Watson Gilder—were all present. Gus drew up the menu card, with a caricature of Stan, who was then sporting a bristly, bright red beard. Saint-Gaudens drew his friend as a porcupine and composed the ditty "who Builds Aright: Honor his Art, his Head, his Heart." Following a series of toasts by Gilder and others, some spirited Spanish dancing began on the tabletops. David Farragut's son, Loyall, known for his great legs and love of dancing, was at his best, winding green vines of White's favored smilax around the guests. The late-century party of the circle would grow out of evenings like this.

The wedding itself was far more sober. Bess's aunt Cornelia Stewart's favorite Episcopal bishop, Abram N. Littlejohn, performed the ceremony, assisted by Bess's sister Kate's husband, the Reverend James B. Wetherill. A reception followed, with the newlyweds then departing for a post-wedding jaunt south through Charleston, which they loved, and into Florida. The flower girl was now a bride.

Stan's parents were pleased that at least one of their children was on his feet. Dick came east to see the family, staying through the winter. This visit would be the last time Richard Grant White would see his elder son.

The wedding gifts may not have been as lavish for the couple as those given Nellie and Prescott years before. We do not even know what Aunt Cornelia gave the couple, but Stanford's parents gave them a soup tureen and Gus made a relief portrait of Bessie preparing her wedding veil for the ceremony. The portrait with a frame by the groom is quite remarkable, but perhaps not endearingly rendered. White disliked Gus's wife, and Gus was never interested in Bessie; perhaps this mutual disrespect goes back to the young artists' tangled life in Italy several years earlier.

The other stellar gift of the wedding was Stanford's first known venture in jewelry design—a necklace for Bessie with two golden crabs holding a large, bright pearl. The necklace design was most novel, but one cannot help wondering if the two claws grasping the prize was not a subliminal response to the four-year courtship of a woman whose aunt still lived a few blocks below the church on Fifth Avenue in that huge, white "Marble Shanty." Perhaps by this year the rather simple woman who seemed to spend nothing after her husband's death except on the Garden City cathedral was too forgetful to give a lavish present.

After the wedding reception, as Bessie and Stanford left the assembly and sped off on their first trip to the American South (only then becoming a place to visit in winter), life for Richard Grant White and Nina resumed a normal pace. It may have been more peaceful at home, as the family cat, Nimrod, had been the victim of Stanford's displeasure, and many confrontations resulted in the noises of a howling feline. Stanford would never return home to live; he and Bessie stayed in a hotel between the first wedding trip south and the second, slightly later honeymoon trip to Europe. When the young couple returned to New York City some six months later, they briefly set up housekeeping in an apartment. A short time later, after Aunt Cornelia's death, the couple moved to a house that was part of the Rhinelander real estate holdings on the south side of Twentieth Street at the eastern corner of Sixth Avenue.

White recognized the severing of his life from his mother's world. As he set out for the wedding, he wrote a touching note to his mother reassuring her that the link between mother and son would not be weakened. White assured her of his constant affection and availability to her when she felt a need to see him. The thoughtfulness of this gesture was in keeping with the old, pre-affluent White, who would always take care of his mother, even having his artist friends do portraits of her. J. Alden Weir and Abbott Thayer painted Mrs. White. When she was widowed, Alexina came to live with Stanford and Bessie, and later lived in St. James with Bessie until her death in 1921.

In March 1884, the newly married couple left for Europe for a six-month tour, probably Bessie's first trip abroad. Her elder sister and parents had accompanied the Stewarts to Europe, but Bessie, still a child, had not gone with her aunt. White, with his lengthy stay in France, became the cosmopolitan guide to his young wife. The couple began the wedding trip in France, which White knew well. The wedding trip was made much easier with adequate funds. Once in Paris, Bessie's uncle Charles Clinch, who often spent much of the year in Paris and out at Versailles, took the couple to several dinners. It was at this time that White first began to buy antiquities to bring home to sell to his clients.

Stanford White had purchased small items on his first trip abroad, including some medals, reproduction casts, and old rugs and textiles. Earlier in New York, as we know, White had discovered the goods Henry Duveen could offer and may have purchased elements of old Breton beds for the Isaac Bell house in Newport, as well as woodwork and perhaps reproduction furniture for Goelet's Newport house. Now, in Europe, encouraged by his own decent earnings and Bessie's potential income, White began what would become a pattern: the purchase of artworks, antiquities, and curiosities to go into houses in the United States. This first venture, begun in Paris with tapestries bought for the Charles Osborn house in Mamaroneck, was modest and probably did much to cement White's relationship with the Osborns, who remained grateful to White for his European purchases.

The purchases White made for the Osborns would help to establish the architect's reputation as a knowledgeable force in the antiques world. White would cultivate this legend carefully, situating himself as a bridge for old items to come to the United States. After a decade, as White's financial situation began to become precarious, he found profit in these buying trips, as he could charge Americans prices that reflected his services and brought him extra income. Indeed, as White's career surged forward and went out of control, he found it useful to falsify information to encourage lucrative sales.

Stanford White was hardly a trained expert on antiquities. In fact, he had no training at all. White worked with dealers, some good, some not, and purchased the works that appealed to his eye. He became, in effect, a major dealer in antiquities, buying great numbers of objects that he then sold to his clients and friends. The work White bought was not always genuine. Indeed, he bought a great deal of reproduction or replicated work as original. He also purchased married pieces that mixed genuine elements with replicated portions. White was not a connoisseur; he was an enthusiastic lover of things that appealed to him. White bought what he loved, which included good, bad, and indifferent pieces. He had a visual attachment to all he bought; those items that White was drawn to, he bought without questioning their provenance too closely.

Indeed, White would enter into the replication world himself. He would buy chairs for a client, then have copies made. Did he always sell the replicas as copies? Well, perhaps not always. But many museum collections today are far richer for White's travels: By the end of the twentieth century, most of his masterpieces from earlier eras were held by museums or protected historic houses. White's good selections are substantial. A visitor to New York City's Metropolitan Museum, to the Cloisters, to the Hyde Collection in upstate New York, or even to Hearst's San Simeon can today see treasures brought to the United States by Stanford White.

After spending several weeks in France, the Whites continued their honeymoon in Bavaria and Austria. White then saw cities he had not visited before and did the culturally expected things. Bessie seems more to have tolerated the tours and music, but no comments about her observations or enthusiasms are made in White's letters. The couple then traveled to Constantinople, up the Bosphorus, and to the bazaars, which, White writes, "alone are enough to set you crazy." There White purchased a mass of old tiles and rugs from beneath the praying bottoms of some old Turks.

By the middle of May, the Whites had returned to Europe, where cholera was once again raging, and they were obliged to alter their plans to avoid disease-affected places. As their travel plans were erratic, contact with home was sometimes missed. A letter of April 15 from White's mother must have been filled with the details of an attack made on

Richard Grant White in *The Century*, which had then been picked up by the newspapers. The incident involved some critical comments questioning R. G. White's musical supremacy in New York City. Professor Frederic Louis Ritter took issue with White's accounts and judgment on music. In *The Century* of April 1884, White responded by belittling Professor Ritter and dismissing his judgment as that of a gentleman from "Alsatia" and therefore incorrect. The public humiliation had hurt the elder White, whose health was declining. Although Stanford White threw away all letters he received, his mother kept her mail, so we have his reply in which he tried to reassure her, advising her to pay little attention to the attack as all figures who have achieved any prominence must expect negative reaction.

After leaving Turkey, White and Bessie toured Greece, where White encountered Heinrich Schliemann, a German-born U.S. citizen who devoted himself to the pursuit of Homer's tales. He visited the archeologist's house, which White found humorous as Schliemann gave the story of his life on frescoes outside his abode. The Schliemann house has been restored by the Greek government and is now a museum.

From Athens the couple went off to Sicily, then up to Naples and to Capri and the Blue Grotto before lodging in Rome for several weeks. By mid-July the heat settled into Italy. The newlyweds went off to St. Moritz before traveling north to cool off in the Alps. The cholera fears were still present, and White boasted of avoiding a mandated fumigation given to tourists at the Swiss border. He then plotted to escape the Austrian fumigation without a dose of the sulphurine mixture that border guards happily dusted over all travelers. White was enjoying this trip as he and Bessie were now blessed with introduction letters and could visit and be entertained by very grand people, thanks to the Smith, Butler, and other connections. White was now truly in the world of the social elite that had shed his father a half century earlier. He would dance his days in a mixture of "sassiety" folk, as he often wrote, and artists, in some periods sojourning only with the well-connected but often mixing the groups, bringing artists to society. Much as White liked being in the social swim, his true soul was still with his artist friends.

In August 1884 the Whites were in England complaining about the cost of living in London and preparing to return to the United States at the end of the month, sailing on the *Aurania* on the thirtieth. White's letters to his parents had now become now briefer, and at the end of one he penned a postscript. In the letter White had forgotten to mention Bessie other than her unhappiness at having to pay six dollars for an umbrella in

London. Bessie forced White to add to his letter of August 22 the news that she was six months pregnant and would have a baby before Christmas. The pattern had now begun: White flying through his days shopping, buying, touring, meeting people; Bessie at home, out of White's world.

The couple returned to their apartment at 2 East Fifteenth Street and White went back to work. Bessie was taken to Smithtown by her family before returning to the city. The couple's son, born December 22, 1884, was named for White's father, Richard Grant White, although he was called Tommy. The baby was christened in Long Island and doted upon by both sets of grandparents. Richard Grant White senior believed the family was back where it belonged—in the city's first ranks.

Encouraged as he was by the success of one son and the better life Stanford and Bessie would have compared to his own, Richard Grant White was not well. A month before the baby would arrive he suffered a heart attack at home, which, although serious, did not kill him. Stanford, who was visiting, caught his father as he passed out and carried him to his bed. The elder White briefly rallied, and even managed to play in his string quartet, before congestive heart failure and pneumonia took his life on April 8, 1885. Richard Grant White was buried in Rosedale Cemetery in East Orange, New Jersey, close to the grave of Miller McKim.

The death of his father was a blow to White; though closer to his mother, he was still very much in the circle of his family. As the elder White left little money and a lot of debt, Stanford had to pack up things from their rented house, then prepare to sell the remaining books, prints, and pictures in his father's collection. Two earlier sales had taken away many of Richard Grant White's books, but some remained. R. G. White had a large collection of old musical instruments, many by famous makers but all at least partly damaged. For a year Stanford White's letters were filled with hopes of selling the broken instruments to defray some of the family debt. In the end, the instruments were sent to London for sale, damaged yet more en route, and sold for a pittance. Alexina moved in with her son and daughter-in-law for life.

In the summer Bessie took the baby out to her parents' house in Smithtown, intending to rent a thirty-year-old farmhouse on a hill in nearby St. James, which she had always admired on her walks to the Sound. Her sister, Nellie, resided just west of the hill, which was called Carman's Hill after a local builder, Isaac Carman. In the midst of the summer, on August 9, in Smithtown, the seven-and-a-half-month-old Tommy suddenly expired, seemingly of a local cholera. Bessie was devastated. After avoiding the disease through Europe, she had lost her son to it while safely at home. Both Richard Grant Whites were now dead.

Although we have no record of the grief White experienced at the loss of his son, it was surely not as intense as that felt by Bessie and Alexina. Both women would always remember the sudden blow that removed the child from them and would spend their many remaining years mourning the lost boy.

# 17. Wedding Bells for McKim and Mead

The office of McKim, Mead & White had clearly been bitten by a marriage bug in 1883–85. William R. Mead, the core of the firm about whom we know so very little, met a Hungarian woman, Olga Kilyeni, in New York City, marrying her in Budapest on November 13, 1883. The Meads would remain together throughout their lives, though they never had children. Little else is known about the marriage, which makes one wonder about the happiness of the couple. We never read about any parties or dinners with Mrs. Mead. We do know she had a father and sister and lived with her sister in New York after Mead's death. Mead's own life was in the office, where he was able to joke with all but would put up an invisible wall if anyone ever tried to enter his life. The Meads were private to the point of mystery. Indeed, when Mead died in Rome, he requested to be interred next to his sculptor brother, Larkin G. Mead, at the Protestant Cemetery in Florence. Was there another story about the Meads? If so, it stands lost.

Charles McKim was now also making a difficult reentry into marriage. In May 1883 at a dinner probably given in Lenox, Massachusetts, in the house called Gusty Gables that the firm had designed for Miss Carey, McKim was introduced to Julia Appleton, a young woman who belonged to a celebrated family of established, genteel Boston. The Boston elite were known for a local clannishness. Julia Appleton was the second child of Charles Hook Appleton (1833–1874) and Isabella Mason Appleton (d. 1869) of the same city. The couple lived on Beacon Street and had four children, two girls and two boys, although illness plagued the family and both sons, Arthur Mason and James Cutler Appleton, died young. Shortly thereafter, Mrs. Appleton died, leaving the father with two young daughters. Julia Amory Appleton was the elder, born in 1859; her sister Mary Alice, born in 1862, had been only seven when their mother died. The combined sadness of too many deaths and their father's ill health brought the Appletons to Nice in the south of France, which was only then being established as a resort of choice. The sun and warm weather should have helped, but Charles Appleton expired there in April 1874, leaving behind his fifteen- and twelve-year-old daughters, who returned to Boston.

The Appleton girls, devout Episcopalians unlike many Brahmin families who retained allegiance to Unitarian beliefs, huddled together in their home on Beacon Street. The sisters matured and began to consider joining the summer colony in Lenox, long popular with a more intellectual Bostonian group than the other summer resorts. Indeed, Julia Appleton, whose aunt had married the poet Henry Wadsworth Longfellow, arrived in Lenox on literary wings. A. W. Longfellow Jr. (1854–1934) had been at the École in Paris training to be an architect, and he knew McKim, Mead, White, and Joe Wells. At the dinner given by Miss Carey and an undetermined member of the Sands family, McKim met Julia Appleton and began speaking with the sisters about perhaps building a house in Lenox. Charles McKim, then thirty-seven years old, stood about five feet nine inches tall, with a fringe of sandy hair around a prominent head. McKim always kept a neat mustache, was blessed with clear and bright blue eyes, and was always perfectly dressed. Though not yet fully confident as to many aspects of the class he was now working with, McKim made sure to use the tailor favored by the well-bred men whose consideration he desired and was careful to follow their style. He had grown up without a wardrobe as fine as his college friends had, and now took delight in buying good clothes as an adult. His insistence that every detail be correct was part of the perfectionistic streak already affecting much of his behavior. Yet, as nicely dressed and polite as he was, McKim knew Julia Amory Appleton was well above his station in life. She was part of social Boston, a group of people not known for adding newcomers to their ranks. Indeed, the tight social world of Boston partially explains the rise of affluent New York; Bostonians who made fortunes would not be accepted in the upper-class circles of their own city, but could gain superior standing in New York City. When Julia Appleton and McKim began to spend time together, many of her old friends looked down on her for favoring a New Yorker.

Julia Appleton was tall, pretty, and far softer than Annie had been.

Julia did not insist on her way as McKim's first wife had; she was happy to remain in the background of McKim's career. As Julia Appleton was slowly brought into the house at Llewellyn Park still headed by McKim's kindly mother, then caring for the three children of her daughter Lucy, who had died so young, and Wendell Phillips Garrison. The two women formed a bond of happy pride in Charlie's accomplishments. Sarah McKim was pleased that her son could now have a hint of happiness.

In September 1883 the Appleton sisters had asked McKim, Mead & White to build them a good-sized wooden summer house on a fine hilltop site at Lenox. Well aware of their patrician history, they must have asked for a house in a revived eighteenth-century style to complement their heritage. The site for the house had full-grown trees, which in earlier days would have been felled for construction. The first generation of resort houses in the years after the Civil War were always built on cleared plots, leaving the houses on completion with an odd, barren quality as if on some planet in outer space. As soon as they moved into the houses, families began to contemplate how best to plant their properties. The Appleton sisters were in the forefront of the newer thinking by sparing the trees.

The sisters insisted upon the retention of a specific tree. To design the house around a particularly tall elm tree required a remarkable plan. The architects were beginning to envision a house plan beyond a rectangle with an angled wing. In August 1883, the architects had taken Charles Osborn's house in Mamaroneck and made it into a sort of opened paper clip. Now in September, they would compose a house one big room wide and turn it around the tree to become a sort of half octagon. The house was entered at an asymmetrical point, which let guests into a triple room arrangement: a hall with a parlor to one side and the stairwell and then dining room to the other. The triple entertaining room formula was widely used by the architects at this time. That portion of the house remained straight as the rest of the rooms bent around the tree. The house must have been McKim's primary responsibility, but in these early days at 57 Broadway, when everyone worked together in the drafting room, we can imagine White arriving at a dull moment in McKim's thinking. McKim, who had learned to plan in the Beaux-Arts axial way, may have lamented the problem of reconciling the triple rooms with the tree and maintaining the axis. Is this the moment when White shouted out a much-quoted remark: "Well, damn it, then bend the axis"?

The remarkable plan would be repeated two years later for Wave Crest, the seaside shingle cottage built for the Cheever-Cowdin marriage in Rockaway Beach outside of New York.

*The Appleton house, the Homestead, at Lenox, Massachusetts, 1884–85. The house bent around a tree was a novel concept in an era when land was routinely cleared before new construction took place. Demolished.*

The Appleton house encircled the elm—a bench was even placed around the tree—but the entertaining rooms faced out over the valley behind the house on a large landscape done by the architects' old friend Frederick Law Olmsted, who was currently the major force in park design. The windows on the driveway façade are detailed to give character to the unpainted shingles, but the windows opening out the back of the curved, two-story house were the ones placed to maximize the view.

The detail on the Appleton house, especially the frieze under the roof, was ornamented with sharply cut eighteenth-century-style garlands and other motifs of the Colonial Revival. The thick white ornament is very much like that on windows of other houses designed by the architects about this time, such as the H.A.C. Taylor house in Newport. The Colonial detail identified the Appleton house with New England, but this is not a replica of any house of the previous century. It is a fully modern house, not dissimilar to those at other resorts, but the identifying hallmarks lure us to the core of the Massachusetts town squares.

*The rear façade of the Homestead.*

As the house was being built, Julia and Charles were forming a bond. At about the moment the house was first commissioned, in September 1883, Charles McKim, of Presbyterian and Quaker background, stood before an Episcopal priest in the small temporary Stockbridge church he had created for the Butlers and became an Episcopalian. Miller McKim was gone, as was his sister Lucy, so no conscience-rending objection could be made to his joining a church not highly admired in his household. McKim's mother, kindly and tolerant, probably recognized the sadness of her son, who was now not even able to see his six-year-old daughter and had little hope of ever doing so. Sarah McKim, who always remained true to her Quaker upbringing, looked the other way as Charles took a big step into the well-bred world of wealth. With Julia and the Butlers close by, McKim became a part of the faith for which he had designed the church. He would continue to build the Stockbridge church in the next year.

Along the way in that year, Alice Appleton became engaged to a Boston-born man who would have a distinguished career with the State Department, George von Lengerke Meyer. As Alice and George contemplated their future, they realized that the summer house at Lenox probably would not be a part of their life. The Appleton house was now

*Interior of the Homestead, briefly the country house of McKim and his new bride.*

becoming Julia's, and it was likely she was going to share with Charles. In the spring of 1885, as thoughts of marriage for Alice and George became serious, McKim and Julia followed along, but with far more difficulty. McKim was a divorced man and a New Yorker. Julia's world held both counts against him, and the Episcopal priest in Stockbridge was willing to receive McKim into the church but would not marry him in it. Instead the wedding would have to be performed in the new Appleton house by a judge. To give the ceremony theological validity, the Reverend Thomas S. Hastings of New York City's Union Theological Seminary, a Presbyterian like McKim's father, performed the ceremony, with the Reverend R. S. Howland of nearby Lee, Massachusetts, standing by. It is not known if Miller McKim had known Hastings, but Hastings's effete son, Tommy Hastings, was then in McKim's office and already a close friend of McKim and White, and he may have arranged for his father to officiate to save McKim from a secular service.

On June 25, 1885, both sisters married in Lenox. The first wedding, that of the younger sister, was held in the Lenox church at 10:30 a.m. A large crowd of Boston and Berkshire people followed the couple to the new house, called the Homestead, where at 11:15 a.m. Charles McKim and Julia were married. Overwhelmed by the problems of arranging the ceremony and probably a bit embarrassed, McKim and his bride left immediately for what would become the mandatory trip to Europe. The McKims would visit England, Holland, Belgium, and Switzerland. Interestingly, the couple did not go to France (where each had spent time a decade earlier) or Italy (which would become McKim's professional home later).

Once back, the couple divided their time between McKim's rooms at Dr. Derby's house in New York—he had rented extra space there—and the Appleton house on Beacon Street in Boston. McKim recognized that Julia preferred to be near her friends and family and actually considered moving to Boston. In December 1885, he wrote a letter to Charles Rutan, whom he had met thirteen years earlier in Richardson's New York office. McKim may have been trying to subtly woo Rutan from the ailing Richardson by asking him for help finding a partner in Boston. In a most confidential letter, McKim asked Rutan to help him find a man "whose experience and training might resemble your own." McKim wanted a practical man with business abilities, about thirty to forty years old, to join him in a Boston office.

McKim's letter to Rutan strikes one as being rather traitorous to the members of his New York firm, who were unaware of his thoughts about "doing a Richardson." Given Mead's patience with Charles in all his illnesses and White's loyalty even now, suffering after the death of his first son, this makes McKim seem a bit dishonest, though he was most likely just giving in to a desire to make his wife happy. Indeed, McKim also looked into renting a summer house in Manchester-by-the-Sea, Massachusetts, to keep Julia content.

By the spring of 1885, these plans were put on hold as Julia became pregnant. The couple stayed in New York City at McKim's apartment in the house at 9 West Thirty-fifth Street. The Appleton family had been frail; both of Julia's parents died at a young age, as did Julia's two brothers. Although we do not know the full details, the baby arrived stillborn and Julia died during the delivery. McKim had been struck by personal tragedy again.

McKim's second chance at happiness had disappeared, along with the child he had hoped to keep with him. McKim was inconsolable and had a full breakdown after burying his wife and child at Cambridge's Mount Auburn Cemetery. The effect of the first stage of the breakdown was odd: McKim decided to move to Boston to live in Julia's house and again corresponded with Rutan about opening an office in Boston. A great commission for a major building, the Boston Public Library, fell into his lap in March, pushing McKim to live in Boston for a time to carry out the work. But after living there briefly, he abandoned the thought of remaining in the city, and moved back to New York, selling the Homestead in Lenox to Anson Phelps Stokes and commissioning John La Farge to create a window in Julia's memory for Trinity Church in Boston. Julia McKim must have wanted children, as the theme of honor to her is that of maternity. The proceeds of the sale of her property were divided, with monies going to the obstetrics wing at the Boston Lying-in Hospital and to Columbia University in New York City to establish a traveling scholarship in architecture. McKim kept the last third of the proceeds, later giving it to Harvard to establish a similar traveling fellowship in architecture in Julia Appleton McKim's name.

McKim's private life died with Julia. Never again would he establish a romantic relationship. McKim would now avail himself of company from couples he knew and from a group of single men with high-minded sentiments who had formed around John Lambert Cadwalader, a clubman and attorney who came from heroic American stock and was McKim's neighbor on Thirty-fifth Street.

The McKims had also faced tragedy at Llewellyn Park. The year before, James Dennis, Annie McKim's husband, had died in Auburn, New York, leaving her alone. Annie, too, had had a tragic decade. She had lost her two children: James McKim Dennis died in 1882 at the age of eighteen, and her second son died in 1884 at seventeen. Annie came home to the house of Sarah McKim and Lucy's widower, Wendell, and helped to raise Wendell's three children. After Sarah McKim's death in 1891, Annie would marry Wendell for the sake of propriety and the three children.

When Julia died, Sarah McKim had been devastated to see her son struck by tragedy again. Although Mrs. McKim was still well, she began to prepare for her own death, wrapping items precious to her in cloth and labeling them for appropriate distribution after she was gone. She was one of the rare people in the world who was so deeply good that she did make the world a better place for all who knew her.

Miller McKim's genetic heritage was not as fine as his wife's had been. Lucy, his daughter, died very young. Lucy's son, Lloyd McKim Garrison, who became the apple of his uncle Charlie's eye, died as his mother had at about age thirty. Annie McKim—not Miller's biological child but a niece—died at about forty in 1893, and her children did not even live to college age. The McKim heritage also carried with it the common mental health disorder of acute depression. McKim, a victim of this condition throughout his life, was surprisingly frank about discussing it. Sadly, when he finally met his long-lost daughter at the end of the century, he found she suffered from the same condition. There was a tragic strain in the McKim family, which life managed to push further along. One can only wonder if McKim would have been a happier person had he married a traditional wifely person and she survived. A more content McKim might not then have buried his life in work. But with every personal hope scuttled, McKim devoted his life to the creation of the profession of architecture at its most noble in the United States.

Once the Massachusetts properties were sold, McKim brought Julia's bedroom fixtures and furniture to New York and made a private shrine to her at 9 West Thirty-fifth Street. The architect then resumed his New York life.

# 18. THE RAILROAD BARONS

McKim, Mead & White had made themselves into agents for bringing the glories of the Old World back to the New World. They built for clients who wanted to fit in with an international set and not appear as provincials. The partners could be entrusted to create buildings for their clients that would put a spin on their personas and make them, the modern Medicis, look as if they knew who the real Medicis were. McKim, Mead & White built European palaces in America, filled them with booty from the Old World, helped their clients enjoy trips abroad, introduced the clients to dealers in Europe, and even helped to establish a foothold for American artists to live in and absorb Rome. Thus, when the clients returned home, they could continue to bridge Europe and America as McKim, Mead & White had done.

The problem was simply that real originality got lost, as every detail had to be found in an authoritative source. At first, during the firm's Renaissance-inspired phase of work, they built imaginative creations based on elements of older buildings, but later their buildings just became well-made clones. With the rise of the modern movement in the later 1920s, opinion on McKim, Mead & White spun around and critics castigated their designs as mere copies of older buildings. But in the eyes of the members of the firm in the thirty years from the death of Wells to the 1920s, they were not copying anything. They were doing the work as artists four hundred years earlier would have done—and the work was for the princes of the modern age.

It was Villard's houses that became the magic bullet in Joseph Wells's campaign for order. In 1882, while the firm was working with Louis Tiffany on his fortress-like town house, Henry Villard appeared at the office asking for six houses to be built, also on Madison Avenue but far below Tiffany's lots. Like Tiffany, Villard had a large piece of property and wanted more than one family to occupy each of the houses. Villard came to the office through McKim's family.

McKIM'S LATE SISTER, Lucy, had married Wendell Phillips Garrison at about the same time that Garrison's sister Fanny had married the German-born journalist who called himself Henry Villard. Villard had been born in Speyer in 1835, as Ferdinand Heinrich Gustav Hilgard. He moved with his parents to Zweibrücken in the Palatinate, where the young Heinrich and his father fought over an issue relating to the social revolution of 1848. Heinrich immigrated to the United States in 1853, adopting a French version of his name, probably to avoid the social stigma of a German name at a time when there was a backlash against the growing number of German-speaking immigrants. Hilgard became Villard rather easily, and French arrivals were treated a bit better.

Villard settled at first in the German Midwest, where a cousin of the well-known German American family active in politics, the Koerners, brought the young man into the abolitionist world; this in turn led Villard to the Garrisons. Villard had made himself into a successful journalist, switching from the American German-language press to the American papers. In the spring of 1866, Villard married Fanny Garrison in a ceremony in Boston undoubtedly attended by the Harvard student McKim. The newly married couple took off for Europe, where Villard was to report on the 1867 Paris Exposition. This may have meant that McKim visited with the Villards in Paris. Villard's letter to Miller McKim supporting young Charlie's desire to go to Paris had been important in launching McKim's career at the École.

By 1880 Villard had become a railroad titan. As the American railroads pressed westward into territory Villard knew as a reporter, the ambitious man hoped to become a Jay Gould or Collis P. Huntington. Villard's business angle would be to act on behalf of European investors, particularly those from his former country, as a trusted agent able to assure them that their money was safe in the United States. European capital had been lost in the early 1870s when Ben Holladay misrepresented his accomplishments in building a rail to the West. Holladay had kept much of the money, a scandal that led in part to the financial collapse of 1873. Investors across the Atlantic were fearful of American manipulations and shenanigans but were eager to invest in an obviously prospering national economy. Villard hoped that a trusted, German-born advisor could lure burned investors back into the market.

Villard clearly modeled himself after George Peabody, the Yankee who came to Queen Victoria's court and settled there as an erudite guide to English and Continental investors eager to prosper with American investments. Peabody succeeded in the 1840s, later bringing in another younger New Englander to assist him, Junius Spencer Morgan. Peabody and Morgan became the trusted conduit for investing in North America. In the early 1870s Villard attempted to gain the same position by convincing the Frankfurt capitalists to trust him. The German businessmen tried out Villard on some holdings in the Oregon & California Railroad lost in the financial panic of 1873. Villard returned to the United States and reorganized the Oregon & California holdings, making himself president of the company. In 1877 the German business community made Villard the receiver of the Kansas Pacific Railroad, which had accumulated major losses. Jay Gould, who controlled the Union Pacific, tried to gobble up what was left of the Kansas Pacific, pitting Villard against the toughest manipulator of railroad stocks. Villard was out of his league with Gould but had been successful with the Oregon Steamship Company, which he reorganized as the Oregon Railway and Navigation Company. He tried to improve the Oregon railroad and to establish legitimate goals, only to find the Northern Pacific Railroad after the Oregon line. Villard did try to work out an agreement with the Northern Pacific's president, but when that failed, he took a giant step in a rather Morgan-like manner: He set out to control the Northern Pacific by buying enough stock to get a voting bloc on the railroad. To do this, Villard wrote letters to fifty capitalists, seeking eight million dollars as an investment that would not be revealed until the money was spent. This tactic, which Wall Street dubbed the "blind pool," was successful beyond Villard's wildest hopes. Not only did he get his eight million dollars, but investors appeared at his door eager to add another twelve million to this nameless and faceless scheme. Villard began to imagine himself as a Morgan, Gould, or Vanderbilt, and he then decided to live like these market manipulators.

The Villards had purchased an 1860s villa at Dobbs Ferry, New York, on a hilltop with a good view of the Hudson. The house, called Thorwood, needed some freshening, which brought McKim, Mead & White into Villard's world in 1880. The architects did some initial updating of Thorwood, which they would greatly expand over the century, and were at work on the house when Villard impressed himself with the triumph of his blind pool. Villard purchased a full block fronting on Madison Avenue, determined to give himself a strong urban presence, just as the Vanderbilt family were then doing on the western side of Fifth Avenue, a block away. The Vanderbilts used domestic architecture to establish the prominence of the second and third generations. The son and grandchildren of Commodore Vanderbilt would build palaces on Fifth Avenue. Villard emulated this technique with a subtle change: He intended to take on the New York business community by projecting a stately, perhaps superior presence. He now dispatched McKim to Portland to begin designing a hotel and company buildings for the new route the Northern Pacific was completing. At the same time, Villard asked the architects to design for him a palace two hundred feet long on his Madison Avenue site from Forty-ninth to Fiftieth Street. Though it looked as vast as the Vanderbilts', it actually consisted of six houses—a large one for Villard and five smaller ones for his associates in the railroad.

When Villard requested the Madison Avenue design, Stanford White was at work on the Tiffany complex, and the story goes that he began the Villard drawings in a similar baronial vein. But at that point White made his first trip to see his brother, Dick, in the Southwest. Probably Villard was distressed when White left and Mead informed him that the next man in the office, Joe Wells, who was not even a partner, had agreed to take on the job. Wells had one condition: that everything except the plan of the six houses around a central courtyard be thrown out. Though Villard must have felt himself to be important enough for a full partner, he was glad to see White's work tossed out. Soon enough Villard and Wells met, perhaps at one of the early quartet concerts. The two men discovered a deep mutual love of Beethoven. Wells then plied Villard with his elegant and dignified renderings of the Italian palazzi. The central courtyard plan resembled the house Villard knew in Frankfurt built by the princess of Thurn and Taxis (now gone), but Wells's elevations could be applied to a German plan. He soon convinced his client to let him build a well-detailed Renaissance palace façade based on his two favorite models, the Cancelleria and the Farnese. It was to contain a tall, double-floored concert hall that would make Villard the master of music in New York.

The only difference of opinion was over the issue of stone for the house. Wells wished to use a white limestone in emulation of the younger Vanderbilt's house. Following Commodore Vanderbilt's death, the wife of his grandson, William Kissam, took on society and used architecture as her weapon to vanquish the old order. Alva Smith Vanderbilt used white limestone for her château on the Fifth Avenue designed by Richard Morris

*The Villard houses, 1882–85. A group of six row houses around a courtyard.*
*The Villard houses were overwhelmed by the New York Palace Hotel in 1980.*

Hunt. There was a fine quarry for such white limestone in Blooming-
ton, Indiana, which Wells probably hoped to use. Yet at the same time
William Henry Vanderbilt, the son of the commodore, requested that his
houses be built in New York's traditional cladding of brownstone. Villard
followed suit, insisting that his Renaissance palace be brown.

McKim, Mead, and Wells recognized that the Villard houses would be
noticed. Tremendous attention was paid to the selection of the craftsmen;
and indeed many of them continued to work on the firm's large commissions. Here was to be an exemplar of artistic décor, as the text on the house
in the subscription volumes of *Artistic Houses* (1883–84) noted: "No
attempt at ostentation appears . . . but good taste as understood by per-
sons of refinement and education and experience." Villard's refined palazzo
was meant to embarrass the more showy houses of the Vanderbilts.

Villard had recognized the potential of the Pacific Northwest by building his link from Kansas to Oregon, but it had been expensive, straining
the capital of the railroad. In an effort to raise yet more investment money,
he put on a public relations display to interest European and particularly
German investors. Villard invited about 350 dignitaries including the
president, Chester A. Arthur, former president Ulysses S. Grant, the most
successful German American, Carl Schurz, and an assortment of wealthy
or titled English and Germans. He made over several Pullman cars into

upholstered suites; stocked the train with lavish food, drink, and cigars; and set off for the great spike ceremony. En route to Bismarck, North Dakota, Sitting Bull spoke to the assembled dignitaries, angrily accusing the railroads of stealing Indian land. The translator reported that the chief welcomed them to his lands. As the train sped through the vast, empty territory, Villard's men had produce allegedly grown in the region placed along the tracks. Even the weather cooperated in this remarkable piece of staging. Mount Rainier, fogged in and impossible to view for four months before, now opened up to sunlight as Villard's escorted guests arrived. Stanford White had journeyed up from visiting his brother in the Southwest along with Saint-Gaudens for this grand event. White reported:

> I arrived here last Monday. Tuesday I saw his royal highness Mr. Villard. I do not know whether the papers have been full of him and his party in New York—but here you think of nothing else. The whole air is full of it: if he was a king there could not be more of a row. I came here on business and have kept clear of the whole affair as much as possible—but I had to go up to Tacoma with him and his collection of English and Yarmen [German] Dukes, countesses and high cock a lorums generally. I cannot say I was much impressed, and I think myself just as good as any——old Lord in his party—don't you? The next time you catch me walking behind a brass band you will hear of it.

Undoubtedly others thought the same. As Villard paraded his party to Puget Sound, many aboard the train telegraphed to New York to sell their shares. Once the hype ended, there was no one to use the railroad. The Pacific Northwest was promising but empty. The older force in the Northern Pacific, Frederick Billings, joined the stock's decline by dumping his shares and creating a panic. Villard tried to stem the run by using all the resources he could command. But his third attempt to increase capitalization failed and brought him down.

He moved into his still incomplete new house in New York City before Christmas 1883. Villard claimed that the hotel suite the family had been using in Seventeenth Street was too costly and insisted he was bankrupt. The failure of the railroad hurt investors badly, so Villard himself had to appear wiped out to avoid charges of keeping his own assets while allowing those who had trusted him to fail. The house on Madison Avenue and the other five lots on the site were put up for sale. Unable to tolerate the disgrace of failure, Villard fell ill. Newspaper stories turned him into a villain, and crowds began to gather outside the house to watch the man who had betrayed his friends live in a splendid palace. In the end, it became not a vehicle for Villard's projection of a baronial image, but a curse pointing out to many the fruits of aiming far too high. He and his family fled to Dobbs Ferry, where the house on the hill was in his wife's name and exempt from the threat of sale. Also in her name was the *Evening Post.* Having bought the newspaper in order to create spin for his enterprises, Villard was not prepared to relinquish it.

Henry Villard was a man with a need to be important but not enough talent to achieve his goals. As a speculator, he followed techniques used by others with an unjustified faith in his own ability. This kept him from becoming a true financial leader. In 1886 his house was sold to Whitelaw Reid, who hired McKim, Mead & White to finish the uncompleted portions of the interiors. But the experience had been an economic disaster for the architects. As the Villard crisis deepened in the winter of 1883–84, liens were placed upon the house by unpaid contractors and artisans. In what McKim thought was a final salute to this house of pleasure and pain, the architects sent in photographers to record the work. The set of pictures reveals empty rooms, a ghostly kitchen, and a man slumped in a chair in the triple drawing room—probably Joseph Wells contemplating the cruel ending to his first opportunity to create a modern house in the manner of Italian Renaissance architects. Wells was perhaps thinking of Villard when he wrote in his notebook, "To all great men who wish their littleness to remain hidden, my advice is. Never sit for a bust or a portrait, or build a house."

Later Villard returned to Wall Street with more capital from Germany and even managed to gain a seat on the new board of the Northern Pacific, but he remained careful and scrupulous; he neither created any further scandal nor made a huge sum of money. Ironically, he rented an apartment on the lower floors of the Tiffany house at Seventy-second Street. Having rejected a design like Tiffany's a decade earlier, he now spent his days there.

The Villard name remained on the houses even though the family had lived there only very briefly. Despite the spectacle of crowds whose savings had been wiped out by the railroad failure standing on Madison Avenue and calling out to Villard, the building was well received. Wells had surprised both McKim and White with his Renaissance design. McKim had little or no part in the house. On his return from New Mexico, White had designed the fine entry hall, bringing in Saint-Gaudens for the great zodiac clock that sits on the marble. Here there was mosaic tile to the vault of the ceiling—an Italian-inspired luxury—and a Roman bench and fireplace probably made by Louis St. Gaudens. The great triple drawing room with its complex, inlaid woodwork was designed by the architects' old mentor, George Fletcher Babb, and executed by Joseph Cabus. This German-born woodworker had designed furniture with a partner as Kimball & Cabus, but was now on his own and well able to create work like that at the palace of the princess of Thurn and Taxis in Frankfurt, which both he and Villard knew. Cabus would be McKim, Mead & White's cabinetmaker for the remainder of his life and produced Stanford White's early sets of picture frames. Wells himself designed the impressive triple-floor stairwell, frequently repeated in later houses. The credit went to the partners.

The mounting critical acclaim the Villard houses received made the partners stop in their tracks. The work being done by McKim and White had far less notice, leading them to reflect upon the kudos they received for Wells's work. One can imagine that the partners now began to thumb through Letarouilly themselves. White and McKim agreed that Wells may have opened a new door for them. Italy would provide the key to many future works, and it would help the firm to learn more about Italy by paging through architecture books. Henceforward the partners began to stick their toes in Renaissance waters.

ROSS R. WINANS HAD SPOKEN WELL of his new house in Baltimore, and his friends and fellow railroad owners in that city, the Garretts, called upon McKim, Mead & White. The Garretts were principals in the Baltimore and Ohio lines, one of the Winans family's investments. Several generations of Garretts ran the railroad, working closely with the banker George Peabody. They wanted work done on a pair of houses at the center of fashionable Baltimore, a mile or so south of Winans. One was 11 West Mount Vernon Place, bought by John Work Garrett in 1872, when it was about twenty years old. John Garrett's son Robert and his wife, Mary Sloan Frick Garrett, had lived there for about a decade. Then the couple decided to expand their house into No. 9 next door. The architects were asked to combine the houses.

The commission began in the summer of 1883, when Villard's brownstone house was complete and visible. The row houses had simple brownstone fronts, which the architects modified with a grand new entrance porch and a balustrade on top. A carved lozenge made the houses look newer, but the major commission was for the interiors, which were grand. Francis Lathrop did murals for the dining room and picture galleries,

George Maynard painted the ceiling in the tiled room, and Joseph Cabus came in to install some older European panels as well as sideboard and fireplace surrounds. The carved Renaissance-style fireplace and other wooden antique or faux antique pieces were purchased from D. Stewart & Co. This may mean that the pieces came from the collection of David Stewart (1810–1891), a New York importer and manufacturer who had been married to a Smith from Long Island, a relative of Bessie's father. The Stewarts married in 1830; among their children was Isabella Stewart, who married Jack Gardner of Boston and was to create the famous Isabella Stewart Gardner house on the Fenway in Boston.* In 1883, White and Saint-Gaudens made a mausoleum for David Stewart's wife in Greenwood Cemetery in Brooklyn. Perhaps some of the items sold to the Garretts came from the estate of this Mrs. Stewart.

Far more interesting is a mantel for the entrance hall and a carved fumed oak sideboard that McKim, Mead & White purchased for the Garretts from H. V. Duveen in New York. McKim and White seem to have used Duveen for real woodwork from European houses, reproductions of Elizabethan/Tudor chairs, and Dutch tiles. The Garrett house is among the first in which White's name appears in connection with them. But within a year or two, White was to rival Duveen's business.

Baltimore took notice of the interiors of the Garrett house. In 1886, just a short walk westward, Harry Guinand asked the architects to create public rooms in a brownstone house that he had purchased and transformed into the Mount Vernon Hotel. But the building returned to private use in 1900, when it was purchased by Waldo Newcomer.

*It is most curious that Mrs. Gardner commissioned a Stanford White–like palace in the Fenway and conspicuously avoided calling on White.

# 19. SHIFTING DYNAMICS
## IN THE 1880s

The early 1880s brought McKim, Mead & White new commissions and further changed the always-fluid dynamics of collaboration among the members of the firm.

In August 1883, the Reverend John F. Goucher asked White to design the First Methodist Church of Baltimore, often known as the Lovely Lane United Methodist Church. The congregation was a famous one, and it hosted American Methodism's annual Christmas conferences. But its downtown site had led to a dwindling of the congregation, to the point that the Sunday school had to close. In March 1853, John Franklin Goucher (1845–1921), a former Methodist circuit rider, was appointed as the new minister. Goucher had married the daughter of a wealthy Baltimore physician and landowner, and the Gouchers were generous contributors to missionary work in Asia. He immediately set about moving the church to the emerging first-class residential district north of Ross Winans's new house. Goucher moved quickly, purchasing the land for the new building before seeking support. He also bought land to the north of the site for a women's college, the future Goucher College in Baltimore, also to be designed by McKim, Mead & White. He ended up footing many of the bills for the eventual building of the church.

McKim, Mead & White were probably selected because of the Winans house and the work they were about to start for the Garretts. Previously they had worked on church buildings only for the Episcopal faith, for which the Gothic Revival was recognized as suitable and traditional. But

Gothic seemed wrong for a denomination that had little connection with medieval church traditions. The point of departure for their thinking was probably Trinity Church in Boston, where McKim and White had both worked for Richardson on a preaching church for a broad variant of the Episcopal faith; for that structure Gothic had been eschewed in favor of Romanesque. Phillips Brooks, the minister there, was a great orator and desired to reach a more inclusive group of Protestants. That made the Trinity commission an obvious precedent for the Methodists, especially since Goucher was also a preacher of great ability. But McKim, Mead & White now went farther back, beyond Richardson's Romanesque to the Early Christian period. The tower that dominated their design was an imitation of the famous tower at Pomposa on the eastern Italian seaboard, which neither McKim nor White appears to have seen personally.

The pace in the office that summer was frantic, with Henry Villard pushing hard to get his work done. White could not have completed much of the design before he and Saint-Gaudens set out for Chicago. Indeed, the visit to the church trustees in early August was made by Mead, and subsequent work on the design was done in the second half of August and throughout September, when White was away. This was to be an increasing pattern in the later 1880s, with White delegating what he felt to be lesser commissions to the abler men in the office.

In these circumstances, the idea to use Pomposa as a basis for the design seems to have come from Mead or Wells. Mead had lived in Italy with his brother, the sculptor Larkin G. Mead, whose wife was Venetian, and had therefore probably been to Ravenna and Pomposa. Wells had also traveled in Italy, although his letters after he reached Florence were destroyed by Lawrence Grant White.

They also had photographs available to them, since from the early 1870s forward, firms like Alinari offered for sale images of notable Italian buildings. At this time, the windows of the tower at Pomposa were sealed up, giving it a curious winking pattern, which the architects copied. Pomposa was later restored and its blocked windows opened, giving the church a different appearance than it had in the days when McKim, Mead & White used it as a source for their Baltimore commission.

Even though the First Methodists were building a church in a new section of the city, the architects wished to suggest history. White wrote that he wanted the church to look as if it had already had changes made over time. He and his helpers wanted the new building to have an instant patina of age, even if it was all new. A difference from Pomposa is in the rough-hewn quality of the stonework, a faint nod to Trinity Church, Boston,

*The Reverend Goucher's church, Lovely Lane Methodist Church in Baltimore, 1883–87, a cornerstone of American Methodism.*

though here the stone is a lighter, off-white color. To complete the Italian Early Christian theme, the architects insisted that the roof be covered with thin red tiles, not the usual slates. There had been no tile making as yet in Baltimore, so the roof tiles proved a major ordeal. When the formal commission for the church was made, the church trustees had insisted on a set fee for the job. This the architects agreed to with great reluctance, as McKim usually insisted on the normal percentage of the building cost plus travel fees. Recognizing that future disputes could arise over the site visit fees, they insisted that the church hire a local architect, Charles L. Carson, to supervise the builders. It was he who would have had to see to the roof tiles.

As first built, the First Methodist Church lacked congregational comforts or a heating system. But it was an eye-catching landmark with a tower that advertised Methodism, and a dramatic interior. White insisted that Frank Lathrop be called down from New York to oversee colors and the choice of fabrics and to supply his glazing for the clerestory. A motif popular at the time was the signs of the zodiac, which White and Saint-Gaudens had used for a clock in the Villard house hall. Here Goucher decided he wanted a zodiac theme on the vault, with the stars set as they would be at three o'clock on the morning of the church's dedication. This was duly carried out. To amplify the experience of the auditorium, White circled the room with 346 gas jets. When lit, these provided dramatic tongues of flame and doubtless heightened the drama of the service.

A fourteen-page letter of September 1886, written in the name of White, responded to a request by Goucher to explain the church's style. This rambling letter, discussing the periods of church building in history, probably came from the hand of George Martin, the loyal secretary to the practice. But its contents were perhaps from McKim, Mead, or Wells, who knew more about the history of architecture than did White. The letter concludes: "The problem, therefore, offered by this church is essentially a modern one. . . . The Congregation becomes the main factor and

*Goucher College, 1887–94, next to the Lovely Lane Methodist Church.*

as the congregation's attention is concentrated upon the minister . . . the whole architectural treatment should concentrate and lead up to this point." A similar explanation of the Protestant style reappeared when White designed his third church, the great and short-lived Madison Square Presbyterian Church in New York.

THE BOND BETWEEN MEAD AND WELLS grew with the work on the First Methodist Church. To Mead, writing at the end of his life, Wells was the fourth partner, one of just four who produced the designs in the early days. He kept an oil sketch Thomas Wilmer Dewing had made of Wells in 1884 on his desk as a memento of his friend. He also made a great effort to have a corner of the library at the American Academy in Rome named for Wells. The two worked well together and did several buildings with Wells as the designer and Mead making the engineering and practical decisions.

In the summer of 1883, McKim, Mead & White received a commission from Henry E. Russell Jr. and C. B. Erwin to build in the precision-tool-making town of New Britain, Connecticut. The Russells, senior and junior, were closely connected to Mead. They knew Mead's brother Charles, president of the Stanley Rule & Level Company. Charles Mead had gone to work for a Brattleboro ruler company, E. A. Stearns & Co., which was taken over by Stanley in 1863 and moved to New Britain, a city well known for its iron factories, blacksmith shops, cooper's sheds, and lock factories. The Stanley Rule and the Russell & Erwin Company were close to each other in New Britain. So Charles Mead was able to steer the younger Russell to his brother's office for the new headquarters of Russell & Erwin, high-grade lock manufacturers, on a site in the center of town not far from the factory and next to the New Britain National Bank, which the Erwins controlled. It was to be an office building with club rooms on the ground floor, of brick, simple in form, but housing the area's first passenger elevator. As the building rose, various local companies, clubs, and fraternal organizations, along with New Britain's mayor and city clerk, took space, making it the city's first true commercial block.

The design of the building posed a dilemma as the site was sandwiched between two small older shops. The new building rose to twice the height of its neighbors, and stretched well back, making it difficult to provide the interior with adequate light and air. Accordingly, Wells made the building U-shaped, introducing a light court at the back. This formula was to become a feature of a slew of office buildings the architects would construct for the New York Life Insurance Company.

The Russell & Erwin building has a brownstone base above which rise red-brick arcaded floors ornamented with early Renaissance flourishes in the same red clay as the bricks, but in molded terra-cotta. This detail gives the simple building distinction at moderate cost.

The Russell & Erwin building was modest, but it boasted fine detail as well as subtle proportion and organization. It proved that McKim, Mead & White could do a modest building sensibly and well. After its completion in 1885, larger buildings were constructed in New York in a similar vein, notably the De Vinne Press on Lafayette Street by the firm now known as Babb, Cook & Willard, and McKim, Mead & White's virtually concomitant commercial block for Bob and Ogden Goelet on Broadway at Twentieth Street.

For the Renaissance details, Wells adapted restrained fifteenth-century Italian forms, perhaps done from memory aided by hours paging through Letarouilly. The echo of the Farnese palace is faint but tasteful. Wells was a master of understated decorative flourishes. Stanford White, however, was addicted to ornament. This made their relationship more difficult. The two men had a great deal in common.* Yet, starting in the 1880s, there were always problems between them.

Once Stanford White became secretly engaged to Bessie, he underwent a change in character that was noticeable to many who knew him. By 1883, professionally successful beyond his dreams, he now had the addi-

---

*Both men matured in an architect's office; both worked their way up within the office. Neither had attended college. Both loved music.

tional security brought on by the expectation of Bessie's inheritance. The thoughtful interludes in White's letters begin to disappear as he stops thinking about people's reactions and focuses only on himself. His letters from his European honeymoon fail to inquire about the routine of his parents in New York and record only what he and Bessie have done. He was swiftly becoming a self-indulgent personality, living (as he later remarked he hoped to do) a short and happy life. He started to spoil himself with purchases, allowed himself fits of temper in the office when assistants did not please him, and permitted others to do work in his name. The change would increase steadily as White relinquished his old milieu in favor of the excitements at the top of "sassiety."

Wells was friendly with Cass Gilbert, the able young assistant who had worked at Newport and on the Winans house before settling in St. Paul in 1883. After Gilbert moved west, Wells kept up a correspondence with him, and a letter he wrote in July 1884 pretty much sums up the story. Wells reports that White has gotten married and is off on his honeymoon. Imagining him settling down into domesticity, Wells realizes that White will be quickly bored. What, he writes, will happen when "all new sensations will have been exhausted"? Others as well as himself had noticed that White was now treating his old friends coldly, "a person capable of great things allowing himself to be led away by small things until it becomes a worship."

By now White had pulled away from Babb and probably Wells also, and was spending time with figures in fresh social worlds. Increasingly he straddled the line between the world of New York smart society and that of artists, undecided as to which group was truly his circle. He was now happy to be invited to parties and the annual Patriarchs' Ball. Stanford White was now a member of the gentry, the world that had been lost when his grandfather failed in business. But he returned, off and on, to his friends in the arts. White's solution was to lift up the artists and make them part of the clubs. He forced Saint-Gaudens into all the clubs that he joined. His personal favorite became the Players on Gramercy Park, where artists could enjoy club life. The conflicting pull between art and society that White endured was not dissimilar from Edith Wharton's battle between literature and the world of her class in America.

In the same letter to Cass Gilbert, Wells noted that without White the office was now quiet but did not function as effectively. Wells now had the role of supervising the men in the drafting room and recognized that he was not as good at it. He realized that the more forceful White could command better attention from the office men. Indeed, White would become very dominant and impatient in the drafting room. In due course he became famous for the harshness of his criticism of those who did his work. He frequently exploded in anger and used strong language to express his displeasure at their inability to understand his cryptic instructions.

Wells now saw that he and White were

finally in different boats in an architectural stream. Differences not merely superficial but radical. These qualities which I recognize as the highest in our art, are just the ones he seems to care the least for. I mean simplicity, proportion and unity of effect. These qualities are especially valuable in architecture more than the other arts. I almost regard him as a brilliant decorator not an architect. He is not equal to the mental strain necessary to gradually form a good style; and from recent developments, I should say cared more to make a social figure, than art or friendship. This may seem severe but is the general verdict. He is fast losing those qualities and traits of character which made him one of the best of friends. Bobby Dufais [architect John DuFais] and some others are more severe than I am myself as I knew him but slightly before coming into the office. Consequently, I do not look for any further art development in him.

Wells then gives an account of his new work in hand, the Russell & Erwin building and the Villard houses, and promises to send Gilbert a photo of these new buildings, which he has "passionately" been working on to the point of ill health. Wells's life was architecture. He did enjoy music and infrequently watched birds, but never took time off and virtually lived in the office.

IN THE FALL OF 1882, McKim, Mead & White developed a new response to urban commissions by means of a relationship with the Perth Amboy Terra Cotta Company. The ancient Italian material of terra-cotta had undergone a vigorous revival for the exteriors of buildings in Britain since the middle of the nineteenth century. It offered the attraction of molded ornament, in theory less expensive than stone carving. This appealed to American architects, and the British-born Richard Upjohn made some attempts in the medium in New York at mid-century. But most Americans had felt that the climate was too harsh for the material and resisted its use until the 1870s, when experiments were made in Boston. The success of terra-cotta in New England winters encouraged McKim, Mead & White to experiment with it at the works in Perth Amboy, New

Jersey. They appear to have been the first New York architects to work consistently in terra-cotta. The use of brownstone veneer had become passé. Brick was obviously the logical material, but red brick was associated with early nineteenth-century New York. They collaborated with the Perth Amboy works to create a custom-made brick with subtle colors and variation at a small price above the ordinary red brick. The same clays were then used in an architect-designed mold to provide the building with modestly priced ornament.

The Perth Amboy Terra Cotta Company began to experiment with architectural terra-cotta in the 1870s. Perth Amboy, rich in clay from the Raritan Foundation, was the site of the works of Alfred Hall's brick and yellow-ware company. In the 1870s, a British terra-cotta expert, James Taylor, joined with Hall to create the new product.

*The American Safe Deposit Building at Fifth Avenue and Forty-second Street, an early commercial building designed by McKim in 1882–84.*

Taylor was likely to have talked up the medium in Boston and New York, where McKim, Mead & White are likely to have heard him.

The first appearance of the new brick was on the Tiffany house in the spring of 1882. Six months later, the architects designed a new headquarters on a remarkable site at the southeast corner of Forty-second Street and Fifth Avenue for the American Safe Deposit Company and Columbia Bank. The safe deposit and banking building was an interloper. Fifth Avenue was for residential use only in the view of those who lived there, although some tailors and dressmakers had invaded the boulevard above Fourteenth Street. The honor of bringing the Columbia Bank to Fifth Avenue fell to Charles T. Barney, client and friend of the firm, who was able to offer banking services to the city's gentry. The dilemma for the designers was how to create an acceptable commercial building in the smartest residential streets. Their answer was to design a brownstone and brick building, using the new colored bricks on the flank elevation. As Forty-second Street was wide, the building had a prominent second front on the cross street.

The new bank was to be a restrained and neighborly building, not meant to stand out dramatically from the houses. The bank itself took up the first three floors with the mandatory double-height banking hall, but expressed

*The Goelet Real Estate Office at
9 West Seventeenth Street, 1885–86.
The Goelets and the Astors both had real
estate headquarters for their operations. This
echo of Dutch New York has been demolished.*

itself discreetly toward Fifth Avenue. Above it rose another five stories in brick, needed because of the cost of the site. As offices would not have been welcome on Fifth Avenue, the bank turned the upper floors into that category of premises used when no one knew what to do with the upper floors of a commercial building in a smart district—bachelor flats.

The brick with an ornamental panel motif was repeated in two row houses just below the bank. For the brothers Phillips and Lloyd Phoenix, who inherited their uncle Stephen Whitney's vast fortune made in merchandising and real estate, the office built a row house at 21 East Thirty-third Street (since demolished), two months after the bank was begun. The Phoenix house (1882–84) was also of amber brick set on a brownstone base. It differed from other row houses of the period in its severe edges and clean lines. The building had a low ground floor, omitting the usual New York high Dutch stoop. The two middle floors had a pair of windows in triplets, between which was a terra-cotta panel with a restrained Renaissance motif. The top story of bedrooms had only two windows, set well apart and embraced by three terra-cotta panels as big as the windows, carrying a square interlaced quilloche pattern.

FOUR YEARS LATER, the architects built a house in a similar vein at 30 East Fifty-first Street (now demolished). The Gibson Fahnestock house (1886–89) was made of the same distinctive amber and gold bricks but without the crisp feeling of the Phoenix house. The door frame is no longer square but now sports a Renaissance hood of the kind Alberti had designed in Mantua, a feature popular with the firm in the mid-1880s. The terra-cotta panels in the midsection of the house have been replaced by the brick corner, with a nail-file-like motif, and the panels of the bedroom floor appear as bare frames.

The firm made another foray into the commercial building world using a related style in the spring of 1886, when White's close friend Robert Goelet and his brother Ogden asked him to design a business building on family property abutting their uncle's old house at Broadway and Twentieth Street. There had been peacocks strutting in the garden, but the new generation was keen to turn the family's holdings into income-producing buildings. The corner site was used for offices, the prime tenant becoming Archer & Pancoast, masters of the well-crafted lamp and the lighting specialists used exclusively in McKim, Mead & White buildings. The Goelets themselves had asked White to design a real estate office for them a year earlier on family land at 9 West Seventeenth Street (demolished). That office, which extolled the family's Knickerbocker origins as early settlers in a city filled with recent arrivals, was a small Dutch-gabled building. The Goelets did not want space in a commercial building, even their own, as they must have wished to appear distinct and grand. The major property-owning dynasty in New York was the Astors, who had their own real estate office building on Twenty-sixth Street. If they had a "house" for the real estate empire, so too would the Goelets. Besides, commerce had invaded Broadway hereabouts. The cross streets from Eighteenth to Twentieth Street had taken on a new cast as the center for the decorating trades along with some art and antiquities dealers. The obvious tenants for the Goelet commercial block were companies in the decorative world, as was proven when Archer & Pancoast settled in.

The Goelet block completed the evolution of the panel style of brick begun at the American Safe Deposit Building four years earlier. Moderate in height still, with a double-height display of shopwindows, the building presented its entry at a rounded corner so as to face Twentieth Street and Broadway equally.

By the 1880s America was regarded by those in the know as a potential source for a new commercial architecture. A smattering of architects were beginning to make a reverse pilgrimage: not Americans going to absorb the Old World but Europeans coming to see industrial and commercial buildings and structures. McKim, Mead & White, like Hunt a generation earlier, started out as players in the commercial building world. By the mid-1870s Hunt had settled into a comfortable pattern of acting as the amanuensis who could transcribe European grandeur for the American wealthy. McKim, Mead & White settled into the same role at about this time. The Goelet building represented the firm's last major commercial success. Over the next twenty years, McKim, Mead & White became image people, bringing European splendor to the New World. They entered a number of office building competitions without success. The work they did do for the Goelet estate and other commercial investors became banal and halfhearted. Only the New York Life buildings by

Wells and Mead rose above the perfunctory. Indeed, McKim, Mead & White would give up entering competitions unless they were certain they would succeed.

By his later years, McKim himself would rail against skyscrapers. The partners were busy, successful, secure, and could now relax a bit in the drafting room. Instead of challenging themselves, they began to rely on Joe Wells's search for precedent in Letarouilly. It became easier for White and McKim to look at book plates and photographs and to make European historical architecture modern by adapting features based on older buildings, fitted out with billiards rooms, boilers, and elevators. After all, the mid-century when the architects began their careers, had been a time of design by precedent, when the High Victorian Gothic of Russell Sturgis, Calvert Vaux, and Frederick Withers had become an assembly of medieval elements. Now McKim, Mead & White did likewise with buildings of the Italian and Spanish Renaissance period and forward. Their drafting room moved from creativity to conformity, with each detail being verified to ensure it had appeared in the office library of Renaissance architecture books. Wells had created Mr. Hyde.

In about 1886, perhaps following the death of Mrs. A. T. Stewart in October, Stanford White and Bessie, along with his widowed mother, moved into a rental house at 56 West Twentieth Street just east of Sixth Avenue. The property belonged to the holdings of the third real estate family in the city after Goelet and Astor, the Rhinelanders, who arrived to bring sugar but ended up a real estate dynasty. The Rhinelanders and Astors owned a lot of row houses, both brick and brownstone fronted, and rented them to "suitable" families. The house was not particularly large, but well located for White, who could take the new elevated train on Sixth Avenue south about three miles to 57 Broadway. White's mother had begun what would be more than thirty-five years of living with her son and his wife. To Bessie and his mother the neighborhood might have been a bit less pleasing, as it was plagued by the noise of the elevated trains and the hubbub of the women shopping along Broadway and Sixth Avenue.

Bessie, still grieving over her first child's death, had begun her pattern of summering in Smithtown. On her return to New York in the fall of 1886, she was first consumed by the ritual of Mrs. Stewart's funeral. There followed the beginnings of a decade-long exercise in frustration—the settlement of the Stewart estate. Just as the lawyers received notice that A. T. Stewart's relatives in northern Ireland were going to contest the widow's will, Bessie learned she was pregnant with a second child.

The Whites and Bessie's family were then recognizing the depths of Judge Henry Hilton's duplicity. Mrs. Stewart, who was described as "simple minded" by Prescott Hall Butler, as we know trusted Hilton as her husband had. In widowhood, she kept her faith in him. The vast property holdings of Stewart's estate were not disposed of until Mrs. Stewart's death. Hilton had been instructed to sell the Stewart retail and wholesale businesses, and the great factories he had built up, including interests in the Cheney silk mills of Connecticut, the great Glenham woolen factory, and mills in Manchester, England, and northwestern Germany and France. Experts on Stewart's retail operations estimated the value at about twenty-five million dollars. Hilton, never true to his word, went against his instructions. Instead of selling the retail operations, he and his children ran them so badly that A. T. Stewart Company was driven into bankruptcy in record time. In effect, Hilton had robbed Mrs. Stewart and her heirs of the second-greatest American fortune of the 1870s.

It is difficult to know when the family really recognized the extent of Hilton's looting. In the early 1880s Prescott Butler remained close to the Hilton family, but by the time of Mrs. Stewart's death, suspicion may have turned to certainty. As yet, however, the Smiths had hardly realized how small their shares of the estate would be. The Irish relatives conducted a lengthy case. The Butlers' firm mounted opposition, but White along with others felt that Charles E. Butler made a mess of the case. Butler remained active in the protracted affair for years. Once the initial payout was made to the heirs, the extended battle was largely about dividing up the fifty or so parcels of real estate among the Irish heirs and the core American group of Judge and Mrs. Smith and their five surviving children.

On March 24, 1887, the Stewart pictures were sold at the Chickering Hall. Stewart had bought paintings in bursts, spending great sums on the collection, which he housed in the huge "museum" or picture room he had built in the Marble House. To our eyes, Stewart bought very well. A great Meissionier and a Rosa Bonheur now in the Metropolitan Museum were part of his collection. He had also purchased American works shunned by more socially correct families who only bought work done by contemporary painters in Paris: a Gilbert Stuart Washington as well as work by contemporary American artists such as Eastman Johnson. Bessie's mother bought a picture at the sale for almost $18,000, displaying confidence in her financial future. Stanford White bought a Boldini, *Washerwoman,* for $1,500. The Stewart heirs did not yet know how little they would ultimately inherit.

Flush with well-being in his Twentieth Street house, White saw the summer approach with joy. Bessie had been renting the Isaac Carman house in St. James. She was expecting their child in the fall, the new Boldini began White's art collection, and life was fun.

In the fall of 1887, the British architect Harold Ainsworth Peto (1854–1933), a partner in the firm of Ernest George & Peto, London architects with a specialty in domestic work, arrived in the United States. The son of one of the great railway builders of the mid-century, Samuel Morton Peto, he seems to have come to the United States to look at recent domestic buildings. Armed with a letter of introduction from his British relatives, Peto charmed Boston. There he met McKim, who took him to the newly built Algonquin Club and gave him a letter to present at 57 Broadway when he reached New York.

Peto was not prepared for the nation's greatest metropolis. He immediately disliked the aggressive city, which he described as "struggling, squeezing, filthy, mean." The new tall buildings, such as George B. Post's Equitable Building, which had been expanded that year, seemed mountainous to him. The business district was, he felt, overpowering, its air darkened by thousands of telegraph wires which lined the streets so thickly that firemen had no hope of putting ladders up against the wall of a burning building.

Peto's views on New York moderated with his hospitable reception. David King, then beginning Madison Square Garden, had him to dinner at Delmonico's, inviting him with several architects, including Stanford White. White immediately invited Peto to his home at 56 West Twentieth Street two nights later, where Peto particularly enjoyed speaking with Bessie. He found her sweet and interesting, and praised her beyond all the women he met on the trip. Shortly thereafter, Peto joined New York's top set at the annual Patriarchs' Ball, where he again spent the evening with Bessie, whom he most regretted leaving. He even reflected on Bessie as he left New York, sad to think that he might never see her again. White, eager to expand his reputation, gave the visiting British architect introductions to everyone he could think of, and Peto particularly singled out White's work for praise. He found the domestic work of McKim, Mead & White better than that of their older rival, Richard Morris Hunt, and judged the Villard houses to be exceptional. He also praised the lavish interior work White had completed for Mayor Abram S. Hewitt, the son-in-law of Peter Cooper, at 9 Lexington Avenue. Peto, coming from Europe, found the houses amazingly modern, with technical conveniences that clients had demanded. American houses were a revelation to a builder from the Old World.

# 20. MADISON SQUARE GARDEN

A ll cities need places for entertainment, and New York had a number that grew in design and sophistication as the city itself grew. The early nineteenth-century citizens took their nights out at Castle Garden, which had been created from the unused shell of the 1811–12 Battery at the tip of Manhattan. As the city grew northward, Niblo's Garden became the entertainment center on Broadway in what we today call Soho. It had been part of the property owned by A. T. Stewart, and all the Smith girls had season passes to Niblo's during Aunt Cornelia's lifetime. White once remarked that he never used his ticket, an indication that Niblo's was no longer exciting. Its place had been taken by Madison Square Garden. But by the late 1880s, that too had become shabby and in need of restoration.

Madison Square Garden was a transformation of the old freight yards of the Vanderbilt-owned New York, New Haven & Harlem Railroads. The yards had been created in 1837; a passenger terminal was added twenty years later. Located just above Madison Square, really a rectangular park, they functioned until 1871, when the area had too many fashionable people to permit even a few trains down to the site, which stretched from Twenty-sixth to Twenty-seventh Streets between Madison and Park Avenues. In 1871 the railroad company leased the property to P. T. Barnum, who created a huge arena and opened it three years later as the Great Roman Hippodrome. Soon after, the popular bandleader Patrick Gilmore tried his luck at making the arena pay by turning it into Gilmore's Garden, where band concerts, dog shows, exhibitions, the circus, and boxing matches were held. After four years his lease expired and the railroad took over the property, calling it Madison Square Garden and adding the Horse Show to the agenda.

The Garden, which was anything but a place of nature, proved to be neither successful enough to continue nor worth the effort to rebuild. The Vanderbilts intended to tear down the structure and create a huge, block-sized multiple dwelling unit. But the city had just enacted an ordinance in 1885, the Daly Law, which restricted the height of new apartment houses to seventy feet on the side streets and eighty feet on the avenues. Passed just as the apartment house started its slow rise to acceptability, the measure effectively snuffed out the multiple dwelling unit for sixteen years, until it was repealed. The Vanderbilts now found themselves stuck with a dirty and rickety arena known to be a firetrap. They were rescued by the National Horse Show Committee, which bought the old arena for four hundred thousand dollars and formed the Madison Square Garden Corporation, offering stock to build a new arena. William F. Wharton and J. P. Morgan bought up shares in the new company, as would Stanford White, who lived just a few blocks below the Garden.

White had taken Bessie to the Horse Show in the old Vanderbilt arena, and he was one of those most interested in creating a new facility for large-scale events in the city. After all, he had created the Casino in Newport, and he was most caught up in entertainment in the evenings. White threw himself into the meetings of the corporation with the attitude that he was the only person to build the new Garden. His power of suggestion proved persuasive: He was asked to be the architect for the Madison Square Garden Corporation, which gave him great delight. In due course he would inhabit his own creation and end his life within its walls. The design that he prepared was made official in July 1887. Other architects were solicited, and by rights White should not have been chosen. Probably Francis H. Kimball should have been, as he was the recognized theater architect in the city; Kimball was skilled at designing performance spaces and had created New York's only roof garden in his Casino Theatre of 1881. White was lucky to get the job. He had no experience with a large amphitheater or a roof garden, although he did design a modest theater for the Newport Casino.

As the Madison Square Garden Corporation raised capital for the building, many McKim, Mead & White clients—from Victor Newcomb to E. D. Adams—joined the shareholders. Stanford White began to prepare a series of sketches for the building, with a very elaborate façade on Madison Avenue and an eye-catching tower to act as a landmark. It was to be built in the wonderful tawny brick made by Perth Amboy with lavish detail in white and brown icing-like terra-cotta. White's thoughts turned to Spain, a nation he had never visited. It had furnished the idea for the tower at Trinity Church in Boston, and now once again he considered Spanish prototypes. To White, Spain seemed gay, musical, in love with evening activities, and most important, relatively unknown in America. Samuel Colman's paintings had influenced White years before, but the selection of the Giralda Tower of the Cathedral of Seville as the model for the tower at Madison Square Garden probably came from an article by George P. Lathrop in *Harper's* in 1882, which was accompanied by an illustration. Lathrop was the brother of a friend of White's, the glassmaker Francis (Frank) Lathrop (1849–1909), who often made glass for McKim, Mead & White buildings.

The Lathrop brothers had become a major part of the firm's life. McKim and White had known Frank Lathrop since the early 1870s, when they met while working on Trinity Church. Frank and George Parsons Lathrop (1851–1898) were descendants of old-line New England families, although the brothers were born in Hawaii, where their father had established the Marine Hospital, Honolulu. On the family's return to New York, the boys went to Columbia Grammar School. George went to Columbia Law School but never practiced law; he became a writer and married Rose Hawthorne, the daughter of Nathaniel Hawthorne and sister of Julian, who had hosted Richard Grant White in England and visited the family in Brooklyn years earlier. George Lathrop wrote an interesting book on Newport in 1884 that deals with the life of the resort during McKim, Mead & White's heyday there. George and Rose Lathrop settled in New York just as the *Harper's* series "Spanish Vistas" was coming to a close in 1883. Perhaps Richard Grant White gave his son Lathrop's articles.*

The Lathrops were White's social equals but better educated. Frank Lathrop had studied in the 1860s at the Royal Academy in Dresden, then in London with Ford Madox Brown. Through this connection he came to know Edward Burne-Jones and then William Morris himself, who let Lathrop work with him on stained glass. Doubtless he regaled White with stories about the Morris circle in the mid-1870s. Once settled in New York, Frank Lathrop provided the illustrations for Clarence Cook's 1877 *House Beautiful,* the bible for tasteful decoration. From his studio at Washington Square South he produced some art glass, including the *Apollo* win-

---

*Sadly, the talented George Lathrop became an alcoholic and died young.

*Madison Square Garden—the famous pleasure palace once at Madison Square, occupying a full block between Twenty-sixth and Twenty-seventh Streets, Madison to Park Avenues, 1887–91. The huge entertainment complex was the design, home, and place of death of Stanford White.*

dow over the proscenium in the new Metropolitan Opera House and his *Light of the World* for the old Church of St. Bartholomew's (the Renwick designed building on Madison Avenue at Forty-fourth Street). He also painted the detail in the ceiling of the principal rooms of the Villard houses, and at the time of the germination of Madison Square Garden was just finishing up work at the Lovely Lane United Methodist Church in Baltimore.*

The selection of a tower for the signature portion of Madison Square Garden was a bid by White for recognition. If the Garden building was simply a new version of the Harlem freight yards, it would not be noticed. White insisted that a tower be built to elevate the presence of the Garden in the city. The problem for the corporation was that they had no need for it. The Garden was meant for mass entertainments; a slim skyscraper tower provided no return at all. White's opponents repeatedly tried to eliminate this costly but unimportant feature. But he fought fiercely for the tower, which was finally completed after the Garden itself opened in November 1891.

Once the tower was almost complete, it was relegated to that ever-present category of failure: to be rented out as bachelor apartments.

The hotel managers were the main force in getting the central block of Madison Square Garden started. This only began in the late summer of 1889, following the shock caused by Andrew Carnegie's defection. The city's biggest players had been investors in the Garden. In the spring of that year, Carnegie had pulled out of the investment corporation, dumping seventy-five thousand dollars' worth of shares. After this major loss, the public was allowed to invest in the building.

Carnegie, the Scottish-born industrialist from Pittsburgh, had begun to settle into a life of importance in New York. Eager to distinguish himself from the raw, new money barons, he used a professed interest in music

---

*Lathrop was clearly in McKim, Mead & White's circle in Newport. He did a portrait of Thomas and Ross Winans.

*The tower of Madison Square Garden with the Diana atop acting as a weather vane.*

and literature as the vehicle to reform his image. When Carnegie huffily pulled out of the Madison Square Garden Corporation, he spouted rhetoric about building a music center for more serious concerts than those discussed for the Garden. He bought the property for the future Carnegie Hall shortly thereafter.

The Madison Square Garden Corporation faltered on Carnegie's loss, as it had no "select" person to buy his share. The corporation put forth a call for an open company beyond the select shareholders, but few takers

*J. P. Morgan, the American titan of industry,
understood the role of building and the arts
as image creators for this new nation.
His path intertwined with that
of the architects several times.*

arrived. In the end, J. P. Morgan and Stanford White were the true believers in bringing a populist entertainment center to New York. To White and Morgan, New York was ready for theaters like the bigger European centers, the Empire in London or the Parisian Hippodrome. Indeed, the costumes the female ushers were to wear at the opening of the Garden were based on the Parisian example, although made in England. With the hotel pressure continuing but no immediate start for construction in sight, White took Bessie, his mother, and the baby to Europe to check out theaters and music halls in 1889. One newspaper account has White boasting that he had visited every theater in the world, an impossible task, but he did see as many as he could, including Bayreuth, which was much discussed in the newspapers as the exact model for the Garden.

At the time he sailed, White had the Giralda model and golden brick with white terra-cotta trim in mind for the Garden tower, but there were no drawings yet ready for construction nor had a date for ground breaking been set. To his embarrassment, construction began immediately after he left. Mead therefore had to front for White. He telegraphed White, who replied asking "Wellzey," Joe Wells, to begin the final design for the base of the tower.

The contractor, David H. King Jr., had agreed to begin on the rectangular block amphitheater and entertainment spaces, with a promise to have the main spaces ready for use in March 1890. Though he was three months late, the Garden's main space was completed in record time, ten months, for the original estimate of a million dollars.

David H. King Jr. was unusual for contractors in the Gilded Age. Born in 1849 to a socially well-connected family, related to Rufus King and the Van Rensselaers, he was admitted to New York's pretentious *Social Register,* making him often confused with Newport's David King Jr. for whom White had built at Kingscote.

David King had already enjoyed a distinguished career. He invested in and developed residential properties in Manhattan but also built as a contractor. He had been the contractor for Richard Morris Hunt's base for the Statue of Liberty and the early commercial Mills buildings. His first connection with McKim, Mead & White came in 1883, when he asked the architects to build a shingle-covered summer house for him at Premium Point, New Rochelle, on Long Island Sound, later expanded into a big house. They were then asked to design a quadruple tenement house on the north side of Eighty-third Street in New York's then-emerging Upper West Side. These modest but remarkable

*Most likely David H. King's larger house at Premium Point.*

tenements, begun sometime in 1885, were among several done by McKim, Mead & White during that decade, and still stand today as a handsome response to middle-class New Yorkers' need for affordable housing. Another example survives today at 359 West Forty-seventh Street. King also built residential hotels and middle-class row housing in Upper Manhattan with some apartment blocks on the avenues. The King Model Houses, popularly known in the twentieth century as Strivers' Row, were designed in 1891–92 by three prominent architectural firms, with McKim, Mead & White taking the north side of 139th Street between Seventh and Eighth Avenues. These striking blocks of housing are often included on architectural walking tours.

As King pressed on with the great entertainment block at Madison Square Garden, he pushed the architects for a hasty completion. This may have prevented the inclusion of some of the equipment for spectacular entertainments. From Europe, White urged Mead to provide a big tank under the stage for aquatic events in the future amphitheater, in imitation of the Roman Colosseum. Besides the huge amphitheater, a smaller concert hall and a roof garden were to provide multiple venues for entertainment.

Cost was a continual problem. The building was to be built for under a million dollars, which was a small sum for such a big space. Brick and terra-cotta were reasonably priced materials. White, though conscious of expenses, wanted to perfect his golden brick and white terra-cotta ornament with all the elaboration he had imagined. At an early stage, he con-

*The roof garden at Madison Square Garden. The turrets are topped with a multipronged star motif, resembling that used at the Vatican. Perhaps another one of White's architectural jokes.*

sidered creating less ornament, but reverted to his original design on the grounds that the public expected a rich presentation at the entrance on Madison Avenue and a round of ornament on the other three sides. In any case, the decoration helped to distinguish a building that was actually a large, cheap barn.

This rich Spanish ornament greeted the city above an internal covered arcade meant to afford visitors a sheltered area to await pickup on a rainy day. The covered arcade, unusual in New York, was borrowed from Parisian streets such as the Rue de Rivoli. The entrance halls were lined in marble, usually said to have been White's favored yellow Sienna, though some newspaper accounts speak of a lavender marble. The remaining walls of the theater were white brick with golden trim. This kind of décor contributed to a new nickname for McKim, Mead & White's work: "McKim, White & Gold."

Getting the body of the building open for June 16, 1890, was a trial. The exhausted White had to be more than the architect, almost the presiding host. He played a major role in orchestrating the glittering opening, which was hyped up to keep New York's gentry from leaving for their summer homes until afterward. He selected the costumes and had a role in the opening program. He asked Eduard Strauss, Johann's brother, to provide a Viennese orchestra as had been done for Queen Victoria's daughter, Alice, in London. A somewhat amateurish ballet performance followed, as some twelve thousand visitors inspected the hall. The critical reception of the music and ballet was unenthusiastic, but the press's main venom was saved for the flagrantly overdone ushers' costumes of orange cutaway, swallowtail coats, orange trousers, and cardinal-colored red waistcoats with huge silver buttons. The U.S. Customs Service, White's father's old agency, held the ushers' outfits for a very high duty, reluctantly paid just before the opening day. Given the negative comment in the papers, White may have wished he had never bailed out the costumes.

As the city's glittering ranks inspected this unique municipal entertainment space with its 180-foot span and high ceiling of glass and what was called steel,* they barely noticed in the evening light the exposed beams of the roof, which were hung with hundreds of small electric lightbulbs. As the ballet finished, the mechanism of the steel skylight was started, so that over the fifteen slow minutes it took to accomplish the silent rolling movement, to the astonishment of the crowd in the amphitheater, the skylight opened to the June night air. The sliding roof goes back to 1877 in London's vaudeville and music halls.

The Eduard Strauss orchestra played for the entire summer, although a heat wave at the end of July forced the whole building to be closed until the temperature dropped. The novelty of the Garden faded over the summer and audiences dwindled, setting the stage for the future dilemma of Madison Square Garden. The entertainments aimed at the swells needed fancy refreshments—indeed, Sherry's and Delmonico's were asked to open a restaurant in the southwest corner of the building and were promised rent-free space. But the restaurateurs recognized that the gentry came to

---

*The terms "steel" and "iron" were used rather interchangeably in this era, so we cannot be certain that the roof trusses were really made of steel even if newspaper reports insisted on using that word.

the Garden only a few nights a season and could not provide a steady clientele. The greater populace, absent at the opening evening, came over the summer but required a different restaurant service. Stores and food sellers could not survive with only a partial season of big-event evenings. The Garden, though launched with hoopla, was poorly attended on ordinary days and never became a financial success. The return to the investors was low—in fact, the Madison Square Garden Corporation lost money all but one year in its thirty-five-year history.

The second-tier rooms opened at the end of the summer of 1890 with the concert hall, a ballroom for fashionable dances, and supper rooms available for hire. The corporation, already noting the financial returns from the summer, thought twice about White's unbuilt tower. It made sense only as a visual anchor, a player in the new race for tallest tower in the United States, and as an advertisement for Madison Square Garden on the city skyline. Its intended height of over three hundred feet came to just under the footage of Joseph Pulitzer's newly finished skyscraper for the *World* newspaper. To battle Pulitzer, Stanford White turned to his old friend Saint-Gaudens and suggested a weather vane figure just over eighteen feet high, in order to make Madison Square Garden taller than the World Building. Yet the tower had no function. It was to be built with conventional load-bearing walls, making the interior only thirty feet wide including an elevator breaking up the middle of each floor. What could the corporation do with an extra six to eight (the number varied) floors of small rooms? On these grounds, they rejected the idea of building the tower after all.

Later, when an ailing McKim tried to persuade J. P. Morgan to accept White as his architect in his place, Morgan remarked that White was "crazy." Perhaps his opinion of White was formed in the winter of 1890–91, when the latter put on a manic performance insisting on the need for the tower. He badgered every director of the corporation about the tower until David King gave in to "shut him up somehow" and agreed to put up half the money himself. With King's generous offer, the corporation went ahead and built the tower. The idea was to have a café in the open area under the elaborate top of the spire. It probably never opened, but visitors did have a great view of Manhatttan. To thank everyone involved for building the tower, White agreed to pay for the casting of Saint-Gaudens's weather vane.

Even though no payment was involved, Saint-Gaudens responded eagerly to White's request, as the commission promised to put his work on the skyline. The pair decided upon Diana, the huntress, as the theme of the weather vane, ushering in a Diana cult for the next few years. The figure was to be nude, an increasing preoccupation of White's at this time. He was just beginning to acquire nude portraits of women that he planned to donate to the staid, and then rather paintingless, Metropolitan Museum of Art. The original figure of Diana had just a flutter of draping as well as a bow and arrow and was intended to spin on a moon of glass filled with numerous small lightbulbs.

The selection of the female huntress as a subject for the crown on the Garden tower was an odd one. Saint-Gaudens was deeply involved at the time with his model, Davida Clark, with whom he had an illegitimate son, Novy; the Diana may have been inspired by his mistress's character. There may also have been a message in transforming the Giralda, a monument to religious belief, into a secular palace devoted to pleasure and topped by a pagan goddess, Diana, rather than the Spanish figure of Faith atop the Seville tower.

The opening ceremony for Diana and the tower took place in October 1891, when the 1,800-pound gilded copper figure was hoisted to the top of the tower and covered in cloth for an electrical unveiling. White used his now-seasoned technique of outlining the Garden and the tower with small electric lightbulbs; he also added a searchlight to the top of the tower so that the golden girl would be bathed in its rays. The electrical tricks extended to the next election evening, when the lighting was used to indicate shifts in the voting. Once the figure was unveiled, a few objected to the display of female nudity, but most New Yorkers accepted the figure happily, giving White tremendous satisfaction at a moral victory won. The only problem was that the Diana was too tall.

The size of the female finial had been determined by a need to win the war of building height, not aesthetics. As preparation for placing the Diana atop the tower, Saint-Gaudens noted a fear that the statue was too tall. Once it was in place, White also recognized the fault. On the Saturday afternoon following the placement of the statue, McKim went over to White's desk in the office to tease him, remarking that White had made a great base for Gus's statue, but had not White intended the Diana to be a finial? White's good-natured explosion provided office merriment. But he now extended himself personally once again—this time to remake the Diana five feet smaller, at his own cost. White and Saint-Gaudens worked over a smaller Diana, even considering using aluminum, a new material, rather than the heavy gilded copper of the first statue. Having stood on her perch just short of a year, the first Diana was taken down and prepared for a position atop the projected Women's Building at the 1893 Chicago World's Fair. There was a tepid scandal in the Midwestern press about the female nude statue, quickly overcome. But in the end, no place to put the Diana was found. So McKim came to his friends' defense by placing the figure above his Agriculture Building at the fair. At the end of the summer, the Diana was removed and, somehow, lost.

The second Diana, set above the tower at Madison Square Garden in November 1893, is the image more familiar to us today. The self-contained goddess was less threatening than her predecessor and became a much-admired figure on the New York skyline. She now lives in the Philadelphia Museum of Art, a gift from those who demolished the building.

The last element of the complex was the roof garden on the Madison Avenue side of the building, where three hundred tables allowed visitors to sit and enjoy musical entertainment. The roof garden opened May 30, 1892; it was the second in the city, following the Casino Theatre. Many summer evenings were enjoyed atop the city on the cool terrace where new vaudeville routines were constantly performed. The rooftop theater was to play a major role in White's life, and he saw many shows from a table near the tower elevator. His last moments were spent watching a new musical, *Mamzelle Champagne.*

The decision to base the tower design on a Spanish source began a new phase of White's working life. He was moving at a pace that left him little time for contemplation, and working beyond one person's capacity. The speed and pressure began to weaken his imaginative work. From Wells White had learned to trust the library for sources of his designs.

White's career and life had moved into a new pattern as the Garden project developed. Getting this plum job ensured that his career was a success. Comfortable now in his work, with a more than able set of assistants in the office, White could be confident. Further, the economic stability secured by his marriage freed him from the need to work as hard as he had in the past. White could now devote himself to the pleasures life offered. In the summer of 1887, he was truly carefree for the last time. With Goelet's loan for membership in the Restigouche Club, he had an assured place in New York's upper reaches, which had been the dream of his late father. The thirty-four-year-old architect had all he could hope for.

Bessie, awaiting her second and last child, had retreated to Smithtown to be with her family and to the house on Carman's Hill, which was becoming the center of her life. She began a pattern in the summer of

1887 that would continue for the rest of her married life: she stayed at St. James for several months each summer, even bringing Nina White, her mother-in-law, to the home she so loved.

Now alone in the city for the summer, White began the life Wells had predicted, throwing himself into new sensations. Bessie's departure gave him a feeling of freedom and detachment from the family. He began to become self-indulgent, hiding behind the work of others in the office. He was preparing to let the enjoyable parts of life take over.

White's son, Lawrence Grant White, was born back in New York City on September 26, 1887, to everyone's joy. Even Dick, out in New Mexico at his disappointing mines, wrote a note of congratulation to his brother. Poor Dick already realized no one wanted to be with him, noting that he had to drink alone to the baby's good health. Lawrence Grant White would be blessed with a long life, perhaps made difficult early on by his mother's and grandmother's concentration on him. Bessie and Nina coddled the surviving child to such a degree that Lawrence and his upbringing put a severe strain on the by now rather empty marriage. Stanford White dismissed the care of the baby to his wife, justifying his withdrawal from their daily life by promising to take full charge of the boy once he reached manhood—a task White felt he could better handle. Indeed, he was to assume a stronger role in his son's life when the boy reached eighteen, as the two of them were fascinated by the newly popular automobile. Tragically, it was just as White began to take on his portion of his son's education for the future that the architect's life was snuffed out by a madman.

As White embarked on his quest to create and to enjoy the delights of life, he began to indulge in thoughtless and even cruel gestures. He forgot or became competitive with old friends like George Fletcher Babb, blackballed people from clubs he belonged to, and took credit for the work of others. But in moments of self-realization, perhaps motivated by guilt, he could become his old self. The story is often repeated of White surreptitiously sneaking into the apartment house hallway of an old friend, long forgotten, a painter down on his luck and about to be evicted from his home. He stuffed a substantial amount of cash under the door frame without identifying himself to his old, lost friend. This was probably Homer Dodge Martin (1836–1897), whom White had known in the Tenth Street Studio building many years earlier. When a witness to this action commented on his kindness, White remarked that it was done solely to justify his own life, not to aid a former friend. As he spun into his own world, he did have moments when he returned to his old personality. His partners endured much from White, yet the humanity the three men shared was never lost. In his next-to-last winter White would live with McKim. At a time of great trial, despite his suffering, White's letters to Bessie, then in Europe, always contain hints of thoughtfulness. In a reflex of consideration, he finished letters to her with the promise of money for a fancy dress in Paris. Bessie's life did not focus on clothing, but the offer, if not deeply felt, showed that he appreciated his old world and old friends. The friends from the world of art would win in the end over the world of wealth.

Just months before the roof garden's opening, White had approached the Madison Square Garden Corporation about taking one of the tower apartments. By now he had become a summertime bachelor, living alone in his Twentieth Street house. The Rhinelander estate, his landlord, was going to demolish the row he lived in for a huge loft/store building. White and his family had to vacate the house in 1892 on Manhattan's once-traditional moving day, May 1. He therefore decided on one of the suites in the tower for a summer home. Each consisted of a living area with spectacular views of the city, two bedrooms, and a bathroom, all arranged around the elevator: perfect for a "summer bachelor." The news accounts of the time refer to White as a bachelor, one even asking where the pretty little (not appropriate to the statuesque Bessie) woman was who had presided over the Twentieth Street house.

White initially selected floor six of the tower as his studio, painting the walls in somber shades of Italian umber, sienna, vermilion, and later chrome yellow. So strong a treatment was to be expected from a master of decoration. Some other artists and architects joined White in the tower—Daniel Chester French, then rising to prominence as a sculptor, also had a studio, and the architect Thomas Henry Randall had a fourth-floor apartment and an office two stories below. White furnished his studio apartment with everything he needed for entertaining and feeling at home there. Plants were delivered to the flat, then removed and replaced if palm fronds discolored. The city's best restaurants happily delivered cooked meals at his request. The elevator must have made frequent trips to apartment 6.

In truth, he and his wife had grown far apart. Bessie accompanied White to fewer and fewer evening events. They did take long trips together a few more times, and shared money in various ways. But White by now regarded himself as a bachelor open to many sensations. Bessie had probably already recognized that he had an active personal life beyond their marriage and had made her peace with his need for freedom. In 1891, when she asked for her bill from Tiffany's jewelry store to pay her account, the accounting department made a foolish error and gave Mrs. Stanford White Mr. Stanford White's bill. The bill must have included gifts for women that had not gone to anyone she knew. Whatever then happened at home, it culminated in Stanford White's angry letter to Tiffany asking the store to be careful in giving out bills.

When White's close friend Robert Goelet died in 1899, his widow, a patron of artists and herself a painter, gave up her studio on the top (eighth) floor of the Madison Square Garden tower. White moved up two stories to take her space. It was apartment 8 that guests described in recollections of the turn of the century. Here he continued to entertain and work under the cardinal's cap, which had a lightbulb set within its folds. In Stanford White's day, the cardinal's cap had an association with a male body part—likely an understood bit of humor. After a festive night, White would settle in and produce drawings, often cryptic and with numerous variations and no direction or label, which he would throw on the ground before sleeping. Office boys were expected to arrive early in the morning and deliver the drawings for the next day's work. By this stage White was rising about noon, arriving at the office late in the day, then staying up virtually all night attending dinners and parties; solitary work began still later, and finally the office boys arrived, tiptoeing around the sleeping redhead.

# 21. THE FREE CLASSICAL STYLE

Brownstone, the pervasive building material of New York City, fades from favor during the 1880s. McKim, Mead & White had rarely used it, favoring brick for urban buildings. Their only notable work in brownstone was the Villard group, for which the client had specified the material. From the time of the Tiffany house and the Edgar house in Newport, the architects turned to lighter-colored brick, often working with the terra-cotta companies to achieve specific and unusual hues. In the later 1880s they particularly fancied a golden color as seen at Madison Square Garden. The buildings of this phase could be called the "golden greats" and are notable for attaining a new dimension in American architecture. Far from depending on European contemporary design, they are a modern variant devised by the architects themselves.

America, long dependent on borrowing architectural styles from Europe, had emerged from the Civil War years deriving inspiration from abroad. Long followers of England, builders and architects in practice in the United States were now also copying Second Empire French and contemporary German buildings. A sense of freedom and coming-of-age seemed in the air to Stanford White as his European travels and blossoming career added to his confidence. Perhaps not able to design without precedent, White turned to a version of the now old-fashioned High Victorian Gothic used so well by Russell Sturgis and others. If the High Victorian Gothic, which came from England, had the freedom to blend together Gothic forms to achieve a new building, not just a replica of an English medieval building, why not create an even freer version of the same style?

The Victorians had blended elements of Gothic from Italy and Spain to create a historical building that was not a reproduction of any specific monument. White took the asymmetry of the High Victorian Gothic, calmed it down to a much more balanced building, but left in the off-axis tower. If the High Victorian Gothic used permanent polychromatic materials for buildings of red and black brick set with stone and tiles, White would use golden brick set with terra-cotta of a different color. If the High Victorian Gothic could turn to forms of southern Europe, so too would White, but he would adapt elements of Italy and Spain to create a new style not based on any specific European monument.

The Giralda Tower in Seville, which White had looked to as a source, was created over several time periods. Seeming to offer proof that different styles could be mingled in a successful work of art, it was the perfect summation of his new version of the High Victorian.

In 1888, White obtained his second opportunity to design a church, the Judson Memorial Baptist Church in New York's Washington Square. How the job came to him is not clear. It seems likely that the minister, Edward Judson, looked to the city's most prominent younger architect. White was then much in the papers because of the projected Madison Square Garden.

Edward Judson wanted an eye-catching building with a tower to attract notice for his church. Both were to be built of White's golden brick and encrusted with white terra-cotta detail. As at the Garden, the materials were to be cheap but the effect was to be spectacular. In a red brick and brownstone city, the golden-colored, iron-spotted, thin Roman bricks made quite an impression at the notable location Edward Judson had selected for his new church, Washington Square, the center of life for New York's prosperous merchant class.

Judson was the son of Adoniram Judson, a Massachusetts-born Baptist who gained fame as a missionary in Burma for forty years. He learned Burmese, translated the Bible into that language, and actively promoted the faith. Edward Judson was born in Burma, returned to the United States for his education, and then followed his father into the church, starting in Orange, New Jersey. He then decided to do his own missionary work in the slums of New York, picking an area where new and impoverished immigrants settled, at Downing and Bedford Streets below Washington Square. The streets were home to numerous poor as well as the city's prostitutes, the latter plying their trade at Twenty-third Street, where the gambling establishments thrived below Madison Square Garden.

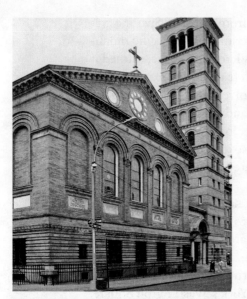

*Judson Memorial Baptist Church, White's creation of the Free Classical style, 1888–93. An inventive design on a budget.*

Judson's work at the Berean Baptist Church was successful enough for him to baptize more than seven hundred people in just seven years. He then sought out a noteworthy location close by, selecting an underutilized frontage on Washington Square South at Thompson Street. The property had one old red brick row house of the type that had enclosed the park in the 1830s, as well as a small store. The southern side of the park had long since fallen into poor condition, and the land was inexpensive. For thirty-eight thousand dollars he acquired a site poised between his mission neighborhood and the gentry on the still-exclusive northern side of the park and above. Judson's dream was to serve the poor and mix those downtrodden but saved souls with the city's wealthy. The site on the park was perfect for this connection; Stanford White was surely the man to bring it alive. An apartment tower was to follow to the west of the church as soon as the congregation could afford to build a second phase of the campaign. This was to house the working poor, even if its real function was to act as a visual beacon, attracting the residents to the north. Although the finances for the church were low and the purchase of the land was already a strain on the congregation, the design for the church was begun in late 1888. The only known donor in McKim, Mead & White's world was Jesse Hoyt, who gave five thousand dollars to the church. The Hoyt family had commissioned two houses from the firm but were not part of the architects' social circle, and the donation was not vital to the building.

The body of the Judson Memorial Baptist Church was constructed in the early 1890s. The apartment tower followed in 1895–96. The park now had a golden icon on its south side, with a great slate and tile roof topped by a large copper cross. The complex did not achieve Judson's goal of uniting the socioeconomic groups above and below the park, but it did usher in other architects' acceptance of White's Free Classical style.

What did this Free Classical style consist of? White's basic sources for Judson's church were similar to those he had employed for John Goucher's Methodists in Baltimore. Here too he resorted to Basilican rather than Gothic styles, spiced up with references to stages of the Renaissance. More specifically, the Judson Church is an assembly of Roman brick with features from several well-known Italian ecclesiastical buildings. The body of the church was based on the Tempio Malatestiano at Rimini and the hooded doorway was based on Alberti's famous basilica of Saint Andrea in Mantua. The tower seems to be a version of Santa Maria in Cosmedin in Rome, a much earlier building. But both appear to be refracted through the lens of modern German architecture, most specifically that of Karl Friedrich Schinkel (1781–1841), which White can have known only through books.

It is likely that White had access to and knowledge of Schinkel and other German architects, and turned to them when he ran out of ideas. It is possible that White looked to Schinkel for his 1880s use of brick in arcade form for tenement buildings that he had designed for David H. King Jr., O. F. Harrison, and James C. Miller. Miller, a contractor like David H. King, commissioned McKim, Mead & White to build several speculative buildings for him. The German architects' economical solution for practical building was to work in brick and terra-cotta, organizing the masses into round-arched arcade forms. When White began to consider his second church, he tried to obscure his sources in a subtle way. He likely based his designs on Italian buildings as well as looking at Prussian versions of Italian-appearing buildings designed by Schinkel and his followers, such as Ludwig Persius, whose Friedenskirche of 1845–48 may have had some influence on White's thought process while designing the Judson Church. Schinkel, working with the Prussian crown prince, had puzzled over the appropriate form for this Protestant church in Potsdam, which was intended to be visually distinct from a Catholic church. Schinkel suggested the Early Christian basilica form as the true meeting point of antiquity and the Christian Middle Ages. The building was to be rendered in brick and terra-cotta.

If White was likely studying Berlin and its region in book plates, so too was his friend Saint-Gaudens. The two artists must have shared new visual discoveries in their hours together. Saint-Gaudens clearly knew the Prussian War victory column in Berlin, the Siegessäule, which is the source for his angel leading General Sherman in the New York monument. Saint-Gaudens must have observed the crowning finial figure at the Schloss Charlottenburg in Berlin; it is clearly the inspiration for the Diana atop the cupola at Madison Square Garden. The two artists probably pored over source material together in the 1880s.

The two designers must have found the German book plates, such as Karl Boetticher's volumes on Schinkel, helpful and may also have gained some inspiration from the French architects Percier and Fontaine's book pages on design,* which assemble historical detail with a panache that echoes White's most creative work. The two also knew the work of the late eighteenth-century Scottish family of architects, the Adams, whose designs were published but no longer well known to American patrons, making the Adam brothers a perfect, obscure source. The figures of flattened angels with arms outstretched that Saint-Gaudens used for his theme of "Amor Caritas" appear first at the tomb of the E. D. Morgan family at Hartford. He continued this as a motif through his life. Saint-Gaudens may well have based the flattened angel on the figure for a bridge at Syon House just west of London, drawn and published though never built by the Adams. The Adams and Saint-Gaudens angels are most similar. Saint-Gaudens was looking to English country houses of the eighteenth century at the time of the Villard houses, and the pink marble fireplace there, with its fish-detailed shell fountains on either side, is an English motif that he must have seen in book plates. There is even a cryptic letter in White's papers that seems to refer to his owning an Adam fireplace surround in 1889, although the reference may be to another Adam, his client E. D. Adams, and not to the great eighteenth-century family of architects.

White's inventive style for the church was copied by other architects, such as Robert Henderson Robertson and DeLemos & Cordes for their Siegel Cooper department store built just below the Whites' home at Sixth Avenue and Twentieth Street. The Free Classical, which might be called White's only stylistic creation, remains a little noticed but effective American style of the late 1880s.

White's loft building for the Goelets on Twentieth Street was just being completed when he began the Hotel Imperial for the family at the beginning of 1889. The hotel, now gone, stood on Goelet family property at Thirty-second Street and Broadway, north of most of New York's hotels but in the midst of its musical and theatrical establishments. It was not as distinctive as the earlier buildings of this style, but its properly grand appearance was enhanced by large murals in the lobby and dining areas. As eating out in restaurants by family groups had still to be socially accepted, meals in hotel dining rooms were deemed fashionable just about this time. To make the public spaces grand, White commissioned one mural from his friend Thomas Wilmer Dewing (who was always in need

---

*The book is Charles Percier and Pierre François Leonard Fontaine, *Recuell de décorations intérieures, comprenant tout ce qui a rapport à l'ameublement* (Paris, 1801).

of money) and another from Edwin Austin Abbey. He had known Abbey from the Tile Club days. Like McKim, Mead & White, Abbey was in the business of creating images of credible history for an American cultural elite.

The Goelet brothers were different in temperament: Ogden was elegant, shy, and scholarly, while Robert was sallow and good-humored. They had inherited their Manhattan property holdings in the late 1870s, found a much improved urban economy to their benefit, and were able to redevelop much of their land, transforming moderately valuable sites into income-producing property of dauntingly high value.

Among the Goelet family holdings that McKim, Mead & White rebuilt was a site at Sixteenth Street and Fifth Avenue, where they reverted to the style of their earlier Goelet office building (1886–87) at Twentieth Street and Broadway. This new building of 1888–89 is still extant. Called the "Judge" building, it was the headquarters of a popular satrical magazine. Then, in 1889, White designed for the Goelets a large commercial building on the southwest corner of Fifth Avenue and West Thirty-seventh Street. As Fifth Avenue was a prime address, they leased the building to Sherry's, the fashionable caterer, as a ballroom and dining establishment, where New York's growing elite could hold their ritual parties and events. Louis Sherry occupied a grand, spacious set of rooms at the street level for rental use, decorated by McKim, Mead & White, probably after J. P. Morgan made an investment in the caterers. The remainder of the building was an apartment house. The acceptance of apartment houses by the city's social elite was still new at this time, but a small number of fashionable people did live in French flats, notably on Fifth Avenue.

Goelet enjoyed his role as landlord to the Hotel Imperial and Sherry's. He and White were close companions in these days. Privately, White decorated Goelet's houseboat in 1890, and with Saint-Gaudens worked up a family memorial tablet of yellow Sienna marble as a gift to Bob in the fall of 1892. The Goelets even had their mausoleum at Woodlawn Cemetery made for them by McKim, Mead & White. The mausoleum remains, although both Sherry's and the Hotel Imperial have fallen to the wrecker's ball.

# 22. THE BOSTON PUBLIC LIBRARY: McKIM SEARCHES FOR INSPIRATION

While White was developing his golden Free Classical style in the 1880s, the last major creative architecture from his own hand, McKim was having career difficulties. Devastated by the death of his wife and baby, he again became subject to severe depression. After the final tragedy of his family dream slipping out of his life in his second-floor rooms on Thirty-fifth Street, he was fortunate to still have his mother, who was out in Llewellyn Park raising her dead daughter's children. Mrs. McKim gave him some comfort, but he was confused and unable to settle on his future path. Before Julia Appleton McKim died, he had as we know considered moving like Richardson to Boston. But to Julia's family and friends he was an outsider, a New Yorker. Many had frowned on the marriage and were ungenerous in accepting McKim. On returning from their honeymoon abroad, the McKims lived in the Appleton double house at 53 Beacon Street. But it was difficult to abandon an office that was doing very well and people with whom he could work happily for an uncertain future in a limited city with very fixed social boundaries. The year and a half of marriage had ended with her death on January 3, 1887. Unable to find comfort in his New York home, McKim continued to think of Boston and of returning to Beacon Street, where he could remember Julia alive.

At this point, fate in the form of a very difficult Bostonian knocked at his door. Boston, the intellectual capital of the United States, had built a true public library in 1854, but it had become too small. The Massachusetts legislature therefore granted the City of Boston land in the newly created Back Bay, provided a new building was promptly begun. At first a large public school building was considered for the library site; then a competition was held, but without an inspiring result. With time running out, the city architect, Arthur H. Vinal, dug foundations to hold the legislature to the expiring promise. In March 1887 the library's trustees were given the power needed to get on with the building. Immediately Samuel Appleton Browne Abbott, an attorney in the city very remotely related to Julia Appleton's family, pushed to get nationally known architects for the job. His choice was McKim, Mead & White. He took a train to New York and raced up to McKim's home at 9 West Thirty-fifth Street, ringing his doorbell on a Saturday afternoon. McKim and Abbott spoke for hours, then, on Sunday, took a long walk past the Villard houses, which Abbott knew and admired. On the basis of Wells's designs for the Madison Avenue houses, McKim was selected to be the architect of the Boston Public Library. Abbott was an admirer, as many New Englanders had been, of the Italian Renaissance. For him, the cool intellectual façade of the Villard group suggested the solution for the Boston building.

In March 1887, the Boston Public Library entered the office bill books and the contract was signed. For some months McKim continued to commute and agonize about Boston versus New York, but as the job moved forward, he recognized the future lay in New York. At that point he sold the Boston house and returned to the fold of McKim, Mead & White. His ties with Abbott continued: The two men, then single, traveled to Europe together and kept in close contact; Abbott later became one of the first directors of McKim's great cause, the American Academy in Rome, until he had to be removed for misconduct. By then the Boston Public Library was long finished—a monument to the goals, dreams, visions, and failings of McKim as architect.

At the start McKim had to contend with the foundations that the city architect had dug to keep the funds from being lost. The peculiar site faced Richardson's Trinity Church, which he and White knew so well. The powerful masterpiece by the Great Mogul, dead only a year, stood on the other side of Copley Square, an imperfectly shaped open zone bisected by an angular boulevard and already lined with Boston's Museum of Fine Arts (since demolished) and another church. Great as the commission was, gloom hung over McKim's mind as he tried to think of what to do—and wrestled with the complex task of competing with Richardson. Working at first from the Appleton house, McKim found himself unable to make progress. A few days after the contract was signed, his sister-in-law and her husband, the von Lengerke Meyers, took him to Florida for a break. Florida was just becoming acceptable as a winter vacation place for the nation's wealthy in the 1880s. George von Lengerke Meyer was beginning a career in the diplomatic corps, becoming ambassador to Italy in 1900, much to McKim's delight.

ON HIS RETURN FROM FLORIDA, McKim found himself still devoid of inspiration. He therefore called upon his old friends to come to Boston for some design sessions. Wells came promptly and invited his friend C. Howard Walker, then settled in Boston, to help with the work. McKim, at his most desperate, also called Sidney Stratton to Boston. McKim now turned to a model that he, Wells, and Stratton all knew well: the Bibliothèque Sainte-Geneviève (1843–50) in Paris by Henri Labrouste. This may have been Wells's suggestion. The other design source for the sides and main façade of the building was the Tempio Malatestiano at Rimini (White's source for the Judson church).

The library committee had accepted McKim's plan for the building, but the design was still pending in December 1887. McKim, in a panic, wrote to his New York partners from Boston that he felt it necessary to go to Paris for inspiration and to consult his old patron, Honoré Daumet. McKim had come to find the solution to his incapacitating depressions in travel to Europe. In a stern reply of December 19, 1887, Mead told him that neither he nor White would take over McKim's role at Boston if he ran away to Europe. "I tell you, with your temperament you are in great danger of getting in doubt about the design and suggesting all manner of changes . . . but nobody but yourself can take care of the Library in the next three months," he wrote. He makes it clear that the partners often tired of his breakdowns and the burden placed on others when he could not function. The letter also reveals that Mead truly was the head of the office. He was the one who—as was suggested by the famous, lost caricature that shows Mead holding two balloons flying off in different directions, one labeled McKim, the other White—kept his partners from making "damned fools of themselves." The letter allowed no room for flight.

In the somber Boston house, McKim worked over the façade with Wells, Walker, and Stratton, then settled down to take elements of the three men's solutions into account and make a final proposal. He had in the house a young assistant, William T. Partridge, who left a report on the work. The uncertain McKim had taken Partridge to dinner before returning to work again late that night. As the two men started up the stairs to the drafting table, McKim turned on a light at the staircase, which threw its illumination on a tinted Alinari photograph of the Roman Colosseum. McKim, startled, looked up at the photograph and accepted it as the sign he needed that he could cease looking for a better solution. He could now put his troubles behind him and get on with his career.

The next stage was to present his design to the board of trustees, which he recognized would be a partly hostile group. One trustee, William H. Whitmore, had opposed McKim's appointment and indeed the entire expensive scheme, and he was doing his best to sabotage the plans. McKim therefore laid on a practice at which he came to excel: a dramatic, festive presentation well oiled by food and drink. The young men in his Boston annex office at 53 Beacon Street created flawless presentation drawings, helped by the French architect Eugene Letang, who had come from the École des Beaux-Arts to head the school of architecture at MIT; his assistant, the handsome German architect Paul Gmelin; and various students. McKim also contrived a replica of the old-fashioned camera obscura, the pre-photographic viewing device, to capture the trustees' attention. McKim cleverly created a "virtual reality" performance for his well-staged assault on the Boston blue bloods. For the party, McKim invited the young students, an unusually democratic gesture for the day, in order to display the artists at work on the library to the audience. The finale for the event was a huge cake made to resemble the library and presented to the trustees as Gmelin sang. The presentation was a triumph. Even the prospect of a million-dollar overrun did not faze the trustees, except for Whitmore, who resigned from the committee in defeat. The public library was ready to go ahead.

The Boston building successfully restored McKim, Mead & White's finances, which had been strained by the state of the economy. McKim himself had spent the office's money wildly trying to accomplish the goal of securing the commission. It was at this stage that Mead seems to have told McKim to close up shop in Boston and return to New York. But McKim returned to the fold as a gentleman. Julia's money enabled him to behave as he had always wanted to do. As he prepared to close the drafting room in Boston, the chief draftsman left for a honeymoon. McKim quietly gave the young man an envelope, asking that he not open it until he got home. Perhaps thinking of his own trip abroad with Julia, he had given the young man a large check that enabled him to take his bride on a full tour of Europe. McKim could see himself now as a mature master, fostering the education of a future generation of American architects. He had joined those he had felt were his natural companions. In marrying into the Brahmin class, McKim had joined the Episcopal Church and let his family heritage of politically based idealism go. Indeed, when he was courting Julia and the family of William Lloyd Garrison had asked McKim to design the base for a monument to the great abolitionist, he declined the job. He instead gave it over to Joe Wells, who completed the monument in 1888.

Once back in New York, McKim settled into relationships with friends both single and married, but he seems to have never again courted a woman. His world became one filled with civic leaders and appropriate causes. In a sense, he returned to the high-mindedness that had characterized his family, only his goals were not political. His cause now was art and beauty, and he was to devote the next twenty years to creating an America able to accept the heritage of European culture, something he believed a new nation ready to take its position as a world leader required. McKim and his circle were the cultural equivalents of Teddy Roosevelt. He hoped that America would be ready to assume leadership in the world of the arts.

For the Boston Puublic Library commission, McKim needed to add to architecture the allied arts, painting and sculpture, as he had contemplated from the day that Abbott had come to see him in New York. This was the first job of a scale commensurate with his Beaux-Arts training in which all the arts could combine to create a great public monument. He immediately summoned White and Saint-Gaudens to discuss the complete work of art falling into their laps. He wanted Saint-Gaudens to make a bronze group for the entrance to the library and his brother Louis to do a pair of Sienna marble lions for the great staircase. White wanted French painters for the mural work, while Saint-Gaudens insisted that American artists were able to compete with the French. Over the next five years, McKim and Abbott on their travels to Europe tried vainly to engage the expatriate American, Whistler, but they did succeed with the other great American painter abroad, John Singer Sargent. The Frenchman Puvis de Chavannes was engaged to paint the murals on the staircase and Edwin Austin Abbey those in the library.

McKim's great monument opened on April 25, 1895. But a day that should have been sublime ended as a sad one. Two of the local newspapers fussed about the opening party and took aim at Abbott for too much lavishness. Abbott, having given up much of his own career to create the library, resigned and moved in due course to Italy. McKim's pleasure at a great accomplishment was soured the next year following a contretemps

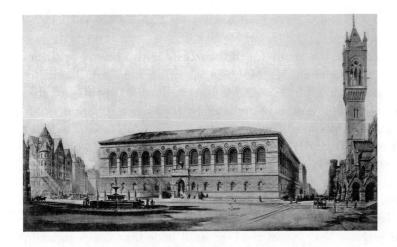

*The Boston Public Library, a great commission and personal battle for McKim, 1887–95.*

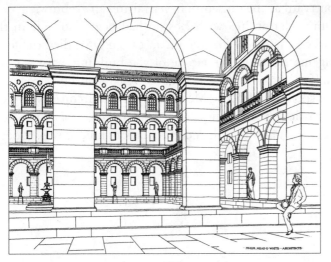

*The Boston Public Library, June 9, 1888.*

*The Boston Public Library courtyard in the manner of Letarouilly.*

over his personal gift, a fountain for the courtyard with a bronze by Saint-Gaudens's pupil Frederick MacMonnies, showing a naked Bacchante dancing with a bunch of grapes. MacMonnies had made it while in Paris, and a replica of the fountain was purchased by the French government for the Musée du Luxembourg. The original was given to McKim, who in turn gave it to the library. But the Bostonians did not like the work at all. Professor Charles Eliot Norton led a campaign against the gift, which was widely taken up by the press and the local clergy. In May 1897, McKim withdrew his gift and instead bestowed the bronze on New York's Metropolitan Museum of Art. The nude and tipsy figure was too much for Boston, but in New York it was received with little fuss. It sits today in the American courtyard at the museum, never raising an eyebrow.

In fact, McKim's relationship with Boston had begun to sour in the spring of 1892, when the *Boston Evening Record* carefully studied the fourteen names being inscribed on the façade of the building, as was often done on libraries. If the first letter of each name were taken alone, together they would would spell out McKim, Mead, White. The architects humorously intended acrostic of their names created such a furor that the names had to be cut out of the granite wall. A certain lack of humor was evident.

# 23. THE MEN IN THE OFFICE

If Mead was the center of the office and McKim and White the balloons pulling in different directions, Mead nevertheless needed someone to carry out his orders. To free the partners from trivial tasks, the firm followed the custom of employing young, often poorly educated men as office boys. These youths would arrive early to the office, light the fires in winter, grind up the materials to create India ink, and so forth. On mornings when clients were expected, an office boy would come to the partner's room and wait as he took off his wrinkled trousers and continued to work in long johns while the pants were taken out for a pressing. The lot of an office boy might be menial, but for one such boy, the kindness of Stanford White could make dreams come true.

Royal Isaac Cortissoz (known to his friends as Robert) came into the office as such a menial worker in 1883. The small, bespectacled youth came from an unhappy home, although he was unlikely to have ever spoken of it. He had been brought up by his mother after his father's mental illness destroyed his wine business and then split the family. The father, Francis Jacob Cortissoz, was the son of a Portuguese Jewish family that had settled in Britain. Cortissoz came to the United States in 1860, settling in Brooklyn, where he married a woman from Martinique named Da Costa, another common Sephardic name. Francis Jacob Cortissoz ended up in the insane asylum on Blackwell's Island and was in and out of asylums until 1880. Cortissoz gave his address as the Fulton Hotel, but Mrs. Cortissoz and her son were probably elsewhere, living in conditions of poverty.

*Mead and Royal Cortissoz in the office as young men.*

Robert Cortissoz went to work as soon as he was able, becoming an office boy at McKim, Mead & White. The partners noticed that he spent his lunch hour in their library and seemed to love music. One afternoon White asked him if he had ever heard an opera, and the boy answered that he had not. White produced an extra ticket and brought Cortissoz to the performance, no doubt remembering that he had begun his career at one small notch above office boy. Eventually, Cortissoz studied enough music and art to seek a newspaper position writing about culture. When he asked for an introduction, White did him one better. Saying that he knew a newspaper editor who was landing in the harbor that afternoon from a trip abroad, he grabbed Cortissoz, hurried to the docks, waited to greet his friend—probably Whitelaw Reid of the *Tribune*—and thrust Cortissoz at him.

Robert Cortissoz rose as a cultural commentator in New York and had a long and productive career, often writing about the artists he had met with McKim, Mead & White. Cortissoz lived until 1948, and in the 1920s he and Mead formed a sort of survivor band. They greatly admired Joe Wells and tried to get a memorial alcove for him set up at the American Academy in Rome; this seems never to have been done. Both wrote often about his importance in creating the climate for Renaissance forms in American architecture and his role at McKim, Mead & White.

Before the mid-1880s Wells had worked equally with McKim and White, but thereafter he seems to have moved to White's projects. William Mitchell Kendall, who came to the office in October 1882, increasingly took his place with McKim, and by the time McKim returned to New York from Boston, Kendall had become his right-hand man. Kendall seems to have been a silent and loyal assistant when McKim was present, but Cortissoz, Partridge, and others regarded him as mean. He was fiercely jealous of Wells, who commanded more respect in the office than he ever would, and did as much as possible to destroy Wells's reputation later on.

Kendall had been born in Jamaica Plain, Massachusetts, in 1856, the only child of a teacher. He graduated from Harvard in 1876, then spent two years at MIT before going to Italy and France. On his return he joined McKim, Mead & White. Kendall married Grace Eliot Endicott of Detroit in 1897 in Switzerland, but the marriage was odd and doomed. Mrs. Kendall spent most of her life in a private sanitarium. Kendall, the architect of the current portico at Plymouth Rock, was a dull sort whose design skills never rose above the mundane; he was content to be known as McKim's right-hand man until 1906, when he became the first new partner in the firm.

With Kendall helping McKim, White and Wells grew even closer. The relationship was a rocky one, with White alternately trying to bring Wells into his "sassiety," on outings and at clubs, then rejecting Wells as being not adequate for a leadership role at the firm.

The relationship between White and Wells went through several stages. There was a close intimacy while Wells was in Europe in 1880–81. During that period Wells wrote frequently to White; his later letters from Italy were destroyed, as we know, by Lawrence Grant White in the early 1930s. The relationship at this stage may have been more than friendship; there is a possibility that an intimate relationship existed. Then White got married. Wells noticed the change in his personality in 1884, and may have been jealous of White's success. Later, in 1887 or 1888, White's relationship with Saint-Gaudens changed when the latter took on his Swedish mistress, Davida. This may have pushed White back toward Wells.

In November 1888, White, Wells, and the painter Thomas Wilmer Dewing began paying for rooms in the Benedick, which they shared for some pursuits not related to the profession. Here they formed a private club, the Sewer Club, whose membership included Wells, White, Dewing, Gus Saint-Gaudens and his brother Louis, and Frank Lathrop. The club lasted for two years, until Wells's death, and was then carried on as "the Morgue" by White in the Holbein studios at 146 West Fifty-fifth Street.

What went on in the Sewer Club? Clearly no records survive. The rooms at the Benedick were used for purposes that implied secrecy and unwillingness of club members to find themselves observed by others not part of the circle. The pursuits shared were probably scandalous by the convention of the day and may have included homosexual encounters.

New York's first known gay community was located quite close to the Benedick. The first gay bar we know about, Columbia Hall (also known as Paresis Hall), was on the Bowery at Fifth Street; the second bar belonged to Frank Stevenson and was called the Slide. The Slide, known to have begun about the time the Sewer Club started, was at 157 Bleecker Street just below the Benedick. The names of the two clubs, the Slide and the Sewer, seem of a similar connotation. Could adventurers at the Slide then return to the Sewer? Although the Saint-Gaudens brothers, White, and Dewing all married, it is likely that they sought male adventure along with the bachelors Wells and Lathrop. The role of the Sewer Club was meant to be and remained private, but Wells and White grew closer through it.

# 24. CLUB LAND

Clubs were a great phenomenon of life in the nineteenth century. They ranged from those loose associations of a private nature such as the Sewer Club or the Tile Club to clubs for sportsmen, yachtsmen, gun fanciers, or religious groups such as Catholics. The club with its own building was especially attractive; some fifty thousand people in the greater New York region claimed club membership in the early twentieth century. Social clubs as opposed to special focus clubs were a defining feature of late nineteenth-century life in New York. With their exclusivity and fine buildings they set a self-congratulatory tone for the privileged members. The British clubs, which the New York clubs copied, on the whole defined a person by a singular affiliation. But New Yorkers after the Civil War created clubs constantly and belonged, if they were able, to a number. Indeed, a sign of popularity or good personality was to be defined as a "clubman" or to be "clubbable." To be considered of a high social rank at one's death, one had to die a member of numerous clubs, particularly those of an exclusive nature, and have the club names run in one's obituary column.

The accepted clubs enjoyed increasingly opulent clubhouses, which grew from private homes converted to club buildings into purpose-built clubhouses. The club offered its male-only members relief from the domestic scene. Although there were a small number of women's clubs, and one or two clubs did admit wives, most were male bastions devoted to the appearance of conviviality. At a club, a man would be welcomed and offered alcohol; he might then then find an agreeable person or two to join in the dining room for dinner. A man could avoid all talk of the ritual of climbing into or remaining important in the social world of the city, an enterprise that often dominated the discussion at home in the brownstone-fronted house. At a club, men could relax and avoid the war games socially conscious women played with gowns, flowers, decoration, food details, parties, balls, stationery, and the other items of social currency. Clubs did have regulars, who might range from the acceptable single fellow trained to be polite to such men as Sidney Stratton or William B. Bigelow, both of whom lived at the University Club. Was there at the first-class clubs a group of bachelors who, after the family men had left, continued to find comfort in evenings spent with each other? Probably so. The club, with its private mailing address, could also be a place to receive letters not welcome at home or to arrange a secretive rendezvous after hours.

McKim and White were part of the club world and built for it. McKim once rejected club life in the difficult early days in New York, when his membership at the University Club was little used, but later, once he had overcome the Bigelow divorce, he found company and solace there.

The issue of religion in clubs is a complex one. New York society was challenged by successful Sephardic and German Jews early in the city's development. Sephardic families had been prominent and accepted in New York for two hundred years when the club world developed. Sophisticated German Jews such as August Belmont were also able to join the city elite from the 1830s forward. Belmont had opened the doors of admission with his European table manners, which seemed in advance of American behavior. He also spent lavishly, which was the second route to acceptance, throwing glorious parties everyone wanted to attend. He introduced the English court affection for costume parties, but they went out of favor after an unfortunate elopement of two costumed guests, to be reintroduced by Alva Vanderbilt in the early 1880s. Men of the last decades of the nineteenth century were often forced by their family into suits of armor, leather tights, and inordinately large hats with plumage and heraldic seals. No wonder men fled to clubs to avoid such experiences.

THE THIRD KEY TO ACCEPTANCE was to marry a woman of established family. This Belmont did with aplomb, marrying Caroline, daughter of Admiral Perry. With the Perry social credentials and the money to stage clever entertainments, Belmont joined the clubs along with a few other successful German-born Jewish men and a scattering of Sephardic families. Newer settlers in the city who were not native English speakers were not welcome in the clubs, and even those newly arrived Germans

*The Freundschaft Club, 1885–89. The American architects' first clubhouse
was for German Americans and was located at Park Avenue and
Seventy-second Street.*

who had achieved some financial success were turned away. But New York's elite club for old-timers, the Knickerbocker Club, founded in 1871, admitted Belmont and Moses Lazarus on the basis of their social cachet.

August Belmont and Henry Villard changed their names, married well, and used entertaining as a method of social advancement, but few other Germans were able to rise to such a prominent level. Excluded from the clubs of the establishment, they created a number of social and musical clubs that catered to their own niche in the city. The premises of these clubs were usually built or altered by German architects, who arrived in great numbers starting in the 1830s and were the first professionally trained architects to come to America.

The first of these clubs, the Deutscherverein, was created in 1842. German Jewish citizens created the Progress Club in 1864, and the Harmonie Club came shortly after. The Harmonie allowed wives in the clubhouse, a rare departure from the all-male norm. Then came the Freundschaft Society, which was organized in 1879, probably after a split from another club, and dedicated to promoting friendship among German speakers in the New World. In need of a visual identity, the Freundschaft Society hired McKim, Mead & White to create a clubhouse for them in 1885. The club must have had ambitions, as it charged the same initiation fees and dues as did the elite clubs and hired a non-German architect. The in-

*Boston's Algonquin Club by McKim, 1886–89, on Commonwealth Avenue. McKim built a clubhouse for those who had initially shunned him.*

vitation came from Max Nathan to Stanford White. Did the membership hope for American friends to join the club, or did they turn to White because they admired his design for the Henry Villard houses?

Whatever the case, the Freundschaft Society started White's career as the greatest of New York's club builders. The society needed a fine new building to strengthen its identity as a club. The site was on Fourth Avenue at Seventy-second Street, once the border of an open cut for the tracks of the New York Central Railroad but now covered over so that the tracks ran beneath the street. But the central strip of Fourth Avenue's fragment of the open cut remained, allowing the steam engines to release smoke from trains on their way south to Grand Central Depot. The smoke and noise of the trains prevented the street from gaining ground as an address for the elite, but once the road was covered and its name changed from Fourth to Park Avenue, it gained favor from the middle classes. The Freundschaft Society clubhouse was the first of several buildings McKim, Mead & White designed on the avenue.

Long gone, the Freundschaft Society clubhouse was probably an effort of all the partners. Stanford White designed the notable Louis XV ballroom within the building, called in its day the white room. This, White's first venture into the French interior, may have been inspired by his honeymoon trip to Europe. It is difficult to guess how the other rooms in this large building were to be used, although a German beer hall was probably the main space used daily. The society overbuilt its quarters with a huge building beyond club needs. Perhaps a continuing German immigration was expected.

The style of the club is difficult to understand. Instead of anything Germanic, the large rectangular block faintly resembled the Union League Club competition design of 1879. The base was of Scottish sandstone and the upper two thirds consisted of a speckled Roman brick not dissimilar to the brick on the Tiffany building nearby. The building was not overly ornate—it may be the large expanse of the exterior was an issue—and the terra-cotta trim around the windows was restrained compared to the lav-

*The Players club, 1888–89. Edwin Booth's house became the most
sociable of clubs to Stanford White.*

ish ornamental terra-cotta on the buildings of a few years later. The cornice and frieze of the club, on the other hand, were quite elaborate and
gave the block an Italian Renaissance character from afar.

The second club, in Boston, was awarded to McKim during his marriage to Julia. His plan of the interior rooms was said to be superior to the
other competitors' designs. The commission for the Algonquin Club came
in October 1886. It was for a five-story building on a residential section of
Commonwealth Avenue, built of a light gray stone, which blended well
with the existing row houses. The Algonquin Club is not one of the
office's better compositions and is probably really from the hand of
McKim. The disjointed elements recall McKim's work of the 1870s,
before Wells blended motifs to a better composition. The street front has
five bays with three areas of different stonework on the façade. It faintly
resembles McKim's Columbia Bank building on Fifth Avenue at Forty-
second Street, but turned into stone. The double-height canopied terraces
over the entrance porch are also an awkward feature. The Algonquin Club
was not a major triumph for McKim, Mead & White.

THE MOST UNUSUAL TALE of the founding of a New York club is that
of Stanford White's favorite club, the Players. This was the creation of
Edwin Booth. John Wilkes Booth and his brother Edwin had been celebrated stars of the stage in the mid-nineteenth century. But it was John
Wilkes Booth who assassinated Abraham Lincoln in Ford's Theatre. The

burden of being part of a family now notorious sat heavily on Edwin Booth as he grew older. His acting career had brought him rewards and failures. He had suffered, as actors often did, through financial reverses; and both his wives died young. When the economy picked up after the 1873 depression, Booth purchased a brownstone house at Gramercy Park, a few blocks east of his Twenty-third Street theater.

In 1887 Booth announced his plans to leave his house to fellow thespians, especially those with children, as a happy and sociable place to stay when the going was rough. How Booth selected Stanford White to carry out his wishes is uncertain. White's interest in the theater was growing in 1887, but he was not yet a fixture in that world.

Booth and White devised a remodeling plan for the house with the expectation that it would become a clubhouse immediately, before the former's death. Booth had rooms of his own at the top of the house, but he was willing to let the building become a private institution during his last years.

The creation of the club involved some major structural changes to the house. The goal was to be as economical as possible and to reuse the stone of the original house. In the fall of 1888 the basic work was done, a new full basement being added with a strong foundation of iron columns on stone bases and with iron or steel wedges and hard brick under the house.

The front walls of the building all had to be rebuilt, and in the end it was not possible to reuse the stone blocks. A double-story porch was to be created to give institutional presence to what had been an ordinary brownstone row house, so a good deal of new stone would be needed. A debate arose over using the original Belleville, New Jersey, "gray stone" or the newer Connecticut River brownstone Richardson had favored. The builder, Smith, had to write to the architects to get them to use the Belleville stone, as otherwise the two sandstones would not match. The porch area created when the 1846 stoop was removed was then built entirely out of Belleville stone. Letters in the McKim, Mead & White files and a history of the club make it clear that Wells did the stonework and the porch.

To the architects at this time, the signifying mark for a club was the double porch, used rather artificially by McKim in Boston but done well here at the Players. The entry was brought down to street level, with the club rooms in the lower floors. The visual direction given by the building was the two-story entry, which told visitors that No. 16 was not just a row house. The exterior of the double porch had elaborate ironwork, and bronze masks of tragedy and comedy were placed on the balcony in a salute to the ancient use of masks for performances. Rumor has always had it that Saint-Gaudens designed the masks; the records reveal, however, that the design came from White and was actually drawn by a young man of talent in the office, Henry Bacon. Bacon and his older brother Francis were major figures in McKim, Mead & White in the first two decades of the firm's existence. Henry Bacon, who remained an architect, eventually became a partner in Brite & Bacon and would design the Lincoln Memorial in Washington, D.C. He had an important role in White's practice in the late 1880s—White could tell Bacon what he wanted and trust him to execute the design skillfully. It was he who drew the masks here, and John Williams made the model for casting, as Gus did not participate at the Players except as a member. Henry Bacon would also design the first-floor hall with office assistant Louis Kemper.

Another young man in the office also began to move up the ladder during this project: Lionel Moses, who would become a trusted site man for White for some years and would oversee companies working frequently with McKim, Mead & White. As ever, Archer & Pancoast would create the lighting fixtures, with W. H. Jackson supplying fireplace equipment. Fisher & Bird sold White older American black marble fireplaces from the 1830s for the club. All the woodwork, including the mantels, were done by the tireless Joseph Cabus, who worked extensively in the library and billiards room. The house was wired for electricity by the Edison Illuminating Company, although the initial wiring proved to be a problem and had to be redone five years later.

White, through the dealers John Chadwick and Henry Duveen, bought bric-a-brac and some antique furniture for the club, with Duveen likely supplying the Dutch tiles for the dining rooms (this would become a signature gesture for White). Frank Lathrop, the glassmaker, supplied windows and the skylight. Lathrop would frequent the club with White after it opened.

Ample records for the rebuilding of the Players club and its decoration survive, allowing us to note White's revisions, which would drive up the cost of the building. White's mind, increasingly impatient, now begins to fly, racing over work in process, redesigning it before it was made. White's restless mind would become a source of contention with others as he became unable to control his urges to keep revising a work. White would pencil changes over drawings, photographs—anything to make his designs better.

On the last night of the year of 1888, more than a hundred men, including White, gathered in the friendly rooms of the Booth house, which were covered in Japanese wallpaper. They were there to greet Edwin Booth, who came downstairs at about midnight to give a speech to the assembled crowd. Booth spoke very graciously, passed around a loving cup filled with wine which each member shared, and then handed the club members the deed to the building. The genial presence of Booth in the house would continue until his death in June 1893. White and other members of the Players would honor Booth by forming a procession from the club to the Little Church Around the Corner (the Church of the Transfiguration) a few blocks to the north, which had begun to conduct funerals for actors still being shunned by other local Episcopal churches. White, as a friend, designed a grave marker for Booth's body at Mount Auburn cemetery in Cambridge, Massachusetts, working in kindly cooperation with Booth's only child, now married and living in Newport. Booth's rooms in the house were closed but not dismantled; they survive intact to the present day.

The mood of the club was indeed jovial. The magical quality of the club was its intimacy, and its homelike surroundings were made all the more natural by Booth's presence. The unpretentious club with its amazingly varied and democratic membership was filled with creative people in arts well beyond the theater. White's friends were drawn into the Players, which, with its members' mailbox, offered an address to use for mail one did not want to have sent home. As the 1890s progressed and White moved close to Gramercy Park, taking rooms just six blocks to the north in the Madison Square Garden tower, he considered the clubhouse his personal annex. The Players became the place White came to settle down virtually every night, relaxing with friends, perhaps planning for an excursion to a music hall or vaudeville performance, or meeting Gus or Dewing or Lathrop for some talk. To White, the Players club was alive, while the Century Association, the older and established club for artists and patrons, had gone dead.

The Century Association had rejected Richard Grant White in the 1860s. Knowing well the value of a club, White joined the Century in 1886, just four years after McKim had been elected to its ranks. White had considerately waited until a year after his father's death; he also had the funds to join now that his financial security was assured with marriage. White became a Centurion, but it would never be his favorite place.

The Century Association took its name from its initial number of members—one hundred. The club began in 1847 and was devoted to the creation of a flowering of artistic production in the United States. The mission of the Century was to introduce artists to men of commerce, with the aim of creating a market for the artists' works. The club prospered with artists who were finally finding success. The Century would help to create America's first generations of artists able to sustain themselves in their profession. The Century was at 109 East Fifteenth Street at the time the architects joined the club, in rooms that had been decorated by Richardson and visited by notables including Charles Dickens.

The old clubhouse was venerable and beloved, but far too out-of-the-way for fashionable people. The world of club life was in its greatest decade, and many clubs, eager to give their new members social affirmation through a grander house, were building new quarters on or near Fifth Avenue farther to the north. The dilemma for the Century was that its mandate was to be affordable and more democratic than many other clubs; the issue of a new house raised eyebrows with those members who wished to keep the dues at a modest level. Others crying out for the status quo were nostalgic about the events that had already taken place in the Fifteenth Street clubhouse, giving the building a patina of history. For a decade the club was torn apart by those wishing a new and fancier clubhouse to be paid for by increasing memberships and initiation fees versus those wanting to leave the club as it was.

One can only wonder if the admission of White might not have been part of a plot to stack the deck for a new building. Richard Morris Hunt and McKim nominated White, who came aboard just after Theodore Roosevelt and Loyall Farragut (1884). The membership included many clients, so White's admission may have been an attempt to balance the votes. In the next three years the club made several attempts to improve the old clubhouse, which was on a block going downhill. The club had its water closets built into the old building in an awkward place, which kept the light from penetrating the dining room. Clearly, something had to be done. The club site committee considered land on Fortieth Street, the house of Dr. Ward on Forty-seventh Street, property at 15–17 West Thirty-eighth Street, and a household plot directly north of the existing clubhouse at 110 East Sixteenth Street. The club even considered the site of a church at Thirty-ninth Street and Fourth Avenue, but the offer was withdrawn. In 1887 the now old-fashioned architect Frederick C. Withers put forward a plan for an enlargement of the Fifteenth Street clubhouse, but it was rejected.

In 1888, as the battle for a new clubhouse raged, the photographer of motion Eadweard Muybridge spoke on animal movement, which must have been fascinating to the members. In that same year, after some internal political shenanigans to bypass the membership on voting for a new site, the club purchased four twenty-five-foot lots on the north side of Forty-third Street just west of Fifth Avenue from Louisa M. Lee for $150,000. The street had one club on it already and would soon become home to several. The membership, including Theodore Roosevelt, did agree to the purchase, voting to increase numbers tenfold to a thousand and to raise the initiation fee to two hundred dollars per person.

After the new site was purchased, the job seemed automatically to go to McKim, Mead & White, with no vote taken. Charles C. Beaman, the attorney and old friend of the firm, was head of the site committee and probably steered the commission to the architects. As White was more the man of the evening and McKim was in Boston consumed with the Public Library, White was given the job. While White began work on his design, the literary crowd of the club, those most opposed to the change, fumed.

The source for the design of the Century Association came from the oldest of the London clubs, known for its card games, wagering, and drink. It was begun by an Italian, probably called Bianco, who changed his name to the English version and opened his club as White's at the end of the seventeenth century. White's is on St. James Street in two older buildings that were converted into the clubhouse in 1787–88, probably

*The club White's in London. The humorous source of Stanford White's design for the Century Association.*

by James Wyatt. In 1811 the original central door was closed and turned into a bow window, with a new door opening to its right. It was in the bow window that the dandy Beau Brummell held court as a member of the club. The present façade was completed in 1852 with some new terra-cotta work by a minor architect, James Lockyer. Stanford White must have known the club, which was the grandest in London. As an in-joke, White based his design on that of the English club, though he changed the materials and centered his door as had been done originally at the London club.

The two clubs, the Century and White's, are mid-block buildings that need to hold their own between neighboring buildings. Both achieve a decorative arrangement of features with a symmetrical balance of the buildings around a large arched window on

*The Century Association on Forty-third Street, 1889–91. Stanford White's father was blackballed at this club.*

the second stage of each. Both have a rusticated base, pilaster strips that double on either side of the center of the building, five bays each, round ornament in four of the upper-story bays, and a crowning balustrade. Lost at the Century was White's famous 1811 bow window. Instead, the Century has a tall central arched entrance. Above the entry at the Century was an open, Italianate loggia formed by a great Palladian window. The resemblance is amazingly close, but the details vary, as do the materials.

At the Century, White had the great Worcester, Massachusetts, builders Norcross Brothers do a granite base. As the building had to be inexpensive, the upper stories were constructed of White's golden-hued Roman bricks from Perth Amboy Terra Cotta Company. Structural steel strengthened the floors and was supplied by Post & McCord, who became regular steel suppliers to McKim, Mead & White. The building process must have been a nightmare—there is a small note in the firm's papers listing a bill of $61.25 to George Bayer, who may have been a contractor, but the note indicates "aspirin," surely a bit of internal humor.

The Century club façade was given over to Joe Wells, who adapted White's source to an Italian Renaissance set of forms. Wells worked ceaselessly on the Century building, dying just as he finished the loggia. William Mitchell Kendall completed the top of the building, sniffing many years later that Wells was "not a Centurion" like himself, an indication of Kendall's hostility to Wells, as one did not have to be a member to design a club: "White designed it. Joseph Wells—who was not a Centurion—died after finishing it to above the loggia. I then finished it." The fine detail at the club is a testimonial to Wells's design skill.

The Century interior, with its gallery space and dining room, had marble work by James Sinclair, who had done the marble at the Players. The Herter Brothers firm, now run by William Baumgarten after the departure of the Herters, did some decorative work, and the architect's favored painters, Sarre & LeLacheur, painted the walls in their usual excellent way. McKim, White, and Stratton all thought Sarre, a French-born painter, was the best in the country and would mourn his passing five years later.

The Century club was completed by increasing the membership, raising the dues, and taking out a second mortgage to pay for the building. The city as a whole now had one of the finest and most cheerful clubhouses yet built, one that is still treasured today.

In 1893, the Century Association needed to redecorate the club interior, a plan that seemed to anger White, who refused the job, leaving McKim to suffer the members' displeasure. John La Farge, the painter and glassmaker, wrote McKim on the issue of wall color and coverings. The artists who showed their work there seem to have considered White a difficult man, and they felt their paintings were hindered by the décor. La Farge tried to maintain a polite deference to White through McKim, but while redoing the gallery he complained about the brown "stuff" on the walls with an aluminum-leaf ceiling. There were also complaints of a leaking roof, probably from the skylight. McKim, then working on improving his rooms at Dr. Derby's house at 9 West Thirty-fifth Street, had a young man in the office, Terence A. Koen, make daily visits to the Century and to McKim's house to ensure that both jobs finished up well. White would bear a grudge against the Century from then on, calling it a sleepy place and insisting that the more vibrant artists frequented the Players club, although White with La Farge and the young architect in his office, Thomas Hastings, would join the Twelfth Night revels for a few years at the Century.

The pressure of building the club rapidly and inexpensively was a major burden on the office, as Wells's health was failing. Wells was working at a faster pace, which seemed now to be taking a toll on the thirty-six-year-old architect. The leisure he once had to contemplate a difficult design solution in peace was now gone; the office pressures were constant. His relationship with White was still complex: White continued to

depend heavily on Wells, and by 1889 the frail man was working inces-
santly to the level almost of hysteria. Wells was balancing the Century
and the renovation of the Plaza Hotel, both of which were at a hectic
stage, flying between the sites too rapidly for flawless work. He was further pressed in the summer of 1889, when White took his family to
Europe, leaving Wells to manage these two difficult jobs while completing other projects. Norcross's office complained that Wells had gotten
sloppy with his orders for cutting the granite of the base for the Century,
further pushing up the costs of the building. J. Hampden Robb, the treasurer at the Century, acting for club members unhappy about the increase
in dues required to support the new building, fussed over the costs. Robb,
a client of the office who had a house built in Southampton in 1885, now
also commissioned a city house from McKim, Mead & White at 23 Park
Avenue, making him a client as well as a boss at the club—an uncomfort-
able closeness for the architects. When the building came in roughly seventy thousand dollars over estimate, almost half again of the total budget,
it would create friction for Robb at the club.

J. Hampden Robb, a Philadelphian, may have known McKim as a
young man. The two were at Harvard at almost the same time. In Boston,
Robb met Cornelia Van Rensselaer Thayer, a daughter of one of New England's wealthiest men, Nathaniel Thayer. The couple moved to New
York City and established a home in Murray Hill, then a section of town
popular with an inherited money set rather than a newly wealthy group.
Cornelius Vanderbilt, grandson of the Commodore, lived on railroad land
at Thirty-fourth Street and Fourth Avenue in this neighborhood, but Cornelius Vanderbilt's wife, Alice Gwynne Vanderbilt, was the link to the
older gentry of the neighborhood. Indeed, Robb's connection to the
neighborhood may have been through Vanderbilt, as Robb's father held a
good deal of stock in the New York Central, the Vanderbilt rail line.

Robb was a merchant in the cotton business until he was able to retire,
still quite young, in 1886. Mrs. Robb had inherited a substantial fortune
in 1883. After building a good-sized house in Southampton on Lake
Agawam, which McKim probably designed in 1885, the Robbs felt prosperous enough to leave business behind. Robb would become a commissioner of Central Park as well as treasurer of the Century.

The couple purchased a large tract of land on Fourth (now Park) Avenue
at the corner of Thirty-fifth Street, and the ample corner site gave them a
double house width. Robb, a collector of art with a good liberal arts background, had wanted to design his own house before giving in to McKim,
Mead & White in May 1889. One cannot tell how much of the house came

from Robb's suggestions and how much came from the office, but the results seem very awkward and beneath the standard of work being done by McKim, Mead & White at the time. The house is a big rectangle and has a brownstone base with the upper floors of Perth Amboy brick, but not the golden color then favored. The wine-colored brick used here gives a grim appearance to the heavy house. There are no indications that Wells or any of the other larger talents in the office worked at the Robb house, which probably explains why the house did not succeed as a major commission. Robb planned to entertain in his new home with its two big floors of public rooms, but we know little about Robb's parties, which may have been for the political crowd he favored. He was a friend of Theodore Roosevelt and other New York politicians. The Robb house, long a club, was turned into apartments and stands today a New York City landmark.

# 25. NEW YORK
# LIFE INSURANCE BUILDS

Whom Wells had completed the Russell & Erwin building in New Britain in 1883 with Mead's backing, the two men had found that they could work well rather quietly in the background on projects that did not enter the Newport–New York social scene. In the late 1880s Mead and Wells formed a bond with the large New York Life Insurance Company. We do not know how New York Life selected McKim, Mead & White, but the initial contact was with Mead and may have come from a relative of Sidney Stratton's late mother, a Vanuxem, since the family figured prominently in the company. Their first commission from New York Life was for two almost identical buildings as headquarters for the company in Kansas City and Omaha. Perhaps the location of the buildings, which could not be easily seen by the usual clients, put McKim and White off designing the relatively low-budget buildings. For both these Midwestern locations in January 1887, Wells designed what would become the largest (and only) tall building in these growing cities. The office buildings would serve as investments for the insurance company, allowing them to rent space to other companies and to lawyers, dentists, and other local professionals.

The New York Life buildings clearly derive their form from Wells's earlier New Britain building. The insurance buildings are far taller, but also clad in brick, using a similar arcade treatment to make the floors a cohesive visual unit. The buildings open in two projecting wings around a narrow light well at the center, a design that would allow the maximum

*The New York Life Insurance Company in Kansas City, 1887–90. Louis St. Gaudens's wonderful bird still adorns the courtyard.*

daylight into an office complex. The central feature was a projecting Italian-appearing tower, which gave both buildings an identity on the horizon.

The buildings went up slowly and well with the contractors Norcross Brothers doing the work. Mead was obliged to make the trips to the site, as Wells believed America's western border was the state of New Jersey. But Mead refused to allow Wells to remain in New York, insisting that Wells go with him to Kansas City and to visit Cass Gilbert in St. Paul. Wells asked Louis St. Gaudens to create a huge bronze eagle to roost over the door of the New York Life building in Kansas City, which Louis did without visiting the site. Amazingly, the Kansas City building, truly beautiful, was almost a demolition candidate. After having been abandoned, it was restored in 1996, and even made the subject of a short video program.

New York Life must have been pleased to see steady, fine-quality work on their new office buildings. When the Plaza apartment building fell heavily back in their hands after a foreclosure, the company asked McKim, Mead & White to create a hotel out of an unfinished shell. The work came to the office in December 1888, and Wells took charge of the project. The two Midwestern buildings were ongoing when the Plaza, a very big job, came in, and the Century Association followed, burning the life out of Wells.

The Plaza story was already complex when New York Life had to take it over. The large block on which it was built, once a skating rink, was deemed too valuable a parcel for private homes, even palatial ones. The property was purchased in 1880 by Jared Bradley Flagg, who had hoped to build a large cooperative apartment house fronting on an unbuilt Grand Army Plaza and the Central Park to the north. The Flagg project, based on selling apartments, became subject to rumors of excessive profit for Flagg. The building was not completed. John Charles Anderson bought the property, then took a mortgage from John C. Pfyfe and James Campbell, who wanted to revive Flagg's idea for a great apartment hotel. To build the block, Pfyfe and Campbell hired the German-born architect

Carl Pfeiffer and took a large loan from New York Life Insurance Company. When Pfyfe and Campbell ran out of money, the developers tried to finish the large brick building themselves, capping it with a massive, spiky mansard roof. The developers were unable to complete the building, however, and New York Life was compelled to foreclose. The insurance company, then beginning to build some apartment houses in the city, decided to make over the building into a hotel and to use McKim, Mead & White to transform this ugly duckling into a swan. As this work was in New York, visible to all, White took a leading role with the clients. Most of the actual work, though, he turned over to Wells.

THE CONCEPT OF THE MULTIPLE DWELLING UNIT for wealthy people run as rental property was still a new one on the few fashionable blocks. In the 1880s in New York City, there was a brief flurry of building what became known as a cooperative property.* The developer would sell shares representing each apartment, enabling people in search of homes effectively to buy out the developer in a successful building. The developer would then be free, in theory, to build another building. Jared Flagg had such a scheme in mind, but the cooperative movement of the 1880s fizzled. When Pfyfe and Campbell built their apartment hotel, they had intended it as a venture to get around the Daly Law's height restrictions, which did not affect hotels. Pfyfe and Campbell's building never took in visitors, and it looked woefully out-of-date, dark, and foreboding when New York Life took over. The insurance company realized that major renovation would be needed to change the image of a gloomy building associated with failure. The architects were to make over the building and create a 448-room hotel for transient guests and, it was hoped, for a few wealthy people to live in as permanent residents. It took McKim, Mead & White about a year and a half to accomplish the task.

The architects promptly lopped off the mansard, creating a flat Italian cornice with a delicate garland-faced band under the deeply projecting eave. The hotel's public rooms were in the lower two floors with the guest rooms on the upper floors. The hotel was given the 1880s McKim, Mead & White double-story columnar porch, which the firm had used at the Algonquin Club and the Players. They then went to work on glorious public spaces vital to lure upscale guests into the new hotel.

The interiors of the original Plaza must have been truly stunning. The venture of transforming the image of a failed structure came with a high

*The city's enchantment with co-ops is now in its third incarnation: 1880s, 1920s, and today.

price tag. The New York Life work was a true blessing for the office as the jobs were adequately funded and came in at well over a million dollars each, making the New York Life commissions the firm's best. The architects' fees were based on a percentage of the commissions, and as McKim, Mead, and White each took a third of the profit, the New York Life work brought the three partners a large sum. Indeed, it was the New York Life work that probably allowed White to go abroad with his family to see the Paris Exposition in the summer of 1889.

The interiors at the Plaza were White's most lavish to date. Judging by the accounts in the newspapers of the day, the opulence and sense of European grandeur must have been incredible. With a full budget White was able to create effects that recalled to travelers the greatest buildings of Europe. The interiors at the Plaza, while different from the creative work White had done a decade earlier at the Seventh Regiment Armory, were still White at his best. The Plaza work now opened the door to the path White would take for the future as the American decorator who could give his clients the opulence of a historical building belonging to a titled European family. White was now the conduit for making an image of a hereditary nobleman for American nouveaux riches. The great rooms, torn down when New York Life's lease with the hotel management was up less than fifteen years later (1905), do not survive in adequate photographic form, but they must have been remarkable work. White, it seems, would talk over his ideas with Wells, who would then actually create the effects, running every day between the Plaza rooms and the Century, both buildings reeking of wet plaster as the fall of 1889 progressed.

Wells and White brought in their friends and usual artisans for the work. Frank Lathrop, their companion in the Sewer Club, did extensive leaded glasswork for the hotel. The Tiffany company also supplied elements for the lower floors. Joseph Cabus, as ever, did the finer woodworking, and David Maitland Armstrong helped with tiles. The elevators were supplied by the Otis firm and were sufficient in number to keep guests from having to wait too long to get to the upper floors. The crowning theme was the fine mosaic work on the floors, including the head of a lion rendered in huge form as a symbol of the insurance company.

The painter George Maynard completed murals as all the artists and craftsmen worked together, pushed by never-ending deadlines. The work at the Plaza, where money flowed freely, seemed to go better than at the Century, where budget constraints created the friction that led to the need for aspirin. The Plaza job went pretty happily as the companies creating the interiors, all fairly used to each other, worked cooperatively. This harmony was in contrast to the next major interior at the Metropolitan Club, where a French decorative company was inserted with the New York firms, causing a less than happy atmosphere.

At the Plaza, as had been the pattern in large commissions for twenty years in the New York region, multiple decorative firms did rooms at the hotel. It was customary to ask the top decorative companies to do one or more rooms in a big job, putting each company side by side with rivals, but since it was an accepted practice, the even-handed gesture usually worked well. Pottier & Stymus did several rooms working with George Schastey's company at the Plaza. The two firms had created the best rooms of the Aesthetic taste, then just over. The quality of work Schastey and Pottier & Stymus could produce, relying heavily on European-born and trained workmen, was incredible. The artisans who created the pieces of furniture and decoration were often German immigrants capable of exceptional work. One is struck today at how quickly, once tastes changed, the work of Schastey and Pottier & Stymus was discarded. The Plaza fittings and furnishings were all sold for fifty thousand dollars in 1905, during the lifetimes of the architects. Indeed, McKim, Mead & White would see much of their early work destroyed in the first years of the twentieth century. H. J. Hardenbergh's Plaza Hotel replaced the first hotel, and the building still stands today.

The office at 57 Broadway was now far too small for a firm with as much work as they had, and the pressure there must have been intense. The rooms were overcrowded, and the location of the office was now most inconvenient, given that the bulk of their work was uptown and not in Wall Street. Moods and tempers grew heated. White and Wells, locked together on their two New York commissions at the Century and the Plaza Hotel, were also still completing the Madison Square Garden's upper reaches. They worked all day, and they often spent evenings together investigating the pleasures in the Sewer Club at the Benedick. Some nights White took Wells with him, as he had Gus, to the clubs he frequented. Wells, with his prickly demeanor, was less comfortable in a social setting than Gus had been, perhaps bringing White some embarrassment. White had decided that Wells did not have the personality for success even if he did have the needed talent. White felt his own people-pleasing skills and his upbringing, even if impoverished, put him in a class above Wells. He found it convenient to see himself as socially better than Joe. Wells felt the slight and must have grown to resent his position at the office, where he did more and often better work than the partners for no share of the profits or prestige. Indeed, Wells was quite poor—as were all the employees of the office.

There must have been a blowup in the office after Thanksgiving 1889. Wells surely pointed out that he was doing the work of a partner without any of the rewards, while White was more and more absorbed in the world of parties. Wells felt used by White and probably created a scene in the partners' rooms. White must have pulled rank and left the office. McKim then thought over the incident, perhaps with the input of Mead, though we have no record of Mead's interaction here. In December 1889, McKim wrote White a most thoughtful letter stating that he felt Wells should be made a partner. McKim argued that the change in name to McKim, Mead, White & Wells would not create any major difficulty, citing the frequent partnership name changes at Prescott Hall Butler's firm, which did seem to rename itself constantly with no loss of business. McKim pointed out that Wells was terribly poor and had none of the better things in life. His final point was that he would welcome Wells's elevation to partner with delight. McKim had taken the high road, which would be characteristic of his behavior for the rest of his life. He concluded with a light touch, remarking that he had taken Wells to dinner after the scene and Wells had regained his good humor, especially as McKim had included George F. Babb in the party and Wells had done all he could to tease Babb all evening. McKim invited White to approve the partnership offer, saying that Wells had agreed that the incident earlier that day should not be taken too seriously; this created an avenue for White to join McKim in the partnership offer, which he then did. Around Christmastime, Wells was offered the first full partnership in the firm since White had joined a decade earlier. Wells turned them down flat with a characteristically caustic remark. He said he would not put his name on a firm that turned out "so much damn bad work."

It is difficult to imagine why Wells would turn down the acknowledgment of his years of high-quality design and supervision on much of the work produced by the office. The partnership would allow him to move from very tight financial circumstances to comfort, but that did not seem to be a matter of concern to Wells, who was quite accustomed to living in straitened conditions. Architecture was Wells's entire focus: He lived in a visual world, with bird watching and music his only hobbies.

The private world White and Wells and the other artists enjoyed in secret may explain Wells's refusal to accept the partnership. The most reasonable explanation of his rejection of the offer was personal spite. Wells was probably satisfying his feelings toward White by refusing to join his own work with that of lesser talents, perhaps specifically White's work. Wells's remark was meant to hurt White. It was likely made with expectation of another offer in the future—but Wells had no future.

Overwork had been constant in Wells's life, and even as his health deteriorated, the frail soul forced himself to keep working at an exhausting pace. He may have had tuberculosis as an underlying condition, but it was pneumonia that began to invade his lungs by late December, when Wells had to take to his bed and summon a doctor. In the new year he returned to work, supervising the wet plaster in the unheated in Plaza Hotel, a task that only intensified his congestion. Wells kept working now with an almost insane urgency that frightened people. Wells's old friend C. Howard Walker called on him about the first of February in 1890 and found him in a terrible state. Wells insisted on taking "Howdie" Walker through the Century and Plaza dining rooms. His friend's condition so alarmed Walker that he left Wells on the elevated tracks, insisting that Wells return to his room in the Benedick for a rest. Wells wrote a letter to his doctor a few hours later, reporting that he felt much worse and asking the doctor to visit as soon as he could. Wells died February 2, 1890, in his room at the Benedick.

The details of Wells's last days are not recorded, but someone from the office was surely with him, as Babb wrote to the office saying that he had heard Wells was very sick and might not live. Babb asked if he might go to see Wells if Wells wished. Yet Babb seemed reluctant to visit, as he could not bear to see Wells suffering. Stanford White seems to have been the companion to his dying friend, since the correspondence bears his name as if he were the observer of the patient. White telegraphed Wells's father and brother in Boston with the news of his illness and then death. Howdie Walker met Professor Webster Wells on the street in Cambridge and told Wells he had seen Joe a few days before in New York, only to be interrupted by the mathematician who told Walker he had just had a telegram informing him of his brother's death. Walker was one of the last to see Wells alive. McKim may have been in Boston, and White telegraphed Mead in Europe with the sad news. Mead, who greatly respected Wells, was deeply saddened and kept the telegram as a memento. As we know, Mead would keep Dewing's oil sketch portrait of Wells on his desk for the remainder of his life.

The New York City papers and the professional press wrote obituaries for Wells, with the best one appearing in Villard's newspaper, the *Evening Post*. The funeral was held in Boston, with burial at Oak Grove Cemetery in Medford, Massachusetts. Wells was interred on April 4, 1890, a Friday, at 4 p.m., in plot 209. His father would be buried near him on January 15, 1903, when he died at age eighty, as would Sarah M. Wells, who died October 20, 1897, at the age of sixty-eight. Wells's brother Webster was put in the plot May 25, 1916, at sixty-four, and Webster's wife, Emily Walker Wells, had her ashes placed there in 1943.*

The Saint-Gaudens brothers created a stele for Wells with some help from Stanford White. Wells's friends helped to pay for the tall, Greek leaf-detailed monument, which was set in the cemetery under McKim, Mead & White's direction in 1894. The monument, now fallen over, sits in pieces in the cemetery today, lost rather as was the reputation of its owner.

Cass Gilbert, a friend of Joe Wells's and now a promising architect in St. Paul, Minnesota, wrote his condolence letter to White as the person closest to Wells. White rather gracelessly wrote that Wells was "an architect whose ability was of the highest order . . . and his hand was seen all through our work while he lived . . . [Wells] had the temperament which makes artists unfit to cope with the world, and which, therefore, kept them always as assistant rather than principals."

McKim, far more graciously, responded to Wells's premature death by trying to get a library of architecture named for Wells at the new Boston Public Library; this did not materialize, but McKim had made a serious attempt to create a lasting memorial to his friend.

Saint-Gaudens was truly devastated, and in Wells's honor he held two memorial concerts for his lost friend and likely lover on the anniversary of his death. Only those at the original concerts were to be allowed to attend these fitting memorials.

Charles Howard Walker penned a fine notice of Wells for posterity in *The American Architect and Building News,* which established Wells as an architect of genius to readers who may not have known of him. Walker wrote for the ages. He remained true to his friend and in 1929 wrote a profile of Wells for *The Architectural Record,* championing his work to a new generation of architects. Many others, such as Royal Cortissoz, wrote in praise of Wells, as would Will Low and Homer Saint-Gaudens, all of whom make a strong point about Wells's role in the office and his development of the Italian Renaissance as a suitable historical vehicle for new American buildings of their day. The accounts of all those in the office in

*For years I tried to determine if Emily Walker Wells might be related to C. Howard Walker, but I have been unable to ascertain if this is true.

*Banquet for H. Siddons Mowbray, May 26, 1888. White does not appear in this image but was at the party. Saint-Gaudens sits at the center of the table. Next to him might be McKim pulling away from the photographer.*

the 1880s extol both Wells's gift and the kind person under the shell of acidic commentary.

Wells's wit was highly regarded by his peers, with remarks of his recorded in several places, including passages of his daybook mainly inscribed in 1886–87. Wells wrote of popular music of the day: "We have plenty of patent exterminators for rats, fleas, bed bugs and other vermin; but none for amateur pianists." On genius, Wells wrote, "A great genius is a godsend to humanity, but a terrible burden to his family and friends." On artists, he noted, "Artists have the genius of wrongheadedness." Wells wrote of architectural style that "the classic ideal suggests clearness, simplicity, grandeur, order and philosophical calm—consequently it delights my soul." Scanning the daybook reveals more of his insights and idiosyncrasies:

The Medieval ideal suggests superstition, ignorance, vulgarity, restlessness, cruelty and religion. All of which fill my soul with horror and loathing.

Success hardens the heart.

New York Life is a carnival of vulgarity. Nothing short of a great man can successfully resist its disintegrating influences.

Superstition is deep—Reason is shallow.

Saint-Gaudens and I differ in this—labour is a drudgery to me and thinking to him.

I wouldn't change brains with any man living, though I doubtless might make many good bargains in so doing. But I am perfectly willing to change teeth, bowels or legs, these being my peccant parts; I am a frequent sufferer from tooth-ache, dyspepsia and gout.

The Renaissance ideal suggests a fine and cultivated Society, with its errands of gay ladies and gentlemen devoted to the pleasures and elegances of life—which excites my admiration, but not my sympathies.

Even if he was building for the newly elegant America, Wells was not himself in sympathy with the new persona that wealthy Americans were now affecting.

# 26. THE OFFICE AT WORK

The loss of Wells at McKim, Mead & White was profound. The office had come to depend on him to make their designs coherent. Wells, the ultimate arbiter of design, was now gone. The number of commissions McKim and White accepted reflected their habit of depending on younger talent in the office to work with them on both the design and the building site. Commissions came in quickly during good economic times, a bit more slowly in the frequent financial slumps. The number of men in the office would surge in the good days, then dwindle as work slowed and layoffs followed. The frantic pace of the office at the time of Wells's death prompted White to set up his own studio around the corner from his red brick home at Twentieth Street.

The house at 1 West Twentieth Street was once a mansion belonging to the great sugar-processing king, Robert L. Stuart (1806–1882). Stuart, with his brother, had brought steam power to the processing of sugar, radically lowering the price of sugar products. After making a fortune and perhaps ruining the teeth of generations of children, he began to collect contemporary paintings made by the Parisian circle of the 1870s. Stuart's collection, notable in his day, hung in his house on Fifth Avenue at Twentieth Street until about 1880, when the Stuarts moved up the avenue to a house designed with the aid of William B. Bigelow. Stuart's picture collection was promised to the new Metropolitan Museum of Art, but with the stipulation that the museum be closed on Sundays. Stuart was an ardent Presbyterian. When the museum found it needed to be open for the working class, who only had Sundays to visit, the Stuart paintings were removed and given to the Lenox Library, then to the New-York Historical Society, where they still hang. The Stuart house on the corner of Twentieth Street was then leased to the Herter Brothers, the decorative arts firm Bigelow worked for in the early 1880s, probably as an in-house architect. By the late 1880s the Herter brothers were dead and the firm was preparing to move to another building nearby. Stanford White liked the neighborhood for its concentration of decorative firms as well as the antiques and art dealers clustered around Twentieth Street. White leased space in the Stuart house at 1 West Twentieth Street. He could now do his own private work with Saint-Gaudens and be near the decorative arts dealers and still be able to walk home or to the Players club. White would still travel to 57 Broadway for firm work, but he now had a private office.

There is no question that a distinct identity to all work once done by the partners had evolved. Mead did oversee the firm to some degree, but White and McKim each had a group of young men to assist him. The design processes were now individual: for instance, McKim worked with his "right-hand man," the nasty William Mitchell Kendall, who was subservient to McKim but to no one else. The men in the office at 57 Broadway almost suffocated, as Kendall would not let them open even one window in the summer. McKim and White shared the other assistants. Indeed, the men in the office must have spent many hours on the elevated railroad line between White's rooms on Twentieth Street and the Battery, where McKim worked.

The design process was quite different in McKim's spaces than in White's studio. McKim had given up drawing early on. His drafting skills were never of virtuoso level, although he was ambidextrous and in his early years was able to draw with either hand. The luxury of turning the drawing over to Bigelow and then Wells had become a habit. When working on a building design, McKim, fastidiously dressed, would sit down with a draftsman, and as Richardson had done twenty years earlier, he would call out with a rich vocabulary of terms as the draftsman labored to produce the image. After hours of work, the session often ended with McKim smudging the cornice line so often to lower or raise the proportionate balance that the draftsman was left with no idea of what to do. McKim then dispatched everyone to the library to consult the volumes of Letarouilly, or, later, those of Joseph Gwilt, to find a precedent. Gwilt's architectural volumes, especially *The Encyclopedia of Architecture* (1842 onward) became an office bible. McKim, Mead & White's post-Wells work would have far more recognizable features drawn from book plates as a result of this method. The architects were often criticized for their "borrowings," which they would justify as part of their mandate in the 1890s and early twentieth century—to adapt the heritage of European culture to the needs of the new American wealthy class and thus to help prepare for the Americans to lead the world as European princes had before. The McKim, Mead & White designs were exemplars of this philosophy—buildings derived from European models, rendered into a new, modern form for the New World.

McKim's manner with his assistant was to use praise and kindness as a method of achieving the best work possible. He softly acknowledged every draftsman's effort, then would gently nudge the man over and over again until the result he desired was attained. McKim would not settle for a result he did not like. He would quietly, flatteringly rephrase the conversation endlessly until he had his result. Beneath "Charles the Charmer" was a rod of steel. McKim backed and filled until his goals were achieved. By the 1890s, however, the goals would veer to education, not design. McKim would devote his last two decades to the establishment of training and standards for future generations of American architects. He fashioned himself as the dean of American architectural training.

Stanford White worked in a very different manner from McKim's. He also followed Richardson's practice of quick sketches to be worked up by draftsmen. White drew anywhere, not only in the office as McKim had, and he made multiple sketches, often late at night after an evening on the town. Each morning an office draftsman would tiptoe into his studio, pick up the piles of paper, and deliver them to the office, where the staff endeavored to figure out which of the several designs White had decided upon. This was done nervously, as White, unlike McKim, could be harsh and angry in his work with the men. Impatient and overcommitted, White expected the draftsmen to be able to produce his imagined results from a confused set of directions. He was unable to be patient with the men, and if he found the results unsatisfactory, he was given to bouts of anger involving ample amounts of foul language. With far too much on his plate to become bogged down with details of office work, he soon became known as a workplace terror. One can imagine Mead now had the extra job of soothing many ruffled feathers after each of White's outbursts.

The office did indulge in some high spirits. In 1888, McKim, Mead & White played a do-or-die baseball game in Central Park with the office of the architects J. C. Cady. The office was then challenged by that of R. H. Robertson, and the story of the partners playing the game has often been retold. McKim was still a fine player, but White was terrible at sports. The Robertson team hit a ball with such force that in catching it White injured himself, and he was sent home by taxi with a wounded foot. White later insisted the game was lost due to Robertson's hiring a professional pitcher. Baseball games among friendly but rival offices were popular in the 1890s, and the firm played summer games against the offices of Robertson, Cady, and even Richard Morris Hunt.

Inside, office merriment was a release for overworked men on Saturday afternoons. The firm's success in gaining a big commission was also heralded with a parade of homemade costumes and props. When the office won the competition for the Rhode Island State Capitol, the draftsmen decided to celebrate with a high-spirited parade led by a bevy of office men who would later be stars of the profession in their own careers. Frank Hoppin (of Hoppin & Koen), John Mead Howells (William R. Mead's nephew), and Henry Bacon dressed up as High Churchmen of Architecture performing an architectural Mass. Hoppin played pope wearing a mitre and holding a T square as a substitute for a crosier. The acolytes followed swinging an old Venetian lamp as if incense. Henry Bacon carried a cutout of the winning design while the office sang a hymn to the tune of "Onward Christian Soldiers":

> Onward, All ye Draughtsmen.
>   Marching as to War,
> With our office T. Square
>   Going on before.
> We are not divided
>   All our office, we,
> In all competitions
>   Ours the Victory . . .
> Foes may struggle vainly,
>   We will Vanquish all,
> For they are not in it,
>   They will have to crawl.
> Providence is with us
>   Thro' the darkest night;
> In our blest profession
>   We're simply out of sight.

A SEVERE BREAK IN WHITE'S LIFE had come with the death of Wells. White had become a member of New York's fashionable circles almost as a single figure, exactly as Wells had expected him to do. Bessie preferred a less public life, and with the toddler, Larry, to care for, retreated from White's social life. White began to attend balls and events on his own more frequently. In 1889, Bessie's father, Judge John Lawrence Smith, died at the New York house on Fifth Avenue at Thirty-fifth Street, which he had used for several years. The Stewart estate held a number of houses in the Thirty-fourth Street area that Mrs. Stewart had rented to her family. Judge Smith had once lived on Clinton Place, today called Eighth Street, in the vicinity of the big Stewart cast-iron store before taking a Stewart house on Fifth Avenue, which White redecorated for the Smiths' brief years as heirs to the Stewart estate. The Stewart legal tangle was barely undone when Judge Smith died, followed just months later by his widow, Sarah Nicoll Clinch Smith. Bessie's parents never had the chance to really enjoy the long-awaited wealth.

Bessie was very close to her parents and was likely to have taken the lengthy ritual of mourning seriously, keeping her out of the social whirl. White now really was left alone to live his city life as a bachelor.

Following Wells's death, the Sewer Club rooms were closed and the furniture sent to a studio building, the Holbein, at 146 West Fifty-fifth Street, where White and Dewing had rented a hideaway for some years. In room 8, which they called the Morgue, they must have continued their search for new sensations. With Bessie in seclusion, such experiments may have been frequent. To hide the quarters from others, the rent checks for the Holbein studio were made out to a John Hay. For White, there was an air of death at home and in the Benedick, and he may have been making a joke with the nickname of the club, as it was full of life.

With Wells gone and Gus occupied with his second family, White and Dewing may have begun their fascination with young women, particularly those belles coming to New York to become part of the theatrical world. White would settle down to a pattern of courtships and brief liaisons with young actresses, chorus dancers, and artist's models. Dewing was more of a womanizer than many of White's other friends. White probably still participated in "sprees" with homosexual men, but he began to settle into a pattern of evenings with increasingly young women. His companions in these evenings included James Breese, Bob Goelet, Henry Poor, the Astor grandsons (the Chanlers), and the Cheney boys. The sprees with homosexual overtones seemingly involved Tommy Hastings and Whitney Warren, both of whom would become famous architects, as well as Arthur D. Weeks of Oyster Bay, the Saint-Gaudens brothers, Frank Lathrop, and other artists.

At the Players club, White became friendly with the painter Edward Simmons, who had been a friend of Henry Casey years earlier. Simmons became part of White's artist group known as "Simjaks." Simmons described White at this time as being very tall and awkward, always rushing and walking with short steps "like a girl." In his view, White was true as ever to being an artist, but he was childlike: Like Peter Pan, he had never grown up. Perhaps White's attraction to young women was part of this adolescent behavior described by Simmons.

# 27. THE WASHINGTON SQUARE ARCH AND PUBLIC CEREMONY

White's public life in the city had been one of celebrity for some years. His artful blend of decoration and upholding of the banner of high art had equated his name with visual displays in the city. As White began his second life as a bachelor, albeit a part-time one, he was the toast of the town with the success of the Madison Square Garden and the unveiling of New York's greatest work of street "furniture," the Washington Square Arch.

The Washington Square Arch story goes back to the mid-1880s, when New Yorkers realized that the centennial of George Washington's inauguration would take place on April 30, 1889. As was typical, given the long-established demolition pattern of New York, the building where the first president took his oath of office was long gone. On the place where Washington stood was a customhouse building, then the Federal Reserve Depository of the city. On the steps of this Grecian temple, the current president, Benjamin Harrison, could re-create the ceremony. Proud New Yorkers could promote the city by enhancing the centennial with a full set of celebratory events. In effect, New York could reclaim, even if just for a few days, the glory of being the national capital. Several groups formed dedicated to the idea of hyping New York, including one begun in 1887 by William Rhinelander Stewart, an attorney well known in the city and a principal in the Rhinelander real estate empire. The sugar-importing Rhinelanders had been active figures in New York life for a century, and maintaining this position may well have been Rhinelander Stewart's

*Washington Square Arch, 1890–93, which became the symbol of the rise of the arts in America.*

motivation for climbing aboard the centennial bandwagon. The Rhinelanders had been re-developing their properties for some time; indeed, Stanford White lived in a rental house at 56 West Twentieth Street that was part of the Rhinelander estate. The Rhinelanders' property was not as large as that of the Astors or Goelets, but they were major players in the real estate world, happy to see the city beautified and given a public relations boast.

Rhinelander Stewart probably knew White personally as a tenant and certainly as a creator of impressive visual effects. White's interior decoration for former mayor James Harper's widow and the grandchildren of Peter Cooper would have been noticed by Stewart, who was of the old New York world. Thus, it is not surprising that Rhinelander Stewart turned directly to White in 1887, inviting him to serve as director of the festivities.

Almost immediately, the idea of triumphal arches was raised as a visual focus for parades and fireworks displays. Such arches, re-creations of Roman triumphs, had been popular civic ornaments since the late eighteenth century in Berlin, Paris, and London. There had not been a stone arch in the United States as yet. Stewart and White settled on a temporary set of arches for the city inexpensively created out of wood with a thick icing of molded white plaster over straw, then called "staff." The temporary arch would have been in people's minds in 1887, as Queen Victoria, Britain's dowager monarch, was being celebrated for her fifty years on the throne with public displays focused around temporary triumphal arches. It is unknown if Stewart or White was inspired by the British anniversary arch, but one tends to think White kept up with the goings-on in the English court. White's selection of Edward Strauss for the opening of Madison Square Garden seemed to indicate his awareness of the celebrations at Queen Victoria's court, where Strauss had played for the queen's daughter's party.

The arches were actually built just before the event, as the wooden structures would have blocked the sidewalks. White did a trellis arch at

Twenty-second Street over Fifth Avenue, but he was primarily recognized for his Washington Square arch, which was actually on Eighth Street across Fifth Avenue at its first block northward from the park. The Stewart committee had raised $2,500 for the Washington Square arch. Stewart lived on Washington Square North, so the Eighth Street arch got the greatest attention.

The parade arch was covered with garlands and laurel wreaths of staff, then freshly painted white. Bunting and flags brought color to the arch, which had stuffed American eagles at the keystone and a larger-than-life wooden statue of George Washington on top. The statue of Washington had turned up in an antique dealer's rooms, where it was brought to White's attention. This wooden figure survives and is now in a Washington, D.C., museum.

For the spectacle, White outlined the arch with his favorite strings of little white lightbulbs. The small white lights strung around buildings and trees today, particularly at Christmastime, are a Stanford White gesture, introduced here at the arch and at the Madison Square Garden festivities. To power the bulbs, White arranged for a generator to be placed close by, magically lighting the arch at night. The city's population, rich and poor, stood transfixed by the arch with its temporary grandeur— though the staff material melted in repeated rainstorms and the electric lights and generator were noisy, sometimes startling the observers.

The success of the wooden arch encouraged the prominent men in the city, particularly those close by the park at Washington Square, to call for a permanent arch at the base of Fifth Avenue. A special committee was created with William Rhinelander Stewart as treasurer charged with finding the funds needed to make permanent the wooden arch. Richard Morris Hunt, who lived nearby, and his patron Henry G. Marquand, the art collector and first president of the Metropolitan Museum, joined the committee, along with the aging portraitist Daniel Huntington, who had painted White's parents at the time of their wedding. Also on the committee was the journalist and client of McKim, Mead & White, Richard Watson Gilder; another client, Levi P. Morton, then vice president; and former president Grover Cleveland, who had just completed his first term.

The initial impulse was to build the arch across Fifth Avenue on the footprint of the old arch, but it was quickly deduced that stone piers would take up too much space on the avenue. White agonized about the proportions for the new arch in a manner reminiscent of his placing of the Farragut statue in Madison Square. He tried out three designs on the committee, which refused to help him decide on the best arch and instead returned the proposals with the tactful excuse that they would entrust White with full authority for the final design. A year after the centennial, a ceremony was held to break ground in the park for the permanent arch. Workmen quickly encountered the remains of an early nineteenth-century graveyard, making the foundation laying a macabre experience. On Decoration Day, a month later, a larger celebration was held for the setting of a cornerstone officially completed by the grand master of the Masonic order. Washington himself had been a Mason.

Public events kept the arch in people's minds, but pocketbooks were not opened very widely. The money needed for the arch, over $150,000, was not easy to secure. David H. King, the contractor, donated his services as did White, but these gestures did not help Rhinelander Stewart secure the money he needed. Richard Watson Gilder had a close friendship with the highly regarded Polish pianist, Ignace Jan Paderewski, who was convinced to play a concert at the Metropolitan Opera House as a fund-raiser. McKim's old friend from Newport and Boston, Colonel Higginson, a great supporter of the Boston Symphony Orchestra, donated the symphony's services for the Washington Square Arch concert, which turned out to be a great success.

On April 5, 1892, the construction of the arch was completed as Gilder, White, and Rhinelander Stewart climbed up on ladders to "finish" the stonework. It was claimed that the three men's initials were carved on the stones, with another one marked "P." and placed in honor of Paderewski, who had returned to Poland.

The sculptural areas on the north side of the arch would not be completed for some time—the large images of George Washington were not installed until World War I. The carving of the lintel was given to the young sculptor Frederick MacMonnies, then living in Paris. It was said that Rhinelander Stewart suggested to MacMonnies that his wife's face be used on the head of the angel facing west toward the Stewarts' house, with Bessie White's face used as the model for the east-facing angel. White did write MacMonnies requesting him to work on Mrs. Stewart's face for one angel, but left the identity of the other angel to the sculptor's discretion. In the final design, both women's heads were used for the figures of War and Peace—Mrs. Stewart for Peace and Bessie for War. It is difficult to know if the placement of Bessie as angel over George Washington as military commander was convenience or a statement. MacMonnies would be one of White's companions on his evening sprees in Paris and New York and may have added a bit of personal judgment on Mrs. White's personality in his selection of an image.

THE ARCH WAS DEDICATED on May 4, 1895, after the previously scheduled dedication on April 30 had to be postponed due to heavy rains. Following a parade down Fifth Avenue and numerous speeches, New York City now had its own "Roman" arch, which gave civic presence to Washington Square at a time when its eastern flank had been populated by the garment and textile businesses that would force New York University out of its birthplace and north to the Bronx. The southern quarter of the Square sat above a slum, the same one the Reverend Edward Judson was trying to improve with his ministry. The arch might be seen as the last hurrah for the old families still at the Square, now very much below the fashionable folk whose homes on or near Fifth Avenue stretched far north. The arch became a link between upper Fifth Avenue and the denizens of Washington Square despite the miles that separated them.

The arch would become a major landmark in a city with no ancient history of its own. It would indicate to the world that New York was a major city like Rome, Berlin, London, or Paris, with its own urban arch. As New York had only one main boulevard then, Fifth Avenue, the Washington Square Arch did not radiate out grand streets as did the Arc de Triomphe, but it did begin Fifth Avenue with style.

# 28. THE STEWART BUBBLE BURSTS

J ust as White's recognition in the city rose, his life at 56 West Twentieth Street may have been under a severe strain. The settlement of Mrs. Stewart's holdings had begun. The primary assets left were in real property, which would require a lengthy and complicated partitioning. The first phase of affluence came in the year when Judge Smith died, 1889. In the summer Bessie had been allotted property on Bleecker Street and Greene Streets in the area below Washington Square, which had gone downhill in the years since Stewart had purchased the properties.

Mr. and Mrs. Stewart had lived, once their dry goods business had prospered, in one of the city's first distinctive row house groups, De Pau Row, built in 1829–30 on Bleecker Street west of Mercer and Greene Streets. The Stewarts lived well there until mid-century, when the neighborhood started to deteriorate. The Stewarts had purchased the properties at 110 Bleecker and around the corner on Greene Street,* and they retained them when they moved uptown to the Marble House. Bessie received these properties outright, and she cleared the lots and had her husband build five-story, yellow brick commercial buildings with lofts above to produce income for her. Bessie and White recognized that the Stewart estate holdings were her properties, but White was quickly mixed up in the development issues as he was an architect and could produce a better

---

*These buildings were demolished to make way for New York University's Silver Towers apartment blocks.

image for the buildings of the estate. White, of course, liked the world of real estate and property that his father had lost out on after his own father went bankrupt. White put himself in the center of the story as the architect for the Stewart estate and as Bessie's spokesman in the meetings he attended for her. White was now able to greatly benefit from the Stewart estate.

Inspired by White's improving the 110 Bleecker Street property, Isabella May asked him to build on Third Street at Mercer with a similar yellow brick commercial building in July 1889.*

Encouraged by the first stage of the Stewart estate settlement, Stanford White took the family to Europe to see the 1889 Paris Exposition. White loved the international fairs, but Bessie must have been miserable to be away from her beloved Long Island summer and fall activities.

Bessie had yielded to White's desire to keep up with the international fair, but on her return, with the death of her parents, the marriage became further strained. Perhaps Bessie, now older, had realized she preferred a man more like her father—a wise, judicious man she could trust. White was occasionally brilliant, but he was also erratic and difficult to rely upon. Certainly after the 1891 Tiffany bill debacle, Bessie realized that she could not trust White's fidelity any longer. She began to drift toward the sedate attorney she had known since childhood when her father had taught the young man—Prescott Hall Butler. The White marriage would become perfunctory, though they retained some of the outward trappings of a proper couple with two homes. The absence of Bessie from much of the New York social whirl could be explained by her need to oversee the Long Island property. The choice of placing the face of Bessie over the figure of George Washington in his warrior mode may have had a real significance: by the 1890s the couple may have had genuine battles.

Perhaps some of the disintegration of the couple's relationship stemmed from the stress of the Stewart case as it moved into more complex stages after the early partial settlement. The Stewart properties were numerous and of great value as a whole but difficult to divide into ninety-five shares. The real estate empire built up between the 1840s and Mr. Stewart's death had remained static for more than fifteen years. Some pieces of the estate had fallen in value during this time, making assignment of property to individuals quite difficult. The properties below Washington Square had

---

*A search for the early life of Isabella May has not been successful. In 1905 she would marry the principal of the George A. Fuller construction company, which belonged to White's world, but I cannot account for her presence with the Whites here on Bleecker Street at this time.

decreased in value, while those in the Thirty-fourth Street area had risen. The purpose of Stewart real estate had also changed. Stewart's Broadway hotel housed Niblo's Garden, once the city's premier nightspot; but by the time of Mrs. Stewart's death, Niblo's Garden had long been replaced by the music halls between Fourteenth Street and Twenty-third Streets. The Women's Hotel, almost completed at Mr. Stewart's death, would need updating if it was to have value. The baronial suburb planned by A. T. Stewart for Garden City, Long Island, had a railroad station, hotel, and some dozen mid-century houses with mansard roofs that now looked woefully out-of-date.

Following Mrs. Stewart's death, only the great Episcopal cathedral in Garden City and its related buildings had been added to the Stewart holdings. The legal team recognized that Garden City, the Park Avenue hotel, and other properties would need extensive reworking to increase their value. Also problematic was the overbuilt Marble House, which had already been shorn of its artworks and was difficult to sell. In the early discussion of Stewart's house as it was being built, the newspapers quoted the childless Stewart as intending the Marble House to be turned into a clubhouse after his wife's death. Stewart, while not himself a clubman, was following the example of the Jerome mansion built on Twenty-sixth Street and Madison Avenue by the horse fancier Leonard Jerome. The Jerome family had been driven abroad when Leonard Jerome's womanizing became overly public. The vacant house was made into the University Club and used for several decades until the great McKim-designed clubhouse was opened.

Stewart's plan to have the Marble House become a club building was realized when the Manhattan Club, an organization devoted to politicians and supporters of the Democratic Party, purchased the house in 1891. The Stewart estate may have held the the Manhattan Club's mortgage on the building, as the property came back into McKim, Mead & White's office when the architects' friend, Charles T. Barney, bought the site for the Knickerbocker Trust Company.

As is obvious from these pages, the Stewart estate was a complicated set of properties, owned by an equally complicated group of heirs. A. T. Stewart's long-forgotten relatives left behind in northern Ireland sixty years earlier had sued for a share of the estate. The Butlers also had a role as both attorneys and beneficiaries. Charles E. Butler, now aging and cantankerous, acted for all the heirs. One of the principal inheritors was his son, Prescott, whose late mother and wife were also heirs. Among the executors was Judge Horace Russell, who was married to Hilton's daughter.

Russell was an agreeable sort, useful as everyone now blamed Henry Hilton for depleting the resources of the estate. The Smith faction, which had included eight family members, was down to six after the death of Bessie's parents. By the late spring of 1890, the remaining Smiths were Bessie, represented by her husband; her brother, a bachelor often in Paris or New York; James Clinch Smith; and Bessie's four sisters. The eldest sister, Louise Nicoll Smith, had married one of Judge Smith's students, Frank Osborne, and had moved to Chicago.*

Frank Osborne had serious financial problems, which he hid by insisting he needed cash for a major investment opportunity. Osborne pressured the executors for an immediate settlement, which made the planning sessions very tense, as the other heirs wished to get better prices by rehabilitating the properties before sale. The second sister, Kate Smith Wetherill, was married to an Episcopal minister; the Wetherills were devoted to the church and did not play much of a role in the Stewart estate. Ella Batavia Smith who had married one of the highly regarded Emmet brothers of heroic Irish ancestry, also played only a minor role in the planning of the estate. The major players boiled down to Judge Russell, the Butlers, the impatient Osborne, and Stanford White, who logically became the designer for the reworking of the properties.

The Garden City land, totaling some ten thousand acres, and buildings, then woefully low in value, were made into a syndicated corporation, with the idea that it would be a long time before the property values rose on those empty plains. White built a small wooden casino, which is still there, as a focus for the future community, rather like the casino at Short Hills, New Jersey. The Garden City Casino was designed for the Stewart executors as one of his off-the-books ventures. McKim, Mead & White bill books do not contain any record of this modest gabled building of 1895, but White was used to working on decorative commissions and monuments in his private practice, so the casino, simple to build, was an independent work. White would do a few more such off-the-books works, such as the design for the William Merritt Chase house in Shinnecock Hills.

The old Garden City Hotel, built two decades earlier by Kellum, was perceived as a hindrance to the syndication efforts, so White, now working with the office, replaced the modest Kellum building with a bigger hotel in a vaguely Colonial style. Built in 1894–96, the new hotel projected a stately image vital for creating a better tone for the community.

*Osborne was not related to Charles Osborn, the client of a few years earlier.

The hotel was built around a courtyard as had been done for Villard's house and hotels of the Pacific Northwest. White, increasingly interested in fireplaces and fittings, extracted all the fireplaces he could from the Stewart properties in New York, placing them in the Garden City Hotel, which tragically burned five years later. The firm redid the hotel in 1899–1901 with the aim of attracting an upper-class clientele. As the building was near a new golf course, many would take rooms in the Garden City Hotel for the summer months. In the early years of the twentieth century, Charles McKim spent several months in the new hotel. After World War II, Long Island grew rapidly as a suburban community, and the hotel was demolished in 1973.

White's relation to the Garden City venture would continue with various small commissions. He gave designs to a developer for a prototype house in 1893. The Garden City saga would go on for many years with, in the end, little benefit for Bessie's family.

In New York City, White worked for the heirs to the Stewart estate in an effort to make the Women's Hotel a bit more fashionable. The hotel had been built on a problematic site just south of the new Grand Central Terminal at Forty-second Street across the old Fourth Avenue. The section of Fourth Avenue from Thirty-fourth Street to Grand Central had been picking up starting in the 1870s. Commodore Vanderbilt's namesake grandson lived at Thirty-fourth Street and Fourth Avenue (later, of course, Park Avenue). The character of the avenue would continue to improve with two houses by Richardson and, later, the Hampden Robb house. In the 1890s, Charles T. Barney would also move there.

WHEN STEWART PLANNED HIS HOTEL as a respectable place for working women, the section of Fourth/Park Avenue he purchased at Thirty-second Street was just below the fashionable area and had foundation problems, owing to the railroad tunnel that ran beneath it. Stewart's hotel site was a difficult one to use, and Kellum gave him a rather ungainly building with big mansard roof. To the press of the day, the concept of Stewart putting up a subsidized or low-profit building for anyone was greeted with disbelief. Stewart died before the cynics' views could be tested. Now fifteen years later, in 1890, the hotel had to have an improved appearance. In the grim winter months, White and the office put on a new portico and fixed up the public spaces to create the Park Avenue Hotel. The architects would redo the hotel again a decade later. The hotel never achieved a major place in the city and has long since been demolished.

The circle of Smith heirs to the Stewart fortune met frequently and with great hope of wealth from 1889 to about 1895, when plans for the future were made and the legal issues were put on a back burner. The income would pour out in 1893, prompting Bessie's two sisters, Kate Wetherill and Ella Emmet, to build near Nellie and Prescott Butler and Stanford and Bessie. The four Smith girls clustered homes either designed or enlarged by Stanford White in 1893 around the Cordwood Path above the harbor in St. James. The four houses, a unique study of a singular family, time, and architect, all stand today as major monuments to the long-awaited fortune, which would never really arrive.

After the flurry of activity in the mid-1890s, the Stewart properties yielded only modest incomes, and Garden City would be lost. The riches of the wealthiest couple in America never really made the Smith family as rich as expected. Hilton's treachery, legal costs, the passage of time, and some family miscalculations left the Stewart heirs unexpectedly poor. Rather like the vision of a waterfall in the desert, the Stewart estate proved to be a mirage.

The course of White's marriage would flow with the dream of wealth in the early years, then close as the dream proved to be faltering. The marriage finally became a forced companionship held in place by convention as each partner developed a romantic world that brought them, separately, comfort. Stanford White became a man on the town, while Bessie spent more and more time in the orbit of her brother-in-law, Prescott Butler, who was, her family believed, the love of her life.

# 29. THE WORLD OF THE PAST

S ince its founding, the United States had boasted a forward-looking culture. Settlers looked to the future as they cleared land and built homes. With rare exceptions, Americans did not begin to contemplate the past until the years after the Civil War, when greater numbers of citizens began to travel to Europe and be introduced to the triumphs of history revered by Europeans as part of their culture. Americans began to recognize that to appear sophisticated, the appreciation of an earlier culture was a requisite part of behavior. As American visitors to the Old World came to admire artifacts, paintings, and buildings done in earlier ages, their eyes also turned to the American past and to the Colonial period in particular. The great collector Ben: Perley Poore had a great influence on McKim, Mead & White as they too began to look to artifacts of the past.

The discovery of Henry Duveen's business above the artists' supply shop, with his Dutch tiles and reproduction Colonial chairs, helped foster the taste for antique furnishings. Indeed, McKim, Mead & White's first good furniture for the reception area at their office was a set of Colonial chairs that the firm valued enough to insure.

Stanford White, with his great decorative sense, absorbed furnishings at an earlier age during his year abroad, but, as his purse was small, he came home with only a few tattered textiles. When he returned to Europe on his honeymoon with a far larger wallet, he was able to buy lavishly, bringing home carpets from Constantinople and many other treasures. Indeed, when Harold Peto visited the Whites' house in 1887, he was impressed with the artifacts he saw there. On his next trips abroad, White would discover he had a taste for antiques that was almost as strong as his love of new experiences. He would buy and buy with an almost uncontrollable appetite, filling his city and country houses with wonders of the past. Indeed, a minor theme of White's life became his obsession with import duties and the Custom House.

In the pre–income tax era, duty at the port was the major source of revenue for the nation, a fact White knew only too well, as his father and Bessie's uncle, Charles Clinch, had been in the Custom House. Bribery by merchants was common, and indeed Charles Clinch was discredited in an 1877 scandal that forced his retirement; the stigma of the accusations may even have hastened his death a few years later. Clinch had probably looked the other way at Stewart's massive textile imports from Manchester, where he was a leading customer, as well as from Parisian and German factories. Through his father White must have been aware of the techniques of pressuring the customs authority and tried many campaigns to go around or reduce the duty assigned to his objects.

Mayor Abram S. Hewitt, who as a Democratic Party leader had taken part in investigations of wrongdoing in the Custom House in 1871, was aware of the favoritism displayed at the Wall Street headquarters of the authority. White wrote many letters to Hewitt, whose house at 9 Lexington Avenue he had decorated in 1887–89, asking for his acquisitions to be given a different status for a different rate. The age of items was a key issue in the process; at the time, older objects were seen as an asset to the nation and given favorable status at the Custom House. White quickly taught his dealers in Europe to claim his items came from the favored periods, so that when the boxes were shipped to New York, they could clear customs easily. White also often made a case for importing antiques as templates for his work or as his "artistic" tools. Painters had been given leeway with props an artist might need for work, an exemption White tried to claim for his own work.

Back in New York by 1888 or so and now living at 56 West Twentieth Street, just around the corner from the city's better decorative suppliers and art importers, White began frequent visits to the newly relocated Duveen headquarters and other importers. Since he was known to be married to a Stewart heir, White was a favored customer for the dealers. With his purchases, he was beginning what would become a full-fledged second career.

By the time of his 1889 trip to the Paris Exposition, White had begun seriously making the rounds of the better antiques showrooms, establishing relationships with dealers in Paris and Florence and with agents as far away as Naples, where Charles C. Coleman was instructed to keep an eye out for items in White's taste. Coleman, an American painter living in Naples, was instructed to buy for White interesting items that came on the market anywhere from Rome to Sicily. He proved a very useful source.

On his 1889 trip, White again carried a letter of credit for a client whose house he was decorating: William Collins Whitney. Whitney would become a major patron of the office and a key figure in the lives of McKim, Mead & White.

William Collins Whitney was born in Conway, Massachusetts, in 1841. He was a typical New Englander of old family but little fortune. Born to a Congregationalist father active in Democratic politics, Whitney began his studies at Yale just before the Civil War, with the class of 1863. At Yale Whitney made two important connections: He met Oliver Hazard Payne and Henry F. Dimock, who would be lifelong figures in his world and would enable the well-born but impoverished Whitney to enter the American baronial class.

Whitney's roommate in his senior year was Oliver Hazard Payne of Cleveland, Ohio. Payne was the son of one of the elite Western Reserve men who had left New England for Ohio to make a fortune. Payne's father had joined John D. Rockefeller's Cleveland-based oil exploration, and the Payne fortune soon blossomed into almost unimaginable sums. Oliver Hazard Payne, Dimock, and Whitney became inseparable at Yale. After graduation, Whitney spent a year at Harvard Law School, then joined Dimock in a legal partnership in New York City, the place of choice for young men on the rise in the 1860s. During the trio's youth, they all met each other's families, with most unusual results: Dimock married Whitney's sister, and Whitney married Flora Payne, sister of Oliver, in 1869.

Will Whitney was tall, handsome, and very bright, but he understood that facilitating success could require a certain amount of corrupt dealings. Flora Payne Whitney was a young woman afflicted with a weak heart, a medical problem she shared with one of her brothers, but she had all the social skills and money needed to launch the couple, now Episcopalians, into the top rung of New York society. Flora's father bought the young couple a house at 74 Park Avenue near the house of another young couple with Ohio connections, Cornelius Vanderbilt and his bride, Alice Gwynne. The Whitneys and Vanderbilts lived in this special section of what was now Park Avenue, just a few blocks south of Grand Central Depot. The house at 74 Park Avenue was designed by McKim's friend Russell Sturgis, who was also a friend of Whitney's.

In the 1870s, Whitney solidified his New York power base with the few members of the gentry who were solid Democrats: Samuel Tilden, August Belmont, and Abram Hewitt. Whitney carefully built up his political and business connections by becoming a close friend of the railroad Vanderbilt just down the street. Both Whitney and the Paynes had aspirations to the presidency. To gain some Washington experience, Whitney gave a twenty-thousand-dollar campaign gift to Grover Cleveland, using Flora's family money. He was promptly given the position of secretary of the navy, for which he was totally unprepared. Will and Flora moved to Washington, where they became known as the city's most charming hosts, but his career was cut short after he decided to oust a long-term major supplier of the U.S. Navy. The action brought criticism to Whitney, particularly from Whitelaw Reid, the editor of the *New York Tribune* and a friend of Whitney's. Stung, Flora and

*W. C. Whitney, one of the most colorful and corrupt of the late nineteenth-century monied men. His life is a perfect exemplar of the Gilded Age.*

Will returned to New York and to the house doting matchmaker Oliver Payne had bought for them at 2 West Fifty-seventh Street, directly across the street from the new house Cornelius and Alice Gwynne Vanderbilt were building, keeping the two men neighbors. The Whitneys' house had been built by Frederick Stevens, the man who had hired McKim, Mead & White to decorate his newly purchased Newport house at this moment. Perhaps the sale of the huge city house inspired the lavish decoration of the Newport house. The Whitneys had made a modest show of redoing the Stevens house in 1883, but on their return from Washington in 1889 they began contemplating a major redecoration. Naturally enough, Oliver Payne offered to pay for the redecoration, and Stanford White was asked to carry it out. The redecoration bills in the firm's bill books are for an expenditure of fifty thousand dollars, but biographies of Whitney suggest it was four times that sum. Whitney asked White to personally shop for him on the trip of 1889—which may account for the difference in price.

The Whitneys had clever children, great promise, and plenty of money, but it came with a price. Will felt a fair amount of discomfort in living off Payne family money, so he set out to make his own fortune. Using his political and Vanderbilt connections, he set up a New York street railway company—the Metropolitan Street Railway—with the young Thomas Fortune Ryan and the Philadelphia Widener family. Whitney, now more eager to make money than to be president, worked the politicians to make the street railroad possible. He avoided overt bribery, instead handing out huge legal fees to those whose help he needed or offering insider tips on the stock market. With his partners Whitney was able to create the cable cars of New York City; the Cable Building by McKim, Mead & White still stands at Houston Street and Broadway.

Flush with success, Whitney began a career as a stock waterer, surpassing Morgan and Vanderbilt in audacity. He drained the railway company monies into his own pocket. For a decade Whitney was able to live like royalty, watering stock and bribing politicians in more and more overt ways until his empire came crashing down with his death in 1904. As Whitney's ploys became more obvious, many old friends, particularly Abram Hewitt, turned on him, viewing him as hopelessly corrupt.

During the days when Whitney lived it up, he did so with great style. He loved the opera and music, and often entertained with wonderful concerts in the house at Fifty-seventh Street. The Stevens-Whitney house was so large that Will invited the confirmed bachelor Oliver Payne to live in an apartment within the house. Payne may have asked Stanford White for some help decorating this apartment, but it would have been done privately, as there is no record of a commission.

In 1893 tragedy struck: Flora's weak heart gave out and she died, leaving three teenage children and a young daughter. The Paynes and Will mourned for the expected three years. By 1896 Will was madly in love with the beautiful Edith May Randolph, a Baltimore-born widow who was the sister of James Gordon Bennett's fiancée decades earlier. Edith's sister, Caroline May, had been the subject of the antisocial living-room behavior on New Year's Day that had forced Bennett to Paris. Edith May had a second odd connection to the story. She had been aboard Thomas Garner's yacht when it capsized, drowning Garner, his wife, and others. Miss May survived the boating disaster that killed Sidney Stratton's friends and in which the sailing trophy made by the young Saint-Gaudens for the New York Yacht Club was lost.

Edith May was far too beautiful for Will Whitney to resist. In 1896, after the proper period of mourning for Flora, he married Edith. Oliver Payne, still very much affected by his sister's death and well aware that Whitney and Edith had been romantically involved before Flora's last illness had begun, became enraged over Whitney's remarriage, especially to a woman who had caused Flora such misery. Their great friendship was severed, and they may even have become mortal enemies. Payne demanded that Whitney's three children abandon their father and champion the memory of their late mother—in return for becoming his financial heir. The wedge Payne created was permanent and did sever the Whitney family: Two children went to Oliver Payne's camp, while two remained with their father.

Whitney could not bring his second wife into Flora's house, so he gave the Stevens-Whitney house to his son Harry, who would bring to it his bride, the daughter of Cornelius and Alice Vanderbilt from across the street. For his own new bride, a great horsewoman, William Collins Whitney purchased a house at

*871 Fifth Avenue, the Robert Stuart mansion before Stanford White transformed it into a palace for W. C. Whitney.*

871 Fifth Avenue, across from Central Park. The house had been rented for some years to Levi P. Morton, a vice president and governor who had invited Whitney there as a guest. It had been built some fifteen years earlier for Robert L. Stuart, the sugar manufacturer, whose previous house was now the headquarters of the decorative arts trade at Twentieth Street.

Oliver Payne moved out of the Fifty-seventh Street house, taking a long-term lease on the "little" Havemeyer house on Fifth Avenue at Sixty-sixth Street, just two blocks below Whitney's house.* In what was a pattern of the day, both Payne and Whitney had McKim, Mead & White work on their houses, with the commissions going to Stanford White in each case. That the two men were at war and had to be seated far apart in club dining rooms did not extend to decoration. White worked for the truly wealthy Payne at a grand scale, and for the now sliding-back-down Whitney, whose finances were compromised by his rate of spending, White truly was in the major league. The firm records reveal that Whitney paid close to a million dollars for the wing on the existing house and the interiors. Moreover, as he had done since 1889, White went shopping for

---

*The Havemeyer family built two houses on Fifth Avenue, living in the larger house with its amazing Tiffany-designed interior. The famous Havemeyer painting collections were in the big house.

*The Whitney house, rebuilt in 1897–1902, with its new entry porch from the Palazzo Doria in Rome. Whitney would die here.*

Whitney, turning the house with its spoils from Europe into one of the architect's most sumptuous works.

For Whitney and a growing list of clients, White was now becoming known not only as a skilled architect but as a purveyor of image and connection. He was buying historical detail from European houses, a novelty to the self-proclaimed barons of the American nouveaux riches. White gave the captains of industry ammunition for social climbing by putting a pedigreed fireplace, ceiling, or wrought-iron fence into an American house for its new owner to brag about.

Following the trip of 1889 for Whitney's Fifty-seventh Street house, White found a new venue. He was discovering the agents used by the New York dealers and was able to go directly to the French, Italian, and Spanish dealers for items. White met the dealers and gave the European houses an idea of the type of things he wanted to buy for himself and his clients. He also warned the dealers about the policies of the New York Custom House and how to label shipments so as to avoid duties. As White's practice at buying treasures in Europe grew, he began to move about more, using one dealer and appearing to be loyal to that supplier while looking for another agent who might offer him a better buy.

His relationship with Stefano Bardini of Florence was a fine case in point. White probably became aware of Bardini while on his honeymoon. The next year in Paris, there was a large sale of Bardini's collections, which White would likely have heard about in New York from the dealers there. The sale would have reinforced his sense that virtually all kinds of material goods from the past were available for sale and transport across the Atlantic. Bardini, whose taste in collecting was varied, as was White's, had in his palazzo on the Via de' Mozzi in Florence a wide range of items including architectural fragments, furniture, tomb slabs, pulpits, chimneypieces, columns, picture frames, textiles, paintings, and sculpture. White may well have formed his eclectic taste after visiting the Palazzo

Bardini.* White worked with Bardini for twenty years, buying Tuscan and Italian Renaissance furniture, sculpture, decorative pieces, and such. He would receive a discount on purchases, and if a sale for a client was directly negotiated with Bardini or another dealer, White would get a commission. He began to play with his dealers, asking for extra discounts and even going around a loyal contact to look for another man in town who would give him a better deal. At one point White sneaked into Florence to see Arthur Mario Acton, an English antiquarian dealer of mysterious background. He began to work closely with Acton, who would marry a wealthy Chicagoan, Hortense Mitchell, at the beginning of the twentieth century. White would then not let Bardini know he was in Italy.

European dealers such as Bardini would play tricks on White as well. Bardini was trained as an artist and ran a "restoration studio" for his pieces in Florence. There is probably an issue of authenticity in the works he sold to White, as Bardini may also have sold high-quality partial or full forgeries. Recognizing that White bought impulsively by eye but did not have connoisseurship training, Bardini might take one good leg of a four-legged table and reproduce it into four, creating a new table with only one real leg. The dealers often did this trick of "marrying" antique furniture with replicated parts. Indeed, recognizing that Americans demanded pieces that looked new even if they were old, dealers had taken to "restoring" works by supplying modern versions of missing parts. In addition to cleaned-up antiques and married pieces, some dealers even sold Americans—including Stanford White—fully modern work billed as antique. There was said to be a man in Paris who could duplicate medieval woodwork, producing modern pieces that fooled almost everyone. There were similar men in Italy who could make most effective restorations, which dealers might sell as old work to naïve American customers. The nephew of Henry Duveen, Joseph Duveen, may have participated in such sales or been aware of them.

Yet another commodity that White could import was the period room. With urban change and railroad expansion, some older houses were scheduled for or appeared to be candidates for demolition. Entire rooms were taken out of these houses and sold to the Rothschilds in Britain and to numerous Americans.

White began his buying career as an amusement before becoming more

---

*Bardini's palazzo and the remains of his collection may be seen by the visitor to Florence as the Museo Bardini.

serious about purchasing for himself and for clients. By the end of the century, White would enter a new phase, buying desperately as he sought a solution to his increasing financial instability. The last years saw him shamelessly manipulating his friends to make profits on his sale of antiques. White's career shift to dealer almost overwhelmed his architecture practice. Though he was known as the creator of interiors for a number of palatial houses, there was a small group who did not like White's taste or effects. To Edith Wharton and her friends Ogden Codman, Henry James, and Henry Adams, White was too flamboyant and not erudite enough. He had not lived in Europe as long as they had, nor was he knowledgeable enough about history to sit comfortably with such sophisticates. To these patricians, White was the designer for the new rich. Indeed, some major creators of grand American houses totally ignored him.

McKim, too, flirted briefly with antiquarian elements. When he worked on the pulpit of New York City's Church of the Ascension in 1885, he based his decoration on forms from a piece of Gothic ornament he bought from Henry Duveen. McKim was not acquisitive by nature, and he would not purchase much in the future. He did buy a reproduction Georgian silver pitcher on a trip to England and some American pieces for his dining room at Dr. Hitchcock's house on West Thirty-fifth Street, which was decorated heavily with Julia Appleton's effects. As McKim aged he cared less for objects and traveled abroad as a scholar rather than a shopper. William Mead seems to have had no interest in objects and was not known as a collector. At McKim, Mead & White, it was only White who loved to shop.

# 30. BACK AT THE OFFICE

The crowded drafting room at 57 Broadway was truly bursting at its seams, but the firm was still capable of bringing in immense amounts of work. For a grand client, the rickety afterthought of a cage elevator did not present an auspicious overture to the office of America's now-leading architectural firm. Yet the older architects who had led the profession, H. H. Richardson and Hunt, had been replaced by this trio who were just over and under the age of forty. Richardson had succumbed to kidney failure in 1886, and Hunt, afflicted by gout, was aging and pretty much out of creative energy. It was now McKim, Mead & White's time for being the center of the profession.

Some clients did not make the trek to the actual office, as McKim, Mead & White had a number of repeat customers who provided commissions without having to be freshly sold on the merits of the firm. The New York Life Insurance Company kept sending work, which Mead handled. The work brought money to the office and was generally rather routine. The firm supplied some row house designs for East 107th Street and worked over two early apartment houses New York Life had invested in at 1054 Fourth Avenue, at the southwest corner of Sixty-second Street, where the architects had to virtually replace a multiple dwelling unit, Holbrook Hall, with a seven-story apartment house, the Yosemite. These early apartment houses are long gone (demolished in 1916). The insurance company asked the architects to create a silken purse out of the Plaza property, but would continue to rebuild their New York City headquarters under the direction of Stephen D. Hatch, a commercial architect of an

*The New York Life Insurance investment apartment*
*house, the Yosemite, 1887–90. Demolished.*

earlier era. The New York Life headquarters were in a long, narrow street
that ran east from Broadway just above City Hall. The insurance compa-
nies were located around City Hall on Broadway at that time, and New
York Life had an earlier building that they were rebuilding and enlarging.
In 1894 Hatch died, and New York Life turned this building over to
McKim, Mead & White, who would finish the earlier building and give it
grand public spaces, a clock tower, and a directors' room. When New
York Life decided to move northward to the streets above Madison Square,
the company turned to Cass Gilbert, who had begun his career with
McKim, Mead & White. For New York Life Gilbert would tear down the
masterpiece of his dead friend Stanford White, but would insert the old
directors' room into the new building in 1926–28. The old New York Life
at 346 Broadway still stands, owned today by New York City.

THE PARTNERS CONTINUED to be absorbed in club life both socially
and professionally. McKim altered the Jerome mansion at Twenty-sixth
Street for his own club, the University Club. The alteration was begun in
1889 and continued for several years.

Stanford White was asked to redo the public spaces at James Gordon Bennett Jr.'s club, the venerable Union Club. In 1890 a fire at Christmas had ruined the dining room and hall. Though not then a member of the club, White was very much a neighbor, living on Twentieth Street just one block south of the Union Club and working on the same block. Was White selected for his interior talents, or did the erratic Bennett, who spent his days and evenings in New York exclusively at the club, promote White? In any case, White redid the interiors in a French manner, an early venture into the French styles of the later Renaissance. The rooms were done up in a manner that was far from sumptuous, as at this time club rooms were still expected to be friendly and not overly decorated environments. This would soon change at the Metropolitan Club, which would bring club-room décor up to the same grand level as that of the finest houses of the day.

Just as the designs for the Union Club rooms were being considered, the office finally decided that the overcrowding at 57 Broadway could no longer be tolerated. On May 1, 1891, McKim, Mead & White jumped the miles from Manhattan's tip to the floors of 1 West Twentieth Street, where White had camped for almost a year. Both Mead and McKim lived above Washington Square, although not just down the block as did White. The office practice would fit in well with the decorative arts dealers who had a strong identity in the neighborhood. The old center of architectural prac-

*James Gordon Bennett Jr.'s yacht, the* Namouna. *Julius L. Stewart's painting shows one of many boats decorated by Stanford White.*

tice, long believed to be best located in the Wall Street district, had vanished and moved uptown. The three partners decided to work beside the galleries and designers, not the Pinkerton Detective Agency. One reason for the move to Twentieth Street was that a big commission had come into the office in June 1890 for a new building for James Gordon Bennett Jr.'s *New York Herald*. The office had worked with Bennett for more than a decade, but the new building was to be large and elaborate, and the project would put a strain on the office staff in tight quarters. The office gave up its venerable home and moved to James Gordon Bennett's own neighborhood.

James Gordon Bennett Jr. carried on his father's paper with aplomb. He also continued to maintain his father's New York City residences and real estate investments. Unfortunately, Jamie Bennett carried on his father's pugnacious behavior and his mother's alcoholism as well. Bennett's infamous rejection of conformity in Caroline May's parlor had forced him to Newport and ultimately to Paris. When his parents' marriage had failed, Bennett and his sister were taken to France by his mother, so he felt comfortable living in that country. Bennett came back to the United States often in the 1880s, although less frequently later on. Thanks to managers carrying out telegraphed orders, Bennett was able to run the paper and the real estate investments from Paris.

On his return trips to New York Bennett lived at his father's house at 425 Fifth Avenue, which he kept until 1896. He had also bought a house on Twenty-first Street near the Union Club, where he spent all his time when he was in the city of his birth. It does not seem that Bennett ever really lived at 28 West Twenty-first Street, although it was mercifully close to the club for a rest after a long drunken night. In 1887 he had Stanford White spend an enormous amount of money on the house interior—almost forty thousand dollars—though it is difficult to determine what was actually done.

The Twenty-first Street house may have been divided up into the proverbial bachelor flats, as several single men lived in the house at different times. The primary tenant, however, was Hermann Oelrichs, of the German family from Bremen who ran the Lloyd Company's shipping business in the United States. The Oelrichs family had settled in Baltimore and quickly became part of America's elite through good marriages and a dash of culture. In Baltimore, Hermann Oelrichs had married Miss May, yet another member of the beautiful blond family to which Caroline May belonged. Hermann Oelrichs's move into Bennett's house at 28 West Twenty-first Street did present a curious dilemma. How could the May family, whose handsome son Frederick had seemingly fought a duel for the honor of his sister with Jamie Bennett in 1877, allow a May girl, now Oelrichs, to live in Bennett's house? Was there some sort of deal between Fred May and Bennett that might explain the lack of injuries in the duel and the enemy in Bennett's house?

Bennett and White had much in common in the 1880s: Each was a member of the club elite, and each carried on in the late night hours with drink and adventure. The two men shared the same social world and friends and even used the same attorneys to keep them out of trouble— Howe & Hummel—but they probably did not spend their evenings together. Bennett did call on White for two other interior reworkings before the Union Club redecoration and the new Herald Building. In 1884 he had asked White to do a major interior renovation of his building on Ann Street at Fulton. This speculatively built, seven-story iron-fronted structure had been created by the respectable architect Arthur Gilman in 1873 as a family real estate venture. Bennett would have White redo the public spaces, probably as an attempt to prop up rents in a building going out of style on what was becoming an out-of-the-way block. White's $21,500 alteration may have included an elevator, which the eleven-year-old building lacked.

Bennett seemed glued to the Twenty-first Street neighborhood even in 1885. He did not like to go far from the friendly environment of the Union Club, so he asked White to fit up a small private office for him in the Western Union Building, just completed at Twenty-third Street and Fifth Avenue only two blocks above the Union. Joseph Cabus provided the cabinets for that office.

Bennett enjoyed boats and seems to have kept one his entire life. In 1882 he had asked White to decorate the *Polyana* for a modest flat fee— but in 1885 White was asked to do a serious decoration of the *Namouna*, including Cabus woodwork, installation of "antique" fireplaces in the cabins, and some Aesthetic taste features. There is a painting of the *Namouna* in the collection of the Wadsworth Atheneum at Hartford, and an illustration of the cabin appeared in *The Century*.

When Bennett's father began the *Herald,* he understood the value of a tabloid paper for the bored public. For a long period of time the *Herald* owned the market niche for a gossip-laced paper, and the younger Bennett continued this tradition. If a rival paper attempted to compete with them in sensationalism, Bennett would dispatch a reporter to "make" news, as he did when sending Stanley after Livingstone or sending the *Jeannette* into the ice. His papers also reported on New York's social scene with a liberal dose of scandal. Though the *Herald*'s gossip was served on a daily schedule, Bennett had an inner circle who were not considered fair game. To keep life friendly in his only refuge in the city, Union Club members were excluded from mention. Also sacred were his old friends the Lorillards, as well as the Vanderbilts and Astors. Stanford White would be in the protected category too—he belonged to the Union Club, even though he never went there—until the end when Bennett, in an effort to generate massive newspaper sales, let his dogs loose. Bennett turned on White, the man he had asked to design his crazed mausoleum on the bluffs of Washington Heights, where his father had lived. From Paris, Bennett had worked with White on a huge owl in which his remains would be placed and hung two hundred feet high suspended on two steel chains. Bennett, who hated former president Ulysses S. Grant, demanded that the owl with its beacon eye be bigger and more prominent than Grant's tomb on the Hudson bluffs. Bennett's owl would never be built.

Bennett disliked rivals and dispatched them when he could. By the end of the 1880s rival papers such as the *World,* built by the Hungarian immigrant Joseph Pulitzer, had established a firm position in the city's singular newspaper district, the eastern border of City Hall Park on Park Row. To celebrate the success of the *World,* Pulitzer had George B. Post build for him one of the tallest buildings in the city; a replica of the dome of St. Peter's—of course, reduced in scale—crowned the lavish building. Bennett had to upstage Pulitzer. Within months of the completion of Pulitzer's building, Bennett had asked Stanford White to create a new Herald Building.

Bennett's decision was daring as he asked for his newspaper headquarters to be built away from "newspaper row." Bennett, who worked by cable, recognized that telegraph and telephone would free newspapers from direct sources of news and that a newspaper could be published miles above City Hall. Since Bennett had no heirs to enrich, he did not buy a new site for the third Herald Building, but instead took a thirty-year lease on a site at Sixth Avenue on the elevated line at Thirty-fifth Street. The site had been briefly an armory, but was now available. The location was an odd one, as that stretch of Sixth Avenue and Broadway was an extension of the popular music district known as Tin Pan Alley. Bennett, who might well have frequented the music halls of the street, may have decided that the location would be fun for his paper, as tourists could walk by the newspaper on a tour of Manhattan's night life district. Bennett also saw that the nearby elevated transit system would give his reporters the flexibility to cover news uptown or downtown rapidly.

*The Herald Building of 1890–95, which, although gone, gave its name
to the area of the city where it briefly stood.*

To skeptics, Bennett's selection of a site miles above newspaper row was insane. They also argued that the expiration of the lease in thirty years' time would leave the newspaper in difficulties, but Bennett countered, "Thirty years from now the *Herald* will be in Harlem and I'll be in hell."

White and Bennett met to discuss the new Herald Building. Bennett, modestly, wanted to attach the imagery of the Doge's Palace in Venice to his paper. He seems to have had a penchant for the louche life he associated with the Adriatic city. For Thirty-fifth Street, Bennett wanted a low-scale building that would rival Pulitzer not in height but in style. White, stung by having his sources discovered by an increasingly sophisticated and well-traveled population, finally convinced Bennett to let him base the new building on a less well-known building, the Loggia del Consiglio in Verona. The selection of the model for Bennett's Herald Building was also surely a private joke on White's part, rather like his choice for the model for the Century Association clubhouse. White selected the Loggia del Consiglio, a late fifteenth-century seat of the local city council, as his model, not a palace of the Renaissance prince Bennett had wished to evoke. The Veronese council building sits in a square dedicated to Dante and is adorned at the top with statues of famous citizens including the ancient Roman poet Catullus, known for his earthy and sometimes obscene poems. Surely White was making a jab at the plebeian nature of Bennett's newspaper and the lewdness of its financially successful advertisements. The Bennetts, father and son, had thrived off revenue from scandalous ads.

After two years of discussion and preparation, the new Herald Building was begun in 1892 and completed three years later. The newspaper headquarters was constructed by the firm of David H. King Jr. and clad in Atlantic terra-cotta. The building, with its subtle colors and elaborate detail, was very much noticed, and its acclaim gave the corner a new name. The oddly shaped site became known as Herald Square, an identity that survives today, almost a century after the Herald Building was demolished.

Although the Herald Building was based on the the Loggia del Consiglio, it is not a literal copy. The architectural designs now emerging from the McKim, Mead & White offices were heavily based on prototypes found in Europe and viewed on visits or, more often, seen secondhand in book plates in the expanding office library and in photographs now easily obtained from commercial photography houses such as Alinari. Though models such as the Loggia del Consiglio may be clearly visible in the executed building, the McKim, Mead & White buildings always differ from the originals. They are given different detail to fit the new building into its site and to provide the architects an opportunity to display their decorative flair. Stanford White, particularly, would work this way: He would pencil in changes to the model, then "redecorate" the prototype with his adaptation of Renaissance forms, creating a "new" old building for the United States. The message being given was that the power of the Old World building was being transferred to the New World, where it was adapted for its new home in a safe and erudite way. To White and many of his clients, the United States was now the inheritor of European culture, and the new princes of business would absorb and be inspired by the achievements of European history then placed on American soil. Such transplantation would create a rich new artistic flowering. Stanford White believed that he was not copying a building, but cultivating a fertile new entity to grow in the United States. His Renaissance buildings may have had roots in the past, but they were always modern.

The new, old buildings that McKim, Mead & White were designing always included all the new technical innovations possible. The buildings were equipped with modern heating systems, elevators, plate glass windows, and, in the case of houses, built-in closets. One of White's pet peeves was the insistence of his women clients on internal, built-in closets, but he agreed to do them. The work of McKim, Mead & White in the last third of their career would be highly derivative in appearance, but always aware of the technological innovations of the era.

Like the Flatiron Building on its triangular site, the Herald Building occupied an angle created by Sixth Avenue and the diagonal of Broadway. But instead of creating a triangular building, White designed a trapezoid set back from the corner. The narrow front of the building faced south and had a five-arched arcade, within which was the door to Bennett's occasional office. The entrance led to a circular space with a staircase on an axis. Bennett, an inveterate stair climber, would run up the steps to the office on his visits to the building. As a form of self-promotion and public relations, he insisted that the great presses be placed on the Broadway side of the building, one floor below ground but within a double-height space, so passersby could watch the presses run through the big windows under the arcade. In rain or snow, the public could huddle under the arcade and be reminded of the paper's presence.

Bennett brought his own iconography to the Herald Building and he had his chance to evoke a Venetian reference. The bronze bell ringers were inspired by those atop the great clock tower at the Piazza of St. Mark. In Paris he commissioned a figure of Minerva, the goddess of wisdom, to stand atop the roof with the bell ringers. While purporting to be a symbol of the paper, she also justified his personal obsession with owls, since owls were an attribute of Minerva.

Bennett believed that an owl's call had saved him during the Civil War, so he made that bird his personal symbol. The eaves of the Herald Building had a regular flock of bronze owls wired for electric lightbulbs. At night, the light from their eyes created an eerie presence. Two clocks showing the time in New York and Paris were also embedded in the façade.

Although the newspaper is long gone (it lingers as the *International Herald Tribune* in Paris), the French-made bronze features of the building survive. The figure of Minerva and the bell ringers known as Stuff and Guff sit atop a triumphal arch with the clocks in the small triangular park where Bennett once dashed into his buildings. The owls were moved to Shimkin Hall at New York University, but without the electric lights in their eyes. Two lovely owls from the building now greet visitors to the Brooklyn Museum.

A COLLEAGUE OF BENNETT'S who was also a continuing client of McKim, Mead & White was Whitelaw Reid. His large alteration and decoration commissions came into the office at the same time as the Herald Building. In June 1890, Reid asked the office to carry out residential work for him on three properties. The work was given to Stanford White.

Reid may well have known Miller McKim, as he had covered the Civil War for an Ohio newspaper and been a staunch supporter of the abolitionist cause. He came to New York in 1868 with Horace Greeley, the dynamic editor of Bennett's rival, the *Tribune.* Reid worked well with Greeley, helped him in his unsuccessful bid for the presidency in 1872, and remained at the paper after Greeley's final illness and death. In 1882 he married Elisabeth Mills, the daughter of Darius Ogden Mills, who had made a fortune in the American West before establishing himself in New York. Mills bought the paper and immediately made Reid its editor. The Mills fortune allowed the couple to purchase Henry Villard's New York town house in November 1886 for $350,000, so that McKim, Mead & White could carry on with their work there. In 1887 the Reids bought Ophir Farm in Purchase, New York, a large, ungainly, medievalizing country mansion built by the notorious railroad builder Ben Holladay, whose failure had been a major force in the great stock market collapse of 1873. The Reids may have wished to concentrate on the city house before beginning work on Ophir Hall, as they renamed it, but a fire there in the summer of 1888 precipitated the renovation project. After the fire, the

Reids had a commercial architect, E. Raht, begin to rebuild, but Mr. Reid probably insisted on grander architects.

The Mills money allowed the Reids not only to manage two houses at the same time, but also to move beyond journalism. By the time that Ophir Hall burned, Reid was in Paris as the U.S. minister to France. In 1892 Reid ran on Benjamin Harrison's presidential ticket and lost, but he would later be rewarded for his party loyalty. His last seven years were spent as ambassador to Great Britain.

Reid was too busy and important to manage Stanford White's work, but Elisabeth Mills Reid did play a role in the decision-making process. At the Villard house, White brought in John La Farge to create two large oil canvases for the lunettes of the unfinished music room. He had a great regard for La Farge and respected his artistic judgment, though La Farge was a difficult man and often fought with others. In this case a row developed when White switched the music room's color scheme to gold and white, effectively ruining La Farge's painting work. La Farge was not asked to work at Ophir Hall. Instead, the commission for the ceiling mural was given to a young artist whom everyone seemed to admire, Dennis Miller Bunker. Then Bunker died suddenly. The mural was taken over by the young Frederick MacMonnies, who was then striving to be a sculptor and had studied with Saint-Gaudens. As the story goes, MacMonnies did not do the painting himself but took the design back to Paris, where Parisian painters, then out on a strike against the government, executed the work. A professional muralist, George Maynard, did the mural for the library.

The Reids saw their New York house as an effective stage for Whitelaw Reid's career. In 1891 they decided the elaborately inlaid woodwork of the triple drawing room was out of style. It had been made by Joseph Cabus under the direction of George Fletcher Babb and was rather German in its appearance, with inlay containing both Henry and Fanny Villard's initials. It was replaced by White with a more French interior, the look now preferred by wealthy Americans.

Nevertheless, the Reids recognized the splendid work done by Cabus and his men. They therefore had the architects remove the panels and install them in the main-floor rooms of Ophir Hall. The work there was overseen by two young talents in the office, H. Van Buren Magonigle and Lionel Moses, while the Reids were absent.

An article written by Magonigle years later gives an account of the work at Ophir Hall. The story may have been a bit embellished in the telling, but the article does provide an account of White's working habits when the

*The Pierre Lorillard house at Tuxedo Park, 1887–91.*
*Never a success for either architect or client.*

money flowed and the client was away.

In the early 1890s Purchase was still remote, and the architects had to travel by rail to White Plains, then take a horse and buggy to the house. A horse called Walter was hired for the ride there. Magonigle evidently dreaded the ride, as Walter liked to gallop downhill, terrifying most riders. When White made one of his inspection trips, Walter duly flew down the first hill. But instead of expressing fear, White jumped up, leaned forward, and urged Walter to go even faster. After the adrenaline rush of the ride, White inspected the elaborate coffers for the drawing-room ceiling. For the intersection of the coffers, Magonigle had designed rosettes, which were at this point hanging from the ceiling, ready for fixing. Already in a state of excitement, White called out for a ladder and hammer, jumped up on the ladder, swung wildly, and knocked the rosettes to the ground, where they smashed to bits. Magonigle admitted White's hammer improved the design, but the wild spree damaged the ceiling coffers and made a mess. The workmen thought White was "loony."

Ophir Hall survives today as the center of Manhattanville College. Its spectacular interior is belied by the dour, gray, medievalizing exterior of stone inherited from Holladay's house. The awkward castellated style of Ophir Hall matched the original house. Yet White also used it for other commissions, with the same unfortunate results. An example is the medievalizing castle built in 1887 for Pierre Lorillard in Lorillard's new planned elite community, Tuxedo Park.

Pierre Lorillard's fortune came from snuff and tobacco. He had had a summer house in Newport designed by Peabody & Stearns and called the Breakers. Lorillard was a horse fancier and had other properties near racecourses. Finding that Newport did not suit him, Lorillard sold the Breakers to Cornelius and Alice Vanderbilt and bought an undeveloped tract of hilly lakeside land about an hour northwest of New York. Lorillard intended the property for development as a private and gated compound with a central club facility: a cross between Hartshorn's Short Hills and Stewart's Garden City. Those considered for Tuxedo Park would have to be of a correct social standing.

The key ingredient for all these planned communities was a rail link to New York. There was no station in the early days, but Lorillard secured a train stop outside the gate. He would hop off, often accompanied by Bruce Price, a talented and well-connected architect with a sense of style rather like White's. Price designed many of the houses at Tuxedo Park in a late and fine shingle-clad resort style. Photographs of Price's houses there were pasted in the McKim, Mead & White office scrapbooks. And yet, when Lorillard and his wife Caroline commissioned their own baronial house, he asked White (whom he probably knew through Jamie Bennett and Robert Goelet) to design it. The outcome slightly resembled Bennett's Newport house, the Stone Villa, perhaps at Lorillard's request. A stone castellated house with shingle-covered projections, set on the highest point of the Ramapo Hills in Tuxedo Park, it was not a success. White was probably not pleased with it himself as it does not appear in the firm's picture books. Lorillard complained that the windows leaked in a heavy rain, despite attempts to line the sills in copper to prevent water damage.

White did not build again for Lorillard, though later, in 1902, he did design lavish New York showrooms for the American Tobacco Company's Havana Tobacco Company at 1137 Broadway. Lorillard lived on at Tuxedo Park where he managed to create an inward-looking "suburban" community for an upper-class population who liked a country-like setting. The houses are set in the woods without lawns and avoid the sense of tamed nature one expects in a suburb. The restricted community, where style was set by Lorillard and Frank Gray Griswold, long continued to thrive despite the scandal when Caroline Lorillard was found dead in her bathroom one night in 1909 after a party she had attended with Pierre. The couple must have had a fight before she went to bed. Pinned to her undergarments was a white envelope containing her own old, modest jewelry, which she had before she married her rich husband. A note supposedly explaining her suicide was also attached but was never opened to the public. She may have killed herself by turning on the gas jets.

# 31. EVARTS, THE BUTLERS, CHOATE, AND BEAMAN

I n the circle of McKim, Mead & White from its early days had been a
law firm started a few years before them. Like the architectural firm,
the practice was a partnership—then a recent development in both
the legal profession and architecture. With offices in modest buildings
just three blocks from each other at Wall Street, the law firm grew in size
and importance along with the architects, and the close relationship was
maintained from the 1870s through the 1890s.

The law office began with Charles E. Butler and William Maxwell
Evarts in 1842. Evarts was a Bostonian by birth who had taken a degree at
Yale before an apprenticeship in the law office of Horace Everett in Windsor, Vermont. After a year there, Evarts set up practice briefly with Daniel
Lord, a major New York lawyer at the time, and then went into partnership with Butler. A decade later the austere Charles F. Southmayd joined
the practice. The partners were active after the Civil War. Evarts was
involved in the impeachment case against President Johnson and in the
Hayes-Tilden election case. He rose to be secretary of state under President Hayes, Mead's cousin.

It is impossible to pin down all the personal interconnections. McKim,
as has been said, had met Prescott Butler at Harvard, but their friendship
did not bloom until they lived next door to each other in 1875. Miller
McKim may have known Evarts through abolitionist cases he had handled
or through Mead and President Hayes. Perhaps the major connection was
Saint-Gaudens, who had met Evarts while still an impoverished sculpture

student in Rome and made a bust of him in 1872–74. Evarts was able to introduce Saint-Gaudens to his friends, who gave commissions to the young artist. He owned a farm on Paradise Heights, in Windsor, Vermont, as a country home for his large family.

In 1879, an attorney who had worked with Evarts on the Alabama Claims Commission in Geneva, became a partner. This was Charles Cotesworth Beaman. Born in 1840 in Maine, Beaman was the high-minded son of a Congregational minister; he went to Harvard and then settled in New York. During the summers Beaman visited Evarts in Windsor, and he bought a large farm in nearby Cornish, New Hampshire, when he married his partner's daughter, Hattie Evarts, in 1874. Known as Blow Me Down Farm, the place was home to the Beamans from early July through September and greatly loved by the family.

C. C. Beaman was kindly as well as able; though he made a great success of the law, it never affected his behavior. He belonged to the clubs, but did not go to them, preferring life at home and with people he truly cared for. Like the Butlers, he gave McKim work early in his career. In 1878, McKim added a mansard-topped extra floor to Beaman's Manhattan house at 27 East Twenty-first Street, and he made further alterations a year later. McKim probably also designed Beaman's modest house at Wave Crest, Far Rockaway (a speculation on the Atlantic side of Long Island involving Beaman and various partners), as well as a rental unit for Beaman there. Beaman knew E. N. Dickerson, who was both a business partner and neighbor at the inlet called Wave Crest. Dickerson, Beaman, and, a few years later, John Cowdin all spent the first weeks of June and last weeks of summer at Far Rockaway.

Over the course of his friendship with McKim and Saint-Gaudens, Beaman came to know White, George Babb, and Joe Wells, all of whom came to Cornish to visit in the summer. In 1885, he also lured Saint-Gaudens there, renting him a parcel of his property with an old brick tavern that could be used for a house. The connection probably

*Augustus Saint-Gaudens. A close friend of the architects, he lived life to the fullest. He often wore a beard. At the time this photograph was taken, he was balancing his life between two families.*

*Joseph Choate, the silver-tongued attorney and diplomat who knew McKim for most of his life. Choate beat back the concept of income taxes in the 1890s.*

came through his wife, Augusta Homer, whose family knew Evarts and Beaman from Boston. Saint-Gaudens was at first tentative about Cornish, but in 1891 he took up Beaman's offer to buy the place he called Aspet, which the sculptor came to love.

By 1886, a small summer artists' colony had evolved at Cornish, with the muralist George de Forest Brush in a teepee pitched at the edge of Saint-Gaudens's property and Thomas Wilmer Dewing close by. Saint-Gaudens eventually moved to Aspet full-time, and he died there in 1907. The house was given to the nation. Today a National Park Service site, it is one of the greatest treasures in New England, filled with the works of the sculptor.

Beaman enjoyed inviting, helping, and hiring people. At a time when some of his partners and clients had baronial ambitions, Beaman chose his friends and companions for values other than that of enhancing his career. Among his guests was George Babb, who designed a wonderful shingle-covered mill at the base of the property in 1891, still extant and easily viewed today. Then there was Wells, who designed the Blow Me Down bridge and a casino for the family's recreation. Both of these survive, but the main Beaman house burned down in 1926.

THE FINAL PARTNER in the office was Joseph H. Choate, the ablest trial lawyer in New York. Each man at Evarts, Southmayd & Beaman (later Choate's name was added to the firm) had a specialty. Beaman, a nervous man, solved disputes privately through conciliatory skills. Choate was a great public figure, a natural after-dinner speaker, and a man given the credit for defeating the first effort to establish income tax in the United States. He served as American ambassador to Britain from 1899 to 1905.

Joseph Hodges Choate was almost a generation older than McKim and White, but both knew him well from their early days. He had given the address when White and Saint-Gaudens's Farragut statue was unveiled in Madison Square. They must have met often at the Butlers' house in Stockbridge, where all the legal partners seemed to visit. Southmayd was said

*Joseph Choate house, Naumkeag, in Stockbridge, Massachusetts, 1884–87.*
*This house can be visited thanks to the generosity of Mabel Choate.*

to be fond of Butler's daughter Rosalie, and he was frequently in the
house. Southmayd and Choate rented places in Stockbridge several times.

At about the time McKim met Julia Appleton, Choate decided to purchase land for a permanent summer house and garden at Prospect Hill,
Stockbridge. The planning for a large shingle-covered house for Choate's
family began around Christmas 1884, but the actual building was delayed
a year due to the death of their twenty-one-year-old son, Ruluff Sterling.
The house was built in 1886–87 and called Naumkeag, the American
Indian name for Salem, Massachusetts, where Choate had been born. He
was very proud of his New England heritage. To reinforce his venerable
roots, the house was filled with American antique pieces rather than the
contemporary furniture popular with most wealthy Americans. Consequently, there are just a few touches of high-fashion taste in the house,
such as in the paper of the dining room.

Choate was particularly close to McKim, and eulogized him in a tender
fashion after his death, claiming to have known him since boyhood. So the
Choate house was probably by McKim, with White working on the interiors. It is quite close stylistically to the English Norman Shaw houses,
having twin gables and strips of small-paned windows on the garden side,
and towered Norman features on the entrance front. The Choate house
sums up houses built in the partially shingle-clad manner by the firm over
the previous five years. It is a fine example of how McKim, Mead & White

had fused different elements into an American resort style of great credibility, but it was not innovative. It would seem that the more creative versions of the resort house style were done for newer-money clients. For those who wished to appear better bred, the examples of the resort style are more balanced.

The Choates hired Nathan Barrett to lay out a series of terraced gardens at Naumkeag about 1888. For a garden fountain, McKim suggested that White's friend Frederick MacMonnies provide a figure; this became *Young Faun with Heron.* McKim and White were just then completing a house of similar style for Edward Dean Adams in Red Bank, New Jersey, called Rohallion. It was a much larger version of Naumkeag on flatter land. At Rohallion, MacMonnies created a figure of Pan, which is now in the Metropolitan Museum.

Later, the Choates' daughter Mabel added to the gardens at Naumkeag, hiring Fletcher Steele to create some remarkable instances of twentieth-century garden design. At Miss Choate's death in 1958, the house, furnishings, and gardens were left to the Trustees of Reservations, and they are now open to the public in summer and fall.

Choate and his partners became more closely tied to McKim, Mead & White after 1884, when White married Bessie and became a brother-in-law to McKim's old friend Prescott Hall Butler. McKim had begun and White joined in to assist Butler and his family on the St. James house, which was altered and extended in the year of White's marriage and again a decade later.

Prescott Butler loved the theater and often hosted visiting thespians. One such was Helena Modjeska, the great stage star who had visited the United States several times. In the winter of 1877–78, Modjeska gave a season in New York, where she met Saint-Gaudens, Richard Watson Gilder, Edwin Booth, and Butler. In 1883 she returned to the New York stage in *As You Like It* and cemented her relationship with Butler.* In 1885 her son Rudolphe completed his training as an engineer at the École des Ponts et Chaussées in Paris, where he graduated first in his class. He was later to become famous as the bridge builder Ralph Modjeski. With her son settled, Modjeska went to California, where she bought property twenty-three miles from Santa Ana. Butler asked Stanford White to send out sketches for a house, Arden, which he did in about 1888. Needless to say, no one was overseeing construction, so White's hand was only partly in this work. Mme Modjeska later introduced White to the family of

*Her performance was reviewed by Richard Grant White.

*House for Mme Modjeska in Santa Ana, California. A design given the client by White to carry to a local builder. These generous portable designs made by White probably led to the number of houses attributed to him by modern real estate brokers.*

Maurice Barrymore, who were close friends of hers. In this way the Barrymores were added to White's list of party guests.

THE ARCHITECTS AND ATTORNEYS stayed close to one another as friends, clients, and legal counsel through the 1890s. Indeed, White and Prescott Butler talked of buying a double house together in 1892, but they never followed through on this plan. Butler remained White's attorney and friend until his final illness. It seems probable that he had a romantic association with Bessie, but, if so, White left no record of conflict over their relationship. The Evarts, Butler firm represented McKim, Mead & White in practice-related disputes, such as the two-year-long difficulty with Townsend Burden of the Burden Iron Company, who did not pay his bill until pressured by the attorneys. But for personal legal matters Mead and McKim turned to Mead's classmate at Amherst Dwight Herrick of Peekskill, New York. By the time of Butler's illness, McKim had become friendly with a neighbor on Thirty-fifth Street, John Lambert Cadwalader, a civic-minded attorney. They became best friends, and Cadwalader may well have taken on some of McKim's legal issues.

# 32. STANFORD WHITE'S ARTISTS

S tanford White had begun his career thinking of becoming a painter. He had left his brushes behind by the time he joined McKim and Mead, but he kept up with the painters and sculptors who remained the heart of his social world. They were his preferred companions.

One of the places where White and the artists met was the home of Richard Watson Gilder and his wife. The Gilders had taken as a house a stable at 103 East Fifteenth Street, where they entertained Mme Modjeska and Paderewski as well as many members of the Tile Club. Though not affluent, they asked White as a favor to assist in the conversion, which he offhandedly described as "turning a stable into a high art palace." The date was about 1882. The façade was supposed to contain that symbol of the Aesthetic movement, a peacock, but the bird was abandoned. Nevertheless, the result was rich and artistic enough to prefigure the role the Players club would have a decade later. All artists were received: painters, actors, musicians, writers, and their admirers. The Gilders had White as a frequent guest as well as Saint-Gaudens, Albert Pinkham Ryder, Will Low, Frank Lathrop, and many others, including Thomas Wilmer Dewing (1851–1938).

Dewing was a painter of White's generation. Tall and good-looking, he had been born in Boston and raised in a house dominated by the difficulties of an alcoholic father. He left the security of an instructorship at the Boston Museum of Fine Arts for New York in the fall of 1880, when one of his paintings was exhibited and praised at the National Academy of Design. In New York Dewing met and married Maria Richards Oakey

(1845–1927), a fellow painter of much higher social standing and with a fine education.

Dewing's pictures often displayed women in enigmatic settings. They were well received by critics such as Clarence Cook, who had the Dewings provide the illustrations for two of his books on beauty. In the days before his marriage and just after, White promoted the young artist to his friends. Charles T. Barney bought Dewing's picture *A Prelude* in the spring of 1883, giving it prominent placement in the hall of his new house on an easel in a frame made by White. At this time White frequently designed items of daily use in an artistic way, including picture frames for his own personal pictures and for friends.

Dewing's pictures, with their limited color palette and metaphoric themes, were considered to be of a very advanced taste in America in the 1880s. White spoke about Dewing to Bob Goelet and his wife, Henrietta Louise Warren Goelet (1854–1912), who was a painter herself and in due course took one of the studio floors in Madison Square Garden. In 1885 White convinced the Goelets to commission Dewing to paint Henrietta's portrait. Dewing made his sitter both aristocratic and artistic. She wore a high-style dress and a prominent hair ornament, making her resemble the Greco-Roman figure of Diana, the huntress, whom White and Saint-Gaudens were to place upon the Madison Square Garden tower finial. Diana was a popular motif for fashionable women in those days, often featured on pins or ornaments made by silversmiths. The symbol perhaps reflected the gradual assertion of competence by women like Henrietta Goelet, the mother of two children, but also a painter.

The Goelets must have been pleased with Dewing's picture, for they immediately asked him to paint their son, Robert Walton Goelet.* The two portraits were given frames by Stanford White with the family crest worked into the design. These carvings are probably not from the hand of White, although in those days he sometimes enjoyed helping artists or craftsmen to execute his designs.

In 1886, White himself commissioned a portrait of Bessie from Dewing following the death of their baby. It has a darker palette than Dewing usually selected, which might be a gesture toward White's increasing interest in Old Master painting, but might also be expressive of Bessie's darkness of spirit as she mourned her firstborn. The wonderful frame with its intricate pattern was by White, inspired by a piece of lace he had noticed in Dewing's studio.

---

*John Singer Sargent had just done a portrait of the Goelets' daughter.

The success of this portrait led White to commission a portrait of Bessie's sister, Ella, who was about to marry Devereux Emmet. It was meant to be a wedding gift, but White kept the picture on his own walls. The two portraits were hung facing each other, as if the two sisters in that tightly knit family were in conversation.

White's relationship with Dewing was close in this period. The painter had joined the men's club at the Benedick, and he became part of the Wells circle there. He was quite close to Wells and painted the 1884 oil sketch that is our principal image of the architect. He also became a founding member of the Sewer Club with Lathrop, White, and the Saint-Gaudens brothers. Dewing was so taken with the evenings that he later convinced White to move the club to the Holbein building as the Morgue. In 1895, when the Morgue no longer existed, he wrote to White, "I sometimes, think of those scenes of mirth and physiological interests and investigations," a comment that still leaves us in the dark.

It was White who dragged Dewing into club life, not caring that Saint-Gaudens and Dewing were both poorly educated and not of the accepted social order usually found in clubmen. White convinced the other members that the presence of these artists enhanced the social clubs. He was able to get Lathrop and Dewing to join the Players in 1889, though Wells must have refused. As artists like Dewing and Wells could not afford to belong to a club, White may have added Dewing's dues to his own account.

Dewing soon found a wealthy patron to help him sustain his career. This was Charles Lang Freer (1854–1919) of Detroit, who had made a substantial fortune in railway cars. Freer had retired to devote his life to art, meaning Oriental pottery and pictures by Whistler and Dewing. The two met through the good efforts of Freer's business partner Frederick S. Church, not to be confused with the artist Frederic E. Church. Freer would be a lifelong friend and client of Dewing's. He was clearly homosexual and may have visited the New York clubs. The nature of Dewing's relationship with Freer is not known. Freer also brought White to Detroit to design a colossal civic monument, but to his chagrin it was never funded. White did design a mausoleum for Freer's partner and neighbor, Frank J. Hecker in Detroit.

Dewing needed Freer's encouragement after his work fell out of favor in the 1890s. His career was not helped by a bristly personality. Like Wells, Dewing had a caustic wit and took great offense at the words of many journalists. There is an interesting exchange between White and Harper Brothers, the publishers, in which he admits Dewing's difficult nature and suggests Marianna Griswold Van Rensselaer, an old friend of his and his circle, as the only writer whom Dewing could work with.

Dewing's reputation fell after his death, when the wits of the period called his work "Nothing Dewing." There has recently been a revival of interest in his work, however, with a large retrospective exhibition at the Brooklyn Museum in 1996.

At the old Hotel Imperial, Dewing worked with another painter, Ned Abbey. Edwin Austin Abbey (1852–1911) was born in Philadelphia, where he began his career as an illustrator before moving to New York in 1871 and going to work for Harper Brothers. He became a founding member of the Tile Club in 1877. But in December 1878 he sailed for England for the first time to illustrate a volume of poetry by Robert Herrick. He was quickly taken with the country. In his first year abroad, he met Francis D. Millet and Alfred Parsons, fellow artists who conjured up the past in their paintings. Millet, an American, became part of the artists' circle around Stanford White. Parsons, a British painter, was in the circle of John Singer Sargent, but Abbey introduced him to the Tile Club. In the spring of 1882, Abbey returned to England. He joined Millet and, for a time, Sargent and other Americans at Broadway in Worcestershire for five summers as part of the colony there. Abbey became engaged to Mary Mead of New York while working on the mural for the Hotel Imperial. They married in New York in 1890. Mary Abbey turned out to be a good promoter of her husband's work and was soon pressing the architects for his inclusion in big commissions. He was immediately asked to do a mural for the delivery room at the Boston Public Library, which became *The Quest and Achievement of the Holy Grail*.

In 1891 Abbey, together with his wife and her mother, finally settled in at Morgan Hall in Gloucestershire, where they were eventually visited by McKim, Mead, and White. For a time Sargent joined the expatriate group there, where Henry James and many others making the rounds of artists at work abroad also visited. In 1896 White wrote Abbey that he would try to get Whitelaw Reid to commission Abbey to paint a panel for his house at 451 Madison Avenue. He succeeded, but the panel, *A Pavane,* is now in a private collection.

The historical images of earlier times created by Abbey, Millet, and painters like them were meant to make the past come alive for Americans. In their way, McKim and White were doing the same, creating an architectural version of the past for the impoverished spirit of the late nineteenth century.

Francis Davis Millet was born in 1846, the same year as William Mead.

He came from a prominent Massachusetts family, went to Harvard, and began a career in journalism before going to Europe to study art. He returned to Boston in 1876 to work on Trinity Church, where he fell in with Saint-Gaudens and the entire circle. Millet returned to Europe as a journalist in the Russo-Turkish war before marrying the sister of a Harvard classmate, Elizabeth Lily Greeley Merrill, a descendant of John Alden. The wedding in 1879 had an interesting mixture of guests including Mark Twain and Saint-Gaudens. The Millets were able to survive financially without working, which gave Frank Millet the opportunity to develop his career as an artist. He was proud of his English heritage and his family's settlement in the New World in 1633, but Britain offered a window into an earlier era not visible in America. Having settled there, Millet carved out a unique artistic niche as a painter of historical moments accurate in detail, elaborately staged painted vignettes.

Millet was the first of the Americans to settle in the Cotswolds village of Broadway, which still looked as it would have a century earlier. Here he purchased Russell House, which became the center of the American community from 1885 to 1890, when Abbey, Sargent, and Henry James all spent time there.

Mary Gertrude Mead, a graduate of Vassar who had taught in Roxbury, Massachusetts, visited Millet and met Abbey, whom she would marry. Mary Gertrude was, it would seem, a most determined woman, who after breaking up Abbey's close friendship with Alfred Parsons did the same with Millet. Millet had been more the fine artist of the two Americans, as Abbey was still an illustrator. After Abbey married Miss Mead, she transformed him into a painter, a peer to Millet, doing similar work but setting his pictures in an even earlier time than Millet's England of Queen Anne. Mary Gertrude moved Abbey to Gloucestershire and ended the Broadway group.

Millet remained in Broadway, happy and popular after Abbey and his wife left. Charles Moore, the biographer of McKim, called Millet an artist in friendship, which was probably true. Though he and his wife retained Russell House, they often crossed the Atlantic, keeping up with McKim, Mead, and White and watching the American art scene. They tried living in New York part of the year and had White remodel a modest house for them in 1887 near Washington Square at 92 Clinton Place. They never really became New Yorkers, but Millet did participate in the evenings out. Though he did not receive many commissions from the architects, he was given a tremendous opportunity when he was chosen as director of design for the World's Columbian Exposition of 1893 in Chicago, on which he worked with McKim. The two had shared a taste for the time of Queen Anne for twenty years, and the months of planning for the Chicago fair kept them close friends.

One of Millet's friends in England was the American stage star Mary Anderson, who was performing in London in the 1880s. The pressures on Anderson were intense at this time, and she suffered a breakdown. She had met Antonio de Navarro, the charming son of a Cuban-born developer. The elder Navarro had a bit of an unsavory reputation in the New York real estate world, where his eight large apartment blocks of the 1880s, just south of Central Park, called "Navarro flats" or "Spanish flats," earned good money.* Anderson married the younger Navarro in North London, and in 1895 the couple settled near Millet in Broadway. When McKim visited Anderson and Millet there, she wrote that he preferred his time in Broadway to building palaces for American millionaires. Mary Anderson may have brought McKim closer to two important figures in his life, both great friends of the actress: McKim's neighbor John Cadwalader, whose house she stayed at in New York, and Mrs. J. P. Morgan, whom McKim had likely met on the steps of the Bigelow house in Newport twenty years earlier.

By all accounts, Millet is reported to have lived life to its fullest. At times he seemed to be living in the United States for extended periods with specific men. This may just indicate friendship, or possibly a connection to the undercurrent of homosexual attachments common in this set. His life ended when he was traveling back to the United States with a friend aboard the ill-fated *Titanic*. He was said to have been heroic in assisting people into lifeboats as he and his companion faced the end of their lives. A friend of Millet's from the Chicago Exposition days, Jim Hunt, kept his diaries and letters and intended to use them for a book that would have enhanced Millet's reputation. But Mrs. Millet demanded all the materials, and when she got them destroyed everything. So Millet's career was forgotten; he is still awaiting rediscovery.

The last of the favored artists of this era was Frederick William Mac-Monnies. His father was a New York merchant who had fallen on hard times. MacMonnies joined the circle of artists as a lowly sixteen-year-old assistant to Saint-Gaudens in 1881. Through his skillful work he gradually rose in Saint-Gaudens's eyes. The watchful McKim then helped Mac-Monnies go abroad to study at the École des Beaux-Arts. On his return to New York in 1887, White found work for him on a modest decoration job

*Navarro, like Jared Flagg, was said to have "sharp," or dishonest, business practices.

he was doing in the chancel of the Church of St. Paul the Apostle on Sixtieth Street and Columbus Avenue. It was a great success and is still so today, a remarkable contrast to the grim walls of an earlier building. MacMonnies was a more willing worker than Saint-Gaudens and better able to produce work on a schedule. White began to give him a number of small commissions, such as the bronze fountain pieces for Edward Dean Adams at Rohallion and Joseph Choate at Naumkeag. In due course he introduced him to Whitelaw Reid for Ophir Hall in 1890.

By the time MacMonnies asked White to design the base for the Nathan Hale monument in City Hall Park, Saint-Gaudens was becoming jealous. He probably resented the close relations between White and MacMonnies, which mirrored his own relations with White a decade earlier. He may also have been envious of his former apprentice. White had high praise for the accomplished Nathan Hale monument, but in the end he probably felt that Saint-Gaudens was still the greatest American sculptor. The strains among the three men continued for a decade, but abated when MacMonnies moved to Paris and settled down there.

The Nathan Hale monument is a fine work for such a young sculptor. The handsome figure of Hale appears to display the homoerotic quality that one perceives in the lives of many of the men in this artistic circle. Although no written evidence seems to have survived, one has a distinct sense that these artists felt free to experiment in different ways before settling into marriage. Even when the artists were attached to wives, their occasional sprees might be of a rather wild sort. Once MacMonnies was settled in Paris, when White or Whitney Warren or others of this circle visited him, their evenings out were, as Warren wrote, "truly debauched."

MacMonnies also hosted McKim in Paris in 1893. We can assume that his vices were, as he often proclaimed, "cigars, wine and late nights," without any of White's sexual adventures. It was on this occasion that MacMonnies presented McKim with the dancing figure he had completed that year, probably to repay McKim for helping him get to the École nine years earlier with a present of fifty dollars.

A MUCH LESS SUCCESSFUL COLLABORATION with White came when MacMonnies was asked to participate in the design of a monument for Civil War soldiers to be placed on a bluff above the Hudson at the U.S. Military Academy at West Point. The Battle Monument was a triple disaster, and White probably regretted ever having anything to do with it.

At the end of the Civil War, a collection was made to create a monument for West Point soldiers lost in the war. But not enough funds came in and the money was banked. In due course, as leading figures in the war died, a spate of monuments appeared. McKim, Mead & White were involved in several, including Saint-Gaudens's and McKim's Shaw monument in Boston and the Sherman monument at Grand Army Plaza, Manhattan. In 1890 officials at the Military Academy reinvigorated the old plan and were delighted to find the small sum of 1863 was now sixty-three thousand dollars. They decided to hold a competition for the monument.

A panel consisting of Saint-Gaudens, too busy to be a part of the sculpture team, the aging Richard Morris Hunt, who often now assessed competitions, and Arthur Rotch, the Boston architect, agreed to judge the allegedly anonymous entries. McKim, Mead & White usually lost in genuine competitions and were becoming allergic to them unless, as McKim wrote, they had a personal connection. With Saint-Gaudens on the selection committee, a friend did exist, and not surprisingly White won the competition. The drawings he prepared were poorly done as he was in a mad tizzy of work over the Madison Square Garden. The drawings were based on the idea of a polished granite column with a figure at the top, an old tradition in battle monuments. Their inadequacy offended other competitors such as George F. Babb, White's old mentor, who wanted the commission. White wrote an apologetic note to Saint-Gaudens admitting his haste and promising to do a good job with the final work. White shed some light on the process in a letter written the same year to William Rotch Ware at *The American Architect and Building News.* The professional journal had requested a photograph of another competition entry White had done. White replied, "You will kindly understand that in a competition for a commercial building an architect is unfortunately led to do a great many things which he thinks may take the eye of the committee but which he would not be so proud to lay before his professional bretheren." The monument competition ended the friendly rivalry White and Babb had enjoyed for years. Babb was angry enough with White to speak to William Mead about White's behavior. White in his turn wrote to Babb: "Your remark to Mead that if I had a chance to take a slight advantage in a competition I would not hesitate to do it, unless you meant it as a joke, was as ungenerous and unlike you as it was untrue."

White asked MacMonnies to carve the image for the top of the column, a figure of Victory. But as was now becoming common, he was too rushed to respond to MacMonnies's letters begging for particulars about the figure, pose, materials, and dimensions. He had become accustomed to Wells being able to take over from his vague guidelines and produce exceptional results. MacMonnies, far away in Paris, now went on with the work and got it wrong. His figure was far too large, out of proportion to the column it surmounted. White paid absolutely no attention to the job, and it was not until he arrived at West Point to see the Victory placed atop the monument that he realized how out of hand this job had become. White had not even looked at the Victory figure until it was being hoisted onto the column. Then he was horrified by its proportions and the immodest pose. He therefore wrote MacMonnies that the figure of Victory would have to come down and be replaced, at White's expense, with a smaller figure in a more severe and architectural pose. The new figure, Fame, was dedicated three years later, in 1897, and proved a great success. West Point was pleased with the work and called White back several times.

As regards the architecture, White soon forgot his promise to do a good job and gave the work over to office assistants. The person who really designed the monument was the young Henry Bacon. Word of this leaked out to the writers at *Harper's,* who reported that White had not done the design. True though it was, White immediately recognized the danger to his reputation and wrote the magazine demanding a retraction. He must have longed for the days of Wells, who had kept his mouth shut about his role in White's work. But the pattern of giving over work to assistants in his name without providing clear guidance continued. If the assistant could not create a work as he had imagined it, his patience wore thin, and he would become impatient, then angry. To the amazement of the office, he would curse freely.

# 33. THE METROPOLITAN CLUB

If there is one building that sums up the confidence of a new American aristocracy—men of merit who achieve a noble status by accumulating wealth—it is the Metropolitan Club. In an era of opulence, when princely spending was rampant and membership in multiple clubs made ambitious men feel wanted and successful, many new clubs were formed. Often the new clubs had missions as a cover for maintaining group exclusivity—education, encouragement of the arts, Dutch colonial ancestry, German background, music, theater, religion, or politics. But in late 1890 and early 1891 a new club formed that didn't bother with any justification. The new, nameless club was a sort of eat-your-heart-out organization, where money alone got you in or kept you out.

The beginnings of the club go back to about 1889, with two important men who had tasted rejection and didn't care for it. The first was the now middle-aged John Pierpont Morgan, shedding the presence of his very able father and feeling real power on his own; the second was William Kissam Vanderbilt, grandson of the Commodore, named in the will and brought up as the first Vanderbilt to have an upper-class childhood. Morgan, used to giving orders and controlling men, had attempted to use a club membership to reward John King, president of the Erie Railroad, which Morgan was then using to contain the expansion of a rival, the Pennsylvania Railroad. Morgan strode into James Gordon Bennett's Union Club and put the poorly mannered King up for membership. King was promptly blackballed, and Morgan was furious, as he was not used to losing his battles. At just about this time, William K. Vanderbilt's brother-in-law, Dr. W. Seward Webb, was blackballed as well. Webb, a Columbia-trained physician, was greatly disliked at the time he married Eliza Vanderbilt. Eliza's father so disapproved of Webb that he made his daughter wait until she was thirty to get her share of his money and the mandatory Vanderbilt house on the west side of Fifth Avenue. The rejection of Webb seemed to be based on some well-known incident in a college society, although the gossip sheets reported too that Dr. Webb was unbearable. Another rejection took place about then when Austin Corbin, a self-made financier who was very important to the creation of the image of Long Island as a pleasant, resort place, was also blackballed at the Union Club. Somehow Morgan and Vanderbilt spoke, and Morgan, whose railroad manipulation depended on keeping his own image all-powerful, probably did say something to the effect of "Hang the expense; let's build our own club."

Morgan, then used to working with White (Morgan had not yet decided he was crazy), called in the architect and demanded his services. White was of course thrilled to be the chosen man for the top of America's self-appointed princely class. Where the club would be located, what to call it, and how to begin were the issues. As the club had no purpose, the name could be anything: the Park Club as the city's swank area was near Central Park, or the Hudson Club, or the Metropolitan Club. The outraged men selected the Metropolitan Club, even though a German Jewish men's club had used the same name. The Metropolitan Club was to be for wealthy "gentlemen"—but what Morgan and Vanderbilt really meant was rich men, as there were few qualifications for inclusion other than an up-front payment of $350 to be a founder of the club.

The founders—Morgan, Vanderbilt, William Watts Sherman, Bob Goelet, William Collins Whitney, D. Ogden Mills, and H.A.C. Taylor—were all clients of McKim, Mead & White. The first call flushed out 650 men, including White and McKim. With powerful names like these, the committee could raise a mortgage, buy the land, and build the clubhouse. The figure of two million dollars was thought to be about right for this fine club building. At a dinner party on the night of February 20, 1891, the club was officially brought into existence during a light snowfall. The dinner was held in another club, the Knickerbocker, and the active founders came forward. Morgan, the force behind the club's creation, retreated, leaving Watts Sherman, Goelet, Vanderbilt, and Taylor as the principal movers. Watts Sherman, who like Morgan was a second-generation financier, worked for Duncan, Sherman & Co., of which Morgan was also a part. Watts Sherman probably acted for Morgan in the club's early days. Goelet would be named treasurer for the club, and his name appears on the bills paid for the new structure. William Kissam Vanderbilt took on the role of committee man in charge of the building. Goelet, as an old friend of White's, allowed the architect great freedom in making costly changes to the design. Goelet indulged White as he began to spin into overspending on a job that would become a major difficulty in his late career. Vanderbilt, who had allowed his first wife to build her great château on Fifth Avenue, now believed himself to be a virtual architect and wished to take a strong role first in design, and later in the decoration of the club.

The committee had decided on an uptown clubhouse and purchased a prime portion of John Mason's famous real estate venture of 1820. The early New York speculator had bought several blocks in the upper Fifties and Sixties just east of Fifth Avenue well before Central Park was imagined. Mason purchased the empty blocks miles above the city, which was then just about to reach Washington Square, for two thousand dollars. This seemed a substantial sum for something to be used in what would be a very distant future. After Mason's death various family members sued for their inheritances, and the block on Fifth Avenue running from Sixtieth to Sixty-first Street on the not-yet-paved boulevard went to Andrew Gordon Hammersley, with other blocks to Mary Mason Jones and her relatives. The Hammersley block went to the sickly heir Louis Carré Hammersley, who had married Lily Price, the beautiful daughter of a naval officer. Louis Hammersley was a strange man, feeble of nature, and he died in 1884. With Hammersley's fortune, Lily married the eighth duke of Marlborough, becoming one of the first American women of fortune to snare an English nobleman. The earlier marriages of Jennie Jerome to a lesser member of the Marlborough family and of Consuelo Yznaga to the Viscount Mandeville had already brought money to impoverished English aristocrats. Lily's money helped the duke of Marlborough warm up the drafty halls of huge Blenheim. The club bought about half the Hammersley block for $480,000, with E. T. Gerry purchasing the northern half for his château designed by Richard Morris Hunt. The Hunt house and the Metropolitan Club went up at about the same time. This caused friction, especially from Gerry, who was arbitrary and difficult, but Hunt and White always managed to get conflicts resolved. Gerry, who had been an attorney earlier in his career, inherited extensive real estate holdings in the city from his mother, a Goelet.

The first records book for the Metropolitan Club is missing, but the McKim, Mead & White records give the specifics quite well. The build-

*The Metropolitan Club in New York, 1891–94.*
*White's best Italian palazzo.*

ing footprint is 90 feet on Fifth Avenue and 142 feet east on Sixtieth Street. The club building includes an almost perfect square courtyard (57 feet long and 57 feet 9 inches wide) to the east of the building. The private courtyard could serve as a carriage turnaround and almost as an outdoor room. No other club and few other buildings were as extravagant with unbuilt space as was this millionaires' club. The only New York buildings with front courtyards were the Lenox Library at Seventieth Street and Fifth Avenue (replaced by the Frick mansion in 1911–14) and McKim, Mead & White's own Villard houses, which were a direct ancestor of the Metropolitan Club building.

The designs for the clubhouse were worked out by October 9, 1891, when some fifty sketches of the proposed building were shown to the press. Great secrecy had been kept until that date, probably so that the club would be brought before the public as a fully thought-through project. The original plans called for the building to have a primary entrance on the Fifth Avenue side, but this was eliminated by December.

The design for the clubhouse is a very restrained work by White's standards at the time. It is an Italian palazzo form adapted from book plates and done in white marble, which was Wells's idea for the Villard houses but overruled by Villard in favor of brownstone blocks. White's hand is particularly evident here in the elaborate six-foot projecting cornice, which displays his skill at creating a new decorative form based on the assembly of existing Renaissance forms. White's cornice, like his frames, is a unique blend of motifs. The building presented a stately front to the city, giving the newly created club the dignity of older clubs such as those done sixty years earlier in London on Pall Mall. Despite its sober exterior, the interior of the clubhouse was the grandest ever created. The club committee faced a difficult problem in selecting the decorators who would create the opulence reserved for members' eyes.

The American economy fluctuated several times in the 1880s and '90s. The committee recognized that the public should not be overly aware of the extravagant sums being spent on the club interior, but there was still debate over which committee member's favored decorators should get a slice of this rich pie. The solution was to be inclusive and give everyone's favorites some of the work. The Solomon-like solution had been achieved in some great houses, where the patron gave a room to each of the major firms. Here at the Metropolitan Club, all the established companies shared the work, along with a newcomer from Paris, Gilbert Cuel, of 20 Rue des Capucines. William K. Vanderbilt had wanted to be in charge of the interiors, but had been forced to bow to Stanford White's presence. Once Willie K. lost the battle, he promoted Cuel, who arrived in New York and set up a branch at 510 Fifth Avenue. The Cuel firm did the main lounge and dining room, with much of the work done in Paris and shipped to the United States. When some of Cuel's work was installed in the club building, American labor organizations cried foul as the economy was poor and the American plasterers and others resented the work done on the other side of the Atlantic. Cuel did not know the ropes of working in America and may not have liked working with a rival Parisian firm, Allard & Fils, which then was well established in the United States. Cuel's work came in slowly, and the completion of the club interiors became a painful saga. It ended as an unpleasant episode with some of Cuel's workers urinating on the finished floors. His firm did not continue to have great success in the United States, although Cuel did work at Marble House and the Breakers—two Vanderbilt houses in Newport.

The old favorite firm of Allard did the front and vestibule doors as well as main entrance and passage halls. Allard also did the second-story loggia. The Herter Brothers firm, now in different hands, did a table, the coves of the library ceiling, and the preparation of the ceiling for the fine arts painter, White's friend from the Players club Edward Simmons. The remaining interior jobs were given out to the same firms as had worked at Villard's own house, and there is a strong echo of the Villard interiors here at the club. Frank Lathrop, as ever, did the leaded glass; Frances Beck did the wallpapers, including White's new favorite, aluminum leaf; Ellin & Kitson did the interior marble work; Yandell supplied the leather and leather panels; Francis Bacon did the fourth-floor members' bedrooms; and Pottier & Stymus & Co. supplied furniture and woodwork.*

Special features for the interiors were all reserved for White's own touch. Otherwise, assistants supervised the execution of much of the design. Kendall apparently did the exterior of the club and Terence A.

---

*Other suppliers were W. & J. Sloane, and Davenport. The linens for the guest rooms came from Lord & Taylor, while the tablecloths had to be imported from Maison de Blanc in Paris.

Koen the interior with help from one of the Sickles brothers, Frederick. White seemed to do the details, Koen the hard work. For example, Koen labored to get the Otis elevator fitted and installed, while White selected the color for the leather of the seat. Both Koen and Frederick Sickles left the office immediately after the club was completed. White also sold a few decorative items to the club, including several lanterns for two thousand dollars. White's growing career as a supplier must already have been known, since Archer & Pancoast, the lamp makers, refused to give the building committee a list of specifics, fearing that White would take the list to his Paris sources and have the lamps made abroad. Clearly, something had happened to anger Archer & Pancoast, who would go out of business during this job. The established antiques company of H. B. Herts & Co. of 242 Fifth Avenue supplied the clubhouse with clocks and a sideboard that had been in E. D. Morgan's Newport house. The Duveen firm is listed here for antique clocks, a pair of Empire vases, and a set of onyx vases. Everyone seemed to work here, with David Maitland Armstrong doing the art windows and Joseph Cabus the woodworking in some of the rooms. Cabus would die during this job and his son Alexander would take over the firm. Alexander Cabus was neither as fine a craftsmen nor as honorable as his father, and White would pull away from the Cabus firm in the next few years.

If the club was about the interiors, it was well served. The exterior was expertly handled, as usual, by David King, with only one delay—from the Cornell metalworkers, who did not finish quite in time. The interiors bogged down immediately, as the marble firm was carving marble columns around the internal metal frame. The saga of the interiors was made more difficult by long periods when White did not have time to reply to questions. His inattention forced suppliers to make their own decisions, and yet he would have a fit when he discovered something completed without his "touch." White would then demand that the work be redone, which the jolly Bob Goelet would authorize for payment. The situation escalated to a point that even Goelet lost patience. The committee became so upset that a stiff letter (now lost) was sent to White putting him on notice that the club needed to open in February 1894 and the building had to be completed.

White went into overdrive in January 1894, spending night and day in the building trying to get it ready. To finish in time for the press view, White had the club hire a small battalion of nonunionized workers who would convey the marble fireplaces from the Hudson River docks to the club and install them there. The issue of union versus nonunion work was a very hot one in the economically depressed winter of 1893–94. A second corps of cleaners picked up after the workers had completed the installation. The final push was enough to get the building done. It was said, however, that a bet that White could not get it done on time had served as a catalyst.

The opening was held on February 27, 1894, with Morgan, flanked by White, proudly receiving guests into their quarters. A friend of Stratton's, James Breese, a trained architect working as a photographer, was called in to photograph the building with a series of platinum prints.

JAMES BREESE SOON BECAME a friend of White's, and a number of White's evening entertainments were held in Breese's photography rooms, known as the Carbon Studio. Breese's sisters had asked Sidney Stratton to design a carriage house for the them at 150 East Twenty-second Street in 1893. The carriage house looks rather like the Goelet estate office that McKim, Mead & White had designed a few years earlier. Breese hired White in a private commission of 1894 to redo the Carbon Studio. Later, in 1898, Breese had the office create and alter the Orchard, a large house in Southampton, Long Island, an ongoing work that White toyed with over several years.

The Breese children were friendly with Fernando Yznaga, the Natchez companion of Sidney Stratton.* The Breeses, Yznagas, and McKim would have noticed Sidney Stratton's mental decline in these years. When Stratton left, Fernando Yznaga asked White, in another private commission, to design the Yznaga family monument.

In his private work White did monuments for many of his friends. The Yznaga monument was one; another was for the Warren family. As White worked with Bob Goelet on the Metropolitan Club, Goelet's wife approached White to create a memorial panel for her parents. Since the Goelets were among White's closest friends as well as excellent clients, he could hardly say no. White always found it very difficult to deny his friends' requests, especially those whose favor he wished to hold. Despite his extremely full workload, he took on the job, agreeing to work gratis and asking Saint-Gaudens to work for a modest fee on the Warren family monument. The Goelets were related to the Warrens by marriage, and Stanford White had designed a rather florid-looking, income-generating commercial building for the Warrens on the opposite corner from the

---

*Yznaga worked for the Henry B. Hollins investment company, which kept the younger generation in contact with each other and thus with McKim, Mead & White.

Goelet building at 903–7 Broadway in 1890–91. These two small office buildings by McKim, Mead & White on Twentieth Street are apt reflections of the opposite directions in which the partners were sometimes flying. The Goelet building, with its simple and well-proportioned façade, contrasts with the overly ornamental Warren Building. The Warren building has overscaled terra-cotta work—actually a bit of family detail, as the molds for the terra-cotta on the Warren building came from those created for the Goelets' new Hotel Imperial. Whitney Warren, determined to have a career as an architect, would enter White's circle at roughly this time and follow the lead of, if not compete with, the more established firm. Warren's financial and social position gave him the assurance to be arrogant, which cost him his American career. In his younger days, Warren had used his sister's Madison Square tower studio as his architectural studio; draftsmen such as Eugene Bourdon, a fellow architect trained in Paris at the École des Beaux-Arts, worked for him there.

# 34. THE ACCOMMODATIONS OF SUCCESS

By 1890 McKim, Mead & White were surely America's premier architects. As the new decade began, the nation's economy was once again robust, and the architects were working for all the powerful players in it. Although the concept of tall office buildings had originated in New York when McKim and Mead began their association and was refined with construction techniques developed in the 1880s, offers to build tall office buildings eluded the firm. Instead, the architects did everything else. McKim, Mead & White did create some tall buildings for the Goelet and Warren families, and in 1892 would design a modest commercial building for the Vanderbilt family on Beekman Street, but for the most part, the firm walked around the skyscraper. They failed to win the American Surety Company competition for a prominent skyscraper in 1893, and by the end of the decade McKim no longer felt comfortable with skyscrapers. White, by the end of his career, probably was frustrated that he had never had the opportunity to design a mammoth tower. White attempted to convince New York Central Railroad that they needed a skyscraper tower over their proposed station, but New York Central rejected this concept.

Though McKim, Mead & White did not get to build that important American contribution to architecture, the skyscraper, the architects were the image makers, creating significant structures for wealthy individuals and their social world. The houses and club buildings the architects designed convinced their clients that they were the true recipients of the historical mantle of accomplishment and were now American princes. As part of such an honored class, the clients could endow and support institutions devoted to art, music, education, and high-minded ideals. For these elevating buildings, the patrons called upon the three partners to give the correct visual spin to their generosity. McKim, Mead & White's architecture could really create the new, improved America.

As premier architects, McKim, Mead & White could now begin to reject the smaller jobs, such as additions on buildings, that had sustained them in their early years. By 1899, correspondence reveals the office rejecting the smaller alterations and doing such work only for established clients. In 1892 White had also rejected commissions for country or resort houses built of wood. White would turn his back on perhaps the architects' greatest and most original contribution to American architecture, the wooden summer house, which they had done so very well a decade earlier. White now proclaimed, to strangers at least, that wooden houses lacked dignity. Times and tastes had changed, and McKim, Mead & White now provided the bridge to the past for their clients.

In the years when the office made a good profit, and as steamships had made Atlantic crossings faster and smoother, we begin to see the individual partners going abroad for several months on a sort of learning vacation. In 1891 and 1892, McKim went to Europe, this time exploring Italy, which would become his architectural home. Each partner would return with books and purchased photographs to share. Architectural history became a common bond in the office, as each partner tried to find new sources for a current design project. The goal had become one of finding the best model to use as inspiration for a new building. McKim, Mead and White were now repositories of historic buildings.

In this era McKim would move toward his career as an ambassador of beauty, an educator of America, a person to put the nation on a par with the great past cultures of Europe. He became more of a spokesman and educator of the profession than a designer. As for Mead, he would strain even harder to keep the men in the office focused on doing the work that had come into McKim's or White's hands. White would turn into a human whirlwind, doing far too much in the office, in his growing antiques business, and in his public life in the city. McKim and Mead had more restrained personal lives, but White's was crowded with business meetings and social events every day. Dinners, parties, music, and the theater consumed White's evenings. He was now happily following his motto of making a short and happy life. The growing popularity of the telephone would make the social events easier to set up, as everyone now had a phone and evening arrangements could be made directly.

The living accommodations of the partners were about to be upgraded. McKim, on Thirty-fifth Street, was taking over more of Dr. Derby's house. He would rent all the upper floors, and by 1894 he had the office install an elevator to the top floor in the back of the house. McKim would privately re-roof the house and make improvements to give himself a pleasant home.

Stanford White, whose city home had been a speculative row house that was part of the Rhinelander holdings, found himself a victim of the changing neighborhood. The Rhinelander houses were some fifty years old by 1892. When the brick row was built, the natural renters were a slightly second-tier set of New Yorkers, members of old families but perhaps not from the most well-off part of the family. The row houses were built with churches close by and low-scale commercial shops on Sixth Avenue to serve the daily needs of the householders. As Fifth Avenue progressed northward, brownstone fronts joined the brick houses and a more fashionable clientele moved in. It was during this phase that White and his family took the house, even though the western border of Sixth Avenue was at that time under siege by the elevated railroad.

The elevated train helped to create an extension of the most favored shopping district in the city, the new Ladies' Mile, which would march up Sixth Avenue from Fourteenth to Twenty-third Street. The push of the stores would even call in White, who in 1886 would enlarge the iron front of Benjamin Altman's dry goods store with a further iteration of its earlier ironwork. The pressure to expand similar stores became increasingly intense, and the Rhinelanders finally succumbed. In January 1892, the family decided to give up the houses, tear them down, and build their own loft building, which would give the Rhinelander estate more revenue. The Rhinelander commercial building would become the famous shoe department store Cammeyer's. Although the shoes are gone today, the building still stands on the southeast corner.

The White household included Stanford, Bessie, Lawrence, and varying servants, as well as Stanford's mother and, often, his uncle. The house had to be emptied in four months. White immediately launched a real estate campaign, reading the professional paper daily, making contact with brokers, and visiting houses. He set himself a range of ideal locations for a new house between Park Avenue on the east and the Elevated on the west. White was hoping to find a house in need of work, as he intended to create his own home and preferred to have a shell—and a less-than-expensive one at that—to make his own.

The frantic search broadened when Prescott Butler agreed to consider joining households with a double house. Putting two houses together had limited popularity at the time, but it had been done and might give the potential purchasers an edge to buy a well-priced larger property. The houses White and Butler visited were never appropriate to their needs. By the late spring of 1892, perhaps during conversations with H.A.C. Taylor at the Metropolitan Club meetings, White had decided to rent a house on the north side of Gramercy Park at 119 East Twenty-first Street, next to Taylor's own home at 121 East Twenty-first Street.

H.A.C. Taylor was an old friend of Charles McKim's, who had been given his first large commission by Taylor's father, Moses, in Elberon. McKim had then built a house for H.A.C. Taylor at Elberon and another at Newport. Taylor had recently bought a two-story, thirty-foot-high stable at 121 East Twenty-first Street, and on October 4, 1887, he had filed a permit to have the building made into a house. The work was primarily internal, and the decorative firm Marcotte & Co. executed the job. Taylor owned the house next door, which he rented, and White took the lease starting in May 1892. White would rent the house at 119 East Twenty-first for about six years, until Taylor was ready to move into a much more stylish new house in the high-fashion neighborhood just east of Fifth Avenue, at 3 East Seventy-first Street. Taylor, who conferred with White often on the club issues, was beginning discussions with McKim for an Italian-styled palazzo in 1892. Before moving into the house next door, White would have been aware that Taylor eventually intended to move from 121 to Seventy-first Street. Perhaps White even planned for Butler to take Taylor's house under their double house scheme. The new Taylor house was not ready until about 1897, by which time Butler had built his own house at 22 Park Avenue. White tried to buy Taylor's property, to no avail, before leasing the corner house at 121 and constructing a temporary wooden passage between the two houses. Later on, White would lease the older house at 119 to his sister-in-law, Kate Wetherill, and expand 121 East Twenty-first Street northward. White's own house was truly the summation of his design skills at the turn of the century.

Both White and McKim now lived as members of the set they served. Through club experiences they expanded the firm's client base, but they also saw their older friends. McKim and White, two mismatched people, always enjoyed each other's company and would remain close even in White's darkest days. They often arranged dinners with the members of their old circle, which White usually set up at a club restaurant. The dinners "for just the old gang" often specified daytime attire, as Louis St. Gaudens and Babb would refuse to wear black tie. The dinners were probably great fun and a chance for all to drink, smoke cigars, and stay up late, McKim's self-proclaimed vices. If the evening then became a "spree," McKim probably left the party and returned home, but this seemed never to present a problem for either man.

The old friends were still granted favors, such as White's unofficial designs. His old love, Anaïs Casey, now Mrs. Bliss, asked him to design an altar for her beloved church, St. Francis Xavier, just a few blocks below White's old house at Twentieth Street. White did a lot of private work that year, altering the Stewart Marble House into the club building, designing a banking interior in the Metropolitan Opera building on Thirty-ninth Street for the Bank of New Amsterdam, and, with clubs on the mind that year, doing over the clubroom for the Knickerbocker Club at 319 Fifth Avenue. White was burning the candle at both ends, working for the office and behind its back as well. He was setting up the house at 119 East Twenty-first Street, his hectic social life was becoming more than any one person could handle—and then there was Columbus to commemorate.

As 1892 dawned, plans were well under way for a national celebration of the four hundredth anniversary of Columbus's voyage. New York and the nation's second city, Chicago, each wanted to host the exposition celebrating the date. Although Chicago won out, New York decided to have a street celebration anyway and asked White to organize the Columbian Celebration. White was to be in charge of the decoration of Fifth Avenue, the boulevard of the parades, and with Hunt and La Farge to choose a young person to design the arches. White, Hunt, and La Farge selected an architectural student, Henry B. Herts, the son of the importers and antiques dealers who were supplying the Metropolitan Club with clocks, as the winner. Herts would build a wooden and papier-mâché triumphal arch at the top of the route at Fifty-ninth Street, while White would himself create a trellis arch at Twenty-second Street supported by twelve twenty-foot columns. White then planned for one hundred sixty-foot poles topped by spheres and eagles to line Fifth Avenue from Twenty-second Street to Thirty-fourth Street; the poles would be decorated with streamers and hold Venetian lanterns strung across Fifth Avenue.

During the summer of 1892, with Bessie out in St. James, White spent his first month in his studio in the Madison Square tower. He planned the Columbian decorations there and spent much of the time with a young man from the office, Thomas Hastings. Tommy Hastings had joined

McKim, Mead & White in the same month as John M. Carrère, October 1883. After two years, the two architects struck out on their own, but Hastings maintained his ties to McKim, Mead & White. Hastings was the son of a New York City minister from a fashionable Presbyterian church and was on a friendly social level with White. He enjoyed the nights out with White and often participated in White's sprees, particularly those with an all-male cast. Hastings loved to design decorative effects, and so must have shared with White the planning for the October celebration. Indeed, the two were so enjoying the planning that in August they decided to take a quick trip to Europe together. The push of work forced White to cancel the vacation, however.

Hastings had long been a friend of Wells; with Longfellow and a few others, the two had been a part of the Parisian circle of architectural students around the École des Beaux-Arts, and on returning to New York they had kept up these friendships. Their circle included Saint-Gaudens and White and was especially active in the evening. Tommy Hastings was a recipient of love letters from Saint-Gaudens, which were similar to those sent to White and Wells. Hastings's love affair with Saint-Gaudens probably was going on in the mid-1890s after Gus settled his second family in Connecticut. Hastings was often described as finding women neither interesting nor tempting. The obviously homosexual Hastings decided to make a social cover marriage, a common practice for the period, when he met the immensely rich Helen Benedict, who was most likely a lesbian. To keep their families at bay and provide a public face, the two married in an elaborate ceremony in April 1900 at Greenwich, Connecticut, the bride's hometown. A choir of twenty-six boys from Trinity Church sang; Charles McKim served as best man and White, who planned the decorations for the wedding, stood by as usher. The bride, perhaps not very interested in a traditional set of wedding customs, had no attendant other than Larry White, then an adolescent boy, who served as a page. Helen Benedict Hastings would set herself up in Old Westbury, Long Island, where she lived with a companion, Miss Jessie Mann, and dabbled in Christian Science. Hastings remained in New York. The gossip paper of the era, *Town Topics,* which, like *Herald* under Bennett, could sometimes be persuaded to ignore events, had two very overt references to the couple, particularly to the bride, making her lesbian identity clear.

White had collapsed from overwork once before, in the spring of 1889, when he had created the decoration for the Washington Centennial. In October 1892, he was more than exhausted. He began to experience stomach pain, which he called "the little buzz-saw inside of me." White would not again undertake a program of massive public decorations and would have periodic bouts of illness. It is difficult to know exactly what caused him to be put in bed in ice with morphine given as a pain reliever, but a common explanation was that he had driven himself so hard that he may have had a perforated ulcer. White did consume a vast quantity of food and alcohol, which may not have helped matters; his stomach or intestinal problems would appear again several times in the next fourteen years. White's battles with digestive disorders forced him on an all-milk diet— a health disaster for him. After that he tried drinking massive quantities of Contrexeville (spa) water, a bottled water he had sent to every one of his haunts. White's poor health had begun to interfere with his life.

The exhaustion was amplified by McKim's removal to Chicago, where he was a principal in creating the World's Columbian Exposition. With a partner away, the others pitched in on the missing man's work. White was acting for McKim when he became ill. After weeks in bed, he was told to take a vacation. In January 1893, White decided to take the trip abroad he had canceled in August, but this time he took Bessie and Larry. With Stewart money still seeming real, the Whites planned a special holiday to Egypt with Bessie's sister Ella and Ella's husband, Devereux Emmet, the future golf course designer. The Whites set sail for a four-month holiday on January 14 on the French ship *Champagne*. The voyage was quite different from the trip White made with McKim fourteen years earlier, as transatlantic crossings were now much less stressful.

Once in Paris, White found MacMonnies, who was then working on the relief panels for the Washington Square Arch. White spent time with MacMonnies and met with Jamie Gordon Bennett. He then consulted a series of French physicians—Guyana, Gautrelet, and a Dr. Clark—before setting out for Florence and meetings with Stefano Bardini, then his principal antiques supplier. Bardini had a vast selection of items available for sale, including the largest assortment of the architectural pieces and decorations White liked, such as fireplaces, ceilings, vases, and statuary.

In March the Whites met the Emmets at Brindisi and set off for Cairo. Each couple had a child, so a Scottish nanny was hired to accompany them. Egypt was a popular destination for New York gentry at this time. Theodore Roosevelt's honeymoon was spent on the Nile, and many others of White's class visited this exotic destination. Mrs. Robb was just leaving Egypt as White arrived. While White was visiting the pyramids, he ran into the writer Richard Harding Davis. Halfway around the world, New Yorkers could bump into each other atop the Cheops. In Cairo White fell into the visiting nobleman role easily. He went shopping with delight, buying artifacts and even unmentionable parts of a mummy. The Egyptian exotica made it back to America and after the usual battle at customs were shipped to St. James.

The Whites and Emmets arranged with Thomas Cook & Co. to hire a larger Nile boat, a dahabeyah, and a guide, a Syrian Christian named Joseph Haik whom White had heard about in New York, perhaps from Hampden Robb. Haik was an exceptional guide and thoroughly pleasant on the Nile journey, which, despite the expensive boat, involved a bit of roughing it. The Whites traveled with a rifle but probably needed a rat-trap more, as the rodents consumed Bessie's shoes. At the end of the voyage, White presented Haik with his rifle as a gift. This kind gesture landed Haik in jail after the guide requested some extra cartridges for the gun, which he could not get in Egypt. White sent him empty extra cartridges, but either White or the delivery company attempted to smooth over delivery by labeling the cartridges as china. The deception brought suspicion on the innocent Haik, who begged for White's help and was given it. White wrote several letters explaining the delivery to the Egyptian envoy in Washington, D.C., and Haik was finally sprung. White spoke so highly of his Nile voyage that others followed. In 1896, McKim and the diplomat Henry White journeyed up the Nile.

The Whites returned to Paris on their way home, visiting Stewart relatives who lived in Versailles and touring the palace. The Whites saw Richard Harding Davis again in Paris. White seems to have gone shopping again in Paris before the couple went to London, where they attended the wedding of Robert Winthrop Chanler, an American Astor grandchild whose brothers and sisters would become great friends of White's. The Whites visited Parliament and the historic sights before going to visit Edwin Austin Abbey and his wife and John Singer Sargent. White, caught up in excitement, seems to have lost his wallet, but other than that traditional tourist complaint, the four-month trip was a success. It restored White to good health, and when he returned to work he found the office and the nation much caught up in the excitement of the Chicago Exposition.

# 35. THE WORLD BEGINS TO SPIN

S tanford White was not the only member of the old gang suffering from nervous strain. By the early 1890s, Sidney Stratton's emotional problems were becoming more intense.

Stratton had joined McKim at 57 Broadway in the late 1870s. He would remain in rooms in the office until 1896. Stratton used the reception area of the McKim, Mead & White offices, and his work was displayed with that of the partners. During these early years of unofficial partnership, Stratton had brought in a dozen commissions from a higher class than McKim, Mead, or White was able to reach. He'd brought in C. Oliver Iselin, Bartow, Colgate, Frederick Roosevelt and the Roosevelts' cousin, J. K. Gracie. Stratton knew Archibald Rogers, Stuyvesant Fish, Daniel Lord Jr., and others. He also did some work for James Gordon Bennet Jr., but exactly what he did is lost. At Narragansett Stratton built a big shingle house for Henry De Coppet and another for Willard P. Ward. For John Cleve Green, the merchant who greatly benefited colleges and the Presbyterian Church in New Jersey, Stratton designed an alcove at the old New York Society Library, then on University Place. He designed summer houses in Bar Harbor, including one for a member of Charles T. Barney's family, and another at Navesink, New Jersey. By about 1887, however, Stratton's career was coming to a halt, with some of his clients now part of McKim, Mead & White's world. In that year, McKim summoned him to Boston to help out during the crisis on the Boston Public Library elevation. Stratton probably helped McKim with the Parisian solution.

McKim and Stratton were not only very old friends and colleagues, but also fellow sufferers from nervous disorders who shared the services of Dr. Charles Hitchcock. Stratton probably had anxiety difficulties as well, which caused him to have uncontrolled tremors and bouts of irrationality. He began to spend extended periods of time with his father's sister in Bridgeton, New Jersey, going there in 1889 and again in the early 1890s. Stratton's aunt Eleanor took him home to his father in Natchez in 1889, when the Reverend Stratton was still recovering from the death of his second son, Joseph Buck Stratton Jr., a year earlier. The aunt and nephew returned to New York, but from then on Stratton would retreat to Bridgeton every time he felt nervous.

In 1890 Stratton had his last big job, the Brooklyn Riding and Driving Club near Prospect Park. The large commission was a severe-looking brick structure with two corner towers. The building was a cross between Babb, Cook & Willard's De Vinne Press building and McKim's inspiration for the Boston Public Library, the Flavian Amphitheater in Rome, the Colosseum. During the 1890s Stratton moved from 55 West Thirty-third Street to 9 East Tenth Street, but he still visited McKim at Thirty-fifth Street. Stratton returned to New Jersey in 1893 after a severe anxiety attack. He had finished the carriage house for the Breese sisters at 150 East Twenty-second Street but was considering giving up his practice.

In the summer of 1894 Stratton reappeared at McKim's house, where he enjoyed playing McKim's Steinway piano. Stratton had no office, so McKim promised him that he would always have a corner at the new offices at 160 Fifth Avenue and also offered to display photographs of Stratton's work with that of the office in the reception rooms, including a small house on Madison Avenue Stratton had recently completed. On August 22, 1894, McKim wrote to Dr. Hitchcock in Narragansett that Stratton had come by and that his hand was steady and mind clear, but that he seemed to be thinking of returning to his father in Natchez. McKim had told Stratton to drop by for dinner anytime and that a place for him was always ready, but Stratton went back to Natchez for a visit in 1894–95. In 1895, McKim wrote Stratton in Natchez that he had seen Henry White in Washington, D.C., and "our old friend, Sam Ward." McKim wrote that he and Dr. Hitchcock had tried to find Stratton's father when he visited New York, looking in Reverend Stratton's favorite hotel, the Marlborough, to no avail. He passed along the news that the French-born painter Mr. Sarre, whom Stratton had particularly enjoyed working with, was dying. As a final note to cheer Stratton, McKim promised him that Cornelia Butler would soon write him about her admiration for Stratton's chancel in the Church of the Transfiguration, known as the Little Church Around the Corner, on East Twenty-ninth Street. Stratton had designed the church's building on West Sixty-ninth Street a few years earlier, then had created the chancel for Dr. Houghton's Little Church. Mrs. Butler must have visited the actors' church and liked Stratton's chancel and intended to write him her praise.

In 1896, Stratton moved back to Natchez permanently. He regained his composure but gave up architecture. In the days after McKim's memorial service, Mead wrote to Stratton that they were the only two of the old guard still left. Stratton may have visited New York and Mexico during his second career in Natchez. At times his sometime partner, Frank Quinby, in New York, sent him clippings about old friends, passing along news of McKim, Thomas Garner's daughter's marriage, and the death of Henry Brevoort in Europe.

Henry Brevoort, a mechanical engineer and an old friend of Stratton's, may have met Stratton during the Civil War. Brevoort was a single man involved in club life in New York, who lived at 36 Brevoort Place in Brooklyn. He seems to have not worked as a mature man but instead lived off his grandfather's fortune. Exactly the role Brevoort played in Stratton's life is unknown, but it is likely that he helped Stratton get some jobs. Stratton was a youth of accomplishment and promise whose difficulties in New York brought his career to a premature end. "Friend Stratton," as Louis Sullivan described him, had to return to his own world of protected acquaintance in his hometown.

IN THE EARLY 1890S, as friends of McKim, Mead & White from the early days such as Wells and Stratton fell away, Stanford White's life began to move so rapidly that for a time it seemed to cover over his losses. His career as an architect was at a pinnacle of success, and his second career as an antiquarian object dealer had also shifted into high gear with his 1893 trip to Europe. White had learned the rules of the game and how to bend them to deceive the customhouse and his clients; he had moved from the friendly purchase of objects with a 10 percent premium for his services to operating as a genuine dealer who falsely reported prices to his clients. Aware of the possible loss of status should his clients begin to think of him as a supplier of artworks rather than as an architect, White worked hard to hide his business arrangements from the public. While depending on men in the office to create his buildings, he was fully absorbed in the antiques trade.

That White was interested only in objects of the past was clearly expressed by his decoration and even the remarks he made to friends. In his absorption of design, he never noticed the modern work of England or Paris. White was oblivious to the sensuous design of the Art Nouveau, which might well have enticed him earlier on. He did not see Mackintosh or Liberty in England, or the work of Parisian designers; he looked only at fireplaces, ceilings, fabrics, tapestries, vases, statuary, and oil paintings of European history up to the days of the painter Salvator Rosa (whom he disliked). While it was true that White bought contemporary American paintings, he seemed unaware of other art movements of his era.

White had become the supplier of image to a fast-moving group of America's newly and greatly wealthy. He supplied people who lacked inherited pieces with the homes of Renaissance princes meant to over-power the old wealth with show. White's work, based on his excellent sources for shopping in Italy, became Renaissance in style unless a client specifically asked for a French or English interior. His formula for design from the 1890s forward would depend on the insertion of imported fire-places and ceilings, with a profusion of objects, many of them gilded, set against red brocade walls.

White's third passion was his life, which he staged with as much relent-less energy as he did his dual career as an architect and antiquarian dealer. Now part of the world that had rejected his father, White made sure he was well set by giving frequent, amusing parties and attending every-thing he could. White was, as someone put it, "ubiquitous." He was everywhere each night—at the opera, at parties and benefits, and then with the artists at the Players club in the wee hours. He was juggling three full careers, and his failings began to show. Unlike Stratton, White did not give up, but he became increasingly impatient with the staff in the office, and his health began to break down. The pace of his life, as well as his overindulgence in food and drink, surely did not help White main-tain well-being.

Sidney Stratton had brought to McKim, Mead & White some of the venerable pillars of New York society, but these old gentry families did not need White's advice on interiors. White's clients were those of con-temporary fortune but with enough knowledge to wish for a merchant prince. The self-confident families of the Patriarchs did not call on Mr. White.

White's position as ambassador of European culture to the newly rich called for hard work both during the day and at night as he tried to main-tain and extend his list of social contacts and possible clients. To accom-plish his goals, White had gradually slipped off the brakes on his personal life, and now a new problem arose. Fueled by the thought of the Stewart millions and the letters of credit from his clients, he began to lose control on a second front—his desire to acquire. Perhaps feeling a bit as Will Whitney did with Flora Payne's money, White turned to the stock market, at first buying stocks under the guidance of his friends. White then plunged full tilt into the market, buying on margins, winning sometimes, but then going further, until he lost control here as well. By the end of the 1890s he was out of control in his personal life, in his desire to buy artworks, and in his need to cover his stock market losses. White was spinning like a dervish.

AS MIDDLE AGE REVEALED White's and Stratton's failings, Mead seemed to continue on impervious to change. McKim also suffered from stress and depression, and had begun to remove himself from the world of the practicing architect. By the end of the 1890s, McKim would place himself above the fray, focusing on the future. He would become interested in, then obsessed by, the training of American architects and artists. McKim emerged as the serene dean of the profession, working to create schools of architecture and the concept of a place for Americans to study abroad, an American school in Rome. Mead really did have a difficult job balancing the two partners and keeping the practice on its feet, as McKim soared to the cerebral and White plummeted into a more material world. McKim had taken up his personal time with the people he longed for at Harvard, his "natural" peers, the old families of the Northeast. White had turned to the new world of the immensely rich. Each partner pulled in work from these different branches of American life. Mead had to get these jobs accomplished. How one longs for Mead's recollections, which were never set down.

# 36. THE CHICAGO FAIR

McKim, Mead & White's view of an alabaster city recalling great European capitals took form, if only as a summer's illusion, when the nation decided to honor Columbus.

With the four hundredth anniversary of Columbus's voyage to America, many local celebrations were planned, but a larger homage seemed daunting—what could be done to honor Columbus, and where? A competition was held for the site of the festivities, with St. Louis, Washington, D.C., New York, and Chicago all wishing to host the Columbian Exposition. Chicago, the largest city in what was then the American West, had been growing faster than any other American city in the 1880s. In the spring of 1890, Congress selected Chicago as the host city for the Columbian Exposition, also known as the Chicago World's Fair, and asked Frederick Law Olmsted to give the city's Fair committee guidance on the best place to construct its buildings. The local architects Burnham & Root, a firm with wealthy and well-connected partners and a hand in all types of buildings, were to be in charge of the plans.

Burnham & Root recognized that a fair held in a city only recently rebounding from a consuming fire had to offer a lot to attract visitors. The city itself lacked the riches of earlier World's Fair cities, such as London, Paris, or even Philadelphia, which had been the host to the American Centennial in 1876. The Fair would have to offer all things to all people, surely more than the architects could provide in the short time until it was due to open. Daniel Burnham realized Chicagoans might be accused of being provincials trying to do too much, so he wisely decided to turn his eyes eastward to the established centers of architecture. Prominent architects from New York and Boston as well as from Chicago and Kansas City would each be in charge of a major theme building at the Fair. Jealousy probably did play a role in the balking of the invited architects, who expressed what was then a major issue in the profession: a fear of losing control of their designs to local authority. Burnham promised the fraternity full design control, and in the committee's first meeting in December 1890 at the offices of McKim, Mead & White, the assembled group agreed to work together toward a common goal. The work would proceed surprisingly well, and it may live on as something close to the apogee of architectural collaboration in the United States. It was McKim who ended up devoting his attention almost fully to the Fair, and acted as the coordinator of the participants. His high-minded nature and absolute lack of egotistical needs encouraged the others to participate with grace, sharing designs and taking out strong features of a building if it would upstage or hinder a colleague's design. McKim was indeed on his way to becoming the force for good architecture.

That the earlier World's Fair cities had built innovative buildings for their displays is well known. Naturally, the metal sheds and engineering marvels of London and Paris were built as inexpensive solutions to the high cost of building a temporary structure any other way. But in cities with lots of traditional buildings, the Fair could look new. In Chicago, which had no panoply of important buildings, the goal of the Fair seemed to be to appear *old.* The designs for the principal buildings to be built along a lagoon created at the edge of Lake Michigan appeared intended to capture the spirit of Europe's major capitals by replicating, at least for a short while, the great buildings of Europe. The symbolism was clear: The culture of Europe had now been transplanted and flourished on American soil. To some the Fair was a step backward, away from the nation's great achievement in skyscraper building, but to Burnham and the other architects assembled, this was the affirmation of America as a world power.

The Fair was to be a city with a short life. The major buildings would be sheds of metal and glass clad in wood and plaster "houses" that hid the utilitarian display areas beneath the guise of white stone-appearing buildings of a classical style. The city, with its own electrical plant, Westinghouse turbines systems, and multiple transportation links, was an immaculate vision with its public faces lined up on the lagoon and a popular paradise back along the Midway. A jumble of tastes could be satisfied on the grounds. The rapidly constructed city of illusion, with armies of cleaners picking up after the crowds each day, taught the nation that architects

could plan for a city that all would enjoy. The Fair created the urban planning movement in America, especially the aspect known as the City Beautiful, which was held as a standard from the 1890s to the 1930s. The
wonder city at the lake's edge with its educational exhibits on the lagoon
and its exotica at the Midway was surely seminal in creating the self-
contained city of amusement that Walt Disney and his forces would build
in California and Florida. Indeed, Disney's father, Elias, worked at the Ferris wheel of the 1893 Chicago Fair and would have been most aware of the
visitors' enchantment with this "perfect" city.

The role that Chicago architect Daniel Burnham carved out for the Fair
and for himself was national in scope. Burnham was active in the professional association for architects, the American Institute of Architects, and
would serve as its president, as would two others selected by Burnham for
the team. In selecting the five non-Chicago architects invited to participate, Burnham turned to those with the greatest name recognition and
good contacts. He surely chose the members of the profession who were
thinking of the position of architecture in American culture and were
looking to establish the utility of this fine art in the mind of the general
public. Burnham wanted emissaries of art to spread throughout the
nation; he wanted the committee's vision of architecture, planning, and
landscape design, as well as the role of painting and sculpture on buildings, to be taken home by all visitors. In Burnham's vision, the theme for
the lagoon-area buildings would be drawn from the goals of the École des
Beaux-Arts, with its dependence on the allied arts to make grand buildings that would carry a historical flavor and project the importance of the
nation. The five nonresident architects Burnham chose had been at the
École or had worked with men who had been in Paris. The Chicago Fair
was the École transplanted to America's heartland.

AT THE FIRST MEETING of the architects at 57 Broadway, McKim
himself may have brought forward the concept of a uniform classical style
around a watery Court of Honor on the shore of Lake Michigan. The following year, 1891, would see the Fair postponed a year to open in 1893.
By 1892 McKim had virtually given up all other work, traveling twenty-
three times—by his own account—to Chicago. During the vital portion
of construction, he lived in Chicago and spent enormous amounts of time
in a log cabin Burnham had built on the fairgrounds. In Burnham's cabin,
the artists warmed up in front of a roaring fire and had evenings to talk. It
was here that Burnham and McKim created the concept of an academy for
American architects in Rome, where they could study and absorb Italian

architecture and bring its principles back to America. McKim and Burnham formed a very close relationship that would endure for their lifetimes; both men were devoted to the idea of the betterment of the profession and the education of the next generation. The Chicago Fair would set Americans' minds on historical grandeur as a necessity in important buildings.

In January 1891, just as McKim prepared to go to Chicago, he was greeted with the sad news that his mother, long the strength of the family, had passed away on January 9 in the house at Llewellyn Park.* Much of McKim's depression can be found rooted in the decreasing life spans of his family members. Sarah McKim outlived everyone, achieving seventy-eight years, but her own daughter had died fourteen years earlier. The McKim household fell away quickly, making McKim, now a confirmed bachelor, a profoundly lonely person. He would devote himself to the educational concepts he and Burnham had begun around the blazing fire. McKim's great final role, which would fully consume him, was that of education for the architect. He would become a zealot in his cause as his parents had been in the abolitionist movement. McKim did return to his parents' fold, but in his own way.

The Fair forced McKim to work quickly, as Columbus Day 1892 had to see buildings begun, even if the Fair would not open until late spring of the next year. McKim threw himself into the Fair and worked tirelessly; Burnham himself declared McKim his "right-hand man."

AT THE JANUARY 1891 ARCHITECTS' MEETINGS in Chicago, Mead represented the grieving McKim. The Fair site, then a swamp, discouraged the architects briefly before their imaginations took hold. The meetings had a touch of tragedy, as Burnham's partner, J. W. Root, had caught a cold during the visits and died within days of pneumonia. Somehow, everyone managed to keep meeting, despite the untimely early death of the talented Root. By agreement, the buildings were given out to the participants. The first École-trained architect, Richard Morris Hunt, now miserable with gout, was given the principal building on the Court of Honor, the Administration Building. McKim's old Boston pal Robert Peabody selected Machinery Hall, while the the great skyscraper designer George B. Post took Manufactures and Liberal Arts. Van Brunt & Howe had Electricity, and McKim, Mead & White were given the unlikely assignment of the building to house exhibits pertaining to Agriculture.

---

*Sarah McKim was remembered by her family with a small volume published privately by the De Vinne Press in 1891.

None of the partners had ever showed the slightest interest in the produce
of the earth. Four Chicagoans did the remaining Court of Honor buildings.

The following month brought McKim, Peabody, and the École-trained
Saint-Gaudens to Chicago. The architects showed one another their preliminary designs, actually agreeing to give up features of their own buildings for the others in a true collaborative effort.

McKim's building on the Court of Honor was a wood and plaster shell
built over a steel shed. The creation of a fictive Roman building of great
size around the exhibition shed was similar to what had been done at the
two Parisian World's Fairs. McKim certainly had seen enough of the 1878
Paris Exposition and would have known about the 1889 Exposition as
White would surely have brought back pictures. McKim's building had
an approximation of the Pantheon set in the center, which then extended
out with long wings focused on Roman thermal windows. McKim created
the Baths of Caracalla welded to the Pantheon—all festooned with flags
and a host of sculpture. Saint-Gaudens had come to Chicago to advise; his
own working habits were not sufficiently subject to the clock for him to
be considered for work at the Fair. His former student MacMonnies would
be given great public work at the Fair, while an admiring Philip Martiny
would do some of the sculpture for the Agriculture Building. Mary
Gertrude Mead Abbey insisted that Larkin G. Mead get a piece of the pie,
which would become the pediment group. In the end, in an unplanned
effort, White and Saint-Gaudens would have a place on the Agriculture
Building, as the rejected, eighteen-foot-high Diana was removed from

*World's Columbian Exposition, Chicago, 1893. McKim's New York
State Building. The Villa Medici meets Elias Disney.*

*In Remembrance of the World's Columbian Exposition, 1893. The Agriculture Building
by McKim. A building on the lagoon devoted to American farming, just as people
were moving to the cities.*

Madison Square Garden and shipped to Chicago to top the dome of
McKim's building. A second version, five feet shorter, was then installed
in New York.

McKim, Mead & White did three other buildings in Chicago. The
humor magazine *Puck* had a pavilion, as did the White Star Line shipping
company, and the State of New York asked McKim to build its home state
structure. The New York State pavilion was intended as a resting place
and clubhouse-like building for those visiting Chicago from New York.
The state that had lost the Fair to Illinois had to project its presence in a
building at Chicago. The pavilion does show McKim's mind already
turned to the idea of an academy in Rome, as the New York State pavilion
was based fairly closely on the Villa Medici, the home of the French Academy in Rome for almost a century. McKim was thinking about joining
the French with a base in a Roman villa for Americans to reside in while
absorbing the city as the French had done so well since the days of Col-
bert. McKim had cheered himself and gathered ideas for his American
Academy by visiting Rome in the summer of 1891 with Samuel A. B.
Abbott. On his return, the pavilion in Chicago was decorated with sculpture and set with potted trees, making the building appear very Roman.

Henry Bacon, the brother of Francis Bacon, one of the first men to join
the office, was sent to Chicago for the building phase as the office's representative. The Bacon brothers were both men of great talent. Francis
Bacon was an archaeologist who supported himself doing furniture
design. Henry Bacon was able to design well enough to garner the support
of both McKim and White. McKim dispatched Henry Bacon to the Fair,
and White also used him on a small commission he was given in Chicago.

That Stanford White had little to do with the major buildings of the Chicago Fair is testimonial to the École concept of Burnham, who chose the Parisian student McKim over the self-taught White. White's main work at the Fair was the smaller special pavilions, such as that for *Puck* magazine, and the display for the American Cotton Oil Company, whose booth White was hired to design. Edward Dean Adams, whose Rohallion had been designed a few years earlier, asked White to do the Cotton Oil job. It was probably done as a private work, as records of it do not appear in the firm's bill books. Adams commissioned White in due time, but White did not bother with the design. As the deadlines drew closer, Adams wrote White about the booth, and White responded with an elaborate explanation of the lack of perfection in the design he was working on. The truth was that White had done nothing at all and was not intending to do anything. Instead, he had planned on getting Henry Bacon to do the booth. This exchange reveals a new aspect of White's behavior: He would go to great lengths, lying outrageously, when facing failure.

White's great contribution to the Fair came with his increasing absorption into the world of the dealers. He had begun to promote his own collection of paintings and the work of contemporary American artists by participating in and organizing exhibitions for the Chicago Fair. White sent his own oils by Kenyon Cox and Dewing for display at the Fair. A painter close to the architects, Frank Millet, had been appointed the director of all decoration at the Fair, and Millet was in frequent contact with McKim. The rich assortment of works of art, from the White City itself (as the Fair's shining city was now called) to the paintings and decorative arts shown, corroborate Saint-Gaudens's exclamation as he saw the Fair about to unfold. He remarked that this was "the greatest assembly of artists since the 15th century." Saint-Gaudens had it right: The assembled artists worked as had not been done before, and a spectacular illusion appeared before the public's eyes in May 1893.

At the 1892 meetings, probably with some off-the-cuff advice from Millet, McKim realized his design for the Agriculture Building was out of proportion to the dome. He therefore argued for adding an attic story. But the bottom line was that the budget had been spent and there was no money for another story. The more Burnham pronounced on the lack of money, the more ardor McKim brought to his argument on the need for the attic to make the building beautiful. This was the technique McKim would perfect: He would quietly and humbly reiterate his vision, stopping to nod at reality before resuming his campaign via another set of responses. Eventually, unable to stop McKim and more and more anxious to leave the meeting, the participants would be worn down and McKim would get his way. His tactic almost always succeeded, and as the delivery was carried out so modestly, no one ever became angry with him; rather, they were simply resigned to giving McKim his goal if they ever wanted to go home.

The third technique McKim developed here was derived from Stanford White's amusing dinners. McKim now began to stage dinners with battlefield precision, taking great care with the food, wine, flowers, and location. Far more sober than White's dinners McKim's were always mounted to sell an idea by softening up the unwary during a good meal, then making a low-key pounce for results. On March 25, 1893, at White's Madison Square Garden, McKim gave a dinner for Burnham with the aging Richard Morris Hunt in the place of host. The Chicago Fair crowd— Millet, the architects, and Saint-Gaudens—joined Joseph H. Choate, Henry Villard, William Dean Howells, R. W. Gilder, and other artists and sculptors assembled for McKim's meal. McKim honored Burnham with this celebration and also displayed his appreciation by obtaining an honorary degree for him—McKim's version of client pleasing, which fit exactly into his character. McKim wrote to college and university presidents asking that people he especially wished to favor—E. D. Morgan and Daniel Burnham, for example—be given honorary degrees. In 1893 both Harvard and Yale awarded Burnham a master of arts degree. These degrees were particularly sweet to Burnham, who had failed to gain entry to those institutions when he was a youth. McKim was becoming the prince of education, so the awarding of a favor in an academic manner was appropriate from him.

Stanford White's manner of showing favor to his friends tended to be of a more pleasurable nature. He would escort his clients into the artists' world or the vaudeville world or to a party with elaborate surprises and lavish food and wine. A White party might include a young woman with blond hair serving white wine, while a redhead served red wine. White also favored his clients with gifts. A classic gift was a salmon caught at the Restigouche Club, then packed in ice and shipped. Many times the ice would melt en route and the fish arrived spoiled, but White kept up the practice. McKim and Mead lived in two far-removed worlds, but they remained White's true friends and good colleagues.

Stanford White, with Bessie and Larry in tow, jumped off a transatlantic liner and onto the train to Chicago, where everyone was bowled over by the White City. The Venetian ambiance and the use of small lightbulbs outlining buildings in the darkness were his own concepts, now imitated by others, and White loved the effect. His first visit stretched to ten days and included some festive evenings. He would return in October at closing time to once again see this living version of a historical novel's setting.

Stanford White's enjoyment of the Fair was dampened by his brother's outrageous behavior. Having had little success in his mining ventures, Dick White came to Chicago as a representative of the Territory of New Mexico. While in the city Dick wrote some inflammatory letters on behalf of the territory without obtaining permission, and Stanford White had to write the president to try to undo the damage. His brother was removed from the New Mexico delegation.

The general public, particularly in agrarian areas, was initially overwhelmed by the effort and expense required to see the White City. But as friends returned and tales of the wonders grew, people took their burial money out of its hiding place and journeyed to Chicago. The Fair convinced the population that great buildings and great art were worth the expenditure and were of value to the nation.

With the Fair, McKim sharpened the diplomatic skills he would need to carry out his ambitions for the future. Working with Frank Millet, McKim spoke quietly to the other nonresident architects, helping them refine their designs. No detail was too small to let go, even for a place with a life of only five months. Hunt was privately given advice to improve the floor of his Administration Building. Millet was everywhere, making McKim even more a part of his circle and bringing him closer to his neighbor at 13 East Thirty-fifth Street, John L. Cadwalader, who was often Millet's host in New York. Millet's role in the Fair is surely worthy of a separate study, as he was a major power in the creation of the Fair even if he is forgotten today. The very appearance of the city was Millet's choice. The buildings were to be painted different colors, but construction was completed too late for paint, so Millet had a compressor hooked up and had the buildings spray-painted white.

# 37. OLD COLLEGES AND NEW BUILDINGS

That the two architectural partners had gone in different directions is clear. Ironically, in the early 1890s their distinct identities won them commissions for a pair of strikingly similar projects. Each of the two private colleges of New York City needed an architect to create a new campus in a different part of the city: one chose White, the other McKim.

New York had never been a college town. The city's oldest school, King's College, later patriotically renamed Columbia College, and the University of the City of New York, later New York University, were the city's elite colleges. Neither was particularly well regarded. The trustees of the two colleges rarely sent their own children to the schools. The two colleges were not part of the life of the city, and each sat in a neighborhood that was becoming increasingly noisy and bothersome. Neither college had much in the way of financial resources, and the pool of alumni produced little revenue. Each college was on the prowl for contributors, but in New York, the pool of wealthy men to be tapped was rather small and both schools were after the same donors. Indeed, several names would appear as good contributors to both schools.

Both colleges were beset by identity problems in a changing world. Columbia with its roots in New York's Episcopal Church was in its 136th year and on its second campus. The University of the City of New York was not yet sixty years old and still in its first building. Columbia had a sense of being the school of the older and more entrenched families of the gentry, while the University of the City of New York had been founded by a group of merchants who were relative newcomers to the city and often Presbyterian in belief. Both schools faced the difficulty of continuing to attract students and dealing with children of the newer arrivals to the city who were Catholic and Jewish. The two colleges accepted some applicants from these groups but did hope to see Catholic and Jewish colleges take over and admit greater numbers of students of their faiths. Neither of the older colleges wished to broaden its outreach beyond the successful families of the city.

Columbia College had been in its midtown campus at Forty-ninth Street between Madison and Fourth Avenue for some thirty-five years when its new president, Seth Low, was appointed. The campus was crowded and there was no possible place to expand, as the area on Madison Avenue had been built up with houses, including the Villard houses just to the north. The eastern border was the troubling one—it stood at the side of the railroad tracks that every day seemed to bring even more trains into Grand Central Depot. Columbia College had eyed some land along the Hudson River at 161st Street but had decided the Upper Manhattan location was too distant.

The University of the City of New York had also looked at land near 161st Street, but had not selected the area either. The university sat at the eastern side of "the reservation," as the center of the old mercantile families of the city was known. But the red brick row houses of Washington Square were being quickly replaced by tall loft buildings created to serve the burgeoning textile and garment industries of the city, lately moving north from older and smaller quarters on Worth Street. The workers in the buildings alongside the university were clearly foreign, and their presence pushed the administration of the college to look uptown much as the railroad noise was pushing Columbia northward.

With both colleges weak, poorly endowed, and in unsuitable locations, the head of one of the city's most important private banking houses, Jacob Schiff, proposed combining them into a single institution, which Schiff promised to richly endow. Neither college wished to merge, but neither school could afford to anger Schiff and his friends. So the two schools had to engage in a polite, yearlong dance to avoid consolidation, even if—as eventually happened—Schiff retreated from his offer. Each college would then use the vigor of a new top administrator to push the institution into a new, image-projecting campus and buildings.

The University of the City of New York had been Richard Grant White's school, and he had toyed with the thought of teaching there in mid-career. In the 1870s, when the school was almost at the point of closing, Dr. Crosby approached former governor E. D. Morgan for a million-dollar donation. Morgan, who had no university tie, was startled, then angered, and avoided the university for the remainder of his life. In 1881, Richard Grant White would petition Dr. Crosby for an honorary degree for Stanford. Granting this request was one of Dr. Crosby's last acts before stepping down and may have been the return of a favor. In 1891, Henry Mitchell MacCracken stepped up to the position of chancellor and turned his full energy toward creating a new campus for the college. Dr. MacCracken would select a section of 1850s country houses above the Harlem River on a high plateau in the Bronx, ten miles above Washington Square, as the new site for the school. The college would purchase the Mali estate for the new campus.

As the New York gentry was a rather small group in the nineteenth century, the buildup of the university involved many of the people whom McKim, Mead, and White had known in the course of their careers, both as friends and as clients. John Taylor Johnston, a son of two founding families of the University of the City of New York, had a gatehouse done by McKim, Mead & White in 1885. Johnston was surely one of the heroic figures of the nineteenth century, an American who bought significant works of art without an advisor, an early client of Louis Tiffany's decorative firm, and a key figure in the creation of the Metropolitan Museum of Art.

The university had recently been saved from near financial disaster by the widow of Robert L. Stuart, whose old house was then the McKim, Mead & White offices.* Another staunch supporter of the school was Loring Andrews, whose residence in the Montauk Association group had been an early resort house by the architects. It was in the company of the family connections that Chancellor MacCracken approached Stanford White in 1891, asking him to become the architect for the university out of respect for his father's memory rather than for pay. White agreed to the proposal and began thinking about the university and the new campus at what would become University Heights.

White loved the bounty of Europe's past. He also had a high regard for America's history, from the old wooden statue of George Washington that had sat atop the Washington Centennial arch to the 1830s Collegiate Gothic Main Building designed by James Dakin for the architectural firm

*As we know, her current house would be sold to William Collins Whitney after Mrs. Stuart's death.

of Town & Davis. White immediately drew up plans for the Main Building to be modernized. White considered the Main Building a treasure of the university and assumed that it would be taken apart and rebuilt at University Heights. Like his father, Stanford White was an admirer of early nineteenth-century New York. He wanted to save the Main Building. He also tried to preserve City Hall, the Croton Reservoir, and the Merchants' Exchange at 55 Wall Street. White was remarkably ahead of his time in his attitude toward New York landmarks and was happy to provide solutions for their adaptive reuse. When an old building was doomed, White would do as the descendants of Peter Cooper did and bring the stones out to their country houses. He saved elements of demolished buildings at the St. James house, just as the Cooper heirs did at Ringwood in New Jersey. An entire study could be done on White's remarkable preservation record, but at University Heights his effort fell on deaf ears. Chancellor MacCracken refused to save the old building, claiming the costs of taking it apart and then reassembling it would be prohibitive. The truth probably was that the chancellor wished to build an entirely new campus with his stamp on the buildings.

White's advice to the university had been to remove the college building to the new campus and have a commercial loft building constructed at the site of the Main Building to produce revenue for the college, with three small divisions of the university—law, pedagogy, and a graduate division—located at the top of the loft building. The rest of the school would go to the glorious country-city edge at the Mali estate. The problem here would be the distance above the city. The University of the City of New York (it would become New York University in 1896) went too far north. Eighty years later, in a remarkable reversal of New York's northward logic, New York University fully returned to its original site at Washington Square.

As money for the new campus would be hard to raise, many of the older buildings on the site would be used until new buildings could be afforded. White's first building was a Hall of Languages, then a dormitory necessary to house students at this distant location, and a science building. The focus of White's campus would be the library building, the symbol of an academic community. The library White designed in the winter of 1894–95 was perched atop the reinforced bluff of the escarpment over the Harlem River, giving the building its greatest visibility to the city below. White's first proposal was for a round, domed, golden brick library in the tradition of college campuses from Union College to Jefferson's University of Virginia.

To White's dismay, MacCracken did not like the library design. The chancellor was probably fearful of the cost of the building, but he was also perturbed by the interior of the rotunda, which seemed to him to have little use. MacCracken asked White for alternate plans for the library, which White felt was an insulting request. Richard Morris Hunt, at the end of his years, was called in to moderate the dispute between MacCracken and White. True to the principles of the American Institute of Architects, Hunt backed White's position.

The library was begun in 1897 with monies from the daughter of the notorious robber barron Jay Gould. The late Gould had not been much of a philanthropist, but his daughter, Helen Gould Shepard, would try to shine up his image with a large donation to create the Gould Library. White, trying to create a campus that projected authority, added the concept of the Hall of Fame to the library. His ambulatory was not only a wonderful visual tool that linked the buildings of the college, but also enhanced the university's image. White's Hall of Fame was a covered walkway decorated with heads of famous figures from history. The pitch was that students who studied at the university and sat among the greats would go on to magnificent achievements after college. The Hall of Fame

*New York University, the Bronx Campus, ca. 1892. The campus and library as finished, 1902.*

*The New York University library and Hall of Fame in the Bronx.*

remains a great work, which inspires both by example and by its setting high atop the city below.

It is difficult to be certain that the Hall of Fame was White's idea, but it appears to have been his, based probably on the suggestions of Mac-Cracken, who wished a projection of importance for the university. The original notion probably came from the Great Galleries of Immortals at the Ruhmeshalle in Munich, Germany, a nineteenth-century Grecian temple where sixty-four busts of famous people sit on bases along the walls, in honor of Ludwig I. White would have seen this Hall of Fame (as the German name translates) on his trips to Munich. The Bavarian temple was probably based on the eighteenth-century Hall of Worthies at Stowe in England, recently restored. The Ruhmeshalle was badly damaged in World War II.

White's campus was a modestly priced group of buildings for a strapped university. Only the Gould Library had a large budget, and its great effect was lost on the city, which was too far south to be able to see the campus. Columbia's location was more expensive, but more adroit, as the city did see that university on a hill.

It would appear that White and Chancellor MacCracken may not have been getting along too well by the time the campus work began. Mac-

*The interior of the library, now named for the Gould family.*

Cracken did get one further favor from White—the NYU logo. The image of the torch comes from a suggestion White gave to the chancellor. It is the logo to this day.

MacCracken took White's concept for a plain commercial building for the old college building site and gave it to the German-born architect Alfred Zucker, who had a good number of commissions in the area. The building would house the American Book Company, which produced textbooks, on the lower floors; the upper three floors were slightly embellished and housed the law, pedagogy, and graduate programs of the university. New York University sought to create a new campus and identity for the school on a budget. The institution was careful to not go too deeply into debt, perhaps remembering its flirtation with financial collapse in the late 1870s. Columbia, with roughly the same set of problems, went out much farther on a limb for more expensive property and buildings; in the end, its efforts probably made it able to create a better spin for the school.

COLUMBIA COLLEGE, jammed into its small Victorian Gothic campus, was badly in need of image enhancement. A solution to the college's woes came in 1890, when the Brooklyn-born Seth Low was installed as president of the college. Low did have Columbia ties and had been a trustee for almost a decade, but he had no academic credentials. His selection had been based on two factors—he was rich and politically well connected. Columbia put its future in the hands of an ambitious man, mayor of his home city of Brooklyn and eager to rise. The school was a good podium for his ambition and Low's connections could help the college solve problems with the legislature. And, of course, Low's father had been one of the most successful of the China traders. Low's wealth would act as a magnet for other donors—or so the school hoped.

Seth Low probably spent his Sunday afternoons as MacCracken had, riding through the northern parts of the city in a carriage, looking for a suitable place for a new campus. In the summer of 1891, a Columbia attorney who acted as clerk of the trustees, John B. Pine, undertook secret negotiations with New York Hospital for a site on the escarpment along the Hudson called Morningside Heights. Pine, a mysterious person who left behind little information that would flesh him out other than a history of his home neighborhood, Gramercy Park, certainly played a major role in the selection and development of the Morningside Heights campus. Pine was an excellent image creator and probably had ties to other legal firms in the city; he may have been able to act on inside knowledge to start the negotiations with the hospital for a site running from 116th Street to 120th Street between Broadway and Amsterdam Avenue.

The property in question, a large tract of land in a bucolic state, had long been the grounds of the Bloomingdale Insane Asylum, a part of New York Hospital opened as a mental hospital in 1821. The Bloomingdale Insane Asylum functioned well into the 1880s, when local real estate investors decided the asylum was holding down land values. With speculative development in full swing on the West Side below Morningside Heights, a few landholders wanted to open up the area, but needed transportation to encourage development. The new Ninth Avenue elevated trains came up the West Side, then veered east at 110th Street, isolating Morningside Heights.

Clearly, a horse car route was needed on the section of upper Broadway then known as the Boulevard, but the asylum blocked the path. The Realtors and their politicians took on the patrician board of New York Hospital, represented by John L. Cadwalader and Elbridge T. Gerry. The real estate forces won. The Bloomingdale Insane Asylum had to remove to White Plains. New York Hospital put the 116th–120th Street tract up for sale. Through the efforts of John Pine, a deal was finally made for the property go to an institution, not a private developer, but with a hefty price— two million dollars. This was far more than Columbia College could afford or was likely to be able to raise. As with the clubs, the funding would have to come from selling the old site and taking out a mortgage.

The Bloomingdale tract was of varied topography, with a high point at the south end and middle ground, then a decline to street grade at the north. The college now faced two problems: how to deal with the grading, an expensive proposition, and how to create a beautiful and image-enhancing campus with almost no resources.

The trustees appointed two professors from its School of Architecture, the second in the nation, and the head of buildings and grounds as a committee to reflect upon the site and future buildings for the new campus. Three New York architects were asked to prepare a preliminary study: the dean of the profession, Richard Morris Hunt; the son of a trustee and architect to the midtown campus, Charles C. Haight; and Charles Follen McKim, already known to Seth Low as the donor of a traveling prize for architects, which McKim had created when he liquidated Julia Appleton's assets. The Columbia trustees were probably hoping to gain a plan from the three architects that the two professors might execute for them as a kind of collaboration, but the three outsiders refused to cooperate with this money-saving scheme.

Charles C. Haight must have expected to have the job and would have been most distressed when the Collegiate Gothic style he had used successfully earlier at the Columbia midtown campus was not selected; Haight's arrangement for the campus was also passed over. Hunt, who had no college design background, may have given up easily even if he would have liked to gain a commission for his sons to finish after his passing. McKim really wanted the job. He was moving toward education as his vocation anyway and had endowed the new (1881) School of Architecture at Columbia with the traveling fellowship announced by the new president in his 1890 inaugural address. McKim's plans for Columbia were truly important to the architect, who might well have seen this commission as a real test of his ability.

McKim's original design has been lost, but we know he envisioned the campus buildings atop an even more built-up plinth at the southern side of the campus, with access by a staircase from 116th Street. The four-block campus, as it was envisioned then, would be a sacred, closed-off precinct that could be seen by the city below. McKim seemed the most likely of the trio to conceive a scheme of the ambitious nature Seth Low expected. The two Columbia professors did try to effect a plan that mingled ideas from the trio of invited architects, but the outside architects objected and demanded the commission be given to a single competitor.

At this point in the tale, the Chicago Fair was to open and Seth Low traveled to the White City to make the announcement of Columbia's move to Morningside Heights from the ballroom of McKim's New York State building. Ironically, Morningside Heights had been proposed as the site for the World's Fair in New York's entry to the competition. The New York bid had, of course, been lost to Chicago. As fall set in and the three outside architects refused to work together, Columbia was forced to select one of the three.

Clearly, all the committee members had agreed that Haight's design was far out of date. Low knew McKim and at Chicago had seen that his role had been more vigorous than that of Hunt. By November 1893, the job was McKim's, which brought him the double satisfaction of keeping many of his office staff busy in a bad economic time and enjoying a personal triumph. Despite the selection of a campus architect, the effects of the deep economic recession were enough to put off Columbia's move from 1895 to 1897.* The time would prove a blessing for McKim as he could now revise his work and think carefully about buildings that he knew would be his legacy to the profession.

Raising money for the new campus buildings would prove very difficult for the trustees. The interim solution would be to use the old Bloomingdale Insane Asylum buildings temporarily while looking for donors for the new buildings.

Not only was McKim working for the ages; so too was Seth Low. Low had staked his reputation on this campus move and buildup of the college, even to the point of declining an offer to run for mayor, which was a continuing theme in Low's life. He promised to stay with Columbia until its new campus was well in hand. Indeed, Low would continue to flirt with the mayoralty, running unsuccessfully in 1897 and again in 1901, when

*Columbia's great first day in the uptown campus would be October 4, 1897.

he won the race. A key factor in Low's mayoral image was his success in creating a new Columbia.

One of Low's two qualifications for the job of president of the university was his father's wealth. In 1893 Abiel A. Low died, leaving his son a good sum for the day. Low viewed the national economic news and reflected on the low level of fund-raising possible, and then he did what the trustees must always have hoped he would. In the summer of 1894, Low had decided to put up the most important of the planned buildings, the library, as a signal of stability, hoping that having a major building under way would inspire other donors to follow. Further, his generosity in donating a library would cast a saintly light on candidate Low for a future election.

Low had to make his plan for Columbia work or his credibility would have been ruined. He probably spoke with McKim in the summer months of 1894, letting the architect know that a donor was secured so McKim could work with the hope of the library really being built, even if Low would make the announcement to the trustees and the city much later.

McKim's and Low's library was to be a symbol rather than a comfortable place. The library was the sign of scholarship and thus represented a college moving toward a higher reputation. It was placed on a platform above the city as a symbol of this striving institution. The library would be the center of the campus, surrounded on three sides by classroom buildings, the chapel, and the assembly halls.

Low Library, a memorial to Low's recently departed father, was to be far more prominent in the four-block campus than the other buildings, so a different material was to be used. McKim seems to have originally favored marble, but, given the number of unemployed in a bad economic time, this would likely have appeared extravagant, so Low rejected marble for a granite-based limestone building. The classroom buildings would be brick with stone trim, making the library the singular limestone building, a building that owed a great debt to the Columbian Exposition with its simulation of white stone and the overall Roman character of its buildings. McKim's low dome, his white building with its references to the Roman Pantheon and Roman baths, seemed an outgrowth of the Fair.

Once McKim was appointed as the architect for this self-improving university, he took the role of educator almost as seriously as he did that of architect. McKim lectured the trustees about architecture and history to secure his goals. His role as architect/architectural historian was so well recognized that a successor to Seth Low, the virtually immortal Nicholas

Murray Butler—president for forty-three years—as one of his first acts asked McKim to consider the directorship of the School of Architecture. McKim rejected the position, although he would agree to run an architectural atelier for the school.

Construction on the Low Memorial Library began late in 1895. The Library would have an equal-armed Greek cross plan with a rotunda in the center to be used as a great, domed reading room rather like the British Library. The design for the dome over the rotunda created a delay until a solution was reached with the contractor, Norcross, still the premier construction company in the nation.

McKim worked on the Low Library interior with great care. He shared this absorption with the donor, who was also looking for a perfect building. The great rotunda ceiling was painted the deep blue of the night sky, with a hanging globe emulating the moon. McKim would wax poetical to the trustees on the role of moonlight in the room. To inspire future scholars, the rotunda was to have sixteen Greek figures in the upper galleries as guardians of the classics, but only four were completed—one a gift of McKim.

McKim and Low wanted to have massive columns of green Connemara Irish marble as White had done in the Gould Library. To Low's great disappointment, only two green marble columns could be made, giving Stanford White an opportunity to gloat to Chancellor MacCracken on their success with the rare marble. To some, Gould's money was less pure than Low's, making for jokes at the office, but White could at least take comfort in having the better marble.

The Low Memorial Library reading rotunda was surrounded at north and east arms of the cross by special libraries devoted to law and architecture. Offices for the president and dean of the college were also located on the main floor. Sadly for McKim, as wonderful as the great library was, it worked poorly for its purpose. The reading room would prove too small for the college, which would grow both in quality and in size. In the 1920s a new library was built in the south third of the Bloomingdale campus, from 114th to 116th Streets, a second parcel of land purchased in 1903. The books traveled to other locations, leaving Low Memorial curiously hollow in its center.

To complete his campus plan, McKim had a topographical model of the contours of the tract made and studied it intently, perhaps because the trip to the site was most difficult. Columbia's new campus, originally a non-residential one, relied on students and everyone else making their way to the campus without good transportation routes. The eastward swerve of the great elevated line forced McKim and all others to get off the El at Ninety-sixth Street and take a horse-drawn car to the campus. The university would not be well served by mass transit until the IRT subway opened in 1904, with a stop at the campus.

Models of the tract would quickly be joined by models of the buildings. To be certain of the proportions of the planned buildings, McKim ventured into the expensive construction of scale models. At 160 Fifth Avenue, a model-making area joined the blueprints as a new sign of professionalism in America. Models would now often be made when McKim was uncertain and no longer could rely on Babb's or Wells's superb sense of proportion. Sadly, as is usually the case, the models did not survive, as they present major storage problems.

The classroom buildings that define the quadrangle of the campus were to be built as donors appeared and were to be flexible, practical structures. To keep costs to a minimum, these buildings were to be of brick, but "Harvard" brick was selected—the dark, hand-pressed brick used in the Cambridge, Massachusetts, college buildings and in the New York City Harvard Club building McKim had just built. The Harvard brick gave the buildings an old-time American air. Columbia College had begun in 1754, and the dark brick and vaguely Georgian massing of the classroom buildings may have been intended to link the college to its past, two campuses back. The classroom buildings have white limestone trim and huge

*The Columbia campus in an 1897 image from the Columbia Archives.*

*Columbia University, ca. 1999. The modern campus, woefully too small today.*

windows with some Renaissance feeling. They are a hybrid image vehicle, harking back to the Bostonian colleges as well as to the penchant for travel to Italy: American Georgian meets Rome, and Harvard meets the Tiber. The design of the classroom buildings permitted great flexibility in their use, allowing a maximum of light and air to enter through the large windows. Further classroom buildings would be added steadily over the next decade as donors appeared.

Columbia's great gamble to move to an empty tract of land in a region with poor transportation actually paid off. Seth Low's great campus and the next president, Nicholas Murray Butler, would re-create the school as a university of the first tier. Indeed, the enlargement of the university has been so great that today it is as hamstrung by its confining campus as it was more than a century ago in its small cloister on Forty-ninth Street.

Columbia was one of McKim's personal triumphs. He was pleased to have the opportunity to contribute to the educational and civic uplift of the city of New York, which he was beginning to find an overly harsh place. McKim could well follow Seth Low's goal of an enlightened city and Nicholas Murray Butler's emphasis on a more rigorous education. It is as a kindred spirit that McKim is remembered on the great plaza before the Low Library, as his campus did create a new world for the college. An inscription in the plaza paving echoes Sir Christopher Wren's epitaph: "Si monumentum requiris, circumspice."

McKim's ties to Columbia were formed on the basis of his professional achievement. His single college year had been at Harvard, which had begun to notice their short-term student when McKim married an Appleton, built the Algonquin Club, and began the Boston Public Library. McKim's benefactions after his wife's death to establish traveling fellowships for students interested in studying architecture abroad gave him a presence at his alma mater. At the graduation ceremony of 1890 at Harvard, McKim, Richard Watson Gilder, and Columbia's brand-new president, Seth Low, sat on the dais together to receive honorary degrees.

For McKim and Gilder, who had known each other for decades, the honor was significant. For McKim especially, whose year at the Scientific School had been so unfortunate, the recognition was truly pleasing, since it showed he had now joined the ranks of those who had done well and become part of the college. In the festivities surrounding the honorary degree (that medium of favor McKim would soon bring to those he wished to encourage or thank), he must have solidified his relationship with Seth Low, who would soon call him to begin thinking with the others about Columbia's new campus.

McKim's work at Harvard had begun the year before with the first of what would be a series of gates donated by college alumni. Indeed, McKim would go on to build so many Harvard gates that he virtually became the gate man of Harvard. McKim's first venture for Harvard was a gate paid for by a Chicago graduate, class of 1855, Samuel Johnston. The goal was a gate, but what would it look like? President Eliot had warned McKim that the simple issue of a new gate would be likely to split the alumni—no matter how it was designed, a good portion of the community was sure to dislike it. McKim agonized over the design, finally settling on the idea of blending the materials of the new gate, a dark New Hampshire brick, with the buildings of the university. He made several experiments with the texture and color of brick until he came up with his "Harvard" brick. The gate was a great success and spurred a donation from George von Lengerke Meyer, class of 1879, who would maintain a lifelong affection for his former brother-in-law. McKim's solution for the gates showed a way around President Eliot's fears and the problem of yoking past and present. McKim would receive three full commissions at Harvard in 1899—for the new School of Architecture building, the stadium, and the Harvard Union, the latter done for Henry Lee Higginson, who loved music and Harvard equally.

Henry Lee Higginson was at the top of the list of McKim's great supporters at Harvard. Higginson was tied to McKim's childhood world of William Lloyd Garrison. Born in 1834, he belonged to the ninth generation of the American-born family of Higginsons. His family was from Cambridge, Massachusetts, but they had moved to New York City, where Henry Lee Higginson could have known Miller McKim. Higginson studied briefly at Harvard and in 1868 married the daughter of the highly revered Harvard professor Louis Agassiz. Higginson then had a double Harvard connection. Henry Lee Higginson was an ardent abolitionist and had served in the Civil War as a major in the First Massachusetts Cavalry. His cousin, Thomas Wentworth Higginson, served as the commander of the first regiment of African American troops commissioned for service by the United States government. A true zealot in the antislavery cause, Thomas Wentworth Higginson was badly wounded in the war. Colonel Higginson retired to Newport, Rhode Island, where he became a key figure in the intellectual life of that city. He was one of McKim's first friends in Newport during his courtship and married days on Mrs. Bigelow's bully piazza.* The two men often read aloud to the summer visitors.

The Higginsons were important to McKim's career, with F. Lee Higginson asking McKim for an addition on his house at Beverly Farms, Massachusetts, in 1879. Two years later F. Lee Higginson's brother, Major Henry Lee Higginson, would have H. H. Richardson build his half of the Higginson/Whittier house in Boston, while McKim designed the Whittier half of the house for Higginson's business partner.

After Richardson's death, Henry Lee Higginson gave his work to McKim. Higginson would ask McKim to build a new Symphony Hall for Boston as well as the Harvard Union. Higginson would even back McKim's American Academy in Rome in its early years, giving money in Harvard's name. He had been happy to have McKim in Boston and must have felt like cheering his friend with some work as McKim wrestled with his future after Julia's death.

---

*Higginson would introduce McKim to Colonel Waring, the sanitary engineer then running H.A.C. Taylor's model farm. Colonel Higginson boarded at Mrs. Dame's house with the author Helen Hunt, whose Indian tales would inspire Stanford White when he went out to New Mexico to visit his brother.

# 38. McKim's New York Clubhouses

McKim had returned to New York when Harvard called upon him to build their New York City clubhouse in the summer of 1893, opening the door for McKim's entry into clubhouse design in New York City. The urban clubhouses had thus far been designed by White, who had been viewed as the ebullient man on the town. McKim had built the Algonquin Club in Boston and the Germantown Cricket Club for his old team, where he had been a stellar player in the 1860s. McKim had never built a New York City club until the Harvard Corporation asked him to build a New York base.

Individual colleges and universities had an interest in maintaining quarters in the nation's major city. A club could be a vehicle for keeping the profile of the college before the public and for extracting donations from proud graduates. However, real estate prices in New York were prohibitive, obliging graduates from different colleges to share a university club, as individual colleges could not count on enough alumni to maintain a separate clubhouse.

It would seem that the first individual college club in New York was the Harvard Club, begun in 1887 in a row house at 11 West Twenty-second Street. The Harvard Corporation was ready to proclaim its presence in New York in a bigger way by 1893 and asked McKim to design a purpose-built clubhouse at 27–29 West Forty-fourth Street, a block above the Century and several other clubs. The challenge for McKim was to make Harvard in Manhattan. McKim echoed the Harvard quad with his now-acceptable Harvard brick.

To make the club more sophisticated for the city, McKim turned to recent work in Britain done by his once favorite British designer, Norman Shaw. Shaw's career, like McKim's, had progressed into a more pronounced historical style that favored the same era in British architecture as Harvard's buildings in the United States. McKim borrowed from Shaw's Bryanston for some of the elements at the Harvard Club, but he still produced a rather modest building. Later McKim, and then his assistant, William M. Kendall, would enlarge the clubhouse twice to today's much larger size.

Before the arrival of the single college clubs, New York's university men had formed a multiple-school club, in emulation of the 1821 United, All University Club in London. The University Club of New York came into being in 1865 at University Place; the institution justified itself as an influence on the domain of learning. Its standards of inclusion were rather loose, with admission given to men who had graduated from a college or resided in one for three years. Interpretation of this rule was generous, and McKim and Saint-Gaudens would offer their years at the École in Paris as their basis for admission. The standards were lax enough to allow honorary degrees as an equivalent.

The University Club was reorganized and reinvigorated in 1879 when it moved into a house at 370 Fifth Avenue, which was part of the John Caswell estate. The fitting of the house as a club was done by Robert Henderson Robertson, one of many architects in the University Club. Robertson, both well·born and well mannered, would be a friendly rival to McKim, Mead & White in the next two decades. He would share space with the firm at an office building he designed, 160 Fifth Avenue, in the 1890s. Robertson's work often shared a design sense with that of McKim, Mead & White. The architects were on friendly social terms too; indeed, famous—or infamous—summer baseball games were staged between the two offices.

At the University Club's new quarters, the young McKim, backed by his friends Sidney Stratton and Prescott Hall Butler and his old mentor Russell Sturgis, was given the honor of designing the club flag, regrettably now lost. For a few years after that, McKim avoided the clubhouse, probably to avoid Bigelow, who was active in the club. When McKim began to spend time at the club again, he joined the library committee with John Jacob Astor, Brayton Ives, Frederick Stevens, W. C. Whitney, and the publisher Henry Holt. McKim, Mead & White would design houses for all these men. The club was a wonderful environment for gathering clients.

In 1884 the University Club took over a bigger house, the Jerome mansion, almost ten blocks south of the Caswell house. At the Jerome house, Charles Coolidge Haight did the alterations for the clubhouse. The club grew in the next few years, causing the club committee to consider leasing the Stokes house next door. McKim's stature in the club members' eyes had grown, and in 1893 he was asked to design the enlarged clubhouse. He made elaborate plans, but the lease fell through. The committee with charge over the clubhouse decided to look to an entirely new club building in keeping with the new houses being built by the Century Association and the new Metropolitan Club.

The committee, under Charles T. Barney, studied three sites on Fifth Avenue, deciding on lots at Fifty-fourth Street recently placed on the market by the trustees of St. Luke's Hospital. The club purchased the

*The University Club on Fifth Avenue in New York, 1896–1900. McKim's synthesis of architecture and education.*

125-foot-by-100-foot plot from the hospital, which had been located on this site from 1848 until the sale in 1896. St. Luke's Hospital was about to open its new facility at Morningside Heights and no longer needed the old site.

As the club committee studied the site, a decision was reached to purchase yet more lots from William Rockefeller, who, along with his brother John D. Rockefeller Sr., had established homes on Fifty-fourth Street and bought a few of the hospital lots. The Barney committee was determined to keep the University Club a premier club and was conscious of having been upstaged by the "no purpose" Metropolitan Club. The University Club had the opportunity to use the world of education as a theme. To Barney's committee, the clubhouse, much like his peers' own homes, was a weapon in the wars of upward mobility. The University Club needed as grand a house as the Metropolitan Club had.

McKim's appointment as architect continued to the new clubhouse. The official appointment was made on June 25, 1896, with plans submitted on February 8, 1897; a month later the plans were approved. He now had his chance to design a major club building. As White had, McKim turned to Italian Renaissance source books to select his model of the palace. Working from an initial pencil sketch in his usual fashion, McKim drew a Florentine palazzo with a Palladian window. In a sense, the sketch was McKim's version of White's Metropolitan combined with the entrance from his own Algonquin Club. The office men were duly dispatched to their library to find Florentine palace details to create McKim's new building from a host of sources.

The office had now become a practicing library with all the men able to name Italian palazzi and architects with authority. The new club would be a learned pastiche on the exterior and a very modern building on the inside. McKim sought a different color from White's building, selecting the pink Milford granite he had used at the Boston Public Library. His Renaissance palazzo had a bolder texture than White's smooth white stone club building. McKim's building is also taller than White's club—the University Club, though it appears to be three stories, actually has more than double that number of floors subtly hidden behind its façade.

In the end, McKim rejected the inappropriate Palladian window, creating a sort of Palazzo Strozzi with a soupçon of five other palaces on the outside. The interior, with its fully enclosed grand hall, exchanged the anticipated staircase for an elevator. The club boasted a swimming pool, large sitting room, dignified dining rooms, and a truly magnificent library.

The University Club members were not all in favor of a two-million-

dollar-plus new building. The club had to expand its membership to justify the expense, which also presented a problem to old-timers. However,
the decision was an excellent one as it brought the club back to the first
rank in the city.

Once the new club was planned, the membership, which included a
good number of McKim, Mead & White clients, overwhelmed the
naysayers and helped keep the fine new building on course. C. T. Barney,
an early and continuing client, acted as Goelet had done at the Metropolitan, making certain McKim's wishes were funded.

The only difficulty with the commission was one similar to that at the
Boston Public Library: The committees were unwilling to pay for artists'
work. To McKim, the library was the appropriate place for murals to be
painted by the best contemporary artists. It had been a struggle to get the
artists properly set for the murals in Boston, where Samuel A. B. Abbott
had proved the most effective in getting the monies agreed upon.

Now, at the University Club library, McKim had Barney to back his
dream of Pinturicchio-like murals on his vaulted ceiling. McKim wanted
to send H. Siddons Mowbray to Rome to gather inspiration for the ceiling. The house committee faced opposition to the expense. As a fear tactic, McKim had the library ceiling painted a glaring white to give club
members a sense of the unfinished. In the end, with Barney's aid, McKim's
ploy won out, and Mowbray was sent off to Rome.

The completed library was one of McKim's greatest triumphs, and the
club stands today as one of his best surviving works. McKim's École des
Beaux-Arts training for the grand building was exploited here, as the
University Club was a synthesis of the arts. His professorial role came out
in the wonderful detail, which even the modernist architect Le Corbusier
found better done in New York than in Italy.* The glaring loss of the street
proportion and balustrade, removed when Fifth Avenue was widened in
1907, makes the base of the building seem a bit tall today, but the University Club remains as one of New York City's best buildings.

The widening of Fifth Avenue, done in McKim's last years, was as dis-
tasteful to him as were the proportions of the tall city with its new, noisy
underground railroad. McKim was particularly saddened to see several of
his own buildings come down and his Fifth Avenue fronts filled in for the
street widening.

---

*The great architectural historian Henry-Russell Hitchcock repeated this comment to me often.
Hitchcock was a host of Le Corbusier's first visit to the United States. The comment was supposed
to have been made after seeing McKim's University Club.

# 39. The American School in Rome

From the days following Julia's death, McKim had given thought to using her assets for charitable purposes, and he had created the traveling scholarships with the money gained when he sold the Lenox house. As had French students, the young architects were to go to Rome to drink in all the sights, with time for measured drawings and even contemplation. While in Burnham's wooden cabin in Chicago, in front of the roaring fire, McKim began to think of an American School of Architecture in Rome. He enlisted Burnham in the cause and, eventually, everyone he could buttonhole. The creation of the American School evolved into the American Academy in Rome, which became the focus of McKim's life for his last twenty years.

McKim believed deeply that the future of the United States rested on artists and architects studying in Rome, then coming home to move the New World forward wih the principles they had learned there. He gave the American Academy his heart, soul, health, and money as he almost single-handedly pushed it into existence. McKim, diffident and shy, had to ask men for money and speak, briefly but in public, to create his dream. He enlisted his partners, particularly Mead and his friends John L. Cadwalader, Frank Millet, Augustus Saint-Gaudens, Burnham, and many others. Even Edith Wharton, who wove in and out of McKim's world in Newport in the 1870s and later took part in disccusions of issues of decoration, agreed to give parties for the American Academy effort in 1889.

Did McKim's friends all believe deeply in the Academy? Seemingly not. McKim's dogged work enlisted the respect of his friends who, unable to deny McKim his dream, went along with the vision. Many friends later remarked that their loyalty had been to the man more than the Academy.

In the early days of the Roman school, McKim counted on his old ally from Boston, Samuel A. B. Abbott. McKim and Abbott remained close in the 1890s, even traveling to Europe together in 1891 to sign on the artists for the Boston Public Library. By the mid-1890s, Abbott must have run out of money, as McKim's letters often seem to suggest Abbott for jobs, noting that SABA, as he called him, had given years of service to architecture with no reward. In 1896 Abbott met a wealthy American woman who had lived in Rome then for two decades. SABA married the woman and was appointed the first full director of the American School of Architecture in Rome in 1897. Abbott and his wife then seemed to have begun to live far too grandly, almost causing the new school to collapse. Mr. and Mrs. Abbott left the school, and from then on the personality of the new directors would be carefully studied in New York before the appointment was made.

During McKim's years of hard work on the American School, he was also juggling his projects for Columbia, the University Club, and the Rhode Island State House at Providence. For relief from this labor, the architect began a new sport. The Parisian days on a flying trapeze were well behind him in the 1890s, but McKim took up the new craze of gear-driven bicycles. On weekends, often with Kendall, McKim rode his "wheel" around the city; he also bicycled at Newport when he visited there.

A spill from his bicycle made McKim miserable with an inflamed hernia. By the fall of 1895, the discomfort of the hernia seemed to be creating the anxiety attacks and sense of depression McKim had long battled. His friend E. D. Morgan took him out on his steamboat to Newport after a stop at the newly fashionable horse country section of Long Island's North Shore at Wheatley Hills, where McKim was building him a weekend and country house. In Newport, McKim visited Beacon Rock, the large summer house recently completed for Morgan. McKim's client Frederick Vanderbilt then picked him up by boat to take him up the Hudson to Hyde Park, where McKim had begun Vanderbilt's substantial country house.

The efforts at cheer were to no avail, and McKim had to undergo surgery for the condition. Prescott Hall Butler's college classmate William T. Bull performed the operation in October, and McKim had recovered enough to travel abroad in early December. The architect wanted to look over, and even, as he wrote to Howard Walker, attend the American School in Rome.

McKim then followed the footsteps of Stanford White, although seemingly without the same boatman, by sailing to Egypt to travel on the Nile. He went with Henry White, a respected diplomat who would become a stalwart friend to McKim later in London. Henry White and his wife met Lord Kitchener at Luxor, and McKim must have been with them at this meeting. Following his travels in Egypt, McKim made a trip to the Parthenon, his first visit to that important temple. Afterward he went back to the American School, visiting with Burnham, also then in Rome. McKim's letters on his return are fixed on the topic of the American School. Though his Egyptian trip must have been discussed at dinners, no account of the voyage seems to have survived—but then, McKim did have Rome on his mind.

As McKim pushed for his American School of Architecture in Rome, he hosted many carefully planned dinners where artists could speak to donors on the importance of the school. As at the party for the Boston Public Library trustees years earlier, McKim planned surprises and decorations fitting the purpose of the party. That such a shy man who spoke haltingly in public and with great reluctance should need to put on these elaborate entertainments indicates the importance of setting the tone for a success with his likely supporters. Much of McKim's work creating the American Academy in Rome came from the dinner table.

McKim's vision for educating American students of architecture grew out of his gifts to young men to see Europe and discussion with his friend Professor William R. Ware at Columbia in 1889. Further talks with Burnham inspired his being able to take action in 1894. McKim began by attempting to create an American version of the Rome Prize, which had been awarded to the outstanding French student at the École. Now American students could have an equivalent prize. So that they could study Rome as their French counterparts did, McKim set up an academic structure in rented rooms at the Villa Torlonia in January 1895. There they would measure and draw the buildings of the past, even if only a handful of drawing boards could be mustered. Three years later, the American School of Architecture in Rome dissolved in favor of a broader learning environment in which students of other subjects could participate. Saint-Gaudens and the artists who had lived in Rome were convinced to aid the new school. American university presidents and patrons of the arts were also brought in to create a larger, more varied, and better concept: a happy place where Americans could live in the world of the past and become artists for the future. McKim would work, beg, plan, and continue his expanded vision to create a base for Americans in Rome. Although his dogged pressure sometimes upset his friends, out of loyalty to the man, his world created the Academy.

The fund-raising, governmental permissions, and decisions regarding the location of buildings would consume McKim for the next decade. With help from Columbia donors J. P. Morgan, who loved the "eternal city," his once brother-in-law Meyer, Daniel Burnham, and Mead, McKim would establish the American Academy in Rome. Although the final element—the primary building for the Academy—would still be in planning stage the year after McKim's death, William Mitchell Kendall would finish it in 1914. The building continues to stand today.

When McKim began his education, travel abroad was rare and difficult. He had read the classic texts in his room in Germantown. Now Americans could transform book pages into a living experience. Mead would bring the Academy into the modern world, taking an active role in the school's affairs and its library. Curiously, White showed little interest in the project. White lived in the present, McKim had retreated to the past, and Mead got it all to work. The roles of the triumvirate remained on course.

# 40. THE SWAN SONG OF THE WOODEN HOUSE

The careers of McKim, Mead, and White all began with domestic buildings built of wood in rural or resort regions. The reputation of their firm rose from commissions for new timber buildings or additions to existing ones. By 1889, however, when potential clients appeared at 57 Broadway requesting alterations on a house, which a decade earlier had been a mainstay of their business, the newcomers were turned down flat. White would refuse to do alterations unless it was on an established client's house. The architects could now decide to refuse a work if it was of a modest nature and unlikely to lead to any great future building.

Wooden resort and country houses would continue to be built for a few more years, although the houses from 1889 forward would usually be of an American Colonial style. As Wells had taught McKim and White to use the library for details in urban Renaissance-style buildings, so too did the architects consult books on American domestic buildings of the eighteenth century. When McKim's very old family friend and remote cousin, Samuel Longstreth Parrish (1849–1932), asked for a resort house in the new summer colony developing in Southampton on Long Island's eastern end, the office, particularly in this case Mead, happily complied. Samuel Parrish's father was part of Miller McKim's Philadelphia abolitionist circle. The McKims were very close to the Parrish family and to Samuel Parrish's uncle, Joseph, who had been a teacher before retraining for a career in engineering in the 1860s. Miller McKim constantly put "cousin" Joe Parrish forward as a role model for his son when Charles was wrestling with the decision about his future. Samuel Parrish and his brother James Cresson Parrish (1840–1887) moved in a higher social set than Miller McKim, but the ties were clearly there. Samuel Parrish was in the Harvard class of 1870 with Prescott Hall Butler, Millet, and Dr. Bull, putting Parrish in the McKim circle, although the two men do not seem to have socialized together.

The Parrish brothers both moved to the Southampton area, a resort colony within commuting distance of New York City, now growing in popularity as Elberon declined. For Samuel Parrish, a bachelor whose business in New York kept him close to the city, McKim, Mead & White built an English-styled Colonial house far more contained than the earlier summer house built in the seaside resort style at Southampton. The Parrish house, an enlarged version of an American Colonial theme, looks rather like the ancestor of so many early twentieth-century "good taste" houses in the American suburbs. Parrish lived in the house with his mother until her death. In later years he would remain in Southampton, living in a genuine eighteenth-century house and creating the Parrish Art Museum and the Southampton Hospital.

McKim would also create a house on Long Island for E. D. Morgan Jr., a yachtsman and close friend who had tried to assist him when he fell from his bike. Morgan was a graduate of Harvard, class of 1888, and he had a fine house designed in the year of his graduation at Newport, Beacon Rock, happily still standing. Two years later, McKim began a country house of wood in Wheatley Hills for Morgan's spring and fall season. The large wooden houses were built, as was Samuel Parrish's house, in an American Colonial style. The Morgan house had a wing in a Dutch Colonial style, which probably related to the older houses in the remote agrarian region now popular for polo and equestrian activities. Morgan's house was the first of several McKim, Mead & White would build in this region and appears to have been designed to be part of the landscape, not to stand out as a palace. Several years later, Morgan would enlarge the complex and add gardens.*

IN 1892 IN SHINNECOCK HILLS, just west of Southampton, Stanford White was consulted about building a clubhouse for a new game brought to the United States from Scotland via Pau in France—golf. The

---

*The Morgan complex was demolished, but just to the south of the Long Island Expressway at Wheatley stands a smaller copy of the Morgan house. It is not the original house but replicates the little Colonial house wing to the side of the main house wings.

*The Shinnecock Hills golf course clubhouse of 1892–95.*

Scottish golf professional thought the Shinnecock Hills perfect for the game and laid out a course. When White was asked to design a club building for the sport, he was unfamiliar with the game, which seemed to be called "goff" at the time. White had not a clue about the sport or a precedent, so he created a wooden building that looked like an enlarged version of a dovecote. It calls to mind those the office had studied in the early 1880s for their ventures in the design of seaside resort cottages. The Shinnecock Hills Golf Club became the nation's first golf club with a clubhouse; it stands today greatly enlarged, but still extant.

Shortly after the golf house was begun, on a neighboring hill White made one of his unofficial designs for a wooden house in a quasi Dutch Colonial style. The house was a favor for his friend, the painter William Merritt Chase, whose art colony would border on the James Cresson Parrish house. The William Merritt Chase house and studio, often seen in the artist's paintings, survives to this day.

In 1892 Stanford White would pronounce his reluctance to build in wood again. White wrote that wooden houses, the genre of his own most fully artistic work, were too modest for his current vision. White was now beginning to be ashamed of his early work, as tastes changed by the office's recent work had moved to a grander historical aesthetic.

Despite White's own words, he would work in wood for his wife's family in the early 1890s, as four Smith daughters enlarged their houses in St. James. It was Prescott and Nellie who first lived in St. James, asking the young McKim to design phase one of their house. Over the years, Butler, McKim, and White tinkered with the house, enlarging and refining the great shingle gable. Bessie had particularly enjoyed walking up on Carman's Hill, the high ground next to the Butler house. Judge Smith is said to have told his son-in-law that Bessie would not be really happy until she could live in the Carman property. The Carman family often rented out a small, plain 1850s farmhouse for the summer, and the Whites began to lease the house about 1887. As expected, Bessie did love the property with its view of the Sound below.

In the next few years, White and Carman played games over the property, with Carman implying he would not lease it for the summer of 1892, then suddenly agreeing to a sale offer rejected earlier. With Bessie's inheritance, Carman's Hill was set to become Box Hill. White with his partners and friends would spend the next fourteen years overwhelming the farmhouse, creating a long, low, Shavian gabled house covered in pebble dash and detailed with some American references. The family was invited to join in one day when White offered piles of pebbles to be tossed onto the wet cement. White had used areas of pebble dash at several much earlier houses, but here the entire façade was to be covered, giving the house a most curious texture.

White worked on the interiors, adding many of his treasures to the rooms. He even repeated his Henry Duveen trick of Dutch tiles in the dining room. White's creativity at his own houses was higher than the work he was then doing for clients. He really was his own best client. In one principal room, White covered the walls with split reeds. The house and the grounds became a haven for the architect's dreams, with potted trees from Europe, elaborate clay containers, cast-off elements from New York City buildings including bits from the Croton Reservoir he had helped to save, and marble slabs from Aunt Cornelia's Marble House. By the early twentieth century, the partners had taken up "goff," and White had a partial course laid out at Box Hill. Two men in the office, Lionel Moses and Jules Crow, oversaw most of the work at Box Hill.

In 1894, two other sisters, Kate Wetherill and Ella Emmet, had White smarten up their newly purchased houses. For Kate, a widow with two small children, White worked at a costs-only fee scale. He helped create a hilltop house, highly dramatic with its central octagonal presentation. The Wetherill house is a bit of a throwback to White's picturesque aesthetic, but the details are now an academic version of Colonial elements. White constantly worked over his designs and updated earlier work in the now-fashionable Colonial style. He even went over to the Butlers' house, where as a suitor for Bessie's hand he had once carved the Shavian ornament on the window frame of the great gable section of the house. White would now redo that window, giving it "Colonial" detail. At Box Hill, White toyed with the idea of dormer windows in the roof, pencil-sketching these thoughts over a photograph of the house. He did not rework the attic at Box Hill, but at the stately Emmet house below Box Hill on the way to the harbor White redid the wooden balustrade detail. The Emmets had bought a house that was far grander than the mid-century farmer's cottages the Whites and Kate Wetherill had purchased. The Emmet house alterations, a gift of White's to his in-laws, were of a sophisticated eighteenth-century taste, rather in the manner of the great Scottish architect William Chambers. For Bessie's family, White created a four-house complex that kept the family happy and close, occupying Bessie's time as White's life in the city had now little reference to her existence.

Amazingly, all four houses in St. James survive today. The story of the houses, their interesting owners over the years, and the treasures within make the complex worthy of a National Register nomination. The plantings of the houses further amplify the spatial quality of this unique district. The landscape of the Emmet house was partly designed by Devereux Emmet, who took up the new game of golf and lived to become a renowned course designer. Golf rapidly became an activity of choice for many of America's gentry, rivaling yachting and racehorses as an acceptable sport.

# 41. ON TOP OF THE WORLD

As Stanford White was creating a corner for Bessie's sisters and their families, life was at its peak for him. Work of the most appropriately important sort had come into the office, which was now recognized as the nation's leading architecture firm. In the late afternoons of winter, when darkness fell and the three partners looked up from their projects, one can imagine the men joking with each other about their success and how naïve arrangements had blossomed into unimagined growth. The office could turn away unwanted business and survive several losses in office building competitions, such as that for the American Surety Company. The work continued to flow in, often with budgets to match the desirability of the jobs.

McKim would settle into the position once occupied by Richard Morris Hunt, that of dean of the profession, choosing to do only noble commissions. McKim tried for, and lost, the competition for New York City's Public Library, but he won many other plum commissions: the renovation of the White House; the plan for Washington, D.C., undertaken by Senator McMillan; the Morgan Library; a few private houses for wealthy men known for their philanthropic efforts; and the American Academy. Like White, he also designed for his friends off the record; McKim did the ground floor of his friend Henry White's house near the Albert Hall in London, and he created a beautiful interior for the house of John L. Cadwalader. McKim even harked back to his childhood roots, working with Saint-Gaudens on the great monument to the Boston Civil War hero Robert Gould Shaw and his African American regiment, one of the best public monuments in the nation. McKim would assist Saint-Gaudens on the great golden Sherman monument at New York's Grand Army Plaza in Manhattan. For McKim and Gus, whose fathers had worked for the cause, the slipping away of those who remembered the war made them feel vulnerable and renewed the two men's desire to create monuments to those their fathers had so admired.

STANFORD WHITE'S WORLDVIEW was quite different. White was now a human bridge across the Atlantic, bringing splendor and purchasable portions of nobility to a group of America's best makers of fortune. His commissions would mainly be residences of baronial size and importance built to create a virtual peerage for the captains of commerce, who would then pass along their ancestral lands to many generations to come. White was asked to build immortal houses for the ages, which he happily did. Ironically, almost all of these great houses were sold within decades and the majority bulldozed for suburban tract houses just after World War II. The American fortune-makers saw themselves as America's newly created aristocracy of wealth. How quickly their illusions were forgotten!

As a couple, Stanford and Bessie White had particularly close friendships with two somewhat eccentric families: the Cheneys of South Manchester, Connecticut, and the Chanlers of the Upper Hudson Valley. The Cheneys and Chanlers came from distinguished families with many siblings who would reside together in their large family house, which White would alter and decorate over the years.

The Cheney family had connections to both Stanford and Bessie White. The family were America's first and best manufacturers of silk fabric. The Cheney mills were built outside Hartford, Connecticut, in South Manchester, and what would become thirteen family houses were built near the factory. The Cheney family factories worked closely with A. T. Stewart, supplying his store with their silks. The Smith children may have known the Cheneys through the Stewarts. Bessie was very friendly with the Cheney women and visited them frequently, as did Bessie's sister, Nellie Butler. The friendship between the Smith girls and the Cheney girls continued for a lifetime, and the women made small mentions of each other in their wills.

Stanford White knew the Cheneys through H. H. Richardson, who had worked on a commercial block building for the Cheneys in Hartford, a project White had been in charge of completing. The family had asked Richardson for designs for houses in South Manchester in 1876 and 1878,

The parlor of the
Cheney house, which
White continually
updated.

A paneled room at
the Cheney house.

The Cheney house, South
Manchester, Connecticut,
ca. 1887. It was one of
several the family owned.
The Cheneys were the best
silk manufacturers in
America. All the Cheney
houses are gone.

which White had prepared in his most Shavian English style. The two Richardson/White houses were probably not built, but the relationship between White and the Cheneys lasted and may well have been strengthened when White married Bessie Smith.

It is difficult to be absolutely certain about the houses White may have built for the Cheneys, since White's work for the family is now gone. In 1881 White built a moderately large house for Rush Cheney. In 1887 he designed a second house nearby for Anne W. Cheney, which he would be asked to alter in 1902–3. Anne Cheney had tremendous faith in White and consulted him continually about changes in the interior, from wallpapers to drapes. She had an 1880s taste, which White served very well with a stunning interior of carved and turned wood created by the architect's best woodworker, Joseph Cabus, who was a master of fine cabinetry and wood design. Through White, the Cheneys met the painter Thomas Wilmer Dewing, who did portraits for the Cheneys as well as a mural, *The Days,* which was mounted above a pseudo-Renaissance bench built into the wall by Cabus in a design created by Joe Wells. The bench now is on display at Hartford's Wadsworth Atheneum, together with the painting. The Aesthetic movement interior design specialist Daniel Cottier also worked on details for the house.

It is difficult to sort out the Cheney story, as the family lived together in these houses and the photographs of these two lost houses are hard to distinguish. It is likely that the unmarried Cheney boys joined White in New York on some of his sprees. (The Cheney boys were blackballed at the Players club when they first went up for membership, but White was able to gain admission for them on a second try. One can only wonder why the Cheneys were blackballed, a thing that did not often happen with such wealthy potential members who lived a distance away.) The Cheney sisters probably also socialized with the Whites. There is clearly far more to the relationship of the Cheneys and White, but the destruction of many of White's letters in the early 1930s makes it hard to discern the full story.

IN THE WHITES' LIFE, there was another unusual family group who were, and would remain, close friends—the Chanlers of Rokeby. Rokeby, a villa on the Hudson River near Barrytown, is one of New York State's great houses. The stone house with a French roof and a cupola was built in 1811–15 probably by the architect, J. J. Ramée, who would lay out Union College. The early nineteenth-century villa was built for John Armstrong and his wife, Alida Livingston. The Livingstons were patrician Americans whose landholdings in the region went back to 1688.

The Livingstons must have been mortified when, in 1818, the Armstrongs' only daughter, Margaret, married William Backhouse Astor. Astor was the son of the original John Jacob Astor of Waldorf, Germany, who had come to New York to sell musical instruments. Astor expanded into fur pelts and real estate, becoming New York City's largest private landowner. The elder Astor was far from refined—he was coarse, loutish, and often bypassed the truth—but he was rich. The Livingstons could only hope that their family's genes would overwhelm the Astor genes and that their son-in-law's family could be improved over time.

In 1836 Margaret and W. B. Astor bought the house that Margaret named Rokeby after a poem by Sir Walter Scott, who was then at the height of his popularity. The Astors enlarged the house, laid out gardens, and raised a family. Their children included Emily Astor, who married Sam Ward, a gifted intellectual and banker. Emily died early, and their daughter, Margaret Astor Ward, led the life of a princess raised by her father with Astor money. That ended when the widower Sam Ward fell for the charms of a beauty living on Staten Island.

The Astors grabbed Margaret back into their fold. Margaret would marry John Winthrop Chanler and have ten children, dying soon after her last child was born. Then, rather tragically, her husband followed her to the grave, leaving the Chanler children Rokeby, where the "Astor orphans" had only Irish nannies and lots of money for comfort. The Astor brood were isolated, educated at home by tutors, and known to be wild. The eldest, John Armstrong Chanler, known as Archie, did go to the Rugby School in England and Columbia College before joining in the New York whirl.

In 1887 Archie visited Newport, where he met a beautiful woman from the South, Amélie Rives, the child of an equally grand family with a large country house near Charlottesville, Virginia. Archie fell madly in love with the Southern belle, who in 1888 managed to turn out a quickly written romance, *The Quick or the Dead,* featuring a man who was clearly Archie. The two married in June. Amélie rapidly discovered that Archie was leaving a state of eccentricity for true delusion. The marriage foundered and the couple eventually divorced. Amélie found herself afflicted with migraines, which she "cured" by using morphine. She descended into drug addiction, but was able to recover with the assistance of the well-regarded Philadelphia physician S. Weir Mitchell, John L. Cadwalader's brother-in-law.

The Archie/Amélie saga continued for a few years until she met Prince Troubetskoy, whom Archie teased her to marry, which she did promptly.

The Rives family would continue to weave into the story as Amélie's brother, George Lockhard Rives (1849–1917), would become a close friend of McKim. George Rives, who had a house at Newport called Swanhurst, had McKim build a stable at the house in 1892. Rives lived in New York in the winter, having been educated at Columbia as a college student and in the law school before studying at Cambridge in England. His scholarly bent gave him common ground with McKim on both the Columbia campus buildings and the projected New York Public Library. Rives had been a trustee of the Astor, Lenox, and Tilden foundations and would prove a key player with John L. Cadwalader in the creation of the huge new public library at Forty-second Street.

Even after Amélie Rives divorced Archie Chanler, she remained active in White's life. White's early acquaintance with Archie in the club life in 1887 led to a full friendship between all the Chanlers and Stanford White's family. The Chanlers and Whites would participate in each other's family events, with a first union of the families made in the fall of 1896, when Alida Chanler married Christopher Temple Emmet, a nephew of Bessie White's. The second great family solidification came when Lawrence White, Stanford's son, married Laura Chanler in 1916.

As Stanford White and the Chanler boys became close friends, the Chanlers might join White at the Players, meeting his friends. Indeed, Saint-Gaudens was able to convince the Chanlers to fund a prize that would support an artist studying in Paris for a year. The Chanler Paris Prize Fund gave an annual fellowship to an artist in Paris for fifteen years, until Stanford White's death. The artists were sent to study under the direction of Jean-Léon Gérôme, by 1890 a rather out-of-date traditional academic painter, reminding us how little inclination White had for advanced painters of his era. White was never abreast of innovative artists such as the Post-Impressionists, whom he seems never even to have noticed.

As the White/Chanler lives entwined, Rokeby came under discussion. The family home was truly in its original state, which was a virtue to White if it was the exterior, but intolerable in an interior. The house needed a modern heating system and new plumbing for the creation of indoor bathrooms. White would radically modernize the house, digging a basement for a heating system and bringing the house up to date before decorating the interiors. On this job White broke the code of conduct of architects, as the Chanlers had contemplated modernizing Rokeby and had already contacted the firm that the Astor family often used, Clinton & Russell, to do the work. In 1894 White wrote to William H. Russell of

Clinton & Russell explaining that he had become so friendly with the Chanlers that it was natural that they would ask him to take the job rather than Russell.

The renovations at Rokeby, made in 1894 and 1895, were accomplished by the time the Chanlers began preparation for Alida's wedding to the young Emmet. Stanford White, in one of his generous gestures, helped to design the October 1896 wedding reception held at Rokeby. Guests from New York City were brought up on a special train. They found the house covered in hangings, including some of the tapestries then so popular. White probably loaned the family objects and fabrics for the event, as he often did. White brought everyone to the wedding including his own mother, who was treated to the strolling musicians and the Hungarian band. The Emmets were of Irish heritage, so it is difficult to imagine how the Hungarian theme came into the event, but the wedding was most successful. Perhaps Mead's music-loving wife supplied the program.

During the time that Rokeby was being reworked, Archie, now without Amélie, and his brother Winthrop became interested in backing a water-driven textile plant that made cotton fabric along the Roanoke River in North Carolina. The Chanler boys set up the Roanoke Rapids Power Company and brought White aboard, first as a professional, then as an investor. White designed the spinning mill in 1894, then some workers' cottages the next year. White's work at the Roanoke Rapids was a rare venture for him into mill design and working-class housing issues, but here the work was done for his friends, not as a designer with a specialty in industrial complexes.

White did only one other factory/workers' housing complex, for Edward Dean Adam's Niagara Falls Power Company in 1892–95. Perhaps this experience left White feeling confident enough to join Archie and Winthrop Chanler in the Roanoke Rapids venture. The three partners tried to run the business, which was made more complicated in 1895 when Amélie divorced Archie and her portion of Archie's investment was caught up in a legal battle. In the next year, the two brothers fought, and Archie took over as president. Later in 1897 Archie decided to leave the company to devote himself to his experiments in psychological phenomena. He turned the entire business over to Stanford White, along with his power of attorney.

Archie set himself up in his house, Merry Mills, to conduct his experiments in changing the color of his eyes by meditation. Reports about Archie's mental state alarmed the family. Stanford White traveled to

Merry Mills with a physician and persuaded Archie to come back to New York for treatment. Once there, Archie insisted on showing that he could go into a trance and reenact the death of Napoleon. Winthrop and their brother Lewis insisted that Archie be committed to the Bloomingdale Insane Asylum, then at White Plains, having departed from Morningside Heights to make room for the new Columbia campus. The family asked White to use his power of attorney to have Archie declared insane, which White, to his credit, refused to do. Lewis and Winthrop did get Archie declared insane by 1899, when Archie thought himself to be a silver box whose finish had been tarnished by magnetism. Prescott Hall Butler was declared guardian for Archie's estate. The problems with Archie continued for the rest of White's life. There was always the nagging possibility that Archie might harm White; despite White's refusal to participate in the declaration of insanity, Archie bore a grudge, which, fortunately, he kept to himself as he dealt with his delusions. The Chanler family continued to be a part of White's life, even if Archie was a bit of a wild card.

One of the sons, Winthrop, would become engaged to a remote cousin, Margaret Terry, who had been raised in Rome by her parents, then by her mother and stepfather, the sculptor Thomas Crawford. Margaret's family had converted to Catholicism in Rome, a rather grand, papal variation of the Roman ritual. When Margaret returned to the United States as the bride of Winthrop, she brought Catholicism into a portion of the Chanler family. Her first child, Laura, was born at Rokeby in 1887 and would be reared as a Catholic, which did make for family conflict with Alida Chanler Emmet, who was a convinced Protestant. The young Laura and Larry White would meet and spend their youth together before marrying when Larry White was a productive member of the architectural firm. Indeed, the courting couple were even together on the evening of Stanford White's murder.

The Chanlers and Whites had two connections beyond this friendship, as was typical of the small society of the day. Prescott Butler had grown up around the corner from the Astor orphans and was Archie's pal, along with Stanford White. It is even likely that Butler introduced White to Archie. After Archie's health deteriorated and his brothers got him declared insane, Butler handled Archie's affairs until Butler's death.

The small world factor played a role in the McKim story, as McKim's close friend, Henry White, had married Margaret S. Rutherford of the distinguished New York family, the Stuyvesant/Rutherfords. Margaret S. Rutherford White was a cousin of the Chanlers. McKim sailed on the Nile with Margaret and Henry White.

THE CLOSE CIRCLE of Stanford White included his early patron, Charles Tracy Barney, who remained a good friend for life. Barney, who had built his wonderful McKim, Mead & White house in 1880–82 and had opened up his West Fifty-fifth Street stable to provide cheap space for practicing American artists, became too successful for his house. Barney had been a key figure in the Knickerbocker Trust Company from its organization in 1884. The Knickerbocker Trust grew rapidly and Barney's career rose with it, and in 1898, the relatively young Barney was appointed president. Barney, whose Cleveland-based father had made a substantial fortune, was also an investor in the stock market and the real estate worlds. Barney remained close to his brother-in-law Will Whitney, and in 1890 the two formed the New York Loan and Improvement Company, which was dedicated to developing the northwestern portion of Manhattan, particularly Washington Heights.

Barney's success made him eager to have a bigger house for his Gothic and Renaissance pieces, some of which had been bought with Stanford White's aid. Barney expected to rise to the top of the city's movers and shakers. He sold his house on Fifty-fifth Street to Joseph Pulitzer, the Hungarian-born newspaperman, and purchased an existing town house at 67 Park Avenue, upon which he planned to improve. The new house was almost a mile south of his earlier house in that peculiar space between Grand Central Station and Thirty-fourth Street at Murray Hill. This was just a block south of his brother-in-law Whitney's old house, so the Barneys knew the neighborhood.

*Helen and Charles Tracy Barney at her coming-out party. The debutante dance was held in the house newly completed by their friend Stanford White.*

Barney would ask White to get the house in shape for them that year, paying the architects about thirty-five thousand dollars. Five years later, when Barney was not only president of the Knickerbocker but a backer with Whitney and August Belmont Jr. of the first substantial underground rail line, the Interborough Rapid Transit (IRT), he felt flush enough to call White back for a thoroughgoing redecoration of 67 Park Avenue, on a scale ten times that of the earlier work done at the house. He did not reach Will Whitney's scale of building, but the 1901 renovation was substantial. Barney's

*The second C. T. Barney house at Thirty-eighth Street and Park Avenue, 1895–1902. Demolished. Another palace for a peer.*

house had sustained some damage when his own company, the IRT, harmed its foundations while blasting the subway toward Grand Central Station. He needed to have the foundations repaired and the improvements made by January, as his daughter was planning a fine coming-out party at the house.

In the end, Barney's work fell behind schedule, and he had words with White on the issue of cost overruns—by now always a feature of White's work—and the ever-present delays. White, very dependent on Barney for financial advice, loan arrangements, and tips on the market, humbly apologized and cut the firm's fee by five thousand dollars to keep Barney happy.

Barney had become even closer to White after Bob Goelet's death in 1899. He had tried to help White dig out after the architect's recent stock market disasters. In the mid-1890s, White needed more money to keep up his extravagances and had taken tips from others and gambled on the market with serious mistakes, which plunged him into debt. At each disaster, Barney helped White with special consideration on his account at the Knickerbocker and with personal loans. White could only hope to right the situation by making extra money dealing in art, or so it must have seemed. In 1901 he sold Barney a ceiling he had bought from Heilbronner in Paris, which came from a palace in Cremona. White also sold Barney a set of fine exterior marble doors from Stefano Bardini's shop in Florence, which would come in very handy when Barney faced the press in 1907. White placed Harrie Lindeberg, a talented young man in the office, in charge of Barney's house, making sure the work was done well. Lindeberg would later have a good career building country houses on Long Island's North Shore and in Connecticut.

White brought Louis St. Gaudens to Barney for the tombstone of his father, Ashbel H. Barney, in 1891 and for a figure of Pan to be placed at 67 Park Avenue. Barney's house became one of the city's most exalted residences.

Barney, like E. D. Morgan Jr., James Gordon Bennett, and Royal Carroll Phelps, was a yachtsman. For all these men, White worked on the interior cabin spaces of the boats. For Barney, whose boat the *Invincible* was a famous race winner, White placed a stock of old wooden mantels in the cabins. It seems likely that the fireplaces came from the Marble House of A. T. Stewart. The Knickerbocker Trust, perhaps to assist the Stewart heirs, bought the Marble House for demolition, which took place in 1900–1901. Fireplace mantels from the less important rooms of the Stewart house may have found their way aboard the *Invincible.*

In 1901, McKim, Mead & White built a bank and safe deposit building on the Stewart site, ending the troubled forty-year life of the city's first "show off" house. For all the magnificence of the thick walls and sturdy building techniques, meant to support the building for the ages, it fell in a generation and a half, wiping out part of the image of A. T. Stewart.

White replaced the Marble House with an elaborately detailed, classical-appearing safe deposit company and bank of about the same size as the Stewart house, but now with an entrance on Fifth Avenue. Barney and the board at the Knickerbocker Trust ended up keeping the Thirty-fourth Street corner low by building only a banking facility without any rentable space above. The original plan called for a thirteen-story building, but the investors for the top nine stories pulled out of the project. At the earlier Knickerbocker building on Forty-second Street, also a bank and safe deposit company, McKim, Mead & White had put bachelor flats above the banking facility. Now Barney felt that the bank could stand alone, buying the cachet of a low-rise building at this valuable corner site. Indeed, the Knickerbocker buildings would be widely admired and copied by others building fine banks in the early twentieth century.

BARNEY AND WILLIAM COLLINS WHITNEY were powerful figures in New York City. Barney was the more retiring of the two, prone to bouts of melancholy which his financial success could not quiet. Will Whitney lived life far more flamboyantly than did his brother-in-law. Whitney let little stop him as he sublimated any political career he had once dreamed of having into a frenzy of financial gain. Whitney, Barney, and White all needed more money for their lives than they had. White had gambled with stock, Barney would play a financial game or two with individuals eager to corner markets, and Whitney, well, watered stocks.

After Whitney married Edith May Randolph, they moved from the Payne-connected property at 2 West Fifty-seventh Street to the Robert L. Stuart house at 871 Fifth Avenue, where McKim, Mead & White did over the entire house between 1897 and 1902. The scale of the remaking of William Schickel's somewhat ungainly mansion was truly princely. The house required two to three million dollars to finish, decorate, and fill with art. Whitney had to pay the bills for the new house, his horses, and his Medicean standard of living. As the relationship with the Payne family of his late wife was entirely severed, Whitney needed to use un-Payne-tainted cash for the house for his new wife. He seems to have adopted the strategy of expanding his interests in street railway systems, including cable transit. He used his political machine tactics mercilessly, covering his removal of company assets by taking care of Tammany Hall political regulars. Will Whitney had made a number of enemies and lost the respect of most friends. His old ally and fellow Democrat Abram Hewitt went from friend to foe as Hewitt's doubts about Whitney turned to fear, then outrage. Hewitt called Whitney "sinister" and "corrupt."

When Will took on the Stuart mansion, he left the old house at 2 West Fifty-seventh Street to his loyal son, Harry, who had married the girl across the street, Gertrude Vanderbilt. The Cleveland-born mothers, Flora Payne and Alice Gwynne, would have enjoyed the symmetry of their children's wedding. Will's other two mature children, Pauline and William Payne Whitney, sided with Colonel Oliver Payne and broke from their father. Colonel Payne, with young Harry and Gertrude moving into 2 West Fifty-seventh Street, leased a house uptown for his own use. This was the "little" Havemeyer house, just down the avenue from the "great" Havemeyer house.

Colonel Payne demanded full loyalty from Whitney's children, but not from their architect. Payne allowed White to work on the Fifth Avenue property even while working on his former brother-in-law's place a block away at 852 Fifth Avenue. Payne did not require as elaborate a house as Whitney did, but we do not have figures for this off-the-books decorative work. Colonel Payne remained pleased with White, as he hired McKim, Mead & White in 1898 to build the Cornell Medical School on First Avenue at Twenty-eighth Street at his expense. Walking the tightrope across Sixty-seventh Street to keep both parties happy must have been very difficult for White, but it became a major triumph that would result in his being commissioned by Colonel Payne to build a wedding-present house for Payne Whitney and his bride, Helen Hay. Both Colonel Payne and Will Whitney kept White well employed.

The house White rebuilt for Will Whitney was close to Central Park, an attraction for Edith, who was a superb rider and would be able to go across Fifth Avenue to ride on the bridle path. As White completed the house, filling it with treasures from his trips to Europe and booty garnered from faithful dealers, Edith Whitney suffered an accident while riding, injuring her head on an unseen tree limb. She lived, but she had suffered severe cerebral damage and it was clear she had only months left. Edith was brought back from their plantation in Aiken, South Carolina, to New York City in a private railroad car and taken home to rest. Edith, who had tried to be a mother to Will and Flora Whitney's youngest daughter, Dorothy, spent her final months with the child. She died before she could move into the house Whitney was building for them. Later, the opening party was hostessed by Edith's own daughter for her stepfather, Whitney.

Will Whitney and little Dorothy moved into a palace in 1900. The house had a Fifth Avenue frontage of nearly fifty-five feet and a longer side going east on Sixty-eighth Street, double the usual length of New York City plots—two hundred feet. Thus the house was more than two times the size of the usual corner house. The brownstone-clad house with its five stories rivaled the biggest in the city. (See page 324.)

The entrance was set on Sixty-eighth Street with a huge protective iron gate bought from the Palazzo Doria in Rome. Hidden behind the gate was a vestibule, then the door to the main house. The reception hall featured a mosaic floor patterned with constellation circles. The floor design was one that Joseph Wells had developed for the New York Life Building in Kansas City. The entry and reception areas were splendid, in what had become White's formula for the big spender. The Renaissance ceiling was bought from Bardini and installed in the room. The Henry II–style fireplace came from a French château—Sieur Frac de Conseil at Piques-Mortes—and had been purchased by a dealer in Paris, M. Worms de Romilly, for his own house before he sold it to Whitney. The hall was dominated by a great sweeping marble staircase that featured glass from a Renaissance chapel supplied by a dealer, Kopp. The dining room of the house was fitted with treasures purchased from the Parisian house of Vicomtesse de Sauze, bought with the aid of Joseph Duveen. The ballroom was enormous, with a ceiling panel from the Château Phoebus d'Albret.

All the great dealers worked to supply this house of trophies. Allard provided ceilings, Carlhian sent over furniture, and tapestries came from many dealers. White shopped without mercy to make the house more full of art than any other house in the city, except for J. P. Morgan's, whose collections, magpie-like as they were, remained in London when Whitney set out to rival him. With no wife left and two of his four children on their own, Whitney was buying as Morgan did—for the sake of the hunt, not for the effect or for the family. Whitney wanted to be seen as one of the handful of great collectors of the early century.

Whitney favored, as Morgan did and Frick would, the Rococo French room, available for purchase to those brave enough to consider a time period regarded as "thin" by others of the day. The fortunate aspect of this was that the purchaser could have a superb-quality work without the staggering competition that then existed for tapestries. Whitney and Morgan were following the lead of the marquess of Hertford, a British collector who had lived in Paris and had bought available interiors and other treasures. The works were installed in his London house, today known as the Wallace Collection. The Wallace was greatly admired by another American magnate, Henry Clay Frick, who would use it as a model for the fine house he would build on Fifth Avenue.

The Whitney house also featured Stanford White signature elements—such as twisted Solomonic columns, which White always included—and a lot of Frank Lathrop's leaded glass.

Whitney did not shy away from publicity. The house was illustrated widely and the architects created a photograph album for their own records. Curiously, the photo album includes a picture of a main reception room where Jean-François Millet's painting *The Sower* was hung, yet Whitney neither bought this picture nor was it in his royal style.

In 1901 Henry Adams wrote from New York City to a friend, "The new rich are impossible here and Stanford White is their Moses, Aaron and Mohamet." Adams, who had fallen out with White over the constant delays in the memorial to his wife, Clover Adams, probably still bore White a bit of a grudge, but was likely describing Whitney's new house and his gargantuan taste for treasures. To the older, established American patricians, Whitney and Morgan's purchases seemed out of control with White acting as an impresario.

The American taste for binge buying was much frowned upon by members of the established social order in Europe and America. However, the American robber barons were following a small but already established European circle whose leading members were the banking family the Rothschilds. "The Rothschild taste" was a distinct visual statement formulated as members of the family established themselves in England and France after their expansion from their Frankfurt roots. The goal of the Rothschild taste was to create "tradition" in their new homes and bring the new and important banking family to a more level playing field with the old order of merchant bankers. The Rothschilds bought rooms and parts of older buildings, establishing a practice that the marquess of Hertford and his son, Sir Richard Wallace, followed in creating their London house. The supply of rooms and architectural elements was enlarged in the century when the cutting of transportation routes including railroads went through old houses, leading to their demolition. Dealers bought up the sections of older buildings, placing them in houses of the newly rich who were looking for a distinguished interior. Americans became a part of this antiquarian business at the end of the nineteenth century and prime customers in the twentieth century.

FOR STANFORD WHITE, the best clients were very rich and sophisticated men such as Will Whitney and Henry William Poor. White often had to deal with the wives of wealthy men, something he was seldom happy about, since wives, he wrote, were overly concerned about remembering closets and other mundane items when he wanted to soar into dazzling effects. When White had a male client dominating the commission, he was at his best. Henry William Poor (1844–1915) would be one of White's best clients. Poor's father had come down to New York City from Maine in 1839 to edit the *American Railroad Journal.* The young Poor took an undergraduate degree at Harvard in 1865 and a master's degree there in 1872. He was described as being of scholarly tastes; he was able to read in Greek and Latin and made studies of texts in Sanskrit, Hebrew, Icelandic, and Russian. Poor built up a fine personal library, which he was known to enjoy. He went into business with his father in railroad securities, and by the 1880s he had set himself up in a publishing business, putting out *Poor's Manual of Railroads* and *Poor's Manual of Industrials.*

White had known Poor from the early 1890s. By 1894 Poor figured in White's after-hours pursuits of young women, belonging to the circle who socialized as bachelors with a bevy of the young pretty women now flocking to New York City in search of riches and glamour. The young women often joined music hall groups, theatricals, and vaudeville chorus lines, where wealthy men saw and followed them. White's circle would devote themselves to these young women. Will Whitney, well known as a womanizer, seems to have pursued wives of his social peers instead of these rather consequence-free young women.

Once White had established his house at Gramercy Park, he wished to hold up the tone of the neighborhood. The real estate pressure of the upper reaches of Fifth Avenue was now drawing fashionable folk northward. Across Gramercy Park from the Whites, Mr. and Mrs. Stuyvesant Fish had had their house decorated by Sidney Stratton in 1887–88. But they had now commissioned White to build them a new, large, corner house on the northwest corner of Madison Avenue at Seventy-eighth Street. White was concerned that such departures meant the neighborhood was losing its cachet. The house at 125 East Twenty-first Street, one of the two neighboring houses belonging to Cyrus and David Dudley Field, had recently been run as a boardinghouse by Mrs. Henry Briggs. The boardinghouse was a most fashionable one, but White did not wish to see these alternatives to the newly emerging building type in New York, the apartment house, appear in his block. White was happy then to help sell Henry Poor on the idea of purchasing 125–127 East Twenty-first Street as a double town house much like White's own on the corner across Lexington Avenue. The site was particularly large, 66 feet by 109 feet, and was sold for more than two hundred thousand dollars to Poor.

The first idea was for White to demolish the older houses and build a grand new house, but the two friends were impressed by the quality of the existing houses, which White knew well as he had worked for the Abram Hewitts there a decade earlier. White was never eager to demolish older buildings. His very early preservationist streak, which had led him to try to save the old Main Building at NYU and would later prompt him to try to save the Merchants' Exchange at 55 Broadway, allowed White to rebuild Schickel's house for Whitney and to save the corner houses at Gramercy Park for Henry Poor.

The connecting of the houses, done between 1899 and 1901, came to more than $130,000, but the major expenses were those of the interiors. White and Poor grew quite close as they worked on the house, and the project mounted. Poor gave White a general mandate to fill the house with treasures on a scale not as lavish as that of Whitney, but neither did he hold back on prices. White put Charles Coleman in Capri on the lookout for items for Poor. He wanted to do an especially good job for a man who was his friend, his sometime broker, and his host in a secret hideaway over Poor's stable at 134 East Twenty-second Street.

When White began working on Poor's house, Poor had him create a stable and squash court a block away. At the end of the renovation, the two decided to put a "secret" room in the stable. In 1901 White sent in furnishings for his and Poor's private room. Poor knew of White's secret rooms and must have visited the hideaway White shared with a man in Poor's firm, J. D. Cheever, at 22 West Twenty-fourth Street. In 1897, Cheever and White had taken the top two floors in a small commercial loft building. In 1899 White had rigging put up on its exterior and hoisted furniture and some antique marble fireplace surrounds onto the roof. The furnishings would then be installed on their floors, which would become famous as the location of the red velvet swing. The studio was shared by White and Cheever until May 1, 1903, when they left the loft.

The treasures of Poor's fine house included a rare baldachino, once in the conservatory and later at the Cloisters in New York City. (This ritual ciborium, or stone covering, was removed to the Metropolitan Museum in 2009.) Sadly, Poor's wonderful, treasure-filled house had to be sold when his stock market holdings collapsed in the panic of 1907.

One purchase made for Poor's New York house was particularly controversial and may be the first round in a higher-stakes game of antiques selling that White now needed to resort to. White had suffered heavy financial losses in the last years of the 1890s, putting him deeply into debt. With his good friend and notably nice client Henry Poor, he may have ventured into the creation of a market for his personal stock of goodies.

In his recollections about McKim, William T. Partridge recounts the story of a ceiling for Henry Poor's house. Versions of this tale were obviously circulating widely by the early years of the century, suggesting that White's successful cornering of Poor may have tempted him to do it again. The story goes that White had been storing a lot of his purchases in an abandoned riding academy. One such item was an elaborate Renaissance ceiling White had found with the help of his Venetian agent. White was said to have had the ceiling unpacked, perhaps for one of his own spaces, but it was not used. A young man in the office, Philip Merz,* was asked to draw it, but the ceiling itself remained in Tattersall's Riding Academy. As Poor was a great collector of books, the library was a prime room in the house White designed for him. White seems to have used the Venetian ceiling's measurements as those for the room, unbeknownst to Poor. Once the house was well under way, White went abroad to purchase objects for Poor's house. Legend has it that White then cabled Poor, telling him that, amazingly, he had found a perfect ceiling for his library but that it was expensive. Poor replied that White should do as he thought fit. On his return to New York, White had the ceiling sitting at Tattersall's boxed and delivered to Poor as if it had just arrived from Venice. White thus made a great profit.

Tales of this sort of behavior sprang up and were known by everyone. The items involved were usually fireplaces. White would create an unusual opening that happened to be the size of one of his own pieces and

*Merz worked in the office from March 1897 until November 12, 1908.

would then "find" the perfect fireplace, undoubtedly very expensive, to fill the hole. Some clients would refuse the expensive item, but many fell for this confidence game.

IF STANFORD WHITE GOT ON BETTER with his male clients, there were nevertheless a few women who tried to take on a major role in the design process, usually without the good results of an agreeable male patron. White would meet his match with two ladies who wanted to make a major statement in New York's social whirl.

The Oelrichs family was prominent in fashionable life in the later nineteenth century. They were among America's few German families who were part of the social scene. The Oelrichs and the sugar-making Havemeyers were close friends and were the apogee of the German American wing of high society.

McKim and White had known two generations of Oelrichses, but were closer in age to the younger Hermann Oelrichs (born 1850), who was part of Jamie Gordon Bennett's circle in New York and Newport. Hermann Oelrichs had married one of the two beautiful Fair sisters, whose father had made a great fortune in the Comstock Lode. The sisters were brought up in San Francisco, but took on New York, where each married very well. Theresa Alice Fair married Oelrichs, and her sister married the young William Kissam Vanderbilt Jr. Both would hire Stanford White to design their New York City houses.

Theresa Alice Fair Oelrichs launched her New York career by convincing her husband to lease a trophy property for women wishing to become key figures in the social order. The Oelrichses took on the great corner house of the Mary Mason Jones row. In 1867, amid the "howling wilderness" with only red cows as neighbors, Mary Mason Jones had a tall row group created, stretching from Fifty-seventh to Fifty-eighth Street on the East side of Fifth Avenue. Mrs. Jones, a patrician widow, asked Robert Mook to build these white stone houses with great mansard roofs, and she chose to live in the seven-story corner house at 1 East Fifty-seventh Street. Guests had to ride two miles above the city to visit the redoubtable Mrs. Jones, whom Edith Jones Wharton, her niece, selected as the model for Mrs. Mingott in *The Age of Innocence*.

After the death of Mary Mason Jones, the house was leased to Marietta Reed Stevens, a self-made socialite who rose, it was said, from the ranks of housekeeper to marry the older hotelier Paran Stevens. The Stevenses had a beautiful daughter who married well, thanks to Mrs. Stevens's assault on the social order. Mrs. Stevens propelled herself and her daughter through the troubled waters of New York and Newport. She became a marriage arranger for wealthy American mothers trying to create a union with European nobility. By the time the Oelrichses bought the house once occupied by Mary Mason Jones and Mrs. Paran Stevens, the city had surrounded the Marble Row and moved farther to the north. The houses were no longer isolated and grand, but now established with a legacy appropriate for the new queen on Fifth Avenue.

White knew the Oelrichses fairly well before Mrs. Oelrichs asked him to renovate the house at 1 East Fifty-seventh Street. He worked on the interiors in this house, spending about as much as Henry Poor had on his double house.

Just as the city house was almost complete, the Oelrichses purchased the former house of the historian and statesman George Bancroft at Newport. The small house Bancroft had built was inadequate for Tess Oelrichs's ambition. Tess and Hermann hired White to do his last major work at Newport.

The early seaside resorts that were the proving ground for the young McKim, Mead & White had been left behind for urban buildings. Little new building was going on in Newport, with no new work in Elberon and none for McKim, Mead & White at Lenox. The new seaside houses the firm was building would be on Long Island's North Shore, the new chosen area. White would build a ballroom at Beechwood for Mrs. Astor at Newport in 1901–1902, but the Oelrichs house was his last big house in America's premier, and now rather overdone, summer colony.

The Oelrichs built on the established avenue, Bellevue, at Marine Avenue. The design was agreed upon in 1897 and the house actually built between 1899 and 1902. The house, Rosecliff, which continued Bancroft's attachment to rosebushes on the site, was not as extravagant as the houses built nearby by the Vanderbilts. Rosecliff is not as tall as the behemoths and built of a less expensive material. The house was intended as a summer home and was meant to appear at its best in strong summer light. It is a U-shaped house, with double columns and prominent ornament used to create areas of light and shadow. The light hit the house in a brilliant, almost limelight-sharp way. The house was built of terra-cotta bricks covered with a flat, icing-like, glazed white coat. The press of the day likened the surface to a glazed teacup's surface. The sun would reflect on the glaze and bounce off in a way that recalled the effect of light on the temporary staff surface of the exhibition buildings at the 1893 Chicago White City.

Rosecliff was to be a "gem" house meant to show off the hostess

*Rosecliff, Newport, 1897–1902. A house with the surface of a teacup. Open to the public.*

who would use the house for parties. White built a large heart-shaped staircase at the end of the hall, much as he had for the Hewitts' New York City house at 9 Lexington Avenue and at the J. Hampden Robb house on Thirty-fifth Street. The house here is a stage set for Tess Oelrichs's campaigns.

The style White selected seemed to reflect his visits to the French houses at Versailles. White had visited Versailles frequently, as Bessie's uncle lived much of the year near the palace. The source for the new Rosecliff was the Grand Trianon, an image meant to flatter the Oelrichses.

The Oelrichses were less open to White's suggestions about furnishings for the house. There is an elaborate fireplace that was meant to be a pedigreed work, although there seems to be a possibility that the fireplace was a reproduction. White did try to fill Rosecliff with select pieces, such as a large tapestry he had placed on a conveniently empty but perfectly sized blank wall panel. Amazingly, Tess rejected the tapestry, concerned about the cost overruns at the summer house.

Tess Oelrichs preferred parties to objects, staging her famous White Ball in which every detail was executed in white, from jewels to gowns to the house. She even planned the party on the embankment to spill out toward the sea, where she had a series of small white boats placed in the water to create the illusion of a flotilla.

If Tess Oelrichs was able to be independent of White's sales techniques, she was a pleasure to deal with compared to Katherine Duer Mackay, the wife of Clarence Mackay, son of one of James Fair's partners. John William Mackay left the world of Catholic charity in New York City to become lucky with Mr. Fair in the Comstock Lode. He then invested very cleverly, buying along with Jamie Gordon Bennett the cable companies that sent messages across the Atlantic. White was approached by the Mackays for a huge new house on the North Shore of Long Island near Roslyn. It was located on the highest point of the shore, at the top at what the Mackays would call Harbor Hill.

In terms of design, it is clear that in his great last houses White was pretty much copying from a book plate. Designing exteriors no longer seemed to excite White now; his creativity was directed toward objects, works of art, architectural fragments, and the like. The design of the

*Harbor Hill, Roslyn, New York, 1899–1902. Great estates quickly gave way to suburban houses.*

*Clarence Hungerford Mackay. The son of a self-made man, he lived grandly for a time, but the castle and illusion crashed just after World War II.*

house had given way to the arrangement and decoration of the rooms. It was thus, perhaps, a bit less than devastating when the iron-willed beauty marched into 160 Fifth Avenue to tell White the style she wished for her house. Katherine Mackay was looking for a style not widely in use for mansions at the time and had settled on a mid-seventeenth-century château with a form more austere than was currently popular.

One can only wonder if she found her model on wine bottle labels. Replicating the French château was the specialty of Richard Morris Hunt, who launched the style for the American pseudo-barons. The houses made famous by Hunt were done by others, such as Francis H. Kimball, who rendered elaborate details in a manner similar to Hunt's. White did look to unusual Norman châteaux, but he did not create the Loire Valley variety unless specifically requested to do so. White would do an expected Loire Valley château for Mrs. William K. Vanderbilt Jr. when she doubled her husband's family house, done by R. M. Hunt a generation earlier.

When Katherine Mackay insisted on this severe style, White obliged, after a few halfhearted attempts to dissuade her, with a house heavily copied from François Mansart's Château de Maisons near Paris, and with details taken from other houses. The debt of the design to book plates is obvious in the letters exchanged by White and the Mackays.

The house was to be built of America's finest building limestone, Indiana limestone, a considerable extravagance for a private home. The house construction included some steel I beams with vaults of Guastivino thin shell tile covering the steel for spectacular open internal spaces.

The house was probably Katherine's overcompensation for her family's financial reverses, which she had been all too conscious of during her girlhood. The Duers were proud of their ancestry, but had run out of money. The new house was meant to put her on the map, where she believed she belonged. Katherine controlled the aesthetic decisions, while Clarence sent the checks.

It was clear from the earliest days that Katherine and Clarence Mackay were not well suited to each other. She suffered from an imperious streak, which allowed her to taunt her Catholic husband by making him pay for a new Episcopal church near the entrance to their house. Katherine Mackay remained Episcopalian and acted as a principal of the building committee for the Roslyn Church, thoroughly tormenting White who was the architect of the church complex. The church complex survives on Northern Boulevard today, clearly visible from the road.

Katherine Mackay stressed her English heritage in the Harbor Hill interiors, which were remarkably un-French and much more English in style. The Mackays' house was formidable, smaller than only one of Hunt's last works, Biltmore, the great house at Asheville, North Carolina, for George Vanderbilt. In creating what was to be one of the very finest American country houses, White did think big, and he was constantly trying to promote lavish purchases at Harbor Hill. At times, Katherine Mackay sided with White, but at other times Clarence put the brakes on the money.

In 1902, Mackay's father died, leaving the couple an estate valued at five hundred million dollars, but Clarence had tired of the huge bills Harbor Hill kept generating. Mackay complained that he could not afford such items, since he was not able to command income as Carnegie and Rockefeller did. And yet the Mackays enjoyed playing king and queen of Roslyn. The couple were active in local events, and there is even a small drawing showing Katherine Mackay dressed as a nurse—expressing her generosity and benevolence to the town—standing before Harbor Hill. The Mackays got to be the lords of the area the way A. T. Stewart had wanted to do at Garden City, but it would be short-lived.

Harbor Hill would become a famously lavish home where important people were entertained at almost royal levels, but the couple would ultimately divorce. The Depression eroded Clarence Mackay's capital, and after falling into disrepair, Harbor Hill would be demolished in 1947 to make way for suburban housing. It is almost impossible to imagine a house of this quality of materials, construction, landscaping, and interiors leveled in one generation.

Despite the flare-ups between White and the Mackays over the cost of the house, the relationship between architect and client remained tolerable. The Mackays sent a check to White, joking that the payment should go to some of White's bills and not to his supper parties, which indicates that they knew of his precarious financial situation. They even seem to have known about White's womanizing, as one invitation to visit appears to include an offer to bring a special girl for him. Though they knew about White's weaknesses, the clients must have felt the results he obtained for them were worth the annoyance.

White was content to work within the constraints of historical build-ings for the Oelrichs, Vanderbilts, and Mackays, but when he was asked to create new buildings in a historic setting without a book to turn to, he was overwhelmed. His creativity had focused on interior effects, and the thought of building new buildings in a historic setting, not just replicat-ing what was there, unnerved him.

THE UNIVERSITY OF VIRGINIA, Thomas Jefferson's academic vil-lage of the 1820s, had outgrown its original buildings by the 1890s. The university wished to remain at the site, but the faculty had already requested a new library when a natural calamity occurred. In the early hours of October 27, 1895, a fire broke out in an unloved 1850s building and quickly spread to Jefferson's central Rotunda where it damaged the upper levels of Jefferson's core for his campus. The fire was a disaster, but despite little abundance in their coffers, the university decided to keep going and use the fire to achieve a more ideal campus. Initially, the univer-sity employed regional firms to clear the damage and begin repair of the Rotunda, but the faculty was afraid the local firms were not skillful enough to do the job well and appealed for a nationally known firm.

In the fall of 1895, the most nationally known campus architects of the moment were McKim, Mead & White, then working on Columbia and New York University. Indeed, McKim, Mead & White may have been approached before the fire to consider work on the campus. After hearing of the fire, Mead wrote a friend in the Medical School, but the pressure for Stanford White's selection surely came from the local family, the Rives, who owned nearby Castle Hill.

As McKim was going down the Nile in January 1896, the university gave the redesign of the campus to White, who hastily visited Char-lottesville. White was to restore the Rotunda, reconfigure it as a library, and build several new buildings in Jefferson's three-sided campus. On White's return from Virginia, Edward Simmons came upon him at the Players club, lost in thought and silent. "Simjaks" managed to get an explanation. White was overwhelmed by Jefferson's original plans for the university, remarking, "They're wonderful and I am scared to death. I only hope I can do it right." White faltered facing a problematic design which required an original solution rather than an easy model found in the useful office library.

White worked on the Rotunda, taking more liberties with Jefferson's design than he perhaps should have. The Rotunda was refitted in a man-ner somewhat like New York University's Gould Library, rather than returning the building to Jefferson's design. The White library displeased modern historians, and his work was removed in 1972–85. White's new buildings, Cabell Hall and two laboratories, were built at the formerly open fourth side of Jefferson's design, which seemed to close the vista Jefferson intended to leave open. White's work at the University of Virginia was done in good faith and in the taste of the era, but his confession to Simmons spoke fully about this work.

With the University of Virginia commission in hand in 1896, White once again tried to do something to help his brother, Dick. Dick White had been in New Mexico for years, but his dreams of finding a rich mine seemed hopeless by this time. After his disastrous visit to the Chicago Columbian Exposition as a representative of the New Mexico Territory, White had been obliged to send Dick back to the West. Three years later, Stanford brought Dick east once more to see their mother, then placed him at Charlottesville as an assistant to the superintendent of the works for more than a year. Dick White was instructed to stay silent on the job, which somehow he was able to do. In the spring of 1898, Stanford staked Dick to go to the Yukon, where another gold strike had started a gold rush. Dick went out to the Northwest Coast, where he would settle for the remainder of his life. When he spoke with his mother, Dick would later claim a family, but there is no evidence that he ever found anyone to marry. Although Stanford White was frequently annoyed by carrying the burden of his brother, he never let Dick down. His willingness to keep trying to find Dick a place was extraordinary, beyond what most people would do, and exhibits the young Stanford White's thoughtful behavior.

JUST AS WHITE LAUNCHED his brother westward again, his close friend James Breese commissioned the office to build him a summer house in Southampton, Long Island. The Breese house, called the Orchard, was begun in 1898 and done in stages over the next eight years, whenever Breese had some luck in the market.

Breese—like White, Henry Poor, and many of White's personal circle—had a family at home, but he enjoyed the company of young women in the theatrical world of New York. They all had pretty much abandoned their earlier sexual experiments and given in to a pattern of chasing young women. Evenings spent with young, beautiful women were an indiscretion popular with many well-off citizens. It certainly was not a harm-free pastime, but Stanford White and his friends were part of a widespread group of womanizers. The custom was not always fair to the young women taken up by the fast crowds, as they were were often tossed away once the fun was over. Stanford White was far more thoughtful to his young women, whom he often helped for years. His perception of these evenings was perhaps rather childishly based on pure enjoyment, but White was one of the most honorable of the chorus-girl chasers of the day.

Perhaps the most famous of the boys' nights was the dinner White planned with Henry Poor and Jimmy Breese in the Carbon Studio on May 20, 1895, for the birthday and anniversary of John Elliot Cowdin, whose wedding house, Wave Crest, at Rockaway had been designed a decade earlier. The dinner had more than thirty guests, including Charles Dana Gibson, John Twachtman, Whitney Warren, Gus Saint-Gaudens, Peter Cooper Hewitt, J. Alden Weir, Edward Simmons, McKim, and Nicholas Tesla, the inventor with whom White became most friendly. The dinner came in twelve courses with champagne at each course. As the dessert course was reached, the banjo players began the children's song, "Sing a Song of Sixpence," and waiters carried out a huge pie covered with a great crust. When the pie was set down, Susie Johnson, a sixteen-year-old girl, and some canaries popped out of the crust. Ms. Johnson was dressed in a filmy black gauze wrap with a stuffed blackbird hat. The "pie girl" dinner was infamous and quickly leaked to the popular press, creating a massive storm of publicity that reflected poorly on the guests. It is difficult to imagine McKim at the party. Did he leave early? What then went on with some of the men who stayed at the Carbon Studio?

The men at the "pie girl" dinner were probably not great fathers to their children. Larry was cared for by Bessie and Stanford's mother, Nina, who coddled and babied the boy, dressing him in extravagant finery and keeping him away from vigorous play and dirt. Whenever White heard an account of the "sissified" treatment Larry was getting, he would return home, fire the nanny, and promise a more normal life for his son. Larry White did grow up as an overprotected dandy who was sometimes tortured by street kids. The elaborately dressed Larry was once dangled over an open Third Avenue manhole by a group of tough kids. Considering Larry's childhood, it is a miracle that the young man turned out as well as he did. McKim and White each had only one child survive, and the two men's methods of raising their children differed as widely as did their lives and work.

# 42. McKim Meets His Daughter

In the early months of 1897, McKim's self-image had grown. True, he was lonely, having not seen his daughter in two decades due to the very unfair ruling of the Rhode Island courts, which forbade visits except in Newport and in environments controlled by Annie Bigelow. McKim's own family continued to shrink with the death of his adopted sister Annie after a long illness. During her lifetime, McKim had sent her financial support. In 1899 he created a small private chapel in Auburn, New York, the town where Annie spent her married life; the chapel was commissioned by Thomas Mott Osborne, but it was probably a memorial to Annie's family, all now dead.* Wendell Garrison spent time in Westchester near Fanny Villard, his sister, as he too tried to dig out from the loss of so many. McKim's family depended on his beloved nephew, Lloyd McKim Garrison, Wendell and Lucy's son, who had gone to Harvard, been active in the Hasty Pudding Club, and was preparing for a legal career in New York City.

McKim was still at Dr. Derby's house, which was beginning to seem a bit dilapidated to him, though he had made over his apartment a few years earlier. His relationship with Dr. Derby had cooled. McKim must have made noises about looking around for a new, larger home, as Dr. Derby seems to have offered him the entire house at 9 West Thirty-fifth

---

*Thomas Mott Osborne, part of Lucretia Mott's family, made an Osborne/McKim/Dennis chapel a family project. Osborne was a renowned penologist.

Street for forty thousand dollars. McKim toyed with the idea but decided that he wanted a more fashionable, English-appearing house without the tall stoop. He preferred the more genteel effect of what is called an English basement house, with a door at the center of the ground floor reached by two or three short steps, not the high Dutch stoop with its asymmetrical door. Further, McKim wanted a house with an internal central staircase, not the side stairs of an old-fashioned brownstone. He was looking to keep pace with the old-line friends of his mature years, the Henry Whites, the Augustus Jays, the Philip Schuylers, the Thomas Newbolds, John L. Cadwalader and Frank Millet. Cadwalader, who was becoming McKim's closest friend, had a house just across Fifth Avenue at 13 East Thirty-fifth Street, part of the Astor estate rental houses, many of which had been made into English basement houses. The Astor family had investment row houses on both sides of Fifth Avenue in the Thirties, which were leased to well-connected New Yorkers.

McKim, living alone, did not really need more room, but he must have felt his life needed an upward boost. He had let Mead and White live in his house when each was renting out his own place. McKim did entertain his old friends at his home, but he was clearly lonely. About this time, he took singing lessons. One can imagine this quiet, solitary person singing in his now well-appointed, tasteful rooms.

In 1897, McKim was asked to join the second round of a competition for a fine, large public library for New York City. He was very proud to participate, as he truly expected to win. McKim was elated with the success of his Columbia work and his American School in Rome, and now the prospect of another educational building of a huge scale promised another feather his cap.

The idea of learning and reading in a well-stocked library is an ancient, if elite, concept. In the nineteenth century, when the movement to provide public education to all children gathered momentum, so too did the notion that all people should have access to a good public library. The genuine public library in the City of Boston had a long history, and McKim had been given the job of building its new, grander quarters at Copley Square on a silver platter, despite the competitions held. McKim turned the library commission into his "perfect" work, with a full Beaux-Arts program of painting, architecture, sculpture, and woodwork. McKim was fiercely proud of what he and Samuel A. B. Abbott had been able to do, including the great murals by Edwin Austin Abbey, Puvis de Chavannes, and John Singer Sargent. With the Boston Public Library virtually finished, McKim received a request from his and Stanford White's old friend George L. Rives to compete for the New York Public Library. McKim expected to be handed the New York job.

New York City did not have as strong a sense of fairness to the general public as did Boston, America's intellectual city. New York had two "public" libraries, the Astor and Lenox libraries, but these benefactions were really gentlemen's libraries hiding behind the word "public." In the 1880s the public library issue became even more complicated when Governor Tilden's bequest left most of his fortune to establish a free library. Those connected to the three library legacies decided that a single library would solve their problems.

In New York City a clean, safe, drinking water resource had been available for a half century at the Croton Reservoir between Fortieth and Forty-second Street on Fifth Avenue. When Central Park's reservoir was completed, the Croton Reservoir became redundant. But what to do with the city property on Fifth Avenue? Stanford White had been involved in the schemes for the Croton Reservoir, including a new City Hall and other ideas. Now the site seemed to be thought ideal for a large public library.

McKim, working for the firm, had reason to think that he would win the job. He was usually wary of competitions, since the partners had lost a large number of commercial building competitions and had vowed in their correspondence never to enter another competition unless they had a friend at the bar. But to McKim, Rives was one friend, Cadwalader another.

McKim's neighbor John Lambert Cadwalader (1836–1914) was his closest friend in these years. Cadwalader was born into two celebrated families, the Revolutionary War hero Cadwaladers and, on his mother's side, the Gouverneurs. Cadwalader graduated from Princeton in 1856 and Harvard Law School in 1860. His family connections could easily have established the young attorney in Philadelphia, where his family was well known, but he preferred the anonymity of New York City and begged his father to write to the mid-nineteenth century's best attorney, Daniel Lord. Cadwalader was with Lord for two years, then moved to the firm of George Bliss in the early 1870s.* Cadwalader then joined President Grant's cabinet as an assistant secretary of state during Grant's second term. The Grant administration was not known for its admirable causes, and Cadwalader's tenure there earned him the lifetime nickname of "Slick Old John." It was said that Cadwalader could see directly to the core of a complex legal problem, a skill that would serve him well for the rest of his life.

---

*Bliss, of course, would marry Anaïs Casey after the death of his first wife and be the customer for the altar in the Church of St. Francis Xavier on Sixteenth Street in New York City.

On returning to New York, he was careful to stick to high-minded causes. The hours Cadwalader spent on public projects after work in his legal firm led to his reputation as a civic leader.

Cadwalader was known as a perfect gentleman by all. His former partner, Henry W. Taft, described him as being "slender and delicate." He was also said to have a high, nasal voice and "an almost feminine sensitiveness and delicacy of perception." As a trustee of the Astor Library, Cadwalader moved into a house at 13 East Thirty-fifth Street that was part of the Astor estate. He furnished the house tastefully and with his collection of mezzotints.

Cadwalader and McKim's worlds circled each other for decades, but when McKim found an Astor house to rent at 9 East Thirty-fifth Street in 1899, he and Cadwalader became constant companions. After Prescott Hall Butler's death, Cadwalader acted as attorney for McKim when problems arose with the Bowery and Knickerbocker banks and Pennsylvania Station. Cadwalader could do litigation, but his great skill was settling complex cases out of court. He settled the disastrous Knickerbocker Trust case following the panic of 1907 and the complex issues in the estate of department store owner Benjamin Altman.

Cadwalader remained unmarried, allowing Mrs. Cadwalader Jones and the actress Mary Anderson to act as his hostesses. He spent the time many men devote to family doing good work for the city. It is impossible to tell by surviving information if he was actively homosexual or just part of the New York bachelor scene. Cadwalader belonged to every club in the city, joining most in 1868. He was a fixture in the late evenings at the clubs popular with single men, but no more can be definitely stated. It appears that Cadwalader was very close to Benjamin Altman and his partner, Michael Friedsam, and other men who were likely homosexual. Cadwalader's circle included Frank Millet, who was in these years probably also living as a gay man. Were McKim and Cadwalader more than best friends who traveled together to Europe every summer and to shooting clubs in the American South in the fall and winter? Likely not. There is no reason to think that McKim was anything but celibate, even if he was most comfortable with Cadwalader's high-minded civic activities.

As an Astor Library trustee, Cadwalader had been dealing with the lack of funds for the library, as after John Jacob Astor II's death the funding had ceased. With the Tilden estate, Cadwalader saw the solution to be a full library to rival Boston's. After the first competition for the library produced uncertain results, Rives and Cadwalader added invited firms to the second competition, including McKim, Mead & White and Carrère & Hastings. McKim wrote Cadwalader that the office could not complete the scheme within the guidelines of the competition, suggesting he would go beyond the competition rules. McKim, Mead & White fully expected to be given the job on their terms. The whole office was shocked when they came in third. McKim was personally devastated, but he nevertheless wrote a charming letter to his onetime pupil and friend Tommy Hastings, who won the competition. Stanford White was grim about the results, fearing the office might now be facing a decline. Fortunately, the firm continued to get jobs and the defeat remained personal. Cadwalader and Rives consoled McKim by telling him it was their exceeding the bounds of the competition that had cost them the job. A similar event would occur in 1903, when Stanford White entered the Grand Central Station competition with a design that went far beyond the rules, probably done because McKim had the Pennsylvania Station commission and White thought he could expect Grand Central.

McKim's thoughts about moving house came to a head around Christmas 1898. He had been told that his twenty-one-year-old daughter, now called Margaret Day after Annie Bigelow McKim's new husband, had moved in with Annie's mother, Mrs. Bigelow, in Cambridge, Massachusetts, to prepare for college in the Harvard Annex, later Radcliffe College. Margaret began college preparation at the Gilman School in 1896, but the next year she had a complete breakdown. Mrs. Bigelow took her to Europe in 1897 for a year, but her health did not improve.

Early in January 1899, McKim was summoned through the intervention of Wendell Garrison to the home of Dr. R. T. Edes in Jamaica Plain, Massachusetts, to see his daughter for the first time in twenty years. Margaret likely shared McKim's depression and anxiety disorder. It would seem the physicians suggested Margaret meet her father. The meeting must have been a most emotional one, with Margaret giving herself over to her father, taking back his name, and agreeing to come live with him in New York City once she was able. McKim had Margaret brought to the home of Dr. Bowman in Greenwich, Connecticut, where she would live with the doctor's family and other patients until her depression lifted. It would be five long years before Margaret was well enough to leave Dr. Bowman.

McKim, elated over the reunion with his daughter, moved into 9 East Thirty-fifth Street and prepared for life with Margaret. Annie, now the mother of three sons, reacted as arbitrarily as she had when she divorced

McKim. Annie Day cut off her daughter fully, despite the young woman's serious mental illness, never communicating with her firstborn again.

One can only think how strained Margaret's life had been with the Days, where she was an outsider. Once her depression began, and Margaret tried to sort through her troubles by learning if her father was the bad person her mother had claimed, Annie Day rejected Margaret.

McKim tried to help Margaret as best he could, keeping her in comfort in Greenwich, visiting her, and writing her a series of loving, supportive letters. "I shall think of you constantly and wish for you whenever I have any pleasure. Farewell for a while, dear child," he wrote on August 1, 1900. His letters in the decade he had with Margaret reveal a man whose character was of the highest order: He always put Margaret first, treating her as a special, beloved person. Even when the burden of her continued ill health depressed him, he never let Margaret know about his fears. McKim became the ideal parent to Margaret, whom he clearly treasured. Her presence in his life was the more valuable as the next year McKim suffered another searing blow: his family's greatest hope, young Lloyd McKim Garrison, just thirty-three years old and newly married, fell ill suddenly and died while McKim was making the transatlantic crossing. McKim arrived in New York to learn of his beloved nephew's death, having landed one hour after the funeral. Llewellyn Park had become an empty house.

McKim had been in Europe with Cadwalader shooting birds at a house his friend rented every summer from 1900 forward, inviting McKim, the Augustus Jays, the Philip Schuylers, Beatrix Jones Ferrand, Edith Wharton, Mrs. Cadwalader Jones, and Henry James. The house, Millden, was a many-winged house over the Esk River near Brechin in North Berwick, Scotland.* Cadwalader rented the house during the shooting season in August and September, filling the house with friends intent on killing grouse. McKim would cross the Atlantic each summer for the next seven years to go to Scotland.

Shooting birds seems less in character for McKim than observing them, but the Edwardian era followed the aristocratic pastime of shooting hapless birds as a social event pursued with friends under the guise of sport. McKim and Cadwalader often went to Georgia and South Carolina in the late fall and early spring. The aspiring shooters had a difficult time find-

---

*Millden is no longer standing. Professor Gavin Stamp kindly searched for Millden and reported its demolition.

ing a good location for their sport. The first location they tried was Garrett, South Carolina. Then they began a club—the Pallashueola Club—in Columbia, South Carolina, but it seems to have failed. The shooting trips to the temperate parts of America were meant as a health restorative to counter McKim's anxiety. While on a trip, McKim recognized that he had to relax and not think of his maddening concerns. McKim did seem to enjoy the hunting trips.

In the year 1900, McKim was pleased to see that his former brother-in-law, George von Lengerke Meyer, was appointed the American ambassador to Rome by President Theodore Roosevelt. As McKim had now turned his thoughts to the American Academy, it was a joy for him to have a close friend in a most convenient place. The night before the Meyers sailed, McKim hosted a great party in New York City for the couple. Every summer McKim would visit the ambassador, who was of great assistance when the American School needed to buy the Villa Mirafiore.

At the summer exhibition of the year 1900 in Paris, McKim, Mead & White received their first international recognition. The architects were given a gold medal for their work, an honor to McKim, who as a young man from the New World found so much to study in Paris. Now, Europeans were looking to America and bestowing an honor on the nation's most important architectural firm. The Atlantic Ocean, once a mighty barrier, was now becoming a pond, with more Americans joining in European events and Europeans coming to inspect the houses of Newport and New York. McKim came to see himself as part of this transatlantic world with the Harry Whites settled in London, the Meyers in Rome, and friends such as the Abbeys and Cadwalader renting houses.

Another person who was a part of the transatlantic set—before she finally settled in France—was Edith Jones Wharton. Edith Jones grew up in New York City and Newport before her parents settled in Europe for several years. As we know, the Joneses returned to Newport in 1872, living on the Bayside near the Auchinclosses, Bigelows, and Hunters. This is exactly the set McKim knew in the same years. Indeed, Edith's brother was engaged to Caroline Hunter in the fall of 1873. The Hunters sailed for Europe on the *Ville du Havre,* which was hit by another vessel, killing Caroline and her parents. Edith Jones Wharton swam in the same waters as McKim, but she clearly snubbed him and Stanford White in her book *The Decoration of Houses,* selecting the young Ogden Codman as her coauthor, although she does acknowledge McKim in the introduction.

When Edith Wharton grew tired of Newport and moved to Lenox in search of a more intellectual group, she had Hoppin & Koen design her house, the Mount. Hoppin and Koen had both been in the McKim, Mead & White office, where Hoppin had done some good design work.*

PERHAPS MRS. WHARTON did not find McKim her favorite architect, but the profession did hold the high-minded Charles McKim in esteem. McKim had devoted his career to refining America's aesthetic judgment. He wanted to train future generations to appreciate the potential role of architecture in the creation of an America ready to assume its place in the world order as a major power. McKim wanted to help the nation prepare its buildings and cities for its expected greatness. His unwillingness to compromise, his generosity to young professionals, and his tireless work on the American Academy project, made him the natural leader of the profession.

The American Institute of Architects was formed with some difficulty in the middle of the nineteenth century. By the beginning of the twentieth century, the AIA, as it was known, was increasingly gaining a national membership. It needed to find an appropriate figure for the presidency and determined the learned McKim to be the perfect candidate. Aware that he was busy and did not do well under stress, the members realized McKim would decline the office. So at the 1901 annual convention in Buffalo, McKim was simply elected president, without his having any say in the matter. He held the office for three years. During McKim's time at the AIA, the Octagon House in Washington, D.C., was purchased for the Institute. The AIA used the house for exhibitions.

McKim was no longer just a New York City architect; he was now a national figure. A symbolic moment in McKim's shift to a broader focus came about on a winter's night in late March 1901 when Daniel Burnham, McKim's old friend from the Columbian Exposition days and an active partner in the American Academy project, roared into the Century club looking for him. John La Farge was there, and he greeted Burnham and whisked him to McKim's house just eight blocks to the south. La Farge and Burnham barged in on McKim, and Burnham excitedly told him of the Senate's decision to empower a committee to prepare a plan for the development of the park system in the District of Columbia and the location of future public buildings. The committee had made the younger Burnham the chairman of the commission along with Frederick Law

---

*Hoppin had married Miss Weeks of Oyster Bay, a close friend of McKim and White, who often spent evenings with Arthur D. Weeks.

Olmsted Jr., who was in charge of the landscape end of the project. Burnham, who had helped McKim in the drive for the American Academy, now asked McKim to join him in this national project. The three men became the Senate Park Improvement Commission, prepared to recover as much of Pierre L'Enfant's 1792 plan as possible.

To gather inspiration for the plan, Burnham, McKim, and Olmsted put together a trip in the early summer of 1901. Joined by Charles Moore, the future biographer of Burnham and McKim, they set off for a study tour of Europe's great capitals. In England the president of the Pennsylvania Railroad, Alexander J. Cassatt, met with Burnham as the other commission members waited nervously. Cassatt's railroad had an ungainly railroad station in L'Enfant's park, which the commission hoped to convince Cassatt to move. The jittery Burnham knew Cassatt's decision about the station's location would be the key to the success of their planning work. The decision was quickly reached and better than Burnham had imagined. Cassatt and the other railroad directors agreed to build a "union" station north of the Capitol, provided that Congress came up with an appropriation for a tunnel under Capitol Hill. Burnham, McKim, and Olmsted were thrilled, as their hopes for an improved Washington blossomed before their eyes.

McKim's goals seemed secure, as later that year plans for expanding the Executive Mansion were put forward during the AIA's annual meeting in Washington, D.C. The AIA was afraid that an enlarged office building might be created at the cost of the venerable presidential mansion. President McKinley and his wife put the lid on these plans as neither wished to live with work going on in the house. Following McKinley's assassination, the Roosevelts were willing to allow work to be done on the mansion. McKim, when asked, was eager to restore the venerable mansion. Probably about this time most architects would have agreed with Burnham that the president might as well move to another house. McKim in reverential tones proposed, "Let me take it down stone by stone . . . and rebuild it; and not an architect in the country can make a finer or more appropriate residence for the President of the United States."

The eagerness of Senator James McMillan to further the work of the Senate Park Improvement Commission and the cooperation of the Roosevelts made the mood friendlier for renovating and expanding the mansion, soon to be known as the White House. McKim got his wish to rebuild the White House, which he worked on from early 1902 to late in that year. The prestige of having the AIA president do the White House probably helped to open tight purse strings in Congress, which agreed to a half-million-dollar renovation and to a McKim, Mead & White Executive Office Building wing at 1600 Pennsylvania Avenue.

McKim, the early student of America's historic architecture, made some decisions that did not stand the test of time. Soon after the Second World War, McKim's White House was gutted and a new version of the building was created. He was greatly criticized for selling off the old furniture of the White House and creating a "good taste" presidential mansion. McKim had turned his back on the taste of an earlier generation, and even suggested to President Roosevelt that the glass screen made by Tiffany twenty years before should be blown up with dynamite. McKim had rejected his own earlier taste in favor of a genteel Georgian aesthetic.

McKim had become one of the nation's premier experts on eighteenth-century American building. The private sector was as eager to have a distinguished historical expert design a new house for them as were congressional committees. In early 1902, the publisher A. Cass Canfield asked McKim to build him a house near those of E. D. Morgan and Will Whitney, in that growing area of the North Shore where McKim, Mead & White had already designed three houses surrounded by huge tracts of land. For Canfield, who was married to an Emmet girl, McKim created a house that would become commonplace in wealthy areas of the nation about this time. It was an erudite, brick Georgian country house which just happened to be huge by comparison to its models. The colossal Georgian house seemed rather like Alice in Wonderland, growing wildly out of scale, but still the same entity. McKim would do a similar house at the end of 1902 for Thomas Jefferson Coolidge, the father of McKim's friend, Mrs. Thomas Newbold. The two large houses have been demolished, but many in this Georgian good taste mode survive.

McKIM'S CAREER had come a very long way in the thirty years since he timidly had his business card made. It must have been truly amazing for him to look back on his early years, with his poor college record and difficulty in getting started, and realize that he was now helping to produce L'Enfant's plan, building for Vanderbilts, and at work on the White House. McKim had exceeded any likely expectation for his success. Now, at the top of the national profession, recognized at the Paris Fair, and thinking about creating a base in Rome for American artists, McKim could reflect upon how very far he had come to achieve his ambitions. The current number of ideal commissions more than made up for the loss of the New York Public Library. Early in 1902, he summed up his giddy feelings in a letter to Charles Moore, "In these days of miracles, one should be prepared for anything . . . and am writing now in the frame of mind of a man more likely to go off on a spree than home to dinner."

At the apex of his career, McKim prepared for a really miraculous commission. The man he pursued in search of funding for the American Academy—as McKim admitted, he did not even know him—was asking him to build a magnificent private library in the Medici manner. J. P. Morgan at this time was the most powerful man in America and one of the major forces in the world. The ruthless titan of business, whose gargantuan appetite for valuable objects had made him a legend, had come to the quiet McKim. Morgan, whose eyes were said to be so fierce that they burned through people like headlights on a train, was willing to build a splendid building.

Charles the Charmer was able to get along with many people. Mrs. Roosevelt noted that he could charm the bird off the bough, but to be able to work at the same moment for two men dead set against each other was amazing. Roosevelt and Morgan were enemies on almost all issues. Only McKim could have built for each during the war of trusts.

The connections between McKim and Morgan may go back farther than the architect was willing to admit when he began negotiations with strategic friends to arrange to contact Morgan about 1900. McKim claimed to have no personal acquaintance with Morgan, but what he probably meant was no close relationship. He must have known Morgan slightly from the work Stanford White did with Morgan at Madison Square Garden and the Metropolitan Club. Further, McKim may have known the second Mrs. Morgan, Frances Tracy Morgan (1842–1924), whose father was an attorney in New York in Prescott Hall Butler's firm. In the early days, the legal office was Evarts, Tracy & Southmayd.*

The Morgans did not have a house at Newport, but would visit in the summers. In the 1870s and '80s the Morgans were not as powerful or as wealthy as they would later be and thus were more accessible. They lived in a brownstone at 6 East Fortieth Street, next door to William Henry Vanderbilt and five short blocks from McKim's rooms in Dr. Derby's house. It is even possible that because of Mrs. Morgan McKim felt confident enough to brave an entry and ride the Morgan-backed street railroad in 1878. McKim was thrilled by the new elevated railroad controlled by Jay Gould, Russell Sage, and J. P. Morgan. In his later years, though,

---

*There is even a faint possibility that Miller McKim spoke of the young J. P. Morgan, as Morgan's mother's father, the Reverend John Pierpont (1783–1866), was an active participant in the abolitionist movement.

*McKim as a dean of the profession.*

McKim would turn away from technology and express his dislike for very tall buildings and mass transportation.

The business career of John Pierpont Morgan flourished at a time parallel to that of McKim, Mead & White. In both worlds, business seemed wide open. It had been fairly unregulated at the beginning of the 1860s, but by the end of their era, before World War I, it was proceeding in a much more ordered and regulated way. Unlike McKim, Mead, and White, who rose from modest but intellectual homes, Morgan rose from a position of secure power. The Morgans of Hartford, Connecticut, had become successful merchants in partnership with Levi P. Morton, before Morton moved to New York. The Morgans were among the more prosperous Yankee merchants, enough so that when George Peabody, the American banker who had gone to London in 1837 to guide European investors to the New World, needed a partner, Junius Spencer Morgan was called to Britain. The aging bachelor had no successor, and in 1854 Morgan crossed the Atlantic to assist in and then take over Peabody's business. Morgan brought his family with him.

Like the Meads, the Morgans were a family long settled in America; they were upper-middle-class New England gentry employed in traditional mercantile pursuits until Junius Spencer Morgan joined Peabody and rose to a financial level nearly unknown in pre–Civil War America. Junius Spencer's son, John Pierpont Morgan, was educated in England until the age of seventeen, then was sent off to school in Vevey, Switzerland, to prepare for university. The young man, called "Pip" and later Pierpont, but never John, then went rather briefly to Göttingen, where Americans from Emerson to Longfellow and George Bancroft had studied.

Junius Spencer Morgan was thriving in London and had bought a new stucco-fronted house at 13 Prince's Gate, just across the road from where the Great Exhibition had been held a few years earlier. Morgan's neighbors at Prince's Gate would be two rival merchant bankers of the day, Herbert de Stern and Eric Hambro. Morgan and Peabody were now of a large enough size to be able to emulate the big London private bankers, the

Rothschilds, de Stern, Hambro, Seligman, and Baring Brothers, who invested widely in emerging businesses of the new age while underwriting the occasional national war treasury. The investment house that Pierpont Morgan most admired was that of the Rothschilds, whose English branch he studied closely. In 1857, despite his father's worries about the strong-willed young man's preparedness, Pierpont sailed for New York City.

Peabody and Morgan favored the Union cause, trying to support Lincoln from Europe. Many other private bankers became fearful that the Union side would lose and pulled out of the market. Young Morgan had a private telegraph wire put in his office so that he could follow the battles. He seems to have done a bit of rifle selling on the side, which would cost him his reputation for years afterward.* It would seem that Junius Spencer Morgan's fears about his son's strong will and bullheadedness were on the mark.

The younger Morgan's career in New York was carefully controlled by the wiser and more levelheaded father from his base in Britain. Junius Spencer suggested that railroad financing was the best means of wealth expansion in the 1870s and 1880s, and proved the truth of this insight on a spectacular scale. Pierpont's first great success in America with his shared firm, Drexel Morgan, was the secret purchase of the Vanderbilt railroad, New York Central, in 1877. William Henry Vanderbilt, the thick but devious son and heir of Commodore Cornelius Vanderbilt, needed to quickly and discreetly break his major promise to his late father. He needed cash to pay off his sisters and brothers, who had been left out of their father's will and were now laundering some fairly unpleasant family stories in the newspapers. Vanderbilt walked next door to Morgan's house to arrange for this huge sale. Thanks to Morgan's father, English and German investors bought the two-hundred-million-dollar stock package; few others were aware of the transaction until Junius Spencer had completed it in London. With the great profit from the deal, rumored to be three million dollars, Morgan purchased a house on the Hudson, Cragston, and another on Madison Avenue at Thirty-sixth Street, which had belonged to the Phelps family. The brownstone at 219 Madison Avenue would become Morgan's home for the rest of his life.

J. P. Morgan set himself up in the United States as a Rothschild-style banking house, but he was sometimes hasty in his financial speculations.

---

*Morgan and his associates sold defective old rifles to the U.S. Army, making a huge profit and endangering the troops with broken equipment.

To many, Morgan was a "plunger," someone who went too far and had to be bailed out by Drexel and his father. As Pierpont's father aged, the control the elder Morgan had over his son's projects began to fade. Thus, as Junius weakened, Morgan took on riskier investments such as Madison Square Garden, for which, Drexel Morgan supplied the funds, with Morgan himself putting up much of the money. In 1890, the elder Morgan died in Monte Carlo, opening up for his son an unwatched investment career.

Almost immediately, J. P. Morgan began his obsessive, massively scaled purchases of art. It is as if the lid came off Morgan about 1890, when his father was out of the picture. Indeed, Morgan's purchases of books, works of art, objects, and the like were constant—of all time periods and places—and soon got out of control. Morgan bought European and Asian objects, Egyptian to Baroque work, with Rococo thrown in. He stored many of his treasures in a double house at Prince's Gate and in the family villa, Dover House, on the Thames. Morgan's enormous personal profit, made from his stock-backing deals, went into artworks, so much so that at his death his principal capital was in art, not cash. In 1909, when the British began to impose death duties on artworks, and the years of efforts by Stanford White, Morgan, and others finally got the U.S. duties on art removed, Morgan shipped his work to America. His enormous collections were here by his death in 1913, having fortunately just missed being loaded on the initial voyage of a boat Morgan held an interest in, the *Titanic.*

J. P. Morgan set himself up as the king of capital in the 1890s and the early twentieth century. He seemed to create, broker, or stop every major financial move. Sometimes it seemed to be Morgan's will alone that moved the economy, saving it from an even more serious crash in 1895 and particularly in 1907, when he single-handedly limited the financial panic and kept the nation from a deep financial disaster.

In some old verses of the day Morgan's stature is revealed. "Question: Who made the world? Answer: God made the world in 4004 BC but it was reorganized in 1901 by James J. Hill, J. Pierpont Morgan and John D. Rockefeller." A second song, "Morgan, Morgan, the Great Financial Gorgon," included the lines

> I went to the only place left for me;
> So I boarded a boat in the brimstone sea;
> Maybe I'll be allowed to sit
> On the griddled floor of the bottomless pit.

But a jeering imp with horns on his face
Cried out as he forked me out of the place.
It's Morgan's, it's Morgan's, the great financial gorgon's;
Get off that spot, we're keeping it hot;
That seat is reserved for Morgan.

Morgan's appetite for control extended beyond his family. Morgan and his wife drifted apart as stories of his affairs filled the whispered hours. The marriage was damaged so badly that when Morgan set off in 1913 for what was pretty clearly a dying man's voyage to his favorite sites, Rome and Egypt, he went without Mrs. Morgan, who was at home when the cable of his death in Rome was sent to her. His womanizing seems to have been done with little mixing into the demimonde. There is no evidence to suggest White's after-hours circle and Morgan's private life ever coincided. Indeed, Morgan and Will Whitney both had affairs with women from their own social circle, including the sharing of Edith May Randolph. Morgan carried on with Edith Randolph before the widow decided she required a husband. Morgan would not divorce, so Mrs. Randolph, who had had an affair with Whitney before his wife Flora died, returned to Whitney once he had come out of the official mourning period for his first wife. It would be fascinating to know what Edith May Randolph Whitney knew, as surely both Morgan and Whitney shared confidences with her.

Morgan held himself above all others except for George Bowdoin and Charles Lanier, his friends, and the quiet conservative banker George F. Baker. Baker was a robber baron on a grand scale, but one who shunned the spotlight and avoided the dangerous acts Morgan dared to try. Baker, who outlived Morgan by many years, was the one baron who had the respect of his peers and the public. Morgan respected Baker for his prudence and because he considered that Baker, like himself, was of a higher social standing than the others. Morgan carefully insisted he be called Pierpont, not John, to assert his Connecticut heritage. To display his "old" family connections, he remained in a brownstone house when the Vanderbilts were building white stone castles. He lived in that curious stretch of the city just below Grand Central Station that came to be connected with the *old* families, not the new. Morgan was a terrible snob who looked down on some of his peers, those who were not as clever as he or were raw in their behavior, such as John D. Rockefeller (Morgan liked John's much nicer brother, William Rockefeller), Gould, and Harriman. Morgan reserved a special distaste for the Jewish bankers whom he so carefully copied. Morgan emulated but nevertheless felt superior to the Rothschilds and his Prince's Gate neighbors, Hambro and de Stern.

One can see why McKim feared dealing with Morgan. When McKim began to circle around Morgan, whose love for the Eternal City of Rome inspired McKim to hope he might endow the American Academy, he reached the financial titan via Lanier and Bowdoin. Bowdoin was also a client and neighbor to Morgan and McKim at 39 Park Avenue. During the time between Morgan's agreement to help fund the Academy and real evidence he might do so, Morgan tortured the architect with lengthy periods of no communication. McKim looked to Morgan for the Academy and Morgan, to McKim's surprise, looked back at him for a library.

The New York Public Library was rising splendidly to the designs of Carèrre & Hastings, but now McKim would have his library in New York, even if it would be a private one. From 1900 on, Morgan had been contemplating a personal library for his vast book collections and, of course, to act as a setting to display himself as a patrician American and a native-born Medici. Morgan had gathered several sites on Thirty-sixth Street to assemble a super-block. Morgan first approached an American architect of old family, Whitney Warren, to design his library and gallery. Warren's lineage, Morgan must have felt, equaled his own. Morgan knew him also as the architect of the new clubhouse for the New York Yacht Club. Morgan, whose boat was called the *Corsair,* looked for Warren's design, but when it arrived it seemed not to immediately please Morgan, who put it on hold for two years.

Just about the time Warren's design came to Morgan, McKim's campaign for the American Academy began. The protracted siege lasted for two years, until the last days of March 1902, when Morgan telephoned McKim at home just a block away. He summoned the architect to come to his house the next morning. McKim expected to be told something about the American Academy as he stepped into Morgan's presence. But to his shock, Morgan informed him of his land purchases on Thirty-sixth Street, then told McKim that he would like him to build a house for his recently married daughter Louisa, now Mrs. Herbert L. Satterlee, and also to build a small museum for his collections. McKim, the president of the AIA, immediately demonstrated his professional principles, hesitating because Whitney Warren had been asked for plans two years earlier. Morgan justified his abandonment of Warren by saying he had long ago decided to not go ahead with Warren's plans. McKim wrote an explanatory letter to Warren many months later, which does show a certain willingness to do the job despite professional ethics. Morgan probably decided he wanted the president of the AIA and the organizer of the Roman academy, not an old school friend.

McKim was delighted to win another institutional commission, even if it came with a bit of terror inspired by Morgan. But the library would long live on, a monument to the patron and architect. McKim worked out the design for the library building in stages, beginning with a central temple-front design similar to the one the office had just done at the public library in Orange, New Jersey, adjacent to McKim's hometown of Llewellyn Park. As Morgan's favorite location was Rome, the temple front quickly gave way to a box with an elaborate Renaissance-featured entrance. The final work done by McKim and his men must rank among McKim's greatest moments. Inspired to work for the man who could assure the American Academy for life, he rose to the occasion, creating a simple, well-balanced marble block with carefully measured, subtle proportions.

The conceit of building an entire block of marble was already very expensive. As the early meetings with Morgan went well, McKim, becoming a bit more comfortable with the client, bullied up the courage to make an even more costly proposal—he suggested using dry masonry in true Greek tradition. This ancient construction technique necessitated that the marble blocks had to be so perfectly cut that they rested upon each other tightly. McKim explained to Morgan that he had inspected this technique on the Acropolis with the Erechtheum, where he had tried to slip a knife blade between the blocks to no avail. Though McKim's idea of sticking a knife into the masonry of a two-thousand-plus-year-old world monument was not exactly correct behavior, Morgan got the point. When asked how much more it would cost for a feature no one would even be able to see, McKim replied fifty thousand dollars, and Morgan agreed to the expenditure. McKim contacted an old draftsman from the office, then a student of classics in Athens, asking for a sculptural model or a squeeze of the joints. On examining the Greek model, McKim's advisors suggested the addition of a film of lead one sixty-fourth of an inch thick to mediate the greater extremes of weather in New York.

As the jobs for Morgan progressed, the architect felt the headlights of Morgan's personality. McKim's health was beginning to fail by 1904, and he recognized that the Morgan projects were taking a toll. He told Charles Moore that he knew the work would take some years off his life, but he felt the library was more important than the years. Even so, McKim did break and had to beg Morgan for time off for a rest. McKim suggested turning the job over to White while he was away, but Morgan calmed down and agreed that McKim needed a vacation. The work on the library would stop until his return.

The Beaux-Arts principle of sculptural enrichment for architecture was not forgotten at Morgan's library. Edward Clark Potter carved the lionesses, while Andrew O'Connor did the relief work. For the interior, McKim directed Morgan's attention to H. Siddons Mowbray's grand paintings for the library ceiling at the University Club, and Morgan was inspired to have Mowbray do the lunettes and ceiling at the Morgan Library.

McKim even tried to do a bit of Stanford White's art shopping. In 1905 McKim bought from Bardini an Italian ceiling for one chamber of the library. He also bought a mantelpiece from the studio of Desiderio da Settignano, and red silk wall coverings from the Palazzo Chigi in Rome. The building of the library was finished in 1906, with the full completion of the project in 1907.

It is difficult to say, in the end, whether the Morgan Library is predominantly a monument to McKim, as Morgan once angrily thought, or if McKim accomplished for Morgan even more than he promised by creating the greatest monument to the avarice and wealth of America's robber barons. Morgan's decline following the antitrust hearings sponsored by President Roosevelt and pursued by Congress led to his death in 1913; he had been brought down by one of his own class, Theodore Roosevelt. But Morgan's reputation has climbed steadily, based on this marble temple of learning.

# 43. THE PENNSYLVANIA STATION

McKim got another abrupt summons from one of the captains of industry in 1902, just a month after Morgan's telephone call. In April the architect was in Washington, D.C., exploring the site for the new Union Station that Burnham was to build there, when Pennsylvania Railroad president Alexander J. Cassatt telegraphed McKim to come to see him in Philadelphia. McKim is said to have remarked to Charles Moore, "I suppose President Cassatt wants a new stoop for his house."

Shortly thereafter, McKim paid a call on Cassatt in Philadelphia, where he found a very different offer put before him: It was one that threw him into internal conflict. Cassatt had worked with Burnham on Union Station, which to McKim implied an expected loyalty to the Chicago architect for a future station. To McKim's surprise, Cassatt asked him to design a New York City terminal for the Pennsylvania Railroad, which was now to be extended to cross under the Hudson River. Indeed, the Pennsylvania had just expanded in the other direction, east, with the acquisition of the Long Island Railroad in 1901. Cassatt, an ambitious man who had worked his way up through the system, wanted to put the railroad into the nation's premier city with a connection east to Long Island. This was Cassatt's crowning achievement, one he would make possible but not live long enough to see built.*

---

*Cassatt had a remarkable sister, the painter Mary Cassatt, who went to Paris (later with her parents, whom she cared for there), and worked with the great painters of the Impressionist group.

McKim's connection to the Pennsylvania Railroad goes back to his childhood friend Daniel Smith Newhall (1849–1913), his closest friend when he was growing up in Germantown. He was related to Daniel Newhall on the Smith side of his mother's family. The Newhall boys, whose family was in the sugar-refining business, were ardent cricket players, and the teenaged McKim played with them often at the Germantown Cricket Club. The Newhalls' financial position was better than that of the McKims. In 1882, Newhall went to work for the Pennsylvania Railroad as assistant secretary, rising to become the purchasing agent for the railroad. McKim was close to the Newhall family in the 1880s, doing interiors for Daniel's brother in 1879 and a house for Daniel Newhall and his family in 1886. The Newhalls, who by themselves almost totally comprised the Germantown Cricket Club, secured the clubhouse building for McKim in 1889. Perhaps in later years McKim saw the Newhalls less often, but the connection to the railroad brought them back together.

It would seem that Newhall had words of praise for McKim, which may have helped Cassatt choose him for the New York station. McKim's prestige as the president of the AIA certainly also figured in Cassatt's decision. The embarrassed McKim wrote Burnham that Newhall had told him Cassatt wanted a local man as architect for the New York station. The strain between McKim and Burnham did not seem enormous, but clearly both men wanted the huge commission. Burnham had been very helpful to McKim as the second architect pushing for the American Academy, so McKim needed Burnham pretty badly. Burnham occasionally underwrote the expenses of the American school and flushed money out of Chicago area donors, which McKim would not have been able to do. Perhaps Burnham consoled himself with his Washington station and the McMillan Commission plan for the Capitol.

The New York station, the realization of thirty years of trying to connect Pennsylvania and the West with Manhattan directly by train, was to be grand and large. There had been many wars among the railroads, but only the New York Central had been able to build a big station in the middle of the city. Cassatt saw himself in battle with the Central. The two railroads would engage in a competition to have the most important station in the city.

The old Vanderbilt lines, now the New York Central, had a long-held advantage—fairly direct access to Fourth (later Park), Avenue in the middle of the island. The Pennsylvania, United New Jersey Railroad, and others longed for a terminal in Manhattan, but the Hudson River was in the way. The idea of a tunnel under the river was proposed in 1871, with construction begun in 1874. The work had to be abandoned in 1880 when an accident occurred, killing twenty workmen. A few years later the plan was changed to call for a bridge over the Hudson, but this idea failed. The issue was clearly one of transport across the river and of electric engines, which were powerful enough to pull a long train, but would cause no smoke buildup in a tunnel. The solution seemed to have been achieved in France in 1901, when the Orleans Railroad used an electric engine to pull their trains in through a tunnel to Paris.

Cassatt had taken over the ailing railroad in 1899, determined to rebuild and improve the system. To pay for the massive effort, Cassatt turned to the investment bankers Abraham Kuhn, Solomon Loeb, and Jacob Schiff, who floated bonds in Europe as Morgan had done for the New York Central decades earlier. Cassatt contracted more debt than had the other railroads, taking out a huge loan of half a billion dollars—much of it spent on the New York terminal.

With the financial backing assured and the Parisian Gare d'Orsay model in mind, Cassatt purchased property and rights-of-way to Eighth Avenue and Thirty-third Street in Manhattan. The Pennsylvania Railroad also had to get permission from New York City for the terminal, which was granted at the end of 1901. Cassatt was now ready to begin.

The directors of the New York Central must have become aware of the Pennsylvania Railroad's plans in 1901. The New York Central owned the only major terminal in the city. This singular status had made the directors a bit overconfident, and they now felt the hot breath of competition. Commodore Vanderbilt's depot had been modernized in 1899, but not very well. The trains on the Harlem, Hudson, and New Haven lines came south down Fourth Avenue in a deep cut covered over except for rectangular open spaces in the central gardens of the avenue. The open spaces were for the steam to escape, but were not adequate for the number of trains now in the cut. The Central's problems grew at the end of the first week of January 1902, when smoke in the tunnel under Park Avenue was so thick that everyone's worst fear was realized. The engineer of a New York Central train going into the smoke could not see what was ahead of him and plowed into a standing New Haven train, killing seventeen people and injuring many more. The New York State Legislature had no choice but to forbid steam trains to enter New York City. New York Central now had to rebuild its own system. William J. Wilgus, New York Central's chief engineer, proposed rebuilding the entire station on two levels of tracks with a new terminal above the trains. A competition was held for the new station early in 1903, limited to four competitors: Daniel H. Burnham,

McKim, Mead & White, Samuel Huckel Jr. of Philadelphia, and Reed & Stem of St. Paul, Minnesota.

The McKim, Mead & White design came from White's end of the office. As with the two college campuses a decade earlier, each man had his station. White, who now loved the idea of joining the skyscraper march, added to his scheme for Grand Central a huge, sixty-story tower to be the tallest building in the world. Rather as McKim had done at the New York Public Library competition, White put in more than the client wanted. His vast design bridged the north/south flow of traffic at Forty-second Street and would have had five arched roads under the station so that traffic could go right through the station. Traffic, especially automotive traffic, was slight then, making White's street-straddling design possible. The tower would rise at the center of the station; in his plans, the architect returned to his Madison Square Garden design, now with a clock. White's design was far more than the railroad wished, and the award for the new building was given to Reed & Stem, who were experienced railroad station architects. After White's death, the next generation in the office would dust off the 1903 Grand Central design and submit it for the New

*White's competition entry for Grand Central Station, 1903.*

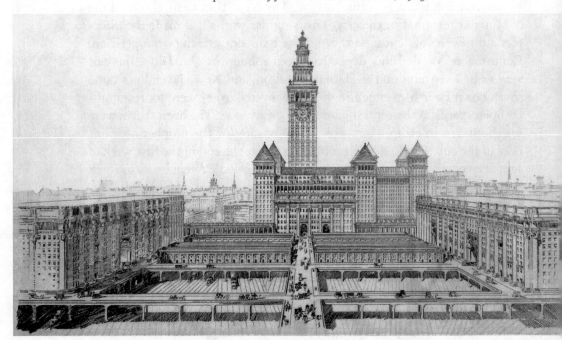

York City Municipal Building, which was built and still stands, a salute to the lost station.

The Grand Central job fell away, but in his last great commercial work McKim was spared from the frustrations of competition. In preparing his plan, McKim concentrated on the design of Cassatt's monumental gate to the eastern metropolis. The Pennsylvania Railroad proposed that its New York station have a large hotel above it, hoping to be able to gain revenue to balance against the costs of building the station. Unlike his partner, McKim had moved away from admiration of the contemporary world's new technology. He no longer liked the vehicles of mass transportation or the host of skyscrapers leaping up around the city. He wanted to create a monument, a worthy building for the "other" terminal. McKim the educator turned to books to prepare for his long encounter with Cassatt. He looked up a series of buildings so that he could battle Cassatt in his usual way. McKim would quietly insist that New York deserved an unencumbered terminal, then buoy his point with precedent. As usual, McKim's technique gently wore out his opponent, and he won the battle. Cassatt agreed to the great station standing alone between Seventh and Eighth Avenues and between Thirty-first and Thirty-third Streets.

The visual marker for railroads since the 1840s had been briefly wood, then an iron-and-glass shed over the trains. Grand Central Depot was an elaborate version of the great shed. But the Pennsylvania terminal would have to keep its tracks below the street, making the signifying shed impossible. The station would have to rely on architecture for its identity.

Stanford White's Grand Central was a big business building with vaulted internal streets. McKim's station was to be a re-creation of a partially lost building type from the ancient Roman world: the bath. McKim combined his Beaux-Arts training with its search for Roman solutions and his admiration for the city of Rome itself.* He set himself the task of solving the perennial question of what the baths of Rome really looked like. McKim and his assistants began work, taking what was known of the Roman baths as their model. McKim's right-hand man on the station was William Symmes Richardson, who entered the office in 1895. McKim and Richardson seem never to have questioned the Roman bath as the source for the station building. The bath had been a source of inspiration for other stations, but here McKim wished to re-create a full version of the Roman bath based on four of the principal sites of the Eternal City.

*Imagining the original apearance of Roman ruins was an exercise for students at the École and at American colleges in the nineteenth century.

*The Municipal Building, 1907–16. The office of
McKim, Mead & White recycled White's railroad station
into a New York City government office building.*

The Baths of Caracalla, Titus, Diocletian, and Constantine were studied for the station.

As Westinghouse's powerful turbines ran and trains came in from the west and then went out east to Long Island, a great granite bath building would rise. As was true of the bathhouse model, luxurious materials would be used for the building. The station was to be lined inside with travertine, the first major use of the material of Rome in the United States, and the exterior clad in Milford pink granite.

The design was worked out and created in drawings, plans, and a plaster model, which was executed down to the most minor detail of the exterior design. The model became the image of the building as McKim's health failed in 1905–6. The pressure of the Morgan Library, the station, his daughter's continuing battle with depression, and Stanford White's financial travails brought McKim to a virtual breakdown. Friends tried to help—Burnham took McKim to the northern woods to camp out in frosty air, for example— but McKim needed a rest. The station was given over to Richardson for building and T. J. Van der Bent for engineering issues.

McKim's application of the Roman bath to the American railroad was most effective. The recreation of travel replaced bathing, but in great splendor. The architect's goal of bringing Roman buildings into modern use had been accomplished. McKim was against modern extremes of technology, but was willing to use engineering wisdom as the prime building factor in his station. The great granite station was actually granite on steel. Its public spaces appeared to be masonry, but really were just cladding over 650 steel columns that supported the upper buildings without exerting too much weight on the fan of tracks below ground.

McKim's great Roman spaces alternated with the concourse, which was an amazing feat of Purdy & Henderson's structural skills. The soaring spaces were capped by a huge latticework of great glass roofs of varied shapes, supported by a network of steel columns. The crisscrossings of metal and glass made a structure remembered forever by anyone who walked within the space. The great glass room was not a copy of the traditional shed, but an almost futuristic version of the bones of the building with light pouring through the glass panes.

McKim did not look only to Rome for his great solution; he also studied stations recently built in France and Germany. The pedestrian "bridge of sighs" came from German railroad stations that followed the Venetian model, only without the water below. The great horizontal external colonnade that marked the stature of this station was very well studied. McKim worried about getting the proportions just right on his rhythm of columns-to-wall, basing the colonnade on a Roman source, Bernini's curving piazza at St. Peter's, and on a London source, the then-extant Bank of England by John Soane. Despite McKim's admiration for Rome, he felt a special kinship with London in his later years and had begun a personal study of eighteenth- and early nineteenth-century English architecture. He kept a picture of Soane's Bank of England above his drawing board.

While McKim remained committed to the total work of art, which he had demonstrated at buildings like the Boston Public Library, there was only modest painting and sculpture at the station. The great architectural painter, Jules Guerin, painted large murals with maps of the system of rails. The sculpture, with eagles and some female figures, was done by Adolph A. Weinman. The building was such a powerful statement that it really did not need sculptural enhancement. The building is a summary of McKim's later style—severe walls with carefully thought-out proportions and little ornamental enrichment. McKim wished to be remembered as a true architect who did not need to rely on ornament for effect. His severity reflected his sense of himself as the spokesman of architecture for the nation, but may have also reflected a reaction to White's love of decorative design. In the architects' later careers, the two men's buildings were very much opposite each other's in appearance.

William S. Richardson carried out the station for McKim. It opened in the fall of 1910, a year after McKim's death and well after the death of Cassatt. Yet this great moment of the historical building created for a new world was a monument to each man.

Exactly how little the nation had gleaned from the teachings of McKim became apparent when Penn Station was destroyed in the early 1960s. As the failing rails gave in to their flying rivals, real estate became the only

*The Pennsylvania Station, 1902–11. The Roman bath becomes a railroad station
and, sadly, lives only a half century.*

asset of the railroads. The permanent monument to the train fell fifty years
after its completion, a casualty of the years before a strong preservation
movement existed in New York. The station's destruction helped to spark
the creation of the Landmarks Preservation Commission, but one wishes
that a less significant building had to be sacrificed to this end. More than
forty years later, the loss of the station still resonates with the public.
After the restoration of Burnham's Union Station, an effort has been made
to transform the McKim, Mead & White Post Office, built after the station in 1908–13, into a railroad terminal. This building sits directly west
of the station and has access to the tracks, as the mail service used the
Pennsylvania lines, so the Post Office could now re-create a bit of the
glory of the old monument.

# 44. THE KING'S MEDAL

E arly in the next year, McKim received a letter from Edwin Austin Abbey with remarkably gratifying news. The letter of January 22, 1903, told McKim of a visit from the British architect Aston Webb:*

> I write this . . . to give away a game that is on here—and to offer you my salaams. Aston Webb came to me last night and wanted my authority for contradicting a rumour that C.F. McK. didn't really do any architecturing himself, but was the social member of the trio, who worked up the jobs, over the wine, as it were. My indignation was well assumed, and unfortunately I was able to cite many instances. I have a kind of memory of stunning things you'd done, etc., etc: and of stunning things you meant to do (like me).
>
> The idea is that you are to receive the gold medal of the Institute of Architects.

Webb had inquired of Abbey about McKim's role in the firm. Webb ran one of the first large practices in Britain, with a range of commissions not dissimilar to those at McKim, Mead & White, including the main buildings for the Victoria and Albert Museum. He was now interested in improving the relationship of the architectural professions in Britain and

---

*Abbey was now very much part of the British establishment. Webb was then the president of the Royal Institute of British Architects, the professional body for architects in Great Britain and a model for the American Institute of Architects; his knighthood came later.

America. After the death of Queen Victoria in 1901, there had been a generalized warming of relations with the United States, and some Royal Institute of British Architects (RIBA) members had visited America on a special bursary (fellowship). Webb saw McKim, Mead & White as standing at the top of the profession in the United States, with an aesthetic sense and range of work rather like his own. Perhaps also motivated by internal politics reasons at the RIBA, Webb wished to give the Gold Medal, the Institute's highest honor, to a non-British figure. McKim seemed the logical choice for this award.

Then, somehow, Webb was told—perhaps by a RIBA member who had worked in the McKim, Mead & White office as a young man—of the firm's heavy dependence on its assistants. The tale of McKim's methods of securing a goal via dinner parties also flew. Webb was told that McKim did not design himself, but was the social member of the firm, bringing in clients over wine. Frankly, the two rumors did have a grain of truth to them, as office assistants did do much of the work, especially for White, and the partners' social friends did bring them jobs. But the rumor that McKim never designed anything at all was quite wrong, and Abbey vociferously defended McKim's talents to Webb. Relieved, Webb cabled McKim the good news directly.

The Gold Medal was, and still is, one of the highest honors in the profession, well above the Paris Prize the firm was given in 1900 at the Exposition. The medal had been given to an American once before—to Richard Morris Hunt, a decade earlier—but to McKim with his shaky start this was truly an enormous gratification. Since McKim was the president of the American Institute of Architects, the Gold Medal reflected on the entire American profession. McKim was also very close to U.S. diplomats in Britain, with both Henry White and Joseph Choate as old friends, so his selection was also affirming to the American legation. Finally, the choice of McKim helped ratify the large architectural office, which was clearly now the modern professional mode, and gave reinforcement to the young architects who wanted to spend some time in an American practice.

McKim, for his part, was familiar with some British architects' work. He had known Richard Phene Spiers since 1869 and had much admired Norman Shaw. McKim would have recognized his similarity to Aston Webb and was careful to arrange a reciprocal honor for Webb with the AIA a few years later. His selection, beyond the joy it brought to him personally, was a true indication that America was now in the same league as the once superior profession in Europe. American architects were now part of the top team.

McKim did enjoy the civilized life in Britain. He relished the extremes of manners, liked the shopping best in London, and really did share Abbey and Millet's love of the England of an earlier age. McKim had remarked to Mary Anderson that he would be happier puttering around with her house in Broadway in the Cotswolds than building for an American multimillionaire. McKim admired and thought Rome appropriate for study, but found Britain appropriate for life.

McKim set off for a month in England, followed by a sojourn at a spa with Cadwalader. He then spent several weeks with Cadwalader in Scotland at Millden before arriving in London for a full and busy week of celebration. The newspapers printed a series of flattering articles about McKim, who was wined and dined by all. Abbey gave McKim the first party in his studio, and there were meals at Henry White's house, followed by the ceremony on the twenty-second of June. McKim was nervous, but with Harry White and Choate on one side and Abbey with Sir Lawrence Alma-Tadema on the other, he made it through the presentation. McKim gave a gracious speech as if speaking for all American architects. He was not a good speechmaker, so the evening picked up when Choate gave the concluding remarks. Joe Choate was widely viewed as America's best after-dinner speaker, able to hit just the right note of warmth and humor. Choate, who said he had known McKim since his boyhood, said with reference to McKim's architectural ambition, "After the Civil War was over . . . there grew up throughout the length and breadth of the land an ambition to improve and adorn the buildings, both public and private—to make them worthy of the municipalities and of the country. This was the universal sentiment, and the result was that America had been and was now, and it was likely to be in the future, a perfect paradise for architects." These remarks were greeted with laughter and cheers.

McKim was enough of a celebrity to be summoned for the last court session of the season at Buckingham Palace. But he had almost no warning. He chuckled at being "commanded" to be at the palace in full court dress, which he did not own. Harry White came by in the nick of time to take McKim to the tailor, who was able to make up the suit in a day. McKim was measured for the black velvet breeches, waistcoat, and tail surtout coat with standing collar. Along with the suit he had patent pumps with large steel buckles, a small sword, and a hat. The outfit came with a man to dress McKim in the very unfamiliar attire. With the hat under his arm and the sword safely sheathed so as to not inflict itself on his leg, he set off for the palace, thoroughly unsure of how to sit down in the suit. McKim was truly dazzled by the evening, from the dinner to his presentation to the royal couple and the stunning apartments. He was up until nearly daylight, awash in the activities of the court.

The next two weeks were filled with evening parties, garden parties, country house events, and great kindnesses shown to the very happy McKim. The description of the month of celebration is best found in letters McKim wrote to his daughter from Carlsbad, where he, Cadwalader, and the Philip Schuylers went to recover from the delights of the earlier months. In his letters, McKim never mentions seeing Spiers, his old friend from his first visit to Britain in 1869, nor is there any mention of his long-favored architect, Richard Norman Shaw. Both Spiers and Shaw were surely at the RIBA dinner.

McKim received the awards and honors which to some extent had been earned by the entire firm. Mead and White apparently never won any awards, but they seem to have been truly happy to share McKim's joy and its reflection of praise for their work.

# 45. THE NEW CENTURY
## FOR WHITE

The early years of the new century found Stanford White without honors and deeply in debt. The strain of White's financial desires did not meet the reality of his share of the firm's profits and Bessie's income from the Stewart legacy. White had continued to take wildly adventurous risks in the stock market, which turned out badly in 1899. Far from helping him out of his difficulties, White's stock market gambles had brought him to the brink of financial disaster. Since White's friend Bob Goelet, who had often helped him, had died, he was now dependent on advice from Prescott Butler and Charles Barney. White's financial problems were so serious that his life took on a truly troubled tone. He worked standing up in the office at a custom-made tall table. At about this time, he put a mirror on the wall near the window, angled to the front door at 160 Fifth Avenue, so that he could see callers before they arrived at the office. If a caller was likely to be asking for money, White could run upstairs to a small, private office, where he would be hidden away from bill collectors and unwanted guests.

Some good news greeted the new century too. At the same Paris Exposition of 1900 where McKim, Mead & White had been honored, the sculptor Saint-Gaudens was awarded the Grand Prize. The young men who had visited the 1878 Paris Exposition with dreams of fame now found their hopes realized.

The joys of the Exposition quickly faded as Saint-Gaudens was diagnosed with an intestinal tumor. The sculptor had been living in Paris, but now would return for an operation in Boston followed by recovery in his house on the Vermont–New Hampshire border. Saint-Gaudens would spend the remainder of his life at Aspet.

As Saint-Gaudens fell ill, so too did Prescott Butler. Butler, who probably married the wrong Smith girl, remained very close to Bessie, who was his true love. He died in 1901 after a long and severe illness. Bessie went into a year of mourning, while White felt the pinch of loss for the man who had continually helped him out of binds.

White's singular enjoyment had become his evenings. In the double-floor studio on Twenty-fourth Street, with its elaborate rooms, White had installed a swing with red velvet covering on the ropes. The red velvet swing was a personal favorite of White's, who liked the swing both for its simple, childlike aspect and because it was part of a canon of accepted erotica known to the Romans and to the aristocrats of the Rococo. White placed the swing within range of a Japanese paper lantern, a favorite device of his since the Columbian Celebration. The person in the swing would try to puncture the lantern while being pushed in the swing.

White's life now revolved around young chorus dancers and actresses who had arrived in New York. He and his peers knew numbers of these young women. On occasion the relationships were innocent, as with Ruth Dennis, later Ruth St. Denis, who did receive help from White with no strings attached. Often White would introduce the young women to artists who needed models. He quite often sent young girls to the dentist, as dental care was not available or affordable in these young women's hometowns. Often, however, the young women were part of an opportunistic exploitation of pretty girls by wealthy older men. Many of the women were well aware of the goals of the men and had their own agenda of trying to marry a millionaire.

Many hideaways were used for entertaining the young women, but the Twenty-fourth Street studio remained the most used until White and Cheever gave up the lease in 1903. Many parties, luncheons, and frolics were carried on in the top two loft floors, which sat above the F.A.O. Schwarz toy store. The studio's location seems somewhat ironic, since the contemporary practice of courting chorus girls, as well as White's own character, could be regarded as childish. White found respite from his economic woes in these juvenile revels with young girls. His pastime of escapist behavior might have him playing a Roman cult figure, clad in a toga and carrying a bunch of grapes, as the girls swung above.

There were many young girls in the various studios over the years. Often dressed in his expensive British-made suits, which were of a rather flashy character and hastily put on, White would attend vaudeville and popular entertainment, searching for new young girls. He would frequently ask an older girl in the troupe to bring a new one with her to a party at White's studio. White, easy to identify with his short, bristly red hair and extravagant mustache, would greet the girls, pour champagne, and attempt to charm the newer, younger one, inviting her to a more "select" party while offering gifts and introductions to all. As the practice of chasing girls went, White was one of the more responsible participants, neither abandoning the girls nor causing them great harm.

One of the girls who was part of this world remains better known to us than the others due to her participation in later events—Florence Evelyn Nesbit. Evelyn, as she would soon prefer to be called, had been born in a small town outside Pittsburgh on Christmas Day 1884. Evelyn and her brother, Howard, were very young when their father died. Mrs. Nesbit was not left with any resources for raising the two children, and from then on she had an agonizing life of poorly paying jobs while trying to raise the children. Mrs. Nesbit tried running boardinghouses, making dresses, and finally working as a salesclerk at Wanamaker's in Philadelphia.

Late in 1900, hoping for a better life, Mrs. Nesbit moved to New York with her daughter. Her son, in poor health, boarded with an aunt in Pennsylvania. Hoping that the pretty fifteen-year-old girl might become an artist's model, Mrs. Nesbit helped promote her daughter's modeling career. A theatrical agent saw Evelyn's picture and offered her a job in a long-running show, making her the youngest of the well-known Florodora girls. Once on the stage, James Garland saw her, picked her up, and began bringing her—and her mother—to fancy restaurants, on yacht excursions, and into the world of wealthy men. Evelyn was delighted with the new, exciting moments of glamour. Mrs. Nesbit may have had her pleasure dimmed by a sense of foreboding.

Garland was the son of an old friend of McKim's, James A. Garland. The senior Garland was a banker with First National Bank and a backer of the Long Branch Railroad. He was also a collector of porcelain. The elder Garland had McKim build a summer house at Elberon in 1880. Garland's son was well enough off to have a trust fund and to be able to contribute to the American School of Architecture in Rome. There is no evidence that Garland knew White or told McKim to tell White about the Florodora girls. It is simply a coincidence.

White seems to have met Evelyn when another girl brought her with her to the Twenty-fourth Street studio in 1901. Edna Goodrich was an "alumna" of White's parties and often brought the new arrivals around.

*Evelyn Nesbit*

White took a fancy to Evelyn. He was quite quick at appraising girls for imperfections and immediately suggested that Evelyn have her front teeth fixed at his dentist and at his expense. Evelyn, then sixteen, demurred for a time until White had Mrs. Nesbit call at the office for precise instructions to the dentist. Mrs. Nesbit, worn out by responsibility, wanted to see the best in White, judging him to be a benign gentleman eager to assist the Nesbits. Evelyn had her teeth fixed. Dinners followed, both on Twenty-fourth Street and in the Madison Square tower. Some of the dinners in the tower ended with White and Evelyn taking the elevator to the top floor and then going up the metal stairs to the roof where the city lay below. Evelyn then would reach up and touch the heel of the Diana as it moved in the wind. Clearly, a romantic liaison had begun.

James Garland seems to have learned that Evelyn was seeing White and warned the young girl that the architect was known to be a "voluptuary." Evelyn was too caught up in White's world to listen to Garland's warning.

In September 1901, Mrs. Nesbit decided to go to Pennsylvania, leaving Evelyn in New York in their apartment. White promised Mrs. Nesbit that he would keep an eye on Evelyn while her mother was away. Wanting to believe that her days of worry were over, Mrs. Nesbit allowed herself to take White at his word. After her departure, White brought Evelyn to his office. McKim was in the office, and White stopped by to introduce the young girl to his partner. He remarked to McKim that "this little girl's mother has gone to Pittsburgh and left her in my care." McKim could only gasp, "My God!" Saint-Gaudens told his wife and workshop that he lost respect for White at this time. Saint-Gaudens, who was very "French" in his Boston-bred wife's eyes, was always in love with someone. He saw himself as a romantic. Indeed, he had by this date effectively settled down with his common-law wife, Davida Clark. Saint-Gaudens felt Mrs. Nesbit had deliberately engineered the virtual "sale" of Evelyn to the generous White. White took responsibility for the family, removing from Mrs. Nesbit the pressure she had found unbearable.

Evelyn was then invited alone to the Twenty-fourth Street studio for dinner while her mother was out of town. In Evelyn's two autobiographies, written twenty years apart, she blames White for seducing her. In the later version of the story, White's behavior is reported in a less accusatory fashion. In her first book Evelyn wrote that after dinner White took her to a different room in the studio, which was lavishly fitted out with velvet-covered furniture and mirrors, and handed her another glass of champagne. She asserted that the drink had a drug hidden in it, causing her to pass out. She claimed to have awakened in a four-poster bed with White beside her. In Evelyn's version of the story, she was a virgin and White drugged her in the studio, then attacked her.

EVELYN NESBIT WAS a beautiful young girl whom Saint-Gaudens would describe as having the face of an angel and the heart of a snake. Was Evelyn really a victim of White or did she continue to walk directly and knowingly into his trap? Evelyn Nesbit surely knew what went on at many of White's parties. The girls of the Florodora chorus would have told her, and she admitted that Garland had as well. Evelyn's story about that September night in 1901 was likely made up later to please her husband, as Evelyn admitted to Abe Hummel, Stanford White's thoroughly disreputable attorney. In 1903, when Evelyn went to Hummel about another matter, she admitted to him that the story of White drugging and then raping her was made up. Of course, Hummel's credibility was nonexistent, so here are two proven liars discussing the details of a night long past.

It would seem far more likely that Evelyn came to the studio fully aware of what might happen, with McKim's exclamation ringing in her ears. She might truly have developed a fondness for the seemingly wealthy older man whose wife was entirely absent from his world. Bessie was attending to Prescott Butler, who was dying. Evelyn, who realized that White was entranced by her beauty, was likely hoping to push him into marriage. That evening, Evelyn was just as likely to have had a plan as was White. The two drank a large amount of champagne and could well have been drunk, which might later have become part of the "drugged" story. White was not known for knocking people out. In truth, the lurid tale Evelyn would tell was a justification of her behavior and her purity made up for the benefit of a later admirer.

Evelyn and White had an affair, which faded. She tried to rekindle White's ardor by taking up with an acquaintance of his. In June 1902, at a party in White's tower studio, Evelyn met John Barrymore, then a cartoonist. When White stepped away, Barrymore asked for and got Evelyn's address. White was going off to the Restigouche Club for fishing, followed by a fishing vacation in the first week of August with Bessie and their son. Evelyn's hope for catching White might have been dimming.

After White left, Barrymore called on Evelyn and began courting her, eventually proposing. Evelyn had Barrymore repeat the proposal in front of White in the tower. Her attempt to make White jealous may have worked, as White was annoyed at the prospect of Barrymore and Evelyn marrying, but her hoped-for result did not occur.

In October 1902 Evelyn must have gone to White to tell him she was pregnant. One of the firm's old clients, T. Gaillard Thomas, was a physician who had become the abortion specialist for New York's top social levels after the jailing and subsequent death of Mme Restell in 1878. Dr. Thomas had McKim, Mead & White build some houses on St. Ann's Avenue on the southern edge of the Bronx, which Thomas may have used for those operations. There is currently no sign of Dr. Thomas's houses on St. Ann's Avenue. Thomas was a specialist in women's medical conditions and wrote the standard books on abortion techniques for his day. He was known for studying European techniques, then claiming to have "invented" the procedures here. The medical community did not believe in Dr. Thomas's innocent invention of techniques done abroad. Although White knew Dr. Thomas, then about to retire, Evelyn did not request an abortion.

The question seems to have been—whose child was Evelyn expecting, White's or Barrymore's? The timing suggests that it may have been Barrymore's, but he was in no position to marry Evelyn as he did not have a good job. As Evelyn must have insisted on having the baby, the answer was to park her out of the public's eye. In late October 1902, Evelyn was sent to a small private girls' school in Pompton Lakes, New Jersey, run by Mathilda Beatrice DeMille, mother of the moviemaker Cecil B. DeMille. White agreed to pay Evelyn's school bills and those of her brother, Howard, in a military school. Barrymore came to visit Evelyn at the school, but she refused to see him. What could this mean? Did Barrymore, in the end, refuse to marry her? Was it White's child all along and Evelyn was angry that White would not divorce Bessie for her? In April 1903, Evelyn had sharp abdominal pains and two physicians were brought in to treat her "appendicitis." The girls were sent away from the school for the afternoon while Evelyn had the baby. Stanford White was at her side when she awoke from anesthesia. Evelyn came back to New York City to recover, ending her short, midyear school career. The baby must have been put up for adoption.

White may have been the father of the baby, but he did not marry Evelyn. He did care for her and her family, and he behaved in a responsible way. Evelyn, however, had a new suitor.

Harry K. Thaw was one of several children born in Pittsburgh to William and Mary Copley Thaw. William Thaw had been active in the Union Transportation Line, the Pennsylvania Railroad, and a large number of coal mines. He died in 1889, leaving an estate of some forty million dollars to his ambitious wife, who was just then moving the family into a much grander new house. William and Mary Thaw had collected pictures, but now, after her husband's death, Mrs. Thaw, sometimes with her problematic son Harry, went to auctions in New York, where she bought several important paintings. Mrs. Thaw married one of her daughters to the nephew of fellow Pittsburgher Andrew Carnegie and another to an impoverished English nobleman who did not like women. Mrs. Thaw married this daughter to a second trophy aristocrat, following the lead of Consuelo Vanderbilt, which brought great value to Mrs. Thaw but condemned her daughter to a life of misery. One son was admirable, Alexander Blair Thaw, a poet and philanthropist who went to MIT and Harvard in the 1880s. He married Florence Dow and had five children.* Alexander Blair Thaw was well known in his day for his poem "An Inaugural Ode" of 1905. In 1890 the Thaws hired McKim, Mead & White to build them a large house in Sparkill, New York, in the stone castellated mode of the Pierre Lorillard house.

Harry Kendall Thaw was the youngest boy and clearly a problem from his earliest days, as William Thaw recognized. Harry Thaw was not to inherit directly from his father's estate; he was to be kept on a small allowance adequate for life, but too meager to get him into trouble. Mrs. Thaw did not abide by her late husband's wishes and extended to Harry an allowance of eighty thousand dollars a year, quite enough to get him into some difficult spots. Young Harry came to New York to live in 1901 and managed to be accepted into high-class social events because of his wealth and his sister's marriage to a member of the English upper class. As Thaw solidified his position in polite circles, he began his life in the fast track.

Thaw was not normal. Even as a youngster he had been known locally as "Mad Harry." In his first months in New York, Thaw accused a young man who worked in the hotel he lived in of taking money from the front room. Thaw beat the young man, then rubbed salt into his wounds. Mrs. Thaw had to make a trip to New York to silence the scandal, a role she would continue to play in Harry's life. She bought silence from the next

*One daughter married Cord Meyer, the developer of much of Forest Hills, Queens County, in New York.

round of young women whom Thaw whipped and was accused of scalding with boiling water. It is most likely that Thaw bought the silence of Colonel Mann to avoid the stories coming out in *Town Topics*. People did hear parts of these lurid tales, however. These rumors, coupled with Thaw's bug-eyed appearance, rapid speech, and odd movements, soon made him known as a person to avoid.

Thaw may well have met Stanford White during the time his brother's house was being built. Thaw did go to the Adirondack League Club in the early 1890s when White and his family were there. Perhaps he also knew White from the art auction houses he and his mother frequented. Stanford White was the clear role model for Thaw in his fast life in New York. White knew the chorus girls, had amusing pastimes, and seemed to be having a wonderful life. Thaw tried to join clubs as White did and was refused. In true Fred May/James Gordon Bennett style at Bennett's home club, the Union, Thaw tried to ride a horse into the building. If the Union Club could tolerate Bennett, Thaw's reputation must have been terrible, as he was rejected. He tried the Knickerbocker Club and was rejected there also.

Thaw fixated on Stanford White about this time and decided that White had blackballed his nomination at the Knickerbocker. White belonged to many clubs, but carried little weight at the "Knick." In Mad Harry's mind, White was becoming his enemy. The event that triggered Thaw's view of White as his tormentor came when another one of the girls in the Florodora sextet, who called herself Frances Belmont, was snubbed by Thaw. Frances Belmont seems to have set up a revenge act directed at Thaw by asking White, who was unaware of her intentions, to have a party for the Florodora girls in his tower studio. White agreed to the party, which Ms. Belmont set up for the same night that Thaw had planned a party at Sherry's. The girls went to White's party, not to Thaw's, forever creating a hatred of White in Thaw's troubled mind.

Thaw began chasing those who had been in White's circle. He made a point of finding Evelyn Nesbit. After two years of paying attention to Evelyn, who rebuffed him, he redoubled his effort in the late spring of 1903 after Evelyn's return to New York City from Mrs. DeMille's school. Stanford White had suggested that Evelyn and her mother go to Europe in the summer of 1903 to recover. Thaw secretly followed. Mrs. Nesbit did not like Thaw, but Evelyn, who must have given up on White, decided his wealth mitigated his problems and went off with him. As the summer progressed, Evelyn learned that Thaw was addicted to cocaine and morphine and that when he used those drugs he became a violent sadist. Thaw severely beat Evelyn in a *schloss* in Austria.

When Evelyn returned to the United States and told White about Thaw's violent behavior, White took her to his lawyer, the bizarre Abe Hummel. Hummel documented Evelyn's accusations against Thaw and, for White's protection, Evelyn's tales of Thaw's obsession with Stanford White. According to Evelyn, Thaw asked her about White constantly, calling him "that beast" and demanding stories about the architect's misdeeds. It is likely that Evelyn then invented stories about White, including the drugged champagne tale of two years earlier. Evelyn's word could not be trusted, but the tales she told Thaw may well have inflamed his hatred of White.

Soon after Evelyn's return to New York in October 1903, she agreed to go back to Thaw. The two would marry in 1905 and go to live with Thaw's mother in Pittsburgh. Evelyn and Harry Thaw seemed to have left White's life.

# 46. PAYNE WHITNEY'S HOUSE

In the early spring of 1902, Stanford White once again had to walk the thin line between Will Whitney and Colonel Oliver Payne, when Whitney's son, Payne, who had sided with his immensely rich uncle after his mother's death, got married. On February 6, 1902, Payne Whitney married Helen Hay, daughter of John Hay, the former secretary of state. Colonel Payne bought an undeveloped lot on Fifth Avenue between Seventy-eighth and Seventy-ninth Streets for his nephew and the new bride. Colonel Payne then asked Stanford White to build the couple a fine house on the lot, which was to be his wedding present.

To Stanford White, smarting from a big stock market loss in the previous year, this commission would be a great boost to his financial situation. Both Colonel Payne and the young couple were likely to order many decorative items and antiques from which White could make a good profit. The Payne Whitney wedding-gift house would be a promising commission, as well as a pleasurable one, since Colonel Payne and the newlyweds at first were uncritical of White's work. This made White far happier than dealing with constantly carping clients such as the Mackays. By 1906, Helen Hay Whitney's patience would be sorely tried by the delays, and she would write to White that she wished she had bought a ready-made house. But all would sort out in the end. This house would be White's swan song in New York City domestic architecture.

Colonel Payne bought the land for his nephew's house while the newlyweds honeymooned at his large residence in Thomasville, Georgia. He paid the Henry Cook estate, which owned the entire block, the relatively huge sum of $525,000 for the mid-block land. White was quickly brought on board and commissioned to design the Payne Whitney house on a lot with a frontage of 45 feet on Fifth Avenue and a depth in the block of 115 feet. The house itself, with a small garden to the south, was 40 feet wide by 93 feet deep and 80 feet tall.

The design called for a combination of a steel framing system and brick party walls, all to be clad in a special Woodbury granite from Hardwick, Vermont, which was very light cream-white in color. The building permit was filed in September 1902, with a special application made to the Parks Department, as the house had a bow or swell front. Stanford White's design was not greatly dissimilar to the very tactile version of a Venetian house he had just designed for the almost-blind Joseph Pulitzer on Seventy-third Street. The Payne Whitney house was far less sculptural, but did seem to grow from the Venetian sources White used for Pulitzer's home. White, however, to give it visual distinction among the flat-fronted builder-created row houses of the city, curved out the façade in a grand London-styled swell front.

Just as the design for the Whitney house was ready, Henry Cook (who had bought the entire block from Fifth Avenue to Madison and from Seventy-eighth to Seventy-ninth Streets) decided to move from just east of Fifth Avenue on Seventy-eighth Street to the empty plot north of Payne Whitney's. The builder for Cook's house was J. C. Lyons, Lyons had come from humble circumstances before he attended the Cooper Union. After his training, he went on to a good career, specializing in boilers and foundations. Lyons did the foundation for the Great Obelisk in Central Park, created at W. H. Vanderbilt's expense. Lyons worked with White to have a continuation of the design of Payne Whitney's house for his house's façade, but with a plain flat front and no swell. After Cook's death, the Lyons house eventually went to his daughter, Mrs. de Heredia, who suffered when Helen Whitney insisted that her house be completed in the spring of 1906 and forced White to put men on the job in twenty-four-hour shifts.

White's real joy with the Payne Whitney house was to carry on his interior work, as he had for Payne Whitney's father, on a baronial scale. The Whitney men were uncritical of White and trusted his judgment in design. A professional decorator, T. D. Wadleton (whose address was the same as the architect's), was hired for the principal rooms at the house, but White bought antiques, accent pieces, and the furnishings. White was not alone at the Payne Whitney house with Wadleton. Allard & Fils, the French decorative house, who were now also antiques dealers, did a room, as did William Baumgarten, late of the Herter Brothers, and several others. White did seem to have control over everyone and the ultimate say on the interiors, which was splendid for him as his commission for the firm of McKim, Mead & White was double that for the building, at 10 percent of cost. White's shopping for Payne Whitney was a private side venture that gave him commissions on the purchase price, as well as the opportunity to sell pieces he already owned that were sitting in storage. Furthermore, in a big commission, White could hide some extra charges. By 1903, this was vital to his survival. He was deeply in debt, indeed hopelessly so. He should have gone into bankruptcy, but he could not face the consequences of such an action and its subsequent limitations on his personal freedom.

White's extravagance was enormous. For years after Evelyn Nesbit left his life, he continued to support Evelyn's brother, Howard, in a military academy in Pennsylvania. White still gave lavish parties. He even found himself a new vice, the automobile, then a luxury for a small number of people. By the first days of 1903, White was thoroughly discouraged about his financial situation. He was torn between his need for the generous behavior he saw in the lives of his wealthy friends, many of whom were also over their heads in their financial circumstances, and his recognition that he was mired in debt.

The collapse of the Northern Pacific Railroad stock, which had been in his life since Villard's days early in the 1880s, caused the final disaster. White lost heavily in the Northern Pacific panic of 1901, putting him in debt to a level of over $700,000, a vast sum for that day. In the next year and a half, he was able to pay off $100,000 worth of obligations, but by March 1903, he was $600,000 in debt, owing money to his partners, the estate of Prescott Hall Butler, Bessie, Henry Poor, Will Whitney, Jimmy Breese, H.A.C. Taylor, and C. T. Barney personally, as well as to the Knickerbocker Trust Company. He also owed florists, art suppliers, Duveen, restaurants, and other companies. Unable to silence the requests for payment, White turned for help to Barney, who agreed to attempt to save him from insolvency. Barney was subject to depression and was under some financial strain himself, but he appeared as a Stanford White knight. Barney consolidated White's debts and advanced him another $100,000, using antiques and art objects as collateral, although many of the treasures were already the basis for earlier loans.

Barney advised White to rearrange his professional salary as well as his personal debt. In June 1903, McKim, Mead & White made a new allocation of profits that acknowledged White's debt to the firm. The firm's

*Madison Square Presbyterian Church in New York City, 1903–6. This was White's final masterpiece, which, like its designer, did not continue long in its place.*

profits would be divided up to give White an income of up to $25,000 a year, with any profit over that sum to go to liquidating White's debt to the office.

Barney further advised White to sign any remaining items over to Bessie, whose house in St. James was in her name. Thus, by 1905, White's financial life had become a constant source of worry for him, even to the point of his giving up the Twenty-fourth Street studio that year.

At this moment, just across Madison Square from the studio building, White received his last major commission, to design a new building for the Madison Square Presbyterian Church. It would be difficult to think of a more unlikely job for White to have been given than the church, which was the pulpit of Dr. Charles Parkhurst, one of New York City's two major moralists. Parkhurst and Anthony Comstock were the voices against vice in the city. Indeed, Harry Thaw had long begged Comstock to concentrate on White's private life. However, Dr. Parkhurst railed against political corruption more than personal vice, and as White had no political attachment, he was not likely to have singled out the architect as an enemy of virtue. Still, White must surely have enjoyed the irony of building a church for the morally pure congregation.

Nominally, White was an Episcopalian. For most of his mature life, he belonged to the Church of the Ascension on Fifth Avenue, where he had helped realize a decorative scheme early in his career. He was not religious at all and described himself so in his letters. White called himself a poor churchman and was sure that Reverend Donald thought of him as a doubtful member of the congregation. The Church of the Ascension was a brownstone Gothic Revival church built by Richard Upjohn, the architect of Trinity Church in Wall Street. Now at the Madison Square Presbyterian Church, White would get to replace a brownstone church in the Gothic Revival style, also built by Upjohn.

The Madison Square Presbyterian Church sat still in its brownstone world. But by the end of the century it was obvious that commerce had invaded the domesticity of Madison Square. The Metropolitan Life Insurance Company had replaced earlier buildings on the southern part of the block. As Metropolitan Life's presence grew, the company made offers to the church. It wished to expand to the northern end of the block. The company offered to build the congregation a new church across the street at Twenty-fourth Street and Madison Avenue. The church insisted that it should be in control of the new building, and this condition was met. In April 1903, McKim, Mead & White were appointed architects.

The selection of Stanford White as architect to the church was remarkable. White had relatively little ecclesiastical building experience, although he had just completed a new porch for the 1870s church, St. Bartholomew's, on Madison Avenue at Forty-fourth Street. White had built a fine memorial to Cornelius Vanderbilt for the church in magnificent materials. The porch was an American version of the church porch at St. Giles du Gard in France, which had dazzled White in Richardson's office and on his tour of France with Saint-Gaudens and McKim a generation earlier. White's porch for an existing Episcopalian church was not much of a reason for this new, large commission.* The likely reason for the selection of White was his presence at Madison Square. He ran across the park many times a day from his house on Twenty-first Street to the Madison Square tower studio, to the office at 160 Fifth Avenue, to the Players club, and, for another month, to the Twenty-fourth Street studio. White's work was all over the area as well. Madison Square Garden dominated the

*The porch is currently on the new St. Bartholomew's on Park Avenue at Fifty-first Street.

Farragut statue, while interiors at the Fifth Avenue Hotel across the street, the Union Club next to the office, and James Bennett's working quarters in the Western Union building showed White's hand. He had even caused the area to glisten in public events like the centennial parade.

The trustees of the church surely included White's friends, who could outweigh the Reverend Parkhurst, who must have wished another architect. Parkhurst had asked Howells & Stokes to design the church house at Thirtieth Street and Third Avenue. For the new church a committee of church members was formed with Robert W. De Forest as chairman. The De Forests were old friends of the architects, who had built for the De Forests in the Montauk Association. Lockwood De Forest, the great expert on Indian woodworking, whom White had long known, was also part of the family. Robert W. De Forest wrote a complete paper on the justification for selecting the firm of McKim, Mead & White, and this carried the day. It is uncertain if De Forest intended the commission to go to White rather than McKim, as would happen. The firm was chosen, but White became the point person.

Once appointed, White dug out his old papers on the role of the Early Christian Church for non-Catholic congregations. White justified his design as an Early Christian/Byzantine church suitable for Presbyterians. It was to be a relatively inexpensive building, done in brick and terracotta as was the Judson Memorial Baptist Church. White's addition to this church was color, which had been absent at the Judson. Working with the Perth Amboy Terra Cotta Company again, White arranged for the creation and glazing of colored tiles in the manner of the Renaissance artist della Robbia. The major design difficulty for the architect was that the church would sit in a great shadow created by the tall campanile being built on its old site by the insurance company that had bought the Upjohn church and its land. White needed to use color to make a little gem of a church that could hold its own against the florid insurance company to the south. White created a Greek cross church topped by a dome, rather in the manner of his work at the Gould Library of NYU a few years earlier. The artist Louis Comfort Tiffany played a major role in the building's interior design but was not, one hopes, told of McKim's remark to President Roosevelt regarding dynamite.

The simple plan, fine proportions, and remarkable use of color made the church a great success at its opening in October 1906. Reverend Parkhurst lamented in his opening address that the architect could not be there to see "the final outcome of his splendid genius." In the following year, perhaps as a statement, the New York chapter of the American Institute of Architects gave its medal of honor to the fine church, thought of by many as White's final significant work.

Praise for the building by the public and the profession had scarcely ended when changing demographics caught the congregation in a business area. Just thirteen years after winning the medal of honor, the splendid work was knocked down to make way for an ordinary tall building. Progress had made its comment on beauty.

# 47. THE GILDED AGE TARNISHES

As the year 1905 began, White was still finding it difficult to manage his many problems, and yet he kept charging up more debt with flowers and parties. He was clearly trying to keep depression at bay as his miseries soared. McKim, pushed by Morgan, the creation of the American School of Architecture in Rome, and the new station, was becoming wobbly again. White's oldest friend, Saint-Gaudens, was weakening in his battle with cancer.

White decided he had to take a radical step to repair his finances. He planned for a huge sale of all his treasures in the spring of 1905. He began to call in his loans of items "resting" in friend's homes and to consolidate his storage areas to prepare a catalogue for the sale. Even White's New York City house was in danger as the landlord, H.A.C. Taylor—who had not had rent paid on 121 East Twenty-first Street since 1898—began to lose patience. White had put a large sum into making over the building, which had appeased Taylor until 1904, when he increased his pressure for a cash payment on some of the debt. As Taylor had been gentlemanly about White's nonpayment, White put Taylor at the bottom of the list of those who were after him. In 1904 Taylor would demand payment of half his back rent. White partly solved the problem by renting out his house the next year, using the large sublet payment to stave off his creditors. While the house was rented, White moved in with McKim, who had the entire and empty row house at 9 East Thirty-fifth Street with only Margaret there. Mead, Saint-Gaudens, and others often visited at McKim's house, but White moved in, indicating the continuing closeness of the two men's long friendship. Bessie went abroad with her sister that winter, as Larry was in school. Only White's mother needed a place, and Stanford put his mother in an apartment in the city for those months.

White was in need of cheer in the winter as an old and loyal friend and client died. Will Whitney, White's loyal patron and close, generous friend, lost his life in mysterious circumstances.

Will Whitney had many enemies. To the reformers, Whitney was sinister and corrupt. To the men of the city's top ranks, he was a handsome wife chaser. To the Colonel Payne side of the family, he was a disloyal husband. To stockholders in companies Whitney headed, he was a stock waterer who ruined their investments. At the end of January, Whitney, who did truly love music, returned from the opera to the great iron gates of his house, brought to New York from a Roman palace by Stanford White. It was dark and late when Whitney stepped into the doorway. Rumors flew that Whitney was then shot or stabbed by someone who was never caught or accused. The family issued a story about appendicitis. Dr. William T. Bull, Prescott Butler's classmate, who had operated on McKim after his bicycle accident, was summoned. Dr. Bull tried to operate on Whitney, but Whitney became worse and died. The public announcement was blood poisoning following the operation. But why was this done at home? The story, as told by Rita da Costa Lydig, an early twentieth-century social figure in New York City who was also a client of Stanford White, was that Whitney was stabbed in the doorway and died from his wounds, which Dr. Bull covered up. Mrs. Lydig, in her remarkable book where identities are absent but the truth spoken, probably reported the real cause of Will Whitney's death. The problem was clearly that there were far too many suspects and the family wished the entire case forgotten. Was Whitney murdered by a jealous husband? Is it even possible that Colonel Payne had a hand in the hiring of an assassin? There is no answer.

As the Whitney scandal and the estate settlement took place, White worked away at the Payne Whitney house. Despite the personal trials the architect was enduring, he was able to create a splendid house for the Payne Whitneys.

By early 1905, Stanford White had joined McKim at Thirty-fifth Street and had filled a top floor in a loft building at 114–120 West Thirtieth Street with all the items he felt he could sell to pay off his debts. The sale was to be held at the American Art Galleries on February 27, 1905, but was postponed until April 23, 1905. The objects were stored for cataloguing in the loft, with many insurance policies on objects having lapsed. White, whose luck had now fully expired, experienced a major blow to his hopes of solvency when, on February 13, 1905, a short in the wiring caused a fire that consumed his floor. The fire devastated White's collection and his last hope. After contemplating the ruins, White went back to McKim's house and sat in "stony misery" for two days. Finally, at breakfast, White accepted the disaster, broke down completely, and sobbed like a child. To his great credit, he turned his head forward and carried on, even though he surely realized how serious his situation had become.

White was urged by his friends to resolve his misery by declaring bankruptcy, but social embarrassment surely kept him from carrying through on this gesture of financial relief. He esti-mated his losses in the fire to be about

*"New" H.A.C. Taylor house in construction at 3 East Seventy-first Street, 1894–96. Demolished.*

$350,000, which, combined with the debacle of the Northern Pacific Railroad panic, left him in debt by about a million dollars, according to an estimate he made in a letter of April 29, 1905.

The pressure became more severe in April, when H.A.C. Taylor again demanded his promised money and threatened to start legal action. White had to act quickly, turning once more to Barney for aid. White catalogued the interior features he had installed in Taylor's house. These items— mantels, columns, tiles, antique ceilings, doors, and accent pieces—were part of the improvements he had promised to Taylor, but they were now assigned to Barney to protect them from Taylor's actions. White's reaction to Taylor's threat included turning over his membership share in the Res-tigouche Salmon Club, his automobiles, and the like to Bessie, while making it clear again that the house and property in St. James were hers alone. White protected his things first, then Bessie, then his partners.

On May 1, 1905, the day that Taylor had demanded payment, White rewrote the agreement with his partners, amending the 1903 arrange-ment. He acknowledged that his 1903 settlement had not been a success and dissolved the equal arrangement of profit sharing at the office. White released to his partners all the assets in the partnership and agreed to

*Stanford White as photographed by Gertrude Käsebier in 1903. White looks far older than his fifty years.*

become a salaried employee with a monthly salary of one thousand dollars. Despite his removal from the partnership, White's name would remain on the masthead. McKim and Mead kept a graceful demeanor as their partner was forced into this difficult position: Word of the change in White's status was not leaked outside the office, payment on White's life insurance policies was continued, and the office even paid a few of his loans. Further, McKim and Mead allowed White to keep the large commissions he charged to Colonel Payne for the Payne Whitney house. McKim and Mead were true friends to their partner.

Even as White was dealing with the shock of his losses in the warehouse fire, a second blow occurred. A private detective, hoping for a job with White, paid a call on the architect at 160 Fifth Avenue. The detective, P. L. Bergoff, told White that he was being followed. White was aware that he had been trailed on occasion, but had not realized the surveillance was continuing. He could ill afford to hire Bergoff, but he quickly did. Bergoff discovered that Thaw was paying for the surveillance. Thaw seemed to have an ongoing pathological hatred for White. He clearly hoped his detectives would catch White in some misdeed that could be prosecuted by Anthony Comstock. Forewarned, White must have been super-cautious.

White must have managed some payment to H.A.C. Taylor, as the threat against his property was not carried out. When Bessie returned from Europe, McKim offered her his house, but she insisted on returning to Twenty-first Street, an extravagant gesture given the circumstances. White surely felt himself on the edge of a sword blade, so he treated himself to his favorite three weeks at Restigouche before returning to the city to prepare for a quick trip to Europe to shop for Payne Whitney. The trip was sponsored by Colonel Payne, who was willing to let White and the couple select some very expensive items for the new house.

White raced over Europe, seeing dozens of dealers and purchasing a king's ransom in art for Colonel Payne and Payne Whitney. He visited all his usual dealers along with a new favorite, Arthur Acton, the British expatriate. Acton seems to have had little training in the field when he set himself up as a dealer. White was given Acton's name by an antiques dealer he had known in Boston and New York, Henri O. Watson, who had been at the Shreve, Crump & Low Company. Watson, a Bostonian, had sold White a number of items, including some old jars, in the early summer of 1893. Watson lived off and on in Florence, where he likely knew Acton socially.

In September 1897, Henri Watson gave White Acton's address in Florence. White wrote Acton that he was on his way to Italy to buy Renaissance pieces and had been assured by Watson that Acton would heed White's orders on shipping—code for avoiding the customhouse duties. White asked Acton to look around for him, except in Venice where he was fully set. He also cautioned Acton to avoid Bardini, whom White knew very well and had purchased from before. White was going behind Bardini's back to Acton, hoping for better luck getting through the customhouse and, perhaps, for cheaper prices. In a letter of December 16, 1897, White wrote to Acton that he would never sell items to outsiders, only to his architectural clients. White, who had learned to fictionalize his character further, wrote about the items he purchased abroad: "nor do I buy them to make a profit on them, as they are always turned into clients at practically their cost."

Acton was very helpful to White in the first visit the architect made to him while looking for items for Will Whitney's house. White returned to Acton twice more, the last time while shopping for Payne Whitney. On the trip of 1905, Acton showed White the villa above Florence he had rented with an eye to purchase. Acton even consulted with White and architect Charles Platt, whom White sent to Acton as a customer, about the gardens for the Villa La Pietra, which Acton would purchase with the assistance of his new father-in-law, a Chicago banker. Acton put his automobile at White's disposal, which clearly indicated how very important a client White had become.

White's shopping trip cost Oliver Payne over three hundred thousand dollars, but Payne did not seem to fuss about the cost. White purchased from Acton, Simonetti, San Giorgi, Durlacher, Bernheimer, Duveen, Ramboldi, Heilbronner in Paris, and many other dealers. Ramboldi sold White a large ceiling, an iron balcony, and more. Heilbronner, a regular source for White, sold him a ceiling and boiserie from the Palazzo Gonzaga, Gothic andiron figures, a large mantel in stone, an iron gate from

Versailles, two Fontainebleau tapestries, woodwork, and more, for what would total twenty-five thousand dollars.

White also had a good deal of new work made for the house. Two sarcophagi with round ends were copied in New York by Batterson & Eisele, intended to be identical except for square ends. White wrote Acton in Florence to duplicate a candelabra he had earlier purchased for the house. McKim, Mead & White's old friend Francis Bacon supplied much of the upper-floor furniture. Bacon had been working with the architects since the Villard houses. Frank Lathrop made skylight glass for the house as he did for numerous other residences.

The work on the house continued with huge sums spent until Colonel Payne seems to have come to a boil. Wayne Andrews quoted White as he apologized to the colonel:

> All kinds of small extras have crept in and . . . the changes I have made in the treatment of the smaller rooms have added over a hundred thousand dollars to the price of the house, and I have dreaded to speak to you about it until the house was far enough finished for you to see the result, as although I feared that you would be angry at first, I thought if you saw the money had been wisely spent and that I had given Payne and Helen a house to live in which is really of the first water.

Colonel Payne joined, if briefly, White's "angry payers" club, although Helen Hay Whitney praised the new house to the skies, which caused Payne to relent in his attack. One can only be a bit suspicious that the extra work did help White's precarious finances as well as reflect a higher aesthetic sensibility.

The final results were truly remarkable, returning White to the level of creativity he had in his early interiors, even if it was in a much more historical vocabulary. The rooms showed White's signature work with bits of Old Rome, medieval clerical devices, Renaissance pieces, fine materials, and a polar bear skin rug. How exactly a polar bear always expired in White's rooms is beyond our contemplation. There were also tiny lightbulbs, a personal stamp of his work. The most imaginative room in the house was his mirrored reception room with its porcelain flowers and bows made by Caldwell here in the United States. Miraculously, the mirrored room was recently put back in the house, giving us two fine Stanford White rooms in what is today the French Cultural Services. Most of the other pieces were sold after Jock Whitney sold the house in 1949.

*Tiffany & Co., New York City, at Thirty-seventh Street and Fifth Avenue, 1903–6. Although Tiffany moved twenty blocks northward, the building still stands.*

*Gorham Silver Company, Fifth Avenue at Thirty-sixth Street, 1903–6.*

WHEN WHITE RETURNED from his European buying trip in 1905, he found McKim in a state of collapse. With Morgan's permission, McKim had a break during the fall, resting for a time in Box Hill with Bessie before going to South Carolina for some shooting. McKim returned to the office in January, giving White some respite as White had exhausted himself in McKim's absence. White was tired, afflicted with arthritis in his hip and knees, and still suffering from kidney problems. He now seemed rather old for fifty-two, puffy in his face and in general discomfort. Paul Baker correctly notes that Gertrude Käsebier's photograph of him shows him in poor health.

In the spring of 1906 White put his last touches on the great shopping palaces for Gorham and Tiffany just above the Knickerbocker Trust building at Fifth Avenue and Thirty-fourth Street.

White was troubled by Saint-Gaudens's health, which had necessitated another surgery. Gus had begun his memoirs, which injected a sense of doom in the air. White's friends were thinking of their mortality. Indeed, while in Paris in July 1905, White had met with James Gordon Bennett about the huge hanging owl mausoleum that Bennett had wanted White to design. Things seemed to be so gloomy that White took only two weeks at the Restigouche in June, as he was preparing to go to Europe in July. He was still being followed by Thaw's agent and the tension was taking a toll on him.

On Monday morning, June 25, 1906, White returned to the city from Box Hill, where his son had been staying for the weekend with his good friend Leroy King, a classmate at Harvard, and Laura Chanler, the daughter of Winthrop and Daisy Chanler, whom Larry White had met in dancing school. The elder White had seemed anxious all weekend, but the boys decided to join him for dinner in Manhattan at Martin's restaurant on Twenty-sixth Street.*

Evelyn and Harry Thaw were at the restaurant that evening with two of Thaw's friends. Evelyn Thaw, now an unhappy wife, knew she could always count on her husband to respond if she mentioned White's name. After seeing White in the popular restaurant, Evelyn passed Thaw a note indicating that White was in the building. She recalled later that Thaw seemed unusually agitated. After dinner, the couple, with Thaw's friends, walked the few blocks to Madison Square Garden, where a new musical, *Mamzelle Champagne,* was opening in the Roof Garden. Thaw wore an overcoat that evening, but one did not question him on such a sartorial issue. The Thaw party sat down in the Roof Garden to watch the show, which included a tenor, Harry Short, singing a tribute to well-off men's behavior in the era, "I Could Love a Thousand Girls."

White had come to the theater himself that evening in time to hear the song. The Roof Garden was White's natural resting place before he ascended by elevator to his studio, where he lived in the summer months more than in the Twenty-first Street house, which had a housekeeper in residence but was virtually closed. White greeted the caterer for the Roof Garden as he watched the revue. Later accounts claimed that White asked the caterer to introduce him to one of the female performers. As White waited for his possible meeting with the singer, the Thaws tired of the revue and got up to leave. Once again, Harry Thaw put on his coat over

---

*Years later, the story changed to include Laura Chanler. It was later claimed that the two boys were really with Laura, but Larry White testified to the above.

his evening suit. As the four neared the elevators, Thaw walked away from the others, then stood behind some tall green plants. He had observed White at his table by the elevator. White was alone and listening to the music as Thaw studied him. By this time, Thaw had become an insane predator. After observing that White was entirely unprotected, Thaw walked out of the shrubbery, at the same time drawing a small gun from his coat. He walked directly to White, stood before him, and rapidly fired three shots at close range into White's head and upper torso. White said nothing, but slumped over and fell to the floor, dead.

*Harry K. Thaw. "Mad" Harry was a lifelong ne'er-do-well prone to whipping both women and men.*

Did White see Thaw or realize that Thaw had a gun? Perhaps not, as he did not acknowledge Thaw's presence. One would hope White was looking at the stage and never saw his assassin. His death was instantaneous. It may well be that White did not even know what had happened as his life ended in his fifty-third year, in the Roof Garden he had created, invested in, and sup-ported. White's life ended as he had lived it for the last decade—at a place of public entertainment, alone in the evening awaiting a meeting with one of the thousand girls who were being sung about on the stage. One could even draw a parallel to Lincoln, who was shot in a place of public entertainment by an obsessive madman.*

After the shooting, it took a moment for people to realize what had happened; then panic broke out. Thaw emptied the gun in the air and walked to the elevators. The conductor tried to keep the music going to reassure the crowd, but the musicians stopped playing. The manager of the Roof Garden attempted to get the audience to leave calmly. A physician came forward, knelt down to White, lying in a pool of blood, his face blackened by the gunpowder, searched for a pulse, and then pronounced him dead.

A Roof Garden engineer apprehended Thaw as a policeman appeared. Thaw handed the gun to the officer as Evelyn, who had witnessed the

---

*White knew well the killer's brother, Edwin Booth, the founder of the Players club.

entire event, reached her husband. Evelyn cried out, "My God, Harry! What have you done? What have you done?" Thaw replied, "It's all right, dear. I have probably saved your life."

The audience left without a full panic, many walking over the body, which was unrecognizable because of the gunpowder. James Clinch Smith, Bessie's only surviving brother, who had been a bit of a family black sheep, had been on the rooftop and may even have had a brief chat with Thaw a half hour earlier. When he left, he stepped over the body without realizing it was his own brother-in-law.

Thaw had lived up to his late father's worst fears. Mary Copley Thaw had ignored her husband's wise words to restrict Harry's access to money in order to prevent an episode of dangerous behavior fueled by the tools of disaster, such as a gun. If William Thaw had been listened to, Harry would not have been on the Roof Garden with an automatic pistol. Mrs. Thaw facilitated the murder of Stanford White and would extricate her son from responsibility for his own actions. Both Harry and his mother were guilty of killing a man for no reason other than psychological delusion. White died because a crazy man irrationally fixated on him. White was completely innocent of pursuing Evelyn after the DeMille school period. White was indeed a victim.

Thaw and Evelyn were taken down in the elevator. Thaw was taken by the arm by another policeman, who told him that he was under arrest. When queried about why he had shot his victim, Thaw was said to have replied, "He deserved it. . . . I can prove it. He ruined my wife and then deserted the girl." Thaw then handed the officer some money, telling the policeman to telephone Andrew Carnegie and tell him he, Thaw, was in trouble. The policeman walked Thaw to the police station on Thirtieth Street, where he was booked. Thaw identified himself, not very imaginatively, as John Smith, claiming to be a student from Washington, D.C.

Word that it was Stanford White who had been murdered spread quickly. Newspaper reporters ran to White's Twenty-first Street house but found just a single housekeeper at home. The reporters waited. Soon after, Larry White returned home alone, having put his friend, or friends, on the train. The young man, who had been pampered and made a bit of a sissy by his mother and grandmother, suddenly found himself in a new world. Larry White was told of his father's death and given the name of his killer, which the young man claimed to not recognize. If that was true, it meant that Stanford White did not confide the information Bergoff had been giving him to his family. White must have suffered alone as Thaw's men stalked him.

Larry White ran to Madison Square Garden, looking for his father's car and driver. It would seem that everyone in New York knew of White's murder because of the police, the hysterical crowd exiting, the undertaker removing the body, and the lights going out on the roof. The chauffeur did not seem to notice, remaining, as he must have been ordered to do, with the car. One can only wonder why White had left his driver outside, as he often stayed over in the tower studio or walked the five short blocks home. Clearly, White intended to go to another location from the Roof Garden, and Larry must have known that, as he knew where the car was waiting.

The driver and Larry headed out to St. James, where Larry posted himself outside his mother's door to await morning. When Larry awakened Bessie, she took the news calmly. One can only wonder if Bessie had already come to terms with Stanford's evening excursions. Naturally enough, Stanford White's mother was overcome with grief. The family would protect and care for Mrs. White, who had no choice but to continue to live in the house of her dead son's wife. The family would screen the news to make certain that Stanford's mother was spared the enormous oncoming scandal. Dick White was summoned from Seattle to comfort his mother during what was likely his last time in the East.

Larry and Bessie dressed that morning to drive to New York to deal with the tragedy. Stanford White's mother was brought to Twenty-first Street, as the initial thought was to have a funeral in the city. When the immense publicity made a New York City service impossible, Mrs. Richard Grant White was left at Twenty-first Street, where she was spared the pain of the funeral and kept from learning of the public nature of the event.

As reporters surrounded Larry at the Gramercy Park house, one of them telephoned McKim at his Thirty-fifth Street house, awakening the household. McKim was told the news and then pumped about Thaw. One can only wonder what went through McKim's head at that moment, as he has left no account. His friend of thirty-six intense years had been murdered by a maniac in a public place. McKim had only just recovered from a severe bout of his own nervous depression, yet was able to fend off the caller rather deftly.

McKim, like Bessie, may have already come to terms with the idea that White would likely incur some scandal, although neither could have ever figured on an incident this horrible. The death of Will Whitney was probably still in their minds. Whitney had tempted many husbands, but White had not; he had carefully avoided married women. Even as McKim staggered under the news, the reporter asked him about Thaw. McKim, probably disingenuously, denied any knowledge of the killer. Of course, McKim would have known Thaw. Indeed, during the winter of 1905, when Stanford had lived with McKim, he surely had to explain to his old friend about the people trailing him. Probably White told McKim about Thaw's bizarre behavior.

McKim would also have known Thaw from the house the office had built for A. Blair Thaw some fifteen years earlier. The large house A. Blair Thaw had commissioned in the year after the death of his father, called, not very imaginatively, the Castle, had the same problem with leaks during rainstorms as did Lorillard's house. The Thaws housed several sisters in the Castle who complained to McKim, Mead & White in 1900 about the leaks. On October 7, 1903, a sister of Thaw, Mrs. W. R. Thompson, wrote a harsh letter to the office, again complaining about the leaks. The office had sent men to survey the water damage at the house, which the men blamed on the local stone the Thaws had wanted used for the house. A reply was sent on October 17, 1903, stating that the stone of the house had absorbed water, doing damage to the interior of the house.

McKim, and then the entire office, would cover for White and not reveal any connection to the Thaw family. Thinking in a legal manner, McKim and the office put up a monolithic wall of silence. McKim summoned Mead to New York the next morning. The two men closed the office until after the funeral, avoided all reporters, and dispatched men who were sworn to silence to White's hideaways to remove all sensitive items. Mead seems to have directed the office cleanup, while McKim, who had long acknowledged Bessie as his best friend, joined the family at Twenty-first Street.

Bessie, Larry, and McKim asked for a death mask to be made. The request seems a bit odd, but may have been done for the purpose of a court trial, although this seems not to have been needed. The family kept the mask, complete with bits of White's hair in the plaster, until recent years, when it was donated to the Avery Architectural Library of Columbia University.

The autopsy results shocked the family almost as much as the murder. The puffy-looking face of the man in Gertrude Käsebier's photograph was telling. White was in terrible health. Indeed, he was dying of kidney disease. Thaw never needed to shoot White. He would have died naturally in a few months' time. White's complaints of poor health were justified. He had what was then called Bright's disease, the condition that killed Richardson. White also had severe liver damage from alcohol consumption. He even had tuberculosis. The autopsy did not reveal his arthritis, which had given him such discomfort. Once the medical work had been completed, White's remains were put in a coffin and delivered to the Twenty-first Street house, where the family had a viewing and then closed the casket. McKim and Bessie initially intended to have the funeral at St. Bartholomew's, where White had just completed the Vanderbilt memorial porch, but the newspaper feeding frenzy made them change their plans to avoid crowds.

As Bessie and McKim—with help from William M. Evarts of Evarts, Choate et al., Prescott Hall Butler's old firm—prepared the funeral, Mead, probably at Evarts's instruction, sent three of White's most trusted draftsmen to White's private office above the firm's offices at 160 Fifth Avenue on the sixth floor. There the men sorted through the books and photographs that White kept private, boxing them and destroying anything that could be used by the press. Any photographs containing images of living people were destroyed.

Some 160 books of erotica, as well as letters, paintings, and likely Jim Breese's own photographs, were sent to Breese at the Carbon Studio. Breese and Henry Poor had been White's pals in the evenings. Neither man ever revealed anything about White or about the precise contents of the shipments. No mention is made of Poor's space over his stable, which also must have been double-checked for incriminating items. Breese, Poor, and the others pulled the shade down tight over the male pastimes of the Gilded Era, which were so commonplace as to be the subject of *Mamzelle Champagne*. White's death silenced the playboy/chorus girl high life. The ensuing trial and negative publicity frightened the participants out of the practice, at least for a while.

Evelyn Nesbit ran off as the police took her husband from the street in front of Madison Square Garden. She hid with an old friend of hers from her single days in New York. She clearly panicked, trying to remain out of view to avoid, most likely, possible blame for her part in the murder. Despite the future course of events in the trial, Harry had planned the murder of White. Thaw had been in the overcoat all evening to keep people from noticing that he carried a gun. Did Evelyn know about the gun? She certainly knew Thaw made wild remarks about White constantly. She also had learned that she could change Harry's train of thought by revealing details about White to him. After a time, Evelyn went into the fiction business, telling Thaw virtually anything that came into her mind to forestall his temper when it was directed at her. Evelyn helped to inflame Thaw's hatred of "the Beast." She may well have feared she would be partly blamed for White's murder.

The funeral was held quickly. On Thursday, June 28, White's coffin was taken from the house to the Thirty-fourth Street East River ferry and carried to Long Island City, then put aboard a Long Island Railroad car for a funeral entourage to St. James. The service was held in the Smith family's small white painted church, below windows White had commissioned from John La Farge. About two hundred people sat sadly in the pews. The unreal atmosphere of the media-driven hoopla brought great discomfort to all of White's friends. Not much of a churchman, White probably would have found the service overdone, but he would have appreciated the sight of the altar banked in orchids, lilies, and roses in June, the best month for flowers on Long Island. All of White's friends attended, except for Saint-Gaudens, who didn't feel strong enough to travel. Surely the entire group felt the wrong that had been done to a person who had been so full of life. They must also have recognized that the days to come would be very unpleasant ones for White's friends. The mourners followed the coffin to the grave site, singing as White was buried. McKim would promptly design a simple grave stele for the spot.

As the sad party returned to the city to attempt to pick up the pieces, the sensationalist wing of the press began a search for scandal to increase the papers' revenues.

McKim devoted himself to Larry and Bessie to help them figure out a course of action. The Twenty-first Street house would be given up and many of its treasures sold. White's disastrous finances were understood best by Charles Barney. White did carry insurance policies on his life, which helped to pay off some of the accumulated debt. Many of White's friends were true gentlemen and looked the other way at White's outstanding obligations. Bessie, Larry, and McKim would survive the murder, but it would deeply affect McKim as the weeks progressed.

Letters of sympathy poured in to McKim at the office. Perhaps one of the more telling ones came to McKim from Harry White, then in Rome. His letter clearly refers to their past discussions of Stanford White's evenings and his risky behavior. Harry White writes: "I have long feared <u>as you know</u> that he would come to an untimely end, but I must say that I did not expect such a tragedy as the incident which has befallen him." White's personal life was obviously much discussed by his friends, even though no indication of these talks remains in our records.

The professional journals wrote about the loss of White as a major setback to America's goal of becoming a place that admired beauty. A few of the young women who had been at White's parties wrote about the evenings as harmless fun, but the press, led by James Gordon Bennett, took off their gloves and went at White. From Paris, Bennett, a man given to far more misdeeds than White, cabled his editors to give White hell. Bennett was quick to turn on a friend—just a year earlier the two men had worked over his hanging owl mausoleum. Colonel Mann of *Town Topics,* whose silence had been purchased by White, recognized that the payments to him were finished and went after the dead man, but in mild form, implying that something like this was expected.

McKim and Mead may have feared that the scandal would destroy the firm. Fortunately, work was still in the office, such as Penn Station, but would new jobs come their way? The contract for New York City's new Municipal Building a year later gave the firm a major new work, which indicated that the office would survive White's death. In 1908 McKim would write to Mead that the office would survive, using their motto "Vogue la Galère": The ship sails on, come what may.

Many of White's friends—especially those who had shared secrets with him—were afraid the scandal might taint them. His close friends fell silent. Richard Harding Davis, the journalist White met at the pyramids, wrote a fine article about him in *Collier's* magazine of August 4, 1906. Davis's heroic article was honest and on the mark, describing White as "a most kindhearted, most considerate, gentle and manly man . . . as incapable of little meannesses as of great crimes. . . . when a man or woman was in trouble, Stanford White was the first man in New York to whom he or she could turn, knowing that, asking no questions, preaching no sermon, it would give pleasure to serve them." Saint-Gaudens was asked to prepare a statement in defense of White, but he claimed he could not find the language he needed to express his feelings.

On August 1, 1906, McKim took Bessie and Larry with him to Europe for a change of scenery. McKim and the Whites went to Scotland, then to Normandy and Paris. Throughout the two-month vacation, McKim tutored Larry in architecture. The young man, now about to enter his senior year at Harvard, must have wondered if he could go into his father's profession after all the publicity. McKim must have devoted himself to high-minded lectures about the beauty of buildings to overcome Larry White's thoughts. His mentoring was a success. Stanford White's son went to the École in Paris after college, returning to McKim, Mead & White, where he stayed for his entire career. Larry White followed McKim's model rather than his father's, practicing as a sober and learned architect.

# 48. THE TRIAL OF THE CENTURY

As the new year began, the most sensational trial of the new century commenced. The trial was the production of Mary Copley Thaw, who probably could have had the votes given to Alva Vanderbilt Belmont transferred to her as the most hated woman in America. Mrs. Thaw took over her family soon after her husband's death in 1889. She moved into a far larger home, begun before her husband's death but obviously Mrs. Thaw's setting for her assault on East Coast society. Mrs. Thaw then went shopping for paintings with Harry, with a view to courting New York City's Mrs. Astor. Mrs. Astor did take on new people, and 1901 brought an invitation to the then-bachelor Harry for the Patriarchs' Ball, the year's most important event.

In the same year, Mrs. Astor listened to the desperate words of the earl of Yarmouth, then in New York searching for a bride while working as an actor. Mrs. Astor probably introduced the earl to Alice Cornelia Thaw, Harry's sister. In April 1903 the ill-fated wedding took place. The earl did not favor women and had some very bad habits. Since the social cachet of having her daughter married to an English earl was enormous, Mrs. Thaw tried to quiet her daughter's misery by sailing for England in late June 1906.*

Mrs. Thaw learned of Harry's actions as she arrived in Britain. She rapidly returned to the United States, hiring a publicist to tar White with as much scandal as possible. The publicist, Benjamin Atwell, did his job

---

*Alice Thaw would divorce the earl in 1908.

very well. The best defense lawyers of the day were hired, while Atwell, with the reports from the detectives who had followed White in hand, went for the ruination of the slain architect's character with relish. Atwell saw to it that several plays were produced with lead characters clearly based on White and Thaw. In the theatricals, White was depicted as a social predator, while Thaw was the all-American good guy, defending his wife's honor. The key to the defense of Thaw would be the same as the theme in the plays: Thaw would be portrayed as defending the honor of his wife.

George Carnegie, Thaw's brother-in-law, advised the family in what should have been the reasonable option—creation of an insanity defense. Carnegie advised, "What the family should do is lock Harry up in the bughouse, where he belongs." Harry and his mother refused to consider an insanity defense.

The trial opened in January 1907 with Evelyn Nesbit, now found by Thaw's family, in daily attendance. In return for Evelyn's loyalty, testimony, and appearance at the trial, Mrs. Thaw promised her daughter-in-law financial support. Evelyn lived up to this agreement, even if Mrs. Thaw did not. Evelyn gave a stellar performance at the trial, dressing as an innocent schoolgirl for months and launching into full-scale lies on the stand that created the picture of Thaw as a defender of his wife. Evelyn told the jury that she had been told White was determined to get her back after her marriage, when nothing could be further from the truth. Evelyn fully sold out to the Thaw team but did not get her reward. The Thaws cut her off, leaving her to a difficult life. In October 1910 in Berlin, Evelyn had a baby, claiming that it was Thaw's child. In 1915, Thaw divorced Evelyn, denying that he was the father of her son. Thaw was likely correct.*

AT THE TRIAL, Evelyn delivered her testimony in a childlike voice to reinforce the concept that White had drugged and then attacked her years earlier. The detail Evelyn gave was duly reported, keeping the newspaper publishers happy with profits, but shocking the nation. Parents objected to the news reports and everyone was scandalized. The adverse publicity was enough to close Mrs. DeMille's academy, driving it into bankruptcy as parents pulled their daughters out of the school.

The case of the people was brought forward by District Attorney William Travers Jerome, a man whose family came from the Whites' cir-

---

*Evelyn Nesbit's life went downhill steadily. She died in a nursing home in Los Angeles in 1967. She later fully reversed her testimony given in 1907 and 1908 to save Thaw from the electric chair.

cle in New York. Having known White, Jerome tried to win the case. He did a good job cross-examining Evelyn Nesbit, even bringing in Abe Hummel to describe his meetings with Evelyn in 1903. Hummel's word was compromised as Jerome had recently won a case against him, convicting Hummel of conspiring to have his client lie on the stand. Hummel was said to have produced fake breach-of-promise contracts for showgirls to use as blackmail. White was said to have had to pay him off twice. White then used Hummel when he needed a sleazy attorney. Hummel was disbarred and sent to prison. Hummel testified that Evelyn told him in 1903 that White had not drugged her. In summation, Thaw's attorney stressed his single moment of insanity while defending his wife, even suggesting that Harry Thaw's pose at the moment of the murder was equivalent to the sign of the cross as he stood for the purity of womanhood.

Jerome summed up his case as premeditated murder. After forty-seven hours of deliberation, the jury reported itself hopelessly deadlocked, with seven voting for murder in the first degree and five for acquittal on grounds of insanity. After twelve weeks, the trial was over.

A year later, a second trial began, again with Jerome prosecuting the case. The new team for Thaw's defense this time stressed his insanity. The number of votes Jerome had received a year earlier frightened Thaw and his mother into the insanity plea. The trial came to a swift conclusion with Thaw declared not guilty on the insanity plea. He was taken to Matteawan Asylum for the Criminally Insane, where he constantly petitioned for release. Thaw left the asylum in 1913 for a brief visit, then fled to Canada. Jerome went after him, eventually getting him back to a New York City jail. Thaw was then given another sanity test, which declared him sane.

On July 15, 1915, Thaw walked out of jail a free man. He rejoined the faster portion of society, unrepentant. In the mid-1920s, when Thaw visited Addison Mizner's new buildings in Palm Beach, Florida, he remarked loudly that he had shot the wrong architect. He lived as a rich man with several incidents of arrests until his death in 1947. Mrs. Thaw had succeeded in beating the system. Thaw really did get away with murder, as well as several other crimes, such as whipping and beating people. He spent 1917–24 in a psychiatric hospital for beating a boy, but the Thaws paid off the victim's family.

FROM APRIL TO DECEMBER 1907, White's collections were auctioned off in three large sales. The sales put White's treasures back into circulation, but the Stanford White interior of his mature years has been lost. White's assembly of objects of all time periods in Western art—he did not buy many Asian pieces—with reproductions of period furniture and imaginative accent pieces, is gone. His tapestries, fireplaces, ceilings, doors, urns, sarcophagi, candelabra, and bearskin rugs, put together for W. C. Whitney, Barney, Payne Whitney, Henry Poor, and himself, were all sold off. Objects can be found in dispersed places, from New York museums to San Simeon in California. William Randolph Hearst bought a number of White's pieces from his house and other houses he decorated.

It would be fun to re-create a White room as a monument to American taste at the beginning of the twentieth century. In any case, sales of White's collections produced about $250,000, which with his insurance policies may have paid off a number of his debts. The financial comfort White thought he had achieved had slipped through his fingers.

# 49. *VOGUE LA GALÈRE*

As White's treasures were being sold off, his best friend from his early years lay in bed dying. In the summer of 1907, Saint-Gaudens became too weak even to instruct his assistants. He had written a memoir that his son, Homer, would turn into a book. Saint-Gaudens rose from the artisan world of New York in the mid-century to become the pride of the nation. He gave his career to creating fine work in America and for Americans. On August 3, 1907, Saint-Gaudens died.

McKim was in Scotland getting ready for the grouse season when he heard the sad news. Still stunned by White's death, he would lose his brother-in-law, Wendell Phillips Garrison, this year also. He was hit very hard by the loss of Gus. McKim remembered that Gus had made a Robert Louis Stevenson relief for Edinburgh's Church of St. Giles, which he went immediately to see. As he stood in front of Gus's panel, listening to the voices of ordinary visitors looking at the work, McKim took comfort in the idea that Saint-Gaudens's work would be there for the ages. The young men of the 1870s who had started out together to bring art to America were now dying, but the goal had been achieved. "Vogue la Galère."

On McKim's return to New York aboard the *Celtic,* he wrote to Margaret on September 12, 1907:

My dear orphaned daughter:
"Lost but not forgotten." How are you? As well and fit, I hope, and as popular as you were a month ago on your birthday? Mine on August 24 was much less gay, partly because I was wretched and

miserable, and partly because when we turn our 60th corner and face 70, the less said the better! Of course, you know I was knocked out of my shooting by the advice of Dr. Blake's Edinburgh colleague . . . I went back to Millden, advised to let the moor alone and stick to golf, walking and motoring.

In a machine which I hired for three weeks, Miss Beatrix Jones* and I scoured the good Scotch roads in every direction . . . the dizziness decreased with the improvement and the noises became less jarring . . .

I sometimes think I am coming to the end of my tether, so low down in the bulb does the barometer go; but I am not ready to give up and propose, if possible, to get well enough, deaf or dumb, to get back to my work and to take care of you for a while longer.

Meanwhile, 13 East 35th Street is yours for the winter, whatever becomes of me! I may go into seclusion, or preferably breakfast with you at the usual hour.

McKim had suffered from a depression during the spring of 1906. At that time he deeply felt the loss of White, then Saint-Gaudens. He returned to New York City to a different house in the Astor estate group, 13 East Thirty-fifth Street, two doors down from his old house. McKim had decorated this property for John Cadwalader, who had lived there for decades. Cadwalader moved north to 3 East Fifty-sixth Street, near his friends Benjamin Altman and Michael Friedsam. McKim took on Cadwalader's house for Margaret and himself in June 1907.

After McKim moved into the new house, he would often speak to Charles Barney about the difficulties in settling White's estate. Barney was McKim's banker also. McKim's money was in the Knickerbocker Trust on Thirty-fourth Street and Fifth Avenue. Many of McKim's friends also banked at the Knickerbocker Trust, which had risen to become the preferred bank for many of the city's patricians, with its beautiful building recently completed by McKim, Mead & White. Indeed, the firm was then completing a new eight-story office building for the bank at 66 Broadway, to be known as the Downtown building.† McKim felt particularly safe at the Knickerbocker as he had many friends there besides Barney, who was really Stanford's friend. McKim was close to Henry Bowley Hollins, who was an organizer of the Knickerbocker with Barney, as well as a bro-

---

*Mary Cadwalader Jones's daughter, the landscape architect later known as Beatrix Jones Ferrand.
†This building would have fourteen more stories put on it by McKim, Mead & White in 1909–11; it was later demolished.

ker in business with Jim Breese's father. In 1899–1901 the office had built Hollins a Georgian red brick row house at 12 West Fifty-sixth Street.* McKim was very friendly with Hollins, who named his son McKim Hollins. McKim's confidence in the bank would soon be tried.

By early summer of 1907, a small number of people connected to the directors of the Knickerbocker Trust had begun to worry about the state of the trust's loans. A great number of loans outstanding were not good. One can only wonder if White's huge loans may have been a factor in this imbalance. It would appear that the Knickerbocker made loans too easily. The worry about the state of the Knickerbocker was known only to a few people and was kept under wraps. The president of the bank, C. T. Barney, had a clear knowledge of the situation, but it was overwhelmed by his participation in the Heinze Copper boom scandal, which had taken a big toll on Barney's personal resources. On the last day of September, Barney met with an upper-level manager of the bank, H. A. Dunn, and gave him a phone number where he could be reached the next day at noon. Barney said he was going off on his yacht to West Point. Dunn thought it odd to go away on the first of the month and noticed that Barney looked very nervous, but he did not question the trip.

The exchanges made soon after Barney sailed on October 1 were not as heavy as they could have been, although demand loans had to be called in to cover the day's calls. Several large deposits were made, which got the trust through the first of the month. Barney returned to his desk.

On the twelfth of the month, a woman customer appeared, demanding cash for her large certificate of deposit. Dunn was surprised that the customer refused to take a check, but gave her the cash.

By the twentieth of the month, Dunn had heard that the bank's assets were a bit short but that J. P. Morgan had been contacted to provide an advance if needed. Dunn sensed that rumors about the bank were beginning and that Barney, Hollins, and another director were in constant conference. At a meeting at 66 Broadway on October 22, Hollins rose to tell those assembled that Barney had resigned from the bank, as he had personal liabilities over the Copper Crisis and his presence might cast a dark shadow on the Knickerbocker Trust. According to Hollins, Barney was depositing additional collateral in the bank. Hollins finished by telling those assembled that the bank was short, but with some help could ride out the difficulties. Just as Hollins finished his remarks, word came that the Clearing House Committee would not aid the Knickerbocker and that

*It is today the Argentine Consulate.

the clearing of Knickerbocker checks would no longer be performed. The New York Clearing House, a private organization formed by the banks to centralize check clearing, examined the assets of the banks. An emergency meeting for that night was called at Sherry's at 9 p.m. The choice of Sherry's restaurant for a serious business meeting is a signal of the nature of Gilded Age life.

The directors and executives met in a small ballroom that night with grave faces. Among them were men from J. P. Morgan, attorneys, and others awaiting the results to facilitate a solution. No true plan emerged in the meeting, so the directors voted to open the bank as usual with as much cash on hand as possible and wait out the run on the bank. The directors, perhaps disingenuously, decided to ask Barney to return to take control of the next day's events (or, perhaps, to take the fall). Dunn rushed to Barney's house, only to find reporters swarming all over even at that late hour. The butler answered, eventually letting Dunn through Stanford White's bronze gates. Barney, once of commanding presence, was lying in bed, surrounded by magazines, holding a novel upside down. He greeted the grim news with "Oh, my God!" but recovered. He dressed himself in immaculate evening attire and went to Sherry's to be with the board. The next day, as the run on the bank proceeded, managers rushed by car, carriage, and subway around the city trying to bring cash from the less affected branches to the more desperate ones. At 12:15 p.m., Dunn gave the order to cease paying, and to draw the shades of the tellers' windows. At 12:26 p.m., the Knickerbocker Trust suspended business. This ushered in the Panic of 1907. J. P. Morgan was to play the major role in calming the panic and limiting the damage. Both Morgan and John Cadwalader dealt with the disaster at Barney's bank.

Barney was miserable, with (it was said) even his wife about to divorce him over an alleged affair with another woman, and he could not cope with the crisis. Barney was by all accounts a good person who, like White, got caught up in the fast life and flew too high. On November 14, 1907, Stanford White's "best friend in the world" put a gun to his head and pulled the trigger, committing suicide in the house White had designed and fitted with treasures.

McKim's account at the Knickerbocker was frozen for months following the bank's failure. He was anxious about his own money, but his greatest agitation was caused by a fear for the account of the fragile American School of Architecture in Rome, which was also tied up by the bank crisis.

The panic of 1907 would take down another of Stanford White's close friends. Henry Poor's personal fortune was lost and Poor, one of the clients who most appreciated White's interior work, had to sell his beautiful house. The collections would also be sold.

McKim's condition, delicate already, was too fragile to absorb the Knickerbocker tragedy and Barney's death. He tried to cheer up with a trip to Pineland, South Carolina, one of several bird-hunting clubs McKim visited in the winters of the early twentieth century, but the trip did not have the intended effect. McKim had reached the end of his tether. He worked over his will, dated November 20, 1907; created a power of attorney for William Mead to use; and left McKim, Mead & White as of January 1, 1908. McKim went off to the sanitarium in Greenwich where Margaret had stayed in hopes of gaining a respite, but none came. Visitors to the office were told that McKim was on an extended vacation, but he had had a breakdown, which he recognized he would unlikely be able to survive. He made plans to close the house at 13 East Thirty-fifth Street, putting the furnishings in storage in his daughter's name. He sent to the Newbolds the last item of Julia Appleton's that he retained—the fireplace mantel that he had made the center of his own room. McKim was in a final cleanup phase, even donating his gold medal from the RIBA to the American Institute of Architects. The AIA realized McKim's health was failing and awarded him the American medal in 1909. McKim even followed his mother's model of setting aside items of jewelry for specific people after he was gone.*

The new year of 1909 found McKim coming out of his torpor. He was consulted about the details of the 1901 McMillan Plan in reference to the placement of the Lincoln Memorial, which obliged him to recall the meeting with President Roosevelt and Secretary John Hay.† McKim was called upon to remember the specific comments made eight years earlier; it was difficult for him to come back into focus, but he did so after a struggle. He was able to recall the words of the agreement and relate them to members of the American Institute of Architects. McKim stayed in Washington at the Hotel Shoreham much of the spring, traveling to Philadelphia to accept a Doctor of Laws degree from the University of Philadelphia. McKim, too ill to speak, accepted the degree with the assistance of Frank Millet, who as a close friend of Cadwalader had again become a constant companion to the ailing McKim. The Newhalls appeared for the ceremony, caring for Margaret McKim as Millet helped McKim sit upon the stage.

---

*Dwight Herrick had written McKim's will on November 20, 1907, with its gifts of Julia's effects to the Newbolds, Stanford White's jewelry to Larry White, and a choice of two of McKim's tapestries to Mead.

†Hay's daughter would marry Payne Whitney the next year, 1902.

By April, McKim had taken rooms in the Hotel Netherland in New York, where he was in better condition for a few months. He exchanged letters with Larry White, who was now in Paris following "Uncle Charlie's" advice. McKim was both optimistic about the role of architecture in the United States and pessimistic about the state of the profession in New York City. In his last exchange of letters, he summed up the success of his lifetime of work to Larry: "When you get through with your work on the other side and come home ready to build, you will find opportunities awaiting you that no other country has offered in modern times. The scale is Roman and it will have to be sustained." McKim perhaps saw the new Washington, D.C., as the vehicle for his views. To him, the skyscrapers with their contest for height represented all that was against his view of a new Rome. The city of his career, which had already removed a number of his own buildings, was becoming too commercial to appreciate beauty. To Larry, he wrote,

> The new Metropolitan Life Insurance tower, seven hundred feet high, makes the Flatiron Building look like a toy and puts every building within a mile in the shade. But all the same, Madison Square tower, one-third of its height, is as far the greater of the two as David than Goliath. The first has the merit of bigness, and that's all. I think the skyline of New York grows daily more hideous. A recent law provides for the widening of Fifth Avenue by narrowing the sidewalks. This involves the removal of areas, front stoops, and all projections into the sidewalk. . . . nobody is spared; and the Knickerbocker, Sherry's, Tiffany's, the Knickerbocker Club and the University are only a few glaring examples.

By the summer of 1909, when McKim and Margaret visited Narragansett Pier under the continued care of Dr. Hitchcock, it had become clear that McKim's heart was giving out. It would seem that the McKim family had a genetic coronary weakness that caused a number of them to die early. Mead, who found himself having to care for his failing partner, remarked with slight annoyance that McKim had no family left, leaving Mead at times as the sole caregiver. Indeed, McKim was the only survivor, except for two of his sister's children, then establishing their own lives. Margaret did attend her father, but her own battle with depression kept her from being able to accept the full responsibility. Once her father's heart started to weaken, Margaret must have felt she could not handle the situation without some help. McKim did have a nurse, so it was likely not the physical care that Margaret feared, but the emotional investment. At this moment, Bessie White, McKim's beloved friend, volunteered to entertain the two until August 15, then to arrange for the McKims to live in a cottage on the Prescott Hall Butler property until McKim died. There are no accounts of McKim's awareness of Bessie's genuine act of love. We do not know if he realized he was back with the family of one of his oldest friends, near the house he designed as a young man. We can hope that the beloved soil of the lands of "Bull" Smith gave McKim comfort.

On the fourteenth of September 1909, with Margaret beside him, McKim died.* His funeral was held back in New York at Trinity Church three days later, with seven hundred people in attendance. McKim was then buried in Rosedale Cemetery in Orange, New Jersey, with his family. In November and December, two memorial meetings were held, one in New York and the second at the American Institute of Architects in Washington, D.C.

The sober, self-effacing dean of the profession had gone. Mead, the lone survivor, had gone to Europe with Frank Millet to attend to, among other things, McKim's beloved American Academy, then at a crucial stage in the search for an appropriate building. Mead's two wildly flying partners, sketched in that now-lost cartoon as balloons flying apart with Mead holding the strings, were gone. Mead had been the rudder of the ship, a position he would continue until 1919 when he retired as an active participant in the firm.

THE OFFICE OF McKim, Mead & White had survived White's trial, led by the young assistants who had done so much for the principals for so many years. The offer of partnership made to Wells years earlier had not been repeated, although several of the more active participants had been given the choice of a substantial raise or a percentage of the profits. Henry Bacon, the brother of Frank, the furniture designer, took the salary raise, boasting to the others for years. The other men—Kendall, Burt Fenner, and Teunis Van der Bent—took a percentage. When Penn Station and the U.S. Post Office behind it came into the office, the three "percent men" were suddenly affluent. Bacon was said to have quit in disgust.

On January 1, 1906, the first new partners were created. McKim's right-hand man, William Mitchell Kendall, known to be hardworking, dull, and mean, became a partner along with Burt L. Fenner, the son of

---

*McKim's daughter, Margaret, would marry the Edinburgh-born neurologist William Joseph Marie Alois Moloney, and with her husband create a collection of papers on nineteenth-century Irish issues, now at the New York Public Library.

Mead's old friend from Amherst. The third new partner was a San Franciscan, William Symmes Richardson. Richardson, perhaps the best designer of the three, took on Penn Station. Richardson had a fine collection of American antiques, which were sold at his death.

The new office carried on, eventually making Larry White a partner in 1920. The second phase of McKim, Mead & White did a number of major works, including many schools and institutions. The second firm carried on the emphasis on quality materials so important to McKim and White and did display McKim's interest in erudite design. There was, however, no spark in the office, which coasted on its reputation as a training ground for ambitious young architects through the 1920s, when the modern movement neutralized the McKim, Mead & White theme. Joseph Wells's book-plate precedent lived on thirty years after Wells's death.

The world of the architects contracted again with the sinking of the *Titanic.* Aboard the ship was Frank Millet, McKim, Mead, and Cadwalader's close friend. Millet still carried McKim's enthusiasm for the Roman school. He was returning to the United States briefly with Archibald Willingham Butt, called Archie, an army aide to William Howard Taft who had lived with Millet for some years. The two men had set up a partnership in housekeeping in Washington, D.C. Also aboard the White Star line vessel was James Clinch Smith, who went down on the boat with the family Bible, ending a phase in the Smith saga.

Mead must have felt increasingly like the only man left on the hill. A number of clients—Henry B. Hollins, J. P. Morgan, and others—faced economic and political trials. Hollins's firm failed in 1913, the year Morgan died after his congressional dressing-down under the Pujo investigation of the money trusts. One can imagine Mead's letter to Stratton, the two old men who were the last to be left. Mead was increasingly dependent on his old office boy Royal Cortissoz, now the grand old man of American art criticism. Cortissoz would carry on for a decade after Mead's death in 1928 as president of the American Academy. The last partner did not return to America in death, asking to be placed next to his brother, the sculptor Larkin, at the Protestant Cemetery in Florence, Italy. In the end, Mead chose to remain in the Old World that his firm had worked so hard to import to America.

McKIM, MEAD AND WHITE all came of age in the years following the Civil War. As individuals, each with his own inherent human flaws, they, like the nation, evolved rapidly, moving from a simpler past toward a more complex, cosmopolitan persona, often with tragic results. As Americans became wealthier, they made important statements about themselves via the built world. They popularized the summer house, cities and states chose to create a grand civic presence through architecture, and businesses demanded taller buildings. McKim, Mead & White's resort houses, in locations from Elberon to Newport, were the first flowering of an independent vein, a wide variety of responses to the wooden shingle cottage. While inspired by English and Norman forms, these houses were not copies of contemporary European practice. The new mode, with its nod to recent internal developments, established the United States as a place worthy of entry on the world stage. European architects now began to come to America to look at our buildings.

As the ocean shrank and wealth grew, McKim, Mead, and White were transformed into modern-day Roman emperors, carrying European treasures back to our shores. While the palazzo precedent had overwhelmed their earlier work, their buildings continued to be modern on the inside. By the turn of the twentieth century, they acted as would their presidential client, Teddy Roosevelt, propelling America into worldwide prominence by importing historic fittings to grace the houses of the nation's self-proclaimed aristocrats. More notice would accrue as Americans purchased homes in Europe and the American School was established in

*Book plate with firm motto from the*
*McKim, Mead & White library*

Rome. American accomplishments now equaled, and at times even exceeded, those of their European peers.

Although many of the greatest works by McKim, Mead & White are now gone, the native baronial country houses, summer cottages, and town houses, as well as the marriage of the old and the new in the now lamented Pennsylvania Station and printing palace for the *New York Herald,* set the stage for the new order. The desire to dress a building's exterior in the past would give way to a type of building that expressed its purpose in a more overt, utilitarian manner.

A century later, we have returned to the fold, mourning the loss of our patrimony but eager to ensure the retention of that which has survived. In our twenty-first-century eyes, McKim, Mead & White surely rank as America's greatest designers from the death of Richardson to World War I. As architects, they gave a distinctive face—at times grand, at times nonchalantly at ease—to a transforming nation.

# APPENDIX

## MEAD'S FAMILY AND EARLY LIFE

The Meads of Chesterfield, New Hampshire, and Brattleboro, Vermont, were typical Yankees of their day. The family may have had some association with the Puritans, as Gabriel Mead arrived in Massachusetts in 1635. Levi Mead, who actually heard Paul Revere speak on that fateful night in Lexington, moved to Chesterfield, New Hampshire, where he purchased a large farm tract. Levi's son, Larkin Goldsmith Mead (1795–1869), was a sensible and sober man who married Polly Noyes in 1821, a sister of the utopian thinker John Humphrey Noyes. Mead left the farm, with its insistent crop of rocks, for the new town of Brattleboro, just east across the state line in Vermont, in 1839. Larkin G. Mead practiced law and was elected for a short time to the Vermont senate.

The Meads had eight children, of whom several moved on to prominence outside Brattleboro. The eldest son died while a student at Harvard College; the second son would have a career in the Stanley Rule Company of New Britain, Connecticut; the third child, a daughter, Elinor, married William Dean Howells, the writer, while he was American consul at Venice. Another child, Joanna Elizabeth, married Augustus D. Shepard, a Vanderbilt relation, in 1862. The Meads joined the ambitious Yankees of mid-century who left the safe towns of New England for the growing urban centers of the coast. New England town fathers of the early nineteenth century saw their sons and daughters recognize the limitations of provincial life and move to the city. Many of these transplanted Yankees would become the backbone of expanded business on the East Coast.

It was the intellectuals of New England who were the first Americans to travel to Europe in search of cultural enrichment. The Meads' third son, who bore the name of his father, Larkin Goldsmith Mead, born in 1835, was to become one of America's first European-trained sculptors and one of the early flow of Yankees to live their lives in Italy as expatriates. The young man displayed an interest in stone carving early on and in 1854 left the dry goods business in Brattleboro for the Brooklyn, New York, studio of the American sculptor Henry Kirk Brown, where he studied for two years. Returning to Brattleboro one New Year's Eve in a very frigid winter, the young Mead carved a tall angel in the snow and ice at the top of the town's main street. The *Snow Angel* made Larkin Mead the talk of the region and may have helped him establish a career in America. Three years later, he yearned to see the work of European sculptors and set off for Florence, where he settled. He married a Venetian woman and would remain in Italy for the rest of his life. He is buried in the Protestant Cemetery in Florence.

William Rutherford Mead was born in Brattleboro on August 20, 1846. The future principal in McKim, Mead & White was the third son of Larkin Goldsmith Mead and his wife Polly. W. R. Mead received a normal education in Brattleboro where his father had tried to maintain standards in the local school. But it was surely in his home with its rich intellectual life that he received the stimulation necessary to propel him forward to college and on to a challenging career. Mead was not as good a student as his elder brother had been, but he was able to enter Norwich University, do well there, and transfer to Amherst College where he took his degree in 1867. He was to be the only member of McKim, Mead & White to complete college and hold a degree. His record at Amherst was not distinguished, however; his records show a failure in "deportment," perhaps the result of a prank at college.

After his graduation, like many ambitious young men in the aftermath of the Civil War, he decided to go to New York, where he was apprenticed in the office of an engineer. The study of engineering did not seem to suit him, as shortly thereafter Mead entered the office of a successful New York architect, Russell Sturgis (1836–1909), then in partnership with Peter B. Wight. The Meads seem to have been supportive of his career change as they paid Sturgis to teach their son the basics of the profession. Mead thus followed the British practice of apprenticing to a working architect. This system was not much followed in the United States in architecture, although it was widely done in law. To enter an architect's office after obtaining a college degree was unusual and may indicate the young man's ambiguity about his future.

Sturgis & Wight were not yet quite at the height of their popularity when Mead arrived. This was before the commissions from Yale University and for the house of Theodore Roosevelt's parents on Fifty-seventh Street arrived in the office. But the Sturgis office did have a tie to the liberal thinkers of the age who had been the mainstays of the abolitionist movement.

Mead seems to have finally found his calling in the office of Sturgis. If he was a bit short on personality and artistic qualities, he forced himself to learn from George Fletcher Babb, the architect in charge of his training. Babb's abilities as a teacher were well known. He had been asked to be the first professor of architecture at the nation's first school of architecture at MIT in 1868, a position he had declined. He was a master of proportion and renowned for his skill at interior designs executed in the high colorist fashion of the mid-nineteenth century.

At the end of his three years of apprenticeship at Sturgis's firm, Mead left the office on lower Broadway in order to journey to Florence, where he spent about two years with his brother hoping to find inspiration. He took classes at the Accademia delle belle Arti, where John Singer Sargent would soon go. Sargent found the classes disorganized. Mead's impressions of Florence are interesting. In a letter to his sister, Elinor Mead Howells, in January 1872, he decries the lack of originality in art in Florence. He calls Italian artists and architects mere copyists. Mead, too, probably did not find the classes in Florence very helpful, as no sign of architectural influence seemed to emerge from his stay in Tuscany.

When Mead returned to the United States in about 1873, he was determined to bury himself in the office of others more able to design than he. He probably recognized that he was not comfortable as an artist. Mead returned like a homing pigeon to 57 Broadway, visiting the offices of several firms, including Gambrill & Richardson, George B. Post, and Russell Sturgis. There Mead encountered his future partner Charles Follen McKim, a year his junior and also an alumnus of Sturgis's office. Mead's and McKim's paths did not cross in their time with Sturgis and Babb, but the two self-reliant young men would later decide to try their luck together as independent architects in small, dark rooms around the stairwell of the building.

Each man had a few family and school friends promising them small jobs, and they hoped that sharing rooms and helping each other might work. This loose arrangement of mutual aid was in place for five years, until a formal partnership was drawn up that would last their lifetimes. McKim, nervous and often discouraged in his private life, was capable of great charm with clients. He provided the greater number of domestic commissions, while Mead ensured the completion of the projects and stability in the dark, small spaces of lower Broadway.

## JAMES MILLER McKIM

James Miller McKim had been born in 1810 in Carlisle, Pennsylvania, of Scots-Irish paternal ancestry and German on his maternal side. The first James McKim, who had been born in northern Ireland about 1756, was in the United States before the American Revolution began. His son, James McKim II, was born in 1779. His wife was Catherine Miller, whose family had immigrated to America from Germany. James McKim II died in 1831. Miller McKim, the third generation of the family born in America, trained for the Presbyterian clergy, graduating from Dickinson College before entering Princeton Theological Seminary in 1831. Shortly thereafter, his parents died and he had to return home to care for his siblings while continuing his studies with a local pastor. It is said that about this time Miller McKim encountered the antislavery pamphlets of William Lloyd Garrison in a barbershop. By Christmas of 1833 he had gone to Philadelphia to join in the formation of the American Anti-Slavery Society. The friends he made at this time would remain the anchors of his life. McKim met Garrison, and the Motts, James and his wife Lucretia, ardent Hicksite Quakers deeply opposed to slavery. James Mott had put conscience before comfort, giving up his cotton business because it made a profit from slavery and dedicating his life to the cause. Mott went into the wool trade while he and his wife devoted themselves to the abolitionist movement. The Motts became an alternative family to Miller McKim in their home, Roadside. They probably introduced McKim to his future wife, and helped open his mind to the women's suffrage movement of which Mrs. Mott was also a leader. Torn between the world of the Motts and his training for the clergy, Miller McKim spent the year of 1835 as pastor in Womelsdorf, Pennsylvania, but his interest in the Anti-Slavery Society gradually claimed his attention. Though he could lecture to his flock, he found himself happier working with the society as a speaker and advocate for abolition. His polite but convinced views had a winning way with those who heard him. McKim's capacity to get his point across in a nonconfrontational manner was a talent his son Charles would also have. The McKims, while appearing to give in to an argument, would patiently circle back their own point of view in an often-successful attempt to convince their listeners.

Miller McKim's internal war between his Presbyterian training and his new fervor culminated in a decision to resign his charge in Womelsdorf and leave the clergy. Shortly after, he set his heart on winning the hand of Sarah Speakman with the quiet blessings of his new friends in the Anti-Slavery Society. Sarah Allibone Speakman was the youngest of five children born to Micajah Speakman (1782–1852) and Phoebe Smith (1785–1832). Soon after her birth in 1813 in Concord, Pennsylvania, her family, who were Quakers, moved permanently to Highland Farm in Chester County, Pennsylvania, where Sarah was still living during Miller McKim's courtship of her. The engagement lasted two years while McKim tried a stint in medical school before deciding to devote his life to the antislavery cause. He was to be a key figure in the preparation of freedom for slaves, and later in the education of those liberated in the Civil War.

Miller McKim married Sarah Speakman on October 1, 1840. Sarah was duly, but gently, "read out" at a Quaker meeting, although she never stopped thinking of herself as a Friend and continued to use Quaker idiom until her death.

But though she was devoted to the best values of life in Quaker fashion and dressed in plain attire, Sarah McKim was at home in the contemporary world. She enjoyed some fashion sense, and had a penchant for singing while she did her day's work. In her girlhood her Quaker aunt had admonished her when she became carried away by song, inquiring if she were in pain. Sarah McKim loved music and dance and gave in to that in contradiction of Friends' doctrine.

The marriage was a good one, and Sarah joined her husband in his life's work. Their union brought Lucy McKim into the world on October 30, 1842. Shortly thereafter, the McKim family finances were strained even further when the couple adopted Annie Catherine McKim, an orphaned niece on the McKim side. Family documents allude to the addition of another orphaned niece, but that child's identity is lost, so perhaps the girl did not survive childhood.

# ACKNOWLEDGMENTS

Kayla B. Stotzky constantly encouraged this book. Sadly, Kayla died before this work was out of draft form. I only wish she had been able to be with me when the work was under way. I miss her deeply as a very close friend. She was the wisest person I ever knew.

To Edward Sullivan go my thanks for making it possible to do this book. His encouragement was vital to this project and I am most grateful to him. As chairman of the Department of Fine Arts at NYU, he even read my earlier studies and gave me a chance to write. Edward provided the vital funds for a typist when I was fearful of not being able to work and write. He has been truly supportive and I am deeply grateful to him.

This book is due in large part to Henry-Russell Hitchcock, who almost knew McKim, Mead, and White. Russell retained a lifelong interest in the architects begun while at Harvard, where he spoke to William King Covell of Newport who knew William B. Bigelow, the one-time partner of McKim. McKim had been Covell's neighbor at the Bayside in Newport. Bigelow later lived in Cambridge, Massachusetts, where he and Covell must have met again. Bigelow must have given Covell his files and told him of commissions in the early days of the firm, which are unique to Hitchcock and Covell's notes. Russell copied Covell's memories from Bigelow onto small blue index cards. Covell must have given Russell Bigelow's collection of Newport and McKim, Mead & White photographs, including a batch of Covell's own snapshots made as he attempted to locate some of these early houses of McKim, Mead & Bigelow in the 1930s and '40s. Russell felt a personal attachment to McKim, Mead & White. Indeed, his 1944 article in the *Journal of the Warburg and Courtauld Institutes* has the best analysis of the work of the architects. Russell and Sarah Bradford Landau brought me to American architecture and encouraged this study. Russell's own work was in a visual analytical vein, but he welcomed alternative approaches to the material and truly understood the nuances of social status presented here. He was a great man, and I only wish he were still here to see the book. Sarah B. Landau shared with me her love of discovery in American architecture, brought me to this topic, and always expected this book. She has been a tremendous source of intellectual encouragement

To Robert Schmitt go my thanks for the many times he drove me in search of phantom buildings and collections of papers. Robert always knew how to find the place, where to have lunch, and how to tactfully do something while I sat reading papers, and then offer reflections on the building.

To Andrew Saint I will always be deeply grateful! He plowed through the first draft of this manuscript and offered suggestions. He made this happen. As a person with a level of knowledge and writing ability far beyond any I will ever attain, he has helped me in multiple ways. He deserves his surname.

To Ann C. Broderick, my thanks for running a great vacation and summer camp and believing enough in me to assist in a crisis at the end of the draft.

To Tim Donehoo, I owe a great measure of thanks for encouragement, major assistance, and bringing books and articles to my attention. Discussions with Tim helped my thinking on parts of the book. I would never have made it without his good-humored assistance when each computer glitch proved too much for a (basically) "quill" person.

Thanks to Madge Cooper Huntington for sharing her wonderful collection of family memorabilia. Thanks also to Rhoda Lerman, Dr. and Mrs. Fallon, and Mary Herbert at the Cazenovia Library. The White family in St. James were generous with their drawings and family materials. Gisela J. Lozada at the Hill Memorial Library at Louisiana State University was especially helpful in Baton Rouge. The late Wendy Shadwell and Janet Parks offered wonderful support in this effort.

Thomaï Serdari, colleague and friend, devised the method of completion of this work and kept me going at the bottom of the effort. She found a way to allow a person with a full-time job to be able to make the most of her time. Sandra Teria Haviland really made it possible to complete this work. A highly intelligent artist and photographer, she has devoted months to helping me round up this lengthy work. I am deeply grateful to her for her rational thinking and decoding skills.

Nina Gray read the manuscript as an expert on interiors, and I am grateful for her comments, especially from her recent work on the Seventh Regiment Armory and the Frederick Vanderbilt house in Hyde Park, New York. Anita Saraceni, Jessica Weglin, and Lisa Charde encouraged, aided, and inspired me write and work this year. One cannot find better friends.

To Veronica Mason, my thanks for being able to endure the chicken scrawl and working numerous weekends to do the project. This talented ceramicist and truly great-spirited person deserves a special place in heaven!

I am deeply grateful to the Humanities Initiative at New York University for a grant-in-aid to help pay for the photograpic rights. To Jane Tylus and Asya Berger, as well as the Humanities Council, I am truly thankful. Sincere thanks to Pepe Karmel, chairman of the Art History Department, for continued solid support of this project.

Hannah Thomas and Linzi Silverman of NYU were wonderful friends to help finish this book. Jennifer Lehe, wizard of the computer and life, keeps sanity in reach at the end of the road. To Maya Dean, I offer deep thanks for wisdom beyond her years and for reformatting the notes brilliantly and rapidly.

To Herb and Camilla, my thanks for putting up with this saga and doing without enough attention and missing many games of Clue. Herb has been a wonderful and stalwart presence as this opus lived for too long a time.

My deep thanks to Victoria Wilson at Knopf, who with good humor waited for me well beyond what should have been a reasonable time period. I am deeply grateful to her for letting me attend to the very long number of last days of Meriam, Michael, and my parents. I think few other publishers would have waited. I am very appreciative of all the e-mails and wisdom given by Carmen Johnson at Knopf.

# NOTES

## INTRODUCTION: McKim, Mead & White

xxii    Mead just worked hard: Letter of August 21, 1917, W. R. Mead file, McKim, Mead & White Collection, New-York Historical Society.

## 1. McKim

4    "Arrived at Harrisburg": C. F. McKim, diary, August 8, 1865, New York Public Library.

4    "We visited the Cemetery": C. F. McKim, diary, August 5, 1865.

6    Modest though it was: The Davis designed-house probably seemed comfortable to Miller McKim as it resembled the William J. Rotch house in New Bedford, Massachusetts, though on a smaller scale. (The Rotch family was closely allied to the Motts, and visits to the Rotches were frequent in the family.) Sarah McKim, however, found it "rather fanciful for my taste; it was built by an artist; it has a funny pitched roof and clustered chimneys and bull's-eye windows, and niches for statuettes, that don't quite suit my plain taste." Letter to Charlie, quoted in Charles Moore, *The Life and Times of Charles Follen McKim* (Boston and New York: Houghton Mifflin, 1929), pp. 14–15. This book is the basic source for facts about the McKim family.

6    "I am not going to enter": Letter quoted ibid., pp. 15–16.

8    "School goes awfully hard": Letter of October 19, 1866, ibid., p. 19.

8    "I have to keep up": Letter of September 15, 1866, ibid., p. 17.

## 2. "A Mighty Serious Thing"

12    ". . . going to France": Quoted in Moore, *McKim*, p. 23.

15    Lucy Oelrichs: Moore, *McKim*, p. 25.

16    "Imagine, reader": Letter of August 31, 1868, quoted ibid., pp. 26–29.

17    The letter offers a wonderful tidbit: See Moore, *McKim*, pp. 29–32, for the full text of the letter. For Jourdain, see Arlette Barre-Despond and Suzanne Tise, *Jourdain* (New York: Rizzoli, 1991).

17 "small inheritance": Barre-Despond and Tise, *Jourdain,* p. 16. I am grateful to Professor Guy Walton of NYU for his help in trying to track down the specific château of Jourdain's aunt. The description places the château on a hill, and a letter from Lucy McKim to her brother uses the name of Joubert, who rescued the tapestries that were found in the château in the 1840s and now attract tourism to the building. For a picture of the château, see books like the tourist manual by Simone D'Huart, Martine Tissier De Mallerais, and Jean Saint-Bris, *Art and History: Chateaux and Cities of the Loire* (Florence: Bonechi, 2002), pp. 154–57. In later years McKim surely knew the famous department store La Samaritaine, built by Jourdain in 1891–1907, and may well have met Jourdain again at the 1900 fair, where he was a player, but we find no further contact then or any anecdotal reference to Jourdain in McKim's life.

18 This must have been discouraging: The first architects to come to the United States from the Continent were able to find jobs as designers behind the scenes at existing architectural firms until some were able to establish a group of prospective clients. The English-born designers often found acceptance quickly, as Americans felt a kinship to Britain. The early letters are found in the McKim Collection in the manuscript collection of the New York Public Library. The letters mentioned here are from May 1869; the letter from Miller McKim about the neighbors in Llewellyn Park, above, was dated June 27, 1869.

20 McKim must have noticed: For an excellent discussion of the earlier Villa Normande houses in America, see Sarah Bradford Landau, "Richard Morris Hunt, the Continental Picturesque, and 'The Stick Style,' " *Journal of the Society of Architectural Historians* 42 (October 1983): 272–89.

### 3. To Become an Architect

26 In addition, McKim worked on: After the death of H. R. Hitchcock, I found in his files a set of blue index cards with notes on McKim's early commissions. Hitchcock probably took these notes in the 1920s during conversations with C. H. Walker, who was in the McKim office in these years and was Hitchcock's drawing instructor at Harvard. The information might also have come from W. King Covell, who while a student at Harvard seems to have spoken with W. B. Bigelow in Cambridge. Bigelow spent his final years in a boardinghouse in Cambridge, where several young students of architecture spoke with him, including Covell and Lewis Mumford.

30 With such a success: These early jobs were all domestic. First came a house for Mr. Criss in Miller McKim's area of New Jersey, Orange; another commission came from a Harvard friend, Joseph Sargent, in Worcester, Massachusetts. Sargent's father, a well-off physician, had presented his son with land just outside Worcester, and the latter called in McKim to design his first house. The Sargent house is gone, and only a drawing of the stair hall survives. The house was described in its day as being extremely odd and irregular, with a very tall and pointed roof; it likely resembled the villas of the coast of Normandy, which McKim had visited three years earlier. We have no description of the Criss house but assume it may have been similarly Norman and tall. Further work in New Jersey followed fast. John Livermore (1838–1925), a banker and broker from New York, began a house at Montclair later in 1872. Two other New Yorkers, the attorney Chauncey Ripley and an unspecified Auchincloss, also asked McKim to build. Ripley's house was in Westfield, where the family owned a large tract of land. The Auchincloss house is unlocated but could be at the Point in Newport. For an image of the stair hall, see Leland M. Roth, *The Architecture of McKim, Mead & White,*

*1870–1920: A Building List* (New York: Garland, 1978), plate 19; for the John Livermore stairwell, see ibid., plate 13. See also the *Architectural Sketchbook,* vol. 1 (Boston: Portfolio Club, 1874).

30 Can this have been the house: The Blake house is the subject of an article by Ann H. Schiller, "Charles F. McKim and His Francis Blake House," *Journal of the Society of Architectural Historians* 47 (March 1988): 5–13. In 1873, a good friend of Joseph Sargent's, Francis Blake of Boston, visited Sargent in his new house and requested a house for himself and his prospective bride in Weston, Massachusetts. Elizabeth Hubbard came from a wealthy family, and indeed her grandfather paid for the house. McKim therefore hoped to make a real name for himself with the Blake house and did every detail here, from bedsteads and bookcases to a Dutch-style settle in the hall. At this stage in his career, McKim believed fervently in the concept of fully designed artistic house. He would happily give furniture design over to White and Francis Bacon, as architect-designed "art furniture" became a bore to the client. The Blake house, now demolished, seems to have been a rather typical wooden house of the period, distinguished by vast, steep roof areas and some fanciful circular holes in the wooden trim.

32 A formal engagement between: The only letter we have from Annie to Charles was written from Paris, which she thought the only place appropriate for her declaration of love for him: "Far from forgetting my promise for these last five months I have been wandering over the world in search of a place good enough to write you from." The curious letter of October 13, 1873, now in the New York Public Library McKim Collection, contains some early misgivings that she will be able to live up to his standards. Her uneasiness reflects Charles's constant striving for perfection. One wonders if Annie, even then, young as she was, sensed that the two were incompatible.

32 Miller McKim was buried: There are no Whites in Rosedale today.

## 4. THE MARRIAGE AND NEWPORT

33 Annie was a beautiful bride: The James Morse Diaries at the New-York Historical Society offer the only known account of Annie and her family. Annie had attended the Morse and Rogers School, a private classical academy run by James Herbert Morse, who graduated from Harvard in 1859. Morse wrote verse and was active in New York City social circles from 1863 until his death. Morse began the school in 1868. Annie was likely an early and prized student. Like McKim, the Bigelows had spent time in France. The family were from Massachusetts, but had traveled to Paris to join an uncle, Dr. Samuel Lee Bigelow, who had studied and then settled in Paris. Dr. Bigelow married Lucy Barton, a sister of Annie's mother in Worcester, Massachusetts, in 1834. The Barton family liked to claim a link to Clara Barton. A Barton had married a Rotch, and it was through this connection McKim and Annie came to be introduced back in the late 1860s, when Will Davis was reported to be "sweet" on the young girl. Dr. Bigelow returned to the United States as a brigade surgeon in the Civil War and died at Hagerstown, Maryland, in 1862.

41 "unnatural acts": Rhode Island Divorce Records.

## 5. MCKIM AND MEAD IN THE EARLY YEARS

45 McKim's two role models: Landau, "Richard Morris Hunt," pp. 272–89.

48 Since Howells was connected: The photo album was given to the Society for the Preservation of New England Antiquities. The Colonial Newport book project probably

failed when Mead's uncle, Edwin Doak Mead, who had been a principal at Ticknor & Fields, left to go to Europe in 1875.

48 The Howellses did not remain: For a picture of Redtop, see Leland M. Roth, *McKim, Mead & White, Architects* (New York: Harper & Row, 1983), plate 33.

49 As a result of their outrage: The Dunn Diaries are in the Newport Historical Society, Newport, R.I.

50 As the exclusions removed: In their search for meaning in form, the young English architects selected a time period then attracting French painters as well. To the Second Empire the eighteenth century was the high point of recent French history. The Impressionist painters turned to a study of eighteenth-century French Rococo landscapes in their work.

50 The building material favored: Indeed, the Channel waterfront districts of cities such as Bremen were filled with gable-fronted houses then being demolished. The gable was associated with the commercial districts of England's trading partners. A characteristic of nineteenth-century architecture was the assembling of elements of older architecture into "modern" buildings. In the mid-century the High Victorian Gothic did not replicate the past in an exact sense. The Queen Anne was rather like the High Victorian Gothic of a generation earlier—a new style that was a mishmash of details from the more recent and local past.

50 A mysterious figure, Remigio Laforte: Christopher Gray, "Streetscapes: The Dickerson Houses; By McKim, Mead & . . . Who?" *New York Times,* June 9, 1991.

50 As for the exterior the Dickerson house: Montgomery Schuyler, "Recent Building in New York, III," *American Architect and Building News* 9 (April 23, 1881): 196.

## 6. STRATTON AND WELLS

53 "Friend Stratton": Louis Sullivan, *The Autobiography of an Idea* (New York: Press of the American Institute of Architects, 1924), p. 190.

## 7. STANFORD WHITE

62 "dear little monkey": Richard Grant White to his wife, letter of July 1852, in Richard Grant White Papers, New-York Historical Society.

65 George Templeton Strong, the great diarist: George Templeton Strong, *The Diary of George Templeton Strong,* ed. Allan Nevins and Milton Halsey (New York: Macmillan, 1952), pp. 147, 163, 425.

65 "in some respects": Julian Hawthorne, *Shapes That Pass: Memories of Old Days* (Boston and New York: Houghton Mifflin, 1928), p. 101.

65 Julian Hawthorne remembered: Ibid.

71 Everyone, he told us: Conversation with Sarah Bradford Landau some thirty years ago.

72 William Maxwell Evarts: Evarts was a partner of Charles E. Butler, who had put together Miller McKim's Freedman's Association.

72 "devouring love of ice cream": Augustus Saint-Gaudens, *The Reminiscences of Augustus Saint-Gaudens* (London: Andrew Melrose, 1913), vol. 1, p. 160.

73 After a while, Rutan reports: Letter of August 17, 1872, Charles H. Rutan Papers, Archives of American Art, Smithsonian Institution, Washington, D.C.

74 It would seem that George Bliss: George Bliss Family Papers, Manuscripts Division, New-York Historical Society.

79 Although a case has been made: The main gable might be a bit more horizontal than

those in Shaw's houses and thus suggestive of an American context. But this is the Shavian house in the United States. It opens the door to the development of an updated wooden vernacular architecture for resort communities, which would give McKim and White their identity as first-rate designers. For a study of the Watts Sherman house as a Colonial model, see Jeffrey Karl Ochsner and Thomas Hubka, "H. H. Richardson: The Design of the William Watts Sherman House," *Journal of the Society of Architectural Historians* 51 (June 1992): 121–45.

## 8. WHITE IN EUROPE

82   this was most likely his first trip: In one letter, McKim refers to crossing the Atlantic four times, which is confusing. Was McKim referring to this trip in the summer of 1878 as the third and fourth voyage, or did he go to Europe another time? It became customary about this time for well-off couples to make a wedding trip to Europe. It is possible McKim and Annie did take such a voyage, but with the poor economic times in 1874, it does not seem likely. McKim's letters of the 1870s are lost, so we have no way of knowing if he had crossed the ocean one time more before he set out on the *Periere*.

83   "As far as pictures go": Letter of July 30, 1878, in Claire Nicolas White, ed., *Stanford White: Letters to His Family* (New York: Rizzoli, 1997), p. 44.

84   Robert Lenox Kennedy: Robert Lenox Kennedy was a nephew of James Lenox, who gave New York the Lenox Library. Stratton, who was with Hunt while the Lenox Library was being built at Fifth Avenue and Seventieth Street, likely then met Kennedy, whose wife was a Philadelphian from the Wurts family. It is possible that Stratton knew the Wurtses, as his maternal grandmother was a figure in a similar set in Philadelphia.

84   "I wish I felt sure": Letter of November 21, 1878, in Nicolas White, *Stanford White: Letters,* p. 70.

87   The thin, rawboned Boston woman: See ibid., pp. 32–81, for selection of White's letters. The letters are part of the collection of the late Robert and Claire N. White. The letter quoted here is from November 21, 1878, p. 75.

90   "I am sure that she": Ibid.

92   "draw like a house afire": Moore, *McKim,* p. 46.

## 9. THE BUTLERS, THE SMITHS, AND THE STEWARTS

102   "Items were chosen": G. W. Sheldon, *Artistic Houses* (New York: D. Appleton, 1883–84; rpt. New York: Benjamin Blom, 1971), p. 7.

106   The Tuckermans had been friendly: But the Tuckermans were also friends of the Bigelows, which put relations with McKim under strain when Annie initiated the painful divorce. After the divorce they may have stayed closer to the Bigelows than to McKim, as there are no further commissions. When Annie married the Reverend Day, she named one of her sons for a Tuckerman.

109   The Tenth Street Studio Building: Annette Blaugrund, *The Tenth Street Studio Building: Artist-Entrepreneurs from the Hudson River School to the American Impressionists* (Southampton, N.Y.: Parrish Art Museum, 1997).

113   McKim surely preferred the anonymity: This information comes from the P. H. Butler diaries and papers, private collection, New York. I am deeply grateful to Madge Huntington Cooper for giving me the privilege of reading this wonderful collection.

114   The Smiths are the ancestral family: Prescott Hall Butler was sent to study with Judge

Smith by his father in the early 1870s. Smith was known to the Butlers in two ways. Judge Smith had gone to Yale in 1832 with both Samuel J. Tilden and William M. Evarts. Evarts was, of course, the early patron of Saint-Gaudens and a partner in Butler's law firm. The family Smith was also well known to the Butlers as Mrs. Smith and Prescott Hall Butler's mother were Clinches.

114 The next daughter, Louise: The couple would move to a Chicago suburb. The second daughter, Kate, deeply devoted to the Episcopalian faith, would marry Reverend Wetherill. A son, Lawrence Smith, would go to West Point, where he died in April 1868. A second son, James Clinch Smith, was a bit of a problem; he was unable to sustain a career, which led to a falling out between Judge Smith and his surviving son, who would live in New York and Europe. Another daughter, Ella Batavia Smith, would marry a member of the distinguished Irish American family the Emmets, while one young daughter, Bessie, remained at home.

117 Judge Henry Hilton: Although Hilton was briefly, in 1859, a judge in the Court of Common Pleas, he used the title throughout his life. Since he was so bad at business and regarded as corrupt within the family, the word "Judge" was used almost humorously.

118 her trust in Hilton was mistaken: Mrs. Stewart's brother, Charles P. Clinch, who had lived in Staten Island until Mr. Stewart's death, had been given a house on Stewart property at 3 East Thirty-fourth Street, which had been fitted out with furnishings from Stewart's store. Clinch lived well briefly, then died, leaving Mrs. Stewart fully in Hilton's clutches.

119 In a letter home from France: Letters in the collection of Robert and Claire N. White.

123 Whatever idea White presented: Many of the letters are in Nicolas White, *Stanford White: Letters.* The hacienda has long since fallen to ruin.

## 10. JOE WELLS

124 Those who worked with him: H. Van Buren Magonigle, "A Half Century of Architecture," *Pencil Points* 4 (May 1934): 224. The recollections of the full circle of artists all stress Wells's important role, including the memoirs by Saint-Gaudens, Will Low, Royal Cortissoz, and the architects Magonigle, E. Swartwout, and E. P. Yorke. Magonigle (p. 223) quotes McKim as saying in 1894 that he owed more to and had learned more from Wells than any other source. Magonigle refers to members of the firm as "all four partners" (p. 224), which clearly includes Wells as an equal.

125 Walker believed that these exquisite works: C. Howard Walker, "Joseph M. Wells," *The Architectural Record,* July 1929.

125 He attributes the great decade of design: H. R. Hitchcock, "Frank Lloyd Wright and the 'Academic Tradition' of the Early 1890s," *Journal of the Warburg and Courtauld Institutes* (January–June 1944): 52–53.

128 Wells was the arbiter of quality: Magonigle tells the tale of the chenille monkey in "A Half Century of Architecture," p. 224. The Parthenon story appears in many places, including Charles C. Baldwin, *Stanford White* (1931; rpt. New York: Da Capo Press, 1976), p. 357.

129 the Sanitary Fair: The Sanitary Fair began with the idea of providing fabric for bandages but grew to more general troop support.

132 The Union League Club façade: This suggestion comes from Andrew Saint, who notes that the École des Beaux-Arts building by Félix L. J. Duban (1797–1870), a French architect, is an early example of the neo-Renaissance. Wells drew the École at about this time.

133 "Italian architecture is great": The surviving letters from Wells to Stanford White and the office are now in the McKim, Mead & White Collection, New-York Historical

Society. This particular letter is dated January 18, 1881. Many were of a more personal nature and were likely thrown away by Lawrence Grant White in the early 1930s. Wells seems to have written a letter to White from the Parisian demimonde, which has vanished. Some of the more neutral letters are reprinted in Baldwin, *Stanford White,* pp. 366–67. The early days of Wells in Paris are chronicled in the diaries of Alexander Wadsworth Longfellow, now in the collections of the Longfellow National Historic Site, Cambridge, Mass. My thanks to L. Spurgin for reading these letters for me. Wells seems to have been in Paris from July 1880 to Christmas of that year.

## 11. THE SUMMER HOUSE AND THE SEASIDE HOUSE

135 Among the vernacular European prototypes: Hunt built chalets on this model in Newport, and Charles W. Clinton, Leopold Eidlitz, and others created similar designs for Rhode Island and New Jersey resorts. The Norman and vernacular chalet styles went out of fashion about the time Richardson and McKim, Mead & White began to design cottages, but the same kind of wraparound porch and high pointed roofs characterize Richardson's early Andrews house at Newport, which both McKim and White helped to design.

136 McKim added another porch: The porch feature of the new seaside-cottage style was also used by McKim in his bigger commissions at Elberon in 1876. At the large Moses Taylor house, he subsumed a double-decker porch under a great round arched screen with prominent gables.

137 Bishop Berkeley's house: For a picture of this house, see Vincent J. Scully Jr., *The Shingle Style and the Stick Style: Architectural Theory and Design from Downing to the Origins of Wright,* rev. ed. (New Haven, Conn.: Yale University Press, 1971), plate 15.

137 Although the Francklyn cottage: There is a small illustration of the Queen Anne detail of the Francklyn house in the article by M. G. Van Rensselaer, "American Country Dwellings II," *The Century Magazine* 32 (May 1886): 216.

139 The house was entered: A latticed porte cochere announced the entry, beyond which were a library and parlor. The Norman turret to the right (north) of the entrance housed the staircase and included what was probably the first La Farge window in McKim's houses. A long, low service wing extended northward in a straight line from the public rooms to include a kitchen with a large open walkway for summer ventilation. As the house might be used in the early fall, five chimney stacks provided a good number of fireplaces, but the house would close for the winter once the weather really became cold.

142 Commissions at Lenox included: The Samuel G. Ward house interiors are illustrated in Van Rensselaer, "American Country Dwellings II," pp. 206–8. More interiors are in M. G. van Rensselaer, "American Country Dwellings I," *The Century Magazine* 32 (May 1886): 15–16.

146 The Newcomb house at Elberon: Interiors of the Newcomb house can be found in Van Rensselaer, "American Country Dwellings II," pp. 210–15.

150 Villard is said to have threatened: Richard O'Connor, *The Scandalous Mr. Bennett* (Garden City, N.Y.: Doubleday, 1962).

152 The house fittingly was called Stone Villa: There is an image of Stone Villa in the *American Architect and Building News,* June 10, 1882. It is likely Bennett had the Philadelphia architect Wilson Eyre decorate the dining room in 1882, as Eyre was going into practice on his own. Like Bennett, Eyre had a caustic wit and had spent much of his youth in Europe, where the two may have met.

154 By then the lawns: Mrs. Van Rensselaer would devote pages to the Newport Casino in

her series, M. G. Van Rensselaer, "Recent Architecture in America," *The Century Magazine* (July 1884): 327–34.

158   King hired the local firm, the Masons: Just south of Kingscote was a stone house built by the Masons on which McKim, Mead & White spent seventeen thousand dollars in 1882 for Frederick W. Stevens (1839–1928). What they did is difficult to determine. It was probably a refitting of the interior. Stevens was an attorney in New York who inherited well from his mother, who was a Gallatin, and became a trustee of the Metropolitan Museum of Art. He seems to have no intimate connection to the architects.

164   As the house neared completion: Bell's younger brother, Louis, a stockbroker in New York, would hire Sidney Stratton to help him with his country house in Cove Neck on Long Island.

164   The Bell house was begun: Large porches—one rectangular, the other a double-decker with a great cone cap—fulfill the breeze-catching function of the cottage. The play of rectangular and round shapes in these open porches balances the Bellevue Avenue face of the house. The porch has an exotic element in the form of bamboo-like posts holding up the roof, an unusual piece of whimsy.

Colonial features abound in the house, from Stanford White's signature double door at the entry to an even-height triple window in the southern gable. The overall asymmetry and texture of the wooden elements give yet more of a Colonial American feeling. Small windowpanes in the sash windows evoke the days when handmade small areas of glass were obligatory, before plating processes made large sheets of glass available. Here was a touch of the "olde fashioned" style used widely in the Queen Anne movement in England. The window areas also have shutters, which help form the pattern of the main façade of the house.

166   The Colman house: A photo of the Samuel Colman house appears in Antoinette F. Dowling and Vincent J. Scully Jr., *The Architectural Heritage of Newport, Rhode Island, 1640–1915* (New York: Bramhall House, 1967), p. 206.

171   Clearly the date here: On the other hand, McKim may have met with Henry Duveen earlier than 1877, as one cannot guess where else McKim could have found the Dutch tiles he used in his Colonial-style restorations of the Robinson, Hunter, and Dennis houses in Newport. These restorations also feature "Colonial" chairs, which have many similarities to the reproductions Duveen was bringing in from Paris. Is it not possible that McKim bought the tiles and chairs from Duveen?

171   Carlhian records do not support: Colin Simpson, *Artful Partners* (New York: Macmillan, 1986), p. 20. The Getty Special Collections now own the Carlhian record books, and there is no attribution to Goelet. Carlhian was from Brittany. Could the Breton bed panels at the Bell house be his?

178   the ocean house of the Cowdins: The Cowdin house is depicted in Scully, *The Shingle Style,* plates 144 and 145.

## 12. THE SUBURBAN HOUSE

181   The Chapins, who were well established: Thanks to Robert Owen Jones for information about the street names in Providence.

182   Her championing of the firm's work: M. G. Van Rensselaer championed the work of the young firm in her series in *The Century Magazine* from 1884 to 1886.

183   The rich, warm woods used: Francis R. Kowsky, "The Metcalfe House: A Building in the 'Early Colonial' Style by McKim, Mead & White," *Little Journal,* Society of Architectural Historians Western New York Chapter, November 1980.

## 13. CITY HOUSES

185  "mad orgy of bad architecture": Schuyler, "Recent Building in New York III," p. 196.

185  White arranged for his old mentor: *New York Sun,* January 14, 1883, p. 2. See also M. G. Van Rensselaer, "Recent Architecture," *The Century Magazine* (March 1886): 681–84.

188  It was said that Charles McKim: Wayne Andrews, *Architecture, Ambition and Americans* (1947; New York: New York Free Press of Glencoe, 1955), p. 197.

190  The Winans house retains: The château tower there takes an off-center position and has slightly different heraldic and shell panels in the gables of the dormer windows and under the roof cap. There is no projecting entrance porch, a feature better suited to Massachusetts, where the weather is nastier. Instead, the entry consists of a simple arch in the brownstone base.

## 14. THE END OF THE PICTURESQUE

197  His widow and children: Letter to White, Osborn File, McKim, Mead & White Collection, New-York Historical Society.

197  The Osborn house itself: My thanks to Vanessa Virgintino for searching the Mamaroneck Beach & Yacht Club for remaining portions of the Osborn house in the summer of 1999.

## 15. SUCCESS

199  Prescott Butler and his wife: Letters of Prescott Hall Butler, Collection of the New York Genealogical Society, New York.

200  His base for the Farragut statue: The fireplace survives in a private collection. For a photograph, see the catalogue by Ronald G. Pisano, *The Tile Club and the Aesthetic Movement* (New York: Harry N. Abrams, 1999), and Gordon Hendricks, *The Life and Work of Winslow Homer* (New York: Harry N. Abrams, 1979), illustration 195.

203  "congenital dislike for eating in the club": Prescott Hall Butler letters, box 3, private collection. The letter quoted here is from April 1885.

205  The letters between the two: Letters in Stanford White press books, Avery Architectural Library, Columbia University, were heavily edited, and some were removed from the books, but a number of White's letters to Saint-Gaudens survive in the Saint-Gaudens Papers, Dartmouth College Library Collection. The letter of December 15, 1898, addresses Saint-Gaudens as "Beloved beauty" and contains the phrases "once more and for the 5999th time you can kiss me." See reel 14, March 20, 1894, frames 7, 148, 222, Saint-Gaudens Papers. Frame 222 has a caricature of Saint-Gaudens with his arms out and White running to him, addressed as "beloved."

205  Gus, happy about White's improved temperament: Nicolas White, *Stanford White: Letters,* pp. 123–26, for White's letters to Bessie on the trip.

206  "a god forsaken place": Ibid., p. 130.

## 16. STANFORD WHITE GETS MARRIED

207  "who Builds Aright": Paul R. Baker, *Stanny: The Gilded Life of Stanford White* (New York: Free Press, 1989), p. 98.

210  "alone are enough": Letter to Mrs. Prescott Hall Butler (Nellie), May 3, 1884, in Nicolas White, *Stanford White: Letters,* p. 134.

211  In *The Century* of April 1884: Open Letters, "Music in America," *The Century Magazine*

(April 1884): 948–54. R. G. White's situation was so strangely impecunious that around 1884, probably during the summer months when Alexina was out of the city, he took a dollar-a-day room in a cheap boardinghouse, likely renting out his own house. He asked his wife not to write to him in the boardinghouse as he did not wish his fellow tenants to know his identity. Letter in the R. G. White Papers, Manuscripts Collection, New-York Historical Society.

211  The Schliemann house has been restored: Nicolas White, *Stanford White: Letters,* p. 136. The earthquake of 1999 damaged the house. I am grateful to Thomaï Serdari for her assistance on the Schliemann house.

212  R. G. White had a large collection: One wonders where the elder White bought the instruments. The first Astor, John Jacob, arrived in the New World with broken musical instruments to sell to Americans. Could any of White's cellos have come from Astor?

## 17. WEDDING BELLS FOR McKIM AND MEAD

220  "whose experience and training": Letters, Charles Rutan Papers, roll 1260. The letters about McKim's possible move to Boston were marked "Strictly Confidential" and mailed from 26 East Thirty-eighth Street.

## 18. THE RAILROAD BARONS

227  "No attempt at ostentation appears": Sheldon, *Artistic Houses,* p. 161. A recent book on Villard paints him in a more flattering light: Alexandra Villard de Borchgrave and John Cullen, *Villard: The Life and Times of an American Titan* (New York: Doubleday, 2001).

228  "I arrived here last Monday": Undated letter (possibly 1883), in Nicolas White, *Stanford White: Letters,* p. 130.

229  The set of pictures reveals: For photographs of the interiors, see Mosette Broderick and William Shopsin, *The Villard Houses: Life Story of a Landmark* (New York: Viking Press, 1980), illustrations on pp. 75 and 84–85.

229  "To all great men": Joseph M. Wells, Day Book, private collection, New York.

229  Wells had surprised both McKim and White: Letter from J. M. Wells to Cass Gilbert, June 30, 1884, Cass Gilbert Papers, Library of Congress. He writes:

> Exteriors: all up and looks quite grand and large about the only building I know of here or in the U.S. since the City Hall which has any scale or largeness . . . I hope that eventually these works will be ascribed to their central author as I do not now think that either White or McKim care a damn about it. It is too difficult in the qualities of a painter to please them . . . I can give almost unqualified praise to White's hall, staircase and dining room . . . [and] Babb's drawing room . . . My own interior work didn't mention side of these. It is not my forte but the three story hall comes out well and is admirable.

230  Wells himself designed: For the full story of the commission, see the sections by Broderick in Broderick and Shopsin, *The Villard Houses,* pp. 21–129.

## 19. SHIFTING DYNAMICS IN THE 1880S

233  Phillips Brooks, the minister there: H. R. Broderick, "Early Medieval Aspects of the American Renaissance in Some New York City Churches of the Late 19th Century," in

*Medievalism in American Culture,* ed. Bernard Rosenthal and Paul E. Szarmach (Binghamton, N.Y.: SUNY Center for Medieval and Early Renaissance Studies, 1987), p. 91.

233   Wells had also traveled in Italy: The destroyed letters would have enlightened us about Wells's travels.

234   "The problem, therefore": Letter of September 7, 1886, Lovely Lane Methodist Church Archives, Baltimore.

235   To Mead, writing at the end of his life: Mead in an exchange with Royal Cortissoz, June 1922, Cortissoz Papers, Yale University, New Haven, Conn.

235   So Charles Mead was able to steer: My thanks to Stephen Bedford for telling me that there was a Mead connection in the Russell & Erwin commission.

236   As the building rose: Pamphlets from Russell & Erwin Company.

236   This detail gives the simple building: The terra-cotta takes the form of round plates placed between the double-story arcades, which comprise the midsection of the building. An ornamental belt course separates the arcaded stories from the top floor of round arched windows. A vast cornice overtops the building and cries out "architecture."

This style of brickwork with Renaissance terra-cotta trim raises the question of Wells's relation to Babb. Could Babb, still sharing rooms at 57 Broadway, have been a party to the Russell & Erwin discussions? The great industrial building Babb & Cook had designed on Duane Street, New York, for Cook's mother's estate holdings was quite similar in appearance. Indeed, both buildings come from the German *rundbogen,* or round-arch, tradition. A plain and economical brick building could be made coherent by means of arched windows linked into an arcade. Such a solution had been used, for instance, by Alfred H. Thorp in his Racquet Club building of 1876, on Sixth Avenue at Twenty-sixth Street (demolished). His arcaded brick commercial architecture was known both to Babb and Cook at Duane Street and to George B. Post. It was Post who took the arcaded brick idiom to its high point in New York with his great brick and terra-cotta Produce Exchange (1881–85), now lost but respected by all aspiring office builders at the time.

237   "all new sensations": Letter of July 30, 1884, in the Cass Gilbert Collection, Library of Congress.

238   "finally in different boats": Ibid.

239   Fifth Avenue was for residential use only: See M. Broderick, "Fifth Avenue: New York, New York," in *The Grand American Avenue 1850–1920,* ed. Jan Cigliano and Sarah Bradford Landau (San Francisco: Pomegranate, 1994), pp. 3–32.

240   As offices would not have been welcome: On both fronts, the upper parts of the elevations were organized by means of triple windows with a curious terra-cotta ornamental rectangle below each triplet. The ornamental panels were to recur in other brick buildings of the next few years, alternating with a nailhead design created by setting the ends of bricks in an angular position. Two square bays extend up the building to the top floor, where they turn into rather jarring terraces covered by a cornice awning supported by paired thin columns. The block then concludes with a deep Italian cornice.

The American Safe Deposit Company and Columbia Bank seems more like Wells's work than White's, with only one clumsy feature on the building—those eighth-floor terraces that jar the viewer. It remained on the corner until the winter of 1913–14.

240   The Phoenix house: For pictures, see *American Architect and Building News,* February 4, 1905, and Roth, *McKim, Mead & White, Architects,* plate 100.

240   The Gibson Fahnestock house: For a picture, see Broderick and Shopsin, *The Villard Houses.* The Fahnestock house was demolished for the Helmsley Palace Hotel.

241   Moderate in height still: The arcade tradition of floors held in subsuming arches had

now fallen to the lowest third of the building, while the middle range of the building took up the theme of windows with panels beneath, with three stories of triple square-headed windows set in three bays toward either street. The use of three as an organizing number here links McKim, Mead & White to George F. Babb. Babb, Cook & Willard had just designed their commercial masterpiece, the De Vinne Press building, which also was organized in triplets. The Goelet office block follows similar thought processes. As is popular in Babb's work, the top story is isolated from the main floors of the building and evenly fenestrated by a row of single windows, with terra-cotta panels like those at the Phoenix house separating the windows. The entire building was crowned with a gloriously complex cornice, removed when the building was doubled years later.

241  The Goelet building: A picture of the Goelet building as originally completed can be found in Benjamin Blom and Leland Roth, *A Monograph of the Work of McKim, Mead & White, 1879–1915,* new ed., 4 vols. in 1 with an essay by Leland Roth (New York: Arno Press, 1977). See also Roth, *McKim, Mead & White, Architects,* p. 120.

243  their five surviving children: The Smith children were Louise, wife of Frank Osborne of Chicago; Kate Annette, who had married the Episcopal minister James B. Wetherill; James Clinch Smith, a bachelor who liked New York and Paris and quarreled with Judge Smith earlier on; Ella Batavia Smith, who had married Devereux Emmet; and Bessie. The sixth Smith child, a boy, Lawrence, had died at school at West Point in 1868.

244  "struggling, squeezing, filthy": Samuel Morton Peto diary, generously shared with me by Hilary Grainger, dean of the London College of Fashion, who will write up the diaries as a book.

## 20. MADISON SQUARE GARDEN

247  an article by George P. Lathrop: George P. Lathrop, "Spanish Vistas," *Harper's Magazine,* August 1882, p. 373.

250  One newspaper account: File of newspaper clippings in the McKim, Mead & White Collection, New-York Historical Society. White surely knew the Eden in Paris and the Alhambra in London.

251  These modest but remarkable tenements: *The Real Estate Record & Guide,* May 2, 1885.

253  The sliding roof: Conversation about theater design with John Earl, British theater historian, July 2005.

254  "shut him up somehow": Baldwin, *Stanford White,* p. 202.

257  He stuffed a substantial amount: The story is retold ibid., p. 278, from the recollection of Edward Simmons.

258  The news accounts of the time: *New York Recorder,* June 13, 1892.

## 21. THE FREE CLASSICAL STYLE

263  It is likely that White had access to: White could well have known Schinkel and his students' work through a Prussian-born New Yorker that his own father was especially likely to have known, Otto Boetticher (1812–?). Boetticher arrived in New York on January 6, 1848, on the *Franklin* with four others with the same surname, probably three children and a brother. Boetticher's occupation was given as economist and his birthplace was listed as Nordhausen. He probably had some military training and had left Prussia for opportunity in the New World as well as to escape the political unrest then sweeping Europe. Boetticher took a studio in New York, where he produced lithographs of military subjects in the city. Boetticher's 1851 painting of the Seventh Reg-

iment Army at Washington Square is very well known and would likely have brought the Prussian into contact with Richard Grant White. He briefly shared the studio with the German architect Charles Gildemeister, who would design New York's Crystal Palace in the year of White's birth. Boetticher served with distinction in the Civil War and was given the rank of lieutenant-colonel in 1865 for "gallant and meritorious conduct." He is well known today for his 1863 picture of a baseball game at a prison in North Carolina. He seems not to have returned to New York after the Civil War, but his son carried on with a pharmacy in Manhattan at 508 Third Avenue.

Boetticher's likely brother Karl (1806–1899) was also born in Nordhausen. He went to the Bauakademie, where Schinkel taught, in Berlin in 1827 and studied the ornamental and structural forms of the Greek temple on Schinkel's advice. In 1868, Karl Boetticher was made the director of the department of sculpture at the Neues Museum in Berlin, where he created the cast collection. Boetticher's work on Schinkel was doubtless known to New Yorkers such as Richard Grant White through his brother. Indeed, White himself may have had in his private library Karl Boetticher's volumes on Schinkel's work and later passed them to Stanford White.

264 The two also knew the work: The Adams were important architects in the second half of the eighteenth century. Their work was widely known in the English-speaking world. A two-volume collection of their work was published in 1773–78 as *The Works of Robert and James Adam;* a third volume was published after their deaths in 1822.

264 There is even a cryptic letter: White would have found a kindred spirit in K. F. Schinkel, who combined great skills as a decorative designer and painter with those of an architect. Schinkel designed a casino in Europe, as White did in Newport, and produced drawings for everything from candlesticks to book covers, showing a versatility that White would emulate. The watercolor White painted for his brother-in-law, Prescott Hall Butler, of their house in St. James has, at the door frame, a curtain rather like a Roman curtain, which might indicate that White was looking at the Schinkel's Römische Bäder (1829–40) at Charlottenhof. One can imagine that White looked at the German book plates and may even have asked for a translation of Schinkel's words in 1886 to write the long justification of his style for the Methodist church, which was sent to Reverend Goucher.

265 The mausoleum remains: White did further work for the Goelet estate in Upper Manhattan in 1896. White built a second-class commercial building and store on Eighth Avenue at 135th Street as well as ten second-class houses on the west side of Eighth Avenue between 135th and 136th Streets. This is close to the area David H. King Jr. was then developing as the King Model properties, or Strivers' Row.

For a photograph of the Hotel Imperial, see Roth, *McKim, Mead & White, Architects,* plate 145.

## 22. THE BOSTON PUBLIC LIBRARY: MCKIM SEARCHES FOR INSPIRATION

268 George von Lengerke Meyer: In 1889, Mr. and Mrs. George von Lengerke Meyer gave a version of the great Copley painting *Watson and the Shark* to the Boston Museum of Fine Arts. The circumstances of the gift are not known, but may reflect the family's recognition that they would be unlikely to have a home in Boston in the future as Mr. Meyer's diplomatic career rose. The museum has no records on the details of this gift.

268 "I tell you, with your temperament": Letter of December 19, 1887, quoted in Moore, *McKim,* p. 65.

272 A certain lack of humor: William H. Jordy, *American Buildings and Their Architects,* vol. III (Garden City, N.Y.: Doubleday, 1972); Roth, *McKim, Mead & White, Architects,* pp. 118–30; Walter Muir Whitehill, *Boston Public Library: A Centennial History* (Cambridge, Mass.: Harvard University Press, 1956).

## 23. THE MEN IN THE OFFICE

274 They greatly admired Joe Wells: The alcove appears not to have been seriously considered, as it does not exist and is not in the annual report. I am grateful to S. Harby and Christina Heuber for their assistance in solving this small mystery. Exchange between Mead and Cortissoz, June 27, 1922, Cortissoz Papers, Yale University.

## 24. CLUB LAND

281 It faintly resembles McKim's Columbia Bank building: Four blind niches flank Palladian windows in the fourth floor of the façade, surmounted by a full band of raised swags that seem out of character on the building. A fifth floor of small rooms is topped by a balustrade rather than a cornice, which is in keeping with Boston tradition but not successful architecturally.

282 The porch area created: The removal of the stoop at the Players is probably the first instance of a stoop being removed from a brownstone in New York City. The goal was to facilitate traffic flow into the club and to create a grander, more public porch. Stoops would be removed widely in New York City in the 1920s, when the brownstones were converted to multiple dwelling units. The stoop cast first-floor rooms into darkness.

282 Letters in the McKim, Mead & White files: The file for the Players exists in the McKim, Mead & White Collection at the New-York Historical Society. There is also a history of the club: Henry Wysham Lanier, ed.,*The Players' Book: A Half Century of Fact, Feeling, Fun, and Folklore* (New York: The Players, 1938).

283 Henry Bacon would also design: McKim, Mead & White Collection, The Players Club file, New-York Historical Society.

283 The house was wired for electricity: McKim, Mead & White Collection, The Players Club file, New-York Historical Society.

288 "White designed it": The Century Association, *The Century, 1847–1946* (New York: The Century Associaiton, 1947), p. 56.

288 La Farge tried to maintain: Letter of July 25, 1893, Century File, McKim, Mead & White Collection, New-York Historical Society.

289 After building a good-sized house: See M. Broderick, "A Place Where Nobody Goes: The Early Work of McKim, Mead & White and the Development of the South Shore of Long Island," in *In Search of Modern Architecture,* ed. Helen Searing (Cambridge, Mass.: Architectural History Foundation, MIT Press, 1982), pp. 185–205.

290 The Robb house: For a picture of the Hampden Robb house, see Roth, *McKim, Mead & White, Architects,* plate 142.

## 25. NEW YORK LIFE INSURANCE BUILDS

292 After having been abandoned: Mary Alice Molloy kindly told me about the video, which has good footage of the building. For Mead and Wells's trip to Kansas City and Omaha, see letter from Mead to Cass Gilbert, April 13, 1889, Cass Gilbert Collection, Library of Congress.

293 As this work was in New York: The two stages of the Plaza Hotel can be seen in Broderick, "Fifth Avenue: New York, New York," figs. 27 and 28.

295 The two firms had created: The two firms may once have been together. Schastey and Pottier & Stymus produced commissions, but the arrangement is unclear.

296 "so much damn bad work": The story is told in Baldwin, *Stanford White,* pp. 358–59, without the interpretation made here.

297 The details of Wells's last days: Ibid., p. 356. Wells was born on March 1, 1853, and died on February 2, 1890.

298 "an architect whose ability": White to Webster Wells, January 31, 1890, Wells file letters M-3, New-York Historical Society; and Cass Gilbert to White, February 11, 1890, frame 335–36, McKim, Mead & White Collection, New-York Historical Society.

298 McKim, far more graciously: Letter of February 27, 1890, McKim Correspondence, Library of Congress. See also WEC (William E. Chamberlain) letter dated February 8, 1890, in *The Nation,* no. 1285, February 13, 1890, p. 130.

298 Only those at the original concerts: Saint-Gaudens wrote some rather ardent phrases in letters to Wells; it is likely that the two had an affair in the mid-1880s. The Saint-Gaudens brothers were members of the Sewer Club, which would have to close its rooms in the Benedick after Wells's death. See frame 508, Stanford White Collection, New-York Historical Society. He wrote Wells, "Mon amoree adore ma belle fille. Je l'aime que toi sut au monde ton beau sourir me fait mourir d'amore." This letter is illustrated with a sketch of Saint-Gaudens carving while naked men play a concert.

298 Charles Howard Walker penned: *The American Architect and Building News* 27 (February 8, 1890): 95, for the obituary. Accounts of Wells's role appear in Royal Cortissoz, *American Architects* (New York: C. Scribner and Sons, 1923), pp. 298–99: "he was both creator and critic, by White's side, the helpful colleague as well as the beloved friend." See also Will H. Low, *A Chronicle of Friendship* (New York: C. Scribner and Sons, 1908). Cortissoz, who had worked in the office during Wells's days, wrote about Wells's role especially in "Some Leaders of Our Architectural Renaissance," *Scribner's Magazine* 86 (July 1929): 105.

298 He remained true to his friend: Walker, "Joseph M. Wells," *The Architectural Record* 29 (1929).

299 Wells's wit was highly regarded: There seems to have been more than one copy of Wells's daybook. These quotes come from a copy of Wells, Day Book, private collection, New York.

## 26. The Office at Work

304 Henry Bacon carried a cutout: P. Baker from Frederick Parsell Hill, *Charles F. McKim, the Man* (Francetown, N.H.: Marshall Jones, 1950), and Philip Sawyer File at the Avery Architectural Library, p. 433, n. 20.

306 Simmons described White: Edward Simmons, *From Seven to Seventy: Memories of a Painter and a Yankee* (New York: Kessinger Publishing, 1922), p. 238.

## 28. The Stewart Bubble Bursts

314 The baronial suburb: Development at Hempstead Plains, which Stewart and his builder-architect John Kellum had renamed Garden City, was, as noted earlier, one of the first suburbs in the United States, predated only by Riverside outside Chicago and the McKim family locality, Llewellyn Park. Stewart and Kellum's evocative place-

name carried the meaning of suburbs and new cities for a century, as everyone dreamed of living in a garden connected to the city by a train. Indeed, when the great urban thinker of the turn of the twentieth century, Ebenezer Howard, returned to Britain, he named his ideal city Garden City, inspired no doubt by the Stewart town, which was begun at the time Howard was living in America.

## 29. THE WORLD OF THE PAST

320  At Yale Whitney made two important connections: Whitney and Dimock, known as Will and Dim, had a remarkable early success in the year of Will's marriage in the famous libel suit of novelist Charles Reade. which the young attorneys found a signal of future success. The chief witness for the case was Richard Grant White, and John La Farge was foreman of the jury. Thus, by 1869, the Russell Sturgis, Richard Grant White circle had already encountered Whitney. Indeed, the prosecutor against Whitney and Dimock was another player in the future story, E. T. Gerry, a Richard Morris Hunt client whose house would abut the Metropolitan Club when Stanford White built the clubhouse. Gerry's wife was a Goelet girl. The number of people in the New York of this period was small enough to reinforce the statement that everybody did know each other. The Whitney family offers more proof of this concept, as Charles T. Barney, the early McKim, Mead & White client and friend, married Whitney's other sister. Barney, another Clevelander then in New York probably knew the Paynes from Cleveland and through them met Whitney.

322  Whitney was able to create: There is a fine biography of Whitney by W. A. Swanberg, *Whitney Father, Whitney Heiress* (New York: Scribner, 1980).

323  It had been built some fifteen years earlier: This was the second Stuart mansion on Fifth Avenue; the first had become the headquarters of the Herter Brothers decorative firm and later an office building, with Stanford White taking on the fourth floor. The second Stuart house had been designed by the prolific German-born architect William Schickel for Mr. and Mrs. Stuart. The primary reception room had been designed by William B. Bigelow right after he left McKim and Mead and was working for the Herter Brothers, then at the height of their fame.

325  White would then not let Bardini: Did White know Acton before he started buying from him at the end of the nineteenth century? Martin Burgess Green, in *Children of the Sun: A Narrative of "Decadence" in England After 1918* (New York: Basic Books, 1976), asserts that White knew and hired the young Acton to work with him at the Chicago Fair in 1892, but this is unlikely, as White seems to learn of Acton later and was not personally active at the Fair. Acton did visit Chicago at the end of the century, when he came to the United States to see a friend from Paris and Florence, Guy Mitchell, who was the brother of his future wife.

325  There was said to be a man in Paris: Books such as Colin Simpson's *Artful Partners: Bernard Berenson and Joseph Duveen* (New York: Macmillan, 1986) discuss Duveen's role in promoting paintings to Americans and indicate the amount of dealer manipulation going on once Americans with big bankrolls appeared on the market. Unfortunately, the lack of sustainable documentation for the assertions made in *Artful Partners* leaves one unable to take the book entirely seriously. See Wayne Craven, *Stanford White: Decorator in Opulence and Dealer in Antiquities* (New York: Columbia University Press, 2005). An active scholar on Gilded Era decorative work is Paul F. Miller of the Preservation Society of Newport County.

325  Entire rooms were taken out: In recent years, Bruno Pons, a fine French scholar-

physician, researched the sale of French interiors and located a number in the United States. Pons's early death may have halted research on the French rooms exported abroad, but it is hoped that future scholars will take up the study.

## 30. BACK AT THE OFFICE

331 There is a painting of the *Namouna:* For the illustration, see *The Century Magazine* 24 (August 1882): 605–7.

334 To skeptics, Bennett's selection: O'Connor, *The Scandalous Mr. Bennett,* p. 223. Books on Bennett and his sacred cows include Don C. Seitz, *The James Gordon Bennetts: Father and Son, Proprietors of the* New York Herald (Indianapolis: Bobbs-Merrill, 1928), and Albert Stevens Crockett, *When James Gordon Bennett Was Caliph of Bagdad* (New York and London: Funk & Wagnalls, 1926).

337 As the story goes: A file from the Reid era work on Ophir Hall is in the McKim, Mead & White Collection, New-York Historical Society.

338 The workmen thought: Magonigle, "A Half Century of Architecture," p. 117.

## 31. EVARTS, THE BUTLERS, CHOATE, AND BEAMAN

342 By 1886, a small summer artists' colony: Keith N. Morgan, *Charles A. Platt: The Artist as Architect* (Cambridge, Mass.: Architectural History Foundation, MIT Press, 1985), and Virginia Reed Colby and James B. Atkinson, *Footprints of the Past: Images of Cornish, New Hampshire, and the Cornish Colony* (Concord: New Hampshire Historical Society, 1996).

342 At a time when some of his partners: The Blow Me Down Diaries, Dartmouth College Library.

344 Choate and his partners: Choate would precede Whitelaw Reid at the court of St. James. He served with the diplomat Henry White, whose second wife was a neighbor of Choate's in Lenox.

## 32. STANFORD WHITE'S ARTISTS

346 "turning a stable into a high art palace": Pen and ink notation inscribed in the McKim, Mead & White Bill Books, New-York Historical Society.

346 The façade was supposed to contain: Rosamond Gilder, *The Letters of Richard Watson Gilder* (Boston: Reprint Services Corp., 1916).

347 At this time White frequently designed: There is an entire study of frames by Stanford White, many of which survive. See Nina Gray and Suzanne Smeaton "Within Gilded Borders: The Frames of Stanford White," *American Art* 7, no. 2 (1993): 32–45.

348 "I sometimes, think of those scenes": Letter from Dewing to White, February 14, 1895, Stanford White Papers, Avery Architectural Library.

348 There is an interesting exchange: White corresponded with the editors of Harper Brothers about Madison Square Garden. In the course of the exchange he noted that Dewing was a difficult subject for reporters. Letters of July 20 and September 10, 1891, and February 8, 1892, in the Misc. American Harper Brothers Papers, J. P. Morgan Library, New York.

349 There has recently been a revival: Susan Hobbs, *The Art of Thomas Wilmer Dewing: Beauty Reconfigured* (Washington, D.C.: The Brooklyn Museum in association with the Smithsonian Institution Press, 1996).

349 Abbey became engaged: Alan Crawford notes on Broadway, Victorian Society Great Britain walking tour of September 15, 1978. Alan was kind enough to send me a set of the notes, now published as Alan Crawford, *Arts and Crafts Walks in Broadway and Chipping Campden* (Chipping, Campden, U.K.: Guild of Handicraft Trust, 2002). The wife of Abbey is often confused with William Rutherford Mead's sister, who was Mary Noyes Mead. I made the mistake myself and was corrected by Abbey scholar Lucy Oakley, who has done extensive work on Abbey and his wife; I am most grateful to her for correcting my mistaken inference about the two Mary Meads. It was because of Mary Mead Abbey's promotion of the work of Larkin G. Mead that I felt certain Abbey had married Mead's sister Mary. Others probably drew the same conclusion in the nineteenth century.

349 They married in New York: For the Mead genealogy to 1882, with a note on the birth of Mary Noyes Mead, see Oran E. Randall, *History of Chesterfield* (Brattleboro, Vt.: Cheshire, 1882). Mrs. Abbey was a relative of the Scribners on her mother's side, giving her good publishing connections for her husband's work. See the DeWitt C. Lockman Papers, Manuscript Collection, New-York Historical Society.

350 Charles Moore, the biographer of McKim: Charles Moore, *Daniel H. Burnham: Architect, Planner of Cities,* 2 vols. (Boston and New York: Houghton Mifflin, 1921), vol. 1, p. 63.

351 The two had shared: *Some Artists at the Fair: Frank D. Millet, Will H. Low, J. A. Mitchell, W. Hamilton Gibson, F. Hopkins Smith* (New York: C. Scribner and Sons, 1893).

351 When McKim visited: Mary Anderson de Navarro, *A Few More Memories* (London: Hutchinson, 1936), p. 125.

351 Mary Anderson may have brought McKim: The Broadway Colony was the subject of Marc Alfred Simpson's 1993 Yale Ph.D. dissertation. Mary Anderson material can be found in the Robinson Locke scrapbooks, vol. 17, at the New York Public Library Performing Arts branch, and in her book, de Navarro, *Memories.*

351 So Millet's career was forgotten: H. Barbara Weinberg, "The Career of Francis Davis Millet," *Archives of American Art Journal* 17, no. 1 (1977): 2–18; The American Federation of Arts, *Francis Davis Millet Memorial Meeting* (Washington, D.C.: Gibson Press, 1912).

352 Once MacMonnies was settled: Letters from White to MacMonnies referring to experiments of some danger shared by the two men, including an adventure with an Italian "Houri," can be found in the Stanford White press books, Avery Architectural Library, e.g., January 8, 1893, January 30, 1899, and February 26, 1900.

353 White wrote an apologetic note: Stanford White to George F. Babb, November 21, 1890, press book 3, pp. 376–77, Stanford White press books, Avery Architectural Library; Stanford White to Augustus Saint-Gaudens, November 6, 1890, Stanford White papers, Avery Architectural Library.

353 "You will kindly understand": Stanford White letter books, Avery Architectural Library.

353 The monument competition: Stanford White to George F. Babb, November 21, 1890, press book 3, pp. 376–77, Stanford White press books, Avery Architectural Library.

354 The new figure, Fame: Baker, *Stanny,* pp. 195 and n. 20, 432.

## 33. THE METROPOLITAN CLUB

355 the Metropolitan Club: The basic tale of the club is in Paul Porzelt, *The Metropolitan Club of New York* (New York: Rizzoli, 1982).

358 The original plans: The building was to have a solid granite base; the lower third was to be white marble, with the upper two thirds of the four-story building to be clad in white Perth Amboy Terra Cotta Company bricks (although White would convince the building committee to use all marble cladding as the building progressed). The lower third of the building was done in Tuckahoe marble, perhaps even from the quarries owned by the Stewart estate, with the upper floors of Vermont marble. The design for the club was accepted in February 1892. See *New York Herald,* February 11, 1892, and *Leslie's Illustrated Weekly,* February 20, 1892. The New York City Buildings Department opened its file on May 4, 1892, with a list of specifications by William Mitchell Kendall, who had become an assistant to White after Wells's death. During the building of the club, two other assistants would handle most of the work, allowing Kendall to turn his full attention to McKim's projects.

361 The final push was enough: Details on the club suppliers and construction are in Boxes 79, 80, and 82, McKim, Mead & White Collection, New-York Historical Society. Letters concerning the commission are in the Stanford White press books, Avery Architectural Library.

361 James Breese soon became: Breese's father, Lawrence, was a partner of Henry B. Hollins in Hollins's banking and investing company. Indeed, Hollins is doubly connected to McKim, Mead & White as he had worked for Levi P. Morton & Co. before starting out on his own. Hollins would become a client of the office. Indeed, Lawrence Breese and Henry B. Hollins were the employers of Fernando Yznaga, which clearly demonstrates the Stratton-Yznaga connection. The carriage house Stratton built for Breese's sisters indicates the family loyalty to Stratton, but as Stratton's health failed, Jimmy Breese became a close friend of Stanford White.

361 Goelet's wife approached White: Mrs. Goelet's mother was a Phoenix, the sister of Phillips and Lloyd Phoenix, whose fine town house of brick was designed by McKim, Mead & White in 1882. Mrs. Goelet's father was George Henry Warren of Troy, New York. The other children of George Henry Warren and Mary Caroline Phoenix Warren were Whitney Warren, the architect, the wife of William Starr Miller, a sometime client of McKim, Mead & White, and George Henry Warren (II), who in New York ran the family real estate holdings and became a partner of Thomas Fortune Ryan in his brokerage company, Lee, Ryan & Warren.

  The Phoenix family were the heirs to the Stephen Whitney fortune. This Whitney was not connected to William Collins Whitney, but rather a New York City–based real estate and merchandising fortune.

362 In his younger days, Warren had used: Gavin Stamp, "An Architect of the *Entente Cordiale:* Eugène Bourdon (1870–1916)—Glasgow and Versailles," *Architectural Heritage* 15 (2004): 80–116.

## 34. THE ACCOMMODATIONS OF SUCCESS

364 White now proclaimed: On the lack of "dignity" of wooden houses, see letter from White to Royal Cortissoz, March 31, 1892, Stanford White press books, Avery Architectural Library.

366 White's own house: Tragically, the house was soon emptied. It briefly became a club, then was demolished. It lives on in Craven, *Stanford White: Decorator,* pp. 181ff.

368 Tommy Hastings was a recipient: See microfilm in Saint-Gaudens Papers, Dartmouth College Library, and quotes in Baker, *Stanny,* pp. 275–76 and nn. 4 and 5, 442.

368    Hastings was often described: David Gray, *Thomas Hastings, Architect* (Boston: Houghton Mifflin, 1933), pp. 4–9.

368    "the little buzz-saw inside of me": Letter to R. Goelet, December 23, 1892, Stanford White press books, Avery Architectural Library.

## 35. THE WORLD BEGINS TO SPIN

371    For John Cleve Green: A plaque survives in the stacks of the present New York Society Library. The librarian, Mark Piel, kindly brought this to my attention.

372    a small house on Madison Avenue: I could not locate this building. McKim might have meant the Breese carriage house. February 20, 1895, McKim Collection, Library of Congress.

372    On August 22, 1894, McKim wrote: Letter of August 22, 1894, McKim Collection, Library of Congress.

372    In 1895, McKim wrote Stratton: Letter of February 20, 1895, McKim Collection, Library of Congress.

373    In the days after: Letter of November 24, 1909, Sidney Stratton Papers, Louisiana State University Archives, Baton Rouge.

374    White was, as someone put it: Baldwin, *Stanford White,* p. 4.

## 36. THE CHICAGO FAIR

379    Sarah McKim outlived everyone: A few years later McKim's adopted sister, Annie, would fall ill and die. The deaths would continue with his favorite nephew, Lloyd McKim Garrison, a few years further on, followed by Wendell Garrison, Annie's second husband, in 1907.

379    McKim threw himself: Moore, *Burnham,* p. 67. Indeed, Moore met McKim in the cabin and would later write the biographies of both Burnham and McKim.

381    On his return, the pavilion: For an image of the French Academy in Rome, which was McKim's source here, see any good modern guidebook to the city, such as *The Blue Guide.*

382    This exchange reveals: Letter of September 17, 1892, Stanford White press books, Avery Architectural Library.

382    "the greatest assembly of artists": Moore, *Burnham,* p. 47.

382    This was the technique: Saint-Gaudens, *Reminiscences,* vol. 2, p. 282.

383    McKim gave a dinner for Burnham: McKim had worked with Burnham in Chicago on the Fair and recognized how much Burnham had done to be certain the buildings designed by the nonresident architects were carried out as planned. Burnham had virtually lived at the Jackson Park site, braving all discomfort to be sure the goals of the architects were achieved. McKim felt the debt to Burnham and shamed his colleagues into a celebration for the Chicago architect, who seemed pleased by McKim's appreciation.

      Burnham arranged to leave Chicago briefly in late March to come east for the dinner. McKim embarrassed Hunt into taking the role of host after writing him about Burnham's efforts to improve Hunt's Administration building. The guests were the usual group of friends—Saint-Gaudens, Millet, William Dean Howells—and clients such as Henry Villard and the ever-popular toastmaster Joseph Choate. The banquet proved a great success, and helped to establish McKim and his partners as leading figures in the profession, able to host a peer event. McKim was also eager to keep Burnham happy to assist him with the plans for the school in Rome. The banquet was a most flattering tribute to Burnham, who was being thanked by most of the East Coast establishment, even if Stanford White was abroad. See "In Honor of Mr. Burnham," *New York Times,* March 26, 1893, p. 2.

384 His brother was removed: Letters in Stanford White press books, Avery Architectural Library.

## 37. OLD COLLEGES AND NEW BUILDINGS

386 So the two schools had to engage in: Theodore Francis Jones, ed., *New York University, 1832–1932* (New York: New York University Press, 1933), pp. 151–55.

387 The college would purchase: Ibid., pp. 92–118.

387 John Taylor Johnston: John Taylor Johnston's family would often summer in St. James, Long Island, in rental houses, so the Smith girls surely also knew Johnston. Indeed, Johnston's daughter would marry into the Mali family, whose country estate in the Bronx would become the new campus.

388 White considered the Main Building a treasure: Letter of January 26, 1892, Stanford White press books, Avery Architectural Library. The archives at NYU have White's plans for modernizing the old Main Building.

389 True to the principles: The basic story appears in Jones, *New York University.* The argument with MacCracken is in White's letter of January 26, 1892, Stanford White press books, Avery Architectural Library.

394 As fall set in: For the Columbia tale, see Barry Bergdoll, *Mastering McKim's Plan: Columbia University's First Century on Morningside Heights* (New York: Miriam & Ira D. Wallach Art Gallery, 1997), p. 41.

394 Low had staked his reputation: Andrew S. Dolkart, *Morningside Heights: A History of Its Architecture and Development* (New York: Columbia University Press, 1998), p. 136.

395 Further, his generosity in donating: The connection of the gift of the library to Low's mayoral aspirations was first suggested in Francesco Passenti, "The Design of Columbia in the 1890's, McKim and His Client," *Journal of the Society of Architectural Historians* 36 (May 1977): 69–84.

396 The design for the dome: Bergdoll, *Mastering McKim's Plan,* pp. 45–49, has a good discussion of the trials of the domed building, along with good illustrations. See also Hollee Haswell, "Constructing Low Memorial Library: A Chronicle of a Monumental Enterprise," in *Mastering McKim's Plan,* pp. 153–84, for a photographic essay.

396 McKim would wax poetical: Dolkart, *Morningside Heights,* pp. 149–50.

## 38. MCKIM'S NEW YORK CLUBHOUSES

405 McKim was particularly saddened: Letters in McKim Collection, Library of Congress.

## 39. THE AMERICAN SCHOOL IN ROME

406 Even Edith Wharton: Wharton's offers to host dinners in the McKim Collection, Library of Congress.

407 The architect wanted to look over: Letter of September 27, 1895, quoted in Moore, *McKim,* p. 153.

408 Much of McKim's work: The architects were not averse to seriously pushing their friends to speak for their firm when new building projects were proposed for compa-

nies in which those friends had a role. Much of this influence shaping must have been done in person, but a surviving letter of March 11, 1892, in Stanford White press books, Avery Architectural Library, demands that Henry deForest, the firm's friend and former client, use his influence at the Bleecker Bank to send the commission for the new bank branch to the office. The commission did not arrive.

### 40. THE SWAN SONG OF THE WOODEN HOUSE

410 "cousin" Joe Parrish: Saint-Gaudens did a bust of Joseph Parrish in 1881, but this must have been an earlier Joseph Parrish. "Cousin Joe" was close enough to McKim to remember the architect in his will.

411 he would remain in Southampton: For the wooden houses of Southampton, see Helen Searing, ed., *In Search of Modern Architecture: A Tribute to Henry-Russell Hitchcock* (Cambridge, Mass.: Architectural History Foundation/MIT Press, 1982), pp. 185–205.

413 become Box Hill: For pictures of Box Hill, see Samuel G. White, *The Houses of McKim, Mead & White* (New York: Rizzoli, 1998), pp. 118ff.

414 At Box Hill, White toyed with the idea: There is a pencil-annotated photograph of Box Hill in the Stanford White Drawings Collection, Avery Architectural Library. The house name, Box Hill, might come from the local hedges, although there is a hill in England just south of London with the same name.

### 41. ON TOP OF THE WORLD

419 "Astor orphans": The Astor orphans are well discussed in the book by Lately Thomas, *A Pride of Lions: The Astor Orphans* (New York: William Morrow, 1971).

419 In 1887 Archie visited Newport: Donna M. Lucey, *Archie and Amélie: Love and Madness in the Gilded Age* (New York: Harmony Books, 2006).

420 In 1894 White wrote to William H. Russell: Stanford White press books, Avery Architectural Library.

426 Hewitt called Whitney: W. A. Swanberg, *Whitney Father, Whitney Heiress* (New York: Scribner, 1980), p. 90.

428 Curiously, the photo album includes: The house was illustrated in *The Architectural Record* 10 (April 1901): 407ff.; *Architecture* 3 (February 15, 1901): 40–45; *Architects and Builders Magazine* 32 (December 1899): 88–89, for the exteriors; *Architects and Builders Magazine* 33 (June 1901): 321. The McKim, Mead & White photograph album is in the Avery Library. A later account of the house is given in the sale catalogue of January 12–14, 1910, under the auspices of the American Art Association with an introduction by Barr Feree. In 1910 the house had been sold to James Henry Smith, who died soon afterward. "Silent" Smith's widow then sold the house and its contents. The house was demolished in November 1942.

428 In 1901 Henry Adams wrote: Henry Adams's quote is the opening for Aline B. Saarinen's manuscript for a book on Stanford White, which she never completed. The manuscript is in the Archives of American Art along with her notes, some images, and fragments of chapters. Mrs. Saarinen's work would have been a great addition to the scholarship on White, and it is sad that it did not get finished. The actual remark appears in *The Letters of Henry Adams,* ed. Worthington Chauncey Ford, 2 vols. (Boston and New York: Houghton Mifflin, 1930–38), vol. 2, p. 312.

428 The American taste for binge buying: My sincere thanks to Guy Walton for his help in discussing this issue and lending me the great work by the late Dr. Bruno Pons.

430  The boardinghouse was: *New York Tribune,* April 15, 1898.

431  The studio was shared: The building was at 22 West Twenty-fourth Street above F.A.O. Schwarz's toy store. Baker, *Stanny,* p. 289.

431  William T. Partridge recounts: William T. Partridge, "Recollections Concerning Charles Follen McKim," unpublished manuscript in the Avery Architectural Library.

432  Some clients would refuse: Conversation with men who had been in the great offices of the early century organized by Catha Grace Rambusch about 1982. Homer Swanke related a version of the fireplace story to me.

432  Mary Mason Jones had a tall row group: For a photograph, see Broderick and Shopsin, *The Villard Houses,* p. 16.

432  Guests had to ride: See Broderick, "Fifth Avenue," pp. 15–19.

436  White would do an expected: After Hunt's death, the junior Vanderbilts went to the Oelrichses' architect, not the sons of Richard Morris Hunt, then in business on their own for the expansion of Hunt's most famous New York City house.

436  The debt of the design: Mackay house files, New-York Historical Society. There is excellent coverage of the service aspect of the house in Richard Guy Wilson, *Harbor Hill: Portrait of a House* (New York: W. W. Norton, 2008).

437  Mackay complained: Letter of February 24, 1903, in Mackay files, New-York Historical Society.

437  The Mackays got to be the lords: The Mackays lived near Will Whitney, E. D. Morgan Jr., and Cass Canfield in this North Shore golden era. When Whitney passed away, Katherine Mackay had a window made in his honor for her Roslyn Church.

437  It is almost impossible to imagine: Outbuildings of Harbor Hill are still standing. The Mackays' daughter, Ellin, married Irving Berlin, much to the misery of her parents. For an article on the Mackay house richly illustrated with images of the principal rooms, see Lawrence Wodehouse, "Stanford White and the Mackays," *Winterthur Portfolio* 2 (1976): 213–33.

437  The Mackays sent a check: Letter of January 24, 1903, in Mackay files, New-York Historical Society.

437  Though they knew about White's weaknesses: See Ellin Mackay Berlin, *Silver Platter* (Garden City, N.Y.: Doubleday, 1957), for an account of the family. The letter about a special girl is quoted in Baker, *Stanny,* p. 300.

438  After hearing of the fire: Baker, *Stanny,* p. 225.

438  "They're wonderful": Simmons, *From Seven to Seventy,* p. 241.

439  Dick would later claim a family: Letters concerning Dick White may be found both in the Stanford White press books, Avery Architectural Library, and in the University of Virginia file, New-York Historical Society.

440  The "pie girl" dinner: *New York World,* October 13, 1895, p. 29. There are numerous sources for this dinner. One version has Susie Johnson committing suicide a decade later, unable to escape the notorious event.


## 42. MCKIM MEETS HIS DAUGHTER

444  His former partner: Henry W. Taft, *A Century and a Half at the New York Bar* (New York: Private printing, 1938), p. 278.

444  "an almost feminine sensitiveness": John Lambert Cadwalader memorial service, New York Public Library, privately printed, 1914.

444  Cadwalader and McKim's worlds circled each other: How did McKim become friendly

with Cadwalader? In ways far too numerous to count. Probably the two met on Mrs. Bigelow's deck for the literary club meetings. Cadwalader was a close friend of Colonel Higginson and Edith Jones Wharton, who visited the "bully piazza." Edith Jones, soon after her marriage to Teddy Wharton, lived at Pencraig and visited the Newport literary scene. She, McKim, and Cadwalader had known each other since those early days. In 1870, another Cadwalader, Mary, had married Frederic Jones, Edith Jones Wharton's brother. The marriage was not a success, leaving Mrs. Cadwalader Jones, as she called herself, with one daughter, Beatrix Jones, the garden designer, later known by her married name, Beatrix Ferrand.

Cadwalader was a close friend of Joseph Choate, who often joked that he had known McKim for most of his life. Cadwalader was also a close friend of Whitelaw Reid, a client of McKim, Mead & White. Cadwalader was also close to his brother-in-law, Dr. S. Weir Mitchell, who was a client of Saint-Gaudens and would cure the morphine addiction of Amélie Rives.

446    "I shall think of you": Letter to Margaret McKim, August 1, 1900, Moore, *McKim*, p. 284.

446    Cadwalader rented the house: Millden was one of many properties owned by the earl of Dalhousie and rented out for income. Cadwalader may have known the earl's father in Washington, D.C., during his days with President Grant.

447    Every summer McKim would visit: Mark Anthony De Wolfe Howe, *George Von Lengerke Meyer: His Life and Public Services* (New York: Kessinger Publishing, 1920). George Von Lengerke Meyer was a third cousin to his wife, Marion Appleton, through the Cutler family.

447    Another person who was a part: Even Henry White weaves into the story, as his wife, Margaret Rutherfurd, lived next door to the Joneses in Newport before the couple married in 1879. As a young woman, Edith Jones considered Margaret (Daisy) Terry her best friend. Daisy would marry Winthrop Chanler. And Edith became close to John Cadwalader in the 1880s.

447    Edith Jones Wharton swam: The circle of connections did truly sum up Allyn Cox's statement that everyone knew each other. Edith Wharton's mother was a Rhinelander. Mary Rhinelander, Edith's mother's sister, married Thomas Newbold. The next generation of Newbolds were Julia Appleton's best friends and the close relationship with the Newbolds continued for the remainder of McKim's life. McKim would leave Julia's things that he had kept to Mrs. Newbold.

448    So at the 1901 annual convention: Moore, *McKim,* p. 174.

449    "Let me take it down": Ibid., p. 205.

450    McKim had turned his back: Ibid., p. 221.

450    "In these days of miracles": Quoted in Moore, *McKim,* p. 206.

451    Mrs. Roosevelt noted: Moore, *McKim,* p. 55.

451    The connections between McKim and Morgan: Ibid., p. 171.

451    McKim was thrilled: David C. Hammock, *Power and Society: Greater New York at the Turn of the Century* (New York: Russell Sage Foundation, 1982), p. 232.

452    Morgan brought his family: Was Edwin Dennison Morgan a member of that family? The sources on Morgan contradict each other, most agreeing that the Hartford-based E. D. Morgan, whose son's tomb was Stanford White and Saint-Gaudens's first major work, was a cousin, but Vincent P. Carosso, in *The Morgans: Private International Bankers, 1854–1913* (Cambridge, Mass.: Harvard University Press, 1987), p. 73, says that E. D. Morgan was not a relative. For an excellent biography of J. P. Morgan, see Jean Strouse, *Morgan: American Financier* (New York: Harper Perennial, 2000); Strouse confirms that E. D. Morgan was not related to J. P. Morgan.

452  sent off to school in Vevey: Morgan in 1854 may have been the first American to attend school in Vevey, but others followed, beginning with William Henry Vanderbilt's younger son, William Kissam Vanderbilt.

453  Pierpont's first great success: Morgan, with his partner Drexel and then George S. Bowdoin, negotiated the railroad stocks through the 1880s and 1890s in the United States. He saved the Baltimore Garretts in 1887, just as they were building their McKim, Mead & White house, when their business debt almost drowned the B&O line. Morgan ran into other McKim, Mead & White clients during the railroad years, including Victor Newcomb and Villard's German investors from the Deutsche Bank, who held a good deal of Northern Pacific stock.

453  With the great profit: Matthew Josephson, *The Robber Barons: The Great American Capitalists, 1861–1901* (New York: Harcourt Brace, 1934), pp. 290–91.

454  To many, Morgan was a "plunger": Ibid., p. 292.

454  A second song: John K. Winkler, *Morgan the Magnificent: The Life of J. Pierpont Morgan (1837–1913)* (Garden City, N.Y.: Garden City Publishing, 1930), pp. 197–98.

456  McKim wrote an explanatory letter: Letter of December 27, 1902, McKim Collection, Library of Congress.

457  He told Charles Moore: Moore, *McKim*, p. 282.

458  The building of the library: On the seventy-fifth anniversary of the opening of the Morgan Library, William Voelkle curated a fine exhibition devoted to the building. The exhibition of 1981–82 is the best study of the library.

## 43. THE PENNSYLVANIA STATION

459  "I suppose President Cassatt": Moore, *McKim*, p. 273.

460  Perhaps in later years McKim saw: Indeed, beginning in 1902, McKim and Daniel Newhall shared a friend, President Theodore Roosevelt, for whom McKim was doing the White House. Newhall knew Roosevelt and was now closer to the president, as Newhall's eldest daughter, Karoline Nixon, was married to George Emlen Starr, who was related to Roosevelt on the Emlen line. McKim acknowledged his friendship with the two men with a gift. Stanford White had long copied period chairs he purchased. As early as 1889, when White bought an antique chair for Will Whitney, he had Joseph Cabus make copies of the chair for White's own use. McKim followed this lead in 1903 or 1904 by having an old Dutch chair, which he thought dated to 1760, copied twice, giving Roosevelt and Newhall each a copy.

461  The solution seemed: William Couper, *History of the Engineering, Construction and Equipment of the Pennsylvania Railroad Company's New York Terminal and Approaches* (New York: Isaac H. Blanchard Company, 1912), reprinted in Fred Westing, *Penn Station: Its Tunnels and Side Rodders* (Seattle: Superior Publishing Company, 1978).

461  Cassatt contracted more debt: Robert Sobel, *The Fallen Colossus: The Great Crash of the Penn Central* (New York: Weybright and Talley, 1977).

464  Friends tried to help: Thomas S. Hines, *Burnham of Chicago: Architect and Planner* (Chicago: University of Chicago Press, 1974), pp. 237–38.

465  McKim did not look only to Rome: W. S. Richardson, "The Terminal: The Gate to the City," *Scribner's* 52 (October 1912): 401–16.

465  Yet this great moment: Books about the station abound. For a recent work, see Hilary Ballon, *New York's Pennsylvania Stations* (New York: W. W. Norton, 2002). Richardson suffered a broken spine in a horseback-riding accident in Princeton, New Jersey, ending his career. He moved to Rome, where he died in 1921. Laura Chanler White, in a

telephone conversation circa 1980, told me about Richardson's role in the station and his fate. She gave the credit for the station to Richardson.

## 44. THE KING'S MEDAL

467 "I write this": Edwin Austin Abbey letter to McKim, January 22, 1903, quoted in Moore, *McKim,* p. 223.

468 Relieved, Webb cabled McKim: Moore, *McKim,* p. 223.

469 McKim admired and thought Rome appropriate: Ibid., p. 230.

469 "After the Civil War was over": Text of the speech of Joseph Choate, reported in the London *Times,* June 23, 1903.

470 He was up until nearly daylight: Letter to Margaret McKim, July 31, 1903, quoted in Moore, *McKim,* pp. 232–33.

470 The description of the month of celebration: Moore uses these letters in his final chapters of his biography, especially in chap. XVII, "The King's Medal," pp. 223–41.

## 45. THE NEW CENTURY FOR WHITE

472 His pastime of escapist behavior: Numerous versions of the story have appeared, from the memoirs of Evelyn Nesbit to the biography of White by Paul Baker. Several full books have been written on White's personal life in this period, including one by Michael M. Mooney, *Evelyn Nesbit and Stanford White: Love and Death in the Gilded Age* (New York: Morrow, 1976). See also Gerald Langford, *The Murder of Stanford White* (Indianapolis: Bobbs-Merrill, 1962), and Charles Samuels, *The Girl in the Red Velvet Swing* (New York: Gold Medal, 1953). The best resource of contemporary articles can be found in the clippings file of the New York Public Library for the Performing Arts, Theater Collection.

474 James Garland seems to have learned: This account depends on Nesbit's second autobiography, *Prodigal Days: The Untold Story* (New York: Julian Messner, 1934). Nesbit's stories cannot always be taken as truthful.

474 He remarked to McKim: See ibid., pp. 37–38, and an earlier version of the story Evelyn wrote as Evelyn Thaw, *The Story of My Life* (London: J. Long and Co., 1914), p. 66.

475 Evelyn Nesbit was a beautiful young girl: Louise Hall Tharp, *Saint-Gaudens and the Gilded Era* (Boston: Little, Brown, 1969), p. 357.

475 Of course, Hummel's credibility: Richard H. Rovere, *Howe and Hummel: Their True and Scandalous History* (New York: Farrar, Straus, 1947), has an account of Hummel's career. He quotes Hummel as saying, "I am a crook and I'm a blackmailer, but there is one thing about me—I am a neat son-of-a-bitch" (p. 40). Mr. Hummel always dressed in black. Howe and Hummel were thought to be adept at bribing judges and advising clients on how to get away with crimes.

476 There is currently no sign: My thanks to Andrew Saint for driving around St. Ann's Avenue with me in a futile exercise to locate these houses; he also helped me try to locate the Davis house in Brooklyn.

476 Although White knew Dr. Thomas: Research on Dr. Thomas was done in the New York Academy of Medicine Library. See Claude Edwin Heaton, *The New York Obstetrical Society* (New York: New York Obstetrical Society, 1963), pp. 24–26; James Pratt Marr, *Pioneer Surgeons of the Women's Hospital: The Lives of Sims, Emmet, Peaslee, and Thomas* (Philadelphia: F. A. Davis Co., 1957), pp. 123–37; and Thomas's obituary of March 4,

1903, in *The New York Times*, p. 9. Mary Alice Molloy and I exchanged some interesting letters on Dr. Thomas in connection with her research in Chicago.

477 William and Mary Thaw had collected: For the Thaw Collection, see Gabriel P. Weisberg, DeCourcy E. McIntosh, and Allison McQueen, *Collecting in the Gilded Age: Art Patronage in Pittsburgh, 1890–1910* (Pittsburgh: Frick Art and Historical Center, 1997).

478 People did hear parts: A good account of Thaw in these days can be found in *The New York Times*, July 1, 1906, pp. 1–2.

478 The girls went to White's party: *New York Times*, February 8, 1907, p. 3.

## 46. PAYNE WHITNEY'S HOUSE

480 By 1906, Helen Hay Whitney's patience: In a letter from Helen Hay Whitney written from Colonel Payne's estate, Greenwood, in Thomasville, Georgia. The undated letter, from the early spring, is in the Payne Whitney file, New-York Historical Society. See also Kathleen Weil-Garris Brandt, "A Marble in Manhattan: The Case for Michelangelo," *The Burlington Magazine* (October 1996): 644–59; and Chrisopher Gray, "A Cupid Renews Interest in a 1909 Mansion," *New York Times*, February 4, 1996, Real Estate section, Streetscapes column, p. 7. The figure is on view at the Metropolitan Museum of Art, 2009–10.

481 After Cook's death, the Lyons house: Letter of March, 30, 1906, from B. L. Fenner to S. White, Payne Whitney file, New-York Historical Society.

484 White called himself a poor churchman: Winter 1889, press book 2, p. 282, Stanford White press books, Avery Architectural Library.

485 Robert W. De Forest wrote: Madison Square Presbyterian Church file, box M-20, 1968, New-York Historical Society.

485 White justified his design: Broderick, "Early Medieval Aspects," pp. 89–114.

485 The artist Louis Comfort Tiffany: Roosevelt and Tiffany were neighbors in their homes at Oyster Bay Cove.

485 "the final outcome": "Dedication of The Madison Square Presbyterian Church: Sunday, October Fourteen Nineteen Hundred And Six," *Morning and Evening Details*, Madison Square Presbyterian Church, New York, 1906, p. 16.

## 47. THE GILDED AGE TARNISHES

488 The story, as told by Rita da Costa Lydig: Rita Lydig, *Tragic Mansions* (New York: Boni & Liveright, 1927), p. 44. Rita da Costa Lydig could well have been the beautiful belle of a ball at Sherry's as seen in Charles Dana Gibson images. A teenager in the Edwardian era, she grew up in New York and married at a young age the rather strange William Earl Dodge Stokes, who claimed to be of Spanish descent, but may have been from a Sephardic Jewish family. Later, as Mrs. Philip Lydig—she had remarried—Rita Lydig became a central figure in New York society. Mrs. Lydig was very smart and a good social observer. Her 1927 book *Tragic Mansions* reveals the sadness within the glitter. Lydig omits the names of the people she discusses, but her stories have all the details needed to clearly identify the participants. This excellent and little-known book fits in well with Edith Wharton's books, which veil the real stories in made-up names. Both women understand the nuances of the era very well. Lydig is at her best on the fashionable churches of the day as being merely social clubs where the members can feel complacent and superior with little interest in the institution.

488 The sale was to be held: The dates of the sales were determined by Baker, *Stanny*, p. 346.

489 Finally, at breakfast: Moore, *McKim*, pp. 295–96.

489 He estimated his losses: Letter of April 29, 1905, Stanford White press books, Avery Architectural Library.

489 White rewrote the agreement: Baker, *Stanny*, pp. 348–49. The details of the new agreement are not fully revealed in the office papers.

490 The trip was sponsored: White was able to dismiss contemporary French painting, although Colonel Payne personally bought two Monets for his own house. One can imagine White and Payne having a good-natured discussion about French painting in Paris during that summer of 1905. White's opinion on contemporary French art can be found in his September 5, 1905, letter to Saint-Gaudens, Stanford White press books, Avery Architectural Library. Colonel Payne's purchases are noted in a letter to Payne from the Durand-Ruel Gallery of August 7, 1902, in the Payne Whitney files, New-York Historical Society. The Monet came to under seven thousand dollars with customs and shipping.

491 Watson, a Bostonian: The story of Watson's sale to White in the year of the Columbian Exposition has been retold in many ways, including a version that has Watson sending his nephew to the Exposition as an assistant to Stanford White. See Green, *Children*, p. 95. White was not active in the creation of the Fair; McKim and Millet were the men on the spot. Watson is buried in the same cemetery in Florence as the Actons and the Mead brothers.

491 He also cautioned Acton: The letters to Acton in White's letter books give one side of the relationship. A telling study could be made of the Bardini-Acton-White triangle.

491 "nor do I buy them": Letter to Arthur Acton, December 16, 1897, Stanford White press books, Avery Architectural Library.

491 White's shopping trip cost: The documentation for the Payne Whitney house is rich and would make a study of White's habits in decorating. Jeni Sandburg began such a study in 1996. The attribution of a work bought by White from Bardini for the fountain at the Payne Whitney house has opened up interest in the house again. There are many intriguing aspects of the story, such as White's purchase of a partial figure of a young boy, which Professor Kathleen Weil-Garris Brandt of New York University and others have tentatively identified as possibly an early work by Michelangelo. The papers for the house list a Clouet portrait of Henry II and a Velázquez. On the Michelangelo attribution, see Peter Plagens, "Miracle on Fifth Avenue," *Newsweek*, February 5, 1996, p. 62; on the house, see Gray, "A Cupid Renews Interest." After the initial publicity, the Venetian Room, one of White's final projects, was reinstalled in the house (*New York Times*, March 12, 1998, House & Home section cover story). For a scholarly discussion of the Michelangelo statue, see Brandt, "A Marble in Manhattan," pp. 644–59.

492 Wayne Andrews quoted White: Wayne Andrews, *Architecture, Ambition, and Americans* (New York: Free Press, 1978), p. 196. The interiors were illustrated in *Architecture* 32 (April 15, 1910).

493 Paul Baker correctly notes: Baker, *Stanny*, p. 354.

493 In the spring of 1906: The Tiffany store at Thirty-seventh Street and Fifth Avenue is extant. The site has an interesting history. Paran Stevens, the hotelier, had purchased the property in 1863 and demolished a thirty-year-old wooden frame house. Six years later, Stevens bought the adjacent property at 2 East Thirty-seventh Street from the father of William R. Ware, the director of Columbia University's school of architecture. The elder Ware was a real estate figure in the mid-century city. Stevens did not

live long enough to develop the property as he must have planned to do; all he did was convert the Fifth Avenue property, which was a stable, into a greenhouse. (As difficult as it may be to imagine today, at that time Fifth Avenue frontages did have stables on the property.) The local florist of fashion, Siebrecht & Sons, used the greenhouse until 1901, when Stevens's widow sold the property to another hotel man, George C. Boldt, manager of the Waldorf-Astoria just down the street. Boldt did not use the property either; he sold it to Tiffany in 1903.

494 White had come to the theater: This version of the story is based on the Stanford White Murder files, New York Public Library for the Performing Arts, Theater Collection, and accounts in Baker, *Stanny,* and Mooney, *Evelyn Nesbit and Stanford White.*

498 A reply was sent: Letters in the A. C. Thaw file, McKim, Mead & White Collection, New-York Historical Society.

499 Some 160 books: Baker, *Stanny,* from A. Saarinen's work in the Archives of American Art, p. 375.

500 The funeral was held quickly: The death of White and the funeral were fully reported in the papers from June 26 through June 29, 1906. This account depends heavily on from the *New York Times* and *New York Tribune.*

500 His letter clearly refers: The letters to McKim are in the McKim papers, Library of Congress; Harry White's letter is dated July 6, 1906.

501 Colonel Mann of *Town Topics: Town Topics,* June 28, 1906, p. 1.

501 In 1908 McKim would write: Letter of June 18, 1908, in McKim, misc. M3, in the collections at the New-York Historical Society.

501 "a most kindhearted": Richard Harding Davis, "Stanford White," *Collier's,* August 4, 1906, p. 17.

501 Saint-Gaudens was asked: Richard Watson Gilder, "Stanford White," *American Institute of Architects Quarterly Bulletin,* July 1906, p. 104. See also Saint-Gaudens, *Reminiscences,* vol. 2, p. 252; letter from Saint-Gaudens to A. Garnier, July 6, 1906, in Dartmouth College Library, Saint-Gaudens's papers, reel 7, home 201: "Un idiot qui tue un homme de génie pour une femme avec un visage d'ange et le coeur d'un serpen."

## 48. THE TRIAL OF THE CENTURY

503 Harry and his mother refused: The literature on the murder and trial is voluminous. In addition to the newspapers, the best collection of material is in the New York Public Library for the Performing Arts. The collection has at its center the great clippings volumes of Robinson Lock, which are invaluable for research. Also valuable are Evelyn Nesbit's two autobiographies; a book by the publicist Benjamin H. Atwell, *The Great Harry Thaw Case; or, A Woman's Sacrifice* (Chicago: Laird & Lee, 1907); and the more sensational Longford, *The Murder,* and Mooney, *Evelyn Nesbit.* The most rational account is in Baker's *Stanny,* pp. 369–93.

504 White then used Hummel: Rovere, *Howe and Hummel,* p. 45.

504 In the mid-1920s: This witty remark seems to stem from a pool of architects' lore. There is no firsthand account of it. I heard it in Brendan Gill's talks on Stanford White.

## 49. VOGUE LA GALÈRE

506 In the summer of 1907: Frances Grimes was taped in her old age recalling her years in the Saint-Gaudens studio between 1901 and 1906. She describes how the terminally ill sculptor was manipulated by his wife and son, who carried the ailing man to work in

the studio to be able to say to committees that the sculptor was watching over the work. The marriage had been a matter of financial convenience for decades. Mrs. Saint-Gaudens liked the celebrity of being the wife of a famous person. She was also rather greedy and wanted every last commission possible. Saint-Gaudens himself seemed to have preferred being "Mr. Clark" when he could stay with Davida and Novy in Connecticut.

506  The young men of the 1870s: Moore, *McKim,* p. 300.

506  On McKim's return: Ibid., p. 299.

509  At 12:26 p.m., the Knickerbocker Trust: Account of July 1913, made by Harris A. Dunn, private collection, New York.

510  He tried to cheer up: McKim owned a share in the club, kept a brace of dogs there, and usually went with John Cadwalader.

511  "When you get through": Letter of April 21, 1909, quoted in Moore, *McKim,* pp. 302–3.

511  "The new Metropolitan Life Insurance tower": Letter of May 18, 1909, quoted ibid., pp. 303–4.

512  Bacon was said to have quit: William T. Partridge Papers in the William Rotch Ware Collection of the Avery Library, box 2.

513  The two men had set up: Glenn Brown, *Memories, 1860–1930* (Washington D.C.: W. F. Roberts, 1930).

## APPENDIX

517  Augustus D. Shepard, a Vanderbilt relation: McKim, Mead & White would build for Augustus D. Shepard at Fanwood, New Jersey, in 1886–87. See *American Architect and Building News* 9 (July 14, 1888), for a sketch of the gatehouse. The Mead family is discussed in Oran E. Randall, *History of Chesterfield, Cheshire County, New Hampshire* (Brattleboro, Vt., 1882), pp. 383–91.

518  Babb's abilities as a teacher: For more on Babb, see my entry in *Long Island Country Houses and Their Architects, 1860–1940,* ed. Robert B. MacKay, Anthony Baker, and Carol A. Traynor (New York: W. W. Norton 1997), pp. 58–61.

518  Sargent found the classes disorganized: Trevor Fairbrother, *John Singer Sargent* (New York: Abrams, 1994), p. 12.

518  In a letter to his sister: Letter of January 16 and 18, 1872, William Mead Collection, Amherst College Archives.

# SELECTED BIBLIOGRAPHY

Armstrong, David Maitland. *Day Before Yesterday: Reminiscences of a Varied Life.* New York: C. Scribner's Sons, 1920.

Baker, Paul R. *Stanny: The Gilted Life of Stanford White.* New York: Free Press, 1989.

Baldwin, Charles C. *Stanford White.* New York, 1931; paperback, Cambridge, Mass.: Da Capo Press, 1976.

Broderick, Mosette, and William Shopsin. *The Villard Houses: Life Story of a Landmark.* New York: Viking Press, 1980.

Chapman, John Hay. "McKim, Mead and White." *Vanity Fair* (September 13, 1919).

Cigliano, Jan, and Sarah Landau. *The Grand American Avenue, 1850–1920.* San Francisco: Pomegranate Artbooks, 1994.

Clews, Henry. *Fifty Years in Wall Street.* New York: Irving Publishing Co., 1908.

Cortissoz, Royal. *American Artists.* London: C. Scribner's Sons, 1923.

———. *The Painter's Craft.* London: C. Scribner's Sons, 1930.

———. "Some Critical Reflections on the Architectural Genius of Charles F. McKim." *Brickbuilder* 19 (February 1910).

Craven, Wayne. *Stanford White: Decorator in Opulence and Dealer in Antiquities.* New York: Columbia University Press, 2005.

Davis, Richard Harding. "Stanford White," *Collier's* 37 (August 4, 1906).

Desmond, Henry W., and Herbert Croly. "The Works of Messrs. McKim, Mead and White." *Architectural Record* 20 (September 1906).

Dryfhout, John H. *The Work of Augustus Saint-Gardens.* Hanover, N.H., and London: University Press of New England, 1982.

Granger, Alfred Hoyt. *Charles Follen McKim.* Boston: Houghton Mifflin, 1913.

Hewlett, J. Monroe. Entry in "Stanford White as Those Who Trained in His Office Knew Him." *Brickbuilder* 15 (December 1906).

———. "Stanford White, Decorator." *Good Furniture* 9 (September 1917).

Hitchcock, Henry-Russell. *The Architecture of H. H. Richardson and His Times.* Rev. ed. Cambridge, Mass.: MIT Press, 1966.

———. "Frank Lloyd Wright and the Academic Tradition of the Early Eighteen-nineties." *Journal of the Warburg and Courtauld Institute* 7 (1944): 46–63.

Low, Will H. *A Chronicle of Friendship.* New York: Scribner's Sons, 1908.

Lydig, Rita de Acosta. *Tragic Mansions.* New York: Boni & Liveright, 1927.

McKim, Mead & White. *A Monograph of the Work of McKim, Mead & White, 1879–1915.* New York: Architectural Book Publishing Co., 1915.

Mooney, Michael M. *Evelyn Nesbit and Stanford White.* New York: Morrow, 1976.

Moore, Charles. *The Life of Charles Follen McKim.* Boston: Houghton Mifflin, 1929.

Moses, Lionel. "McKim, Mead and White: A History." *American Architect and Building News* 121 (May 24, 1922).

Partridge, William T. "Recollections Concerning Charles Follen McKim." Unpublished ms., Avery Architectural Library, Columbia University.

Randall, Oran E. *History of Chesterfield.* Brattleboro, Vt.: D. Leonard, 1882.

Reilly, Charles Herbert. *McKim, Mead and White.* London: E. Benn, 1924.

Roth, Leland M. *The Architecture of McKim, Mead & White, 1870–1920: A Building List.* New York: Garland, 1978.

———. *McKim, Mead & White, Architects.* New York: Harper & Row, 1983.

Saint-Gaudens, Augustus. *The Reminiscences of Augustus Saint-Gardens.* 2 vols. New York: The Century Co., 1913.

Sawyer, Philip. *Edward Palmer York: Personal Reminiscences.* Stonington, Conn.: Privately printed, 1951.

———. Entry in "Stanford White as Those Who Trained in His Office Knew Him." *Brick-builder* 15 (December 1906).

Searing, Helen, ed. *In Search of Modern Architecture: A Tribute to Henry-Russell Hitchcock.* Cambridge, Mass.: Architectural History Foundation/MIT Press, 1982.

Simmons, Edward W. *From Seven to Seventy: Memoirs of a Painter and Yankee.* New York: Harper, 1922.

Sturgis, Russell. "The Works of McKim, Mead & White." *Architectural Record, Great American Architects Series* (May 1895).

Swanberg, W. A. *Whitney Father, Whitney Heiress.* New York: Scribner, 1980.

Swartwout, Egerton. "An Architectural Decade." Unpublished transcript, n.d. Walker O. Cain donation to Avery Library, Columbia University.

Van Rensselaer, Mariana Griswold. "Recent Architecture in America." Series in *The Century Magazine,* vols. 28–32 (May 1884–July 1886).

Villard, Henry. *Memoirs of Henry Villard, Journalist and Financier, 1835–1900.* Boston: Houghton Mifflin, 1904.

Walker, C. Howard. "Joseph Wells, Architect, 1853–1890." *Architectural Record* 66 (July 1929).

White, Claire Nicolas, ed. *Stanford White: Letters to His Family.* New York: Rizzoli, 1997.

White, Lawrence Grant. *Sketches and Designs of Stanford White.* New York: Architectural Book Publishing Co., 1920.

Wilson, Richard Guy. *Harbor Hill: Portrait of a House.* New York: W. W. Norton, 2008.

———. *McKim, Mead and White, Architects.* New York: Rizzoli, 1983.

# INDEX

Page numbers in *italics* refer to illustrations.

A NOTE ON THE TYPE

The text of this book was set in Garamond No. 3. It is not
a true copy of any of the designs of Claude Garamond
(ca. 1480–1561), but an adaptation of his types, which
set the European standard for two centuries. This particular
version is based on an adaptation by Morris Fuller Benton.

COMPOSED BY
North Market Street Graphics, Lancaster, Pennsylvania

PRINTED AND BOUND BY
Quad/Graphics, Fairfield, Pennsylvania